D0214533

MEDIEVAL MUSIC

MEDIEVAL MUSIC

RICHARD H. HOPPIN

The Ohio State University

W · W · Norton & Company · Inc · New York

Copyright © 1978 by W. W. Norton & Company,
Inc. All rights reserved. Published simultaneously in
Canada by George J. McLeod Limited, Toronto.
Printed in the United States of America.

Library of Congress Cataloging in Publication Data
Hoppin, Richard H
    Medieval music.
    (Norton introduction to music history series)
    Bibliography: p.
    Includes index.
    1. Music—History and criticism—Medieval,
400–1500.   I. Title.
ML172.H8   780'.902   78–7010

ISBN 0 393 09090 6

2 3 4 5 6 7 8 9 0

To Jean

for whom, as for
Guillaume de Machaut,

La musique est une science
Qui veut qu'on rit et chante et dance.

Contents

Dame • Musical Forms in the Mass—Gloria and Credo • The Isorhythmic Movements • The *David Hocket* • The Secular Songs • The Ballades • Poetic and Musical Form in the Ballades • The Rondeaux • The Virelais

List of Illustrations

List of Tables

Abbreviations for Bibliographic References

AcM   *Acta Musicologica,* 1928–.

AH   *Analecta Hymnica Medii Aevi,* 55 vols., Leipzig, 1886–1922; repr. New York and London, 1961.

AIM   American Institute of Musicology; publications include CMM, CSM, MD, MSD. For lists, see latest issues of MD.

AMM   Richard Hoppin, ed., *Anthology of Medieval Music,* New York, 1978.

AMRM   *Aspects of Medieval and Renaissance Music: A Birthday Offering to Gustave Reese,* ed. J. LaRue, New York, 1966.

AMW   *Archiv für Musikwissenschaft,* 1918–.

AnM   *Annales musicologiques,* 1953–.

AoM   *Anthology of Music,* ed. K. Fellerer, Cologne, 1959–. The English edition of a series of anthologies originally published in German as *Das Musikwerk,* Cologne, 1951–.

CFR   R. Hoppin, ed., *The Cypriot-French Repertory of the Manuscript Torino, Biblioteca Nazionale, J. II. 9,* 4 vols., CMM, 21, AIM, 1960–63.

CMM   *Corpus mensurabilis musicae,* AIM, 1948–.

CS   E. de Coussemaker, ed., *Scriptorum de medii aevi nova series,* 4 vols., Paris, 1864–76; repr. Milan, 1931, and Hildesheim, 1963. For contents, see MMBb, No. 925.

CSM   *Corpus scriptorum de musica,* AIM, 1950–.

EFCM   G. Reaney, ed., *Early Fifteenth-Century Music,* 5 vols., CMM, 11, AIM, 1955–75. A sixth volume has been announced.

EM   H. Gleason, ed., *Examples of Music before 1400,* 2nd rev. printing, New York, 1945.

FSC   W. Apel, ed., *French Secular Compositions of the Fourteenth Century,* 3 vols., CMM, 53, AIM, 1970–72.

FSM   W. Apel, ed., *French Secular Music of the Late Fourteenth Century,* Cambridge, Mass., 1950.

GC   W. Apel, *Gregorian Chant,* Bloomington, Ind., 1958.

GD   *Grove's Dictionary of Music and Musicians,* ed. E. Blom, 5th ed., 9 vols., London, 1954, and Supplement, ed. D. Stevens, London, 1961. A sixth edition is in preparation.

GMB   A. Schering, ed., *Geschichte der Musik in Beispielen,* Leipzig, 1931; repr. *History of Music in Examples,* New York, 1950.

GS   M. Gerbert, ed., *Scriptores ecclesiastici de musica,* 3 vols., St. Blasien, 1784; repr. Milan, 1931. For contents, see MMBb, No. 926.

HAM   A. T. Davison and W. Apel, eds., *Historical Anthology of Music,* Vol. 1, 2nd ed., Cambridge, Mass., 1949.

HDM   W. Apel, *Harvard Dictionary of Music,* 2nd ed., Cambridge, Mass., 1969.

HMS   *History of Music in Sound,* RCA Victor; recordings in albums 2 and 3 illustrate the corresponding volumes of NOHM.

HWM   D. Grout, *A History of Western Music,* rev. ed., New York, 1973.

IMM   Institute of Medieval Music, Brooklyn; publications include MSt, MTT, PMMM.

JAMS   *Journal of the American Musicological Society,* 1948–.

JMT   *Journal of Music Theory,* 1957–.

LU   *The Liber Usualis with Introduction and Rubrics in English,* Tournai, 1952 (and later editions).

MD   *Musica Disciplina,* AIM, 1946–.

MFCI   N. Pirrotta, ed., *The Music of Fourteenth Century Italy,* 5 vols., CMM, 8, AIM, 1954–64.

MGG   *Die Musik in Geschichte und Gegenwart,* 14 vols., Kassel, 1949–68; Supplements, 1968–.

ML   *Music and Letters,* 1920–.

MM   C. Parrish and J. Ohl, eds., *Masterpieces of Music before 1750,* New York, 1951.

MMA   G. Reese, *Music in the Middle Ages,* New York, 1940.

MMB   F. Ll. Harrison, *Music in Medieval Britain,* New York, 1959.

MMBb   A. Hughes, *Medieval Music: The Sixth Liberal Art,* Toronto Medieval Bibliographies, 4, Toronto and Buffalo, 1974.

MQ   *The Musical Quarterly,* 1915–.

MR   G. Reese, *Music in the Renaissance,* 2nd ed., New York, 1959.

MSB   *Musikwissenschaftliche Studien-Bibliothek,* ed. F. Gennrich, 24 vols., 1956–66.

MSD   *Musicological Studies and Documents,* AIM, 1951–.

MSt   *Musicological Studies,* IMM, 1955–.

MTT   *Musical Theorists in Translation,* IMM, 1959–.

NMM   C. Parrish, *The Notation of Medieval Music,* rev. ed., New York, 1959.

NOHM   *New Oxford History of Music,* London and New York, 1954–. Vol. 2, *Early Medieval Music up to 1300,* 1954; Vol. 3, *Ars Nova and the Renaissance, 1300–1540,* 1960.

NPM   W. Apel, *The Notation of Polyphonic Music 900–1600,* 5th ed., Cambridge, Mass., 1961.

OHM   A. Hughes and M. Bent, eds., *The Old Hall Manuscript,* 3 vols., CMM, 46, AIM, 1969–73.

PalM   *Paléographie musicale: les principaux manuscrits de chant grégorien, ambrosien, mozarabe, gallican,* 21 vols. in 2 series, Solesmes, Tournai, or Berne, 1899–; reprint, ser.[1], vols. 1–15 and ser.[2], vols 1–2, Berne, 1968–74.

PAM   *Publikationen älterer Musik . . . bei der deutschen Musikgesellschaft,* 11 vols., Leipzig, 1926–40; repr. Hildesheim, 1967–68.

PM   *Polyphonic Music of the Fourteenth Century,* various eds., Monaco, 1956–.

PMC   Separate volumes of commentary to PM 1, 2–3, and 4; repr. with revisions and additions as PM 4A.

PMMM   *Publications of Medieval Music Manuscripts,* IMM, 1957–.

RBM   *Revue belge de musicologie,* 1946–.

RISM   *Répertoire international des sources musicales,* 1960–.

RVB   F. Gennrich, *Rondeaux, Virelais und Balladen,* 2 vols., Gesellschaft für romanische Literatur, 43 and 47, Dresden, 1921, and Göttingen, 1927.

SIMG   *Sammelbände der internationalen Musikgesellschaft,* 1899–1914; repr. (15 vols.), Hildesheim, 1970(?).

SMMA   *Summa Musicae Medii Aevi,* ed. F. Gennrich, 18 vols., 1957–67.

SMRM   M. Bukofzer, *Studies in Medieval and Renaissance Music,* New York, 1950.

SR   O. Strunk, *Source Readings in Music History,* New York, 1950. Also published in separate paperbacks (1960), of which the first two are *SR: Antiquity and the Middle Ages* and *SR: The Renaissance.*

SS   E. Lerner, ed., *Study Scores of Musical Styles,* New York, 1968.

TEM   C. Parrish, ed., *A Treasury of Early Music,* New York, 1958.

Abbreviations for Manuscript Sources

Apt Apt, Trésor de la Basilique Sainte-Anne, 16 bis

Ba Bamberg, Staatliche Bibliothek, Lit. 115 (formerly Ed.IV.6)

BL Bologna, Civico Museo Bibliografico Musicale, Q 15

BU Bologna, Biblioteca Universitaria, 2216

Ch Chantilly, Musée Condé, 564 (formerly 1047)

Cl Paris, Bibliothèque Nationale, nouv. acq. fr., 13521 (La Clayette)

F Florence, Biblioteca Medicea Laurenziana, Pluteus 29. 1

Fauv Paris, Bibliothèque Nationale, f. fr., 146

Iv Ivrea, Biblioteca Capitolare (without signature)

Ma Madrid, Biblioteca Nacional, 20486

Mo Montpellier, Faculté de Médecine, H 196

Mod Modena, Biblioteca Estense, α, M. 5, 24 (formerly lat. 568)

O Oxford, Bodleian Library, Canonici Misc. 213

OH Old Hall Manuscript, London, British Library (Museum), add. 57950

Pic Paris, Bibliothèque Nationale, Coll. de Picardie 67, f. 67

Pit Paris, Bibliothèque Nationale, f. ital. 568

PR Paris, Bibliothèque Nationale, nouv. acq. fr., 6771 (Reina)

Rs Rome, Biblioteca Vaticana, Rossi 215

Tu Turin, Biblioteca Reale, vari 42

TuB Turin, Biblioteca Nazionale, J. II. 9

W₁ Wolfenbüttel, Herzog August-Bibliothek, 677 (formerly Helmstadt 628)

W₂ Wolfenbüttel, Herzog August-Bibliothek, 1099 (formerly Helmstadt 1206)

Preface

Writing this *Medieval Music* for the Norton Introduction to Music History series proved to be a much longer task than I had anticipated. I began with the naïve assumption that I need only explain and illustrate everything students had ever wanted to know about medieval music and never been afraid to ask. Much sooner than I did, I should have realized that the amount of music and, even more, the variety of styles and forms to be considered made attainment of that goal an impossible dream. Yet I persisted, quixotically, until I had far exceeded the practical limits of an introduction. My sympathetic editor, Claire Brook, then suggested that the more detailed and technical analyses be extracted and published as a separate collection of essays. We hope thereby to have made the present book of greater usefulness to the college student who wants more information than can be gleaned from a survey of all Western music but may not have time for an intensive study of the entire medieval repertory. We also hope that the book will prove interesting and helpful to the increasing number of amateurs who, through both live and recorded performances, have come to know and love the strangely beguiling qualities of medieval music. Perhaps, in addition, it may contribute to a wider realization that the Middle Ages produced music worthy of the same careful study and admiration long accorded to its masterpieces of literature, art, and architecture.

But reading *about* music is not enough. Full understanding can only come from study of the music itself, from listening to it, and from performing it whenever possible. As a complement to the present book, therefore, a separate *Anthology of Medieval Music* has been prepared. This publication should provide at least the minimum amount of illustrative material for a survey of medieval forms and styles. Similar material may be found in other anthologies listed in the Bibliography, most of which have fewer examples, however, because they are not devoted solely to medieval music.

I make no apology for the fact that this introduction still presents more material than can be assimilated in a survey course lasting three or four months. When it is used as a text, instructors will be free to choose what they will emphasize and illustrate, and it will provide students with suggestions and topics for oral reports or term papers. I fondly hope it may also prove a stimulus to further study after the work of a specific course has been completed. As both a student and an instructor, I have always felt shortchanged when a text's informational content was exhausted by the end of a course. And an introduction, after all, should be the beginning, not the end, of a relationship. It takes time to acquire the wider and deeper knowledge that will turn mere acquaintance into friendship, intimacy, and love. My efforts in writing this book will be amply repaid if it kindles even one lifelong love affair with medieval music.

The author of a book such as this inevitably requires counsel, guidance, and active assistance from untold numbers of people and institutions. Major contributions should be acknowledged, however. First of all, I must express my deep gratitude to the late Nathan Broder, who persuaded me to begin the project and whose invaluable criticisms of the first few chapters set the course I endeavored to follow throughout the remainder of the work. I am equally grateful to Claire Brook and her staff at W. W. Norton and Company, Inc. for their professional competence in helping me with revisions of the original draft and in guiding me through the final stages of publication. Special thanks must also go to John Morris for taking over much of the burden of providing pictorial illustrations.

Students, faculty, and staff at The Ohio State University helped in innumerable ways. Miss Olga Buth, music librarian, met all my demands speedily and with unfailing good humor. I owe a great debt to the Center for Medieval and Renaissance Studies for providing a research assistant, William Melin, who read and checked most of the first draft, offered many valuable suggestions, and assisted in preparing musical examples and transcriptions for the accompanying *Anthology*. Stephen Kelly also read several of the later chapters and was particularly helpful with the Italian Ars Nova. David Cunningham saved me much trouble by supplying some of the photographs appearing in this book. I am most grateful to them all.

Professor Gertrude Kuehefuhs of the School of Music read the chapters on Gregorian Chant, and Professor Hans Keller of the Department of Romance Languages read those on the troubadours and trouvères. I thank them both for sparing me the embarrassment of several egregious errors. Whatever errors and imperfections remain, there and elsewhere in the book, are all my own.

Less tangible assistance usually goes unacknowledged, but I cannot omit thanking my colleagues on the Music History staff for their moral support and understanding forbearance during my time of travail. The contributions of my wife during this same time are even more incalculable and indescribable. She did accomplish the almost impossible task of typing the whole of the original version from a draft for which the word *rough* is a totally inadequate description. Words fail me as to her other contributions, but without her sympathy, encouragement, and occasional goading, the book might never have been completed. For sharing both the pain and the pleasure, therefore, it is only fitting that I dedicate this book to her with gratitude and deepest affection.

Columbus, Ohio
March, 1977

MEDIEVAL MUSIC

CHAPTER I

Historical Introduction (to A.D. 1000)

If art holds—or at least used to hold—a mirror up to life, music too reflects the society that gave it birth. But societies change, and, as they do, their musical image also changes. While we cannot hope to view the music of the Middle Ages with the eyes of its contemporaries, we can at least refrain from judging it by the position and function of music in our own society. We must forget glittering—but not necessarily golden—new opera houses, famous composers conducting their own works around the world, impresarios touting their "great musical artists," festivals proliferating so rapidly that the vacationing traveler can avoid them only with the greatest difficulty. We must forget radio, television, the phonograph, high fidelity, and stereophonic sound. We must forget, in short, almost every aspect of twentieth-century commercialism that has turned music into big business and made it an inescapable phenomenon that sometimes brings more pain than pleasure to weary ears in a noisy world. Music in the Middle Ages was neither as spectacular as this nor as pervasive. Yet it was central to the religious, social, and intellectual life of the times. How music can help us to understand the life of medieval man, this book, it is hoped, will make clear.

Before we begin to consider the music of the Middle Ages, however, the period itself must be defined, or at least its limits established. Boundaries between historical periods are as difficult to draw and as subject to change as any arbitrarily drawn boundaries between countries. Italian writers of the fourteenth and fifteenth centuries believed that their civilization represented a rebirth of the ancient glories of Greece and Rome. Therefore, they designated all the intervening centuries as medieval (literally, "middle age"). Mistaken as the judgment of these writers may have been, their designation has persisted; and modern scholars generally regard the collapse of the Roman Empire in the fifth century as the beginning of the Middle Ages. A study of medieval music, however, cannot begin somewhere between A.D. 400 and 500. Almost no music survives from the first thousand years of the Christian era except the music of the Church, and the history of that music begins with the foundation of Christianity. It is for this reason that a discussion of the Christian liturgy up to A.D. 1000 must take place in Chapter II before we can turn to the proper subject matter of this book.

The close of the medieval period is even more difficult to define than its beginning. The Renaissance did not appear simultaneously in all parts of western Europe, and it manifested itself in different ways in different areas of intellectual and artistic endeavor. Moreover, the revival of learning and letters did not immediately obliterate all traces of medieval ways of life. Learning and letters were, in fact, far from dead; two or three rebirths preceded what we know as the Renaissance. Dates for the end of the Middle Ages, then, vary according to the personal interests and prejudices of individual scholars. Music historians generally accept 1400 as a convenient, if somewhat arbitrary, compromise. The continuity of musical development, of course, neither stops nor sharply changes direction in that year. We shall find, however, that the music of the first two or three decades of the fifteenth century looks both backward and forward. It crowns the achievements of the Middle Ages and at the same time provides a firm foundation on which the great composers of the fifteenth century could build. A consideration of this music, therefore, logically concludes the present book and may also serve as an introduction to the music of the Renaissance.

Discussion of a special aspect of any period must presuppose at least a little knowledge about the general history of that period. Yet between

An example of early Christian art depicting Jesus's triumphal entry into Jerusalem. A detail from a fourth-century Roman sarcophagus (Foto Biblioteca Vaticana).

the beginnings of Christianity and the end of the fourteenth century lies a vast expanse of time. We cannot hope to describe in detail the history of those fourteen centuries, but we can, perhaps, suggest some of the major events that determined the course of that history and the conditions of men's lives. The present chapter, therefore, offers a sketchy outline of the history of western Europe during the first millennium of the Christian era. Against this background, we may then proceed to examine the church music that this millennium produced. Our primary concern, of course, must always be with western Europe and especially those regions in which music flourished. A book devoted to medieval music cannot treat general history to the satisfaction of specialists in the field. May this historical sketch prove useful, however, to those who are not specialists. Above all, may it stimulate further investigation of what is perhaps the most terrible, yet the most fascinating, period in the history of Western civilization.

To citizens of the Roman Empire in the second century A.D. it must have seemed inconceivable that the peace and prosperity in which they lived should ever pass away. Under the five "good emperors," from Nerva (96–98) and Trajan (98–117) to Marcus Aurelius (d. 180), the Roman world gave every indication of being vigorous, healthy, and secure. Yet even before the end of the century, symptoms of decay began to appear. Barbarians were exerting increasing pressure on the northern frontiers, some cities were in financial difficulties, and—above all—the unresolved problem of the imperial succession began to produce ugly civil wars. Imperial rule became, in fact, military dictatorship, and assassination the most common means by which one popular commander succeeded another as emperor. Toward the middle of the third century, when none of the contending generals was strong enough to win, the internal strife left the frontiers open to barbarian invasions. Franks and Alamans moved up to the Rhine and raided far beyond; Goths came down through the Danubian provinces to the Aegean Sea; and control of Asia was lost to the attacking Persians.

Fortunately for the history of the West and especially for the development of Christianity, this first disintegration of the Roman Empire was only temporary. The emperor Aurelian (270–275) overcame all his rivals and regained control of the entire empire except for lands north and east of the Rhine and Danube rivers. After Aurelian's murder, another soldier-emperor, Diocletian (284–305), completed the restoration of the empire so successfully that he insured its survival for another hundred years.

The comparative stability of the fourth century brought with it two developments of major importance. The first involved an astonishingly rapid change in the fortunes of Christianity within the empire. From bitter persecution under Diocletian, Christianity advanced to complete toleration under Constantine (312–337) and became, by decrees of

Theodosius (379–395), the compulsory religion of all Roman subjects except the Jews. In the following chapter, we shall consider the ways in which this sudden reversal of fortune affected the forms and rites of the Christian religion. Here, it is important to note some of the extraspiritual results. Men of established social and political prominence became members of the clergy or achieved prominence by becoming members. Churches throughout the empire acquired wealth and power through extensive property holdings. Most important of all was the establishment of an ecclesiastical government modeled after the territorial organization of the Roman Empire. There can be little doubt that these new-found strengths enabled the Church to survive—as Rome itself could not—the disastrous events of the fifth century.

The second important development in the fourth century was the founding of Constantinople and the resultant division of the empire into a Latin West and a Greek East. This development too profoundly affected the future of Christianity and, therefore, of its music. The political effects were no less striking: the eastern part of the Empire outlived the western by a thousand, not always glorious, years. By virtue of its strategic location on a peninsula at the mouth of the Bosphorus, Constantinople withstood repeated attacks by northern barbarians and Arab Moslems before it finally fell to the Ottomans in 1453. In addition to thus serving as a bastion on the southeast flank of Europe, the Byzantine Empire preserved cultural and intellectual traditions that were temporarily lost in the West. Consequently, it more than repaid any debt it may have owed to Rome by its contributions to the rebuilding of Europe in the centuries following the total collapse of the West.

THE FALL OF THE ROMAN EMPIRE

We cannot even begin to discuss here the various signs of social, political, cultural, and economic decay that preceded the collapse of the Western Empire in the fifth century. All we can do is to record that collapse and the resulting domination of Europe by barbarian tribes.

In its prime, the Roman Empire had successfully held back the Germanic tribes along the northern frontiers. Even so, various pressures had led to considerable infiltration. A chronic shortage of troops forced the Empire to hire barbarian soldiers, many of whom thus became Roman citizens and even rose to high positions in the imperial administration. Moreover, entire tribes became allies of Rome and patrolled the frontiers in return for grants of land. By the end of the fourth century, then, there were many new "Roman" citizens in various stages of Latinization. Finally, military intrigue and the incompetence of the Western emperor Honorius (395–423) led to the invasion of Italy by the Visigothic allies who had been stationed along the Danube. Honorius simply withdrew to the fortress of Ravenna and did nothing, leaving the Visigoths (West Goths) under Alaric free to subdue and pillage Rome itself (410).

Imperial power in the Western Empire having thus collapsed, the frontiers lay open to invasion. Picts and Scots, Angles and Saxons overran Britain; Franks, Alamans, and Burgundians pressed into northern Gaul; Vandals occupied Aquitaine and Spain. Indicative of the confused situation is the Visigothic invasion of southern Gaul and defeat of the Vandals, who fled to Africa where they established an independent state. Eventually, the Visigoths gained control of the Spanish peninsula and parts of southern Gaul.

Perhaps the major factor contributing to the speed with which barbarians took over the Western Empire was the tremendous pressure of the still more barbarous Huns. As early as 376, the Huns had forced the

The Persian god Mithras, whose cult became the prevailing religion among Roman legionaries and the most serious rival of Christianity in the later days of the Empire (by courtesy of the Vatican Museum).

Visigoths across the Danube into Roman territory; by the middle of the fifth century, they had crossed the Rhine and were pillaging the cities of northern Gaul. With the assistance of German tribes in 451, the able Roman general Aetius defeated the Huns in the battle of the Catalaunian Fields near Châlons and turned them away from Gaul toward Italy. The death of Attila in 453 left the Huns without a leader, and they quickly disbanded, no longer a menace to western Europe. It is characteristic that the weak Roman emperor, Valentinian III, jealous of Aetius's glory and power, had him put to death and was then himself assassinated. The Vandals took this opportunity to cross from Africa to Italy, and Rome was sacked for the second time (455). For the next twenty years, a series of emperors, mere puppets of the military commanders, preserved the outward appearance of imperial rule. In 476, the last puppet was deposed, and the Eastern emperor Zeno (474–491) became the theoretical sovereign of the entire empire. In reality, Zeno had no authority at all in the West, and 476 is commonly regarded as the year in which the Roman Empire officially came to an end. Zeno was responsible, however, for establishing the kingdom of the Ostrogoths (East Goths) in Italy. After the death of Attila and the dissolution of the Huns freed the Ostrogoths, they became allies of the Eastern emperor. Theodoric, the son of an Ostrogothic king, grew up in Constantinople and rose to a position of power in the imperial administration. When he became leader of all the Ostrogoths, his ambition caused Zeno to get rid of him by sending him to recover Italy for the Empire. Theodoric accomplished his mission with total success; moreover, despite his professed allegiance to Zeno, he ruled Italy as a sovereign prince from 493 until his death in 526.

In Gaul, meanwhile, the Franks had become tremendously powerful under the leadership of Clovis, a member of the Merovingian family. Totally unscrupulous, and a brilliant military commander, Clovis removed, by assassination or other means, all of his rivals among the Frankish chiefs and thus became the founder of the Frankish dynasty of Merovingian kings. By waging war against the Alamans, Burgundians, and Visigoths, Clovis extended the boundaries of the Frankish kingdom south to the western Pyrenees and north to beyond the Rhine. Only the intervention of Theodoric kept Clovis from reaching the Mediterranean (see Map 1). Perhaps the most significant event of Clovis's reign was his conversion to Christianity around the end of the fifth century. Thereafter, with the approval of the Church, Clovis campaigned against his heathen neighbors to the north and the heretical Visigoths to the south. By taking a Burgundian wife and by giving his sister in marriage to Theodoric, Clovis proved that he also knew the value of political alliances. Despite his cruel and barbarous ways, Clovis was obviously a remarkable man. Yet even he can scarcely have foreseen the long-term results of his endeavors. By the time of his death in 511, Clovis had created a

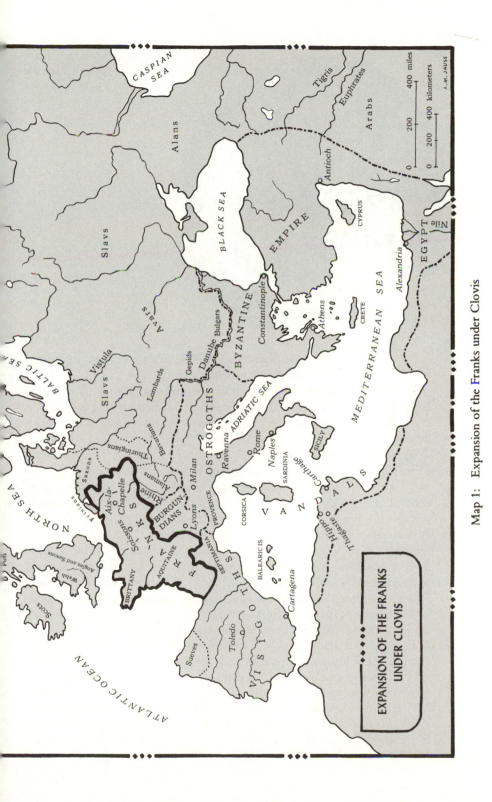

Map 1:   Expansion of the Franks under Clovis

Portrait of Theodoric from a contemporary medal (Museum of the Terme, Rome).

large and powerful kingdom and had, in fact, initiated events leading to the creation of France as an independent nation.

If we have dwelt at some length on the disintegration of the Roman Empire and the establishment of independent barbarian kingdoms in the fifth century, it is because these events determined the social and political conditions that were to prevail for several centuries. We cannot here describe those conditions in detail, but it is important to note their one common characteristic: the mixture in varying proportions of Roman and Germanic elements. The German invaders had no sooner gained control of their new territories, than their assimilation by the conquered populations began. This process was not achieved, however, without a considerable decline in the level of civilization. The higher-ranking members of imperial society adopted the warlike habits of the German leaders and evolved a semibarbarous aristocracy based on military strength and the ownership of land. Similarly, the various elements of lower social levels merged to produce the peasantry of the Middle Ages.

The extent of Roman influence varied greatly in the different barbarian kingdoms. As might be expected, the Ostrogoths under Theodoric in Italy came closest to preserving the forms of imperial life and culture. For the music historian, it is especially important to note that the greatest Latin writers of the age, Boethius (c. 480–524) and Cassiodorus (c. 485–c. 575), served at Theodoric's court. Boethius was primarily a philosopher and Cassiodorus, a historian and statesman; but both men also wrote musical treatises based on Greek sources. The work of Boethius in particular remained the foundation of musical studies throughout the Middle Ages.

In other barbarian kingdoms, Roman influence took much longer to become apparent. That it was preserved at all and that it became increasingly significant may be credited largely to the spread of Christianity and to the rise of the papacy to a position of supreme authority over Western Christendom. The Western Church, with an administrative and territorial organization that followed the imperial model to some extent, became the only stable and unifying element in a confused and confusing world. The common religious element may also have been responsible for the fact that so many of the German tribes abandoned their own language in favor of Latin as spoken by the invaded peoples. At any rate, the assimilation of the conquerors by the conquered is nowhere more obvious than in the survival of Latin and its development into the modern Romance languages spoken in France, Spain, Portugal, and, of course, Italy. With the exception of Britain and the regions along the northern boundary of the Roman Empire, the areas where these languages are spoken correspond almost exactly with the oldest and most thoroughly Latinized parts of western Europe.

THE SIXTH CENTURY

After the reigns of the two great Western leaders Clovis and Theodoric, the European scene again underwent violent changes. On the death of Clovis in 511, the Frankish kingdom was divided among his four sons. When not waging war among themselves, they managed to unite sufficiently to extend Frankish dominion over the Alamans and Bavarians to the northeast and, after the death of Theodoric (526), through Burgundy and Provence to the Mediterranean. Thus the Franks became the most powerful and independent people in western Europe. The other barbarian kingdoms were showing signs of disintegration, however, and their weakness tempted the Eastern emperor Justinian to try to reconquer the West.

Justinian, who ruled from 527 to 565, is generally known as the last of the great Roman—that is, Byzantine—emperors. He is most famous, and rightly so, for his promulgation of the *Corpus Juris Civilis* (Body of Civil Law), the foundation of the present legal system in most European countries and Latin America. Justinian's other achievements were more immediately spectacular but much shorter lived. In 533, he sent Belisarius with a small expeditionary force against the Vandals in Africa, ostensibly in answer to appeals against a usurping king. Belisarius accomplished his mission so successfully that the once proud Vandal nation ceased to exist. The Goths in Italy took longer to obliterate. Taking the murder of the Ostrogothic regent as a pretext, Justinian sent two forces to retake Italy. One advanced through Dalmatia; the other, under Belisarius, took Sicily and in 536 captured Rome without a struggle.

Mosaic from Ravenna depicting Justinian and his court attending Mass.

This did not end the war, however. After a seeming victory in 540, Justinian recalled Belisarius; but the Goths rallied under Totila and recaptured almost all of Italy. They met final defeat in 552 when Totila was slain in battle. The next year the imperial army under Narses destroyed the last pockets of Gothic resistance. Justinian now turned his thoughts toward Spain, where civil war between rival kings provided yet another legal pretext for military intervention. The Visigoths united against the invaders, however, and contained Justinian's forces within a small area on the southeast coast of Spain.

Despite his boast that the Mediterranean was again a Roman lake, Justinian fell far short of his goal of restoring the Western Empire. The net result of his military efforts, indeed, was the exhaustion of the Eastern Empire and the destruction of the little that yet remained of classical civilization in Italy. Imperial power could no longer fend off either the Persians to the east or the new barbarian hordes pressing down from the north across the Danube. The long war in Italy had finally reduced Rome to ruins, and urban civilization everywhere virtually disappeared. As in the rest of Europe, an agrarian aristocracy now predominated, but in Italy that aristocracy had little unity or strength. Neither it nor the Empire could repel the next barbarian invasion that was so soon to come.

The Avars, a horde of nomads comparable to the Huns, had swept westward out of Asia and were threatening the Germanic tribes along the Danube. In about 568, one of these tribes, the Lombards, fled across the Alps into Italy. After occupying the valley of the Po (still known today as Lombardy) they moved southward almost the entire length of the peninsula. Because of its superiority on the seas, the Roman Empire retained control of the more important coastal regions, but the greater part of Italy was in the hands of the Lombards by the end of the sixth century. Unfortunately for the future history of Italy, the Lombards showed little genius for political organization. Their kings, if they had any at all, were kings in little more than name. Each chieftain, later dignified by the title of count or duke, enjoyed nearly autonomous rule over his own small district. These divisions of Lombard territory, combined with the isolated possessions of the Empire, contributed to the patchwork of petty states that Italy was to remain until late in the nineteenth century.

One central administrative authority still functioned in Italy at the end of the sixth century, however: the papacy. Civil administration, indeed, had virtually disappeared in Rome itself, and by default the popes became the political, as well as religious, rulers of the city. Much as they may have been disturbed by conditions throughout Italy and western Europe, the popes had little interest in the restoration of imperial power. By ancient tradition, the emperor was head of both the state and the state religion, and Justinian had reaffirmed this tradition with particular vigor. In attempting to unify all of Christendom under his own leadership, Justinian ran directly counter to the so-called Petrine theory of papal supremacy. According to this theory, first clearly expressed by Pope Leo the Great (440–461), the bishop of Rome, as the successor of St. Peter, was the supreme authority of Christendom. The theory was never acceptable to the Eastern branches of Christianity, and imperial supremacy was equally unacceptable to the popes in Rome. Justinian's despotic attitude thoroughly antagonized the papacy and widened the rift between East and West. It remained for a weak emperor and a strong pope to complete the separation by establishing the independence of the Western Church. That pope was Gregory the Great (590–604). We shall discuss Gregory's contributions to the Church and its music in the following chapter. Here we need only note that under Gregory the Petrine theory became an actuality and the papacy, a world power.

THE RISE OF ISLAM

For men of the seventh century, the rapid spread of a new religion by hosts of conquering Arabs was as unexpected as it was astounding. Nomadic hordes had been sweeping westward from central Asia for centuries, but a similar outpouring from Arabia was without precedent. Still more unprecedented was an invasion under the banner of religion. Most astonishing of all, the Arab conquests imposed a new culture on the conquered peoples, created one of the world's great civilizations, and permanently established Mohammedanism as a major world religion. Even today the underlying causes of these events and the rapidity with which they took place remain difficult to explain.

Fascinating as the story of Islam is, we must confine ourselves here to

A water clock and musicians: page from an Arabic treatise (Isabella Stewart Gardner Museum, Boston).

those aspects that profoundly affected the history of western Europe, especially its musical development. The most immediately obvious aspect is territorial expansion. At the time of Mohammed's death in 632, his authority was scarcely felt beyond the Hejaz region of Arabia, a narrow strip along the Red Sea that included the city of Mecca, Islam's holiest shrine. Within the next hundred years, the prophet's Holy War of Islam had extended Arab domination eastward through Persia and Afghanistan to the Himalayas and westward across the top of Africa to the Atlantic Ocean. All this was not accomplished by Arabs acting entirely alone. Conversion went along with conquest, and the prospect of enjoying the fruits of further conquests undoubtedly brought many adherents to the new religion. Thus it was with the Moors in western Africa. After some preliminary defeats, the Moslems eventually won over the Moors, who then provided thousands of troops for the invasion of Europe. In 711 a Moorish force crossed the strait from Africa under the leadership of Tariq, whose name is preserved in that of Gibraltar (literally, *Jabal,* "mount of," + *Tariq*). Begun merely as a raid for plunder, Tariq's expedition achieved phenomenal successes—the defeat of the last Visigothic king and the occupation of the royal capital of

Toledo. Within a dozen years the Moslems were in possession of almost the entire Iberian peninsula and were pressing northward across the Pyrenees. Their raids into central Gaul were finally stopped by Charles Martel, who won a decisive victory between Tours and Poitiers in 732, exactly one hundred years after the death of Mohammed. For this victory Charles won his surname (*Martel* = "the hammer") and a position in history as the savior of Christianity.

Charles Martel's son and grandson, Pepin I and Charlemagne, effectively confined the Moslems south of the Pyrenees, thus ending the threat to Europe from that direction. In the East, meanwhile, a sadly diminished empire recovered sufficient strength to withstand Moslem attack. After the total destruction of the imperial fleet in 655, the Mediterranean had become a Moslem, rather than a Roman, lake; but Constantinople remained invincible to attack by land and sea. The last major effort to take the city failed early in the eighth century, and the Moslems were thus prevented from overrunning eastern Europe. It was Italy that suffered longest from the threat of invasion and conquest. Moslem control of the sea permitted occupation of the larger Mediterranean islands, including Sicily, as well as allowing piratical raids on the European coasts. By the ninth century southern Italy had been invaded, and in 846 Rome itself was under attack. Whether southern Italy would fall to the Moslems remained in doubt for over fifty years; but early in the tenth century the invaders were finally and permanently expelled.

Christian writers, both in the Middle Ages and later, have tended to exaggerate the menace of Islam. It must be remembered that Christianity not only survived in Moslem Spain but, as we shall see in the following chapter, continued to develop one of the great Western liturgies. To understand how this could be, we must briefly review the basic tenets of Islam as founded by Mohammed. The religion we commonly speak of as Mohammedanism is known to its adherents as Islam, meaning "submission" (to the will of God). Those who have made this submission are Moslems. The creed of Islam is extremely simple: "There is no God but Allah, and Mohammed is His prophet." But Allah was no new creation. He was, as Mohammed insisted, the God of the Jews and Christians, and Mohammed was merely the last in a long line of His prophets. Thus, in the Holy War of Islam, only idolaters who refused to accept the true faith were slain. Jews and Christians were tolerated but forced to pay tribute as subject peoples. Moreover, Moslems were at first exempt from taxation, and complete conversion of conquered territories was therefore undesirable. Under these conditions, it is not surprising that both Jews and Christians persisted and, one might even say, flourished in Spain during the centuries of Moslem domination. Certainly Christianity, and western Europe in general, profited greatly from the richness and variety that characterized the literature and learning of Islam.

Even during its first triumphant century, the Arab world had begun to display the inability to maintain political and religious unity that has since become proverbial. Rivalry for the caliphate—the temporal and spiritual leadership of Islam—led to the establishment of the Ommiad dynasty in Spain and the Abbasid dynasty in the eastern capital of Bagdad. Powerful military governors (emirs) turned Morocco, Tunisia, Egypt, and various provinces in the Near East into virtually independent states. As a result, by the end of the ninth century the Arabian Empire had ceased to exist as a political entity. Despite all this, and despite bitter theological quarrels, the world of Islam continued to be united by a common culture and civilization. The chief agent in preserving this cultural unity was undoubtedly the existence of a common language. Because the Koran, the book of revelations to Mohammed, was so sacred that it had to be used in the original, Arabic became the language of educated Moslems everywhere. Educated nonbelievers also learned Arabic, primarily as a means of improving their position under the Moslems. Of much greater import, however, was the resulting contact between Islam and the accumulated wisdom of earlier civilizations. This contact set off a cultural explosion as astonishing as had been the territorial expansion of Islam.

The Abbasid caliphs, especially the famous Harun al-Rashid (786–809) and his successor al-Mamun (813–833), made Bagdad the center from which waves of culture radiated throughout the Arabic-speaking world. Under their patronage, a magnificent library of manuscripts was assembled and a school for the study of Greek science and philosophy was founded. During the course of the ninth century almost all the Greek literature of medicine, mathematics, and philosophy became available in Arabic translation. The position of Bagdad, with its trade routes to Persia and India, brought the culture and learning of the Orient within the reach of Islamic scholars, who combined this more contemporary information with what they learned from the ancient Greeks. They then proceeded to make important contributions of their own in several fields of intellectual endeavor. Moslem scholarship was by no means confined to Bagdad, for the knowledge acquired there was quickly transmitted to other Moslem schools, including one as far west as Cordova in Spain. It was largely through Spain, indeed, that Arabic learning made its contributions to the "renaissance" of the twelfth century in western Europe. It is one of the ironies of history that many Greek writers first became known in the West through Latin translations from the Arabic.

The extent of Arabic influences on the rebirth of Western civilization is not always easy to determine. Contributions also came from Byzantine sources; and, according to individual prejudices, scholars tend to attribute any unexplained phenomenon of medieval life to one or the other influence. This has been true in many fields, including music,

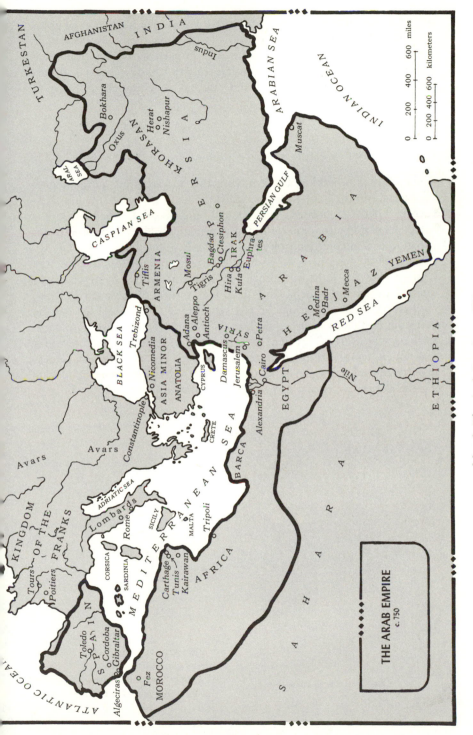

Map 2: The Arab Empire, c. 750 A.D.

where Arab partisans have credited them with the invention of measured note values and even polyphony itself. While these matters remain controversial—and deserving of further, impartial investigation—it is abundantly clear that Arabic scholarship profoundly affected almost every aspect of the intellectual and cultural development of western Europe.

THE DARKEST AGE

While Islam was making its great conquests and attaining a high degree of civilization, the Latin world reached the nadir of its decline into barbarism. Urban civilization had virtually disappeared. The aristocracy had degenerated into illiterate and ignorant landholders, whose only occupation beyond enjoying physical pleasures was waging war. The ignorance of the peasantry, of course, was still more profound. Only the Church kept the light of culture burning, but with a flame that was often unsteady and unbelievably pale. Irish monks of the sixth and seventh centuries were among the last who knew Greek, and few of the best-educated churchmen could boast a real mastery of Latin. Classical learning was nearly forgotten, and the study of pagan authors, when it was not expressly forbidden, was tolerated only because of its usefulness in perfecting a Latin style. Scholarship was essentially utilitarian, educating the clergy just enough to fulfill their functions and serving only to

A monogram page from the Book of Kells (c. 800). In this masterpiece of Celtic art, intricacy of abstract design achieved its ultimate sophistication (Trinity College Library, Dublin).

promote the true faith. As might be expected, the prevailing ignorance was coupled with the most extraordinary superstition, and rational thought was almost nonexistent. It is not surprising, therefore, that the seventh and eighth centuries produced few noteworthy authors and contributed so little to the advancement of European culture.

Unenlightened as it may have been, the Dark Age was by no means uneventful. One development, the effects of which we shall discuss in the following chapter, was the spread of papal influence and the acceptance of papal authority. A second development that momentarily lightened the gloom was the revival of Frankish power under the Carolingian dynasty, named for its outstanding representative, Charles the Great or Charlemagne. Along with this military and political revival, the so-called Carolingian Renaissance took the first tentative steps toward the rebuilding of Western culture.

REVIVAL OF THE FRANKISH KINGDOM

The fratricidal wars of Clovis's descendants evidently exhausted their energies, and the last Merovingians became *rois fainéants* (do-nothing kings). All authority lay in the hands of the so-called mayor of the palace, a position that aristocratic landholders struggled to obtain. One such landholder, Pepin of Herstal, managed to unite the main divisions of the Merovingian realm under his own control and to pass on the office of mayor to his son, Charles Martel. On Charles's death in 741, his son Pepin succeeded to the office now regarded as hereditary. Both Charles and Pepin ruled as kings in all but name, and it was inevitable that the family should eventually seek the title as well. In 751, at Pepin's instigation and with papal approval, the Franks deposed the last Merovingian, Childeric III, and proclaimed Pepin as their king. Thus was founded the Carolingian dynasty that was so soon to reach the height of its glory in the reign of Charlemagne (768–814).

Table 1: *The Carolingian Dynasty*

Pepin of Herstal, Mayor of the Palace (c. 679–714)

Charles Martel, Mayor of the Palace (714–741)

Pepin I, Mayor of the Palace, then King (741–768)

Charlemagne (768–814)   Carloman (768–771)

Louis the Pious (814–840)

(Italy)   (Germany)   (France)

Lothair (840–855)   Louis the German (840–876)   Charles the Bald (840–877)

As the most powerful Christian forces in western Europe, the Carolingians and the papacy were natural allies, working together to their mutual benefit. The religious effects of this alliance we shall discuss in the following chapter. Here we need only mention some of the political and military events that were to have far-reaching results. Pepin, as we have indicated, sought papal approval before assuming the kingship of the Franks, and in 754 Pope Stephen II traveled to Gaul, where he anointed Pepin as king and proclaimed him *Patricius* (Patrician) of Rome. This title, which the pope had no right to bestow, implied that Pepin held authority in Rome as the representative of the Eastern emperor. Pepin confirmed this interpretation when, after driving the Lombards from the imperial territories in Italy, he gave the pope sovereignty over these lands. This famous Donation of Pepin created the Papal States and provided a basis for the papacy's temporal power that endured for well over a thousand years.

Pepin's cooperation with the papacy paved the way for the climactic events of Charlemagne's life. After the early death of his brother Carloman left Charlemagne in full possession of the Frankish kingdom, he turned his attention to the projects left uncompleted by his father and grandfather. First on the list was conquest of the Lombards in northern Italy. This was accomplished in 774, when Charlemagne deposed the Lombard king and took the crown for himself. With it went control of Italy to the north of a line just below Rome. Charlemagne then led his armies north and east, subduing—and Christianizing—the Saxons, regaining control over the too independent Bavarians, and defeating the Avars, who had kept eastern Europe in subjection for two hundred years. By the end of the eighth century, a series of military districts, or marches, protected an eastern frontier that extended in a wide arc from the Baltic to the Adriatic (see Map 3). Of all his undertakings only Charlemagne's effort to conquer the Moslems in Spain ended in failure. Returning from an unsuccessful expedition across the Pyrenees in 778, his rearguard under Roland's command was ambushed in the valley of Roncevaux—not by Moslems but by Christian Basques. The death of Roland in this battle later inspired the greatest of French medieval epics, the *Chanson de Roland* (Song of Roland). Charlemagne's further military activities along the Pyrenees were primarily defensive in nature, but he did acquire an area in the northeast corner of Spain, including the city of Barcelona, in which he established a buffer frontier district known as the Spanish March.

By his military genius combined with inexhaustible energy, Charlemagne thus won control over a territory so vast that it was really an empire in all but name. That deficiency was soon remedied. In 799, an insurrection in Rome forced Pope Leo III to take refuge with Charlemagne, who promptly escorted the pope back to Rome. There, after clearing himself of the charges made against him to justify his ex-

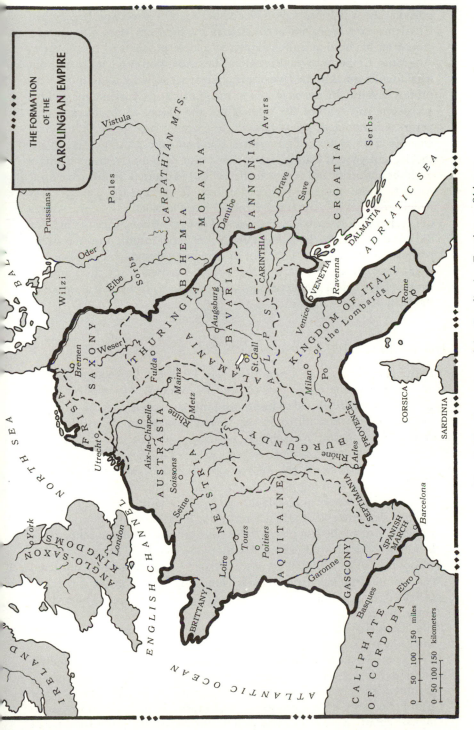

Map 3: The Formation of the Carolingian Empire, c. 814 A.D.

pulsion, Leo was reinstated on December 23, 800. Two days later, when Charlemagne was praying at the altar after Christmas Mass, Leo placed a crown on his head and the assembled people proclaimed him Charles Augustus, Emperor of the Romans. The coronation was totally without legal foundation, but the Byzantine court was too weak to do more than protest. Eventually it was forced to recognize that Charlemagne and his successors had revived the title, if not the glory, of the Roman emperors. Charlemagne's new position as emperor brought with it no real changes in his system of government and no significant increase of authority and power. Rather, it provided him with a title commensurate with the authority and power he had already acquired. It also gave him, so he thought, supreme jurisdiction over Rome and the papacy. This belief produced no immediate trouble, but it was later to be the source of much conflict between emperors and popes, for the office of emperor did not die with Charlemagne. Perhaps the most important result of his coronation was the establishment of a tradition by which Frankish and, later, German kings received the imperial crown from the popes in Rome. Thus began the institution that eventually came to be known as the Holy Roman Empire.

THE CAROLINGIAN RENAISSANCE

Fortunately for the subsequent history of Europe, Charlemagne did not give all of his time and energy to military conquest. Much of his attention, in fact, was devoted to improving the educational system throughout the empire. His efforts in this direction may have been partly inspired by a desire to achieve political and religious unity, but Charlemagne seems also to have been aware of the need for an educated ruling class. Following the example of his father, who had procured scholars to teach young noblemen at court, Charlemagne developed a famous palace school at Aix-la-Chapelle, his favorite residence. Significantly, Charlemagne sought a director for his school not in Italy, but in England, one of the few places where the traditions of Latin scholarship had been kept alive. He chose Alcuin (735–804), head of the cathedral school at York, whose presence at Aix-la-Chapelle quickly attracted teachers and students from all parts of the kingdom. They, in turn, then provided the personnel for carrying out Charlemagne's educational program. By endowing them with high positions in the church—abbacies and bishoprics—Charlemagne enabled them to organize both monastic and cathedral schools.

Training in the Carolingian schools, at least in theory, was based on the traditional seven liberal arts: the humanistic *trivium,* consisting of grammar, rhetoric, and logic; and the scientific *quadrivium,* consisting of arithmetic, geometry, astronomy, and music. In practice—and Carolingian schools were eminently practical of necessity—only the first of these arts—grammar—was or could be studied with any degree of thoroughness. Learning to read and write Latin was itself a major achievement at that time, and material for more advanced study was in short supply. Literature, insofar as it was studied at all, was thought of as being part of grammar, and writings of the church fathers were generally preferred to the pagan classics. For the other liberal arts, a few popular authors—from Boethius and Cassiodorus to Alcuin himself—provided the standard texts.[1] Greek philosophy and science were almost wholly unknown, for very few texts were available in Latin translation. Under such conditions, education inevitably was superficial and consisted largely of learning definitions and familiar quotations. Original thought and new contributions to learning were neither desired nor expected. In the liberal arts depending on mathematics, indeed, no advance was possible as long as Roman numerals remained in use. (To experience the difficulties, one might try multiplying or dividing MCCXLIX by LXVIII.) The development of higher mathematics had to wait for the introduction of the decimal system using Arabic (actually Hindu) numerals, including zero.

The study of music as a liberal art demands particular comment in a book devoted to medieval music. The writings of Boethius and those who came after him were primarily concerned with philosophical speculations as to the nature of music, its effects, and its relation to man and the world in which he lives. Because these speculations took as their starting point the expression of musical intervals by mathematical ratios, music won its place in the quadrivium. This aspect of music is stressed in one of the aphoristic definitions so dear to (and typical of) the medieval mind: Music has to do with number as related to sounds. But, according to the Neo-Pythagorean view, number and proportion regulate the universe and all that is within it. Music, therefore, both represents and includes the universe. In the words of Cassiodorus, "nothing in things celestial or terrestrial which is fittingly conducted according to the Creator's own plan is found to be exempt from [musical] discipline."[2] Thinking such as this, quite obviously, has little or nothing to do with the problems of musical performance. For Boethius, indeed, performers and even composers were "separated from the intellect of musical science," and only the man who possessed "the faculty of judging according to speculation or reason" was worthy of being called a musician.[3] This attitude, which prevailed among the educated throughout most of the Middle Ages, could well have put a stop to all musical development. Fortunately, humble performers and composers continued to evolve new types and styles of music, leaving the critics to

1. For selections from Boethius, Cassiodorus, and Isidore of Seville, the "Big Three" of medieval musical instruction, see Strunk, SR, pp. 79–100.
2. Ibid., p. 92.
3. Ibid., p. 86.

Charlemagne with Pope Leo III, who crowned him Emperor, on his left. From the Imperial shrine at Aachen, completed in 1215.

catch up as best they could. Real progress in music, as we shall see in Chapter II, came from the practical singing schools that preserved and developed the music of the Church.

After these somewhat derogatory remarks, we may well ask whether there really was a Carolingian Renaissance. If an evaluation were to be based solely on immediate contributions to literature and learning, we should have to admit that no rebirth took place. Nothing in western Europe could compare to the cultural explosion among the Moslems or even to the continued, if by now sterile, tradition of classical scholarship in the Byzantine empire. But we should remember how great the darkness was before we carp about the dimness of the light. Alcuin and his associates did rekindle an enthusiasm and respect for learning that kept it from ever again coming so close to extinction. Cathedral and monastic schools continued to grow and became increasingly influential. Manuscript production, moreover, was now a routine part of monastic life, and special rooms (called *scriptoria*) were set aside for the use of scribes. From these scriptoria came the manuscripts that have preserved for us the medieval literature and liturgy of the Church, including its music. Religious works did not constitute the sole output of the monastic scribes, however. Much ancient literature survived only because it was copied in some Frankish monastery. An interesting and important by-product of all this copying activity was the development of a new system of writing, the Carolingian miniscule. The simplicity and clarity of this script, with its rounded letter forms, soon gained it wide acceptance. From the miniscule developed the modern styles of handwriting and the lower case type in which this book is printed.

We may say, then, that the Carolingian Renaissance was largely a renewal of Latin education. If its immediate results were unimpressive, the importance of its long-range effects can hardly be overestimated. The intellectual activity fostered by its schools was eventually to produce the scholars and authors, the composers and musical theorists, to whom we owe a real revival of learning and culture in the eleventh and twelfth centuries. It is tempting to believe that Charlemagne foresaw, however dimly, the far-reaching results of his educational policy. Here, at any rate, he built something much more solid than his territorial empire. The deterioration of that empire was destined to be as rapid and as spectacular as its creation.

DISINTEGRATION OF THE CAROLINGIAN EMPIRE

Only a leader with the strength and energy of Charlemagne could hold together the many disparate elements in his vast empire, and perhaps not even he could have successfully repelled the new waves of barbarian invasion that were so soon to come. Certainly Charlemagne's son Louis the Pious (814–840) was not the man to preserve the empire. Well-educated and devout, but with no military or political skill, Louis was unable to cope with internal rebellion, foreign invasion, or the rivalry among his own sons. On his death in 840, the unfortunate practice of dividing lands among the male inheritors split the empire into three sections. Lothair (840–855), Louis's eldest son, became king of Italy and emperor; Louis the German (840–876) was king of the East Franks; and Charles the Bald (840–877), king of the West Franks. The Peace of Verdun in 843 settled the rival claims of the three brothers by leaving Lothair in possession of a narrow strip of territory between the two Frankish kingdoms. This highly variegated belt of land, which ran from the Low Countries south through Alsace, Burgundy, and Provence to Italy, made no political sense whatsoever. Its disintegration was inevitable; and it did, in fact, begin in 855, when once again a threefold division split the middle kingdom among Lothair's three sons. By 875 all three were dead, and the middle kingdom had disappeared forever. The western and eastern kingdoms, however, despite many vicissitudes, managed to maintain at least a nominal unity. Eventually, they developed into the countries we know as France and Germany.

While the Carolingian empire was thus disintegrating from within, it was also subject to attack from without. This time, the invasions of western Europe came by sea as well as by land and from all directions. We have already noted the Moslem conquest of Sicily and of Italy as far north as Rome in the middle of the ninth century; in addition, Moslem raiding expeditions terrorized the coastal regions of the Mediterranean for many years. At the same time, Viking raids along the Atlantic coast were spreading even greater terror and destruction. These men from the North were magnificent and fearless sailors; we know of their voyages to Iceland, Greenland, and North America. Plundering the comparative wealth of Europe, however, was easier and apparently more attractive. Coastal raids became a yearly event, and in 859 a Viking expedition even penetrated the Mediterranean as far east as Italy. Emboldened by the weakness of coastal defenses, the Vikings turned to systematic conquest of inland regions. Britain and Ireland were completely overrun, and London itself was sacked. The Seine river provided a convenient entry into France, and in 886 the Vikings besieged Paris, which was saved only by payment of an enormous ransom. Being heathen, the Vikings were no respecters of the clergy or of ecclesiastical property. Indeed, cathedrals and monasteries were particularly attractive objects for plunder. The lands they attacked were devastated and depopulated, and colonization was therefore easy. Thus the Northmen, or Normans, as the Franks called them, settled a large area in England north of the Thames and an even larger area in France on both sides of the Seine. The latter area became the duchy of Normandy, a nearly independent state whose dukes nevertheless acknowledged the sovereignty of the Frankish kings. As had happened so often in the past, the new barbarian invaders rather quickly adopted the customs, religion, and language of the lands they had conquered and settled. Early in the tenth century, the Normans ceased to threaten the rest of France, though they had not yet lost their taste for military expeditions. The eleventh century saw the establishment of Norman principalities in both Sicily and southern Italy. In this century occurred too the Normans' climactic exploit in western Europe, the conquest of England under William the Conqueror, Duke of Normandy, in 1066.

While the Vikings were bringing death and destruction to the western shores of Charlemagne's empire, its land frontiers to the east were also under attack. Northmen from eastern Scandinavia (Sweden) had crossed the Baltic and, using the same invasion techniques as their western confreres, had pushed along the rivers into the plains of eastern Europe. Because Charlemagne had broken the power of the Avars, the Swedish invaders encountered only slight resistance. By the end of the ninth century, they had established themselves at Smolensk and Kiev on the Dnieper River and had extended their raids to the shores of the Black Sea. This brought them to the attention of the Byzantines, who called them, among other things, Russians (Rhos). The Russians were more of a threat to the Byzantine than to the Carolingian empire. It was this contact that eventually led to their conversion to the Eastern branch of Christianity and to the dominating influence of Byzantium on the religious and cultural life of Russia.

A much more serious threat to both Eastern and Western empires came at the close of the ninth century with the eruption of still another horde of Asiatic nomads. These were the Magyars, whom Europeans generally called Hungarians because of their supposed resemblance to the Huns. The Magyars followed the routes of their predecessors, leaving the usual devastation in their wake. After crossing the Danube, they moved south to the Adriatic and into Lombardy. The kingdom of the East Franks also was not spared, and the Magyars laid waste to Bavaria, the Rhine valley, and the northern Germanic provinces. Eventually the majority of the Magyars settled in the middle Danubian plains, where the Kingdom of Hungary emerged at the beginning of the eleventh century. Unlike other invaders, the Magyars retained their native language, but under their first great king, Stephen I (997–1038), they began to be Christianized. During the rest of the Middle Ages, Hungary remained one of the most important Christian kingdoms in central Europe.

These developments did not come to pass, however, until after the Magyar raids in the tenth century had contributed to the complete collapse of the old Carolingian empire. Lothair's middle kingdom, as we have seen, had long since disappeared. The Carolingian line in the east died out with Louis the Child (899–911), and dukes of the various Germanic provinces ruled as equal and independent sovereigns. In France, the situation was even more confused, although the Carolingian dynasty lasted longer there than elsewhere. The incompetence of Charles the Fat at the Viking siege of Paris led to his deposition in 887, and the Franks then elected Count Odo of Paris as their king. For a full century thereafter, the family of Odo contested the throne of France with the descendants of Charles the Bald. Finally, the death of the last Carolingian, Louis V (986–987), left a collateral relative of Odo in undisputed possession of the crown. This was Hugh Capet (987–996), the founder of the Capetian dynasty of French kings. By this time, however, France had been divided into a number of feudal states, whose leaders acknowledged—nominally—the sovereignty of the French kings while continuing to act as independent rulers. The king himself ruled only that small area around Paris known as the Ile de France.

Long before the last Carolingians disappeared, they had ceased to hold the title of Roman emperor. By the beginning of the tenth century, indeed, the title had become meaningless, for it brought little prestige and no power to the local princes who held it. The empire of Charlemagne had survived less than a century after his coronation, and by 950 even the imperial title had gone begging for a number of years. The utter collapse of military strength and political unity in western Europe seems to have produced a corresponding decline in the power and prestige of the papacy. At any rate, a series of weak and notoriously profligate popes brought the papacy to perhaps the lowest level of degradation in the history of western Christendom. To all appearances, then, Europe in the first half of the tenth century was in a state of complete chaos. Never had the present looked so dark or the future so hopeless. No one could have foreseen that the process of regeneration would be well under way before the century came to a close.

Three factors were of primary importance in bringing about this regeneration. The first was the revival of the imperial title in 962 with the coronation of Otto the Great. Otto had been King of Germany since 936 and in the intervening twenty-six years had asserted his authority—not always with complete success—over the various duchies in that kingdom. He had also forced the kings of Bohemia, Arles (Burgundy and Provence), and Italy to acknowledge him as their overlord. By thus acquiring actual or nominal control over the central portion of Charlemagne's empire, Otto clearly deserved the imperial title. This was not always true of his descendants or of the long succession of later emperors, who kept the title alive until 1806. The real authority of the Holy Roman Emperors, as they came to be called, lay not so much in the title itself as in their individual talents and forcefulness as military and political leaders. Nevertheless, the revived empire played an important role in the reconstruction of European civilization. One of the most immediate effects of its revival was the rehabilitation of the papacy. With Europe fragmented into dozens of small, nearly independent states, the popes had been unable to maintain their spiritual leadership, and church organization had disintegrated almost to the same extent as the Carolingian empire. Because the new emperors took the traditional position that the Church was a department of state under their supreme control, they were naturally concerned with strengthening the central authority of the papacy. To accomplish this end, they were not above deposing weak or uncooperative popes and securing the appointment of men of their own choosing. Once the strength of the papacy had been restored, however, the old conflict arose as to whether emperor or pope was the supreme authority. Eventually the papacy secured its independence of secular control and rose to new heights of both temporal and ecclesiastical power in the period of the Crusades.

It would be a mistake, however, to credit the rehabilitation of the papacy entirely to the revival of the Roman Empire. That impressive achievement would have been impossible if a powerful reform movement had not arisen within the church itself, for the condition of the papacy in the tenth century merely reflected the general decadence of religious life in western Europe. Bishops and abbots generally owed their positions to feudal lords and acted as feudal lords themselves. Buying ecclesiastical positions—the sin of simony—was commonplace. Many of the secular clergy—those living in the outside world rather than in a monastery—were married and sometimes bestowed church lands upon their children. Even the religious ideals of monastic life were nearly forgotten, and peasant labor on a monastery's estates often supported its inmates in relative comfort and luxury. Yet the credit for initiating reform goes largely to a single monastery, the great Benedictine abbey of Cluny. Founded in 910, Cluny was an independent monastery whose abbot, elected by the monks themselves, was answerable only to the pope. Being thus free of local control, Cluny could devote itself to the renewal of monastic ideals within its own walls. Its growing reputation eventually induced over three hundred other monasteries to become its affiliates, with priors chosen by the abbot of Cluny. The resulting organization, known as the Congregation of Cluny, became a powerful instrument of reform and was the second important factor contributing to the regeneration of Europe in the eleventh and succeeding centuries. But, powerful as it was, the Cluniac reform made little progress until it obtained the backing of the emperor Henry III (1039–56). Then, great strides were made in erasing the scandals of simony and clerical marriage and in reasserting the ecclesiastical authority of the popes. Even more important than these reforms, which were largely of an administrative nature, was the effect of Cluny on religious life at all levels of medieval society. Indeed, to the Cluniac reform must go most of the credit for the renewal of Christian ideals and the wave of religious fervor that swept over Europe in the eleventh and twelfth centuries. To this religious fervor, in turn, the modern world is indebted for many of the greatest monuments of medieval art, architecture, literature, and music.

The third factor contributing to the regeneration of western Europe was the peculiar military and political organization known as the feudal system. This statement may seem paradoxical, because many historians equate feudalism with the disintegration of the Carolingian empire. But feudalism was not the cause of that disintegration. Rather, it developed to fill the vacuum left by the disappearance of a strong central authority. Despite its faults, feudalism provided a workable form of government for the many small states into which Europe was fragmented in the tenth and eleventh centuries. Moreover, it greatly influenced many phases of life in the later Middle Ages and became a point of departure for the development of later forms of government. It is fitting, therefore, that we should conclude this survey of medieval history to A.D. 1000 with a brief description of feudal institutions.

As we have already noted, the decline of urban civilization led to the formation of an essentially agrarian society based on the manorial system. A manor was an estate supervised by a lord who derived his income from a wide variety of "contributions" imposed on the peasants living on the estate. The system seems to us sheer exploitation, but it worked because it provided the mass of the people with a measure of protection and a means of livelihood. By the end of the tenth century, the economic life of western Europe was based almost exclusively on the manorial system, and this, in turn, made possible the development and spread of feudalism. Manors became part of a feudal organization only when they were fiefs held by vassals of an overlord. Because they represent the two most fundamental aspects of feudalism, the terms *fief* and *vassal* require some explanation.

The basis of vassalage was the ceremony of homage, by which a man became the vassal of a lord. In theory, the two men thus accepted permanent bonds of friendship, loyalty, and support. The normal reward for becoming a vassal was an endowment of land—a fief—which the vassal ruled and for which he owed various services to his lord. If the fief were large, a duchy or county, for example, its holder became the lord of numerous subvassals holding smaller fiefs. The subvassals, in turn, received homage from those with still smaller holdings. It should be clear that vassalage in feudal times had none of the implications of slavery or abject servitude that later came to be associated with the term. Instead, it organized the ruling class, the aristocracy, in a network of personal relationships that extended from kings—who might be vassals of the Roman emperor—down to the landed gentry.

As might be expected, the success of feudal organization depended in large part on the personal qualities of individual lords and vassals, and its effects were both good and bad. One noteworthy achievement was the establishment of the principle of *primogeniture,* inheritance by the eldest son alone. This came about because fief holding was, in a sense, an administrative office that could not be divided. Once the principle was established, it put an end to the division of land among all a ruler's sons, the practice that had contributed so much to the dissolution of the Carolingian empire. A less desirable result of feudal organization was its extension to include members of the clergy. Many bishops and abbots were fief-holding vassals of local lords, to whom they naturally felt more obligation and allegiance than to the pope. Feudalization of the church thus weakened its centralized organization and became a major obstacle to the restoration of papal authority.

Ideally, feudalism should have brought a golden age of peace and harmony to western Europe. In practice, however, it produced almost constant warfare. Lords and vassals constituted both the aristocratic and the warrior class, and by training and inclination they came to regard war as the normal condition of life. Troops were readily available, for one of the chief obligations of a vassal was to provide his lord with a specified number of mounted soldiers, or knights. It is not surprising, therefore, that disputes over feudal obligations and rivalries between jealous lords should have become pretexts for the innumerable wars that gave the aristocracy most of its pleasure and much of its profit. The situation became so bad, indeed, that the church attempted, with imperfect success, to impose the so-called Truce of God—periods of the year and even certain days of the week when armed combat was forbidden. Not all wars, of course, were wholly without purpose or completely lacking in significant results. With help from the north, for example, the small Spanish kingdoms gradually expanded, pushing the Moslems ever farther south, until their final expulsion was achieved by Ferdinand and Isabella in 1492. The feudal military organization also made possible those magnificent adventures the Crusades, which temporarily brought the knighthood of Europe together under the banner of the Church.

For the most part, however, feudal warfare was limited to raiding expeditions into the enemy's territory and to small skirmishes in the neighborhood of his castles. Originally rather simple earthworks and a wooden tower surrounded by a moat, these castles developed into the elaborately fortified stone structures that, in different stages of decay, still dot the European countryside. For the upper levels of the aristocracy, at least, castles served as homes as well as military fortresses. Social activities within the castle, therefore, represent an important aspect of feudal life. War was primarily a summer sport; and, in the rare intervals of peace, tournaments provided an almost equally hazardous substitute. In winter, hunting was the chief outdoor activity, although in all seasons it ranked just below fighting in popularity. All hunting was done on horseback, with dogs for the larger game, such as stags and boars, or with hawks for smaller game and birds. Hawking, or falconry, was one of the few outdoor sports in which both gentlemen and ladies participated, and the many medieval books on the subject attest to their great enthusiasm for it. But not all pastimes could take place out of doors. Bad weather and the long winter nights of northern Europe forced medieval gentlemen to stay in their castles for at least some of their waking hours. The age afforded little entertainment beyond eating, drinking, and gambling; but occasionally, wandering minstrels appeared to sing their tales of heroic deeds. A growing taste for this sort of amusement was to have important results. Gradually, the aristocracy began to receive a better education and to enjoy the more refined pleasures. In the later Middle Ages, the courts and castles of the aristocracy became the chief centers for the cultivation of secular literature and music. This development, however, carries us far beyond the limit set for the close of the present chapter. It is now time, therefore, to return to the beginning of the Christian era for a more detailed study of the growth of the Church and the music that forms an essential part of its liturgy.

CHAPTER II

Christian Liturgy to A. D. 1000

The history of Western music, at least for the first thousand years of the Christian era, must of necessity be a history of the Christian liturgy. Although secular music of various sorts must have existed during this long period of time, almost none has been preserved. Only the chants of the Church remain. All of these chants were intended for use in the various rites and services—that is, the liturgy—of the Christian Church. Their history, therefore, forms part of the larger history of the liturgy as a whole. We must briefly survey that larger history if we are to understand the origin of the chant and the influences that shaped its further development.[1]

TO A.D. 300

Christianity began as an offshoot of the Jewish religion, and the first Christians attended both the synagogue services and their own private gatherings. It is not surprising, then, to find that the new sect retained many features of the Jewish liturgy, adapting them as needed to fit the new faith. We shall discuss aspects of these features when we consider the development of individual services in the Christian Church. From the musical point of view, the most important borrowings from the synagogue were the chanting of Bible readings and the solo singing of psalms with congregational responses. Even the Lord's Supper, we must remember, was celebrated within the context of a Jewish ceremonial meal; and in the elaborate ritual of the Passover observance we find elements that were converted into the Christian Communion service, the core of the later Mass.

In Palestine, the liturgy of the early Church continued to be celebrated in Aramaic, the language of Jesus himself. When the apostles began to carry the new religion farther afield, however, they naturally adopted Greek, the international language of the time. Even in Rome,

---

1. Much of the information presented in this chapter is drawn from the two books by Josef A. Jungmann that are listed in the Bibliography.

Greek continued to be the liturgical language of the Church for the first three centuries of its existence. Thus, for a time, Christianity enjoyed a linguistic unity that has never been recaptured.

Two types of services developed very quickly in the young church and were common to all Christian groups: the reenactment of the Lord's Supper—the Communion service or Eucharist—that later became the Western Mass; and meetings devoted to psalm singing, Scripture reading, and prayer. The latter were forerunners of what are now called collectively the Office, or the Canonical Hours. For convenience, we shall designate these two types of services by their later names, always remembering that these names were not in use during the first centuries of the Christian Church.

In both types of services the individual texts were not at first rigidly determined, and important prayers, such as the central thanksgiving of the Eucharist, might even be extemporized. Yet this freedom existed within basic patterns common to the Church as a whole. This is particularly true of the Mass, which has always tended toward a greater fixity of structure than the Offices. In this sense, then, we may speak of a kind of embryo liturgy during the first three centuries of the Christian era. In its subsequent history the liturgy has alternated between periods of consolidation and standardization marked by relative unity, and periods of growth and development marked by great diversity. The first such period of expansion began in the fourth century, concurrent with the changing attitude of the Roman Empire toward its Christian subjects.

DEVELOPMENT OF DIFFERENT LITURGIES

The unified liturgy, such as it was, of the early Church began to disappear shortly after A.D. 300. Perhaps the most important reason for the divergent paths that liturgical development followed was the new attitude of the Roman Empire toward Christianity. During the rule of Diocletian (284–305) the campaign for the suppression of Christianity had been carried on with particular severity. Enforcement of the imperial decrees lapsed, however, during the civil war following Diocletian's abdication, and with Constantine's ascendance the situation changed entirely. According to the legend, Constantine was preparing to do battle with Maxentius, his rival for imperial power, when he saw a blazing cross in the sky with the motto IN HOC SIGNO VINCES (By this sign thou shalt conquer). Resisting immediate conversion, Constantine nevertheless had the sign placed on his banner, and his troops went into battle with the name of Christ on their shields. Constantine defeated Maxentius in 312 and the next year issued the famous Edict of Milan, which granted freedom of worship to all Christians and recognized the Church as an institution with the right to own property. But Constan-

Episodes from Constantine's life: his dream, his victory, and as Roman Emperor. From a ninth-century illumination (Paris, Bibliothèque Nationale).

tine's interest in Christianity did not stop there. He gave Christians positions of trust in public office, brought up his children in the faith and was himself finally baptized. After he defeated Licinius, his coemperor in the East, Constantine built a new capital, Constantinople, on the site of ancient Byzantium. Under the impetus provided by Constantine, Christianity took hold rapidly and achieved official recognition when Theodosius (ruled 379–395) proclaimed it the state religion and forbade all pagan rites.

Until the time of Constantine, then, Christian religious observances had been expressly forbidden throughout the Roman Empire; and even though the attitudes of civil officials varied from time to time and place to place, gatherings of Christians were always viewed with alarm. Christian services, therefore, had to be kept as simple and unobtrusive as possible. During the fourth century, all of this changed. The increasing number of Christians, the holding of services in large buildings, and the establishment of Christianity as the state religion, all contributed to an elaboration of liturgical forms and ceremonial procedures. The great urban centers—Rome, Antioch, Alexandria, and Constantinople (Byzantium)—developed their own rites out of the common liturgical practices of the primitive Church. As these rites spread from the urban centers to surrounding areas and as they became more elaborate, the need for standardization grew. Liturgical texts, with directions for their accompanying ritual action, were written down and gradually disseminated. Gradually, too, vernacular languages—Latin, Syriac, and Coptic—replaced Greek as the language of worship in much of the Empire. Thus emerged the great liturgies of the early Christian Church, their regional identity underlining and even contributing to the declining political unity of the Roman Empire.

From the time of Diocletian, the task of governing had become too much for one man, and a coemperor frequently ruled the eastern part of the Empire. This division reinforced the natural rivalry between the Latin West and the Greek East, a rivalry that became ever more pronounced as Constantinople increased in wealth and power at the expense of Rome. Here, in fact, were laid the foundations of the schism that ultimately divided Eastern from Western Christianity.

Still another factor that influenced the development of divergent liturgies in the fourth century was the spread of heretical views—doctrines that differed from the teachings of the Church. As early as the second century, the Church had had to deal with heretical sects influenced by Gnosticism, a philosophical, ethical, and religious movement of many peculiar forms but unified by the central doctrine that knowledge (*gnosis*) freed the initiate from the "clutch of matter." Later heresies produced more serious effects. In the fifth century, for example, the spread of Monophysitism—the belief that the divine and human in Christ formed but one composite nature—was directly connected with the adoption of the vernacular tongues in Antioch and Alexandria.

By far the most influential heresy of the fourth century, however, was Arianism, named for Arius, a priest of Alexandria. Arius taught that Christ as the Son of God was a created being—not truly God, not truly man—who could only be worshiped as a secondary divinity. The rapid spread of Arianism so alarmed the Church that Constantine summoned all the bishops of Christendom to a meeting at Nicaea in 325. This first general council in the history of the Church forcefully condemned Arianism and prepared a statement of faith that, with some later additions and amendments, became known as the Nicene Creed, the Credo of the Roman Mass. The heresy persisted, however, and was carried by missionaries to the Goths in Germany. Both Visigoths and Ostrogoths were thus converted to an unorthodox Christianity, a matter of considerable consequence when parts of the Empire came under Gothic rule.

DEVELOPMENT OF WESTERN LITURGIES

The liturgies of the Latin West must be our primary concern here, for in them developed the chants that we find—centuries later—in the oldest surviving manuscripts of Western music. As in the East, the fourth century saw the emergence of a number of different Western liturgies, which may have begun even earlier to develop distinctive traits. Unlike

With Constantine's conversion, it became possible for the Christian church to erect imposing buildings for worship. An example of an early basilica may be seen at Santa Maria Maggiore in Rome.

the Eastern liturgies, however, those in the West all made use of the same language—Latin. In spite of occasional efforts to promote services in the vernacular, Latin remained the ritual language of the Roman Church until the Vatican Councils of 1962–65 authorized services in modern tongues. As we have seen, however, Latin was not the original liturgical language in Rome itself, and Latin services seem to have appeared first in North Africa toward the end of the second century. Indeed, the late introduction of the Latin Mass in Rome may have been at least partly responsible for the development of other Latin liturgies in the northern and western provinces of the Empire where Greek was less well known.

Broadly speaking, the Western liturgies divide into two families: the Roman-African and the Gallic, with the latter further subdivided into Ambrosian, Hispanic (Mozarabic), Celtic, and Gallican proper. Since the Roman liturgy was eventually adopted for most of the Western Church, its history must be our chief concern. First, however, we must discuss briefly the Gallic liturgies, for they influenced both the musical and textual development of the Roman Mass.

That the Gallic liturgies do not seem to have emanated from important centers of the West—as the Eastern liturgies did from Alexandria, Antioch, and Constantinople—has puzzled church historians. It has been suggested, however, that Milan may have been one such center, producing a liturgy known as Ambrosian, and influencing the formation of both the Hispanic and the Gallican rites. This theory, though unproved and perhaps unprovable, is attractive, for it explains many of the Oriental usages, particularly those from Antioch, that appear in the Gallic rites and distinguish them as a group from the Roman. Quite properly, then, we may begin our brief discussion of the various Gallic rites with the Ambrosian liturgy of Milan.

As a favorite residence of the emperors during the fourth century, Milan was a city in which Eastern and Western customs met and mingled. Some of her bishops had come from the Eastern Church, for example St. Ambrose's predecessor Auxentius (355–374), originally of Cappadocia, a region north of Syria in Asia Minor. It is not surprising, therefore, that the Milanese liturgy should display a mixture of Oriental and Latin elements. In fact, some of the Latin forms are older than those now in use in the Roman liturgy and are at least as old as elements brought in from the East.

Just how much St. Ambrose had to do with the formulation of the liturgy that bears his name remains an open question. To the general historian, Ambrose is known primarily as an ecclesiastical statesman who numbered emperors among his parishioners. Born in 340, Ambrose was the son of a high Roman official and was trained for a civil career. He was serving Valentinian I as a provincial governor in Milan and was not yet baptized when he was chosen bishop on the death of Auxentius in 374. Ambrose served the Church well until his death in 397, strengthening it against both pagan and heretical beliefs and asserting its supremacy in religious matters over the emperor himself. Moreover, on the testimony of St. Augustine, Ambrose was directly responsible for introducing certain Oriental practices into the Western liturgy. Bishop Auxentius had been of the Arian sect, as was the Empress Justina, who persecuted the orthodox Christians after Ambrose succeeded to the bishopric. To sustain his followers in this time of trial, Ambrose, according to Augustine, introduced the custom of singing hymns and psalms "after the manner of the Eastern Church." Apparently the Eastern manner of singing psalms was antiphonal—that is, with two choirs chanting the psalm verses alternately—and the practice quickly spread throughout Western Christendom.

Even more important was the practice of singing hymns, because these songs of praise introduced new poetic texts into the liturgy rather than being merely a new method of performance (see Chapter IV). As St. Augustine's statement implies, hymns had long been cultivated in the East and were to play an important role in the Mass of the Byzantine rite. Inspired by the Eastern practice, Ambrose apparently created new hymns in Latin to unite his followers in praise of the Lord. In the West, hymns never became an essential part of the Mass in its officially prescribed form, but were introduced instead into the daily Offices. We shall have occasion to return to the hymns of St. Ambrose when we consider the development of Latin liturgical poetry. For the present, we need only remark that, although only four of the many hymn texts ascribed to Ambrose are now agreed upon as authentic, these four are sufficient to establish him securely as the founder of Latin hymnody.

Saint Ambrose, an eighth-century stucco tondo (circular portrait) (Museo at Sant'Ambrogio, Milan).

If we know little about Ambrose's contributions to the liturgy that bears his name, we know even less about the music of his time. The earliest preserved collection of so-called Ambrosian chant dates from the twelfth century, and we cannot safely assume that the chant melodies had remained unchanged from the time of Ambrose. Nevertheless, these later Ambrosian chants represent a tradition that has continued to exist throughout the Christian era. Of all the Gallic liturgies, only the Ambrosian has survived.

HISPANIC OR MOZARABIC LITURGY

The liturgy of the Iberian peninsula (modern Spain and Portugal) is commonly known as Mozarabic, from the designation of Christians living under Moslem rule as Mozarabs. Various objections to this name, as well as to the alternative Visigothic, have been raised. To meet these objections, recent studies have proposed Hispanic as the most appropriate designation for the liturgy developed in Spain and Portugal. It is this term, therefore, that we shall use here.

The Hispanic liturgy remained in use until late in the eleventh century, when, as the Moors were gradually driven from northern Spain, the newly established monarchies imposed the Roman rite. In 1071, the "superstition of Toledo" was officially suppressed throughout Christian Spain; and in 1085, after the recapture of Toledo by King Alfonso VI, the Roman rite was instituted in the ancient capital of Spain. This move did not go unopposed, however, and six Toledo churches received permission to retain the old liturgy. It also persisted for some time, presumably, in the Moorish parts of Spain. (Final defeat of the Moors and their expulsion from Spain did not occur until the capture of Granada in 1492.) Nevertheless, the Hispanic rite must have lost favor rather rapidly, for in the late fifteenth century the great Cardinal Ximenes designated a chapel of the cathedral of Toledo in which the ancient liturgy should be preserved. It is thanks to Cardinal Ximenes, therefore, that the Hispanic liturgy—somewhat adulterated, to be sure—has survived to the present day.

The Hispanic rite as established and printed by Ximenes in 1500 shows a heavy infiltration of Roman elements. Older texts, however, have enabled scholars to reconstruct the liturgy as it was before the Moorish invasion of Spain. Unfortunately, this has not been possible for most of the chant. The little we know about the origins of Hispanic chant suggests that much of it was developed in the cities of Toledo, Seville, and Saragossa during the sixth and seventh centuries. In Moorish times, Cordova also became an important musical center.

Although a number of manuscripts from the ninth to the eleventh centuries preserve the Hispanic chant, they are unfortunately written in a notation that does not indicate intervals and hence cannot now be read. (See Chapter III for the development of notation.) Of the large number of Hispanic chants, only twenty-one have been found "transcribed" into a later, and legible, notation. The absence of later chantbooks with a more precise notation bears witness to the rapidity with which the Hispanic liturgy must have disappeared after its official suppression in the eleventh century. As a result, a unique lacuna exists in the history of liturgical music. We possess the musical repertory of an important Western liturgy, but that repertory remains tantalizingly unrealized.

CELTIC LITURGY

The Celtic liturgy need not detain us long. Apparently it originated in the monastic institutions founded in Ireland by St. Patrick (d. 461) and was also in use, in one form or another, in Scotland, parts of England, and perhaps Brittany. During the sixth and seventh centuries, moreover, the missionary zeal of the Irish monks led them to move eastward through Europe, establishing monasteries as they went. The most important of these monasteries, for the music historian, at least, was St. Gall in Switzerland. Although Irish monasticism imposed a severe discipline, its organization was rather loose and, therefore, displeasing to ecclesiastical authorities. Largely through the efforts of Pope Gregory the Great, Benedictine monasticism replaced the Irish, and the Roman rite replaced the Celtic. This happened even in the British Isles after Gregory, in 596, sent Augustine of Canterbury with a group of Benedictines to convert the Anglo-Saxons of eastern England. The increasing influence of both the Anglo-Saxons and the papacy itself soon led to the disappearance of the Celtic liturgy. The very nature of that liturgy may also have contributed to its rapid demise. From the few documents available, it seems to have been a rather incongruous mixture of Hispanic, Gallican, Roman, and Oriental elements that failed to achieve a distinctive character of its own. No music associated with the Celtic liturgy seems to have survived.

GALLICAN LITURGY

In contrast to the Celtic liturgy, it has been said, the Gallican "shows a magnificent independence and exclusiveness."[2] Moreover, the Gallican Mass in particular "shows a definite leaning towards splendor and ceremonial."[3] While these characteristics may have been introduced initially to impress and convert the still barbarous Franks, they must have suited the temperament of the people well. In its relatively short span of life, the Gallican liturgy developed a rich multiplicity of detail and a ceremonial splendor far removed from the "antique severity" of the Roman rite.

By a quirk of fate, the Gallican liturgy proper became the most influential and, therefore, the most important of all the Gallic liturgies. It flourished in the kingdom of the Franks (see Map 1, p. 7) from the time of Clovis, the first Merovingian king (d. 511), until its suppression by the first Carolingians, Pepin and his illustrious son Charlemagne, in the later years of the eighth century. Much has been made of the political motive behind this suppression: the desire of the Carolingians to make the Church a powerful unifying force throughout their empire. The reasons for the disappearance of the Gallican liturgy as an independent entity are probably not that simple. Anglo-Saxon monks and scholars, such as St. Boniface, who supplanted the Irish as missionaries to the Franks and Alamans in the seventh and eighth centuries, brought with them the Roman rite, which they left firmly established in the monasteries they founded. Both Pepin and Charlemagne seem to have genuinely preferred the Roman liturgy, and this preference may well reflect the growing respect for the authority and prestige of Rome as the center of Western Christendom. Furthermore, lacking important metropolitan

2.   J. A. Jungmann, *The Mass,* 1, p. 45.
3.   Ibid., p. 48.

centers to regulate and standardize its forms, the Gallican liturgy developed so many local variants and customs that it became distasteful to ecclesiastical authorities. Thus the time was ripe for supplanting the Gallican liturgy when Pepin (751–768) began his vigorous support of the Roman rite.

The Gallican liturgy, like the Celtic, disappeared before the development of musical notation could record and preserve its music. Nevertheless, it wrought such profound changes in the imported Roman rite that the eminent historian of the Mass, J. A. Jungmann, could discuss in detail the "Romano-Frankish Mass as a new basic type."[4] In the eleventh century, this new Mass-type even displaced the older Roman rite in Rome itself. Before we can discuss this astonishing development, however, we must go back to the early stages of the Roman-African liturgy.

THE ROMAN RITE FROM THE THIRD TO THE SIXTH CENTURY

The early history of the Latin liturgy in Rome remains almost completely unknown. Most of the surviving documents, particularly for the Mass, come from Frankish scribes of the eighth and ninth centuries and are heavily overlaid with Gallican elements. By comparative study of these various documents, scholars have attempted to reconstruct the earlier forms of the Roman rite but without much success for the period before the time of Gregory the Great (590–604).

The transition from Greek to Latin as the liturgical language of Rome seems to have occurred gradually during the third and fourth centuries. In the process, a major change of attitude toward the ritual of the Mass becomes evident. Within a fixed outline or framework, the earlier liturgy, as we have seen, had allowed great freedom with regard to individual forms. Now, however, the individual forms themselves became rigidly fixed. This prescribing of set forms seems to have originated with the prayers of the celebrant (at first, the celebrant of the Eucharist was always a bishop assisted by his priests and deacons; later on, priests were authorized to preside alone). It involved both those prayers that were the same in every Mass (Ordinary) and those that changed according to the festival or season of the Church year (Proper). Later, the texts of readings and chants were prescribed with equal rigidity. The strict regulation of every detail in the services for the entire year, perhaps an expression of the Roman genius for organization, has remained characteristic of the Roman liturgy almost to the present time. Again and again, however, the rigidity of the Roman rite has come into conflict with the efforts of other peoples to adapt and embellish the Mass to suit

4.   Ibid., pp. 92–103.

their own needs and tastes. Much of medieval music, indeed, is the direct result of those efforts.

In contrast to the Mass, the other regular services—that is, the Divine Office—never achieved the same rigidity of structural outline or fixity of individual forms. These services seem to have originated in private gatherings of Christians who met together for scripture reading, psalm singing, and prayer. To these activities, as we have seen, St. Ambrose added antiphonal performance of the psalms and the singing of hymns. For several centuries, many of these services were not publicly celebrated in church but retained their private character and, hence, their relative formlessness. The greatest impetus toward both a more standardized procedure and the daily observance of the Offices came with the rise of monasticism, which therefore requires brief discussion.

When Theodosius (379–395) established Christianity as the state religion, he inadvertently sparked the great development of monasticism that was to transform the religious life of western Europe. In meeting the needs of a vast number of Roman citizens who had become instant Christians by decree, the Church could no longer satisfy the more zealous members of the faith. Many of the latter, following the example set by St. Anthony in Egypt early in the fourth century, renounced the world in favor of a hermit's life devoted to meditation, prayer, and mortification of the flesh. Although the hermit's lot was not an easy one, particularly in the more rigorous European climate, the movement gained ground to such an extent that soon nearly every cave had its her-

Prayer and manual labor were at the center of the monk's life, as represented in these eleventh-century manuscript illuminations.

mit. As their numbers increased, it became evident that, in order to in-
sure physical survival, religious communities would have to be established. Various methods of organization were tried, resulting,
eventually, in the monastic system as we know it. Thus the word monk
(*monachus*)—which originally and literally meant one living alone, a
hermit—came to designate one of a group living together under one
roof, a monastery, and sharing the duties of daily life.

Although numerous religious communities and even monasteries
were in existence in western Europe by the end of the fifth century,
strict organization of monastic life was the achievement of St. Benedict
(480–543), the founder of the Benedictine order and, in a sense, of Western monasticism itself. The career of St. Benedict, indeed, neatly sum-
marizes the early development of monasticism. He was born of a noble
family in Nursia and was sent to Rome for his education. Dismayed by
the life he found there, Benedict, like so many people of that time, became a hermit. He lived in a cave near Subiaco for several years during
which his growing reputation for holiness attracted many disciples. As
the spiritual leader of a religious community, Benedict had to concern
himself with regulating that community's life. In about 520, he and
some of his followers left Subiaco and founded the famous monastery at
Monte Cassino. Here, during the next decade, he composed the set of
regulations known as the Rule of St. Benedict that was to establish the
pattern for Western monastic life for centuries.

Benedict's rule concerned itself with all phases of monastic life, both
its religious observances and the manual labor by which the community
supplied its physical needs. For the music historian, the most important
aspect of the rule was its establishment of the Divine Office, the eight
services that were performed daily in addition to the Mass. Here, for the
first time, we find a written description of the complete series of Hours
as they would be observed for centuries. The Office will be discussed
more fully in Chapter IV; but we should note here the order of the
Hours in Benedict's Rule: Matins occurred sometime after midnight;
Lauds followed at daybreak; Prime at the first hour, or 6 A.M.; Terce at
9; Sext at noon; None at 3; Vespers in the early evening; and Compline
before retiring at night.

Although the Hours established for the Benedictines became standard
for the entire Western Church, the contents of individual Offices continued to vary considerably. Designed for monastic use, the Benedictine
services did not always meet the needs of the secular churches or prove
agreeable to the secular clergy.[5] As a result, two types of Offices developed: the monastic and the secular. Still further variants in the internal

5.   The ecclesiastical use of the word *secular* may prove confusing. Rather than being the
     opposite of sacred, its meaning here is "living in the world." The secular clergy live
     in the world, while the regular clergy have renounced the world to live under
     monastic rules (*regulae*).

A portrait of St. Benedict writing his Rule for monks, from an eleventh-century Montecassino manuscript.

structure of the Office appear in the later Middle Ages with the rise of new religious orders, such as the Franciscans and Dominicans. For the most part, the existing differences between the secular Offices and the various monastic forms merely involve the number and order of individual items, not the items themselves. Therefore, when we come to consider their musical contents, we may concern ourselves primarily with the secular Offices as they exist today.

To return to our historical survey, then, we may note that the sixth century saw the essential structure of the Roman liturgy established for both Offices and Mass. The latter in particular was to undergo considerable further development and expansion in the next four centuries. Before we can follow that development, however, we must consider the role of Pope Gregory I, Gregory the Great, in creating the chant that bears his name.

GREGORY THE GREAT

Tradition has long credited Pope Gregory I (590–604) with being chiefly responsible for developing the chant of the Roman Church. Specifically, he is said to have established a papal choir, the *schola cantorum* (school of singers), and to have composed a large part of the Roman chant. In a pictorial embellishment of this latter activity, Gregory was often shown receiving the chants from the Holy Spirit in the form of a dove. Unfortunately, Gregory did not begin to receive credit for these achievements until nearly 300 years after his death, and in large part that credit has now been taken from him. Yet so persistent a tradition—one that gave the name Gregorian to the entire chant repertory of the Roman

Church—must have had some foundation in truth. A glance at Gregory's career as a whole may suggest the part he probably did play with regard to the music of the Church.

Gregory was born into a noble and wealthy Roman family and received a good education in Latin but not in Greek. He apparently intended to follow a political career and by 573 had become prefect of Rome. Within a short time, however, he resigned his position, gave away his inheritance, and founded a Benedictine monastery in his home. His political and administrative talents had evidently been remarked by the Church, for in about 578 he was ordained a deacon at Rome and thereafter was sent as papal ambassador to Constantinople. There Gregory remained for about seven years before returning to his monastery as abbot. Again the Church called him to a position of importance, this time the highest, and he became Pope Gregory I.

The achievements of Gregory as pope are too many and too varied to be recounted here. It must suffice to note that under him the papacy became for the first time a world power and the supreme authority of Western Christendom. Up to this time, the idea that the Bishop of Rome, as the direct successor of St. Peter, should be the head of all bishops had remained little more than a theory. It was never accepted by the bishops of the Eastern Church, one cause of the eventual schism between the two branches. Under Gregory, however, the superiority of the papacy in the West was both vigorously asserted and successfully enforced. To maintain its universal authority, the papacy needed sound financial backing, and Gregory devoted much care to the efficient management of its property. In addition to supervising the conduct of international affairs and administering the papal estates, Gregory found time to write so voluminously that he became known as one of the Four Doctors—that is, teachers—of the Church. (The other three were St. Ambrose, St. Augustine, and St. Jerome.) It is not without reason, then, that Gregory is known to historians in general as the first great pope of the Middle Ages.

With all his multifarious activities, it is remarkable that Gregory should have concerned himself with the music of the Church. It is characteristic of his amazing attention to detail, however, that he did. Yet Gregory seems not to have been interested in music for its own sake. Rather he sought, and this too is characteristic, to regulate and standardize its use as an adjunct of the Roman liturgy. Gregory did not found the papal choir. One had been in existence for over a hundred years. In other churches, however, much of the singing was being done by priests and deacons, who, Gregory felt, were cultivating their voices at the expense of their other duties. To remedy this situation, he directed that Roman seminaries should train prospective choir singers, and he established orphanages for the same purpose.

With regard to the liturgy and its chant, Gregory probably played the

St. Gregory the Great, the most influential of early medieval popes, prompted by the Holy Spirit as he writes. From a thirteenth-century fresco at Subia (Foto Biblioteca Vaticana).

part of the efficient administrator interested in regulating and organizing the ritual of the Roman Church. In doing so, he was merely carrying on the work begun by his predecessors and continued by his successors in the papacy. If Gregory composed any chants at all, which is unlikely, they could only comprise a small fraction of the total plainchant repertory.

Perhaps Gregory's greatest contribution to the dissemination and eventual domination of the Roman rite was his establishment of papal influence and authority in Britain. When, at Gregory's bidding, Augustine of Canterbury and forty other Benedictines went to England in 596, they must have carried with them liturgical books that followed the current Roman practice. None of these books survives, but the Roman rite itself was thenceforward firmly established in England. From there, as we have already noted, Anglo-Saxon missionaries carried it back to the continent in the North and East Frankish territories. We may regard the adoption of the Roman rite by the Carolingian kings in the second half of the eighth century as a final triumph of Gregory's statesmanship.

For his nobility of purpose, his practical common sense, and his accomplishments as writer, diplomat, and administrator, Gregory well deserves the epithet Gregory the Great. It is therefore fitting, whatever his actual contributions to music may have been, that his name should have been perpetuated by calling the music of the Roman rite Gregorian Chant.

ROMANO-FRANKISH LITURGY
TO A.D. 1000

In order to understand the intrusion of Gallican elements into the Roman liturgy, we must look briefly at the various types of liturgical books that came into use during the seventh and eighth centuries. It was by means of these books that the essentials of the Roman rite were brought to the Frankish kingdom.

Two factors determined the character and contents of these early liturgical books. First of all, they contained only the great festival services as celebrated by the pope. These services, conducted with particular pomp and splendor, obviously required modification for use in smaller churches with fewer participating clergy. Nevertheless, their influence was very great. Because their details were written down, they provided fixed liturgical arrangements that could be transmitted to other lands.

The second factor determining the contents of liturgical books was their division according to the various performing persons or groups. Thus the *sacramentary* was for the celebrating bishop or priest. Normally it contained only the texts that changed from feast to feast. The unvarying texts were either written separately or were presumed to be memorized. Readings were originally done from the Bible itself; but later, special "lectionaries"—books containing the Epistles and Gospels—were assembled. There were also books of directions (*ordo,* pl. *ordines*) that prescribed in detail the order and the ritual action of the ceremony.

Texts that were to be sung were assembled in separate books. Originally the choirbook for the Mass was called an *Antiphonary,* because it contained only those texts that were sung antiphonally during processions at the entrance, the offertory, and the Communion. A special book, the *cantatorium,* contained solo chants that were sung with simple congregational responses after readings. When the choir took over the responses of these chants—which we know as the Gradual and Alleluia—they too became part of the Antiphonary. From the first of these responsorial chants, the book of music for the Mass later became known as the *Gradual,* the term in use today. Many medieval chantbooks for the Mass still bear the title *Antiphonary,* however, and must not be confused with antiphonaries that contain the chants for the Office. These latter books, which were always kept separate from those for the Mass, were originally divided into different types according to the same general principles—antiphonaries for entirely choral chants, and responsorials for chants involving soloists. Later, all of the Office chants were often brought together in a single antiphonary.

We may now proceed to examine the consequences of Pepin's and Charlemagne's importation of liturgical books from Rome. As far as we know, the chantbooks contained only the texts that were to be sung and were wholly without musical notation. To transmit the melodies, therefore, singers who knew them also had to be imported. From the liturgical point of view, the most important books from Rome were the sacramentaries. Because these books included only the services for special feasts at which the pope himself officiated, they had to be adapted to local circumstances and expanded to include the complete Church year. When Pope Hadrian I sent Charlemagne the so-called Gregorian sacramentary in 785–786, for example, it did not even contain the normal (nonfestival) Sunday Masses. Charlemagne gave Alcuin, the English director of the palace school, the task of supplementing and completing this sacramentary. In fulfilling his task, Alcuin naturally drew on local materials, and thus the Roman liturgy began to incorporate Gallican elements from the very moment of its importation into the Frankish kingdom.

Historians now tend to discount the importance of the so-called Carolingian Renaissance. If we take the term in its widest sense, however, as including both the intellectual activity sponsored by the early Carolingians and the political organization that was to become the Holy Roman Empire, its influence on the further development of both the liturgy and music of the Church can scarcely be overestimated. At any rate, there seems to be no other way to account for the fact that, during several centuries after the death of Charlemagne (814), the growth of the Roman liturgy took place primarily on Franco-German soil. Frankish territory also saw the origin of polyphony and its development to a position of preeminence. It cannot be mere coincidence that the history of music between 800 and 1300 is almost entirely concerned with events occurring in what had been the empire of Charlemagne.

Jungmann has remarked that two "peculiarities which must have been anchored in the very temperament of the new people" were particularly influential in transforming the Roman Mass when it reached Frankish soil: "a predilection for the dramatic and a delight in endlessly long prayers."[6] Although Jungmann was primarily speaking of the Mass as a whole, we shall find again and again that musical developments confirm his observation. Music played an increasingly important role in the dramatic ceremonial of the Mass. Simple congregational singing gave way to elaborate chants for soloists and trained choir. And the addition of both music and words greatly extended existing parts of the Mass. In the twelfth century, further elaboration in the form of polyphony proved that a delight in endless length was not confined to prayers. Details of these developments will provide the subject matter for several later chapters.

If the reasons for the intrusion of Gallican elements into the Roman Mass are obvious, the displacement of the local liturgy in Rome itself by its Gallicized version is more difficult to explain. Apparently the causes

6.   Jungmann, *The Mass,* 1, p. 77.

are to be sought in the contrast between the demoralized state of Rome in the tenth century and the political power enjoyed by the Holy Roman Empire. Manuscript production in Italy had practically ceased, for instance, and the need for new liturgical books was supplied by monastic scribes in the North. From the middle of the tenth century we have records of German Mass books being brought to Italy, and in 998 Pope Gregory V arranged to have a sacramentary sent to him from the abbey of Reichenau. The frequent visits to Rome of such Holy Roman Emperors as Otto the Great (962–973) provided many opportunities for the transfer of manuscripts, and also for German clerics to participate in Roman religious services. In one case, the direct intervention of a German ruler changed the shape of the Roman liturgy for all time. At his imperial coronation in Rome in 1014, Henry II requested that the Credo be sung in the Mass as had been done for some time in the North. From that time on, at least for Sundays and special feasts, the Credo formed an essential part of the Roman Mass.

Once the Romano-Frankish liturgy had been adopted in Rome itself, the Western Church again enjoyed a degree of liturgical unity. One must not, however, overemphasize the extent of that unity. The tenth-century liturgical books from the North outline the structure of the Mass fundamentally as we know it today, but the details of that structure were by no means fixed. Keeping the elements inherited from the old Roman sacramentaries, countries, cities, and even individual churches developed their own variations and elaborations of the basic structure. These elaborations then crystallized into clearly distinguishable customs or *uses,* as they are called. Such, for example, was the Use of Sarum (the diocese of Salisbury), which became standard throughout much of England. The Sarum Use disappeared with the Reformation, but another special use, that of Lyons in France, has persisted—with modifications, of course—to the present day. Not until the liturgical reforms instigated by the Council of Trent in the mid-sixteenth century did the Use of Rome win almost universal acceptance in the Catholic Church. And in determining that use, a conscious effort was made to return to liturgical forms as they had developed during the first thousand years of Christianity.

THE CHANT BETWEEN
A.D. 800 AND 1000

Although we can determine with considerable accuracy the Gallican contributions to the Roman liturgy during the ninth and tenth centuries, we are in a much less favorable position with regard to musical matters. When Pepin and Charlemagne imported the Roman rite, antiphonaries for both the Mass and Offices must have been brought from

Rome along with other liturgical books. These antiphonaries, however, can have contained only the chant texts, for a musical notation had yet to be developed. And even if notation began much earlier than we now believe, its first forms remained unreadable for anyone who did not already know the melody (see Chapter III). Thus, along with the liturgical books, it was necessary to import singers who knew the melodies of the Roman chant. Singing schools were established, of which perhaps the most famous were at St. Gall and Metz. Even during Pepin's reign (751–768), the choir of Metz cathedral was regarded as the equal of the Roman schola cantorum.

The introduction of Roman chant, however, did not proceed without difficulties. Roman singers were not always tactful in concealing their contempt for the singing of the northern barbarians, much to the annoyance of the latter. Moreover, the fame of the northern singing schools aroused the envy and rivalry of the Romans. In such a situation, and with no written music to establish authenticity, the original Roman chant can scarcely have remained unchanged.

It has long been traditional to marvel at the faithfulness with which Gregorian Chant was transmitted orally for many centuries before the development of musical notation. As singers are not noted for their adherence even to written notes, belief in that tradition seems somewhat naïve. Actually, the earliest manuscripts with musical notation are from the ninth and tenth centuries, and none comes from Rome or even Italy. All of them originated in the North. The remarkable uniformity of later Gregorian Chant is in all probability due to the same dissemination of manuscripts that eventually carried the Romano–Frankish liturgy back to Rome itself. The uniformity of the chant, incidentally, has also been overemphasized. In two versions of the same melody coming from widely separated places, similarities may greatly outweigh the differences, but differences do exist. As with the liturgy as a whole, certain types of variants are regional or national characteristics. Others are of a more restricted or even local nature. Recognizable Sarum chants accompany the Sarum Use, and minor melodic variants have identified chants from Notre Dame in Paris.

The most striking departures from traditional Gregorian Chant melodies occur in a series of manuscripts originating in Rome between the eleventh and thirteenth centuries. Considerable controversy has raged over the significance of these manuscripts, but it is now generally agreed that they represent a much older Roman tradition.[7] Their contents correspond to the oldest liturgical sources and lack the feasts added after the eighth century. It is logical to assume, therefore, that their music approximated the chant in Rome as it was before being transplanted to the Carolingian empire. These manuscripts have received neither the li-

---

7.   See Robert J. Snow, "The Old-Roman Chant," in Apel, GC, pp. 484–505.

turgical nor musical study they deserve. Preliminary investigations of the music, however, confirm the supposition that it is an archaic form of the chant as we know it today. This Old-Roman Chant, as it is now called, stubbornly persisted in some Roman churches after the Gallicized chant from the North had prevailed everywhere else. One of the interesting aspects of the Old-Roman Chant is that a number of its Alleluias have verses in Greek. This suggests another influence at work in forming the musical repertory of the Church during its first thousand years. The transition from Greek to Latin as the liturgical language of the West was by no means instantaneous or complete. At first, some parts of the service were performed in both languages, and even today the readings of a solemn papal Mass are done in Greek and Latin. Moreover, later additions to the liturgy came from the East, either with or without translation into Latin. Examples are the *Kyrie eleison* (Lord, have mercy) in Greek, introduced at an early period, and the *Agnus Dei* (Lamb of God), introduced in the seventh century with the text translated into Latin. Numerous chants were created after Greek models, and some were even sung in Greek or in both Greek and Latin.

Greek—or, more properly, Byzantine—influence was inevitable, given the power and importance of the Byzantine emperors after the collapse of the Western Roman empire. That influence was exerted primarily through the constant flow of Eastern clerics to positions of importance in the West and even to the papacy itself. The flow reached such proportions in the seventh and eighth centuries, indeed, that the Roman liturgy was in serious danger of being Orientalized.[8] According to Jungmann, the counterinfluence that saved the Roman liturgy was, curiously enough, its transplantation to Franco-German soil. But the influence of the Byzantine Church did not stop even then. Although opinion is divided as to the Eastern origin of tropes and sequences (see Chapter VI), we have proof that, in at least one instance, Charlemagne was directly responsible for the introduction of Byzantine chants into the Western liturgy. Notker Balbulus tells us in his *Gesta Caroli Magni* (Deeds of Charlemagne) that Charlemagne heard Eastern singers (presumably sent by Byzantine Empress Irene in 802) perform a set of antiphons for Epiphany. Pleased by these chants, Charlemagne ordered them translated into Latin and adapted to the original melody. The truth of Notker's story has recently been verified through discovery of the Greek originals. Although the Latin antiphons do not now form part of the Roman liturgy, they still survive in the Use of Braga (northwestern Spain) and in some monastic rites.[9]

Quite obviously, many influences combined to produce the liturgy

8.   See Jungmann, *The Mass,* 1, p. 74.

9.   O. Strunk, "The Latin Antiphons for the Octave of the Epiphany," *Recueil des travaux de l'Institut d'Études byzantines,* No. 8/2 (1964), pp. 417–26. Reprinted in Strunk, *Essays on Music in the Byzantine World* (New York, 1977), pp. 208–19.

and music of the Western Church as it developed during the first millennium of the Christian era. Moreover, the development continued well beyond the year A.D. 1000, and some of the best-known melodies of so-called Gregorian Chant were written after that year. Nevertheless, the main body of chant had been completed, and the liturgy had been stabilized in approximately its present form. In later chapters we shall consider some of the important additions to the liturgy that constitute a large part of musical history between A.D. 1000 and the end of the Middle Ages. Now, however, we are prepared for a detailed study of liturgical forms, and especially their musical components, as they emerged in the Romano-Frankish liturgy of the tenth century. We shall not, of course, be using tenth-century sources as the basis for our study. Instead, we shall rely on modern publications that contain the officially approved versions of the chants for the Offices and the Mass. The nature of these various chantbooks requires brief explanation.

In the later Middle Ages and Renaissance, the interests of church musicians—both composers and performers—centered increasingly on polyphonic rather than chant settings of liturgical texts. As a result, there seems to have been little concern for maintaining the purity of the chant itself. Manuscript and printed versions, and consequently performances, became more and more corrupt. Finally, after the Council of Trent (1545–63) restored the textual integrity of Offices and Masses, Pope Gregory XIII (1572–85) entrusted the revision of the music to the great composer Palestrina and his colleague in the papal chapel, Annibale Zoilo.[10] Fortunately for his reputation, Palestrina did not complete the task, although there is no reason to suppose that he would have done it differently. Gregory's instructions called for "revising, purging, correcting, and reforming" the chantbooks that were "filled to overflowing with barbarisms, obscurities, contrarieties, and superfluities." The aim was laudable enough, but, as it happened, many of the "barbarisms" and "obscurities" were essential characteristics of plainchant. Their removal merely corrupted the chant still further by making it conform as much as possible to sixteenth-century standards of vocal style (see Chapter III, pp. 86–87).

The "reform" of the chant begun in the late sixteenth century culminated in 1614 with the publication of the notorious Medicean Edition, and the totally corrupt versions there presented remained standard for more than two centuries. Restoration of the chant to its original form, or at least to the form of the earliest known sources, remained a task for modern scholarship. Credit for that restoration goes almost entirely to the French monks of the Benedictine abbey at Solesmes near Le Mans. Beginning in the latter half of the nineteenth century, the Solesmes monks labored with incredible zeal to recover the lost purity of

10.   For an English translation of Gregory's brief, see Strunk, SR, p. 358.

Gregorian melodies "after the authority of the earliest manuscripts." They completed the first stage of their work about the end of the century, and in 1904 Pope Pius X sanctioned the use of their restorations for the official Vatican edition of liturgical chant.[11] Since that time, a number of later editions have incorporated the results of the monks' continuing investigations.

The music for the Mass is published in the *Graduale Sacrosanctae Romanae Ecclesiae* (Gradual of the Holy Roman Church), and for the Offices, in the *Antiphonale Sacrosanctae Romanae Ecclesiae pro diurnis horis* (Antiphonary of the Holy Roman Church for the daytime hours). A third publication, the *Liber Usualis* (Common Book) contains a large selection of chants for both the Mass and Offices. For a number of reasons, all musical references in the following chapters will be to chants that appear in the *Liber Usualis* (LU): it is usually the most readily available of the various chantbooks; in addition to chants for the Mass and the daytime Offices, it contains some examples of the very important chants for Matins that do not appear in the *Antiphonary;* it provides more than enough material for an introductory survey of Gregorian Chant.

In addition to the official chantbooks, two significant by-products of the Solesmes monks' activities deserve mention. Since 1889 they have been publishing facsimile editions of early manuscripts with indices and extensive commentaries. More important from the practical point of view, perhaps, is the standard of performance that the Solesmes monks themselves have set. With recordings now a commonplace, their performances have become the ideal against which all others are measured—and generally found wanting. Whether the Solesmes methods of performance are justifiable historically is debatable, particularly with regard to rhythmic interpretation. It is undeniably true, however, that the polished elegance of their singing has brought to many people a first realization of the great beauty of our most ancient musical heritage.

THE LITURGICAL YEAR AND THE CHURCH CALENDAR

As a further preliminary to the study of Gregorian Chant itself, a brief discussion of the liturgical year and the Church calendar may prove helpful. The structure of the Church calendar is a complex affair that need not be gone into in great detail. Some knowledge of it is necessary, however, because it determines which chants are to be used on any given day. Moreover, the arrangement of the chantbooks follows the li-

11.   The *Graduale* and *Antiphonale* of the Vatican Edition were published in Rome in 1907 and 1912 respectively. Versions of the same books and of the *Liber Usualis* are published by Desclée in Tournai, Belgium. Known as the Solesmes editions, they give the chants with additional rhythmic signs devised by the Solesmes monks.

The calendar page for January, indicating the feasts to be observed during that month, in a late medieval manuscript (Musée Condé, Chantilly).

turgical rather than the calendar year. Thus, a brief explanation of the way the Church calendar is organized should clarify the somewhat confusing arrangement of the *Liber Usualis* and thereby simplify its use.

The liturgical year consists of two cycles that run concurrently, the first and more important of which is called the Proper of the Time. It provides for the liturgical observance and commemoration of the principal events in the life of Christ, as well as all the Sundays of the year. Various problems arise from its organization around the two most important events of Christ's life: his birth, celebrated on December 25, and his Resurrection, which is not observed on a fixed date. Falling on the first Sunday after the full moon following the vernal equinox, Easter may shift its position within the calendar year by a little more than a month.[12] And Easter, in turn, determines the dates for about ten months of the Proper of the Time. Thus the cycle must be adjusted annually around the movable date of Easter and the fixed date of Christmas.

The second cycle of the liturgical year is the Proper of the Saints. Here, the feasts of saints, including the Virgin Mary, occur on specific and unchanging dates, which therefore fall on different days of the week from year to year.[13] As a result of the variable elements in both cycles, then, feasts of saints often coincide with Sundays or other important

12. In 1940 and 1943, for example, the dates of Easter were March 24 and April 25 respectively.

13. Present practice moves some of the more important feasts to Sunday.

feasts in the Proper of the Time. To resolve these conflicts the Church devised an elaborate system of ranking feasts according to their relative importance.[14] The application of this system to specific feasts has often changed over the years and varies considerably from place to place. The ranking of feasts, indeed, is one of the principal ways in which local uses differ from one another. Even in the *Liber Usualis,* the details of the system, as well as the system itself, will be found to vary somewhat in different editions. We need not consider here how the system works when two feasts fall on the same day, but it is important to note that the rank of a feast determines the degree of solemnity and musical elaboration with which it is celebrated.

THE PROPER OF THE TIME

As the chief organizing factor of the liturgical year, the Proper of the Time calls for further comment. The two large but unequal sections of the year that revolve around the Nativity and Resurrection of Christ are further subdivided into periods of preparation, celebration, and prolongation. Quite appropriately, therefore, the liturgical year begins, not on January 1, but with Advent, the period anticipating the birth of Christ. Advent includes the four Sundays before Christmas, the first of which may fall on any date between November 27 and December 3. The period of celebration continues from Christmas Eve to Epiphany, a feast celebrated on January 6 that commemorates the visit of the Magi. There may be from one to six Sundays after Epiphany, depending on the date of Easter. One peculiarity of the Christmas cycle should not pass unnoticed. The week following December 25 includes five feasts from the Proper of the Saints, the only such feasts that appear in the Proper of the Time (LU, pp. 414–40). This is the last remnant of an older medieval practice that did not entirely separate the two cycles, and the Proper of the Time probably still retains the five feasts because of their long-standing and close association with the Nativity.

In contrast to the Nativity section of the year, the Easter section subdivides into such lengthy periods that each is sometimes treated as a separate entity.[15] The period of preparation consists of the nine weeks before Easter and may begin on any date between January 18 and February 22. With little regard for mathematical accuracy, the three Sundays before Lent begins on Ash Wednesday are known as *Septuagesima, Sexagesima,* and *Quinquagesima* (seventieth, sixtieth, and fiftieth). These names apparently developed by analogy with *Quadragesima* (fortieth),

---

14. Simple, Semi-double, Double, Double Major, and Doubles of first and second class. These categories have now been simplified, but they appear in the editions of LU.

15. E.g., by Apel (GC, p. 6 ff.), who considers the entire Nativity Section as the first of four periods in the Church year.

which became the Latin designation for Lent. Actually, Lent has forty-six days from Ash Wednesday to Holy Saturday, but the correct total of forty is reached because the six Sundays in Lent are not fast days and therefore are not counted. The climax of the Lenten season is Passiontide, which begins the second Sunday before Easter and culminates in the increasingly solemn and elaborate ceremonies of Holy Week. During this whole period of penance and fasting, the Gloria of the Mass is normally omitted, and the word *Alleluia* is never sung.

With an abrupt change of mood, Easter begins the period of celebration known as Paschal Time. This period of rejoicing for the Resurrection of Christ includes the Feast of the Ascension and continues until Pentecost, the descent of the Holy Spirit on the Apostles. Other events of the season need not detain us, but some of the terminology is of historical interest. Pentecost, from the Greek meaning "fiftieth," is always the seventh Sunday after Easter; that is, the fiftieth day counting Easter itself as the first. The Christian feast obviously derives from the Jewish Pentecost, which is celebrated on the fiftieth day after the second day of the Passover. Another connection with Jewish religious festivals is suggested by the word *paschal,* which comes from the Hebrew word meaning the Passover. The paschal lamb that was slain and eaten on that feast became the symbol of Christ and the origin of the phrase *Agnus Dei* (Lamb of God). Thus, the Jewish commemoration of the sparing of their first-born in houses marked with the blood of the lamb became Paschal Time, a period of rejoicing over the Resurrection of Christ.

Paschal Time is particularly interesting from a musical point of view because the word *Alleluia* concludes all the important chants of the Proper in both the Offices and the Mass. For feasts with fixed dates that may or may not fall in Paschal Time, the *Liber Usualis* provides separate Alleluias to be used when appropriate (marked T.P. [*Tempore paschali*], or sometimes P.T. [*Paschal Time*]). In the Proper of the Time, the Alleluia appears as an integral part of each chant.[16] The Alleluias for the Introit, Offertory, and Communion of the Mass in Paschal Time are also brought together and arranged according to the eight modes in the *Liber Usualis* (pp. 95–97). No Alleluia is added to the Gradual; instead, that chant is replaced in Paschal Time by the normal form of an independent Alleluia in the Mass (see Chapter V).

Returning to the organization of the liturgical year, we find that the prolongation of the Easter section is the longest period in the Proper of the Time. With little relationship to the events of Christ's life, this period allows the Proper of the Saints to come into greater prominence. Yet numbering the period's Sundays "after Pentecost" implies a continuing connection with the Easter celebration. The varying number of

16. See, for example, the chants of the Mass for the fifth Sunday after Easter, LU, pp. 830–33.

these Sundays—from twenty-three to twenty-eight—complements the
similar variation in the number of Sundays after Epiphany.[17] For convenient reference and to give a clear overview of the Proper of the Time,
its major divisions and most important feasts are listed in Table 2.[18]

Table 2: *The Proper of the Time*

The Nativity Section or Christmas Cycle

Preparation—Advent
    Begins on fourth Sunday before Christmas

Celebration—Christmastide
    Christmas Eve
    Christmas
    Circumcision (January 1)
    Epiphany (January 6)

Prolongation
    One to six Sundays after Epiphany

The Easter Section or Cycle

Preparation—includes Lent
    Three Sundays before Lent
        (Septuagesima, Sexagesima, Quinquagesima)
    Ash Wednesday—beginning of Lent
    First Sunday of Lent—Quadragesima
    Second to fourth Sundays of Lent
    Passion Sunday
    Palm Sunday
    Holy Week

Celebration—Paschal Time
    Easter and following week
    Low Sunday—first after Easter
    Second to fifth Sundays after Easter
    Ascension of Our Lord—Thursday, forty days after Easter
    Sunday after Ascension
    Pentecost—fifty days after Easter
    Week after Pentecost

Prolongation
    Trinity Sunday—first after Pentecost
    Corpus Christi—Thursday after Trinity Sunday
    Second to twenty-third Sundays after Pentecost
    One to five additional Sundays possible

It is no doubt impossible to anticipate all the questions that will arise
when converts to the beauty of Gregorian Chant begin to find their way
around in the *Liber Usualis*. It may help, however, to define some other
terms used in connection with the liturgical year.

17. For the way Sunday Masses are adapted to these variable periods, see LU, pp.
    1074–78.
18. Apel, GC, pp. 9–12, gives a much more complete listing, with titles in English and
    Latin and with page references to both LU and the *Graduale*.

Feria and *ferial*. By a curious evolutionary process, the word *feria,* originally meaning a festival, has come in Church usage to designate a weekday on which no festival occurs. Until the word *dominica* came into use, Sunday was called Feria I. Thus the weekdays were, and still are, numbered with Monday as Feria II, Tuesday as Feria III, etc. Chants identified as "ferial" are therefore used on days when there is no special feast.

Octave. As applied to the Church calendar, the word *octave* means the eighth day after a feast, counting the day of the feast itself. Sundays are sometimes identified as being "within the Octave" of a particular feast. The relation to the musical octave is obvious.

Ember. The adjective *ember* designates days of fasting and prayer and also the weeks in which such days occur. There are four Ember Weeks in the year, one in Advent and one in each of the three periods of the Easter section. In these weeks, Wednesday, Friday, and Saturday are Ember Days.

Rogation Days. The three days preceding the Ascension are days of special supplication marked by processions and the chanting of litanies (see LU, pp. 835–43).

Vigil. Originally meaning a night watch before a feast, the term *vigil* now designates the eve of a feast. *Eve* means the entire day, however, and is further extended backward to include Vespers on the preceding evening. For example, the Eve of the Epiphany on January 5—called a Vigil in LU, p. 454—would actually begin on January 4 with First Vespers.[19]

A first encounter with the organization of both the liturgical year and modern chantbooks can be a confusing experience. It is hoped that the foregoing definitions will materially reduce the neophyte's bewilderment.[20] As further aids to penetration of the mysteries, infinite patience and a good dictionary are indispensable.

19. For an explanation of First and Second Vespers, see Chapter IV.
20. For an outline of the contents of LU, see Appendix A, Part 1.

CHAPTER III

Gregorian Chant: General Characteristics

A number of factors determine the musical style of Gregorian Chant. In the first place, it is exclusively vocal and entirely monophonic. A single melodic line, in other words, is meant to be sung without accompaniment and without harmonic support of any kind. Music consisting of nothing but melody may sound strange and dull to twentieth-century ears. With a little study, much listening, and an open mind, however, one begins to appreciate the marvelous subtleties that lie behind this music's apparent simplicity. Gregorian Chant is music in its purest state, fashioned with consummate skill, and perfectly adapted to its liturgical function.

NOTATION

Some explanation of the notation used in present-day chantbooks is called for before we can begin to examine the general characteristics of Gregorian Chant. Actually, this *square notation,* as it is called, is well adapted to plainchant, for which it was, in fact, developed. With a little practice, reading difficulties quickly disappear, and square notation remains the most satisfactory method of recording the plainchant repertory.

In order to appreciate fully the significance of this plainchant notation, we must look briefly at its historical development. The earliest manuscripts for use by the choir contained nothing but the texts. All the melodies had to be learned by heart and performed from memory. As the number of chants increased, this became a more and more formidable task. The first step in easing the singers' burden came with the introduction of various signs written above the chant texts. These signs, or *neumes,* as they were called, apparently developed from grammatical accents indicating the rise and fall of the voice. The sign for a higher note (/) was the *virga* (rod), but the sign for a lower note (\) was reduced to a short horizontal line or simply a point (– or •) and called a *punctum.* When several notes were sung to one syllable, the single signs could be combined into two- and three-note neumes. Probably for ease of writing, many of these neumes took on the rounded forms found in the oldest manuscripts:

Script	Name of neume	Presumed origin
⌒	Clivis	∧
✓	Pes or Podatus	✓
⌒	Torculus	⋃
∿	Porrectus	∿
⸾	Scandicus	
⋏	Climacus	

Compound neumes of more than three notes could also be written; but if more than four or five notes were sung to one syllable, they were generally divided into two or more separate neumes. In addition, a number of special neumes indicated various peculiarities of vocal performance (see Table 3, p. 61).

The system of neumatic notation seems to have developed no earlier than the eighth century, but by the ninth it was coming into common use. Different regions and important religious centers in Europe developed distinctive styles of writing neumes, so that it is possible to deter-

Introit for Ascension Day from a Bolognese Gradual, second quarter of the eleventh century, written in staffless, unheighted neumes.

Tract for the Easter Vigil from an eleventh-century Gradual (Pistoia), written in heighted neumes.

mine with considerable accuracy the place of origin of a given manuscript.[1] Comparative studies show, however, that all early sources, whatever the style of writing, follow the same notational system and share in that system's limitations.

Early neumatic notation was anything but simple and indicated many subtleties of performance in ways that later forms of plainchant notation found difficult or impossible to duplicate. Yet it gave specific information only as to the number of notes and whether they move up or down. There is no way of determining the size of successive melodic intervals or even the note on which the melody begins (see illustration on p. 58). The notation thus served only as a memory aid for a singer who already knew the melody. For anyone else it was useless. Notation of this type is called a variety of names: oratorical, staffless, unheighted, *in campo aperto* (in the open field), and chironomic (from Greek words meaning gestures of the hands, as of a choir director). Some of these terms suggest the improvements that were soon to be introduced.

The first new development in notation was the appearance of heighted neumes, which indicate by their placement the size as well as the direction of individual intervals. For this reason, notation with heighted neumes is often called diastematic, from the Greek word for interval. (For an example, see Parrish, NMM, Plate VI.) Careful spacing of neumes so that notes of the same pitch always appeared on the same

---

1. Comparative tables of neumes from different regions may be seen in Apel, GC, p. 120, and Parrish, NMM, p. 6. Plates in both books illustrate neumes from a variety of manuscripts.

level quickly led to the use of one or two lines to represent particular notes. These generally had no fixed meaning, and a letter at the beginning indicated the note that they represented. Gradually, however, lines indicating middle **C** (**c'**) and the **f** a fifth below became the ones most commonly used.[2] At first, lines might be merely scratched on the parchment, in which case they are now often invisible. Later, lines drawn in different-colored inks were frequently used, usually red for **f** and yellow or green for **c'**. Obviously, we are embarked on the development of the musical staff as we know it today.

The completion of the four-line staff still used for plainchant notation is generally credited to Guido d'Arezzo (c. 1000–50), one of the most important musical theorists of the Middle Ages. Guido also invented the system of solmization syllables—*ut, re, mi, fa, sol, la*—that has remained, with some modification, a teaching device up to the present time (see below, p. 63). Armed with these new developments, Guido was able to "produce a perfect singer in the space of one year, or at the most in two," whereas previously, ten years of study had yielded "only an imperfect knowledge of singing."[3] The great change, of course, was that singers could now read and perform a melody they had never heard before. Guido was fully aware of the importance of his contribution and of the need that it filled. As he said, with perhaps unnecessary limitation, "In our times, of all men, singers are the most foolish."

Guido's innovations did not escape notice, even in his lifetime, although the older types of notation continued in use for several centuries. Gradually, however, the staff became more and more common, and the form of the neumes evolved to permit accurate placement on lines and spaces. In particular, the regional notation of northern France developed the square shapes that form the basis of modern plainchant notation (see Parrish, NMM, Plate VIII).

GUIDE TO THE READING OF SQUARE NOTATION

Collected in Table 3 are the most common neumes of square notation, together with their names and modern equivalents. Comparison of the two versions will quickly reveal the basic principles of square notation, and only a few words of caution are necessary.

Plainchant notation uses only two clefs. The C clef (—♭—) indicates which line of the staff is middle **C,** and the F clef (—♯—) indicates **F** a fifth below. Notes in ligatures are read normally from left to right, but two notes aligned vertically are read from bottom to top (see the podatus in Table 3). An oblique line, as in the porrectus, merely indicates two notes that are determined by the position of the line's beginning

2.   For the system of pitch identification used throughout this book, see Appendix B.
3.   For the Prologue to Guido's *Antiphonary* and his famous letter concerning the singing of unknown chants, see Strunk, SR, pp. 117–25.

Table 3: *Neumes of Square Notation*

Name	Neume	Modern equivalent
VIRGA		
PUNCTUM		
PODATUS		
CLIVIS		
SCANDICUS		
CLIMACUS		
TORCULUS		
PORRECTUS		

Special Neumes

Name	Neume	Modern Equivalent
a. LIQUESCENT EPIPHONUS		
CEPHALICUS		
b. STROPHIC DISTROPHA		
TRISTROPHA		
c. ORISCUS		
d. PRESSUS	*or*	*or*
e. QUILISMA () WITHIN A NEUME		

and end. Each neume in Table 3, of course, may represent any notes of the same number and relative position. Thus, for example, a podatus always consists of two notes with the second above the first; and a porrectus is always a three-note neume in which the middle note is lower than the other two. Compound neumes produced by the addition of one or more notes to the three-note forms do not introduce any new reading problems (see LU, p. xxi).

The notes of the special neumes are perfectly clear, but their interpretation is somewhat problematical. They represent a variety of vocal ornaments found more frequently in medieval sources than in the editions of the Solesmes monks. Modern directions for performance (LU, p. xxii ff.) are not too successful in describing medieval vocal practices often imperfectly understood. Only the liquescent neumes have a direct connection with the text. They appear with diphthongs, certain double consonants, or i (j) used as a semiconsonant as in *Alleluia*. Apparently intended to facilitate clear enunciation of the text, liquescence is indicated in modern editions by neumes with smaller final notes. The other special neumes are purely melodic ornaments. Strophic neumes repeat the same note on a single syllable. They are now sung simply as a sustained note of double or triple length, but originally they called for a "repercussion" of the voice on each note. (One thinks inevitably of the Italian trill on a single note of the early Baroque period.) Both the oriscus and the pressus also produce notes of double length but in combination with ligatures. Once again, they seem originally to have been more elaborate ornaments, and the pressus in particular may have introduced pitch deviations involving quarter tones. The quilisma, written as a jagged note, never appears alone but always within a neume, where it normally fills in the interval of a third. According to the Solesmes monks (LU, p. xxv), the preceding note is to be "notably lengthened," and the quilisma itself "must always be rendered lightly." More probably, the original effect was some sort of tremolo or trill. Indeed, as far as one can judge from contemporary descriptions, many of the ornaments indicated by special neumes were suspiciously Oriental in character. We can be certain, at any rate, that plainchant in the centuries before A.D. 1000 sounded quite unlike the performances that are so highly prized today.

Square notation in both its medieval and modern forms clearly indicated all the pitches that were to be sung. It utterly failed, however, to indicate rhythmic relationships. As a result, the rhythm of Gregorian Chant has been, and probably always will be, a highly controversial subject. The various "rhythmic signs" in the *Liber Usualis* are based partly on medieval practices and partly on the theories of the Solesmes monks. We may ignore them, therefore, in considering the musical style of Gregorian Chant. Unfortunately, questions of rhythmic interpretation cannot be thus ignored, but discussion of them may be delayed until we have dealt with the less problematical aspects of musical style.

SOLMIZATION SYSTEM OF GUIDO D'AREZZO

The period that saw the development of neumatic notation also saw the theoretical definition of the tonal realm within which Gregorian Chant moved. Basically, that realm consisted of the two octaves from **A**, a tenth below middle **C**, to **a'** a sixth above, with **B**♭ the only permissible accidental. The solmization system of Guido d'Arezzo slightly expanded this range and organized it in a series of interlocking hexachords.

Guido derived his hexachord—a stepwise series of six notes—from the syllables and notes beginning the successive phrases of the hymn to St. John the Baptist, *Ut queant laxis* (Example III–1). All notes in this series are a whole tone apart except between *mi* and *fa,* where there is a semitone. Guido used this pattern of notes to build a system of seven overlapping hexachords on **G, C,** and **F** (Example III–2). The system began on low **G**, which was identified by the Greek letter Γ (*gamma*). Roman letters from A to G identified the other notes of the system, with capital and lower-case letters—single and double—being used to distinguish the different octaves. The hexachord on **F**, which required **B**♭ to produce the semitone between *mi* and *fa,* was named soft (*molle*) because the rounded form of the letter *b* indicated *b-fa.* Conversely, the **G** hexachord was hard (*durum*) because a square letter indicated ♮-*mi* (**B**♮). The original pattern on **C** was known as the natural hexachord.

Example III–1: *Hymn to St. John the Baptist (LU, p. 1504)*

Ut que-ant la - xis re-só-na-re fi-bris Mi - ra ge-sto - rum fa-mu-li tu-o - rum,

Sol - ve pol - lu - ti la - bi - i re - a-tum, San - cte Jo - an-nes.

That thy servants may freely proclaim the wonders of thy deeds, absolve the sins of their unclean lips, O holy John.

Example III–2: *The Hexachord System of Guido d'Arezzo*

Γ A B C D E F G a b ♭ c d e f g aa bb ♭♭ cc dd ee

The hexachord system was designed to facilitate the teaching and learning of plainchant melodies. Its obvious advantages were the association of syllables with particular notes and especially the fixed position of the semitone in the hexachord. Whenever a melody went beyond the range of one hexachord, the singer moved to another by changing syllables on a note common to both, a process known as *mutation*. One would like to believe that Guido is still enjoying the fantastic success of his essentially simple teaching device.

THE CHURCH MODES

Although Guido d'Arezzo's hexachords were first used for singing plainchant melodies, they do not reflect the scalar patterns, or modes, in which these melodies were written. However, the gamut of the solmization system contains all the tonal material of the church modes. One of the ways in which monophonic music achieves variety and subtlety is through the use of more modes than the two—major and minor—that sufficed for the music of the Classic and Romantic periods. Although many modes were to be found in Oriental music, Gregorian Chant used no more than the eight modes shown in Table 4. These modes and their various designations require some explanation.

All the chants in a given mode normally end on the same note, the *final* of the mode (marked F in Table 4). On the basis of their finals on **d**, **e**, **f**, and **g**, then, the modes are grouped in four pairs. Medieval theorists called these pairs *maneriae* (sing. *maneria*) and identified them by the Greek ordinal numbers, *protus, deuterus, tritus,* and *tetrardus.* Hence, modern writers sometimes use the phrase "protus tonality," for example, to indicate modes ending on **d**. The numbering of the modes is always the same and provides the most convenient means of identification. In the *Liber Usualis* and other modern chantbooks, the mode number normally appears under the name of an individual chant. Each pair of modes contains an authentic and a plagal form, distinguished by the range of the melody either above or around the final. Thus, Modes 1, 3, 5, and 7 are authentic, while the even-numbered modes are all plagal. Finally, the modes were given Greek names. The authentic modes are Dorian, Phrygian, Lydian, and Mixolydian; and the plagal form of each maneria is identified by the prefix *hypo-*, meaning "under" or "sub-". These somewhat confusing designations will become clearer, it is hoped, in the ensuing discussion of modal structure and its application to plainchant melodies.

Each mode consists of a pentachord joined conjunctly with a tetrachord. In Mode 1, for example, the five consecutive notes from **d** to **a** form a pentachord, the last note of which is also the first of the four notes from **a** to **d'** that form the conjunct tetrachord. In the authentic modes, the tetrachord is above the pentachord, whereas it is below the pentachord in the plagal modes. Here, then, the common note that joins the tetrachord and pentachord is the final of the mode, which is always

Table 4: *The Eight Church Modes*

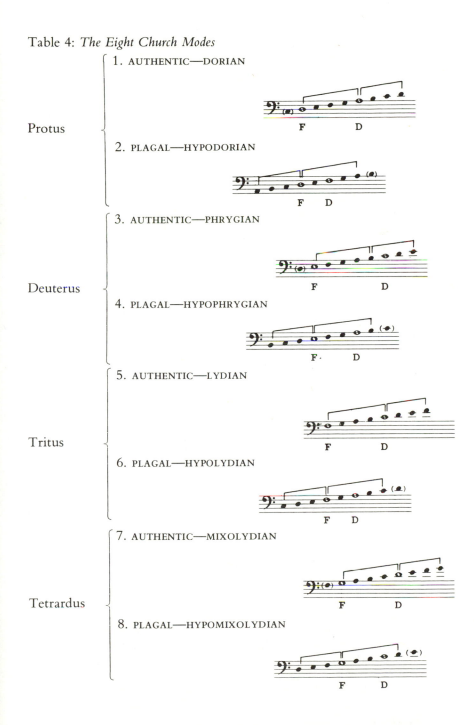

the lowest note of the pentachord. The distinction between authentic and plagal forms ending on the same final might seem to be unnecessary until we realize that the modes were not regarded as being repeatable from octave to octave like modern scales. Instead, the octave of each mode represented the normal range for a melody in that mode. The authentic and plagal modes, therefore, provide a means of distinguishing melodies according to the position of their final in relation to their total range. This purely melodic distinction has no validity for harmonic music, but we could apply it, if we wished, to many familiar, and much later, melodies. The tune of *America,* for example, is clearly authentic, using only the semitone below the final. A well-known plagal melody is *O Come, All Ye Faithful (Adeste, fideles*—LU, p. 1870), which ranges from **c** to **c'**, with a final on **f**. The difference between Modes 1 and 8 should now be clear. Although they have the same normal range from **d** to **d'**, the first mode ends on **d** and the eighth, on **g**. Moreover, the two modes have different pentachords and tetrachords within the same octave, so that the relationships of whole and half tones to the finals are also different.

Not all melodies, of course, have a range of exactly one octave. Many of the chants, especially the older ones, move within the limits of a fifth or sixth. Later melodies frequently have a range of an octave plus a third or a fourth. Even in melodies of restricted range, the note below the final is commonly used in all the authentic modes except Mode 5. For listeners accustomed to the leading tone in melodies associated with tonal harmony, it is curious to discover that plainchant composers evidently disliked the semitone below the final. In contrast to the usage in authentic modes, plagal melodies frequently extend one note above their basic octave. Both of these common additions to the modal ranges are indicated in parentheses in Table 4. Further extensions of the range can usually be explained as combinations of authentic and plagal forms, known to medieval theorists as "mixed" modes.

In their pure form, the modes were written without accidentals, a practice that now makes it convenient to find them on the white keys of the piano. One accidental, **B**♭, was permitted, however, and it appears more frequently than the theoretical forms of the modes might suggest. It is used in Mode 1, for example, in melodic figures such as **d–a–b**♭**–a**; and it is particularly common in Mode 5. Where it is used throughout a melody, as in *Alma Redemptoris Mater* (Fostering Mother of the Redeemer), the result is indistinguishable from our modern major scale (AMM, No. 1).

Although the notes **d, e, f,** and **g** are the normal finals for the eight church modes, some chants end on the notes **a, b,** or **c'**. Medieval theorists called these latter notes cofinals *(confinalis* or *affinalis).* Chants ending on one of these cofinals are normally regarded as being transposed up a fourth or fifth. The reasons for such transpositions will become evident when we consider the historical development of the medieval modal system.

One important aspect of the church modes remains to be discussed: the presence in each of a *dominant* tone identified by the letter D in Table 4. These tones are variously called tenors, *tubae,* or reciting tones; but the designation of *dominants* seems to be most commonly accepted. The choice is perhaps unfortunate, for it suggests a relationship to the dominant of tonal harmony; but there seems to be little point in trying to reform the terminology here. We shall not be led too far astray, if we remember that the dominants of the modes had a purely melodic function. They are, in fact, the reciting tones, or tenors, of the formulas used for singing psalms. These formulas, known as psalm tones, will be discussed in detail when we consider the various types of liturgical recitative. Now we need only note that there is a psalm tone to correspond with each mode, and the tenor of the psalm tone is the dominant of the mode. Originally, the dominants of the authentic modes were all a fifth above the final, and those of the plagal modes, a third above. During the tenth and eleventh centuries, however, the dominants of Modes 3, 4, and 8 shifted up a step to their present positions. Possibly this resulted from the newly standardized notation and solmization systems with their alternation between **B**♭ and **B**♮. In any case, the dominants of Modes 3 and 8 moved up from **b** to **c′**; and, influenced perhaps by its authentic partner, the dominant of Mode 4 became **a** instead of **g**. Although the dominants originated in the psalm-tone formulas, they evidently influenced the composition of many free melodies, which often stress the dominant more than the final.

Having described the various characteristics of the church modes, we may now attempt a definition: *modes* are octave species characterized by different arrangements of whole and half steps around dominant and final notes. To identify the mode of a written melody, the final, dominant, and range are the important determining factors, in that order. The Offertory *Deus, Deus meus* for the second Sunday after Easter (Example III–3) illustrates very well the relative importance of these factors. The total range of this chant is only a sixth, from **c** to **a**, but its final on **d** establishes it as being either Mode 1 or 2. Quite obviously, it is the stress on **f**, the dominant, that determines its classification as Mode 2.

For the listener, the distribution of intervals around the final provides the most obvious means of identification. The position of the semitones and the size of the third—major or minor—above the final make the mode of a particular chant easily recognizable. To illustrate again from Example III–3, whole steps both above and below the final and a minor third above are found only in the modes of the protus tonality. Once more it is the emphasis on the dominant that decides in favor of Mode 2. The student is advised to study the modal characteristics of a number of different chants in the *Liber Usualis* and to practice identifying by ear as many recorded chants as possible. In this way, he will become increasingly aware of both the individual characteristics of each mode and the great variety of modal structure in the total plainchant repertory.

Example III–3: *Offertory* Deus, Deus meus (*LU, pp. 818–19*)

O God, thou art my God; early will I seek thee. I will lift up my hands in thy name.—Psalm 62 (63):1 and 4 (parts).

THE MODAL SYSTEM: HISTORICAL DEVELOPMENT

The modal system, of course, did not spring full-blown from the head of any one man. Instead, it evolved over several centuries before reaching the complete state that we have just described. The course of its development is complex and somewhat problematical, and we need not consider it in detail here. A few remarks, however, should clarify the historical relationships between the repertory of plainchants and its modal system.

Perhaps the most important point to remember is that the modal system did not begin to take shape until the tenth century, at which time, of course, a large part of the plainchant repertory was already in existence. The same period saw the development of an exact pitch notation and the establishment of available tonal material in the gamut of the Guidonian system. These nearly simultaneous developments presented a number of problems. Musicians had not only to classify a large number of chants according to mode but also to write those chants correctly within the limits of the Guidonian scale. That some melodies resisted their efforts is less surprising than that the majority seem to have fitted into the new theoretical system with little difficulty.

Even before the formulation of the modal system, classification of some chants had occurred in chantbooks known as *tonaries*. In these collections, the Office antiphons—chants performed in conjunction with psalms—were grouped according to the psalm tones with which they would be used (see Chapter IV). Although the psalm tones as we know them were standardized at about the same time as the church modes, the earlier tonaries represent a first step toward modal definition by final and reciting tones. Another, and very important, means of classifying antiphons, however, was by their opening melodic formulas. That they, as well as other types of chants, can be arranged in melodically related groups or families suggests the chief reason for the ease with which so much of the plainchant repertory fitted into the later modal system. The different chants of a particular family prove to be in the same mode, but the real basis of their relationship is their common use of certain melodic formulas. The chants of some antiphon groups have only the opening phrase in common. In other groups, especially in other types of chants, the melodies are made up of several stock figures. The process of creating new melodies from combinations of preexisting melodic formulas is called *centonization*.

The modern emphasis on originality in the creative arts makes the idea of centonization seem strange indeed. Yet it is the normal procedure in much Oriental music. For the Oriental musician, modes are not so much octave species or scales as collections of melodic formulas. The originality of the composer or improvising performer consists in his choice and arrangement of these formulas, the way he links them together, extends and elaborates them, and perhaps includes a small amount of free material. Centonization is not to be confused with mere adaptation, in which a complete melody, with whatever modifications are necessary, is fitted to new words. This process too is common throughout the Middle Ages, not only in plainchant but in many other types of music as well. Centonization, obviously, represents a considerably higher stage of artistic endeavor. The composer must assemble, and the listener recognize, traditional melodic formulas in new and individual contexts.

The formation of the modal system, then, was in part an effort to extract the fundamental series of modes from the existing plainchant repertory. At the same time, however, tenth-century theorists tried to relate their modes to the complex Greek system as transmitted by Boethius and later Latin writers. This accounts for the Greek names of the eight modes, although nothing else about them is Greek; and through a misunderstanding of Greek theory—by no means the last— even the names were misapplied. (In the Greek modal system, Dorian begins on **E**, Phrygian on **D**, Lydian on **C**, and Mixolydian on **B**.) Despite their failure to reconstruct the Greek modal system, medieval theorists nevertheless evolved a new system that was to have far-

Boethius discussing music with Pythagorus, Plato, and Nichomachus. From a twelfth-century drawing (Syndics of Cambridge University Library).

reaching effects on the further development of music in the Western world.

These effects first showed themselves in the treatment of chants that did not fit well into the new modal system. A number of chants, for example, used intervals—or notes—that are not found in the pure form of the mode. In later times, of course, these notes would have been indicated simply by accidentals. The medieval solution was to transpose the chants when possible, so that the necessary accidentals came in the only permissible position, on **B**. If a chant in Mode 3 or 4 used both **F** and **F**♯, for example, transposition up a fourth to end on **a** would move the variable notes to **b**♭ and **b**.[4] The opening phrase of the Easter Gradual *Haec dies* (This is the day) illustrates another kind of transposition to avoid a different set of accidentals (Example III–4). *Haec dies* is in Mode 2 transposed up a fifth to end on **a.** As may be seen, the normal position of this chant on **d** would require an **e**♭ and also a low **B**♭ that is found in neither the Guidonian gamut nor the tetrachord below the final of the Hypodorian mode. The upper **b**♭ occurs but once in the present version of *Haec dies* (AMM, No. 10), and its authenticity has been disputed. Throughout the chant, however, the continued use of **f** (**B**♭ if un-

4.   E.g., in the Communion *Beatus servus* (Blessed servant), LU, p. 1203.

transposed) is sufficient to account for the transposition.[5] Such transpositions, it seems, led to the introduction of cofinals into the modal system.

Example III–4: *First Phrase of* Haec dies *in Transposed and Untransposed Positions*

transposed) is sufficient to account for the transposition.

It must be stressed that the need for transposition arose only with the development of an exact pitch notation. The use of staffless neumes had presented no problem, and neither, for that matter, did performance. Singers merely reproduced the correct intervals of a chant at any convenient pitch level. It should be clear, therefore, that the notation of the different modes, and their endings on **d**, **e**, **f**, and **g**, do not represent absolute pitches. In the Middle Ages, as now, well-known melodies were sung at whatever pitch level suited the singers involved. The actual notation of the melody did not matter. We may note, too, that different pitch levels were sometimes specified for different types of occasions: for example, joyful festival days called for higher pitches than did days of penitence or mourning.

One important result of transposition is the beginning of the breakdown of the eight-mode system. Mode 1 transposed to **a**, for example, becomes a different octave species as long as it does not use **F♯**. Similarly, Mode 3 on **a** remains Phrygian only when **B♭** is kept throughout. As soon as **B♮** is introduced, the pure form of the mode, and indeed its essential character, is lost. Moreover, the common introduction of **B♭** in some of the untransposed modes—a practice we have already noted— resulted in the formation of new octave species. Medieval theorists did not admit these modal changes, and it is doubtful that they even recognized them. Nevertheless, the seeds were planted that, in the middle of the sixteenth century, would produce four new modes: Ionian and Hypoionian ending on **C**, Aeolian and Hypoaeolian ending on **A**.

Although transposition solved many of the problems arising from the need to notate the chants, it did not, by any means, remove all the difficulties. This is evident in the rather large number of chants that are assigned to different modes in medieval chantbooks and theoretical treatises. Willi Apel suggests that about one-tenth of the total plainchant

5.   In his discussion of transposition (GC, p. 157 ff.), Apel seems not to have recognized avoidance of low **B♭** as a reason for transposing chants. It applies, however, to many of the transposed chants in his list (p. 159) that do not have both **B♭** and **B♮** (i.e., those without an asterisk).

repertory displays this "modal ambiguity."[6] Most of these chants in their present form fit nicely into the modal system, a result of emendations they received during the so-called Cistercian Reform in the first half of the twelfth century. The Cistercians were noted for the severity of their monastic rule, and apparently they felt that the music of the Church should be equally pure. Taking a fundamentalist view of the Biblical passage "upon a psaltery and an instrument of ten strings will I sing praises unto thee" (Psalm 144:9), they decided that no chant should have a range of more than ten notes. To bring offending chants into line, the Cistercians generally resorted to transposition of the pertinent phrases. Other transpositions of short sections within a chant seem to have been introduced to avoid either chromatic alterations or too many endings on notes other than the final of the mode. Although scholars are divided as to the extent and importance of the Cistercian Reform, there can be no doubt that it marks the nearly successful completion of efforts to correlate the modal system and the preexisting plainchant repertory.

To close these general remarks on the historical development of the modal system, we may note its effect on the later composition of plainchant. In the first place, composers were released from the restrictive technique of centonization. In practice, they had declared their freedom earlier, but the establishment of the modal system sanctioned their right to create entirely new melodies based on the available tonal materials within a given mode. This represents a first and very important break from Oriental traditions of music making that stood in the way of evolutionary development.

In exercising their new-found freedom, composers seem to have taken particular pains to make the mode of a chant obvious from its very beginning. Moreover, they quickly learned how to construct a melody so that it conveyed a sense of tonal organization. This they accomplished in certain modes by stressing not only the final but also the third and fifth above. These notes might appear as a melodic triad, or skips from and to the final could emphasize the interval of a fifth. In addition, phrases begin and end on these notes more frequently than on any others. The Marian antiphon *Alma Redemptoris Mater,* already cited for its constant use of **B**♭ in Mode 5, provides a particularly striking example of this new type of tonal organization (AMM, No. 1). Even in the opening phrase on the first three words, the procedures we have outlined are obvious, and succeeding phrases begin and end only on the first, third, fifth, or eighth notes of the mode.

Tonal organization of the sort displayed in *Alma Redemptoris Mater* is suggested to a certain extent by the structure of the modes themselves. In Modes 1, 5, and 7, the fifth above the final is the dominant of the

6.   Apel, GC, p. 166 ff.

mode; and the octave from the fourth below to the fifth above the final defines the normal limits of the plagal modes. The idea of stressing the third may have come from the second and sixth modes, in which it is the dominant. Composers must have recognized, however, the importance of the third in establishing modal identity. (In Modes 1–4, the third above the final is minor; in Modes 5–8, it is major.) The influence of the primary modal characteristics can only have been strengthened by theoretical emphasis on the pentachords and tetrachords as the basis of modal structure. The limits of these units are again the final with its fifth and octave above in the authentic modes, and, in the plagal modes, the fifth above and fourth below. Many shorter phrases move entirely within a pentachord or tetrachord. Others add a note above or below the limits of these octave segments. (For an illustration of this latter procedure, see the phrases on the words "quae pervia caeli" and "tu quae genuisti" in *Alma Redemptoris Mater*.)

Objection to the foregoing explanation might be raised on the ground that the displaced dominants of Modes 3, 4, and 8 do not correspond with the divisions into pentachords and tetrachords. Paradoxically, however, this fact strengthens rather than weakens our argument. As the feeling for tonal organization becomes more and more evident, it is just these nonconformist modes that fall into disuse. This is particularly true, as we shall see, in both monophonic and polyphonic secular songs of the later Middle Ages. In these repertories, the protus and tritus tonalities predominate, and the deuterus tonality is conspicuous by its rarity. It can be no accident that tonal organization went hand in hand with a concentration on the modes most nearly resembling our major and minor scales. What we are witnessing, in fact, is the beginning of a development that comes to full flower in the functional harmony of the eighteenth and nineteenth centuries.

GENERAL CHARACTERISTICS OF MUSICAL STYLE

It should be obvious by now that the modal structure of Gregorian Chant determines many of its distinctive characteristics. Some of these we have already mentioned, and some we shall expand upon in discussing the general stylistic aspects of the plainchant repertory as a whole. In the following chapters, we may then consider the individual chants of the Offices and the Mass.

RANGE

The entire body of Gregorian Chant is written, and was undoubtedly sung, in the normal range of male voices from *gamma ut* (Γ) to **g'** or **a'**. According to the rule of St. Paul, women were to be silent in church.

This obviously would not apply to a convent of nuns, but in monasteries and secular churches all the singing was done by the monks, the assisting clergy, or the trained choir. Boys were not yet generally included in the choir; and, indeed, before the innovations of Guido d'Arezzo, their voices would have changed by the time they had gained "only an imperfect knowledge of singing in ten years of study."[7] In any case, the performing range of the total repertory was probably even smaller than the written, for no ideas of fixed pitch kept a particular group of singers from adopting the most comfortable level for any chant, no matter what its mode.

No single chant covers the entire available range. Even without a statistical survey, it seems safe to say that the majority of chants have a range of a seventh, octave, or ninth. A rather large number, however, move within the more restricted limits of a fifth or sixth. In general, narrow ranges are found most often among the older and simpler types of chants, such as the Office antiphons. Curiously, however, an unexpectedly large number of highly ornate Alleluias also move within these narrow limits.[8] Chants with a range of more than a ninth are considerably less frequent than those with a limited range. Nevertheless, some striking examples do occur, although they cannot be considered characteristic of the plainchant repertory as a whole. With a range of c–f′, for example, the Communion *Qui mihi* (LU, p. 1141) includes all the notes in both authentic and plagal forms of the tritus tonality. Excessive range is most common in Graduals—responsorial chants of the Mass in which choral responds alternate with solo verses (see Chapter V). The individual sections of such chants are usually normal in range, but the solo verse often lies one or two notes higher than the choral respond. Thus the total range may extend from a third to a fifth beyond an octave. The Gradual *Timebunt gentes* (The nations shall fear; LU, p. 489) provides a typical example in which the respond ranges from **d** to **d′**, and the verse from **f** to **f′**. One of the widest ranges in the present repertory—from **A** to **b♭** and **c** to **e′**—is found in the Gradual *Universi* (LU, p. 320). In Offertories with verses (which were later removed from the liturgy), Apel found even wider ranges and the occasional appearance of such unusual notes as **e♭** and **F** below the gamut. Some, if not all, of his observations must be discarded, however, because they are based on a modern edition in which phrases within chants have been transposed by a fourth, a fifth, or even an octave from their positions in manuscript sources.[9] However interesting the exceptional ranges of some chants may be, it must be remembered that far more remain within the octave or ninth limits of the theoretical modes.

7.   See the already-cited letter of Guido d'Arezzo in Strunk, SR, p. 122.
8.   The Alleluia for Christmas Eve (LU, p. 361) has a range of only a fifth, **g–d′**.
9.   Apel, GC, pp. 151 and 165 (fn. 29). But see Ruth Steiner, "Some Questions about the Gregorian Offertories and their Verses," JAMS, 19 (1966), pp. 166 and 169–71.

MELODIC INTERVALS

In all types of chant, melodic progressions are primarily conjunct—that is, moving by step up or down the notes of the mode. Skips of a third in either direction are the most common form of disjunct motion, and some chants consist of nothing but seconds, thirds, and repeated notes.[10] Throughout the repertory, the predominance of stepwise motion with occasional skips of a third produces a smoothness and uniformity that greatly increase the effectiveness of larger melodic intervals. In general, it is true that the greater a melodic interval is, the less frequently it will occur. Fourths are relatively common; fifths are fewer in number, especially as downward skips. A number of melodies begin, however, with a dramatic upward skip of a fifth (Example III–5). Intervals larger than a fifth are extremely rare, even in late compositions. It is noteworthy that octave leaps have no place in the melodic style, although they, as well as sixths, may appear as "dead" intervals between phrases.

Example III–5: *Introit for the Christmas Mass* (*LU, p. 408*)

Pu - er na - tus est   no - bis

A boy is born to us.

In contrast to the conservative treatment of single intervals, plainchant often displays considerable boldness in combining skips in the same direction. Successive thirds are so common that they cannot be called bold, except, perhaps, when they outline a diminished triad, as in the Easter Gradual *Haec dies* on the word "ea" (AMM, No. 10). Curiously, sixths made up of a third and fourth are rare.[11] Only the downward progression of a fourth plus a third seems to belong to the older musical language. It occurs, for example, in such very old chants as the Gradual for the third Mass of Christmas, *Viderunt omnes* (All . . . have seen), where it closes a repeated phrase that begins a long melody (melisma) on the first syllable of the word "Dominus" (LU, p. 409). Progressions outlining a seventh, on the other hand, are common. Generally, these are ascending formations made up of a fifth and a third or of two fourths, but the limits of a seventh may also be filled in with a number of intermediate pitches (Example III–6). Complete phrases frequently span a sixth or seventh, but formations encompassing a full octave are

10. For example, the antiphon *Hodie Christus natus est* (Today Christ is born; LU, p. 413).

11. The mathematics of music can be as confusing as its terminology. A third and a fourth combine to make a sixth, just as a fifth and third, or two fourths, make a seventh.

rare and seem to be characteristic of later chants, such as Alleluias and Offertories. Perhaps we may see here another effect of the theoretical emphasis on octave species as the basis of the modal system.

Example III–6: *Phrases Spanning the Interval of a Seventh*

a. LU, p. 825

Va - do ad e-um
(I go to him)

b. LU, p. 507

est
(is)

c. LU, p. 827

mors
(death)

MELODIC OUTLINES

Mention of the limits of melodic phrases naturally leads to a consideration of general melodic outlines. Attempts have been made to classify plainchant melodies in whole or in part as variations on a basic arch form. Presumably, "classic" Gregorian melodies, or their individual phrases, should display a gradual rise to the peak of the arch, followed by a gradual descent to the cadence. Although many melodies can be analyzed as consisting of one or a series of arches, deviations from the pattern are numerous and varied. Occasionally a phrase will be an inverted arch, with the lowest point of the melodic line falling approximately in the middle. More often we find phrases that gently rise and fall around a fixed pitch level. Incomplete or half arches are particularly common, with the high point coming either at the end or the beginning of the phrase. Related to the latter variant is the type of phrase that begins with a rapid rise, often of one or two skips, followed by a gradual descent. In this connection, it is worth noting that skips, either single or in combination, occur much more frequently in ascending than in descending motion. All in all, the many varieties of melodic outline make a comprehensive system of classification virtually impossible. One might better cultivate an awareness of the subtle relationships between rising and falling lines as they establish the characteristic curves of a particular chant. The appreciation of curves, after all, rests on the perception of individual dimensions.

CADENCES

As an element of plainchant style, cadence patterns are closely related to matters of intervallic progression and characteristic melodic curves. Cadences in plainchant obviously cannot be defined by the familiar chord progressions of later music. Instead, they are typical melodic figures that lead into the closing note of a phrase or a complete chant. Such figures are far too numerous to permit easy classification, but the most common approach to the closing note is from above, either by step or by a skip of a third. Although an approach from below marks the middle cadence (mediant) in some psalm tones, it appears principally in chants of a later date. On wonders whether there is any connection between theoretical descriptions of modal ranges and the more frequent later use of this most modal-sounding cadence. We have already remarked that the semitone below the final is almost completely avoided, but the semitone above the final is common in cadences in the deuterus tonality (Modes 3 and 4). A few of the more common cadence figures are shown in Example III–7. It will be noticed that by themselves these figures are often insufficient to determine the mode of a chant. In the first place, the same figures appear in both authentic and plagal forms of a given tonality. Moreover, protus and deuterus cadences are distinguishable only when the note above the final is present; and some tritus and tetrardus patterns are identical in intervallic structure.

The study of cadences must proceed with caution because neither the textual punctuation marks nor the phrase divisions of the Solesmes editions are present in medieval manuscripts. Thus, while the endings of major sections and of complete chants are obvious, the internal phrase structure is sometimes open to differing interpretations.

Example III–7: *Typical Cadence Patterns*

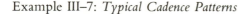

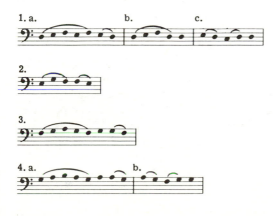

RELATION OF WORDS TO MUSIC

Any analysis of vocal style must include a study of the relationship between words and music. The several aspects of this relationship can be discussed here only in the most general way. It is pertinent to note, first of all, that vocal music of any sort must reconcile two essentially irreconcilable demands: for straightforward and comprehensible presentation of the words, and for purely musical interest and attractiveness. One might write the entire history of vocal music in terms of the varied responses to these conflicting demands. Plainchant itself, despite its rather limited scope, illustrates the extremes that result from yielding to one demand or the other. In addition, we can observe an almost infinite gradation of intermediate compromises.

The conflicting demands of text and music are responsible, at least in part, for the fundamental division of all plainchant into two stylistic categories: liturgical recitative and free composition. The essential characteristic of liturgical recitative is the chanting of a text on a single note—the reciting tone—with upward or downward inflections to mark the ends of clauses and sentences. Thus, any number of different texts may be sung to the same recitation formula. In free composition, on the other hand, each text is provided with its own distinctive melody. (The later adaptation of new texts to preexisting melodies does not invalidate the original "freedom" of composition.)

Within each of the basic styles—recitative and free—there are varying degrees of complexity. Particularly in free composition, these degrees are indicated in a rough sort of way by the terms *syllabic, neumatic,* and *melismatic.* Syllabic melodies have a single note for each syllable of text and are therefore the simplest in style. Neumatic (from the neumes of plainchant notation) implies that each syllable will be set to a neume—a group of from two to five or even more notes. Longer passages sung to a single syllable are called *melismas,* and hence a chant with several such passages is melismatic. Quite obviously, no sharp dividing lines separate the styles designated by these three terms. The difference between one note per syllable and more than one is clear, but the precise point at which neumatic style becomes melismatic can scarcely be determined. Moreover, many chants contain a mixture of two, or even all three, styles. Some chants, chiefly antiphons, are almost completely syllabic, but even they may have several syllables with two or three notes. Predominantly neumatic chants, on the other hand, may have both short syllabic passages and a few longer melismas. Despite this indefiniteness, the terms prove useful in describing the general gradations of melodic style from extreme simplicity to utmost elaboration.

LITURGICAL RECITATIVE

A wide range of styles is to be expected in freely composed chants, but it is somewhat surprising to find an almost corresponding range from simplicity to complexity in the types of liturgical recitative. Because these types appear in both the Offices and the Mass—often in combination with various classes of free composition—it is convenient to discuss them here as a group. An understanding of the general principles of liturgical recitative will make much clearer its relationship with free composition in the various services.

With only a few exceptions, liturgical texts that were not given free melodic settings were sung as recitative. Most of these texts varied from day to day, and it was therefore necessary to devise recitation formulas—usually called *tones*—that could be used for any set of words. In addition, different types of text were sung to slightly different formulas. Medieval manuscripts show considerable variation in the details of the recitation formulas, but we need concern ourselves only with the standardized tones of the modern chantbooks.

The simplest of all recitation tones are those for prayers and various types of readings, Biblical or otherwise. The *Liber Usualis* gives a number of such tones for the Mass (p. 98 ff.) and the Offices (p. 118 ff.), with somewhat complicated and confusing directions for their use. Actually, the tones consist, as we have indicated, of recitation on a single note with various inflections to mark the grammatical divisions of the text. Complications arise only for the performer, who must introduce these inflections at the proper places and adapt them to the accented syllables of the text. The simplicity of the result may be seen in the prayers and readings of the complete Mass for Easter Day (AMM, Nos. 5–22).

In the earlier Middle Ages, the normal reciting tone was **a**, with inflections down to **g** and **f**, as in AMM, Nos. 8 and 13. By the twelfth century, however, there was a growing tendency to recite on the upper note of a semitone interval (**f** or **c′**), as in the tone for the Epistle, AMM, No. 9. Most of the tones in LU call for recitation on **c′**, but some "ancient tones" on **a** are provided as alternatives.

In addition to the indicated inflections of the Epistle and Gospel tones (AMM, Nos. 9 and 13), some tones have a simpler inflection called a *flex,* corresponding roughly to a comma. The *metrum* marks a more important division of the sentence structure, and the *full stop* is the equivalent of a period. A question, or at least its final phrase, normally begins on a lower reciting tone and ends with a rising inflection. Most tones have a special formula to mark the conclusion of the text.

Quite obviously, musical interest in these tones is entirely subservient to sentence structure and word accentuation. We may well agree with Johannes de Grocheo, a theorist writing about 1300, when he says that prayers and readings do not concern the musician. One might even ask why these texts were sung at all. The practice of chanted Biblical readings is, of course, very old, reaching back to the Jewish synagogue. Moreover, the combination of song with prayer and story telling is as old as humanity itself and undoubtedly arose from a desire for the most effective communication. Yet the Church's long retention of such simple recitation must be due in large part to the proven superiority of singing over speaking in terms of projection and carrying power.

Unlike recitation tones to which many different texts may be sung, two tones are associated with special texts for special occasions. One is used for the Lamentations of Jeremiah, the lessons for the first Nocturn of Matins on Thursday, Friday, and Saturday of Holy Week (LU, pp. 626, 669, 715; in later editions, pp. 631, 692, and 754). The second serves for the Passion stories of the four Evangelists, which are the Gospel readings for the Masses of Palm Sunday and the following Tuesday, Wednesday, and Friday.[12] Each of these special tones illustrates different ways in which liturgical recitative was elaborated to meet the needs of particular texts and to enhance the solemnity of the reading.[13]

Similar degrees of elaboration are to be found in the tones for *versicles,* short sentences with equally short responses that introduce or conclude more extended parts of the liturgy. One point should not be overlooked: the *Liber Usualis* (pp. 124–27) gives twelve different tones for the concluding versicle of the Offices, *Benedicamus Domino* (Let us bless the Lord) with the response *Deo gratias* (Thanks be to God). Even a cursory glance at these tones reveals that they have nothing to do with liturgical recitative. They are, in fact, free melodies, at least some of which were extracted from other chants. It is important, therefore, not to be misled by their classification as tones in the *Liber Usualis.*

PSALMODY

The reciting formulas discussed thus far might all be called independent in that they are used for items of the liturgy that have no connection with texts set to free melodies. Psalms, on the other hand, are not normally sung alone but in combination with additional texts—either antiphons or responses—for which the melody is freely composed. This union of recitative and free composition in a single musical item necessitated certain refinements in the recitation formulas. The association with

12. The *Liber Usualis* gives only the texts of the Passions, but the complete chants are included in the *Officium Majoris Hebdomadae* (Ratisbon, 1936).
13. They are described in detail in the volume of essays that complements the present book. See also Apel, GC, p. 205 ff.

free melodies may also have encouraged the tendency toward greater elaboration displayed by the psalm formulas in comparison with the tones for prayers and readings.

According to the method of performance, we may distinguish three different types of psalmody: *direct, antiphonal,* and *responsorial.* In direct psalmody, the verses of the psalm are sung straight through with no textual additions. Antiphonal performance implies the alternation of two half-choirs, either in singing the verses of the psalm itself, or, as was more commonly the case, in singing an additional verse set to a simple, free melody—an antiphon—before, between, and after the verses of the psalm. Responsorial psalmody involves solo performance of the psalm text, with a congregational or choral response after each verse. An interesting relic of the ancient tradition of responsorial psalmody—another legacy of Jewish practices—is the custom still followed in many Protestant churches of having the psalm verses read alternately by the minister and the congregation.

Direct psalmody seems never to have occupied a prominent position in the liturgy of the Western Church, and its modern use is restricted to a few occasions when psalms are sung without an antiphon. For these occasions, simple tones "in directum" are provided (see LU, p. 118 and the references there given). These tones present no new features to detain us, and we may turn our attention to the more complex, and more interesting, formulas of antiphonal and responsorial psalmody.

ANTIPHONAL PSALMODY AND THE PSALM TONES

Antiphonal psalmody played an important role in the daily Offices and in the early form of the Mass (see Chapter V). Now, however, complete psalms with antiphons are sung only in the Offices, and it is for these that the psalm tones are intended. As may be seen in Example III–8, each mode has a corresponding psalm tone with a tenor (reciting tone) on the dominant. In addition, an irregular *tonus peregrinus* (foreign or exotic tone) has a tenor on **a** in the first half and on **g** in the second. This "wandering" tenor is often cited as the reason for the tone's being called *peregrinus,* but the name seems to have been given originally because the Western Church took over the tone from a foreign source.

Hebrew poetry—which, of course, the psalms originally were—was characterized by parallel structures in which an idea is immediately restated in different words, or two related ideas are juxtaposed. This parallelism is generally maintained in Latin (and English) translations and accounts for the structure of the psalm tones. Although these tones are still relatively simple, the way psalm texts are fitted to them calls for some explanation.

Example III–8: *The Psalm Tones*

An antiphon sung at the beginning and end frames the psalm and makes it the central portion of a larger musical unit. The antiphon naturally ends on the final of the mode, and the intonation for the first psalm verse provides a smooth transition to the tenor of the psalm tone. For each of the remaining verses the tone is repeated, but beginning directly on the tenor with the intonation omitted. At the end of the psalm, the Lesser Doxology, *Gloria Patri* (Glory be to the Father), is normally appended. It is divided into two verses and thus adds two more repetitions of the psalm tone before the antiphon is sung once again. All this is simple enough, but complications arise in the cadential divisions that mark the middle and end of the psalm tone. The mediant cadence closes the first half of each verse, and the termination, of course, the second. The flex is used only when the first half of the verse is unusually long and has two distinct grammatical divisions. The great majority of verses do not need the flex and simply proceed on the tenor until they reach the mediant. (As the psalms are printed in the *Liber Usualis,* an asterisk marks the position of the mediant, and a dagger [†] indicates the flex.)

It is adapting the cadential patterns to the accented syllables of the text that creates problems, for the accents must fall on the notes indicated by ′ in Example III–8. This accounts for the optional notes in parentheses. (In the *Liber Usualis,* they are hollow instead of solid black notes.) If the accent falls on the penultimate syllable, the optional notes are omitted. They must be used, however, when the accented syllable is the third from the end of the phrase. Some of the cadence patterns, it will be noted, also specify the position of the penultimate accented syllable. In these cases, two optional notes are required to adapt the formulas to such various rhythms as /—/—; /—/–; /-/—; and /-/-. The way in which this adaptation is carried out, and the use of psalm tones in general, may perhaps be most easily comprehended by a careful study of AMM, No. 2, in which some verses of Psalm 115 (116) are set to Psalm Tone 3.[14]

One aspect of the psalm tones not indicated in AMM, No. 2 is that some of them have several different terminations. Tones 2, 5, 6, and the tonus peregrinus have only the ending given in Example III–8. For the other five tones, however, the number of terminations ranges from three for Tone 8 to ten for Tone 1. These terminations may be seen in LU, pp. 113–17, where each is identified by a letter corresponding to the note on which it ends. From this it is apparent that the psalm tones do not necessarily close on the final of the mode. Indeed, the single termination of Tone 5 ends on **a**, and none of the five terminations of Tone 3 ends on **e**. This may seem surprising until we remember that the performance does not end with the psalm tone but with the repetition of the antiphon. Just as the intonation linked the end of the antiphon with the reciting tone, so the terminations are designed to provide a smooth transition to its beginning. Roughly speaking, the number of terminations for a given tone corresponds with both the total number of antiphons in the mode and the number of different characteristic patterns with which those antiphons begin.

14. The numbering of the psalms is complicated by different divisions in the Latin (Vulgate) and English Bibles. The number given first is that of the Latin Bible as used in LU. For convenience in finding the English version of a psalm, its number—when different—follows in parentheses. The following complete conversion table may also prove useful:

Latin		English	Latin		English
1–8	=	1–8	114 & 115	=	116
9	=	9 & 10	116–145	=	117–146
10–112	=	11–113	146 & 147	=	147
113	=	114 & 115	148–150	=	148–150

OTHER TONES FOR PSALMODIC RECITATIVE

In addition to the simple tones for psalms, other sets of tones are used for other texts or other forms of psalmodic recitative. Biblical songs of praise, called *canticles,* occupy prominent positions in some Offices (see Chapter IV) and are sung like psalms with an antiphon preceding and following. For some canticles the standard psalm tones are used. Others have their own set of eight tones. Indeed, the *Liber Usualis* provides two sets of tones for the *Magnificat,* the canticle of Vespers (pp. 207–18). The first set differs from the psalm tones only in a few details, but the second, the "solemn tones" for use on principal feasts, has more elaborate formulas for the mediant cadences and in most cases for the intonation as well. In addition, a different manner of performance increases the solemnity of the canticles for Lauds, Vespers, and Compline and distinguishes them from the Office psalms. Instead of the first verse alone, all verses of these canticles begin with the intonation.

The process of elaboration that is evident in the solemn tones for the *Magnificat* is carried still further in the special tones for Psalm 94 (95) (the Invitatory Psalm of Matins) and in the different set of tones for the verse and doxology of the Introit, the sole remaining vestige of psalmodic recitative in the Mass. It should always be remembered that elaboration of the chants does not represent a chronological development; it reflects instead the liturgical function and importance of a given text. As might be expected, therefore, elaboration reaches a peak of complexity in the tones for the solo verses of responsorial psalmody. In these tones, the formulas for the intonation, mediant, and termination become so long and so highly ornamented that shorter verses may not even use the reciting tone. We shall return to all of these forms at the appropriate places in Chapters IV and V, but here we must mention two aspects of the tones for the Invitatory Psalm, the Introit, and the Great Responsories (see p. 105 ff). As in performance of the *Magnificat,* the intonation formula is never omitted when any of these tones is repeated. Moreover a second and different intonation is used for the second half of each tone or for the second and third parts when a tone has three instead of two subdivisions. The second aspect of the three sets of tones is even more significant, because musical considerations begin to take precedence over the demands of the text. Instead of having variant forms to accommodate different accentual patterns, as do the tones for the psalms and the *Magnificat,* the terminations in these three sets consist of fixed formulas that disregard textual accents in the final syllables of the verse. Especially in the responsorial tones, musical elaboration has become more important than clear and forceful declamation of the text.

WORD ACCENT AND MELODIC LINE

Fixed cadential patterns that disregard textual accents bring up one of the more vexing problems in the stylistic analysis of plainchant: how and to what extent do the melodic lines reflect the accentuation of the text? It is commonly said that Gregorian Chant is "oratorical" melody based on the grammatical accent of its text. Some scholars have even raised the principle of musical reflection of textual accent to "a very important law of composition." Textual accents, obviously, must always be considered in the creation of vocal melodies. It remains doubtful, however, whether laws can be formulated as to how those accents should be musically represented. [15]

The problem begins, as it always must, with the accentual characteristics of the language involved—Latin, of course, in the case of Gregorian Chant. In classical Latin of the period from the second century B.C. to the fourth century A.D., accent was primarily a matter of quantity—that is, of long and short syllables. In addition, however, accent was a matter of quality or stress and rise in pitch. After the classical period, Latin gradually lost its accents of quantity, and only the accents of stress and pitch inflection remained. This change in accentuation took place during the formative years of Gregorian Chant and was essentially completed by the time the chants as we know them began to be notated. We may safely assume, therefore, that free melodies were composed to fit a spoken Latin in which stress and a higher pitch level distinguished accented from unaccented syllables.

Without going into the rules for determining Latin accentuation, we may note that the accent never falls on the last syllable of a Latin word. Thus, in words of two syllables, it is always the first that is accented. In longer words, the accent falls on either the penultimate or antepenultimate syllable. In an age when almost everyone knows little Latin and less Greek, it is fortunate that the *Liber Usualis* normally indicates the accents in the chant texts.

While there is general agreement as to the accentuation of spoken Latin in the Middle Ages, there is almost none as to how this accentuation is or should be reflected in the plainchant melodies. In syllabic or nearly syllabic style, one of the fundamental "laws" of composition is that the accented syllables, especially of the more important words, should coincide with higher notes or melodic peaks. This does happen in many cases, of which a few may be seen in Example III–9a. On the other hand, it is by no means difficult to find instances when the melody ignores or even contradicts the raised accent of spoken Latin. When several syllables are sung on the same note, as in Example III–9b, accent

15. Apel, GC, pp. 275–97, discusses at length the problems of textual versus musical accent.

results only from dynamic stress introduced by the performer; and in the melodic settings in Example III–9c, the musical stress actually seems to fall on an unaccented syllable.

Example III–9: *Relationship of Melodic and Textual Accents*

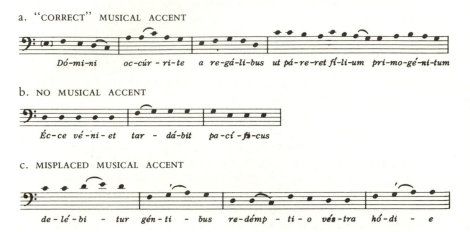

a. "CORRECT" MUSICAL ACCENT

Dó-mi-ni   oc-cúr - ri-te   a re-gá-li-bus   ut pá-re-ret fí-li-um   pri-mo-gé-ni-tum

b. NO MUSICAL ACCENT

Éc-ce vé-ni-et   tar - dá-bit   pa-cí - fi-cus

c. MISPLACED MUSICAL ACCENT

de - lé - bi - tur gén-ti - bus   re-démp - ti - o vés-tra   hó-di - e

Problems of correlating musical and textual stresses become even more complicated in neumatic and melismatic styles. Melodic peaks and higher notes still may or may not coincide with accented syllables; but, in addition, the length of syllables is now determined by the number of notes to which each is sung. Even a slight acquaintance with melodies set to English texts should make it obvious that music often translates strong and weak syllables into long and short notes. This may also happen, of course, in setting Latin texts, with no implication that the spoken syllables have correspondingly long and short values.

In syllabic chants, lengthening accented syllables is impossible, at least in the officially accepted rhythms of the Solesmes editions and performances, but there is considerable evidence that long and short notes did exist in earlier stages of plainchant development. The whole subject of plainchant rhythm is so uncertain and so controversial, however, that any attempt to prove a correspondence between long notes and stressed syllables would be unprofitable, not to say impossible. Stressed syllables can be lengthened, of course, by being given more notes than the surrounding weak syllables. Opinions vary considerably as to whether this procedure, which Apel calls *melismatic accent,* belongs among the structural principles of plainchant.

We must note, first of all, that a common and important stylistic feature of plainchant is the placement of melismas on final syllables, which are always unaccented. This characteristic procedure has been a source of distress for scholars who felt that agreement between word and music was "the supreme law of all vocal music." Around 1600, indeed, humanistic insistence on classical Latin led to "reform" editions of plain-chant that redistributed the text so as to reduce or eliminate melismas on weak syllables. Such reforms corrupted the chant and destroyed one of its most appealing musical aspects. We must accept the fact that vocal music recognizes no "supreme law." For the composers of plainchant, melismatic extensions on final syllables obviously had no connection with the idea of melismatic accent. Instead, they provided a perfectly normal means of achieving free melodic expression.

An investigation of melismatic accent, then, must leave out of account words with melismas on the final syllable. Many more words remain, however, in which the presence or absence of melismatic accent can be tested. Positive examples, in which the accented syllable has more notes than the others, are very common (Example III–10a). On the other hand, the accented syllable and at least one other may have the same number of notes (Example III–10b). Even more frequent are negative instances when the accented syllable has only one or a few notes, while unstressed syllables have longer melismas (Example III–10c). Some scholars have gone so far as to raise this reverse form of melismatic accent to a constructive principle.

Example III–10: *Melismatic Accents*

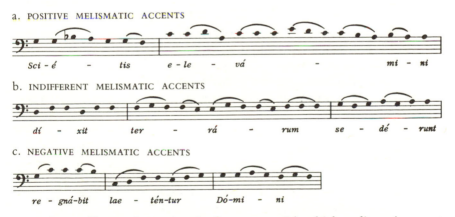

a. POSITIVE MELISMATIC ACCENTS

Sci - é   tis   e - le - vá   mi - ni

b. INDIFFERENT MELISMATIC ACCENTS

dí - xit   ter - rá - rum   se - dé - runt

c. NEGATIVE MELISMATIC ACCENTS

re - gná-bit   lae - tén-tur   Dó-mi - ni

In an effort to determine the frequency with which melismatic accent appears, Willi Apel tabulated the number of words with positive, negative, or indifferent accents in a series of chants from the Proper of the Mass.[16] Apel's findings show that, in Introits, Alleluias, Offertories, and Communions, words with a positive melismatic accent greatly outnumber negative and indifferent cases combined. In Graduals and Responsories for Matins, on the other hand, negative accents alone equal or exceed positive ones. The appearance of elaborately melismatic Alleluias

16. GC, p. 283 ff.

in the first group is surprising, and Apel suggests that their later date may account for their greater use of melismatic accent. The relative rarity of such accents in ornate responsorial chants, however, is only to be expected, given the musical independence we have observed in the responsorial tones. Clearly, music has here asserted its right to develop freely according to its own laws, and the words have become its servant.

The controversies over whether pitch accents and melismatic accents—positive or negative—constitute fundamental laws of vocal composition seem pointless. For one thing, they fail to consider that music can emphasize words and syllables in many more ways than are available in the most high-flown elocution. To cite but one example, it should be obvious that music can stress a syllable by placing it at the bottom as well as at the top of a melodic curve. Although such an accent may have no counterpart in Latin speech, it occurs with some frequency in Gregorian Chant. Approaching the lowest note by a downward skip often increases the effectiveness of this reverse pitch accent (see Example III–11a). Yet this type of accent too does not always control the melodic outline; in some instances the accented syllable falls on a note other than the lowest (Example III–11b).

No composer worth his salt will voluntarily limit himself to one or two types of melodic accentuation. Instead, he will alternate types, combine them, let one reinforce or conflict with another, vary their use, in short, in an infinite number of ways. At times, too, he may ignore textual accents or even misplace them for the sake of his melodic line. All of these things the composers of plainchant did. Let us enjoy the results without trying to raise any type of musical accent to a law of vocal composition. One of the charms of this music lies in the various ways it attempts to reconcile the conflicting claims of words and music.

Example III–11

a. REVERSED PITCH ACCENTS

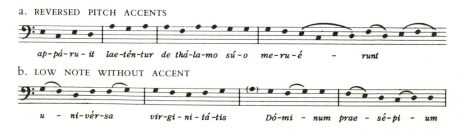

ap-pá-ru-it   lae-tén-tur de thá-la-mo sú-o   me-ru-é   –   runt

b. LOW NOTE WITHOUT ACCENT

u - ni-vér-sa   vir-gi-ni-tá-tis   Dó-mi - num prae - sé-pi - um

THE RHYTHM OF GREGORIAN CHANT

The greatest unsolved—and perhaps insoluble—problem with regard to Gregorian Chant concerns its rhythmic interpretation. Attractive as performances by the Solesmes monks may be, their solution is neither the only possible one nor the one supported by the greatest weight of historical evidence. As we have seen, the square notation of the late Middle Ages—and of modern chantbooks—gives no indication of note values. According to the basic principle of rhythmic interpretation established by the Solesmes monks, then, all notes are of equal value except dotted notes, which normally come only at the ends of phrases and are doubled in length. Such dotted notes are a modern invention, however, and do not appear in medieval sources. Equally modern is the mysterious *ictus* indicated in the *Liber Usualis* by a short vertical stroke called an *episema* (ı). As the Solesmes monks have never satisfactorily described the musical effect of the ictus, and as its placement is determined by somewhat arbitrary rules, it need not concern us further here.[17] One other rhythmic sign in modern chantbooks, the *horizontal episema* (–), does find a precedent in medieval usage. It is generally agreed that this sign, which may appear over a single note or over a neume of two or more notes, indicates a lengthening of the notes; but there agreement stops. For the Solesmes monks, the lengthening is "slight," and the oftener the sign occurs, "the less we must mark it and vice versa" (LU, p. xx). Going to the other extreme, some scholars have interpreted the horizontal episema in medieval sources as indicating a doubling of the note values.

The disagreement as to the meaning of the horizontal episema is typical of the opposing theories concerning the rhythm of Gregorian Chant. The earliest manuscripts with chant melodies contain a number of so-called "rhythmic signs" in addition to the neumatic notation. For the Solesmes monks, these signs merely imply nuances of performance within an essentially even flow. For other scholars, however, the signs coupled with variant ways of writing the actual neumes are clear indications of long and short note values.

The term *mensuralists* provides a convenient label for all those who believe that Gregorian Chant originally used long and short notes in measured values. But beyond this fundamental belief, the mensuralists are rarely in agreement. The difficulty lies, of course, in the inadequacies of early notation. Even if long and short notes are clearly indicated—which is by no means always the case—the notation gives no clue as to their relative values. Are there only two values in a ratio of 2 to 1 (♩ and ♪), or may some longer notes equal three or even four of the shorter value? We do not and cannot know. Mensural transcriptions, therefore, can only be individual interpretations, and their authenticity must always remain in doubt.

Uncertain as the results of mensural transcription may be, historical evidence strongly supports the mensuralists' fundamental belief. Again and again, theoretical treatises of the early Middle Ages make it clear that the chant did use long and short notes. Unfortunately, the treatises, like the notation, confirm the principle without providing sufficient infor-

---

17. For the attempted explanation, see LU, p. xxvj ff.

mation for its application. Although we may feel legitimate resentment against the inadequacies of the theorists, those of the notation are explicable when we remember its original function: to remind the singer of a melody he *already knew*. We may safely assume that the rhythmic indications of early notation were sufficient to recall the known values of the notes, just as the neumes recalled the notes themselves. It is our loss that later and clearer indication of notes and intervals went hand in hand with the abandonment of rhythmic signs and, presumably, of mensural performance.

The practice of using Gregorian Chant as the basis for polyphony was at least partly responsible for the late medieval performance in equal note values (see Chapter VIII). The term *plainchant* itself (*cantus planus* or *musica plana*) first appears in the tenth century with somewhat uncertain meaning. By the thirteenth century, however, the term distinguished the free, unmeasured rhythm of Gregorian Chant from the measured note values of polyphony. It would seem, therefore, that we must regard equal note values—the basis of the Solesmes monks' rhythmic theories—as a corrupt practice of the later Middle Ages, when the tradition of mensural performance had already been forgotten. Undeniably, the subtle refinements and elegant singing of the Solesmes monks result in performances of great beauty. The frequent failure of other choirs to achieve the same effects, however, suggests how far the Solesmes monks may be from reproducing the typical sounds of a less elegant and more robust age.

MUSICAL EXPRESSION OF THE TEXTS

Many books designed to popularize Gregorian Chant—and even, unfortunately, some scholarly writings—have overindulged in descriptive explanations of the way individual melodies reflect the moods of their texts. To a lesser extent, there have also been efforts to discover examples of *word painting,* the melodic depiction of particular words or phrases.

The presence of two consonants after each of the first three vowels in the words "et turtur nidum" (and the turtle dove a nest) calls for a series of liquescent neumes (LU, p. 556). That these neumes may also be thought of as imitating the cooing of doves is merely a happy coincidence.[18] Words indicating height or depth, ascent or descent, are sometimes given appropriate melodic positions. Frequently, however, the implications of such words are either ignored or flatly contradicted by the melodic progressions. Examples of word painting—when and if they do occur—may well have been incidental and perhaps even unintentional.

18. Apel, GC, p. 303.

That individual chants were intended to express such moods as anguish, grief, resignation, reverence, or humility is even more difficult to believe. These descriptions smack of nineteenth-century romanticism and had best be abandoned altogether. Certainly the impartial listener who was not forewarned would be hard pressed to distinguish exaltation from anguish.

Advocates of romantic expressiveness in Gregorian Chant forget two of its most significant aspects. As we have already seen, centonization, or the construction of new chants from preexisting melodic figures, is characteristic of several types of chant. That this procedure precludes any close association with the mood of individual texts is self-evident. Even more obviously, complete melodies to which different texts have been adapted (*contrafacta*) cannot reflect the varying moods of them all. That centonization and adaptation played such basic roles in forming the plainchant repertory surely eliminates expressive relationships between melody and text as a conscious goal of this music.

The second overlooked aspect of Gregorian Chant will answer the question that a rejection of romantic expressiveness must inevitably raise. If the composers of the chants were not concerned with musical representation of the text, what determined the differing styles in which they wrote? Peter Wagner answered this question long ago in his monumental *Introduction to the Gregorian Melodies*.[19] Taking a single text, *Justus ut palma* (The Righteous Shall Flourish), Wagner showed that it might be set in a wide variety of styles, ranging from the simplest recitative to the most elaborately melismatic free melody. The chief factor determining this style, then, is not the meaning or mood of the text, but rather its place and function in the liturgy.

Liturgical function as the determining factor of melodic style does not preclude "expressiveness" in Gregorian Chant. It does mean, however, that the expressive element in the chant must not and cannot be described as a personal interpretation of a particular text. The chants as a whole, rather, must be taken as a musical embodiment of the spiritual values inherent in the various acts of collective worship that make up the liturgy of the Church. In addition to its great beauty, then, the flexibility and the usefulness of Gregorian Chant account for its extraordinary vitality. No other music has endured for nearly two thousand years. No other music has been so long regarded as the ideal adornment of the Catholic liturgy. But no other music has so successfully served every liturgical function from the simplest to the most solemn. For this reason, obviously, an understanding of the liturgy is a prerequisite for an understanding and appreciation of the chant itself.

19. *Einführung in die Gregorianischen Melodien;* unfortunately, only the first volume has been translated into English (see Bibliography). The musical examples of Vol. 3, however, are written in the by-now-familiar (it is hoped) square notation.

CHAPTER IV

The Music of the Offices

The preceding chapter dealt with liturgical recitative and the various tones for singing the psalms and canticles that make up the bulk of the music in the daily Offices. Here, our primary concern will be with free melodies: the antiphons and responsories that are used in conjunction with psalmody, and the Office hymns, which have an independent musical function. First, however, we must review the origin of the Offices and their formal organization. We shall then be in a better position to appreciate the important role that music plays in these services.

During the early centuries of Christianity, its adherents were often forced—for both convenience and safety—to hold night assemblies, or vigils. At first, vigils were held only on Saturdays, beginning after midnight and closing in the early hours of Sunday morning with the celebration of the Eucharist in its primitive form as the forerunner of the Mass (see Chapter V). Sunday, the day of the Resurrection, thus replaced the Jewish Sabbath (Saturday) as the festival day of the week. Vigil services consisted primarily of prayers, Scripture readings, and the singing of psalms, which were traditional activities at Jewish hours of prayer and have remained the fundamental elements of the Roman Offices. To these was added at an early date the apparently Christian innovation of singing hymns.

As Christianity grew in strength and numbers, the celebration of vigils evolved into three separate Offices. Originally, it was customary to anticipate the vigil with a service at sunset, the primitive form of *Vespers*. The central portion of the vigil, celebrated in the last hours of the night, was later called *Nocturn* or, somewhat illogically, *Matins*. A third service, held in the early morning hours before the Mass, developed into the Office later known as *Lauds*. These three, together with the Mass, provided the chief liturgical forms in the first centuries of the Christian era. It is no surprise, therefore, to discover that Vespers, Matins, and Lauds were and still are the most elaborate and musically most important Offices. Moreover, the ancient practice of beginning a celebration on the preceding evening is still followed. The series of Offices for a particular Sunday or feast day always begins with First Vespers on the eve of the feast and closes with Second Vespers on the day itself.

Celebration of the Mass with its preceding vigil in three parts originally took place only on Sunday, but it was soon extended to include the feasts of martyrs and other holy or fast days. In addition, private devotions were often celebrated in the home during the day, particularly at the third, sixth, and ninth hours (that is, at 9 A.M., noon, and 3 P.M.), corresponding approximately to the traditional Jewish hours of prayer. These times were hallowed for Christians by their coincidence with the judgment, crucifixion, and death of Christ on Good Friday. The greatest impetus to the further development of the Offices, however, came with the rise of monasticism (see Chapter II). Daily observance of both vigils and the daytime Hours became a normal part of monastic life. During the course of the fourth century, moreover, public services in the churches began to replace the daily devotions that had thus far been largely private in character.

Many of the early developments in the history of the Offices took place in the Eastern branches of the Church, particularly at Antioch and Jerusalem. Our knowledge of their growth in the West, especially as they were observed by nonmonastic churches, is scanty and uncertain. As we have seen, the first description of the complete cycle of daily Offices appears in the Rule of St. Benedict, dating from about A.D. 530. With some modification of their contents, these Offices quickly became standard for all of Western Christendom. Our present concern is with the order and contents of the Offices as they were celebrated in later medieval times. Their order has remained unchanged, and their contents differ only in a few details from the prescribed modern form.

The eight daily Offices appear in the following order:

1. Matins	Sometime after midnight
2. Lauds	At daybreak
3. Prime (first hour)	6 A.M.
4. Terce (third hour)	9 A.M.
5. Sext (sixth hour)	Noon
6. None (ninth hour)	3 P.M.
7. Vespers	Early evening
8. Compline	Before retiring

As we have said, the three services that evolved from the early vigils are the longest and most elaborate of the Offices. Compline, apparently one of the latest additions to the series, is only slightly shorter than Vespers and Lauds, but it is musically much less significant. The Offices from Prime to None are relatively short and are known, indeed, as the Little or Lesser Hours. The Day Hours, another designation commonly encountered, include the entire series with the exception of Matins. It is perhaps because the service of Matins is now usually spoken rather than sung that it is excluded from the modern *Antiphonary* (see Chapter II). Indeed, the Offices as a whole are rarely performed with music at the present time outside of monasteries. Throughout the Middle Ages and Renaissance, however, they were normally sung in full daily in all monastic establishments and in cathedral and collegiate churches.

THE FORM OF THE OFFICES: VESPERS

Because the celebration of Sundays and other feasts always begins with First Vespers on the preceding evening, we will deal with that service first in discussing the liturgical structure of the Offices. We may thus establish the general procedures characteristic of all Offices and simplify later explanations of the ways in which other services resemble or differ from Vespers.

Offices normally begin with a number of private devotions, after which the versicle and response *Deus in adjutorium* is sung. This text is the first verse of Psalm 69 (70): "Make haste, O God, to deliver me; make haste to help me, O Lord." The response, the second half of the verse, continues with the Lesser Doxology and concludes either with a short Alleluia or, between Septuagesima Sunday and Wednesday in Holy Week, with the phrase *Laus tibi Domine Rex aeternae gloriae* (Praise be to thee, O Lord, King of eternal glory).[1]

For singing *Deus in adjutorium,* three recitation tones are provided: a simple or ferial tone, a festal tone, and a solemn tone that is used only at Vespers of solemn feasts (see LU, pp. 263 and 250). This restriction in the use of the solemn tone confirms the preeminent rank of Vespers in the hierarchy of the Offices. The three tones also provide another interesting example of the degrees of elaboration to be observed in the recitation formulas (see Chapter III).

After this opening versicle common to all Offices, Vespers continues with five psalms, each of which is sung with its own antiphon, one of the two types of free melodies used in connection with psalmody. The next item in Vespers, a short reading normally consisting of only one Biblical verse, is called a *Chapter.* A hymn now follows the Chapter, but in medieval times a Great Responsory came between these two items. Great Responsories, the form into which responsorial psalmody evolved, normally follow longer readings, or *Lessons,* in both the Offices (Matins) and the Mass. Their use in Vespers, despite the brevity of the Chapter, was undoubtedly intended to increase the solemnity of that service, for of all chants responsories are the most elaborate and ornate. Still greater solemnity was later achieved by the Notre Dame composers, who used the Vesper responsories as the basis for polyphonic compositions (see Chapter IX). It is doubly regrettable, therefore, that these responsories have been abandoned except in some monastic rites.

A versicle separates the hymn from the *Magnificat,* now the musical

1.   For the text of the Lesser Doxology, see AMM, No. 2, verses 9 and 10.

All that remains today of the Abbey Church at Cluny, a most influential center of liturgical observance in the Middle Ages, is the right lateral nave and the imposing clock tower.

high point of Vespers. Three New Testament canticles find a place in the Offices, but the Song of Mary (Luke 1:46–55) receives the position of honor as the canticle of Vespers. As discussed in Chapter III, the *Magnificat* itself is sung to tones closely resembling those of the psalms. The antiphon for the *Magnificat,* however, is generally somewhat longer and more elaborate than other antiphons.

Following the *Magnificat,* the service of Vespers concludes, as most Offices do, with prayers and a benediction. Also inserted here at Vespers is the antiphon "Suffrage of [petition to] All the Saints," or antiphons commemorating feasts or their Octaves. These chants deserve mention because they are among the few antiphons in the Offices now detached from psalms and sung as independent melodies (see LU, pp. 262–62[11]). Of the closing versicles, only the *Benedicamus Domino* is sung to one of the elaborate free melodies given in LU, pp. 124–27. These melodies are used regularly for Vespers and Lauds and occasionally for other Offices. The versicle itself, however, is sung at the close of every Office, usually to a simple recitation tone (see LU, p. 233).

To clarify and summarize the foregoing discussion, the essential elements of the Vesper service are outlined in Table 5. Texts identified by their opening words in Latin are invariable and belong to the Ordinary of the Office. Sections indicated by a general title in English have texts that change according to the day of the week or the particular feast that is being celebrated. Here, our primary concern is with the variable musical elements printed in capital letters in Table 5. Most of the important feasts of the Church year have their own (Proper) antiphons for the five psalms of Vespers. Where these are not provided, the Ordinary antiphons of Vespers are to be used.[2] The same situation exists with regard to the Vesper hymn. Sundays and feasts either have a Proper hymn or use the common one for Vespers (LU, p. 256). The antiphon for the *Magnificat,* on the other hand, is always Proper, and its melodies, therefore, are to be sought in the Propers of the Time and of the Saints.

Table 5: *Form of Vespers*

> *Deus in adjutorium*
> Five Psalms with five ANTIPHONS
> Chapter
> (GREAT RESPONSORY)
> HYMN
> Versicle
> *Magnificat* with ANTIPHON
> Prayers and ANTIPHONS of Commemoration
>   or Suffrage of All the Saints
> Closing versicles, including *Benedicamus Domino*

THE FORMS OF THE OTHER DAY HOURS: COMPLINE

In its formal structure, Compline differs little from Vespers, but it proves to be much less important and less interesting from a musical point of view. There are three psalms instead of five, with a single antiphon. The positions of the Chapter and Hymn are reversed, and the Chapter here is followed by a simple responsorial chant called a Short Responsory. The canticle is the Song of Simeon (Luke 2:29–32), *Nunc dimittis* (Lord, now lettest thou thy servant depart in peace). The musical poverty of Compline becomes apparent only when we realize that the same few chants are used repeatedly throughout the year. Not even the most solemn feasts have Proper chants for Compline. In the Ordinary of the Office, each day of the week has a different antiphon for use with the psalms except in Paschal Time, when the same antiphon (Alleluia) is used every day. The antiphon for *Nunc dimittis* is unchanging, as are the texts of the hymn and the Short Responsory. These latter two items, however, have different melodies for different seasons of the Church year. Thus Compline can boast fewer than a dozen chant texts that are set to only a slightly larger number of free melodies. The reason for its neglect in the study of Gregorian Chant is obvious.

Following the *Benedicamus Domino* of Compline, the Offices of the day conclude with one of the so-called Antiphons of the Blessed Virgin

---

2.   They may be found in LU, pp. 251–56 for Sunday at Vespers and pp. 280–316 for Vespers and Compline on weekdays.

A reconstruction of the Abbey of Cluny in about 1157, showing its complexity and size (after a drawing by K. J. Conant).

Mary (B.V.M. or, in Latin, B.M.V.—*Beatae Mariae Virginis*). There are four of these Marian antiphons, one for each season of the Church year. We shall consider their musical characteristics later, but a few words must be said here about their liturgical use. They are rather long and elaborate chants that have no present-day connection with psalmody. Originally, they were not intended for use after Compline, and the *Liber Usualis* still calls for their performance after Lauds, Terce, and Vespers whenever another Office or the Mass does not immediately follow.[3] It is thus a mistake to credit them solely to Compline. Such a limited use would be inconsistent with the popularity these melodies enjoyed in the Middle Ages and the many polyphonic settings they received throughout the Renaissance.

LAUDS

Lauds and Vespers are identical in formal and musical structure, but have two noteworthy differences with regard to their texts. In place of the *Magnificat,* the concluding canticle of Lauds is the Song of Zachariah, *Benedictus Dominus Deus Israel* (Blessed be the Lord God of Israel; Luke 1:68–79). This is the third major (that is, New Testament) canticle to be assigned a fixed position in the Ordinary of the Offices. As with the *Magnificat,* the antiphon sung with the *Benedictus* is always Proper on Sundays and important feasts.

The second difference between the texts of Lauds and Vespers occurs

3. See the directions for their use in LU, pp. 223, 240, and 261.

in the fourth of the five "psalms." The other four are really psalms, but the fourth is always one of the minor, or Old Testament, canticles. The fourteen such canticles are distributed throughout the week in two sets of seven. One set is used for most of the year, while the other is reserved for the period between Septuagesima and Palm Sunday.[4]

THE LESSER HOURS

The four Lesser Hours—Prime, Terce, Sext, and None—are the shortest Offices and the least important from a musical point of view. They all follow the same structural plan (although Prime has several additional items not found in the other three Hours) and may therefore be discussed together. Between the standard beginning with *Deus in adjutorium* and ending with *Benedicamus Domino,* these Offices have a hymn, three psalms with only one antiphon, a Chapter with a Short Responsory, and a versicle. Much of even this small amount of music either is not the exclusive property of the Lesser Hours or remains unchanged throughout the year. For example, the four antiphons—one for each Hour—are often borrowed from Lauds, and the hymns are normally part of the Ordinary. As a rule, only the Short Responsories are Proper to a particular Hour of a given feast.

Before we turn to the structural pattern of Matins, it may be helpful to present in tabular form the essential musical elements of the Day Hours. The arrangement of these Hours in Table 6 ignores chronological succession in an attempt to show more clearly various differences from the form of Vespers and Lauds.

Table 6: *Musical Elements of the Day Hours*

Vespers	Lauds	Compline	Little Hours
Deus in adjutorium ———————————————————————			
			Hymn
5 Psalms	5 Psalms (1 a canticle)	3 Psalms	3 Psalms
5 Antiphons	5 Antiphons	1 Antiphon	1 Antiphon
		Hymn	
Chapter	Chapter	Chapter	Chapter
Hymn	Hymn	Short Responsory	Short Responsory
Versicle	Versicle	Versicle	Versicle
Magnificat with Antiphon	*Benedictus* with Antiphon	*Nunc dimittis* with Antiphon	
Benedicamus Domino ———————————————————————			
(Antiphon of the B.M.V.) ———————————————————————			

---

4. See LU, p. 221, for Lauds of Feasts. Apel, GC, p. 21, lists the fourteen canticles as they are distributed throughout the days of the week.

MATINS

A discussion of Matins has been deferred until now, not only because it is the longest and most elaborate of the Offices, but also because it introduces totally different structural principles. Its form cannot be compared with the forms of the other Offices, although they all have at least the singing of psalms with antiphons in common.

Matins subdivides into four distinct sections that are performed without interruption. After the opening section, which has no specific name, come three Nocturns, each built on the same structural pattern. The whole is framed by the normal introduction to all Offices (*Pater noster, Ave Maria,* Credo, versicle, and *Deus in adjutorium*) and by the usual close with *Benedicamus Domino.*

After *Deus in adjutorium,* the characteristic chants of Matins begin with an antiphon and Psalm 94 (95), *Venite, exsultemus Domino* (Oh come, let us sing unto the Lord). From these words come the designations Invitatory Psalm and, for the antiphon, simply Invitatory. It is because of its appropriate text that Psalm 94 (95) invariably begins the

Pope Urban II depicted consecrating the high altar of the Abbey Church at Cluny in 1095 (from a manuscript at the Bibliothèque Nationale, Paris).

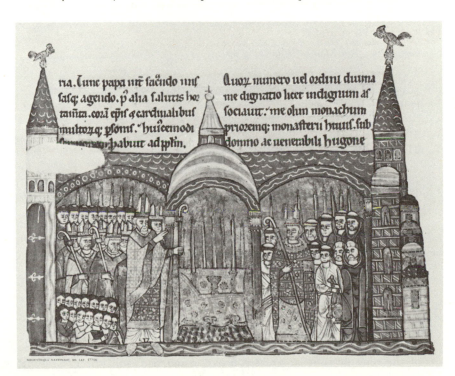

Office of Matins. No other psalm is so honored by a fixed position in the Ordinary of the Offices. Following the Invitatory Psalm, the concluding item in the first section of Matins is a hymn.

The Office continues immediately with the three Nocturns, each of which follows the same pattern. Each Nocturn begins with three psalms, each with its own antiphon, and concludes with three Lessons, each followed by a Great Responsory. The psalms and Lessons are separated by a versicle, the *Pater noster,* an absolution, and a blessing. As the important musical items in the Nocturns, then, we have the nine psalms with their antiphons, and the nine responsories following the Lessons. In the *Liber Usualis,* for no apparent reason, the antiphons are numbered from one to three in each Nocturn, but the Lessons and responsories are numbered consecutively from one to nine.

After the antiphons and responsories of the Nocturns, which are Proper to particular feasts, the so-called Hymn of Thanksgiving, *Te Deum laudamus* (We praise thee, God; LU, p. 1832) completes the chants peculiar to Matins on Sundays and feasts. The entire form of Matins as performed in the Middle Ages is shown in Table 7. It should be noted, however, that modern practice has shortened the Office slightly by dropping the ninth responsory and letting the *Te Deum* take its place. On the other hand, during Holy Week and in the Office of the Dead, it is the *Te Deum* that is omitted.

Table 7: *Outline of Matins*

Pater noster, Ave Maria, Credo
Versicle
Deus in adjutorium
Invitatory with Psalm 94 (95)
Hymn

First Nocturn

Three psalms with their antiphons	(1–3)
Three Lessons, each followed by a Great Responsory	(1–3)

Second Nocturn

Three psalms and three antiphons	(1–3)
Three Lessons and three Great Responsories	(4–6)

Third Nocturn

Three psalms and three antiphons	(1–3)
Three Lessons and three Great Responsories	(7–9)

Te Deum laudamus (on Sundays and feasts)
Versicle
Prayer
Benedicamus Domino

As a final comment on the form of Matins, note that it might be considerably shortened for feasts of lesser importance. Such feasts, instead of the nine Lessons of greater feasts, often had only three, or what amounted to a single Nocturn. The rank of a feast, indeed, was sometimes indicated in church calendars by the number of Lessons in its Office of Matins. In this respect, Matins was more flexible in structure than the other Offices, none of which admits of such variation.

Because the music for Matins is richer and more varied than for any other Office, it is particularly regrettable that so few examples are readily available for study. The Office is not represented at all in the *Antiphonary* for the Day Hours, and the *Liber Usualis* contains the Matins of only eight feasts.[5]

Even these few examples demonstrate the remarkable flexibility of form that is characteristic of Matins. Only the services for the Nativity and Corpus Christi exactly follow the structural outline given in Table 7, with the *Te Deum* substituted for the ninth responsory. The three services of Holy Week omit the Invitatory Psalm and hymn and begin directly with the first antiphon of Nocturn I. The *Te Deum* is not sung on these days. On Easter Sunday, both the Invitatory Psalm and the *Te Deum* reappear, but there is still no hymn and only one Nocturn. Pentecost also has only one Nocturn, which closes with the *Te Deum* in place of the third responsory, but the opening section of Matins is complete. Thus we may regard this Office as the normal form of Matins with one Nocturn. Matins in the Office of the Dead lacks only a hymn and the *Te Deum*. On some occasions, however, there is a choice as to whether it is performed with one or three Nocturns (see LU, p. 1779). It would be difficult to find clearer illustrations of the way services may be varied to meet different liturgical situations.

From the foregoing discussion of the Offices, it must be obvious that the Book of Psalms provides the major portion of their texts. The Offices, in fact, were designed so that all 150 psalms would be sung once each week. In each service, the psalms were originally performed in numerical order; but, for many feasts, psalms deemed more appropriate to the occasion are substituted. However, performance in ascending numerical order is always strictly maintained.

Psalms and canticles, as we saw in Chapter III, are sung to recitation formulas, or tones, that correspond to the eight Church modes. The choice of a tone for use with a particular psalm, however, has nothing to

5.   For convenience in observing the form of Matins and examining its music, page references for the eight examples in LU are listed here. (Page numbers in parentheses are those in later editions of LU with the "restored Ordo of Holy Week.")

Nativity	368–92
Maundy Thursday	621–46 (626–51)
Good Friday	665–88 (688–712)
Holy Saturday	713–33 (752–73)
Easter	765–77 (omitted)
Pentecost	863–76
Corpus Christi	917–39
Office for the Dead	1779–99

do with its text or its liturgical position. Instead, the choice depends entirely on the mode of the antiphon with which the psalm or canticle is to be sung. We must turn our attention, therefore, to the free melodies that regulate and ornament the psalmody of the Offices.

TYPES OF FREE MELODIES IN THE OFFICES: THE ANTIPHONS

If we grant that St. Ambrose introduced antiphonal psalmody to the West (see Chapter II), we still do not know how the psalms were actually performed by alternating groups or choirs. The verses or half-verses could have been alternated without any additional material. Fairly early in the history of antiphonal psalmody, however, it apparently became the custom to alternate a text set to a free melody with the verses of the psalm. This free melody with its text was then known as an *antiphon*. It seems likely that the antiphon, in addition to appearing at the beginning and end of the psalm, was also sung after each verse or pair of verses. The resulting forms would then be:

A V_1 A V_2 A etc.; or A V_{1-2} A V_{3-4} A etc.

One example of this procedure is still used for the unusually long verses of the Invitatory Psalm. After each of these verses, all or part of the Invitatory Antiphon is repeated. In addition, there are further repetitions of the antiphon at the beginning and end. As an example of the complete form, we may cite the Invitatory for Christmas (LU, p. 368). In the diagram that follows, A_1 and A_2 represent the two sections of the Invitatory Antiphon; D is the Lesser Doxology, normally appended to all psalms and canticles.

A_1A_2 :‖ V_1 A_1A_2 V_2 A_2 V_3 A_1A_2 V_4 A_2 V_5 A_1A_2 D A_2 A_1A_2

Obviously, performance of all the psalms in this way required a great deal of time, much more than even monastic establishments were willing to allow. As a result, it became customary to sing the regular psalms and canticles of the Offices with the antiphon only at the beginning and end. In a further curtailment now frequently encountered, only the intonation of the antiphon (the first word or phrase up to the *) is sung at the beginning, with a complete performance only at the close. This practice, abhorred by liturgical and musical scholars alike, makes neither grammatical nor musical sense. Although this barbarism was purged by a decree of July 25, 1960 (see LU, 1961 ed., p. lxi), it is still indicated at various places in the body of the *Liber Usualis*.

As might be expected from their frequent appearance in the Offices, antiphons far outnumber any other type of chant. Medieval books contain thousands of antiphons, and well over a thousand are still in use. With such a large number to consider, it is difficult to make generalizations as to stylistic characteristics, but on the whole, antiphons are the shortest and simplest of the free melodic types. Many are almost completely syllabic, with here and there an occasional two-note neume, as in the setting of *Justus ut palma* (Example IV–1). Even on the most solemn feasts, the style rarely changes in antiphons for the psalms. This is less characteristic of antiphons for the *Benedictus* and *Magnificat,* which tend to be somewhat longer and more elaborate at all times and to approach a fully developed neumatic style on some feasts.[6] As a group, however, the antiphons may reasonably be said to present the principles of plainchant composition in their most elementary form.

Example IV–1: *The Antiphon* Justus ut palma[7]

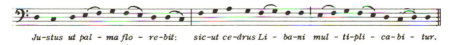

Ju-stus ut pal - ma flo - re-bit: sic-ut ce-drus Li - ba-ni mul - ti-pli - ca-bi - tur.

> The righteous shall flourish like the palm tree: he shall grow like a cedar in Lebanon.—Psalm 91 (92):12.

One of the most interesting aspects of the antiphons is their melodic relationship to the tones of the psalms for which they provide a frame. When antiphons and other chants began to be arranged in tonaries according to mode, further subdivisions grouped the antiphons according to the psalm-tone terminations with which they were to be used. As these terminations were designed to lead smoothly into the repetition of the antiphon, it is not surprising that many antiphons calling for the same termination begin with the same melodic figure. Even for tones with only one termination, different groups of antiphons may be established on the basis of their opening melodic progressions. Medieval theorists were well aware of these relationships, and modern scholars have shown that the thousands of antiphons can be reduced to approximately fifty "themes." In general, we may say that the number of antiphons and of different themes in a given mode is in direct proportion to the number of different terminations for the corresponding psalm tone.[8]

Before leaving the antiphons of the Offices, we should mention a few

6. Degrees of elaboration may be observed in the series of antiphons for the *Magnificat* for Saturdays after Pentecost. These are conveniently assembled in LU, pp. 986–97.
7. After Wagner, *Einführung,* 3, p. 11.
8. See also Apel, GC, pp. 394–404. An explanation of the ways in which modern chantbooks indicate the termination to be used with each antiphon can be found in Appendix A, Part 2.

instances in which they lost their original liturgical function. This occurs most commonly after the canticles of Lauds and Vespers. At these points, feasts that have been replaced by more solemn feasts falling on the same day are "commemorated" by the performance of an antiphon, versicle, and prayer. The antiphons were not originally independent, however. Usually they are the antiphons to the *Benedictus* or *Magnificat* that would have been sung had the more important feast not intervened.[9] For example, *Iste sanctus* (This saint) appears as both a commemorative antiphon for one martyr (LU, p. 262) and the antiphon for the *Magnificat* in the Common of One Martyr (LU, p. 1123). In themselves, therefore, these antiphons present nothing new. Their use as independent chants is interesting, however, because it represents the final stage in the dissolution of antiphonal psalmody, a stage we shall meet again in the chants of the Mass.

A somewhat different situation exists with regard to the four Antiphons to the Blessed Virgin Mary: *Alma Redemptoris Mater* (Fostering Mother of the Redeemer); *Ave Regina caelorum* (Hail, Queen of the heavens); *Regina caeli laetare* (Rejoice, Queen of Heaven); and *Salve, Regina* (Hail, Queen).[10] They date from the eleventh century and later and are among the few chants from that tremendously productive period that remain in the liturgy of the Offices. Originally these chants functioned as normal antiphons, but they quickly lost their connection with psalmody. By the thirteenth century, they were used, as they are today, to close the Offices whenever the choir disperses.

It should be clear from the example of *Alma Redemptoris Mater* cited in Chapter III that the Marian antiphons differ considerably from the style of the older Office antiphons. Not only are their texts much longer, but they are given more elaborate settings, with wider ranges, greater emphasis on tonal organization, and even occasional melismas, which are particularly extended in *Regina caeli*. Undoubtedly, it was this "modernity" that earned the Marian antiphons their prominent liturgical position and their place in the affections of composers throughout the Middle Ages and Renaissance. The texts with their melodies were frequently given polyphonic settings, and the melodies alone served as the basis for many polyphonic Masses.

Renaissance composers apparently preferred *Ava Regina* and *Salve, Regina,* although they did not completely ignore the other two antiphons. In the later Middle Ages, however, *Alma Redemptoris Mater* seems to have enjoyed the greatest popularity. Written by Hermannus Contractus (1013–54), it is perhaps the oldest of the Marian antiphons and may therefore have been the most widely known in medieval times.

---

9.   Examples of such antiphons may be seen in LU, pp. 262–62[11] (The Common Commemorations of Saints), and pp. 1080–1110 (Commemorations of the Sunday or of the Feria on Feasts of the First Class).

10.   See LU, pp. 273–76.

Perhaps the most striking evidence of the medieval regard for *Alma Redemptoris Mater* is the crucial role Chaucer assigned to it in *The Prioress's Tale,* which brings up an interesting musical sidelight. Usually, Chaucer calls the chant an antiphon, but once he uses the term *anthem* (antym). It may come as a surprise to find that the word *anthem* is merely an English corruption of *antiphon.* Before the Reformation, it was chiefly used to designate independent chants such as the Marian antiphons, both in their monophonic versions and polyphonic settings. It is probably for this reason that the *Liber Usualis* with English rubrics calls the Marian antiphons "Anthems to the Blessed Virgin Mary." In any case, we here catch a glimpse of one stage in the development of the Protestant anthem from the humble Gregorian antiphons.

GREAT RESPONSORIES

From the simplest type of free melody, the antiphons of the Offices, we now turn to the most complex—the Great Responsories. It is the soloistic aspect of responsorial psalmody that accounts for its sharp stylistic contrast with the simplicity of the choral antiphons. As performance of the responses passed from the congregation to the choir, and as choirs became more skillful, the responses too became much more elaborate. Finally, in many responsories as we know them now, there is almost no discernible difference in style between the choral responds and the solo verses. The verses, as we have seen, were originally sung to responsorial tones, but the intonations and cadential formulas of these tones were so ornate that only the longest verses made any extended use of the reciting notes. Moreover, some of the same formulas reappear in the choral responds. Eventually, the verses themselves began to be freely composed melodies.

The solo elaboration of responsorial psalmody seems to have been responsible for a method of bringing it down to manageable length that differs from the one we observed in antiphonal psalmody. Instead of reducing the number of repetitions of the antiphon, the psalm itself is normally reduced to a single verse in the responsories. The Lesser Doxology apparently was not an original part of the responsories but was added later, perhaps in imitation of antiphonal psalmody. Even then, only the first half of the doxology was used—*Gloria Patri, et Filio, et Spiritui Sancto* (Glory to the Father, and to the Son, and to the Holy Ghost)—and only for the last responsory of each Nocturn and the now suppressed Vesper responsory.

We thus find two forms of responsories, one with a respond and verse, and one with respond, verse, and half of the Lesser Doxology. The arrangement of these parts into a formal pattern is not an entirely simple matter, however. Because the responds generally have longer

The opening page of a thirteenth-century *Antiphonary*, which begins with the Office chants for Advent and includes the Great Responsory *Aspiciens a longe* (Badische Landsbibliothek, Karlsruhe).

texts than the antiphons, they usually tend to divide into three clearly defined musical periods, although some responds have four periods, while others have only two. The entire respond is sung before the verse, but as a rule only the last period is repeated after the verse and doxology when present. If we indicate the respond with its subdivisions as R_{abc}, and the verse and doxology as V and D, we may represent with reasonable accuracy the basic formal patterns of the responsories. In the following list, one example of each form is cited from the responsories in the *Liber Usualis*.

1. Forms with respond and verse
    A. R_{abc} V R_c
        O magnum mysterium (O great mystery), p. 382
    B. R_{abc} V R_c R_{abc}
        Unus ex discipulis meis (One of my disciples), p. 640 (645 in new editions)
2. Forms with respond, verse, and doxology
    A. R_{ab} V R_b D R_b
        Quem vidistis (Whom did you see?), p. 377
    B. R_{abc} V R_c D R_{abc}
        Hodie nobis (Today to us), p. 375
3. Form with three verses
    R_{abc} V_1 R_b V_2 R_c V_3 R_{abc}
    Libera me, Domine (Deliver me, Lord), p. 1767

The distribution of these forms in the liturgy of Matins depends largely on the position of the responsories. Form 1.A is usual for the first two responsories of each Nocturn, and Form 2.A, with doxology, for the third. With the replacement of the ninth responsory by the *Te Deum,* however, Form 2.A now appears in the eighth. The first responsories for the Nativity and Easter also take on greater importance by the addition of the doxology and the unusual repeat of the entire respond at the close (Form 2.B). Neither the *Gloria Patri* nor the *Te Deum* appears in Matins during Holy Week (Thursday, Friday, and Saturday), but Form 1.B gives distinction to the third, sixth, and ninth responsories on all three days. For responsories in the Office of the Dead, the *Gloria Patri* is again inappropriate, but a different procedure stresses the importance of the last responsory in each Nocturn.[11] In place of the doxology, there is a complete second verse, always with the same text: *Requiem aeternam dona eis Domine: et lux perpetua luceat eis* (Give them eternal rest, O Lord, and may light everlasting shine upon them). Formally, these responsories differ in no way from the pattern for responsories with doxology (Form 2.A).

Finally, we come to the special case of the responsory *Libera me* (Form 3 above). Here, even more than in responsories with the doxology, we find a remnant of the older method of responsorial psalmody in which several verses or an entire psalm alternated with choral responds. The formal details of *Libera me* as we know it now may not correspond exactly with earlier practice, but the essential structural principle is clearly evident. *Libera me* is not a responsory for Matins but is sung at the Absolution following the Mass for the Dead. It is not surprising, therefore, to find that its third verse is again the text *Requiem aeternam.* Polyphonic settings of this responsory were appended to a number of sixteenth-century Masses for the Dead, including two by Victoria; and in the nineteenth century Verdi continued the practice in his *Requiem.*

THE FREE MELODIES OF THE RESPONDS

To call the responds of the Great Responsories "free melodies" is in some respects misleading, for many of them are clear examples of centonization technique. This technique is much more clearly demonstrable here than in the antiphons, primarily because the longer texts and generally neumatic style make melodic formulas much easier to identify. Adjustments to accommodate text lines of different length may be made before or after the standard formulas, which are introduced with little or no modification from one responsory to another. In addition, standard formulas sometimes made their way into freely composed verses, just as the cadential formulas of responsorial tones sometimes

11. LU, pp. 1787, 1792–93, 1798–99.

appeared in the choral responds. The originally contrasting styles of the two sections may thus become nearly indistinguishable.

A detailed study of centonization in the responsories, or any other type of chant, is obviously impossible here. We should have to consider the responsories of each mode as a separate family, with some very close relationships and some much more distant. That such a study would be long and complicated may be seen in Apel's analyses of standard phrases in the responsories of Modes 2 and 8.[12] For the moment, let us examine the characteristic melodic style of responsories as a whole.

In large part, the Great Responsories are written in a neumatic style that here and there expands to include relatively short melismas. The total range of a melody may be a ninth or even more, but standard phrases generally move within the narrower limits of a fifth or sixth and in predominantly stepwise motion. Original melodies, on the other hand, or those that show only slight traces of centonization, are bolder in every way. Individual phrases tend to be wider in range and somewhat more melismatic, with larger and more frequent skips and melodic figures that sweep rapidly throughout the entire range.

The evolution of responsorial style has yet to be described to everyone's satisfaction, and we cannot safely assert that an original melody is necessarily more recent than one constructed from standard phrases. Nevertheless, there seems to have been a general trend toward the abandonment of responsorial tones for the verses and a greater use of free material in the responds. In what is perhaps a related development, longer melismas appear near the close of the respond in some responsories. Not many such melismas are available for study in the *Liber Usualis,* but a few may be seen in the responsories for Corpus Christi.[13] By way of illustration, we may cite the final phrase of the respond in *Coenantibus illis* (As they were eating; LU, p. 931). Particularly striking is the boldness with which the motive on "hoc est corpus" covers the interval of a ninth in a few notes (Example IV–2). Also remarkable is the use of repetition to create a purely musical form (*aab*). We shall encounter other examples of this procedure in the Offertories and Alleluias of the Mass.

Example IV–2: *End of Respond from Fourth Responsory for Matins of Corpus Christi (LU, p. 932)*

hoc   est   cor-pus   me - um.

This is my body.

12.   Apel, GC, p. 332 ff. A supplemental essay will discuss and illustrate the use of such phrases in three responsories in Mode 2, as well as their appearance in a supposedly "free" responsory.

13.   LU, pp. 926–39. See especially Nos. 2, 4, 6, and 7.

The melisma in Example IV–2 is relatively short, but in some responsories these melismatic extensions reached fantastic lengths. Most of the longer melismas, called responsorial *neumata* (sing. *neuma*), have been either drastically pruned or completely deleted from modern chantbooks. Many of them, apparently, were inserted in preexisting responsories to increase the solemnity of the chant for important feasts. The responsorial neumata, therefore, are a kind of trope, and further discussion of them must be delayed until we can devote an entire chapter to tropes and related forms.

SHORT RESPONSORIES

For the sake of completeness, we must not ignore the Short Responsories that are sung after the Chapter in the Little Hours and Compline. As found in the *Liber Usualis,* these chants do not possess great musical interest, but neither do they adequately represent the medieval repertory of Short Responsories. Three main melodies are given, one for use "during the year," one for Advent, and one for Paschal Time (LU, pp. 229–30). By the process of adaptation, different texts may be sung to these melodies as required by the Propers of the Time and of the Saints. In essence, all three melodies are nothing more than ornamented recitation formulas, and thus they confirm the derivation of the Short Responsories from the practice of psalmody. Perhaps their greatest importance lies in their having preserved irregular, and probably very ancient, recitation formulas that would otherwise have fallen into disuse.

A few special melodies, according to Apel, "seem to be limited to a single text."[14] This may be true of *Inclina cor meum* (Incline my heart), the Short Responsory for Sunday at Terce during the year (LU, p. 237). At any rate, this is not one of the three main melodies, although it too is an elaborated recitation formula. Contrary to what Apel says, however, *Erue a framea* (Deliver from the sword; LU, p. 239) does not have a special melody. It is set, rather, to an adaptation of the main melody for use during the year. The relationship between the two melodies may be seen in AMM, No. 3, which also serves to illustrate the forms of the Short Responsories.

Christe Fili Dei is in the form commonly used for responsories with the doxology:

$$R_{ab} \ R_{ab} \ V \ R_b \ D \ R_{ab}$$

Clearly, both the Great and Short Responsories follow the same structural pattern, even to using only the first half of the doxology. The more repetitive nature of the Short Responsories undoubtedly results

14. Apel, GC, p. 245.

from their extreme brevity. All repetition is dispensed with, however, in the least of the Little Hours, Sext and None, and sometimes also in Terce. The form of a Short Responsory with verse and doxology then becomes simply R V D (see, for example, LU, p. 243). In *Erue a framea* and all Short Responsories for Passiontide, the doxology is omitted. The resulting form—R_{ab} V R_b R_{ab}—is identical with Form 1.B that we found in the Great Responsories for Holy Week (see page 106), the distinction between the two deriving only from their lengths and contrasting musical styles.

HYMNS

Great religions normally inspire an ecstatic faith that expresses itself in songs of adoration and praise. Christianity was, and still is, no exception to this rule. Almost from the beginning, both in the East and in the West, its adherents have poured forth a veritable flood of religious poetry. The Middle Ages alone produced thousands of Latin sacred poems that we may classify somewhat loosely as hymns. In view of this tremendous output, the relatively insignificant role of hymns in the official liturgy of the Western Church is nothing less than astounding. As we have seen, a hymn is sung in each of the daily Offices, but this in no way indicates the number of hymns currently in use. One text may serve a number of different occasions or may appear in the same Office throughout most of the year. Thus the *Liber Usualis* contains about eighty hymns, and the complete *Antiphonary* of the daytime Hours has only some forty more. That the Church should have so abandoned one of its richest treasures remains almost inexplicable.

From the start, however, the Church has wavered between approval and disapproval of hymns. This instability seems to have been the result of two conflicting attitudes. On the one hand, the use of hymns by the Gnostics and other heretical sects strengthened the conservative belief that only the Bible could provide suitable texts for liturgical use. At the same time, many churchmen recognized the popular appeal of hymns and their effectiveness in spreading orthodox doctrines. Consequently, Church Councils alternately forbade the singing of hymns and censured bishops for not allowing them to be sung. These controversies had little effect on the Eastern branches of the Church, where hymns soon won a prominent and permanent place in the liturgy. A different situation obtained in the West. Just when Ambrose was introducing Latin hymns, the Council of Laodicea (c. 360–381) prohibited their use. This edict did not stop the composition or performance of hymns, but for many centuries it effectively denied them official status in the liturgy of Rome. It should be noted, however that Rome was often slow to accept practices that were common throughout the rest of Western Christendom. No

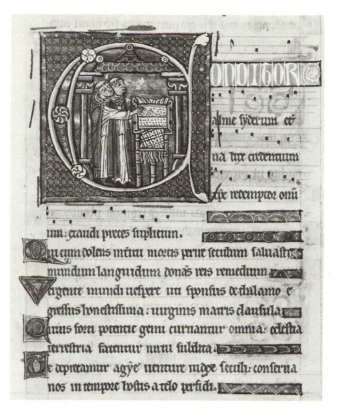

The Office hymn *Conditor alme siderum* from a thirteenth-century manuscript (Laon).

doubt the popular appeal of hymns as expressions of individual religious fervor also contributed to their late acceptance into the severe and somewhat impersonal solemnity of the Rome rite. Except for a few special ceremonies, notably in Holy Week, hymns never gained an official place in the liturgy of the Mass, and their position in the Offices always remained subordinate to psalmody. It will come as a surprise, therefore, to discover in later chapters that hymns and related forms of religious poetry were of great importance in the history of medieval music. For the present, however, we need concern ourselves only with hymns as they appear in the liturgy of the Offices.

Any discussion of hymnody in the Latin West must begin with Ambrose, because the poetic and musical procedures that he established are still the guiding principles of hymn writing. From the time of Ambrose until now, hymn texts have been divided into short stanzas, or strophes, all of which have the same poetic structure. This structure may vary from one hymn to another, but all the stanzas of one hymn will have the same number of lines, the same metrical pattern, and the same rhyme scheme, if rhyme is present. It follows, therefore, that when the melody of the first stanza is repeated for each succeeding stanza, strophic form results. It also follows that all hymns with stanzas of the same poetic structure may be sung to the same melody, and the use of one melody for two or more different hymns was as common in the Middle Ages as it is in present-day hymnals.

Much more unexpected is the use of different melodies for a single text, a practice that distinguishes hymns from all types of plainchant based on psalmody. We have seen that a Biblical text such as *Justus ut palma* might receive a number of different musical settings. The forms and styles of these settings, however, were determined by the differing liturgical positions in which the text appeared. Within one liturgical type, as antiphons, for example, the same text rarely appears with more than one melody. Many hymns, on the other hand, seem never to have been associated with any single melody. Perhaps the most striking example in the *Liber Usualis* is the hymn for Sunday at Compline, *Te lucis ante terminum* ([We beg] thee before the close of day). The *Liber* provides no fewer than twelve melodies for the chant of this hymn, which "varies according to the Season and Feasts." [15] Other hymns may not have such an ample supply of melodies, but few texts always appear in medieval sources with the same musical setting. For somewhat different reasons, the texts of the Ordinary of the Mass also receive a variety of musical settings (see Chapter V). Here, however, the same melody cannot serve for a number of different texts. Hymns prove to be the only type of plainchant in which independent texts and melodies are freely interchanged.

The loose connection between words and music that characterizes hymns probably results from their subordinate position in the liturgy and even more from their semipopular origin. Unfortunately, we know next to nothing about the earliest hymn melodies. With very few exceptions, the melodies as we know them now do not appear in a precise musical notation until the eleventh century or later. Attempts to reconstruct hymns as Ambrose might have sung them must therefore remain conjectural and must be based primarily on the metrical structure of the texts.

For his poetic form Ambrose used iambic tetrameters—that is, lines made up of four groups or feet consisting of short and long syllables in the pattern ∪ – ∪ – ∪ – ∪ – . The complete text normally included eight stanzas of four lines each. On the testimony of St. Augustine, four such texts may be definitely attributed to Ambrose: *Aeterne rerum Conditor; Deus Creator omnium; Iam surgit hora tertia;* and *Veni Redemptor gentium.* [16] Only the first of these was retained in the Roman liturgy (for Sunday at Lauds), but we may use it to illustrate various problems that arise in connection with hymn melodies.

The first melody in *Aeterne rerum Conditor* (AMM, No. 4) is the one

---

15.   LU, p. 266. Four of these melodies appear on pp. 266–69.
16.   Eternal Maker of All Things; God, Creator of All; Now Came the Third Hour; and Come, Redeemer of the People.

now given in the Roman Antiphonary. (The hymn does not appear in the *Liber Usualis*.) It is a simple and syllabic tune that, according to the Solesmes theory, would be sung in even notes. The second melody is equally simple, but it has been given a setting in triple meter, with note values that correspond to the long and short syllables of the text. The authenticity of this metrical version cannot be proved, of course, but there are good reasons for believing that Ambrose intended his hymns to be sung in a regular meter. After all, they were introduced for congregational singing and must therefore have been easy to remember and to sing. Correspondence between musical and poetic meters, especially when combined with syllabic style and strophic form, would obviously contribute much toward the achievement of these goals.

We know almost nothing about folk and popular music during the first millennium of the Christian era except that it must have existed. We may also assume that folk music must have been simple and rhythmic in style. It is not at all unlikely that early hymns were sung to well-known secular tunes. Certainly this procedure was common enough in later periods of music history. The use of secular or secular-sounding tunes, indeed, might well account for much of the animosity toward hymn singing in the early Middle Ages. In any case, the simple hymn tunes preserved by the Church probably constitute the nearest approach we shall ever have to the secular melodies of the time.

Ambrose maintained the long and short syllables of classical Latin poetry with considerable fidelity, and thus his hymns naturally fall into triple meter. Even in Ambrose's time, however, the basis of Latin accentuation was beginning to shift from long and short to strong and weak syllables, and the two systems did not always coincide. This may be seen in the second line of *Aeterne rerum,* where the strong accents indicated in the text fall on short notes. Whether this conflict between the two systems of accentuation confused later poets, or whether they were merely less careful and consistent than Ambrose, their hymns often fail to maintain one poetic meter with strict regularity. These metrical deviations may have been introduced to avoid monotony, but they also suggest that the poets were primarily concerned with maintaining the correct number of syllables in each line. It is entirely possible that early medieval hymn writers knew the principle of construction known as *isosyllabism* (same number of syllables in each line). The Syrian hymns of St. Ephraim (306–373) had abandoned versification by long and short syllables in favor of isosyllabic construction; later, as we shall see, the same principle rules the formation of poetry in French.

As a result of the developments just outlined, it became increasingly difficult to adopt a regular musical meter for later hymn tests. Metrical variants in the poetry would upset the musical scheme, and the placement of accents might shift from one stanza to another. Moreover, as qualitative accents (strong and weak) became established in common usage, medieval singers may well have disregarded versification by long and short syllables, just as the *Liber Usualis* often does today. We are getting back, of course, to the problem of rhythm in Gregorian Chant, where the ground is dangerous and the footing uncertain. It seems probable, however, that hymn melodies experienced the same fate as the rest of plainchant: the abandonment of long and short values in favor of an undifferentiated succession of even notes. This solution of the problem—easy but not particularly interesting—removes the difficulties of using one melody for different stanzas of one hymn or for entirely different hymns. Systems of versification and deviations from the normal metrical pattern become unimportant. Only the correct number of syllables in each line must be maintained, and slight adaptations of the melody can accommodate occasional departures from even this requirement.

The musical style of many later hymn melodies also suggests that performance in even note values had now prevailed. In place of the syllabic settings of *Aeterne rerum Conditor* (AMM, No. 4), we now find melodies in which many syllables are sung to neumes of two, three, or even more notes. This type of elaboration, which we shall meet again in the chants of the Mass, characteristically results when performance is transferred from the congregation to a trained choir or to the assembled clergy. As an example of this more elaborate style, we may cite the melody to which the processional hymn *Vexilla Regis* is now sung (Example IV–3). Two aspects of this hymn should be noted: the strong syllables in the second line ("Fúlget Crúcis") depart from the iambic

Example IV–3: *Ornamented Hymn Melody (LU, p. 575)*

The banners of the King go forth;
The mystery of the Cross shines out,
By which life suffered death
And by death brought forth life.

versification of the other lines; and accented (or long) syllables have from one to five notes. Quite obviously, the difficulties of metrical performance arising from textual problems are greatly increased by the ornamental figures in the melody. Triple meter can still be applied, and it is perhaps significant that short syllables rarely have more than one note except at the ends of lines. This is not true of all ornamented hymn melodies, however, and many of them approach the neumatic style that appears with some prose texts. It may even be that, by disguising the poetic structure of the texts, performance in even note values removed one of the chief objections to singing hymns and led to their eventual adoption by the Church of Rome. All this is mere conjecture, however. As with all types of plainchant, the rhythmic performance of hymns must forever remain a matter for controversy.

A final word should be said about the forms of hymn melodies. As four-line stanzas are most commonly used for hymn texts, so the melodies normally consist of four distinct phrases. In the great majority of melodies, these four phrases are different, producing the form *abcd*. This form, so common that it is sometimes called *hymn form,* is illustrated by the first melody for *Aeterne rerum* in AMM, No. 4. The metrical tune is also in *abcd* form, but its first, second, and fourth phrases are related by the use of musical rhyme. Indeed, the repetition of characteristic cadential patterns to produce musical rhyme is one of the most common structural devices in medieval music.

At first sight, the melody of *Vexilla Regis* (Example IV–3) also appears to have an *abcd* form. Closer examination reveals, however, that phrases two and four are identical for the last six out of eight syllables. Complete or partial repetition of phrases also occurs in a number of other hymn melodies. The most common repetitive pattern is *abca,* but such patterns as *aabc, abab, abcb,* and *abba* can also be found.[17]

Although they are rare in hymns, repetitive forms such as these are of great importance. We shall meet them again both in nonliturgical and secular Latin songs and in the vernacular songs of the troubadours and trouvères. It is not always possible to determine where these forms originated or to trace the lines of development from one class of monophonic song to another. Each class may, in fact, have influenced the other two. At any rate, the presence of repetitive forms in hymn melodies suggests once again that they cannot be far removed from traditions of popular music that are otherwise lost to us forever.

---

17.   For examples of hymns in these and other forms, see Apel, GC, p. 427.

CHAPTER V

The Roman Mass

Throughout the history of Christianity, the reenactment of the Lord's Supper—the Communion service—has been the most important and solemn ceremony of the Church. The Communion rite itself, known as the Eucharist, has constituted the nucleus of liturgical actions in many forms, called by many names. We need not concern ourselves with its various designations in different branches of the Eastern Church, but the origin of the Latin *missa*—in English, *Mass*—warrants a brief explanation. In very early times, the celebration of the Eucharist was either called an *offering* or a *sacrifice,* and in the third and fourth centuries it was often known simply as "the Lord's" (*dominicum*). It is curious that the colorless term *missa* should have replaced these more descriptive designations. The word simply means "dismissal" and appears in the closing formula *Ite, missa est* (Go, it is the dismissal) with which the congregation is sent away at the conclusion of the service. By the end of the fourth century, apparently, the term meant both the dismissal of the assembly and the end of the ceremony, and in the fifth century it designated any divine service, including the Offices. Gradually, however, *missa* was restricted to the celebration of the Eucharist and replaced every other name for that ceremony in the Christian lands owing allegiance to Rome.

As the most sacred part of the Catholic divine service, the Roman Mass developed a ceremonial rite that made it the central artistic achievement of Christian culture. In that achievement, music has always played an extremely important role. Indeed, the Mass has occasioned the composition of more music by more composers than any other liturgical service. This is, of course, especially true in the Middle Ages and Renaissance, but music for the Mass is by no means limited to the plainchant and polyphony of these periods. The ancient texts have continued to inspire composers from Bach and Beethoven to Stravinsky.

Let us consider the basic structure of the Mass in some detail in order to understand the significant contributions of plainchant and polyphony to its artistic evolution. Although the essential framework of the Mass has been fixed for centuries, we should remember, as J. A. Jungmann has remarked, that we are not dealing with a finished art-product that

The celebrant at the altar with his two assistants. From a Sarum Missal of the early fourteenth century (Morgan Library).

has "any consciously determined and accomplished plan," but a living thing, to which "men of many centuries and speaking many languages have all contributed."[1] The latest indications that the Mass is constantly developing are the changes authorized by the Second Vatican Council (1962–63). We must never think of the Mass, therefore, as an artistic achievement in the sense of a completed form, fixed and unchangeable for all time.

We must also remember that, even in a given historical period, the ceremonies of the Mass could and did vary considerably. Although the basic structure might remain the same, a pontifical Mass—that is, one celebrated by a bishop with numerous assistants—would obviously be much more elaborate than a Mass performed by a single priest. Other differences reflected the season of the Church year, the importance of the particular day, or the function of the Mass itself. The Requiem Mass, for example, differs markedly from the High Mass of a joyous festival. Still other differences arose from the size of the congregation, the number of assisting clergy, the presence of a trained choir, the size and physical arrangement of the place of worship, and local attitudes toward the role the congregation should play in the service.

Despite sporadic efforts throughout the Middle Ages to bring about liturgical uniformity in the celebration of the Mass, the Church remained remarkably tolerant of different usages consciously introduced. St. Gregory wrote that "in one faith, diverse usage is in no way harmful to the Church," and his words were echoed over and over in medieval

1.   J. A. Jungmann, *The Mass of the Roman Rite,* 1, p. 4.

times.[2] Not until the Council of Trent in the middle of the sixteenth century was the luxuriant growth of the Middle Ages pruned away and a simplified, uniform Mass liturgy imposed with almost complete success on the Roman Catholic Church as a whole. It is with the growth, not its suppression, that we are concerned, however, and we may now turn our attention to the form of the Mass as it developed during the first thousand years of the Christian era.

THE EARLY FORM OF THE MASS

We do not know exactly how the Apostles and the primitive Church carried out Christ's command to repeat the sacrament of the bread and wine "for a commemoration of me." Apparently they celebrated it at first in connection with a meal at which the Jewish ritual for community meals was combined with ceremonial elements of the Passover feast. The latter customarily began with the blessing of unleavened bread, which was then broken and shared with all present. Similarly, the meal closed with a blessing over a cup of wine from which all present then drank. Another important part of the Passover ceremony was the singing of the *Hallel* (psalms of praise), with those at table responding "Alleluia" after each half-verse.

As Christian groups grew in size, the connection with meals began to disappear, until Communion was finally celebrated only at special religious services. In this process, the leaders of the young religion naturally continued to use the ritual practices of the Jewish faith with which they were familiar. The consecration and prayers associated with Communion adapted Jewish formulas and responses to Christian needs. The "Amen" response (So be it) even remained untranslated. From the Sabbath service of the synagogue came the practice of Biblical readings from the Law and the Prophets, with singing in between. These readings formed the nucleus of the fore-Mass that preceded the Communion ceremony itself. Thus, the outlines of the later Mass liturgy began to take shape.

The fore-Mass usually consisted of three readings from the Bible, but now the emphasis fell on the New Testament, especially the Epistles and Gospels. Although the various liturgies differed widely in their choice of texts, the final lesson was invariably from a Gospel, after which came a homily (sermon) and prayer. Each of the first two readings was followed by the responsorial singing of a psalm. The function of the fore-Mass was twofold: to prepare the minds of the faithful for Communion, and to provide instruction in the rudiments of Christianity. Those receiving such instruction were known as *catechumens,* and hence the fore-Mass is sometimes called the Mass of the Catechumens. After

2.   Ibid., p. 98.

the closing prayer, the catechumens were dismissed, for only the faithful might partake of Communion.

The Communion ceremony itself was celebrated to the accompaniment of special prayers that gradually developed into the invariable form known as the Canon of the Mass. Its beginning, however, remained changeable and became what is now called the Preface. From a very early date it included the threefold Sanctus from the vision of Isaiah.[3] Here we have another element of the Jewish Sabbath service that was taken over with its text adapted and expanded to meet Christian needs. Behind this chant and the prayers of praise lay the idea that the bread and wine of the Communion service was a sacrifice to the Lord, which, in turn, led to the offering of gifts—originally animals and fruits of the field—before the Eucharistic prayers. We find accounts of such offerings by the faithful from the beginning of the third century, and the practice developed into an important part of the early Mass: the offertory procession. Thus began the process of growth and elaboration in the Mass that was to continue for many centuries. In order to make that growth more easily understood, here is an outline of the Mass structure that evolved during the first three or four centuries:

Fore-Mass or Mass of the Catechumens

Introductory greeting
Lesson 1: the Prophets
Responsorial psalm
Lesson 2: Epistle
Responsorial psalm
Lesson 3: Gospel
Sermon
Prayer
Dismissal of catechumens

Sacrifice-Mass or Communion (Eucharist) of the Faithful

The offering of gifts	(Offertory)
Prayer over the offerings	(Secret)
Eucharistic prayers of	(Preface)
praise and consecration	(Sanctus)
	(Canon)
Communion rites	
Psalm accompanying	
communion of faithful	(Communion)
Prayer	(Postcommunion)
Dismissal of the faithful	(*Ite, missa est*)

3.   Isaiah 6:3: "Holy, holy, holy, is the Lord of hosts: the whole earth is full of His glory."

DEVELOPMENT OF THE MASS TO ITS COMPLETED FORM ABOUT A.D. 1000

The most important addition to the structure of the Mass outlined above took place at the very beginning of the service. As late as the fifth century in Rome the Mass began directly with the readings. Gradually, however, a number of unrelated items were assembled into what we may call the entrance or opening ceremonies. These ceremonies apparently developed everywhere at about the same time, presumably motivated only by the idea that the readings needed some sort of introduction. The shape of the entrance ceremonies in Rome seems to be directly connected with the so-called stational Masses of the sixth and seventh centuries. On each of the great feast days, the pope celebrated Mass at a different Roman church (station), to which the papal court came in procession. The congregation normally came in seven processions from the seven regions of Rome, but on certain penitential days, all assembled at a central point and proceeded to the church where the service was to be held. Particularly on these latter occasions, it was customary to sing litanies which used the phrase *Kyrie eleison* (Lord, have mercy) as a refrain. Once the pope had arrived at the church and been vested, a further procession moved from the entrance intoning the Introit, a psalm sung antiphonally.

Rather than being left over from the time when the Roman liturgy was performed in Greek, the Kyrie seems to have been introduced from the East in the fifth century, perhaps by way of Milan. At any rate, in the present Ambrosian liturgy, during the Lenten period, a litany closing with a threefold *Kyrie eleison* follows the *Ingressa* (=Introit). In the sixth century, the Roman liturgy introduced a litany to be used in several places, including the opening ceremonies of the Mass. At times it was complete, while at other times it was reduced to a ninefold invocation that became the standard form of the Kyrie.

Like the Kyrie, the *Gloria in excelsis Deo* (Glory to God in the highest) did not originate as part of the Mass. It is one of the few surviving remnants, along with the sightly later *Te Deum*, of a rich literature of ancient hymns written in imitation of Biblical lyrics. Like the *Te Deum*, the Gloria was a song of praise and was included in the Mass celebrated by a bishop on particularly festive occasions. Later, its use was extended to other feast days and Sundays, even when the celebrant was a priest. The Gloria is still omitted, however, on weekdays (ferias), in Masses for the Dead, and in periods such as Advent and Lent when its text is inappropriate.

It is usual in liturgical rites for both the service as a whole and its major subdivisions to culminate with prayer. Thus we find that the opening ceremonies end with a Collect, "a gathering together, by the priest, of the preceding petitions of the people."[4]

4.   Jungmann, *The Mass*, 1, p. 268.

In contrast to the newly developed opening ceremonies, the service of readings was subject to few radical changes in the later centuries of the first millennium. By the sixth century, the number of readings was reduced from three to two, but traces of the old practice remain in the two intervening chants—Gradual and Alleluia or Tract, which now come one after the other. Originally a chant of the Easter season, the Alleluia gradually came into use throughout the year and on special feast days. It is replaced by a Tract only in penitential seasons such as Lent, when its joyous text, like that of the Gloria, would be inappropriate. Beginning in the ninth century, the Alleluia was often followed by a sequence, a musical and textual expansion of the liturgy to be discussed in detail in Chapter VI.

One other change in the service of readings involves the closing prayers and dismissal formulas. Although the fore-Mass continued to be called the Mass of the Catechumens, its dismissal formulas disappeared as congregations came to consist entirely of the faithful. Eventually, too, the Credo replaced the closing prayers of the fore-Mass. All that remained of these prayers was the single word *Oremus* (Let us pray), followed immediately by the Offertory. It should be noted, however, that the Church has always regarded the Credo as being appropriate only for Sundays and important feasts. Even today, it is not used for ferial Masses.

Although the form and contents of the prayers and ritual actions accompanying the Offertory and Communion changed considerably, only one new item was added to the sacrifice-Mass: the *Agnus Dei* (Lamb of God). It was brought from the East by the influx of clerics from lands overrun by the Moslems, and only became part of the Roman Mass in the late seventh century. The Agnus Dei originally accompanied the breaking of bread, but when the introduction of unleavened bread in small particles made that rite superfluous, it was used to fill the interval between the Consecration and Communion.

A final change came with the substitution of *Benedicamus Domino* (Let us bless the Lord) for the older dismissal formula *Ite, missa est* when the Mass had no Gloria. Apparently unknown in Rome before A.D. 1000, the *Benedicamus* formula may have originated in the Gallican liturgy. In addition to its occasional use in the Mass, it was also the standard dismissal formula for the Offices.

Early in the eleventh century, then, the structure of the Mass had become essentially what it remained until recent returns to some of the older forms. In the following outline of that structure, items with texts that change from day to day (Proper) are marked with a P; the unchanging texts (Ordinary) are marked with an O. Items printed in capital letter are sung to free melodies; asterisks identify those sung to recitation tones. Both kinds of musical items—eighteen in all—are included in the complete plainchant Mass of Easter Day in AMM (Nos. 5–22).

Form of the Mass c. 1000 A.D.

Fore-Mass

Entrance ceremonies
INTROIT	P
KYRIE	O
GLORIA	O
Collect★	P

Service of readings
Epistle★	P
GRADUAL	P
ALLELUIA	P
or TRACT	P
(SEQUENCE)	P
Gospel★	P
Sermon (optional)	
CREDO	O

Sacrifice-Mass

Offertory rites
OFFERTORY	P
Prayers and Psalm 25	O
(Little canon)	
Secret	P

Eucharistic prayers
Preface★	P
SANCTUS	O
Canon	O

Communion cycle
Pater noster★	O
AGNUS DEI	O
COMMUNION	P
Prayers	O
Postcommunion★	P
ITE, MISSA EST	O
or BENEDICAMUS	O

PROPER CHANTS OF THE MASS: FORM AND FUNCTION

The chants that belong to the Proper of the Mass are those whose texts change from day to day according to the seasons of the Church year. For the most part, these chants, or at least their texts, are among the oldest parts of the Mass. They all stem from the ancient practices of psalmody, although in some cases those practices are now unrecognizable. As the Mass developed, the styles and forms of the Proper chants continually altered to fit the changing situations. Some account of their evolution is necessary if we are to understand the chants as they now exist, but it is their final and present form that is our primary concern.

Originally, the chants of the Proper represented the two basic types of psalmody, antiphonal and responsorial, with the choice of type depending on the function of the particular chant. Antiphonal psalmody accompanied various actions in the Mass: the entrance and offertory processions and the Communion of the faithful. Responsorial psalmody, as in the Offices, followed the reading of Lessons. Because the division into types produced distinctive musical characteristics, we shall consider the chants of each type as a unit, instead of discussing them in consecutive order.

ANTIPHONAL CHANTS OF THE PROPER

The three antiphonal chants of the Mass—Introit, Offertory, and Communion—constitute the newer portion of the musical Proper. As we have seen, St. Ambrose first brought antiphonal singing from the East to Milan, and according to tradition Pope Celestine I (d. 432) introduced it in Rome. Apparently the antiphonal chants were always performed by the choir and have therefore preserved their musical style more consistently than other chants of the Mass. Their forms, however, have undergone radical amputations.

Originally, Introit, Offertory, and Communion all consisted of a complete psalm with the doxology and a pre-verse or antiphon at the beginning and end. Whether the antiphon was also repeated between the psalm verses remains an open question, since practices varied from place to place. At any rate, all three antiphonal chants were designed to accompany actions of indeterminate length that might well be different each time. Thus it is that even the earliest Roman ordinals direct the bishop, when a particular action is nearing its close, to signal the choir to skip to the doxology and the final antiphon. As the different ceremonies were themselves changed and shortened over the centuries, the accompanying chants became more and more curtailed. Finally, the Offertory and Communion were reduced to nothing but the antiphon, and only the Introit retained a vestige of its original form.

INTROIT

The shortening of the Introit psalm took place during the eighth and ninth centuries and occurred more rapidly in some places than in others. For many churches, it was not possible or desirable to conduct processions with the pomp of the papal liturgy, and eventually, the Introit came to be sung after the priest reached the foot of the altar. It thus became an independent musical prelude to the service, rather than a pro-

The Introit *Puer natus est,* from an illuminated manuscript c. 1375 (Morgan Library).

cessional chant. Perhaps for this reason, it remained closer to its original form than the other two antiphonal chants. The first verse of the psalm and the doxology were retained, along with the enclosing antiphon. The resulting form is AVDA.[5]

OFFERTORY

Antiphonal psalmody to accompany the Offertory procession seems to have originated in much the same manner as for the Introit. However, the Offertory underwent a curious and unique development: it is the only antiphonal chant that adopted the form and style of responsorial psalmody. We do not know when or why this change occurred, but it was evidently completed before the first chantbooks with musical notation appeared. As with other responsorial chants, musical elaboration of the solo verses led to a great reduction in their number. Instead of a complete psalm, therefore, the Offertories in medieval manuscripts

---

5.   It should be noted that the Benedictine monastic liturgy calls for repetition of the antiphon between the verse and doxology. The Introit is so performed in recordings of various Masses made in Germany by Benedictine choirs (Archive Production, I: Research Period, Gregorian Chant—Deutsche Grammophon Gesellschaft). Modern performances frequently substitute responsorial singing for the original antiphony.

have from one to four verses, with the latter part of the respond (R_b) being repeated after each verse. The complete form of an Offertory with three verses would then be R_{ab} V_1R_b V_2R_b V_3R_b. So extended a form could not be maintained as the Offertory procession fell into disuse, but the Offertory verses do not begin to disappear until the eleventh century. Although they persisted in exceptional cases throughout the Middle Ages, only the respond (originally, antiphon) remained in later times. In the liturgical reform of the sixteenth century the Offertory retained one verse in the Mass for the Dead (LU, p. 1813), and Offertory verses are still present in both the Ambrosian and Hispanic rites.

It is particularly regrettable that the Offertory verses were never restored to use.[6] In their complete form, the Offertories are among the most interesting and unusual chants of the entire repertory. Perhaps their most striking feature (which, in fact, occurs nowhere else in Gregorian Chant) is the frequent repetition of words and phrases. There may be one or several repetitions, with the same or with different music. Although such repetitions are particularly characteristic of the now discarded verses, they are occasionally to be found in the responds as well (see LU, pp. 480 and 514).[7]

Similar repetitions of melody only occur in many of the extended melismas in the Offertory verses. The form *aab* was particularly favored, but other and longer forms were also frequent.

Most of the characteristics of the complete Offertories do not appear in the older responsorial chants—the Office Responsories, Graduals, and Tracts. These characteristics testify not only to the later introduction of responsorial singing in the Offertories, but also to a new creative spirit. Instead of drawing on common melodic formulas that emphasize group characteristics, composers now use both textual and musical repetition to organize each chant into an individual and unified work of art. Perhaps it is just their personal and even dramatic nature that has kept the Offertory verses from regaining their former position.

COMMUNION

The Communion is without doubt the oldest of the three Mass chants sung antiphonally by the choir. Originally, it seems to have had the same form as the Introit, and both chants often used the same psalm, but with different antiphons. However, the Communion lost its psalm much sooner than the Introit or Offertory; and by the twelfth century, it was almost universally reduced to just the antiphon as the congrega-

6. They are published in a book that is neither readily available nor entirely reliable: C. Ott, *Offertoriale sive versus offertorium* (Tournai, 1935).

7. Apel (GC, pp. 366–67) gives an example of a phrase that is stated in some manuscripts no fewer than nine times.

tion came to receive Communion only infrequently. Eventually, the Communion chant came to be regarded as a conclusion rather than an accompaniment and was even called the antiphon after Communion or simply Postcommunion. (The present Postcommunion is a short prayer that is either spoken or sung to a reciting tone—see AMM, No. 21).

It is probably their age, not their concluding function, that accounts for the general characteristics of the Communion chants. As a rule, they are short and relatively simple in style. Many of them are no more elaborate than Office antiphons, although a few are extended with melismas of moderate length (for example, *Panis, quem ego dedero*—The bread which I shall have given—LU, p. 1043). Another indication of their antiquity is a modal ambiguity that led to disagreement among medieval sources as to the mode of certain Communion antiphons.[8]

RESPONSORIAL CHANTS OF THE MASS

As was pointed out before, responsorial psalmody following scriptural readings goes back to practices of the Jewish synagogue. In the early Christian Church, the people sang simple, short responds between the psalm verses sung by a soloist. With the introduction of the schola cantorum, however, the responds became choral chants, the first instance of a procedure that eventually eliminated most congregational singing in the Mass by replacing the simple melodies that the people could sing with more elaborate chants suitable only for a trained choir. Artistic considerations may also have been influential here. Even in St. Augustine's time (354–430), solo singers were becoming notorious for creating richly embellished melodies.[9] Assigning the responds to the choir made it possible to reduce sharply the stylistic contrast between solo and choral sections.

Complete psalms disappeared from the responsorial chants of the Mass even sooner than from the antiphonal, but for different, primarily musical reasons. Never limited by an accompanying action, responsorial psalmody could be of any length. Nevertheless, a complete psalm that would not have been unduly long in the original method of performance became impractical in the extended ornamental style of the chants for choir and solo singer. Another factor that undoubtedly contributed to shortening the texts was the disappearance of the Lesson between the Gradual and the Alleluia. As a result, the two chants occupy a moment when the action of the Mass gives way before a great lyrical effusion. The Gradual and Alleluia are indeed "the jewels of the Roman Mass," and in their richness the plainchant Mass attains its greatest splendor.

8.   See Apel, GC, p. 166 ff.
9.   St. Augustine, *Confessions*, Bk. X, Ch. XXXIII. Part of this passage is quoted in Grout, HWM, p. 26.

GRADUAL

The chant following the first Lesson was originally called a Responsory (*responsorium*). Later manuscripts designate it as *responsorium graduale,* or simply *graduale,* from which it acquired the name that distinguishes it from other responsorial chants. Opinions differ as to the origin of the term *graduale,* but the most commonly accepted thought is that it derived from the position of the soloist on the step (*gradus*) of the pulpit rather than in the pulpit itself, which was reserved for the reader of the Gospel.

In its reduced form, the Gradual came to consist of a choral respond followed by a solo verse. Repetition of the respond after the verse persisted until the thirteenth century, but soon thereafter it disappeared entirely. At this time developed the method of performance common in later times. After the usual solo intonation, the choir sings the major part of the respond. One or more soloists then sing the verse until the final phrase, at which point the choir joins in to provide a more impressive conclusion. Modern chantbooks provide for an optional repetition of the respond "if the responsorial method is preferred" (LU, p. xv). In this case, the cantors complete the verse alone, after which the choir sings the full respond.

As a class, Graduals are the most elaborate and melismatic of all chants. Even in the choral responds, melismas of twenty to thirty notes are not uncommon, and, as befits solo chants, the verses are even more highly melismatic. The verses also tend to lie more frequently in the upper part of the range than the responds. Some characteristic Graduals that we shall meet later in polyphonic settings are *Viderunt omnes* (All have seen), for the third Mass of Christmas (LU, p. 409), and *Sederunt principes* (The princes have sat), for the Feast of St. Stephen (LU, p. 416). An extreme example of melismatic development may be seen in the Gradual *Clamaverunt justi* (The Righteous have cried aloud; LU, p. 1170).

One of the interesting aspects of the Graduals is their use of the centonization technique that is characteristic of the Office responsories.[10] In the Graduals, however, centonization is applied much more consistently and obviously than in the responsories. A number of standard phrases or formulas supply the melodic material for Graduals in a given mode. Certain formulas serve only as introductory or concluding phrases, while others serve as internal links that may be freely combined and rearranged. In some modes, centonization appears principally in the verses, with the responds being freer but occasionally using standard cadential formulas. In modes 3, 4, 7, and 8, however, both responds and verses make use of standard phrases, which occasionally recur in each section to produce a highly unified chant. For example, in *Benedicite*

10. For a detailed discussion of centonization in the Graduals, see Apel, GC, pp. 345–62.

Dominum (Bless the Lord; LU, p. 1654) the melisma after the first "ejus" in the respond reappears intact after the word "Dominum" in the verse. Moreover, the final melismas of the two sections are identical.

The use of standard phrases in combination with extensions, variations, and freely composed passages makes of each Gradual an individual chant that yet bears a strong family resemblance to other members of its group. As we have already remarked, this method of composition is essentially Oriental and was probably adopted from Jewish musical practices. That it is so consistently evident in the Graduals attests to their antiquity as a class in comparison with the Offertories and, even more, the Alleluias, in which centonization is conspicuously absent.

ALLELUIA

Alleluia is the Latin spelling of the Hebrew *Hallelu Jah* (Praise ye Jehovah). As an expression of praise, it was and is used in a great variety of ways in all Christian liturgies. Perhaps because of the association of Alleluia psalms with the Jewish Passover, Western liturgies have made particular use of the Alleluia in Paschal Time—that is, from Easter to Pentecost (Whitsunday or Whitsun). In this season, the word is added at the end of every chant, both in the Offices and the Proper of the Mass. Moreover, from Saturday in Easter Week to Pentecost, an Alleluia replaces the Gradual, so that Masses at this time have two Alleluias between the Epistle and the Gospel (see, for example, the Mass for the fourth Sunday after Easter, LU, p. 827). At other seasons, use of the Alleluia is more restrained; but it functions as an independent chant of the Mass Proper throughout the year, except for penitential days and seasons such as Lent

The Alleluias as they are performed today are even more clearly responsorial than the Graduals. After the cantors sing Alleluia, the choir repeats it, continuing with an extended melisma, the *jubilus* (pl. *jubili*).[11] The cantors then sing the major part of the verse, with the choir joining in for the final phrase. Again the cantors sing Alleluia, but this time, as a closing respond, the choir sings only the jubilus. As in the Gradual, the concluding choral respond of the Alleluia often disappeared in the later Middle Ages. This was normal procedure, as it still is, when a Sequence followed the Alleluia (see the Easter Mass, LU, p. 780). But the repetition also tended to disappear on other occasions, especially days that were not marked by any particular solemnity. Now, with rare exceptions, the *Liber* prescribes responsorial performance as outlined above for the Alleluia.

---

11.   The sign *ij.* in LU after the Alleluia is the Roman numeral two, indicating the repetition. See LU, pp. xv–xvi, for the manner of performing the double Alleluia in Paschal Time.

Much might be said about the historical development of Alleluias, the choice of texts for their verses, and the adaptation of different texts to the same melody. Above all, musical forms in the jubili and melodic relationships between the Alleluia and its verse are particularly interesting and worthy of detailed study.

TRACT

Whether the Alleluia replaced the Tract or vice versa is a question we may leave to the liturgiologists. By the time liturgical Mass books made their appearance, the Alleluia had obviously been deemed inappropriate for the pre-Lenten and Lenten seasons, as well as for some other penitential occasions. Then, a Tract rather than an Alleluia follows the Gradual. This should not be taken to mean, as some medieval commentators concluded, that Tracts were necessarily penitential and sorrowful in themselves. The Tract for Quinquagesima Sunday, for example, consists of the first three verses of Psalm 99 (100): "Make a joyful noise unto the Lord, all ye lands." It is also noteworthy that, on Holy Saturday and the Vigil of Pentecost (Whitsun Eve), the two chants between the Lessons are an Alleluia followed by a Tract (see LU, pp. 759–60 and 860).[12]

Opinions differ as to both the original method of performing the Tracts and the derivation of their name. Medieval commentators saw in the word *tractus* references either to a drawn-out (protracted) style of singing or to a continuous performance without respond or antiphon to serve as a refrain. This was certainly a later method of performance; and, as a result, modern scholars often cite the Tracts as a rare instance of direct psalmody in the Roman liturgy. There is clear evidence, however, that some Tracts were originally sung responsorially and were even identified as *responsorium* or *responsorium graduale* in the earliest manuscripts.[13] It is quite possible, therefore, that the Tracts represent an early stage of responsorial psalmody from which the responses were later dropped. Modern chantbooks compound the confusion by directing that the verses be sung alternately by the two sides of the choir or by cantors and full choir.

In their final form, the Tracts consist of a series of psalm verses, ranging in number from two to fourteen. Only rarely is a complete psalm used, but in any given Tract all the verses come from the same psalm. It is noteworthy that the opening verse is not so designated; the symbol for *versus* (℣) appears only with the second and succeeding verses. In the case of Tracts that were originally called Responsories, the undesig-

---

12. In the revised liturgy for Holy Week, the Saturday Mass is now the "Mass of the Paschal Vigil" (pp. 776_GG-JJ_ in recent editions of LU).

13. Apel, GC, p. 184.

nated opening section must have been a respond, all or part of which served as a refrain between the verses following. Three examples that may be cited are the Tract for Wednesday of Holy Week and the two Tracts for Good Friday (LU, pp. 614, 695, and 697). These were evidently Responsories with several verses in which abbreviation was achieved, not by dropping verses, but by abandoning the repetitive principle of responsorial performance.[14] Even so, Tracts with several verses are among the longest chants in the repertory. On the first Sunday of Lent, for example, the Tract, which includes all of Psalm 90 (91)—He that dwelleth in the secret place—occupies almost three and one-half pages in the *Liber Usualis* (533–36).

One of the features that distinguishes the Tracts from all other types of chant is their restriction to only two modes, the second and eighth. Along with this modal limitation goes a more systematic application of centonization technique than is to be found anywhere else. Willi Apel has calculated that there are only nineteen melodic formulas for the sixty verses of Tracts in Mode 8, and twenty-two for the eighty verses of Tracts in Mode 2.[15] Adherence to these formulas is so strict that each Tract consists almost entirely of a regulated succession of standard phrases.

Melodically, the Tracts tend to be rather ornate. Some of the chants, presumably the oldest, begin many of their phrases with recitativelike passages reminiscent of psalm tones. Almost invariably, however, these same phrases cadence with elaborate melismatic formulas. This style may perhaps be seen most clearly in the five Tracts for Holy Saturday.[16] The majority of Tracts do not combine these syllabic and melismatic extremes but flow smoothly in a neumatic style that frequently expands into melismas of considerable length (see, for example, the Tract for the first Sunday of Lent cited above). Quite obviously a style such as this can only have originated in solo song. It would seem, therefore, that the Tracts preserve that song as it was used in the Mass before its further elaboration in Graduals, Offertories, and Alleluias.

ORDINARY OF THE MASS

The five chant texts that belong to the Ordinary—Kyrie, Gloria, Credo, Sanctus, and Agnus Dei—provided the basis for the many polyphonic Masses composed in later periods. Unchanging texts that could be used

---

14.   In the 1961 edition of LU, the Tract for Wednesday of Holy Week is still so called (p. 619), but the two for Good Friday are identified as Responsories (pp. 721 and 725).

15.   Apel, GC, p. 330.

16.   See ibid., pp. 315–18. In older editions of LU, the Tracts are to be found on pp. 745, 748, 751, 753, and 760. In the revised liturgy (1961 edition) for the Paschal Vigil, the first four are called Canticles (pp. 776$_{R-BB}$) and the fifth is identified only as Psalm 116 (p. 776$_{II}$).

The most solemn moment in the Mass, the elevation of the Host, shown in this miniature from a Sarum Missal of the early fourteenth century (Morgan Library).

repeatedly were naturally more attractive to composers of elaborate musical settings than the texts of the Proper, which appeared but once a year. In the plainchant repertory, however, the situation is entirely different. Here, the Proper chants are of primary concern, especially the responsorial chants between the Lessons, which, as we have seen, form the musical high point of the Mass. The chants of the Ordinary, taken as a group, are generally less elaborate musically, but we must discuss them in some detail nevertheless. Not only do they, or their texts, form the basis of the later polyphonic Mass, but they also represent the continuing development of plainchant composition.

All the musical items of the Ordinary were originally intended for congregational singing. They were introduced at various times over a period of several centuries, the Credo being the last to be officially authorized by Rome in 1014. It is not possible to say exactly when the singing of these texts passed from the congregation to the assisting clergy or to the trained choir. Undoubtedly, this was a gradual process that took place at different times in different places. For some chants it began as early as the eighth century, and it must have been nearly completed by the end of the eleventh, at least in the larger churches and monasteries. It is from such places, from the tenth century on, that we get manuscript evidence of new melodies for the Ordinary texts.

It is not surprising that composers seized the opportunity to write new melodies for these texts. The chants of the Proper had been firmly established, and additions could be made only with the institution of a new feast. Although such occasions were not rare, they provided an inadequate outlet for the upsurge of creative activity that marked the eleventh and twelfth centuries. Moreover, the chants of the Proper, with the exception of the Alleluia, were by this time so rigidly fixed in their traditional forms and styles that composers often merely adapted old melodies to the texts of the new feasts. No such restrictions inhibited composers when the chants of the Ordinary became the property of the choir. Therefore, they could and did write a great many new melodies of which the modern chantbooks present but a small selection.

The Ordinary chants in the *Liber Usualis* appear in groups that we may call Mass formularies or, for convenience, simply Masses (see Appendix A, Part 3). These groups, which do not include the Credo, call for some comment. It used to be thought that they were an invention of modern editors, but recent scholarship has shown that such formularies originated in medieval practice. Most manuscripts put all the chants of each type together, as is now done with the *ad libitum* chants in the *Liber Usualis*. In some sources one finds an arrangement in pairs: Kyrie-Gloria, and Sanctus-Agnus Dei—and occasionally in the later Middle Ages complete formularies correspond to those in the modern chantbooks. Whatever the medieval arrangement may have been, however, formularies existed in fact whenever individual chants were assigned a particular liturgical use. This began to happen as early as the eleventh century.

The usual explanation for the omission of the Credo from the Mass formularies has been that, because of its late adoption by Rome, it was considered an outsider not to be accepted among the other Ordinary chants. Actually, the Credo had been universally adopted when the Mass formularies were assembled, and its omission is probably to be explained on purely practical grounds. Different settings of the Credo were rare in medieval times, and a chantbook might contain up to twenty Mass formularies but only one or two Credo melodies. Obviously, copying the same Credo in several different formularies would have wasted a great deal of time and parchment. The same situation exists in the *Liber Usualis*. There are eighteen Mass formularies, but only Credo I, the "authentic tone," is normally used. The formularies, at least those for use on Sundays and major feasts, are thus incomplete, and the Credo must be added, no matter where it appears in medieval manuscripts or modern chantbooks.

It seems quite obvious that, for whatever reasons the Ordinary chants were assembled in groups, musical unity was not one of them. We will do well, therefore, to avoid using the term *Mass cycles* for collections that are no more true cycles than are the Proper chants of a particular feast. The designation *formulary,* on the other hand, suggests with reasonable accuracy what these collections really are: compilations of disparate chants into somewhat arbitrary and variable groupings with prescribed liturgical functions. In medieval formularies, chants were often interchanged or used more than once, and modern books allow the same procedure: "Chants from one Mass may be used together with those from others"; or *ad libitum* chants may be substituted "to add greater solemnity" (LU, p. 78). This latter statement suggests what is perhaps the basic criterion for assembling a Mass formulary: the principle that the rank of a feast, its solemnity, should be matched by the elaborateness of its chants. Given the permissible variability, however, it follows that we must consider the different items of the Ordinary separately rather than as members of the formularies in which they appear.

KYRIE ELEISON

Of some 226 catalogued melodies for the Kyrie, only 30 are included in the *Liber Usualis*. Nevertheless, this small number proves to be representative of the most important stylistic and formal characteristics of the repertory as a whole. Each of the three acclamations—*Kyrie eleison, Christe eleison, Kyrie eleison*—is sung three times, so that the complete chant has nine sections in all. This textual arrangement obviously provided composers with an ideal framework for creating distinct musical forms. In the simplest, and presumably oldest, of such forms the same melody serves for the first eight acclamations, with either a variation or a completely different melody for the ninth. The only example of this form still in use is the Kyrie of the Requiem Mass (LU, p. 1807). The last "Kyrie eleison" begins with a new melodic outline but closes with the final phrase of the other eight acclamations. The form may thus be indicated as *aaa aaa aaa'*; that is, the final melody may be considered as a repeat of *a* with a varied beginning. The repetitive nature of this form suggests that it may have been the usual one for congregational singing, and some even simpler melodies probably served the same purpose. A characteristic Kyrie of this type is illustrated in Example V–1. It has been suggested that the rather unexpected closing melody served as a link with one of the oldest Gloria melodies, as shown in the example. (In medieval practice, "Kyrie eleison" was normally elided to make a six-syllable phrase.)

Example V–1[17]

Ky - ri - e - le - i - son. iij.
Chri-ste e - le - i - son. iij.
Ky - ri - e - le - i - son. ij. Ky-ri-e -   le - i - son.   Glo-ri-a   in ex-cel-sis De-o

As a rule, the later and more elaborate melodies display more complex musical forms. Almost all Kyries that do not have the simple form

17. After Wagner, *Einführung*, 3, p. 440.

described above are usually classed in one of the following three structural patterns: [18]

	Kyrie	Christe	Kyrie
1.	*aaa*	*bbb*	*aaa'*
2.	*aaa*	*bbb*	*ccc'*
3.	*aba*	*cdc*	*efe'*

Examination of the Kyries in the *Liber Usualis* will quickly reveal that these patterns are often oversimplified and misleading, if not inaccurate, indications of the musical structure.

Two structural principles are at work in the Kyrie melodies, neither of which is indicated by the standard formal patterns. The first and more frequently applied principle is the unification of all melodies within a given Kyrie by means of a common closing phrase. The phrase may be fairly short, as in Kyrie III (LU, p. 22); or it may be greatly extended, as in Kyrie II (LU, p. 19). In some of the more complicated forms, two closing phrases may appear in alternation, as in Kyrie IX (LU, p. 40). Curious to modern ears, this sort of musical rhyme recurs with extraordinary frequency during the later Middle Ages. Whether the principle originated in the Kyries one cannot say, but its occurrence in them probably derives from the repetitive nature of litany responses. The text itself, with the words "Kyrie" and "Christe" both followed by "eleison," suggests the use of contrasting or variant opening phrases leading to a common close.

The second structural principle concerns the typical elaboration of the final invocation. Sometimes this elaboration is achieved by repeating segments of the preceding Kyrie melody (see Kyrie II). Often, however, the final melody proves to be a combination of elements from both Christe and Kyrie sections.[19] Perhaps this procedure stems from the theological interpretations of the Kyrie as symbolic of the Trinity that were particularly common in Frankish territories, from which most of the Kyrie melodies came. Combining Kyrie and Christe melodies in a final acclamation certainly fits such an interpretation. Theological considerations aside, the procedure is particularly effective from a musical point of view. It would be difficult, indeed, to find a better way to sum up and conclude a composition.

GLORIA

Because its first lines are the angels' song on the night of the Nativity (Luke 2:14), the Gloria is known as the *hymnus angelicus* (see AMM, No. 7). (It is also called the Greater Doxology, the Lesser being the *Gloria*

18. As in Apel, GC, p. 406.
19. Examples in Kyries VII, X, XI, XII, XVIII, and *ad lib.* VII and VIII.

Patri.) The rest of the text consists of short phrases praising God the Father and Christ, and petitions for mercy. In performance, the opening phrase—"Gloria in excelsis Deo"—was always sung by the bishop or, later, the celebrating priest. The rest of the text was sung by the congregation, the chorus of assisting clergy, or a trained choir. After congregational singing disappeared, the choir generally performed the Gloria antiphonally.

Unlike the Kyrie, the Gloria does not form part of every Mass but is omitted during Advent and Lent, on some other penitential days, and on ordinary weekdays. Both these restrictions on its use and the nature of its text probably account for the relatively small number of Gloria settings. Only 56 Gloria melodies are known, compared to 226 Kyries. Whatever the cause for this relative neglect, the Gloria text itself limited the possibilities of free musical expression. Its very length prevented expansive melodic treatment, and most settings alternate between syllabic and slightly neumatic passages with two, three, or four notes per syllable. Though they thus maintained its liturgical fitness, composers managed to incorporate the characteristic musical style of their times in melodies that are often strikingly different.

Perhaps the oldest, and certainly the simplest, of the melodies in the *Liber Usualis* is Gloria XV (p. 57). The entire text, with the exception of the Amen, is adapted to what is really a psalm tone, using only the four notes **e**, **g**, **a**, **b**, with **a** as the reciting tone. To this simplicity, Gloria I *ad libitum* (LU, p. 86) stands in the sharpest possible contrast. Covering a total range of a twelfth, from **d** to **a'**, the melody makes especially bold use of wide skips and abrupt changes of pitch level. Also noteworthy is the strong feeling of tonal organization that results from the fact that all phrases but one end on either **G** or **D**.

The textual structure of the Gloria naturally imposes limitations on its melodic setting. With no textual repetitions to produce a musical pattern for the piece as a whole, composers generally set the successive phrases in a continuous flow of ever-varying melody. Parallel phrases in some sections of the text do suggest the use of the same or similar melodic material, which then creates one or more small internal forms. The absence of an overall formal scheme should not lead us to overlook these and other, more subtle relationships present in many of the Glorias. Musical organization does not depend on a clearly recognizable pattern of sectional repetitions but may result from nothing more than the recurrent use of melodic figures or cadential patterns in an otherwise free melody. In a few instances, the Gloria melodies are organized into repetitive structures that have little or nothing to do with the form of the text. Perhaps the most obvious example is Gloria VIII, in which three basic phrases provide the entire substance of the melody (Example V–2). Varied to fit different words, these phrases always recur in the same order, although a single phrase is occasionally repeated before the next appears. Sometimes, two or even all three phrases are telescoped into one, as at the words "Deus Pater omnipotens" and, most remarkably, "suscipe deprecationem nostram." Although Gloria VIII may have originated as late as the fifteenth century, the same technique is used with only slightly less rigidity in Gloria V, a twelfth-century composition.[20] In both Glorias, individual melodic phrases generally correspond with short phrases of text, but the complete melodies are repeated without regard for the larger grammatical units, which may begin on any one of the three phrases. This use of a single reiterated melody, completely independent of the structural patterns of the text, almost seems to foreshadow certain twentieth-century techniques of serial composition.

Example V–2: *Gloria VIII*

CREDO

After formulation of the Credo at the Council of Nicaea in 325 (see above, p. 33), its first liturgical use was as a baptismal creed, hence the singular form *Credo*—"I believe"—instead of the plural "we believe." In the sixth century, the Credo appears in the Mass in Oriental liturgies and also in Spain. Two centuries later, we find it in the Frankish realm, perhaps coming by way of Ireland and England. Not until the tenth century, however, did the Credo come into general use in the North, and the year 1014 then saw its acceptance by the Church of Rome. This late adoption was undoubtedly only one of the factors that limited medieval settings of the Credo to a mere handful of melodies. Another was the Credo's function as a profession of faith by the entire congregation. In many places, therefore, it continued to be sung, or perhaps merely recited, by the people long after the other Ordinary chants had been taken over by the choir. The length of its text—even exceeding the Gloria— must also have acted as a deterrent to the frequent composition of new

20. See Apel, GC, pp. 411–12.

Credo melodies. One is tempted to believe, however, that the most important factor may have been a feeling, even in the Middle Ages, that the melody we know as Credo I was the authentic Credo (see AMM, No. 14). Certainly no other Ordinary text was so widely associated with a single melody. Many manuscripts, and even later printed books, have only the "authentic tone" of the *Liber Usualis.*

As in the Gloria, the celebrating priest sings the first phrase of the Credo alone, and the people, or the choir, begin with the words "Patrem omnipotentem." These are the only phrases in the Ordinary chants to be so treated, which accounts for their being absent occasionally in plainchant books and invariably in medieval and Renaissance polyphonic Masses. Antiphonal singing of the Credo by the choir was sometimes frowned on in the Middle Ages because everyone was expected to recite the whole text. It is now permitted, but the full choir may also sing the text continuously.

The melody of Credo I appears in eleventh-century manuscripts, but it is probably much older and may be of Greek origin. Almost completely syllabic, it is made up of a very few melodic formulas that recur in a number of different arrangements. Although the opening formula on "Credo in unum Deum" is not used elsewhere as a separate and complete phrase, it does reappear at least ten times, either within or at the ends of phrases. As may be seen in Example V–3, it is usually varied to some degree but returns once in its original form to close the phrase on "Et resurrexit tertia die." In the example, the lines of text are numbered to show the order in which the different versions of the formula recur. All but one of these versions are introduced by rising, intonationlike progressions (**e–f–g** or **d–e–f–g**), which lead to more extended recitations on the note **g** in the second half of the Credo beginning with the phrase "Et iterum venturus est cum gloria" (No. 7 in Example V–3). When these psalmodic introductions are not followed by variations of the opening formula, they usually begin shorter phrases that cadence on **g** or **d**.

Example V–3: *Variations on the Opening Motive of Credo I*

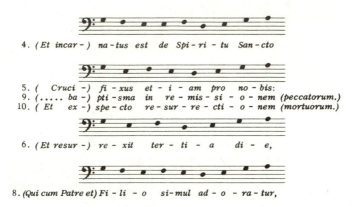

4. *(Et incar -) na - tus est de Spi - ri - tu San - cto*

5. *(Cruci -) fi - xus et - i - am pro no - bis:*
9. *(...... ba -) pti - sma in re - mis - si - o - nem (peccatorum.)*
10. *(Et ex -) spe - cto re - sur - re - cti - o - nem (mortuorum.)*

6. *(Et resur -) re - xit ter - ti - a di - e,*

8. *(Qui cum Patre et) Fi - li - o si - mul ad - o - ra - tur,*

The next most important formula in Credo I first appears on the words "Patrem omnipotentem," immediately following the opening phrase. Whatever variants are later introduced, this formula always begins a–b♭–a and cadences with the rising progression f–g. It usually serves as the closing formula of a section and follows seven of the ten appearances of the opening formula listed in Example V–3.[21] It can hardly be mere chance that most of these ten appearances coincide with textual phrases related either to various aspects of the Trinity or to the incarnation, crucifixion, and resurrection of Jesus Christ.[22]

Credos V and VI are the only other medieval melodies in the *Liber Usualis*. The motives in Credo V closely resemble those of the "authentic tone," and the derivation from psalmodic recitative is even more obvious. The same derivation is still evident in the slightly neumatic style of Credo VI. Both melodies use a limited number of musical phrases; and, especially in Credo VI, their almost unvaried repetitions become somewhat monotonous. For its imaginative and flexible manipulation of melodic formulas within an extremely simple style, Credo I clearly deserves the predominant position it occupied in the Middle Ages and still occupies today.

SANCTUS

The text of the Sanctus combines passages from both the Old and New Testaments. From the vision of Isaiah (Isaiah 6:3) came the cry of the angels, which the Roman liturgy modified somewhat, appending to it the cry of the multitudes that greeted Jesus when he entered Jerusalem

21. It is missing only after Nos. 2, 9, and 10.
22. This analysis of Credo I differs greatly from that of Apel, GC, pp. 413–14. He lists the appearances of "four standard formulae," but—curiously and, to me, inexplicably—he finds that the melody of the opening "Credo in unum Deo" stands "outside of this basic material."

(Matthew 21:9) (see AMM, No. 17). The enclosing Hosannas of this latter cry, with the first changed to agree with the last, gave the complete text a formal organization often reflected in its musical settings.

Finding a place in all Christian liturgies, the Sanctus at first was invariably a song for all the people. This is evidenced in the Roman liturgy by the Prefaces, which introduce the Sanctus with a phrase suggesting that the people join the angels in saying (*dicentes*): "Holy, holy, holy." During the seventh and eighth centuries in Rome, at least for pontifical Masses, a chorus of assisting clergy began to take over the Sanctus, but there is evidence that in some places congregational performance persisted until the twelfth century. In general, however, transference to the assisting clergy and then to the choir occurred during the tenth to twelfth centuries, the same period that produced so many new melodies for the Mass Ordinary. These and the next two or three centuries have left us some 230 settings of the Sanctus, of which only 21 are available for study in the *Liber*. Even this small number, however, reveals a diversity of forms and styles that makes the Sanctus one of the most interesting chants of the Mass Ordinary.

Once again the simplest, most recitativelike melody is probably the most archaic. Sanctus XVIII seems clearly designed as a continuation of the ferial Preface tone (LU, p. 109). After the first two "Sanctus" come four phrases of recitation on **b**, with cadences alternately on **b** and **g**. The melody for the final Hosanna seems to be free but proves to be a condensation of the ferial tone's first phrase, including the Amen. The *Liber*'s indication of the thirteenth century for this Sanctus is surely an error, although earlier sources usually give the melody a step lower with **a** as the reciting tone. The present version, then, may be a later modification, but the melodic principle involved goes back to the very roots of the plainchant tradition.

No other Sanctus makes use of psalmodic recitative, although a few of the available melodies are nearly as simple and syllabic as Sanctus XVIII.[23] The majority, however, are written in a more ornate neumatic style. It would be a mistake to assume that the simpler melodies are necessarily older and intended for congregational use. They could just as well be late compositions whose style was dictated by liturgical purpose or the capabilities of relatively unskilled choirs. Some of the simplest melodies, moreover, display subtle and sophisticated formal structures that are totally foreign to the needs of an uneducated and largely illiterate congregation singing from memory.

The Sanctus melodies provide excellent material for further study of the means by which composers achieved organized and coherent musical structures. Although the text neither suggests nor permits the kinds of repetitive forms characteristic of the Kyries, composers often did

---

23. For example, Sanctus X, XIII, XV, XVI, and *ad lib*. I.

avail themselves of the obvious opportunities for musical repetition. The threefold Sanctus at the beginning sometimes appears as a small three-part form, either *aba* or, less frequently, *aa'b*.[24] Much more often, the two Hosannas are set to the same music. Neither of these practices, however, is sufficient to establish an organizing principle for the complete Sanctus melody.

The one such principle most frequently observable is the adaptation of a basic melody to different lines of text. The second and fourth lines of the Sanctus, for example, are commonly sung to variant forms of the same melody. When this procedure is combined, as it usually is, with identical phrases for the two Hosannas, the form *abcb'c* results.[25] As with the Kyries, careful study of the Sanctus melodies will show that simple representations of the form often conceal more complex and subtly organized musical structures.

AGNUS DEI

The threefold Agnus Dei is related to the Kyrie in a number of ways. Both texts originally formed part of the litany, the Kyrie at the beginning and the Agnus Dei at the close (see LU, p. 758); and both were standard items in Eastern liturgies before their introduction into the Roman Mass. For the Agnus Dei, that introduction apparently took place under the Greek Pope Sergius I (687–701). At first, all three petitions closed with the phrase "miserere nobis"; but during the tenth and eleventh centuries, "dona nobis pacem" became the concluding phrase (see AMM, No. 19). At about the same time, a similar change took place in the Agnus Dei of the Requiem Mass (LU, p. 1815), the first two phrases of which close with the words "dona eis requiem" (give them rest) and the final phrase with "dona eis requiem sempiternam" (give them eternal rest).

Like the other chants of the Ordinary, the Agnus Dei gradually lost its function as a congregational song. Even by the end of the eighth century, it was assigned to the choir (schola) in Roman pontifical Masses. Elsewhere, the people continued to participate until considerably later; but by the tenth and eleventh centuries, performance had generally passed to the assisting clergy or the trained choir. At this time, then, composers began to create new settings of the Agnus Dei, eventually producing about 300 different melodies.

24. For the *aba* form, see Sanctus II and III. Sanctus I and VII have the form *aa'b*.
25. It is curious that Apel makes no mention of the frequent use of common material for these lines. It is present, however, in almost all of the Sanctus melodies listed in the third and fourth of his "four structural types" (GC, p. 417). See, for example, Nos. I, II, IV, VII, X, and XII, among others.

Despite the large number of different melodies, the Agnus Dei does not seem to have inspired composers to the same degree as the Kyrie and Sanctus. A good many of the Agnus melodies prove to be adaptations of preexistent chants, and the musical forms are generally simple and straightforward. Of the twenty Agnus Dei settings available for study, about a third simply repeat the same melody for all three petitions.[26] Even more common is a simple ternary form, *aba,* which appears in half of the Agnus melodies in the *Liber Usualis.* In three cases, the middle section differs completely from the first and third (Nos. XII, XV, and XVI). Six of the ternary melodies, however, have a common ending for all three sections (Nos. II, IV, VIII, IX, XIII, and XIV). In addition, the three sections of Agnus IX have a common opening, so that only the melodies on "Qui tollis peccata mundi" display an *aba* form. The reverse situation obtains in Agnus X, where the "qui tollis" melodies are all the same, and the *aba* structure is evident only in the opening and closing phrases.

Two exceptional forms remain to be mentioned. Agnus VII is arranged in an *aab* pattern, with the same cadence formula for all three sections. A continuous form (*abc*) in Agnus XI is unified by similar, but not quite identical, melodies for the final phrases of each section.

Simple as the forms of these Agnus Dei melodies are, it is striking that none of them reflects the change of text at the close of the third acclamation. Either the closings are identical, or it is the second "miserere nobis" that is differentiated. Once again composers have demonstrated that musical forms need not slavishly follow the organization of their texts.

ITE, MISSA EST

For the sake of completeness, brief mention must be made of the *Ite, missa est* (see AMM, No. 22). It does not form part of the normal polyphonic Mass as it came to be set in the Renaissance, and the history of its development in plainchant has yet to be written. The majority of current Mass formularies, moreover, draw on the Kyrie for the melody of the *Ite, missa est.* For these reasons, perhaps, it is usually slighted or ignored entirely in studies of Gregorian chant.

The celebrating priest or a deacon has always pronounced the dismissal formula, but originally all the people responded with the *Deo gratias.* Singing this response to the rather elaborate melody of the *Ite, missa est* cannot have been introduced until the choir had once again assumed a

---

26. Agnus Dei I, III, V, VI, XVII, XVIII, and *ad lib.* I. Nos. III and XVII have slight variants on the word "Agnus" in the second petition.

congregational function. It is unfortunate that we do not know just when this happened, or when it became customary to complete the Mass Ordinary with a melody taken from its opening chant. With this information, we could speak more definitely about the development of musically unified plainchant Masses.

The alternate dismissal formula, *Benedicamus Domino* (Let us bless the Lord), replaces *Ite, missa est* in Masses that do not include the Gloria. It may be of Gallican origin, for it seems to have been unknown in the Roman Mass before A.D. 1000. During the eleventh century, however, its present use became generally established. In modern chantbooks, *Benedicamus Domino* and its response (*Deo gratias*) are sung to the same music as the *Ite, missa est,* but again we do not know to what extent this represents medieval practice.

CHAPTER VI

Expansion of the Liturgy in the Later Middle Ages: Tropes and Sequences

In discussing the music of the Church thus far, we have been primarily concerned with the standard items of the Roman-Frankish liturgy as it developed during the ninth and tenth centuries. To what extent Frankish musicians modified the older chants is now difficult, if not impossible, to say; but they continued to create new chants and to embellish existing chants in a variety of ways. Most chants for the Ordinary of the Mass were composed in the eleventh and twelfth centuries or even later, as were also the Marian antiphons and many hymn melodies. But these represent only a small fraction of the enormous repertory of chants produced in the later Middle Ages. Begun in the ninth century, stimulated by the Carolingian Renaissance, this repertory continued to grow, even through the appalling times brought by the disintegration of the Carolingian empire and the devastating invasions of Huns and Normans. The period of greatest activity came during the tenth to twelfth centuries—the so-called Silver Age of plainchant—and continued throughout the rest of the Middle Ages and much of the Renaissance. The present chapter will begin the survey of important additions to the liturgy that this later age produced.

But first, some words of caution are necessary. In the middle of the sixteenth century, the Council of Trent decreed that the liturgy should be restored as much as possible to its "original" form. As a result, the Church discarded almost all of the repertory with which we are here concerned. This action, combined with the efforts of the Solesmes monks to restore the official chant melodies, seems to have led many musical scholars to believe that what was discarded must necessarily have been second-rate and therefore unworthy of their attention. Literary and liturgical scholars made no such mistake. Not only have they studied the texts of this later repertory, but they have made many thousands of those texts available in a variety of modern publications, including the fifty-five volumes of the series *Analecta Hymnica*. (This series is limited to poetic texts, but it is by no means restricted to hymns alone.) The music for these texts, unfortunately, has remained almost completely unknown. Only recently have scholars begun serious study of the music; and there are encouraging signs that more and more of it will be published in modern editions. For the moment, however, descriptions of the music must remain tentative, for they must still be based on a small fraction of the total repertory. What we already know is sufficient to ascertain the artistic merit and historical importance of this music. Not all of it, of course, is great; but much of it is good and all of it is interesting. The later additions to the plainchant repertory reflect new artistic ideals and new compositional procedures. They are not necessarily inferior simply because they differ from more ancient chant.

TROPES

Since their rediscovery by modern scholars, tropes have been a subject for heated debate. Most of the controversy has centered around their origin and early development, but there has also been disagreement as to what constitutes the process of troping and what a trope actually is. Part of the confusion arises from the medieval use of different designations for what we now group together as tropes. Moreover, tropes involve a number of different musical styles and compositional procedures. Yet all tropes have one characteristic in common: they expand standard items in the liturgy by the addition of words or music or both. One kind of trope, the sequence, became musically—if not liturgically—independent and will therefore be dealt with separately. With few exceptions, other kinds of tropes remained attached to the musical items they enlarged. They could later be pruned away without damage to the original chants, but the rejected clippings lost their musical function and textual logic. This probably accounts in part for their comparative neglect by musical scholars.

The origin of troping is obscure, but it seems that the practice began in France in the ninth century or earlier. Through a series of historical accidents, the early development of tropes and sequences has been associated primarily with two great religious centers: the monasteries of St. Gall in Switzerland and St. Martial at Limoges in southwestern France. Both institutions undoubtedly did contribute to the repertory of tropes, but they were by no means alone in so doing. Their historical importance can be attributed largely to the zeal of their librarians for collecting and preserving an unusually large number of manuscripts. Rather than being at the center of the new activity, St. Gall and St. Martial mark the approximate outer limits of Frankish territory within which troping was born and nurtured in its formative years. From this territory, indeed, came much of the later repertory of tropes and sequences as well as further musical developments, including many forms of early polyphony. The practice of troping became immensely popular and spread rapidly to other countries, especially Italy and England. New tropes continued to be written, but many of the oldest were disseminated throughout Europe and came to be regarded as a normal part of the liturgy.

It is a little difficult to account for the great popularity of tropes and the process of troping. In part, at least, it may reflect Frankish antipathy to the "antique severity" of the Roman liturgy. It seems significant, at any rate, that the beginning of troping closely follows, or coincides with, the imposition of the Roman rite throughout the Carolingian empire. Because the elaboration of existing liturgical items was tolerated much more readily than the introduction of totally new ones, troping provided religious poets and musicians with an important outlet for their creative energies. That these energies also found other outlets will become apparent in later chapters, but troping and related processes continued to play a role in the production of music for the Church throughout most of the Middle Ages.

Medieval churchmen evidently regarded tropes as a means of emphasizing the solemnity and significance of special feasts; and because the Mass was the most important service of the day, it naturally received the greatest elaboration. New texts were freely added to every musical item of the Mass except the Credo, which, as a prescribed confession of faith, could not readily be expanded. These textual additions occur most frequently at the beginning of the Mass, in Introits and Kyries; but even the concluding *Ite, missa est* was sometimes troped, as was the reading of the Epistle, at first with Latin phrases and sentences interspersed throughout the Biblical text and later with translations or explanations in the vernacular. Of all the Mass chants—except the Credo—the Gradual was least frequently troped, probably because it formed a musical unit with the following Alleluia, a favorite spot for the addition of new texts. Much less common than in the Mass, tropes in the Offices generally occur in the Vesper responsory, the last responsory of Matins, or the responsories at the end of each Nocturn. The *Benedicamus Domino* was also a favorite item for troping.

From a textual point of view, the chief function of tropes was to explain or enlarge on the meaning of the official text, but they might also establish a connection between that text and a particular day or season of the Church year. Because the Ordinary chants were used on many different occasions, their tropes tend to be of the more general, amplifying variety. In some cases, however, tropes of the Ordinary are related to a particular season, to feasts in honor of the Virgin Mary, or even to a specific feast, usually one that celebrates a major event in the life of Christ. The texts of the Proper chants, of course, are already assigned to specific days in the Church calendar. Yet these texts are normally taken from the Bible, especially the Book of Psalms, and their relationship to Christian feasts is often vague and obscure. Tropes of the Proper, therefore, provided an excellent opportunity to identify the feast being celebrated as well as to amplify and explain the meaning of the official chant texts. It is probably this identifying function that accounts, at least in part, for the preponderance of Introit tropes over those for the Offertory and Communion.

Whether they were written in poetry or prose, tropes were rarely independent literary compositions. More often than not they relied on the original text to complete their sense and their sentences. Examples in the ensuing discussion of the different classes of tropes will illustrate the ways in which new and old texts were combined.

THREE CLASSES OF TROPES

In expanding the standard items of their liturgy, medieval churchmen followed three distinct procedures: the melodic (melismatic) extension of an existing chant; the addition of new text to a preexisting melody; and the addition of both text and music. These procedures do not necessarily represent chronological stages in the development of troping. They all appeared at approximately the same time, and they could be and were used in combination. It is probable, however, that the expansion of a melody through the addition of melismas represents an extremely ancient tradition. It may, indeed, be another legacy of Jewish practices, one that perhaps caused the occasional diatribes of the Church fathers against vocal excesses in the performance of the liturgy. Unfortunately, the absence of manuscripts with musical notation before the ninth century prevents us from documenting the practice at an earlier date. Whether it was an innovation or not, melismatic extension formed an essential part of the troping process as we find it appearing in the ninth and tenth centuries.

CLASS 1 TROPES: MELISMATIC ADDITIONS TO EXISTING CHANTS

In studying tropes, literary scholars ignored purely musical additions to the chant. Some musical scholars, however, have claimed that such additions represent the earliest form of troping and the original meaning of the word *trope* itself.[1] The latter part of this claim, at least, is scarcely justified. An added melisma, when it was identified at all in an early manuscript, was normally called a *neuma* (= melisma), *melodia,* or, in the special case of the Alleluia, a *sequentia.* The way these melismas were added depended to some extent on the style of the original chants. In Glorias and Introits, both of which are essentially neumatic in style, short melismas sometimes functioned as a sort of musical punctuation separating phrases or sections of text. More commonly, however, purely musical expansion occurred in responsorial chants that were al-

1.   See J. Handschin, "Trope, Sequence, and Conductus," NOHM, 2, p. 128.

ready melismatic in style. Here, a melisma at or near the close of a chant was either extended or replaced by a new and longer melody. Office Responsories and Alleluias in the Mass were particularly subject to expansion in this way.

Perhaps the most famous example of melismas added to an Office Responsory is the *neuma triplex* (triple melisma) mentioned by a ninth-century writer, Amalarius, in describing the liturgy of his day. According to him, these melodies were of Roman origin and originally belonged in the Responsory *In medio ecclesiae* (In the middle of the church), for St. John the Evangelist. Modern singers, says Amalarius, transferred them to the Christmas Responsory *Descendit de caelis* (He descended from heaven). The last words of the respond—"fabricae mundi" (of the fabric of the world)—were set originally in neumatic style. In its complete form, the Responsory with verse and doxology called for three repetitions of the respond (R_{ab} V R_b D R_b R_{ab}), and the neuma triplex provided a new melisma for each repetition. Later sources eliminate one statement of the respond and use only the three melismas given in Example VI–1. The first two are neither longer nor more ornate than melismas in the same position in other responds, but the third, as Apel says, "is of truly staggering dimensions." The three melodies are entirely different, but they all close with the original setting of the words "[fa-]bricae mundi."

Example VI–1: *The Neuma Triplex as used in the Christmas Responsory* Descendit de caelis[2]

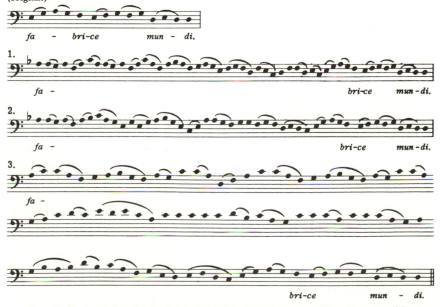

2.   From the Codex F. 160, Cathedral Library of Worcester (PalM, 12, p. 31 of facsimile).

Exceptional as it may be, this neuma triplex illustrates several characteristic aspects of the troping process. In the first place, melismatic extensions could be transferred from one chant to another, apparently at the singers' discretion. Secondly, versions of the neuma triplex differ considerably from one manuscript source to another.[3] However, the same sources transmit the original responsory with only the slight variants usually encountered in the older plainchant repertory. This suggests that purely musical tropes were treated much more freely than the original chants and could be varied at will. The existence of notable variations in a given melisma may therefore be a clue that it originated as a melodic trope, even though an earlier form of the chant without the melismatic extension is unknown. Finally, it is interesting to note that some later manuscripts add words to the melismas of the neuma triplex. They thus become examples of Class 2 tropes, in which texts are set syllabically to preexisting melodies.[4]

Even more than in the Office Responsories, purely musical tropes appear in the Alleluia of the Mass. Here they are more easily recognized, because it is the repetition of the Alleluia and jubilus after the verse that is expanded. This might be done by interpolating a new melody between the beginning of the Alleluia and the end of the jubilus; but, at times, a completely new melisma replaced the repeat of the Alleluia. In both cases, these new melodies were called *sequentiae,* and we shall return to them when we deal with the sequence as a separate form. It is also possible that greatly extended melismas at the close of the now suppressed Offertory verses were later, purely musical expansions of the chant. Certainly the repetitive formal structures in some of these melismas suggest that they represent a late period of chant composition.

Much more research must be done before we can know the whole story of melismatic additions to the chant. From the ninth century onward, such melodic expansion seems to have been the least extensively practiced form of troping and the first to disappear. It is noteworthy, however, that some localities developed standardized repertories of melismas classified according to mode. Thus, a ready-made stock of melismas was at hand whenever melodic expansion of a responsory was deemed appropriate. Collections of melismas in the different modes also provided optional extensions for psalm tones, primarily those that were used for the verse and doxology of the Introit. In these ways, at least, melismatic troping continued to be practiced throughout the Middle Ages.

---

3.   For other versions of the neuma triplex, see Apel, GC, p. 343, and Wagner, *Einführung,* 3, pp. 347–48. NOHM, 2, p. 143 (Ex. 47), has a version that appears in the Responsory *In medio ecclesiae.*

4.   Examples of these melodies with added texts are published in H. Villetard, *Office de Pierre de Corbeil* (Paris, 1907), p. 135. (Melodies 1 and 2 are reversed.)

CLASS 2 TROPES: TEXTUAL ADDITIONS
TO EXISTING CHANTS

The addition of new words to an already existing chant implies that the chant originally had many more notes than syllables, that it was highly melismatic, in other words. Tropes of this type, therefore, are generally found in responsorial chants, where they are usually identified by the term *prosa* (prose; pl. *prosae*) or its diminutive *prosula*. These terms evidently came into use because the first texts added to melismas were in prose, but they continued to be applied to tropes of this class even after poetic texts became the rule. Eventually, they came to designate pieces in a particular style and form in which both words and music might be newly composed. This development we shall explore more fully in dealing with the sequence.

In adding words to a melisma, the normal procedure was to provide each note with a syllable of its own. An almost completely syllabic style, therefore, becomes the distinguishing characteristic of prosae. When one or two prosae appear in an otherwise melismatic chant, the result is a curious alternation between syllabic and highly florid styles. This contrast is still evident, but to a lesser extent, when words are added to a complete chant. In the Alleluia verse *Dicite in gentibus* (Say among the people), we have a characteristic example of a prosa that includes all of the original text in its normal position with regard to the melody. In some cases, words and phrases also keep their original setting; the phrase "in gentibus," for example, retains its original notes but is now imbedded in a syllabic setting (see AMM, No. 23).

This Alleluia and its verse also provide examples of assonance, a frequent characteristic of prosa texts. Assonance—the use of the same vowel sound—is normally associated with verse and later became a characteristic element in Provençal and Old French poetry, where it functioned as a special kind of rhyme. In the Latin texts of prosae, however, assonance seems to result from a desire to reproduce as often as possible the vowel sounds to which the melismas were originally sung. Thus, in the prosa for the Alleluia, the words "caterva," "astra," and "perfecta" fall at normal cadential points on the final of the mode. Assonance in the prosa for the verse is even more complex and interesting. Each added phrase ends either with the vowel sound or the complete syllable of the corresponding section of the original text. In addition, some phrases repeat the vowel of the melisma a number of times. For the melisma on the last syllable of "ligno" (a repetition of the jubilus), the first four and the last two words end with *o,* and the sound appears three more times within words. The preceding phrase provides a shorter example with which we may illustrate the procedure here.

Original: *regna* —————————— *vit*
Prosa: *regna*nt omnia sacra et impera-*vit*

Tropes of Class 2 were not applied solely to melismas in responsorial chants. Long melismas in the Hosanna section of the Sanctus—perhaps examples of melismatic additions—often received textual additions that converted them into prosae. Other tropes of the Mass Ordinary sometimes present special problems with regard to the relationship between text and music. This is particularly true of Kyrie tropes, which are usually regarded as belonging in Class 2. As we saw in Chapter V, most of the melodies for the Ordinary, including the Kyries, were not written until the tenth century or later. It is possible, therefore, that Kyrie melodies may have been written to fit the troped text and only later were converted into a melismatic chant. Priority can rarely be proved, however, for in most cases the melismatic and troped versions appear together in the manuscripts. A further complication arises from the fact that not all Kyrie tropes display the same relationship between text and music. Many of them, it is true, are completely syllabic in the manner of a prosa. The trope *Cunctipotens genitor* (Almighty Father) is a typical example.[5] On the other hand, some Kyrie tropes are set in a richly neumatic style. Typical of this style is the trope *Auctor celorum* (Example VI–2). All nine acclamations are sung to the same melody, and each is followed by a ten-syllable line of the trope. Another melody serves for all nine of these lines, but the two melodies, though obviously related, are by no means identical. In this case, at least, the second melody must have been elaborated as a neumatic setting of the trope.

Example VI–2: *Kyrie Trope,* Auctor celorum[6]

1. Author of the heavens, eternal God
4. Christ, from heaven aid us
7. Holy Spirit, illuminator of hearts
(Complete text: AH, 47, p. 168)

5.   HAM, No. 15. The Kyrie is No. IV in LU, where the titles of the Kyries are the opening words of the tropes to which they once were sung.

6.   From PalM, 15, fols. 129 and 278v.

A similar trope of Kyrie XVIII in the *Liber Usualis* is given in AMM, No. 24. Here too, a line of the trope follows each acclamation of the Kyrie, but in this instance the tropes repeat the Kyrie melodies in settings that are more nearly syllabic, though not entirely so. Occasionally, however, repeated notes accommodate extra syllables.

It should be noted that the alternation of melismatic and troped melodies is not typical of all Kyrie tropes. The longer melodies tend to avoid double repetitions by inserting the trope phrases in the normal nine acclamations. This was done in two different ways. In what seems to be the earlier procedure, a longer Latin phrase was substituted for the words "Kyrie" and "Christe," but "eleison" was kept at the end of each line. Somewhat later, it became customary to retain both words of each acclamation and to insert the trope phrases between them. The two tropes whose first acclamations are given in Example VI–3 illustrate these two different procedures.[7]

Example VI–3: *Different Textual Procedures in Kyrie Tropes*

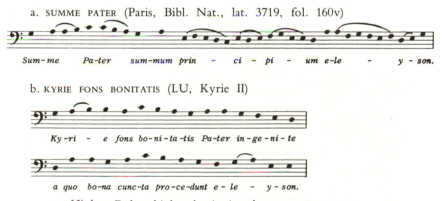

a. SUMME PATER (Paris, Bibl. Nat., lat. 3719, fol. 160v)

Sum- me   Pa-ter   sum-mum prin –   ci – pi – um e–le   –   y – son.

b. KYRIE FONS BONITATIS (LU, Kyrie II)

Ky –ri – e fons bo–ni –ta –tis Pa–ter in –ge –ni – te

a quo bo–na cunc–ta pro–ce–dunt e – le – y – son.

    a. Highest Father, highest beginning, have mercy upon us.
    b. Lord, source of goodness, Father not born, from whom all good proceeds, have mercy on us.

Example VI–3 also serves as a reminder that Kyrie tropes show a diversity of style that prevents their classification as a group. Completely syllabic tropes may have resulted from adding words to a melisma, or they may have been newly composed in imitation of prosae. Tropes in neumatic style, on the other hand, bear no resemblance to the typical tropes of Class 2. Instead, they more nearly approach, both in style and in spirit, the tropes of Class 3, to which we may now turn.

7.   The trope *Cunctipotens genitor* cited above is another example of the first procedure (see HAM, No. 15b).

CLASS 3 TROPES: ADDITIONS OF TEXT AND MUSIC TO EXISTING CHANTS

This class of trope, unlike the first two, did not alter the style or substance of the original chant. Instead, new phrases of text and music were added before the chant itself or were inserted between its phrases. The new text phrases generally served to introduce the old, to which they were grammatically linked in various ways. Similarly, the new melodies attempted to match the style of the original chant, even drawing on it occasionally for some of their musical material. More often, the trope melodies were freely composed in the style of the original but related to it only by unity of mode and by smooth connections between old and new phrases. Because chants to which tropes of Class 3 were attached were usually neumatic in style, these tropes can be readily distinguished in most cases from texts set syllabically to a preexistent melisma.

More than any other chant, the Introit was a favorite vehicle for tropes of Class 3. At first, these tropes only introduced the Introit, but later they expanded to include line-by-line interpolations in the original chant. In some cases, indeed, tropes also introduced the verse and doxology of the Introit. A trope of the Introit for Epiphany (AMM, No. 25) may serve as an illustration of both the most common form of Introit

A troped Introit and Kyrie from a twelfth-century Gradual at Ravenna.

tropes and the treatment of Class 3 tropes in general. Similar tropes appear—but much less frequently—with Offertories and Communions.

Medieval sources consistently apply the term *tropus* only to the words and music added to these three chants of the Mass Proper, but Class 3 tropes are also common in three chants of the Mass Ordinary: the Gloria, Sanctus, and Agnus Dei. Here, they appear under a variety of names. A Gloria trope may be called a song of praise (*laus,* pl. *laudes*), a term that also designates the untroped Gloria itself. Tropes of the Sanctus and Agnus Dei were also known as *laudes,* or sometimes simply as *versus* (verses) on the Sanctus or Agnus Dei. Nevertheless, we find in these chants the same troping process as in the Class 3 tropes of the Proper chants. Occasionally a trope introduces the Gloria, but more often its phrases appear as interpolations in the ancient text. Because the Preface of the Mass introduces the Sanctus, tropes of this chant can be added only within the body of the original text. The Agnus Dei presents a somewhat special case. Here, as in the Kyrie tropes, new phrases sometimes replace the opening words of the three acclamations, and the melodies may well have been written for the tropes rather than for the Agnus Dei text itself. The same is possible, of course, for the Gloria and Sanctus. Textual tropes are clearly later additions to these long established texts, but this does not necessarily mean that new music has been interpolated into old. Instead, it is probable that, in some cases at least, the setting of the original text and its trope was composed as a musical entity.

Because new music could be, and normally was, written for them, tropes of Class 3 were subject to no limitations of size. For tropes of Class 2, the length of the melisma determined the extent of the added text, and these tropes, even at their longest, remained appendages to a chant that preserved its musical and textual unity. Only when the prosae of Class 2 detached themselves from preexistent chants did they become an independent and extended musical form—the sequence. Class 3 tropes continued their function as expansions of preexisting chants, but they often outgrew the chants to which they were attached. Many tropes are far longer than the official chant, which then gives the impression of being no more than a series of familiar quotations inserted in a new and otherwise original piece of music.

MIXED FORMS OF TROPES

The three classes of tropes would seem to be clearly distinguished from each other by the different ways they add music or words or both to the standard items of the liturgy. We may wonder, therefore, why so much confusion exists regarding tropes and the process of troping. Apart from the chief reason—a grossly inadequate knowledge of the total repertory—several others have contributed to the clouding of the picture. Literary scholars, with whom the study of tropes began, regarded all textual additions or substitutions as tropes and did not concern themselves with musical processes. Musical scholars, on the other hand, often gave the impression that adding words to a melisma was the original, and indeed only, form of troping. Even recent recognition of the three classes of tropes has not entirely eliminated the confusion, partly because of associated efforts to restore medieval terminology. But that terminology itself is not entirely consistent or free from confusion. Some terms are too inclusive, others too exclusive, to be presently useful. The restricted use of the term *tropus,* for example, is unlikely to win acceptance, even if it is enlarged to include all tropes of Class 3. On the other hand, the term *prosa* as used in the Middle Ages included tropes of Class 2 as well as the independent sequence. Here a distinction needs to be made, but we cannot limit the meaning of *prosa* without obscuring a relationship that medieval terminology made clear. It seems best, therefore, to adhere to modern usage by applying the generic term *trope* to the products of all three methods of embellishing standard liturgical chants. Further support of this usage comes from a situation already hinted at in the foregoing discussions. However distinct the three classes of tropes may originally have been, they did not always preserve their identifying characteristics of liturgical position or musical style. The Class 3 trope of the Gloria *Regnum tuum solidum,* for example, included a melisma that was later converted into Class 2 tropes by the addition of several different texts. This, and other examples of mixed classes, may serve both as a warning against a too rigid terminology and as further proof of the family ties that relate all classes of tropes.

The right of the Roman Church to reject all tropes as corruptions of the plainchant tradition cannot be denied. To restrict our view of plainchant to the purified editions of the Solesmes monks, however, is to receive a totally erroneous impression of what medieval man heard when he went to church. That tropes occupied an important place in the liturgy, especially for major feasts, is also undeniable. From the ninth century until well after the end of the Middle Ages, they formed a normal and even integral part of that liturgy. If one of the goals of musical scholarship is to reconstruct the music of the past as its contemporaries knew it, then tropes must be restored to the position of prominence they once enjoyed.

THE SEQUENCE

As additions to the Alleluia of the Mass, sequences have generally been regarded as a special kind of trope. Recent objections to this classification stress the fact that the sequence rapidly became—if it was not from the very beginning—an independent composition, complete in itself both textually and musically. Certainly this is reason enough to discuss one of the most popular literary and musical forms of the Middle Ages separately. It is not to say, however, that sequences were born from a different impulse than those that produced other kinds of tropes. With relatively few exceptions, the sequence remained a liturgical appendage to the Alleluia or in some cases, perhaps, to other chants that were traditionally extended by the addition of lengthy melismas. As a class, therefore, sequences fall within our broad definition of tropes as expansions of officially recognized items of the liturgy. We may take the creation of some 4500 sequences in the Middle Ages and early Renaissance as another sign of the enthusiasm with which religious writers and composers seized every opportunity for self-expression that the liturgical practices of the time allowed.

The early history of sequences is even more shrouded in obscurity than are the beginnings of tropes in general. And, paradoxically, the existence of contemporary evidence only clouds the issue further. That evidence comes from the often-cited preface to a collection of sequences written by Notker Balbulus (Notker the Stutterer) about A.D. 884. Notker (c. 840–912) was a monk of St. Gall who was famous in his day as a teacher, poet, and author of a prose account of the deeds of Charlemagne (*Gesta Caroli*). In the preface to his sequences, Notker tells how they came to be written. As a youth, he confesses, he found it hard to remember the "longissimae melodiae" of the chant, and he had often longed for some device to aid his "unstable little memory." Then one day a monk from Jumièges near Rouen came to St. Gall after his monastery had been sacked by the Normans (862). With him the French monk brought an antiphonary in which some "verses" were fitted to the "extremely long melodies," the sequentiae of Alleluias. The idea delighted Notker, but he thought the verses somewhat crude. Attempting to improve on the models, he wrote the sequence *Laudes Deo concinat orbis* (Let the world sing praises to God).[8] After his teacher Iso suggested that each syllable should have but one note, Notker tried again and produced his second sequence, *Psallat ecclesia* (Let the Church sing).[9]

This account seems straightforward enough, and it is difficult to understand why it has given rise to so much controversy and to so many misconceptions. Notker clearly did not claim to be the "inventor of the sequence." He merely tells where he first saw sequences with words and mentions his first attempts at writing better ones. The reference to

8.   The most recent publication of *Laudes Deo* is in N. de Goede, *The Utrecht Prosarium*, No. 19, p. 30. It is also given on p. xxxiii, together with a French version that may have served as Notker's model. Notker's Latin preface is published, together with extensive commentaries in German, in W. von den Steinen, *Notker der Dichter* (Berne, 1948), 1, pp. 154–63 and 504–07, and 2, pp. 8–11; and also in H. Husmann, "Die St. Galler Sequenztradition bei Notker und Ekkehard," AcM, 26 (1954), pp. 7–13.

9.   Published in N. de Goede, *Utrecht Prosarium*, No. 65. Also in Apel, GC, p. 445.

Iso's criticism should not be taken to mean that the French examples were not syllabic. Notker probably intended no more than a graceful compliment to his teacher; but if Iso really made his comment, he must have been indulging in typically professorial fault finding. Notker apparently would have had to change only a few words to make *Laudes Deo* almost completely syllabic. Perhaps the most misleading aspect of Notker's account has to do with the process of sequence composition. It is easy to infer that Notker merely added words to preexisting melismas to make them easier to remember. Indeed, this has long been the standard explanation of how sequences originated. The explanation has been challenged, however, because it does not agree with what is found in the earliest manuscript collections of the music. A thorough study of these collections may eventually solve the many "riddles" that scholars have been able to find in Notker's innocent little story of how he came to write sequences.

Medieval terminology has again been one source of confusion. Melismas that expanded or replaced the repeat of the jubilus after the Alleluia verse were called *sequentiae* (sequences), and presumably this term was not used for melismatic additions to other types of chant. Notker called his compositions *hymns,* but German and, later, Italian sources adopted the word *sequence* to designate the pieces in syllabic style that we know by the same name today. In France, however, such a piece was usually called a *prosa* (prose) or sometimes *sequentia cum prosa* (sequence with prose). French and English sources continued to use the term *prosa* long after sequences normally had rhymed poetic texts. Recent proposals to restrict the terms *sequence* and *prose* respectively to melismatic and texted forms do not seem destined to win general approval. In the first place, neither literary nor musical scholars are likely to change their long-standing habit of designating both texts and music as sequences. A more serious objection to the proposed terminology is that the word *prosa* itself never had such a restricted meaning. As we have seen, it was used, along with its diminutive, *prosula,* to designate many different Class 2 tropes. In this instance, at least, medieval terminology clearly establishes a relationship that a limited usage of the word *prose* would only obscure. For convenience in the ensuing discussion, then, we shall make only two distinctions. The Latin form *sequentiae* will designate melodies without words.[10] Syllabic settings of these melodies will continue to be called *sequences*.

THE EARLY SEQUENCE

We know from Notker's account that sequence composition must have begun in northern France by the middle of the ninth century. Unfortunately, the earliest collections of sequences with music date from a cen-

10. They have also been called *sequelae,* as in A. Hughes, *Anglo-French Sequelae.*

The sequence *Congaudent angelorum chori* from a German manuscript of the second half of the eleventh century.

tury or more later; and, when they do begin to appear, they raise a number of problems. That a good many of the oldest sequence melodies have no connection with any known Alleluia creates the first difficulty. A few texts, moreover, do not even seem to be liturgical in nature. Although we must be cautious in deciding whether a piece was actually used in the liturgy, we must admit that the early sequence was not invariably associated with an Alleluia. It is possible that the collections of sequences even contain some prosae for the close of Responsories or Offertory verses. In at least one instance, a sequentia (and sequence) derived from an Alleluia melody reappears as both a melismatic trope and a prosula for an Offertory verse.[11] Evidently the two categories were not then as sharply distinguished as they later became. Perhaps they were never as distinct in the Middle Ages as modern writers have made them seem.

A second difficulty with the earliest collections of sequences is that they normally contain both the melismatic and the texted versions of the melodies. No manuscript sources exist to prove the greater age of the melismatic sequentiae, and in some cases the melismatic notation reflects various characteristics of a particular sequence text. Thus the origin of sequence melodies remains unknown. Even sequentiae that derive from

11. See N. de Goede, *Utrecht Prosarium*, p. xxi.

specific Alleluias often show only a slight resemblance to the parent chants. They usually begin with the first notes of the Alleluia and, less frequently, close with the final notes of the jubilus. But between these opening and closing motives the major portion of the melodies seems to be newly composed.

To meet these various difficulties, some scholars have recently proposed a complete reversal of the traditional explanation of sequence composition.[12] They suggest that, instead of adding texts to preexisting melodies, composers created words and music together as a unit. Neither theory has yet been definitely proven, and neither accounts satisfactorily for everything we find in the earliest collections of sequences and sequentiae. The two theories, in fact, are not mutually exclusive and may both contain elements of truth. Certainly there is evidence that the traditional explanation based on Notker's preface cannot be dismissed entirely.

Many of the oldest sequence melodies, including several used by Notker, have specific names apart from the opening words of their texts. In some cases, these titles refer to a related Alleluia by giving the first words of its verse. Often, however, they are inexplicable or meaningless to us. Some may indicate a secular derivation; for example, *Puella turbata* (Disturbed girl), *Frigdola* (?), *Duo tres* (Two three), or *Cithara* (Cither or lyre). Others seem to indicate a place of origin, as *Romana, Graeca, Occidentana,* and *Metensis* (Of Metz). The existence of so many titles unrelated to any sequence text strongly suggests that the melodies had an independent life of their own. This impression is confirmed by the fact that the same melody—with the same title—often appears with several different texts. Quite obviously the melody, if it did not already exist, can have been created for only one of these texts; but usually it is impossible to determine which was the original. Even among the oldest sequences we find two or more texts sung to the same melody, and some melodies eventually accumulated as many as twenty or more different texts. More rarely, the same text occurs with different melodies, but this usually happens with later sequences after both poetic and musical forms had become standardized. Whatever the origin of sequence melodies may have been, it is undeniable that writing new words to fit old tunes was a dominant, perhaps predominant, part of sequence composition throughout the history of the form.

It would be a mistake to assume that composers of sequences, because they used preexistent melodic material, were simply literary craftsmen. They evidently did not regard sequence melodies as fixed and unchangeable forms to which they must rigidly adhere. Instead, they treated the melodies as basic material that could be modified in a variety

12. See, for example, the articles of R. Crocker cited in the Bibliography.

of ways. Within a single musical phrase, the repetition or omission of notes and motives accommodated text lines with differing numbers of syllables. More significant modifications involve rearrangement of the basic material to produce entirely different musical—and textual— forms. Two versions of a melody known as *Concordia* provide a particularly striking illustration of these procedures.[13] A longer, more complex, and more symmetrical version appears in French sources with several different texts. German sources preserve a drastically shortened, one might even say mutilated, version with two texts by Notker Balbulus.

Despite their divergent forms, a common structural principle underlies the two *Concordia* melodies. The opening and closing phrases have one line of text and are sung but once, while each of the internal phrases has two lines and is repeated. The chief difference between the two versions of *Concordia* arises from the omission of some internal phrases in both of Notker's sequences. To return to generalities, the two lines of text for a repeated phrase will normally be similar in construction and will have the same number of syllables. This parallelism of textual structure and the musical repetition that goes with it produce a form that is often said to be the distinguishing characteristic of the early sequence: *a bb cc dd ee ff g,* for example. Like most generalizations, this one is misleading. In the first place, designating the forms of *Concordia* and of many other sequences in this manner completely obscures the many different ways in which relatively small amounts of musical material were used to create lengthy sequence melodies. Even worse, the generalization hides the fact that many early sequences deviate wholly or in part from the so-called standard pattern. Some, indeed, have no musical repetitions whatsoever, and consequently no textual parallelism. Such sequences are generally short and may represent an early stage in the development of the form. At any rate, their melodies suggest the type of Alleluia jubilus in which repeated phrases had not yet been introduced.

In a much greater number of early sequences, parallelism is present but incomplete. Departures from strict parallelism take two different forms. The two lines sung to one melodic phrase may differ in length by several syllables, thus necessitating the addition or subtraction of several notes in the repetition. A more obvious departure from the standard form results when some internal phrases have only one line of text and are therefore not repeated. In these cases, the single phrase is often longer than usual and may be given a distinct form of its own by the repetition of melodic motives. The second and third phrases of Notker's first sequence provide characteristic examples of both types of departure from strict parallelism (Example VI–4). In the second phrase, an insertion of eight notes and a repetition of four accommodate the

13.   Both versions are printed in NOHM, 2, pp. 154–57.

added twelve syllables in the second line of text (2b). The third phrase has only one line of text, but the melody subdivides into three smaller units with considerable motivic repetition.

Example VI–4: *The First Three Phrases of Notker's First Sequence,* Laudes
Deo

Sing praises to God everywhere, the whole circle of the earth that has mercifully been set free by the indulgence of the highest father. He, full of pity that mankind was oppressed by the ancient Fall, sent his Son here to earth that with his right hand he might raise to heaven those lying in the mud and restore their fatherland.

Sequences that depart from strict parallelism in one or both of the ways illustrated in Example VI–4 are actually in the majority in the first period of sequence composition. According to recent surveys, less than half of the sequences in both the St. Gall and St. Martial repertories display complete parallelism. In the slightly later repertory of Winchester Cathedral, the situation has changed and more than two-thirds of the sequences exhibit complete parallelism.[14] In its formative period,

14. See N. de Goede, *Utrecht Prosarium,* p. xx, where precise figures are quoted from
H. Husmann's article in German, "Alleluia, Vers und Sequenz," AnM, 4 (1956), pp.
40–41.

then, the sequence is often far removed from textbook descriptions of the type. But we have not yet exhausted the diversity of structure that is perhaps the outstanding characteristic of the early sequence.

SEQUENTIAE WITH PARTIAL TEXTS

Nine sequentiae have double lines of text set syllabically in two or three of their repeated phrases. In every other respect, they appear to be normal, albeit extended, examples of melismas to be sung after an Alleluia. Each of these sequentiae also occurs as a fully texted sequence, some with two or even more different texts. In almost every case, the partial texts of the sequentiae maintain their positions and are thus to be found imbedded in the texts of the sequences. Sequentiae with partial texts seem to be of French origin, and the traditional view has been that they represent an early stage in the transformation of melismatic sequentiae into syllabic sequences. Now, scholars are not so sure. Although the phrases with text are scattered through the sequentiae, they make musical sense when brought together as a unit. It has been claimed, therefore, that they are older songs, well known, well loved, and deliberately preserved by insertion into sequentiae. This could have been easily done, of course, but the partial texts of these sequentiae already have the assonance on the vowel *a* and the double versicles characteristic of the full-fledged sequence. That they were written for any other purpose seems unlikely.

For a better understanding of sequentiae with partial texts, we may examine the melody known as *Adorabo maior* (AMM, No. 26), which also illustrates the characteristics of sequentiae in general. The two phrases with text (5 and 9) have essentially the same melody with open and closed endings (on **c′** and **d′** respectively). It is curious—and typical—that these phrases do not constitute complete phrases of the sequentia. The same short melisma introduces both syllabic phrases, and shorter melismatic cadences reaffirm the open and closed endings. The position of the texted phrases in *Adorabo maior* is also typical. With one exception, the first lines of text appear in the fifth phrase of each partially texted sequentia; and three or four melismatic phrases always follow the last phrase with text. In addition, melismatic interludes of two or three phrases separate the two or three texted phrases. Obviously, a common structural principle underlies eight of the nine sequentiae with partial texts. Whether this common principle is evidence of a common origin remains to be determined. In any case, the systematic achievement of symmetrically balanced musical structures can only have been deliberate.

The title *Adorabo maior* refers to the *Alleluia: Adorabo ad templum,* which was and still is used in the Mass for the Dedication of a Church

(LU, p. 1251). A different and shorter sequentia derived from the same Alleluia was known as *Adorabo minor*. The partial text of *Adorabo maior* is appropriate for dedicatory ceremonies or the celebration of their anniversary, and one of the melody's complete texts, perhaps the oldest, specifically mentions such an anniversary. This text, *Observanda*, is also important because its opening lines establish a connection with St. Martial of Limoges.

1. *Observanda*

2a.	Abunde solemnitas	2b.	Qua pontifex maximus
	nobis omnibus		*hanc Martialis*
	aderit hodierna,		*dicavit basilicam.*

According to a French scholar, the correct meaning of these lines is:

> We must all celebrate the solemnity of this day when the very great pontiff (St.) Martial dedicated this basilica (of St. Peter in Limoges).[15]

It is obvious, at any rate, that the sequence *Observanda* must have originated in Limoges as a trope of the *Alleluia: Adorabo ad templum*. In this connection, it is interesting to note that the sequentia with partial text is normally identified by the word *Observanda* or by the opening word of some other complete sequence text.[16] The fully texted sequences, on the other hand, identify the melody as *Adorabo maior*. These cross references have made their own contribution to our uncertainty about the historical relationship between sequentia and sequence.

The melodic relationship between *Adorabo maior* and its parent Alleluia is typically slight. Only the first few notes are identical, and the rest of the long sequentia is entirely new. Even the mode of the sequentia seems to change. The Alleluia and its verse are in Mode 7, ending on **g**, but the Alleluia of the sequentia ends on **d'**. Thereafter, the melody stays within the range of **a** to **a'**, and all of the phrases end on **d'**, with the exception of the open ending in phrase 5. *Adorabo maior* thus gives the impression of being in Mode 2 transposed up an octave. Such a change of mode, or at least of final, is very common in sequences, although it usually occurs during the course of the melody rather than at the beginning. As one example from many, we may cite *Psallat ecclesia*, Notker's second attempt at writing a sequence. Here, the first five phrases end on **d**, but the last three end a fourth higher on **g**.[17] This practice—ending a melody a fourth or fifth higher than its beginning

---

15. J. Chailley, *L'École musicale de Saint Martial de Limoges* (Paris, 1960), p. 69.

16. The complete text of *Observanda* is printed in AH, 7, No. 221. The first word replaces "Alleluia," and the rest of the text turns the sequentia in AMM, No. 26 into a completely syllabic sequence. Four other sequences that include the partial text of this sequentia are listed in AH, 49, p. 272 (note to No. 519).

17. See Apel, GC, p. 445.

leads one to expect—has never been satisfactorily explained. Perhaps it is related to the custom reported by medieval writers of repeating the Gradual after the verse "on a higher tone."[18] It may also have some connection with the probable performance of sequences in improvised polyphony or with organ accompaniment.

SEQUENCES WITH DOUBLE CURSUS

The presence of a curious formal structure known as a *double cursus* characterizes another small group of eight or nine early sequences. In these pieces, several repeated phrases are themselves repeated as a unit with different words. Within this double cursus, a further departure from normal sequence structure is the occasional repetition of internal phrases as many as four times instead of the usual two. For most of the sequences with double cursus, the notation of the melodies—if it is present at all—is either incomplete or undecipherable. In two or three cases, however, medieval sources preserve the melodies in a notation that can still be read. By their repetition of musical material, these few examples confirm the parallel structures that scholars first recognized in the texts. A particularly important discovery was the complete melody of the sequence *Rex caeli* (King of heaven; AMM, No. 27).[19] The first two phrases of this sequence had long been famous because of their appearance among the oldest known examples of two-part polyphony (see Chapter VIII and Example VIII–2b). But these two phrases by themselves gave no indication that *Rex caeli* was a typical example of a sequence with double cursus. If we disregard minor variants in the repeated phrases, we may indicate its complete form as follows:

A							A							A'	
aa	bb	cccc	aa	dddd	eeee	f	aa	bb	cccc	aa	dddd	eeee	f	aa	f
1	2	3	4	5	6	7	8	9	10	11	12	13	14	15	16

It is self-evident that *Rex caeli* differs strikingly from the usual early sequence, both in the overall form and in the restricted amount of melodic material, only five phrases plus a cadential figure (*f*) of four or five notes. The large- and small-scale repetitions in *Rex caeli* clearly distinguish it from the "classic" forms of the early sequence. It is this distinction that gives the sequence with double cursus its historical importance and interest.

The origin of the characteristic sequence structure has been the subject of much speculation. Some scholars have attempted to prove By-

18. See J. A. Jungmann, *The Mass*, 1, p. 428 and n. 43.
19. J. Handschin discovered the sequence and published it complete in "Über Estampie und Sequenz," *Zeitschrift für Musikwissenschaft*, 12 (1929/30), pp. 19–20.

zantine influence, but without notable success. Parallel phrases of text sung to repeated melodies are not at all characteristic of Byzantine chant, and it is difficult to believe that an exceptional procedure in the liturgy of the Eastern Church could have touched off the widespread and enthusiastic production of sequences in the West. Sequences with double cursus have a much more direct connection with the origin of sequence composition. Most of these pieces date from the ninth century and come from northern France. They are therefore contemporary with the earliest normal sequences and probably developed in the same geographical location. For these reasons, the similarities and differences between the two types become particularly significant.

The chief similarity, of course, lies in their common use of double versicles—paired lines of text sung to the same melody. The differences go far beyond the formal characteristics that we have already observed. Sequences with double cursus have no connection with an Alleluia, and their melodic style is quite unlike that of the normal sequence. In some cases, many repeated notes suggest recitation tones rather than extended melismas. It is significant that their melodies do not appear in melismatic form in the manuscript sources. Their texts also differ from the normal sequence in both style and content. Assonant endings are lacking, but rhymes occasionally appear. Some texts are partly or wholly written in metrical poetry, and three are laments over the desperate conditions resulting from the Norman invasions. Although a few were later assigned a liturgical use, sequences with double cursus apparently did not originate as pieces to follow the Alleluia of the Mass. Instead, it has been suggested that they represent a nonliturgical, perhaps even secular, tradition stemming from the court poets of Charlemagne. In this connection, it is interesting to note the reappearance of the double cursus in the lai and Leich, French and German vernacular songs that bear a structural resemblance to the sequence (see Chapter XII).

SEQUENCES OF LATER PERIODS

All of the sequences that we have been discussing belong to what is sometimes called the first epoch of sequence composition, roughly comprising the ninth and tenth centuries. If this period requires more detailed consideration than later periods, it is because the origin of the sequence is still a controversial matter and because the earliest examples are the least well known—perhaps even the most interesting. As is usually the case, the first stages in the development of a new form display such diverse procedures that it is difficult and dangerous to make generalizations about common characteristics. Only in later periods do we find consistent application of the structural principles that distinguish a particular form. It is the more standardized structural pattern for the sequence that we must now examine.

Evidence of a trend toward greater regularity of formal structure first makes its appearance in sequence texts written during the course of the eleventh century. In place of prose texts either with or without assonance and with lines that varied greatly in length, there is now a tendency to equalize the length of the lines, to introduce real rhyme, and occasionally to alternate strong and weak syllables in a regular pattern. In other words, the sequences of this transitional period show a gradual shift from prose to poetry. It may seem strange that such a shift should have been introduced gradually. Prose and poetry, after all, were rather clearly distinguished from each other in the eleventh century. Why should an intermediate stage that was neither one nor the other have been necessary? Perhaps the answer lies in the conservative attitude of the Church, to which the sudden use of rhythmic poetry and rhyme would have been distasteful. Hymns, as we have seen, were slow to gain general acceptance, even in the Offices; and similar texts could probably be introduced into the Mass only by degrees and surreptitiously. In any case, the changes in textual structure were gradual and were accompanied, inevitably, by corresponding changes in the musical structure of the sequence. The impetus for change, however, seems to have come from the texts rather than from the music.

One of the first examples of the transitional period, and the one that is most commonly cited, is the famous Easter sequence *Victimae paschali laudes* (Praises to the pascal victim). Written by Wipo of Burgundy (d. 1048?), this is one of the four sequences that the Council of Trent (1545–63) kept in the liturgy (LU, p. 780). Unfortunately, the present version alters the original form of the sequence by omitting the first line of text that was sung to the final phrase. The presence of this line gave the form *a bb cc dd* (as in AMM, No. 12); and we may note that the gradual disappearance of single lines at the beginning and end of sequences is another development of the transitional period.

The text of *Victimae paschali laudes* reveals its transitional character in a number of ways. The opening phrase of fifteen syllables is the shortest; phrases *b* and *d* both have twenty-four syllables; and phrase *c* has thirty-one. The latter phrase in particular breaks up into shorter lines with rhyme and occasional suggestions of regular rhythmic patterns. These lines do not yet form typical stanzas of rhythmic poetry, however, for they are all of different lengths.

3a. *Dic nóbis María*   (6)   b. *Angélicos téstes,*   (6)
     quid vidístis in vía?   (7)   *Sudárium, et véstes.*   (7)
     Sepúlchrum Chrísti vivéntis, (8)   *Surréxit Chrístus spes méa,*   (8)
     et glóriam vídi resurgéntis.   (10)   *Praecédet súos in Galilaéam.* (10)

Tell us, Mary, what you saw on the way? "I saw the sepulcher of the living Christ and the glory of (his) rising; the angelic witnesses, the napkin and the clothes. Christ, my hope, is risen. He goes before his own into Galilee."

As a sidelight, it is interesting to note that some medieval versions emphasize the dramatic nature of this dialogue by repeating the question to Mary before each pair of lines in 3b. The textual structure of these lines is also emphasized by division into separate phrases in the *Liber Usualis*. As a result, the form of the sequence as a whole appears to be *a bb cd cd e.*

By the twelfth century, the transition to completely poetic texts had been accomplished, and the second epoch of sequence composition had begun. Indeed, it quickly reached its peak in the skillful and elegant poems of Adam de St. Victor (d. 1192), whose fifty or so sequences set the standard, often providing the models for an enormous number of late-medieval and early-Renaissance compositions. Adam was a monk in the Abbey of St. Victor on the left bank of the Seine not far from the newly begun cathedral of Notre Dame. It is significant that Adam's productive period also coincided with the first polyphonic compositions of the so-called School of Notre Dame (see Chapter IX). The results of all these activities must be counted among the early signs of the emergence of Paris as the intellectual and artistic center of western Europe.

The essential characteristic of the new sequence was the organization of its text in poetic stanzas, with regular patterns of both rhythm and rhyme. In addition, a limited number of stanzaic forms were used for many different sequences, and one or a few of these forms might serve throughout an entire composition. As a result of this standardization of poetic forms, it became even more common—and much easier—to write new texts for preexistent melodies. Conversely, the new sequence texts could be, and sometimes were, sung to different melodies.

None of the sequences of Adam de St. Victor remains in the present liturgy; but, with the exception of *Victimae paschali laudes,* those that do appear in the *Liber Usualis* are representative examples of sequences of the second epoch.[20] Brief comments on one of these sequences will therefore make clear the features that characterize the output of this period, including the works of Adam de St. Victor.

As is so often the case in the Middle Ages, the authorship of *Veni Sancte Spiritus* (Come, Holy Spirit), the sequence for Pentecost, has been attributed to a number of different men. The most likely candidates, however, are Stephen Langton, Archbishop of Canterbury (d. 1228), and Pope Innocent III (1198–1216). Certainly the form of the poem is typical of the late twelfth century. All of the five stanzas consist

---

20.   Forty-five sequences attributed to Adam are available in E. Misset and P. Aubry, *Les Proses d'Adam de Saint Victor.*

of six lines, with seven syllables in each line and the rhyme scheme aab ccb. A further unifying device is the use of the same rhyme (*-ium*) in the third and sixth lines of all five stanzas. Such regularity, of course, makes the sequence text exactly like a hymn, and it is only the musical setting that now distinguishes the two forms. Instead of repeating the same melody for all stanzas, the sequence provides the first half of each stanza with a different melody, which is then repeated for the second half (lines 4–6). In the case of *Veni Sancte Spiritus,* this procedure results in the form *aa bb cc dd ee.* Obviously, the regularity of poetic structure has led to the suppression of single versicles at the beginning and end and to the creation of five melodies that are of equal length and identical structure (Example VI–5). Analysis of this and other sequences in the *Liber Usualis* is somewhat difficult because the repeats are written out and the half-stanzas are numbered consecutively when they are numbered at all. In Example VI–5, the numbers in parentheses are those found in the *Liber.* A less confusing procedure numbers each melody, with the half-stanzas indicated as 1a and 1b, 2a and 2b, etc. To facilitate study, the melodies of *Veni Sancte Spiritus* have been given without text except for the indication of the rhyme *-ium* that appears at the close of each. This textual rhyme is paralleled by identical cadential progressions in the first three melodies. In the last two melodies, the cadential phrases are obviously related, but one ends on the fifth, the other on the final of the mode. Although the five melodies are all different, analysis will reveal other motivic relationships between them and between phrases within a single melody. Compare, for example, the first phrase of melody 3 with the first two phrases of melody 4. The careful way in which contrasts of pitch level are used to produce variety and balance is also worthy of attention.

Example VI–5: *Melody of* Veni Sancte Spiritus

PERFORMANCE OF SEQUENCES

The question of how sequences were performed is difficult to answer, but there is considerable evidence that performances were much more colorful and sonorous than the simple monophonic melodies would suggest. The presence in some manuscripts of both syllabic and melismatic forms of the sequence melodies has led to the belief that both forms were used together, either simultaneously or in alternation. In view of the length of most sequences, simultaneous performance seems more likely, and several sequence texts appear to confirm this judgment. Among the earliest texts we find phrases such as this: "For we celebrate you with the bright melismas of our voices, while with lifted voice we bind together sonorous organa syllable by syllable."[21] A comparable passage from another sequence reads: "Wherefore let us all, joyful, sing melodies, extended melismas."[22] The same sequence begins: "Let us sing organa sufficiently beautiful and fitting" (*Cantemus organa pulchra satis atque decora*). Passages such as these—and many more could be cited—suggest that sequence melodies may have been doubled at the octave, fourth, or fifth to produce the early form of polyphony known as *organum* (see Chapter VIII). Indeed, as we have noted above, one of the earliest and most famous examples of organum used the opening phrases of the sequence *Rex caeli*. Confusion arises, however, because the term *organum* can mean either the early forms of polyphony or the organ as a musical instrument; and, in some cases, performance with organ accompaniment seems to be implied. The eighth stanza of the sequence *Epiphaniam*, for example, begins with the words "Omnis nunc caterva tinnulum iungat laudibus organi pneuma" (Now let the whole assembly join the ringing melody [breath] of the organ in praises; NOHM, 2, pp. 156–57). The phrase "Let us sing organa," on the other hand, suggests polyphonic vocal performance. In either case, the musical result, if not the quality of sound, must have been much the same. As far as we know, medieval organs normally had more than one rank of pipes and probably sounded at least the fifth and octave above each fundamental tone. A melody played on the organ would therefore be doubled in parallel fifths and octaves, very much in the manner of parallel organum. It is even possible that this characteristic of the medieval organ sparked the development of vocal polyphony and eventually gave this new development its name. The first theoretical description of polyphony, be it noted, used the term *symphonia* rather than *organum*.[23]

The organ was by no means the only musical instrument to be men-

---

21.   From AH, 7, No. 11. "Nam pangimus tibi clara dando vocum neumata. Voce praecelsa perstringentes sonora sillabatim simul organa." For other quotations of a similar nature, see W. Waite, "The Era of Melismatic Polyphony," in *Report of the Eighth Congress of the International Musicological Society, New York 1961*, 1, pp. 178–83.

22.   AH, 7, No. 84. "Propter quod laeti omnes decantemus melodias, prolixa neumata."

23.   See Strunk, SR, pp. 126–38.

King David and other, apparently secular, performers illustrating different modes in a tonary, part of an eleventh-century troper from the St. Martial library (Paris, Bibliothèque Nationale).

tioned in sequence texts. We find phrases such as "Let the flute resound" (*Resonet fistula*) and "Let us sing to the accompaniment of the lyre" (*Fidibus canamus*).[24] Liturgical purists insist that references to these and other instruments are merely symbolic and that instruments cannot have been used in the church service. Whether the services really remained that pure is doubtful. Miniatures in an eleventh-century manuscript of tropes and sequences depict both wind and bowed string instruments, with performers ranging from King David to ordinary minstrels. Such illustrations, of course, do not prove that instruments were used in church. More positive indications come from prohibitions of performances by jongleurs during religious services. Laws rarely prohibit nonexistent sins. Whatever unauthorized instruments may occasionally have been used, there can be no doubt that organ accompaniment was a normal procedure in the later Middle Ages. Egidius de Zamora, a Spanish Franciscan who was tutor to the son of King Alfonso the Wise (1252–84), wrote of the organ that "the Church uses only this one musical instrument with diverse chants and with proses, sequentiae, and hymns; other instruments in general are rejected because of abuses by the players."[25]

Leaving the question of instrumental participation, we must return to a consideration of the way sequences were sung. The characteristic repetitive structure of sequence melodies naturally led to performance by alternating groups of singers, a practice that is still followed today. For confirmation of the antiquity of this practice we may turn once again to the early sequence texts themselves. Mention is made of choirs singing alternately (*alternatim*);[26] and one text even names the specific performing groups. The opening double stanza of a sequence for St. Stephen begins as follows:

1a.	*Praecentorum*	1b.	*Psallat Christo*
	succentorumque turma		*neumata regi compta*
	concentorumque pia		*concordi symphonia*
	personet laude una.		*vota reddens debita.*[27]
	Let the devout choir (crowd)		Let it sing to Christ the King
	of precentors, succentors,		melismas adorned with
	and concentors, resound		concordant symphonies,
	with one song of praise.		returning due devotion.

The names of the three groups that form the "devout choir" suggest their different functions, and definitions given by the contemporary

24.   AH, 7, Nos. 55 and 100.
25.   GS, 2, 388b. "Et hoc solo musico instrumento utitur ecclesia in diversis cantibus, et in prosis, in sequentiis, et in hymnis, propter abusum histrionum, ejectis aliis communiter instrumentis."
26.   AH, 7, No. 128, stanza 7b.
27.   Ibid., No. 194.

theorist Regino of Prüm (d. 915) confirm those functions. The fore-singers (*praecentores*) would naturally begin, and the after-singers (*succentores*) would answer. The *concentores* sing *with* one or both groups to form the "concordant symphonies": that is, organum.

All of the texts that we have cited come from a single volume of the *Analecta Hymnica* (Vol. 7), which is devoted to sequences of the first epoch from the region around Limoges and its famous Abbey of St. Martial. The German scholar Bruno Stäblein asserts that the word *organum,* or its synonym *symphonia,* appears in 71 of the 265 sequence texts in this volume.[28] On the other hand, such references are entirely lacking in texts from East-Frankish areas—those of Notker and his followers. Whether this reflects different methods of performance or more rigid standards of propriety for religious poetry is impossible to say. In any case, we may be grateful that French poet-musicians felt free to combine their religious fervor with expressions of delight in the glorious sounds of their new songs. To their enthusiasm we owe most of our information—and little enough it is—about how sequences were performed. From their enthusiasm we gain some insight into the contemporary attitudes that made the sequence a favorite outlet for creative energy during the course of several centuries.

28. "Zur Frühgeschichte der Sequenz," AMW, 18 (1961).

CHAPTER VII

Further Expansion and Embellishment of the Liturgy

Our discussion of tropes and sequences may seem to have led us far afield from the established forms of the liturgy, but it should have demonstrated that those forms were not as immutable as is usually supposed. Tropes as a class freely expanded various items of the liturgy, particularly in the Mass. Sequences, if they originated as expansions of the Alleluia, soon became musically independent pieces, although they still followed the Alleluia on most occasions. The present chapter will consider other ways in which medieval men expanded and embellished their religious services.

Further contributions to the liturgy in the later Middle Ages generally took one of two forms: new services written in the established structural patterns; and new items added to the traditional framework of the liturgy. Both of these procedures produced an enormous amount of sacred music between the twelfth and sixteenth centuries. New services, whether or not they were adopted by the universal Church, were obviously liturgical in nature, and their intended function was never in doubt. New items added to the liturgy, on the other hand, are much less easily recognizable. Even when the Church tolerated such additions, it rarely gave them official sanction. Yet the function of much religious music, in both the Middle Ages and the Renaissance, can be understood only if we recognize how freely the liturgy could be expanded to meet the needs and tastes of individual princes, clergymen, and churches.

NEW FEASTS IN THE LATER MIDDLE AGES

During the first 800 years of its existence, the Church calendar included a limited number of special feasts. Beginning in the ninth century, however, the religious activity which ranged from the creation of tropes and sequences to the construction of churches and cathedrals throughout western Europe included a tremendous growth in the number of feast days in the Church year. The majority of new feasts honored individual saints, either recently created or suddenly popular; but medieval religious fervor also added new feasts to the Proper of the Time: Trinity

Sunday early in the tenth century, and Corpus Christi over three centuries later in 1264. Other contributions to the Church calendar came when the growing cult of the Virgin Mary prompted the addition of new feasts in her honor.

Each new feast, of course, required a Mass and a complete set of services for all the Hours from first to second Vespers, but Rome evidently felt no need or was unable to establish uniform services for use in all of Western Christendom. At any rate, we find—somewhat unexpectedly—a number of completely different services for the same feast. In the case of saints, this occurred because not all churches celebrated their feast days with the same degree of solemnity. Newly created saints naturally received higher honors in the areas where they had lived and worked. Moreover, the feast days of patron saints were celebrated with special pomp in the cities, churches, and monasteries under their protection.

Further impetus for the creation of new services came from the Crusades and the resulting brisk trade in relics. The possession of bones or other physical remains of a saint naturally called for a more solemn celebration of his feast. The complete body of an important saint might make its repository the goal of pilgrims, as happened when St. James was "translated" to Santiago de Compostela in northwestern Spain. This event occasioned the development of unusually elaborate services for the Feast of St. James at Compostela, where the cathedral archives still preserve the famous Codex Calixtinus containing these services with their music. Other kinds of relics also led to the creation of new liturgical services. In the thirteenth century, for example, an impecunious—and enterprising—Byzantine emperor gave the Crown of Thorns to the Venetians as security for a large sum of money that he was unable to repay. Louis IX of France paid off the creditors and in 1239 took possession of the relic. To house this and other relics of Christ and the Virgin Mary, Louis built the Sainte Chapelle in Paris, probably the largest and certainly one of the most beautiful of all reliquaries. Not nearly as long lasting, but important nevertheless in the history of liturgy and music, were a number of special services honoring the Crown of Thorns. Louis himself became the subject of several different services after his canonization as a saint in 1297. The Middle Ages obviously did not lack opportunities for creating new services, and many cathedrals and monasteries seem to have taken pride in developing their own liturgies for special feast days. Medieval men clearly regarded the church service not as something fixed and immutable, but as a living expression of religious faith to which they could make their personal contributions.

The common medieval designation for these new services was *historiae,* probably because they drew the subject matter of their texts from the lives of the saints or from Biblical stories. Now, somewhat confusingly, they are generally known as *Offices.* This term, then, can designate either the daily Hours of the liturgy as a whole or the special set of services, often including the Mass, for a particular feast. All of these special Offices required new texts and new or adapted melodies for the Proper of each service, especially Vespers, Matins, and Lauds. The new chants therefore include hymns, responsories, and antiphons for psalms and canticles. In later Offices, the texts of all these items were normally the same kind of rhymed and rhythmic poetry that characterized the later sequence. That the volumes of the *Analecta Hymnica* contain over 850 such rhymed Offices is a measure of their enormous popularity.[1]

ADDITIONS TO THE MASS

By comparison to the Offices, the Mass showed itself much more impervious to penetration by poetic texts, particularly of the modern, rhymed variety. Tropes and sequences, of course, did introduce such poetry in the later stages of their development, as did on occasion the verses of Alleluias. On the whole, however, the chants of the Mass Proper continued to draw on the Bible for their texts, even for feasts that were newly added to the Church calendar. Only in a few exceptional cases were Proper chants provided with poetic texts. Curiously, the practice seems to have been confined to Offertories and Communions, perhaps because these chants had lost any semblance of psalmodic form. The volume of *Analecta Hymnica* devoted to tropes of the Mass Proper (Vol. 49) includes forty-two "rhythmic Offertories," and twenty-seven "rhythmic Communions." Almost invariably these chants are for feasts of the Virgin Mary or individual saints. Most of them, moreover, come from sources dating from the fifteenth and sixteenth centuries. There are even a few instances when the entire Proper of the Mass is set in rhymed poetry. Peter Wagner quotes one such example as a "curiosity" and comments that "no proof is needed that works of this sort belong to the period of liturgical degeneracy."[2]

A more fruitful and acceptable means of embellishing the Mass had been found long before the scattered attempts to introduce poetic texts into the Mass Proper. Just as tropes expanded individual chants, so introductions, interpolations, and conclusions expanded the form of the Mass itself. The official items of both Proper and Ordinary remained unchanged to form a structural frame that could support a multitude of local additions, some of which themselves became part of the official Mass liturgy. When we recall the form of the Mass as outlined in Chapter V, we may well be surprised to find that the Ordinary in the *Liber Usualis* (p. 1) has a full page of text *before* the Introit. Similarly, the

1.   See Bibliography.
2.   P. Wagner, *Origin and Development of the Forms of the Liturgical Chant* (London, 1907), p. 261, n. 1.

dismissal *Ite, missa est* is followed by a prayer and a final Gospel reading. The Ordinary chants, moreover, begin with what are called "The Asperges" (LU, p. 11), chants to be sung during the sprinkling of altar, clerics, and congregation with holy water. In medieval practice, further additions—both textual and musical—often expanded these introductory and concluding ceremonies to even greater lengths. Interpolations within the Mass also enriched its musical contents. At some points in the service, notably the Communion rites, the insertion of extra music became a generally accepted practice for solemn feasts and even for ordinary Sundays. Added music was also provided for Masses celebrated in connection with such special ceremonies as royal weddings, the installation of bishops, and the coronation of kings. As indicated earlier, the original function of much religious music cannot now be determined. We do know, however, some of the music that was commonly added to the Mass, and scholars have identified a few pieces, both monophonic and polyphonic, that were composed for the coronations of particular French kings (see Chapter X, p. 242 and fn. 2).

LITURGICAL DRAMA

The introduction of dramatic representation is perhaps the most interesting and surely the most unexpected way in which the medieval Church expanded and embellished its liturgy. The recorded history of liturgical music drama begins with a scene depicting the encounter of

The three Marys at the tomb of Christ. A scene from the earliest liturgical drama.

the three Marys with an angel (or angels) at the tomb of Christ on Easter morning. Usually named from its opening words, "Quem quaeritis" (Whom are ye seeking), the "play" in its simplest form consists of only three lines of dialogue:

> Angels: Whom are ye seeking, O servants of Christ?
> Marys: Jesus of Nazareth, who was crucified, O servants of heaven.
> Angels: He is not here. He is risen as He said. Go and proclaim that He has risen.

In this form, however, the dialogue does not appear as a play at all, but in a St. Gall manuscript that dates from c. 950, as an introductory trope to the Easter Introit *Resurrexi* (AMM, No. 5), in which Christ himself announces "I have risen." Another version, the first to have been preserved, is found in a Limoges manuscript dated 923–934. Also attached to the Easter Introit, this version, curiously, is more complex than the later one from St. Gall. It appears to be embedded within another trope of the Introit, but the three-line nucleus is itself expanded by a second speech of the three Marys: "Alleluia, the Lord is risen. Today the strong lion, Christ the Son of God has risen. Give thanks to God, say Eia!"[3]

The manuscripts give no indication that either of these two earliest versions of *Quem quaeritis* was dramatized, although they were probably sung responsorially or antiphonally as was usual for the Introit itself and as a number of later sources specify for the trope. Our first evidence of dramatic representation comes not from a musical source, but from the *Regularis concordia,* a manual of ceremonial usages for the Benedictine order in England. Drawn up between 965 and 975 by Ethelwold, Bishop of Winchester, the *Regularis* gives an unusually full account of how the *Quem quaeritis* play was to be performed after the final responsory of Matins on Easter Sunday.[4]

It is generally assumed that the indications of dialogue in Ethelwold's description are the textual incipits of the chants that were sung. If this be true, the play begins with the three-line nucleus from St. Gall and the added speech of the Marys from Limoges. In two further additions the angel sings a liturgical antiphon, "Come and see the place where the Lord was laid," and the Marys respond with another antiphon announcing that "The Lord who was hung upon the cross for us has risen from the sepulcher, alleluia." The performance then returns to the regular liturgy of Matins with the singing of the *Te Deum* accompanied by the traditional pealing of bells.

Only a few years later than the *Regularis concordia,* the Winchester

---

3. For transcriptions of the first tropes from St. Gall and Limoges (the latter incomplete), see NOHM, 2, pp. 178–79. A later version from Limoges may be found in P. Evans, *The Early Trope Repertory of Saint Martial de Limoges* (Princeton, 1970), p. 155. The first play, from the Winchester Troper, is recorded in HMS, 2, with a transcription of the music in the accompanying booklet.

4. For one translation of this account, see Reese, MMA, p. 194.

Troper (c. 980) preserves a complete version of the play with music. Although this version lacks the detailed stage directions of Ethelwold's description, its contents differ in only two respects. The first is the insertion of still another liturgical antiphon as the angel's final speech. After the Marys have seen that the tomb is empty, he tells them, "Going quickly, tell the disciples that the Lord is risen." The play then ends with the antiphon of the Marys announcing that "The Lord has risen." Omission of the *Te Deum* is the second and more significant difference from the *Regularis* version, for it shows that the play was not performed at the end of Matins. If we can trust its placement in the Winchester Troper—which otherwise gives an accurate sequence of liturgical events—this version of the play served as a prelude to the Blessing of the Paschal Candle, part of the ceremonies of the Easter Vigil service.

In spite of chronological discrepancies that had to be explained away or ignored, the early appearances of the *Quem quaeritis* dialogue just described have provided the chief basis for the orthodox explanation of how liturgical drama originated. According to that explanation, the simplest form—the three-line nucleus—must have been the earliest, was probably composed at St. Gall, and began as a trope of the Easter Introit. When the trope was later expanded and performed as a Visitation to the Sepulcher at the end of Matins, liturgical drama was born. In this view, then, dramatic representation was a direct outgrowth of the process of troping.

Various objections to this traditional explanation have been raised in the past, but only recently have serious doubts as to its validity been accompanied by proposals of more credible alternatives. In a series of brilliant essays, O. B. Hardison, Jr. analyzed the place of drama in the liturgy and examined the numerous "manuscript anomalies" in the transmission of the *Quem quaeritis* dialogue as trope and play.[5] Hardison concluded that the play must have come first and probably originated as an addition to the ceremonies of the Easter vigil.[6] A later article reported Hardison's discovery of remarkable textual parallels between the *Quem quaeritis* play and portions of a ninth-century Easter Vespers that "is emphatically a commemoration of the rites of Holy Saturday."[7] Still later research by Timothy McGee into the liturgical placement of *Quem quaeritis* has shown that, when the dialogue came before the Easter Mass, it normally formed part of a larger processional ceremony preceding but

5. *Christian Rite and Christian Drama in the Middle Ages;* see especially the fifth essay, "The Early History of the *Quem quaeritis*."

6. Following the papal decree of 1960, the Easter vigil is included in the "restored Ordo of Holy Week" in later editions of LU, pp. 776_{1-MM}.

7. O. B. Hardison, Jr., "Gregorian vespers and Early Liturgical Drama," *The Medieval Drama and its Claudelian Revival,* ed. E. Catherine Dunn *et al.* (Washington, D.C., 1970), p. 37.

separate from the Mass itself.[8] From the evidence of some eighty manuscripts of the tenth to twelfth centuries, McGee came to doubt that the little dialogue was ever regarded as a trope directly connected with the Easter Introit. Instead, he concluded that it was "a separate, self-contained ceremony," which might or might not be called a trope, depending on the meaning given that term in various parts of western Europe. It is not unreasonable to suppose that this ceremony may have included representational elements from its very beginning. A number of sources indicate performance as a dialogue, and some specify that it was sung "at the sepulcher" (*ad sepulchrum*) or "at the visitation to the sepulcher" (*ad visitandum sepulchrum*). Transference of the ceremony from the procession before the Mass to the end of Matins, which was supposed to come at dawn, would then reflect a desire to conform more closely to the women's arrival at the sepulcher "very early in the morning" (Luke 24:1).

That McGee's investigations partly confirm and partly modify Hardison's conjectures is obvious. The old hypothesis that liturgical drama developed from the process of troping preexistent chants is no longer tenable. Both representational scenes and tropes, to be sure, resulted from the same impulse to embellish and, perhaps, to humanize the rituals of the Church, but they developed independently. Occasional relationships between them are merely incidental and do not imply lineal descent of one from the other.

Whatever the origin of the Easter play, it obviously served as a model for a Christmas play representing the shepherds' visit to the stable in which Christ was born. This play, which first appears in eleventh-century sources, begins with the words "Quem quaeritis in praesepe, pastores, dicite" (Whom are ye seeking in the manger, shepherds? say!). The shepherds reply: "The Saviour, Christ the Lord, . . ." Two more speeches follow, the second of which is completed by the Introit of the Christmas Mass, *Puer natus est nobis* (Unto us a Child is born; LU, p. 408).[9] That this play so often introduced the Mass seems to confirm the orthodox hypothesis that liturgical drama evolved from tropes. Another Christmas play, *The Visit of the Magi,* again raises doubts, however. Most examples of this play are attached to Matins and appear to be independent compositions. Much more diversified in content than the shepherd plays, they often expanded into highly complex episodic forms. The visits of the shepherds and the Magi were sometimes combined in a single play, which might also include elaborate scenes at King Herod's court. Such scenes naturally suggested dramatization of the Slaughter of the Innocents and the Lament of Rachel. Another play that

8.   Timothy J. McGee, "The Liturgical Placements of the *Quem quaeritis* Dialogue," JAMS, 29 (1976), pp. 1–29.

9.   For the melodies of the first two speeches, see NOHM, 2, p. 196. A complete setting of the text is available in Evans, *The Early Trope,* p. 129.

appeared in the eleventh century, the *Ordo prophetarum* (Procession of the prophets), was also performed during the Christmas season. Based on a sixth-century sermon, it assembled various Old Testament characters, as well as pagans such as Vergil and the Sybil, who prophesied the coming of Christ.

Not until the twelfth century do Easter plays begin to approach the richness and complexity of Christmas plays from the previous century or of contemporary plays on other subjects. Only then were new episodes and scenes added both before and after the central dialogue at the sepulcher. The various episodes related to the Resurrection, like those related to the Nativity, were sometimes performed on different occasions as separate playlets, sometimes combined in a longer, continuous play. Some details of this accumulative process will appear later in the present chapter. The Easter and Nativity seasons were naturally the favorite times for the production of liturgical drama, and they inspired the vast majority of plays that have been preserved. Indeed, fewer than twenty surviving plays from the twelfth and thirteenth centuries are based on other subjects. Dramatized stories from the Old Testament include those of Isaac, Joseph and His Brothers, and Daniel. The number of stories provided by the New Testament was scarcely greater: the Annunciation, the Raising of Lazarus, the Conversion of St. Paul, and the Wise and Foolish Virgins. Curiously, eight plays—almost half of those unconnected with either Easter or Christmas—are not Biblical at all but are devoted to the miracles of St. Nicholas, which seem to have been among the most popular tales of medieval religious mythology.

The expansion of liturgical drama from simple dialogues to lengthy plays with scenery and costumes naturally depended on the introduction of new texts and new music to which those texts could be sung. Throughout their history, the liturgical plays remained sung rather than spoken drama. In a very real sense, therefore, they are music-dramas. Some writers have even gone so far as to call them "medieval operas." The name is misleading only if we think in terms of opera as we know it now. Medieval opera was acted and sung, certainly; but until late in the fourteenth century the few references to instrumental participation mention only the organ and sometimes bells, and then only to accompany the concluding choral chants such as the *Te Deum* and *Magnificat*.[10] Moreover, the music was entirely monophonic, single-line melodies that retained the notation and, to some extent, the character of plainchant. Within these restricted limits, however, the music of medieval opera displays considerable diversity.

Whatever their origin may have been, the melodies of the *Quem quaeritis* dialogues for Easter and Christmas matched the style of the In-

---

10. See W. L. Smoldon, "The Music of the Medieval Church Drama," MQ, 48 (1962), pp. 493–94.

Belshazzar's Feast from the Play of Daniel, as produced by the New York Pro Musica, Noah Greenberg, director, at Wells Cathedral in England.

troits with which they first appeared. In the plays, additional texts taken from the liturgy—antiphons, the *Te Deum,* and, later, sequences—normally retained their traditional and relatively simple melodies. They were thus in perfect accord with the already prevailing style—partly syllabic, partly neumatic—which set the standard for later additions requiring new melodies for nonliturgical texts. More elaborate styles with melismatic passages were usually reserved for laments or other situations in which their dramatic and emotional intent is obvious. It is curious to note, however, that later plays of German origin show a decided tendency toward melismatic elaboration.[11] Interesting and beautiful as some of these German melodies may be, they are often less effective dramatically than the simpler melodic style to which the French plays adhered. Even in medieval opera, apparently, the typically French principle of subordinating music to words was well established.

In the twelfth and thirteenth centuries, a new development came with the introduction of rhymed poetic texts into liturgical drama. This development coincided with the appearance of the new poetic forms in the sequence and in the many rhymed Offices that date from the same and later centuries. The new plays now exhibit great variety in their textual, and consequently their musical, structure. In some of the musically most interesting, poetic forms—often as a sort of set piece—alternate with the prose dialogues and liturgical chants. In others, older prose texts were remodeled into poetry and provided with modified or completely new melodies. The process was occasionally carried to such extremes that almost the entire text was cast in poetic forms, with little or

11. For examples see GD, 5, p. 325, and Smoldon, ibid., p. 487.

no dependence on liturgical texts and melodies. The result of this process is nowhere more evident than in *The Play of Daniel,* perhaps the best known because the most widely performed of all medieval dramas. Except for two concluding items—one stanza of a hymn and the *Te Deum*—the texts and melodies of this play are entirely nonliturgical. Their diverse forms and styles make *The Play of Daniel* one of the most fascinating examples of medieval dramatic art.[12]

REPRESENTATIVE PLAYS FROM FLEURY

Perhaps the most important collection of liturgical dramas is the "Fleury Play Book," so called from the monastery of St. Benoît-sur-Loire from which it comes.[13] The ten plays in this thirteenth-century manuscript presumably formed the dramatic repertory of the monastery and represent all types of the later liturgical drama both in subject matter and in methods of construction. The first four deal with the miracles of St. Nicholas. Then come two plays for the Christmas season and two for Easter. The last two plays are based on the Biblical stories of the Conversion of St. Paul and the Raising of Lazarus. All of the plays close with a liturgical chant, usually the *Te Deum,* but their texts as a whole are of three different kinds: 1) almost exclusively rhymed poetry; 2) almost exclusively the prose of liturgical chants; and 3) a mixture of the two. Comments on plays representative of each can at least suggest the differing musical forms and styles to which each gave rise.

PLAYS WITH LARGELY POETIC TEXTS

The Play of Daniel belongs to the class of plays with largely poetic texts, but its great variety of textual forms and musical settings makes its position unique. As a rule, plays in this class are much more limited in both their textual and musical resources. Frequently, indeed, a single poetic form, and even a single melody, will serve for an entire play. This is the case in the first two miracles of St. Nicholas in the Fleury Play Book and also in the final play, *The Raising of Lazarus.* The practice may have been suggested by contemporary performances of the epic *chansons de geste* (songs of deeds), in which one or two melodic formulas served for hundreds of lines of text (see Chapter XII). The liturgical plays are not

---

12. *The Play of Daniel* is a performing version edited by N. Greenberg, recorded on Decca Records (DL 9402; stereo, DL 79402). An edition by W. L. Smoldon simply gives the original melodies in unmeasured note values.

13. The original name, Fleury-sur-Loire, was changed to St. Benoît-sur-Loire when relics of St. Benedict were brought to the monastery, which is situated on the Loire River some miles above Orléans. The Fleury Play Book is now in the Municipal Library of Orléans (MS. 201).

nearly as long, but the constant repetition of a single melody can scarcely be called dramatic.

A more imaginative procedure lends considerably greater interest to the fourth miracle of St. Nicholas, *The Son of Getron*. The story is a simple one. The servants of a pagan king kidnap a small boy, who serves for a year as a page in the king's household. St. Nicholas then intervenes and miraculously returns the boy to his parents. The text still makes use of a single poetic form: four-line stanzas with ten syllables in each line. Variety comes, however, from assigning a distinctive melody to each character, including the chorus of servants. Departures from this principle of musical characterization are few but dramatically effective. At first it may seem incongruous that the mother should lament, and her comforters console, to the same melody. Yet this unusual repetition of one melody does make a point. From despair and lamentation, the mother gradually becomes more hopeful. Finally, on the advice of her comforters, she concludes the scene with a prayer for the intercession of St. Nicholas. The double meaning that the melody thus acquires becomes clear when it later reappears in the mouth of the boy lamenting his fate as a servant of the pagan king. By abandoning his own melody, the boy recalls both his mother's anguish and her prayer to St. Nicholas. In this subtle way the music prepares the audience for the intervention of the saint that is soon to bring the play to a happy ending. Fittingly enough, the mother's closing song of rejoicing uses a new melody that borrows a prominent motive—a melismatic descent stepwise through the interval of a fifth—from the son's melody. It is perhaps an exaggeration to see in *The Son of Getron* an "early experiment with the Wagnerian *leitmotif*,"[14] but certainly the suggestive power of music has here been used to good effect.

PLAYS WITH LARGELY LITURGICAL TEXTS

A good many plays follow the example of the early Easter plays, drawing their texts largely from liturgical chants. Antiphons were the favored form for use in this class of text, but longer chants, as well as tropes and sequences, were also included. For the most part, of course, these are prose texts, either taken directly from the Bible or elaborated from simpler Biblical phrases. Usually, the plays retain the melodies to which their texts are sung in the liturgy; but now and then a liturgical text will appear with what seems to be a newly composed melody. Because even these new melodies do not radically depart from traditional plainchant style, plays of this kind seem more sober, more severe, and—to us, perhaps—more truly liturgical than plays that use rhymed and rhythmic poetry.

14. *The Son of Getron,* ed. by C. Sterne, p. 1 of Introduction.

Of the ten plays in the Fleury Play Book, only *The Appearance at Emmaus* belongs in the class with largely liturgical texts. According to Rembert Weakland, "almost the whole of [this] Peregrinus Play . . . is composed of chant antiphons."[15] (The term *peregrinus* ["stranger" or "traveler"] identifies plays that deal with the meeting of the risen Christ with two disciples travelling to Emmaus [Luke 24:13–52].) Rubrics in the manuscript tell us that the play was performed at Vespers on Tuesday after Easter, and some of its antiphons are still in use during the Easter season. Christ's first chant, for example, *Qui sunt hi sermones* (What manner of communications are these; Luke 24:17), is now the antiphon for the *Magnificat* at Vespers on Monday after Easter (LU, p. 788). Not all the play's antiphons have remained in the liturgy, and some texts that do remain have different melodies.[16] It is not surprising, therefore, that the liturgical nature of many chants has gone unrecognized. Unfortunately, lack of recognition has led to mensural transcriptions that, to quote Weakland again, "can be seen at once to be capricious."[17] Whatever one's theories with regard to the rhythm of early plainchant may be, by the twelfth century it must certainly have been performed in unmeasured note values. In a play such as *The Appearance at Emmaus,* then, mensural transcriptions, either in free or in triple rhythms, can have no place. The contemporary way of singing plainchant—as far as we can know it—must provide the only basis for modern interpretations of liturgical dramas that draw the bulk of their material from the liturgy itself.

PLAYS WITH A MIXTURE OF POETIC AND LITURGICAL TEXTS

The Easter and Christmas plays were originally mixtures of new prose texts and liturgical chants. At first, expanded scenes and added episodes followed the same procedure. Where chants alone proved inadequate for dramatic dialogue, the new prose texts were given musical settings that matched the style of the chants with which they appeared. Later additions introduce rhymed and rhythmic poetry in different places throughout the plays. Many fully developed plays, therefore, combine liturgical chants and dramatic dialogue in prose with set pieces having poetic texts. This mixture of different textual types has suggested to some scholars a comparison with the operatic recitative and aria. The resemblance becomes even more pronounced if we grant that the poetic texts should be performed in triple meters. The style of the set pieces

15. R. Weakland, "The Rhythmic Modes and Medieval Latin Drama," JAMS, 14 (1961), p. 136.

16. Compare *Videte manus meas* (Behold my hands) in LU, p. 792, with the version in E. de Coussemaker, *Drames liturgiques du moyen âge,* p. 199.

17. JAMS, 14 (1961), p. 136. The edition referred to is G. Tintori, *Sacre rappresentazioni,* a complete transcription of the Fleury Play Book.

then contrasts strikingly with the prose dialogues sung in free, un-measured rhythms.

Two of the more extended Fleury plays illustrate such mixtures of poetry, prose, and liturgical texts: *The Representation of Herod* and *The Slaying of the Children*. These two plays dramatize the entire Christmas story from the vision of the shepherds in the field to the slaying of the children, the death of Herod, and the return of the Holy Family from Egypt. In their modern revival they have been performed and published as a single play under the title *The Play of Herod*.[18] In this edition, an acting version is followed by a literal transcription and facsimiles from the Fleury Play Book. Interested students thus have a unique opportunity to study medieval dramas in their original form as well as in their modern dress. Let us at least mention a few of the items that make *The Play of Herod* characteristic of its class.

One of the first contrasts between poetry and prose occurs when Herod sends a soldier to question the Three Kings. The soldier (*armiger*) addresses the Magi in prose, but they reply in rhymed verse (Nos. 14 and 15).[19] Poetic texts often emphasize the emotional climax of a scene after a series of prose dialogues. Thus in the long scene at Herod's court (Nos. 16–38), the King learns the purpose of the Magi's visit and summons the Scribes to say what they find in the Prophets. When the Scribes report that the Prophets foretold the birth of Christ in Bethlehem, Herod flies into a rage. His son Archelaus interrupts and the two alternately sing four-line stanzas to the same melody (Nos. 39–41). After this outburst, the return to prose for the final chant of the scene is particularly effective. Herod falsely asks the Magi to bring back word of the newborn child so that he too may go and offer homage to him.

The second part of *The Play of Herod* reaches its emotional peak with the Lament of Rachel over the slain children (Nos. 17–23; AMM, No. 28). In this famous scene, as in *The Son of Getron*, the solo lament alternates with ensemble chants of the "consolers." Rachel's lament is much more extended, however, and its structure and style are both more varied and more expressive. The first three numbers—two laments with an intervening consolation—are stanzas of rhymed verse with the same poetic rhythms. They are also related musically through the use of similar opening motives and a recurring cadential pattern. Beginning with the second chant of consolation, another group of three numbers (20–22) draws on a sequence of Notker for its text. The lines are therefore irregular in length and without rhyme. Continuing this re-

18.   Edited by N. Greenberg and W. L. Smoldon, recorded on Decca Records (DXA 187; stereo, DXSA 7187).

19.   Musical items are numbered consecutively but begin again with No. 1 in the second section of the play. The same numbering appears in both the literal transcription and the acting version, but in the latter, numbers with letters indicate repeated or added items. No. 6a, for example, is a motet of the late thirteenth century; Nos. 55a and 56a are repetitions of No. 55.

turn to older textual types, Rachel's final lament closes the scene with a liturgical antiphon. The melody for Notker's text seems to have been newly composed for Fleury, but the antiphon has its traditional melody.[20]

The complete text for the scene of Rachel's Lament may seem a curious mixture of styles, but the progression from "modern" rhythmic poetry back to a Biblical—and liturgical—text can only have been deliberate. It is surely significant, too, that the antiphon was sung at Lauds on Good Friday and thus suggests the coming Resurrection. In the Fleury play, indeed, an archangel raises the children to heaven immediately after Rachel's exit. Excerpts from the lament have often been quoted, but the rather lengthy scene must be studied and heard in its entirety for full appreciation of its effect. In the words of its modern editor, we have here "one of the most remarkable examples of the use of dramatic melody that can be found in medieval times."[21] Smoldon's qualification "one of" might well be eliminated from this statement.

A final comment on *The Play of Herod*: the opening episode is a complete shepherds' play, including the familiar dialogue of the midwives and shepherds. Curiously, however, the first two words, "Quem quaeritis," are sung to the beginning of the Easter melody, which is here transposed to lead smoothly into the traditional melody of the Christmas trope. Thus *The Play of Herod* relates the birth of Christ with His Resurrection and subtly reminds us that liturgical drama began with the scene at the empty tomb.[22]

LITURGICAL DRAMAS AND VERNACULAR PLAYS

The propriety of the term *liturgical drama* has sometimes been questioned, but a number of considerations justify its continued use. With few exceptions, the texts were entirely in Latin. The actors were clerics, and the action took place within church walls. Most important of all, liturgical drama never lost its original connection with the liturgy itself. Plays continued to serve as a postlude to Matins, as an interpolation into Lauds or Vespers, and even, on occasion, as a prelude to the Mass. To deny their function because the Church never recognized them as part of the official liturgy is to misrepresent the attitude of the Middle Ages toward its religious observances. We have seen before, and shall often see again, that medieval men felt free to embellish and expand the universal liturgy of the Church in a great variety of ways. Among those ways, liturgical drama is one of the most interesting and attractive.

20. See LU, p. 690: *Anxiatus est in me spiritus meus* (My spirit is overwhelmed within me), Psalm 142 (143):4. Despite numerous variants, the two versions are obviously the same melody.

21. *The Play of Herod*, p. 78.

22. The same procedure occurs in a thirteenth-century Magi play from Rouen; see Coussemaker, *Drames liturgiques*, pp. 235–41.

The term *liturgical drama* also provides a useful means of distinguishing the Latin plays of the Church from miracle and mystery plays in the vernacular. By the end of the thirteenth century, the independent development of liturgical drama seems to have been completed. In cathedrals and especially in monasteries, performances of Latin plays as adjuncts of the liturgy continued well into the sixteenth century and perhaps even later. After 1300, however, religious plays in the language of the people captured the popular imagination and experienced the greatest development. Modern terminology makes a distinction—not observed in the Middle Ages—between miracle plays, which portray the miracles of the Virgin Mary or the lives and miracles of saints, and mystery plays based on stories from the Bible. Both kinds are found in Latin plays of the twelfth and thirteenth centuries, as we have seen, and the same centuries saw the first appearances of both kinds in French. From the beginning, apparently, vernacular plays were not performed in church as an addition to the official liturgy, although throughout their history the great majority continued to betray their ancestry by ending with the *Te Deum*. Despite the occasional introduction of other liturgical chants, perhaps the chief distinction—after that of language—between liturgical and vernacular drama was the latter's use of spoken rather than sung dialogue. In large part, presumably, this change occurred because the actors were now laymen, not clerics who were trained singers. Minstrels often took part in performances both as singers and instrumentalists, but more and more the miracle and mystery plays became spoken dramas with incidental music.

Freed from the restrictions of the Church, the vernacular plays treated their Biblical or legendary subject matter with great freedom and a lively sense of humor. Scenes with the devil in hell seem to have been particularly popular. More than miracle plays, mysteries grew in length and elaboration until, by the fifteenth century, their performances often extended over several days and covered the entire story of the Bible from the Creation of Man to the Last Judgment. Music continued to serve as an ornamental adjunct to these plays, but little that was composed specifically for them has survived. The texts that were to be sung were often in the poetic forms characteristic of secular song from the thirteenth to the fifteenth centuries, and we may assume that their musical settings were also characteristic of their age. In some cases, indeed, we find no more than a direction that some chanson or motet should be sung. Suggestions for the use of instrumental music are common but even less specific as to what the musicians played. Because of this characteristic indifference to music on the part of playwrights, or scribes, the mystery plays must remain more a part of theatrical than of musical history. And that, after all, is perhaps where they belong. Rather than foreshadowing the development of opera, they are much more the ancestors of Shakespeare.

CHAPTER VIII

The Rise of Polyphony

Thus far we have been concerned with musical embellishments of the liturgy that retained the general characteristics of plainchant. We must now consider another musical embellishment, the simultaneous sounding of more than one melody, which we know as *polyphony*. To call polyphony an embellishment of the liturgy is merely to state its primary function during the first centuries of its recorded existence. Beginning as an elaboration of plainchant, polyphony served almost exclusively as a means of increasing the splendor and solemnity of church services from the ninth century until well into the thirteenth. It may be regarded, then, as a kind of trope in which new music appeared together with the chant instead of being added to it by monophonic extensions. Significantly, polyphony originated and was first cultivated extensively in the same centuries and in some of the same places that produced the large repertories of tropes and sequences. Both types of music quite evidently resulted from the same need to find an outlet for creative activity. Both fulfilled that need in the most logical way by expanding and enriching the only large musical repertory then existing.

The invention of polyphony was undoubtedly the most significant event in the history of Western music. Once the concept had been accepted, organization of the vertical (harmonic) dimension of music became a major preoccupation of both theorists and composers. That it has remained a major preoccupation ever since is evident in the common differentiation of musical styles on the basis of their distinctive methods of harmonic organization. This would seem to be wholly justified, since it is precisely the systematic organization of vertical sounds that distinguishes Western music from all other musics, whether they be the products of primitive peoples or of highly sophisticated Oriental cultures. The distance between a work of the late twelfth century and one of the twentieth may seem immense. But the latter could not have been written if the development of the former had never taken place. And both stand in opposition to plainchant in their concern with the combination of simultaneous musical sounds.

Because the invention of polyphony thus altered the course of musical evolution in the Western world, the circumstances of that invention become a matter of extraordinary historical interest. In this chapter we shall trace the development of polyphony from its earliest manifestations to its first flowering in the twelfth-century repertories of St. Martial and Santiago de Compostela. In the course of so doing, it should become evident that we are dealing with music of much more than purely historical interest. Approached with an open mind and a lively imagination, the polyphony of the Middle Ages reveals itself as a worthy counterpart to the great churches and cathedrals in which it was performed.

THEORETICAL DESCRIPTIONS AND EXAMPLES OF EARLY POLYPHONY

Polyphony began as an unwritten accompaniment of plainchant. We must depend on theoretical treatises, therefore, for knowledge of the earliest stages of its development. This situation gives rise to a number of difficulties. The brevity and ambiguity with which medieval authors described contemporaneous practices often make it difficult to reconstruct those practices after a lapse of many centuries. Even with seemingly explicit musical examples we sometimes find ourselves on shaky ground. As we shall see, problems of accidentals remain unsolved. The examples are generally short and are based on a limited number of simple, often fragmentary chants. They sometimes illustrate specific procedures very well, but we cannot be certain that those procedures would be applicable throughout a complete or more elaborate chant. Indeed, we cannot know how accurately the theoretical examples reflect the actual performance practices of the time. The theorists' need to simplify and systematize must inevitably distort the natural tendency of performers toward complexity and freedom in improvisation. But theoretical descriptions of early polyphony are all we shall ever have, and we must learn from them what we can.

The concept of harmonic consonance was apparently known to St. Augustine and Boethius. Both writers—along with others in the early Middle Ages—made statements that *may* refer to something more than simple monophonic singing. Not until late in the ninth century, however, do we find descriptions of part singing that establish its distinguishing name, organum, and provide decipherable musical examples. Perhaps the greatest value of the earlier writings, however vague and ambiguous their references to part singing may be, is their confirmation of the probability that organum as described in the ninth-century documents was neither a sudden nor even a recent innovation. These late treatises, then, attempt to describe and systematize practices that may well have been widespread and of long standing. With them we pass from the conjectures of prehistory to the written record of polyphonic development.

Two nearly contemporary authors, Regino of Prüm (d. 915) and Hucbald (c. 840–930), wrote treatises with the same title, *De harmonica institutione* (Concerning Harmonic Instruction). Both introduce the term *organum* (pl. *organa*), and both attempt to define consonance and dissonance. Hucbald in particular makes it clear that organum involves the simultaneous sounding of different tones:

> Consonance is the judicious and harmonious mixture of two tones, which exists only if two tones, produced from different sources, meet in one joint sound, as happens when a boy's voice and a man's voice sing the same thing, or in that which they commonly call *Organum*.[1]

More detailed descriptions with musical examples are given in two of the most important treatises of the period, the *Musica enchiriadis* (Music Manual) and the *Scholia enchiriadis* (Commentary on the Manual). Although these works were formerly attributed to Hucbald, their authorship is now in dispute. Dispute has also arisen as to their date of composition, which has been variously placed from c. 850 to c. 900. There can be little doubt, however, that they both describe the organum referred to in the authentic Hucbald treatise as it was practiced in the latter half of the ninth century.

PARALLEL ORGANUM

According to the *Enchiriadis* treatises, the different types of organum they illustrate all derive from the application of one basic principle: the duplication of a preexistent plainchant in parallel motion at the interval of an octave, a fifth, or a fourth. The plainchant is called the *vox principalis* or principal voice. When it is doubled by one other voice, the *vox organalis* (organal voice), the result is *simple organum*. Further doubling of one or both voices at the octave yields *composite organum*. To these distinctions, which are made in the treatises themselves, we must add another that is not named but is implicit in the musical examples. When parallel motion is rigidly maintained, modern writers generally speak of *strict* or *parallel organum*. When parallel motion is temporarily abandoned, usually at the beginning and end of phrases, there is less agreement as to what the resulting kind of organum should be called. Some writers refer to it as *free organum*. Others treat it as a subspecies of parallel organum. The *Enchiriadis* treatises imply that a proper designation would be *modified parallel organum*. To avoid confusion with the free organum of the eleventh century, this designation will be adopted here.

All musical examples in the *Scholia enchiriadis* use the same psalm-tone

1.   Reese, MMA, p. 253.

formula, a variant of the tonus peregrinus.[2] The *Scholia* begins with organum at the Octave above and below (Example VIII–1a), which, "since it is easier and more open, is called greatest and first." Next comes organum at the fifth below (Example VIII–1b). Various octave doublings convert this two-voice structure into different types of composite organum (Example VIII–1c). In the second and third types, dropping the original organal voice leaves the chant in the principal voice as the lowest part.

Example VIII–1: *Parallel Organum at the Octave and Fifth*

a. AT THE OCTAVE ABOVE AND BELOW

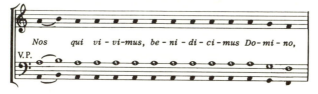

b. AT THE FIFTH BELOW

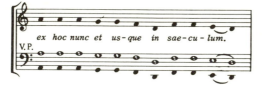

c. THREE FORMS OF COMPOSITE ORGANUM AT THE FIFTH

We who are living will bless the Lord from this time forth and forever.—
Psalm 113:27 (115:18)

Although they use different examples, the *Enchiriadis* treatises agree in all essentials in describing organum at the octave and fifth. When it comes

2.   LU, p. 117. For a translation with complete examples from the *Scholia enchiriadis,* see Strunk, SR, pp. 126–38.

to organum at the fourth, however, their opinions diverge. The *Musica* gives an example of strict parallel motion at the fourth below the chant and says that the voices sound agreeably together (Example VIII–2a). Later, the author says that the fourth is often not suitable for organum because of the frequent appearance of augmented fourths (tritones). To avoid this disagreeable interval, the singer must modify the organal voice as shown in the oft-quoted setting of *Rex caeli* (Example VIII–2b). The *Scholia* takes the position that strict parallel organum at the fourth is never possible, for the organal voice cannot "agree with the principal voice so absolutely as is the case with the other consonances." Unlike the example of *Rex caeli,* modified parallel organum in the *Scholia* begins on a perfect fourth, but it does reach a unison by contrary motion at the end of the psalm-tone formula (Example VIII–2c). As in parallel organum at the fifth, octave doublings then create composite forms of modified parallel organum. These are particularly interesting because of the new intervals and intervallic progressions that are introduced, especially in cases where the lower organal voice is again omitted and the plainchant becomes the lowest part (Example VIII–2d).

Example VIII–2: *Parallel and Modified Parallel Organum at the Fourth*

a. *Musica enchiriadis:* SIMPLE ORGANUM

V.P.

V.O. *Tu Pa-tris sem-pi-ter-nus es Fi-li-us.*

b. *Musica enchiriadis:* MODIFIED PARALLEL ORGANUM

V.P.

V.O.
1a. *Rex cae-li Do-mi-ne ma-ris un-di-so-ni*
b. *Ti-ta-nis ni-ti-di squa-li-di-que so-li,*

V.P.

V.O.
2a. *Te hu-mi-les fa-mu-li mo-du-lis ve-ne-ran-do pi-is*
b. *Se ju-be-as fla-gi-tant va-ri-is li-be-ra-re ma-lis.*

c. *Scholia enchiriadis:* MODIFIED PARALLEL ORGANUM

V.P.

V.O. *Nos qui vi-vi-mus be-ne-di-ci-mus Do-mi-ne,*

V.P.

V.O. *ex hoc nunc et us-que in sae-cu-lum.*

d. *Scholia enchiriadis:* COMPOSITE FORMS OF MODIFIED PARALLEL ORGANUM

a. Thou art the everlasting Son of the Father.—From the *Te Deum*
b. King of heaven, Lord of the sounding sea, of the shining Titan sun and the wretched earth, thy humble servants, worshiping thee with devout song as thou hast bidden, earnestly entreat thee to free them from their various ills.
c. We who are living will bless the Lord from this time forth and forevermore.—Psalm 113:27 (115:18)

The supposed need for modification of parallel organum at the fourth results from the use of a scale peculiar to the *Enchiriadis* treatises. This scale consists of the arbitrary and artificial arrangement of disjunct tetrachords shown in Example VIII–3. Containing no diminished fifths, the scale was obviously designed to accommodate simple organum at the fifth. It works for nothing else, however, because it produces augmented octaves as well as tritones. The author ignored this problem in organum at the octave and in composite forms, and, perhaps through carelessness, he left tritones in some of his examples (marked ⋆ in Example VIII–2a and c). In any case, the artificiality of the scale makes the explanation of modified parallel organum as an avoidance of tritones somewhat suspect. It is quite possible that the *Enchiriadis* treatises confused the picture considerably by attempting to find a common principle in two distinct practices.

Example VIII–3: *Scale of the* Enchiriadis *Treatises*

Singing in parallel octaves was known to the Greeks, who called it *magadizing,* but it is such a natural phenomenon that there is no need to look for Greek influence in the emergence of organum. As Hucbald's *De harmonica* suggests, men and boys singing together would unconsciously produce strict organum at the octave. Parallel motion at the fourth or fifth would probably require a more conscious effort, but even this procedure seems less strange when we remember that the most comfortable ranges for bass and tenor voices lie approximately a fifth apart. Strict organum, whether simple or composite, never needed to be written down, and for performers the problem of tritones would never arise. Once each singer had settled on his starting pitch, he would merely reproduce the intervals of the original melody, just as he would join in unison singing at a pitch level most convenient for the group as a whole. Avoidance of the tritone, then, would concern only the theorist who was trying to explain and *notate* the improvised practices of his time.

Thus the explanation of modified parallel organum becomes further suspect, and we must seek its origin elsewhere. The most likely source that has been suggested is *heterophony,* a practice also known to the Greeks and common in both Oriental and primitive music. Heterophony, meaning "different sounds," results when two or more persons simultaneously perform differing versions of the same melody. Probably introduced accidentally, the different vertical sounds of heterophony must have proved attractive enough to be deliberately cultivated, and heterophonic performance became the basis of ensemble playing in much Oriental music. Because heterophony often involves partial duplication of the basic melody at intervals other than the unison or octave (Example VIII–4), the attempt to explain it as a modification of parallel organum need not surprise us. We may suspect, however, that the *Enchiriadis* treatises give oversimplified examples of a procedure that, in practice, resulted in a more elaborate variation of the original chant.

Example VIII–4: *Heterophony—Modern Chinese*[3]

Whatever the origins of organum may have been and however faithfully the *Enchiriadis* treatises may reflect the practices of their time, it is with them that the recorded history of Western polyphony begins. Quite obviously, the strictly parallel duplication of a melody offered little stimulus for further development. Its chief contribution would have been to familiarize the ear with the sound of perfect consonances as harmonic intervals. Modified parallel organum presents a different picture, for it introduces procedures that constitute the first step in the direction of true polyphony. Strict parallelism is varied by both oblique and contrary motion. Equally important is the appearance of intervals other than perfect consonances: seconds and thirds in simple organum, sixths and sevenths in composite forms. The concept that a given melody could be enhanced by being combined with a new and completely different melody had not yet been grasped. But the technical means by which that concept could be realized were already at hand in modified parallel organum.

3.   After E. Fischer, SIMG, 12 (1910–11), p. 192.

Guido d'Arezzo and Bishop Theobold with a monochord. From a twelfth-century manuscript.

THE *MICROLOGUS* OF GUIDO D'AREZZO

After the *Enchiriadis* treatises, more than a century elapsed before organum was again described, in the *Micrologus* (Little Discourse) of Guido d'Arezzo (d. 1050).[4] Although he acknowledged the continued existence of strict parallelism, Guido concerned himself primarily with modified parallel organum. In its formation, Guido rejected the fifth and minor second, thus limiting available intervals other than the unison to four: the perfect fourth, major and minor thirds, and the major second. Of these, the fourth occupies the highest rank, the minor third the lowest. Guido dealt particularly with the *occursus,* the coming together on a unison at the end of a phrase. He specified that a third progressing by contrary motion to a unison must be major, as must also be a second that proceeds to a unison by oblique motion. These concerns probably reflect the characteristic avoidance of semitone cadences in plainchant, but they also suggest that musicians were becoming aware of both the qualities of intervals and the effectiveness of oblique and contrary motion.

One innovation permitted by Guido was the crossing of the principal and organal voices (Example VIII–5c). That he also permitted more than one note in the principal voice against a single note in the organal voice is a common statement needing some qualification. Guido's musical examples, which are notated in letters, always seem to provide a strictly note–against–note setting. The organal voice sometimes reaches its final note first, however, and then repeats that note (or holds it?) until the

4.   Guidonis Aretini, *Micrologus,* ed. J. Smits van Waesberghe, CSM, 4 (AIM, 1955).

principal voice arrives at the final unison (see Example VIII–5a, b, and especially c).

Example VIII–5: *Examples of Organum from the* Micrologus *of Guido d'Arezzo*

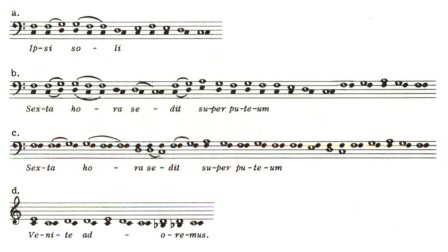

a. To himself alone.
b & c. At the sixth hour, he was seated on the well (see John 4:6). (A traditional melodic formula and text that identify the sixth mode)
d. Come, let us adore.

From Guido's description, it would seem that organum had developed very little in over a century. This impression is contradicted to some extent by his musical examples. In some, the scarcity of fourths suggests that the preeminence of that interval may have been less clear-cut than Guido would have us believe. Even more striking is the tendency to avoid parallel motion in favor of a sort of drone in the organal voice, a tendency that reaches its ultimate in Example VIII–5c. Taken as a whole, Guido's illustration allow us to infer a richly varied practice of modified parallel organum in the first half of the eleventh century.

FREE ORGANUM

During the second half of the century the rate of development accelerated, and by 1100 the restless search for new means of expression that was to characterize the subsequent history of Western music was in full swing. The great achievement of the century was the breaking away from the restrictions of parallel motion that Guido's *Micrologus* had already foreshadowed. The result was a new kind of polyphony that well deserves its common designation as *free organum*.

An example of two–part organum from the *Musica enchiriadis* in the Staatsbibliothek, Bamberg (see transcription, Example VIII–2b).

Two treatises that may be dated c. 1100 present a clear picture of the revolutionary developments that had taken place. The first to be considered, though not necessarily the earlier of the two, is by John Cotton, or John of Afflighem. He evidently did not think highly of organum, for he devoted only one chapter of his *De musica* to a "brief and succinct" account, with a single short example included "for benevolence's sake."[5] Brief as they are, however, John's description and example reveal the giant strides that had been taken toward melodic independence in the added organal voice.

Admitting that organum is practiced in many ways, John declares that the most easily comprehensible involves contrary motion between the voices. Depending on the range of the chant, moreover, the organal voice may end its phrases at the octave above or below, as well as at the unison. John recommends the alternation of these cadences, with preference being given to the unison, however. Even more than the concentration on contrary motion, these new cadence possibilities, with the freely crossing parts that they imply, open up new resources to the composer or improviser of organum. Within its brief span, John's example not only illustrates these new resources but also provides an enlarged vocabulary of available intervals (Example VIII–6). The fifth, excluded by Guido, has been reinstated; seconds and thirds are used as before; even a seventh has been introduced. Despite all these advances, the most important aspect of John's discussion of organum is the clear indication that an element of choice has entered into its creation. With the availability of various alternatives, composition has become a creative act, and polyphony a new form of musical art.

5.   Johannis Affligemensis [Cotton], *De Musica cum tonario,* ed. J. Smits van Waesberghe, CSM, 1 (AIM, 1950).

Example VIII–6: *Free Organum as Illustrated by John Cotton*

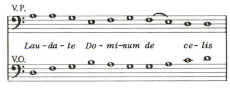

Praise the Lord of heaven.

The element of choice is even more explicit in the second treatise to be considered, the anonymous *Ad organum faciendum* (How to Construct Organum).[6] The newly acquired freedom with regard both to direction of movement and alternation of consonances permits the construction of different melodies above the same principal voice. These advances are self-evident in the musical illustrations within the treatise, two of which are given in Example VIII–7.[7]

Example VIII–7: *Two Settings of an Alleluia from* Ad organum faciendum

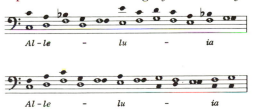

Both the anonymous *Ad organum faciendum* and the *De musica* of John Cotton make statements that seem to allow the introduction of two or three notes in the organal voice to one in the principal. This innovation is not documented in the musical examples, however, and consideration of its consequences must await its appearance in practical sources of organum. The first decipherable examples in these sources represent approximately the same stage of development as the free organum of the two treatises just discussed, but the departure from a strictly note-against-note style is not long in coming.

Later descriptions of organum tend to ignore the radical changes of style that appear in written collections during the twelfth century. Instead, the treatises seem to have been designed as handbooks for beginners in improvisation, and they undoubtedly give a most inadequate picture of an expert improviser's performance.[8] They do remind us,

6. *Ad Organum Faciendum & Item de Organo,* trans. and ed. Jay A. Huff, MTT, 8.
7. One of the longer pieces preceding the treatise is a setting of the famous Kyrie trope *Cunctipotens genitor* (HAM, No. 26a).
8. One treatise, *Ars organi* (Art of organum), is found in a thirteenth-century manuscript but appears to describe the early style of melismatic organum as practiced by the School of Notre Dame (see Chapter IX). This treatise, with extensive commentary, is available only in a German edition: F. Zaminer, *Der Vatikanische Organum-Traktat,* Münchner Veröffentlichungen zur Musikgeschichte, 2 (Tutzing, 1959).

however, that improvisation did not cease with the advent of composed organum. Indeed, the tradition of improvised polyphony persisted for centuries. Occasionally its influence may be seen in written music, but our meager knowledge of it continues to be derived chiefly from theoretical sources. In the Middle Ages, improvisation seems to have remained largely a matter of note-against-note polyphony with a considerable amount of parallel motion, but the extent to which virtuoso performers may have embellished this simple structure we cannot know. From now on, it is primarily in the preserved collections of composed music that we must follow the continuing development of medieval polyphony.

ORGANUM IN PRACTICAL SOURCES

Because there must always be some doubt as to the accuracy with which theorists describe contemporary practices, we welcome with relief the first appearance of organum in manuscripts intended for practical use. Despite the frequent inadequacy of the notation, we can now get a much clearer idea of how organum was performed, and we can follow the stylistic developments that rapidly outdistanced the oversimplified theoretical descriptions. In addition, we can now determine which chants were commonly sung in polyphony.

THE WINCHESTER TROPERS

The first practical collection of organum is found in the later of two English manuscripts known as the Winchester Tropers. The earlier of the two (dated c. 980) is already familiar as the source of the oldest version of the Easter *Quem quaeritis* play with music. The second Winchester troper is an eleventh-century revision of the first, but it also contains a supplement of more than 150 organa, i.e., chants with an added organal voice. That the organa and the Easter play both appear in collections devoted primarily to tropes and sequences is a clear indication of the unity of purpose behind these seemingly disparate forms. The Winchester Tropers also bear witness to the rapidity with which liturgical embellishments, including polyphony, spread throughout western Europe. It is believed that their contents, rather than being of English composition, came from the repertory of a French religious center, possibly in the Loire valley.

That the second Winchester Troper was a revision of the first probably accounts for the curious placement of the added organal voices in a section by themselves instead of with the chants for which they provide

Two-part organum from Winchester, early eleventh century. The page on the left contains the organal voices for the Alleluias.

a polyphonic embellishment.[9] Scholars have attempted to reconstruct some of these pieces, but the notation in neumes without staff lines and only partially heighted creates far greater difficulties than the physical separation of the voices. Only the chant melodies appear in later sources in more precise notation. Reliably accurate transcriptions of the organal voices remain unattainable. Nevertheless, certain aspects of the musical style can be determined. It is clear that the basic style of the organa is note-against-note polyphony. Parallel motion still predominates, but contrary motion is not confined to cadential passages presumably leading to a unison. The occasional appearance of contrary motion within phrases marks a tentative step toward greater melodic independence of the organal voice. More important than these stylistic characteristics are the size and nature of the Winchester repertory. About a third of the collection is devoted to settings of Alleluias, another third to Office responsories. The rest of the repertory includes a few Introit tropes, twelve Kyries and eight Glorias, some of which are troped, seven Sequences, and nineteen Tracts. The concentration on responsorial and other melismatic chants is particularly significant, because it foreshadows the chief concern of Parisian composers in the late twelfth and early thirteenth centuries.

No large body of organa from the eleventh century which dates after the Winchester Tropers is known to exist. Scattered examples, from a single piece to one or two pages, have turned up in some dozen manuscripts.[10] Even this slim repertory remains in part unknowable because of imprecise notation. Only a few pieces notated in letters and a few

9. See Grout, HWM, p. 62, for facsimiles of a troped Kyrie and its organal voice.
10. Listed in L. Spiess, "An Introduction to the Pre-St. Martial Practical Sources of Early Polyphony," *Speculum, 22* (1947), p. 16.

more with neumes on staff lines give some idea of the state of organum at the end of the eleventh century. Among the most important of these pieces is a group of five Alleluias, some of them fragmentary, from a manuscript at Chartres.[11] These Alleluias are of particular interest because they are set in the manner that became standard for responsorial chants in the twelfth century. Organum is used only for the solo sections of the chants. Choral sections, which are not written out in the Chartres manuscript, are sung in their original monophonic form.[12] This alternation of polyphony and plainchant in the Chartres Alleluias marks the establishment of a principle that the Church continued to apply in various ways for many centuries.

Another significant aspect of the Alleluias from Chartres is their increased use of contrary motion and of intervals that contemporary theorists regarded as dissonances. According to the calculations of Dom Anselm Hughes, a majority of intervals in the five Alleluias are perfect consonances, but more than a quarter of the total number of intervals are thirds. Moreover, these thirds appear several times in groups of two or three in parallel motion. Most surprising of all is the presence of 23 seconds, although it should be remembered that Guido d'Arezzo ranked the major second above the minor third.[13] Other surviving examples of contemporary organum are too few in number to permit us to say that the Chartres Alleluias are typical of the later eleventh century. John Cotton's brief example contains two thirds, one second, and one seventh in a total of only ten intervals; but, as we have seen, the examples in *Ad organum faciendum* rely almost exclusively on perfect consonances. Of the twenty-four intervals in the two settings of an Alleluia melody (Example VIII–7), only one is an imperfect consonance, a minor third. In contrast to these more conservative examples, the Alleluias from Chartres, and a few other pieces from the decades just before and after 1100, show that some composers were in advance of some theorists in using intervals other than perfect consonances.

MELISMATIC ORGANUM OF THE TWELFTH CENTURY: THE SCHOOL OF ST. MARTIAL AT LIMOGES

The development of polyphony in the twelfth century takes us back to Limoges and the region of south-central France that had already been active in the creation of tropes and sequences and that will, in the same

11. Transcriptions in NOHM, 2, pp. 282–84. The notation of another set of Alleluias from Chartres cannot be transcribed. For a facsimile of one of these pieces, see Parrish, NMM, Pl. XXc.

12. For a complete Alleluia from Chartres with both polyphonic and monophonic sections, see HAM, No. 26c.

13. Exact figures may be found in NOHM, 2, p. 284.

century, see the birth of lyric song in the vernacular (see Chapter XI). Although the organum of this period is commonly attributed to a "School of St. Martial" at Limoges, arguments for the existence of such a school rest primarily on the large collection of manuscripts from the Abbey of St. Martial now in the Bibliothèque Nationale in Paris. More than twenty musical manuscripts attest to the richness of the St. Martial library, but new evidence supports the contention that only three or four of the manuscripts originated at the Abbey. Some collections of monophonic tropes and sequences came from the Limoges area; others came from as far away as Narbonne and Toulouse. Three of the four manuscripts that contain polyphony belonged to the Abbey library, but we cannot be sure that they are the product of a School of St. Martial. The fourth collection of polyphony, now in the British Museum, never formed part of the St. Martial library and appears to come from a religious center near the eastern end of the Franco-Spanish border. Even the broader designation "School of Limoges" would thus seem to be a misnomer. Limoges may well have been an active center for the composition and performance of organum, and to avoid confusion we should probably continue to speak of St. Martial polyphony. We must remember, however, that the collections of that polyphony are not the product of a single monastery. Instead, they represent a tradition of polyphonic performance throughout southwestern France and the northern regions of Spain.

The sources of St. Martial polyphony contain some sixty-four different pieces that fall into three main groups. The largest consists of strophic poems that some of the sources identify as *versus*. This term is nearly synonymous with *conductus,* and the two terms are sometimes used interchangeably. The versus are Latin sacred songs that functioned primarily as unofficial additions to the liturgy on important feast days. Tropes of *Benedicamus Domino* constitute the next most frequent type of text in St. Martial polyphony. The third and smallest of the three main groups consists of sequences. The scarcity of established liturgical chants in this polyphonic repertory does not necessarily mean that such chants were always sung in their original monophonic form. Considerable evidence points to a continuing tradition of improvised polyphony in the style of free organum. Still operative in the sixteenth century, this tradition seems to have little to do with the stylistic development of organum in the twelfth-century repertories of Limoges and Paris.

THE TWO STYLES OF ST. MARTIAL POLYPHONY

Two contrasting styles of organum are clearly discernible in the polyphony of St. Martial. One, traditionally associated with the School, is known as *florid* or *melismatic organum.* The other, "a kind of developed discant," has only recently been recognized as an important style in St.

Martial polyphony.[14] In melismatic organum, note-against-note writing virtually disappears, and we find instead an organal voice with several or many notes against each note of the chant. The two voices are normally written in score in the manuscripts, but their correct alignment is often difficult to determine.[15] Indications of relative note values are totally lacking. Modern transcriptions of this music, therefore, present no more than personal interpretations that can never be regarded as definitive. There seem to be two possible solutions to the problem of rhythmic relationships between the two voices. Either the plainchant may move in even but extended notes with changing values for the note-groups of different lengths in the organal voice, or that voice may be sung evenly with the notes of the plainchant coming at irregular intervals. The first solution seems preferable when the chant is syllabic and the organal voice has relatively short melismas on each syllable. In the St. Martial repertory, settings of older tropes and sequences usually meet both of these conditions. The sequence *Laude jocunda* (With joyful praise) provides a characteristic example (see AMM, No. 29). Here, the syllabic lower voice, moving at an even pace, maintains its original character and provides the easiest means of keeping the voices together. When melismas of the organal voice are greatly extended, however, that voice must become the controlling factor. Perhaps the most extreme melismatic extension in the St. Martial repertory occurs in the prayer *Ora pro nobis* (Pray for us), the beginning of which is given in Example VIII–8. Here, quite obviously, the lower voice must sustain some notes much longer than others. Less obvious are the exact places where the lower voice should move from one note to the next. The transcription below follows the alignment of the manuscript source as closely as possible.

Example VIII–8: Ora pro nobis, *Beginning*[16]

14. L. Treitler, "The Polyphony of St. Martial," JAMS, 17 (1964), pp. 29–42.
15. Compare the facsimile and transcription of *Viderunt* in Apel, NPM, p. 211, and HAM, No. 27a. See also the facsimile of *Jubilemus* in Parrish, NMM, Pl. XXI.
16. British Museum, Add. 36881, fol. 22.

The different rhythmic solutions for *Laude jocunda* and *Ora pro nobis* seem plausible enough, but decisions are less easy to reach for pieces between these stylistic extremes. Whichever solution is adopted, it is evident that the notes of the original chant become more and more drawn out. As a result of this process, the plainchant, or principal voice, in melismatic organum came to be called the *tenor,* from the Latin *tenere,* "to hold." Thus, throughout the Middle Ages the term *tenor* does not designate a specific type of male voice but refers to one part, usually the lowest, of a polyphonic piece. The nature of these tenor parts suggests that *sustained-note style* would be a more accurate description of melismatic organum. The added voice is melismatic, certainly; but the tenors, as both *Laude jocunda* and *Ora pro nobis* show, may be entirely syllabic. Moreover, extended melismas may and often do occur in "developed discant," the other characteristic style of St. Martial polyphony.

DEVELOPED-DISCANT STYLE

By the twelfth century, the term *discant* was being used to distinguish syllabic text settings in note-against-note polyphony from the sustained-note style of melismatic organum. At the same time, however, a new development began to enrich this simple discant style by what has been called neume-against-neume writing. Both voices, that is, normally have a single note or a neume of several notes for each syllable of text, but they do not necessarily set the same number of notes against each other. Thus, in developed-discant style we may find two, three, or four notes against one, three against two, four against two or three. Departures from this neumatic setting of the text often occur at the ends of poetic lines, where the penultimate syllable may receive an extended melisma. Such passages differ from the melismas of sustained-note style, in that both voices continue in note-against-note polyphony. The most logical solution to the rhythmic problems of discant style, again left unanswered by the original notation, would seem to be an equal value for each syllable of text and for each neume in melismatic passages. This solution has been applied to the *Benedicamus* trope *Omnis curet homo* (Let every man take care) in AMM, No. 30.

The two examples of St. Martial polyphony in AMM require a few further remarks, both individual and general. *Laude jocunda* is so short, and its tenor displays so little variety, that it does not give the impression of being complete. It consists, in fact, of only the first three sections of a much longer sequence in honor of Saints Peter and Paul. The polyphonic version appears in the same form in two of the St. Martial manuscripts. Only the first half of each double versicle is written beneath the musical score. The second half, usually written in a narrow column, follows immediately after the section to which it belongs.

Above these added texts, one manuscript gives the original sequence melody—that is, the tenor of the preceding polyphonic section. In the other, space was apparently left for the melodies, but only the second half of the third versicle has the monophonic chant above it. This disposition in the manuscripts suggests that the polyphonic first half of each versicle was to be answered by the second half in plainchant. How, or even whether, the rest of the sequence was to be performed remains unknown. Quite possibly, the polyphonic version was meant to be a complete and independent piece. The text does not proceed far enough to define its liturgical function and could serve for any joyful occasion.

The *Benedicamus* trope *Omnis curet* presents a different kind of problem. Like many such tropes, its textual and musical forms follow the structural principle of the sequence. In this case, however, neither text nor music is entirely regular. Each half of the first versicle has a different melody and therefore a different polyphonic setting. The second versicle has not one, but two repeated sections to fit the fourfold subdivision of the text. The third and fourth versicles are normal. This still leaves unexplained the line "Est verbum caro factum" (The word was made flesh). Because it fits neither the rhythm nor the rhyme scheme of the text as a whole, literary scholars have regarded this line as a refrain to be repeated after each versicle. The form of *Omnis curet* would then be *ab R ccdd R ee R ff R*. This combination of sequence form with a refrain would not be unique (see Chapter XI, p. 265), but we should note that none of the five versions of *Omnis curet* gives any indication that its second section is to be sung more than once. Perhaps the attempt to regularize the form is a mistake and we should perform *Omnis curet* exactly as it appears in the manuscripts.[17]

Turning from formal to harmonic considerations, we find rather remarkable differences between the sustained-note and discant styles. In the former, elaboration of the upper voice is achieved by melodic ornamentation of notes that form consonances with the tenor. The process of ornamentation naturally introduces numerous dissonances that, in modern terminology, we would call passing or neighboring tones. More unexpected are the occasional appearances of appoggiaturas: seconds resolving to unisons, sevenths to octaves, and sixths to fifths. Because such dissonances do not accord with contemporary theory, attempts have been made to minimize their effect by rhythmic realignment or other editorial adjustments. This seems neither justifiable nor

17. *Omnis curet* appears in all four sources of St. Martial polyphony, twice as plainchant and three times in two-voice polyphony. In one polyphonic and both monophonic versions, all repeats are written out in full. As in *Laude jocunda,* the other polyphonic versions give only the first half of double versicles with a two-voice setting. In the London manuscript, the second versicle is garbled and incomplete (see Parrish, NMM, Pl. XXII).

necessary. In many cases, the dissonances, including appoggiaturas, are clearly present, and we must regard them as an essential element of the style. To that element, indeed, melismatic organum owes much of its historical importance and its musical charm.

The dissonance treatment characteristic of melismatic organum also appears occasionally in discant style. On the whole, however, pieces in this style adhere more closely to procedures outlined by the theorists of the time. Contrary motion predominates, as do consonant intervals, including the third. Counterbalancing this harmonic conservatism is an emphasis on melodic integration of the two voices, particularly in melismas at the ends of poetic lines. To achieve this, composers found various ways to organize and relate melodic motives in the two voices: by sequential repetition, by inversion, by imitation, and by other, more esoteric devices. Because these devices were to remain characteristic of polyphonic writing for many centuries, their appearance in music of the twelfth and early thirteenth centuries is of great significance.

VOICE EXCHANGE

One device, rare in the St. Martial repertory, soon became so characteristic of medieval polyphony that it must be described and illustrated here. Although frequently referred to by its German name *Stimmtausch,* the translation *voice exchange* seems more suitable for discussions in English. Although voice exchange is not present in *Omnis curet,* it does occur in the first section of another *Benedicamus* trope, *Noster cetus.* As we can see in Example VIII–9 below, each voice in measure 2 has the melodic line that the other had in measure 1. The second measure, therefore, merely repeats the first with the voice parts interchanged. Voice exchange also occurs on a smaller scale in the cadential melisma of the same example where two–note cells (x and y) are interchanged, revealing the close relationship between voice exchange and imitation. Taking x and y as a four–note motive (c), we find that the upper voice imitates the lower at a distance of one beat (or neume). Voice exchange, it is clear, is a rather simple process of repetition, in which melodic and harmonic structures remain unchanged. Only contrasting tone qualities in the two voices distinguish between repetitions with voice exchange and those without. Nevertheless, the device was of considerable importance. By itself, voice exchange gave composers one means of controlling the symmetry and design of their polyphony. In addition, it provided a starting point for the development of other, more complex, and more effective contrapuntal devices.

Example VIII–9: *First Section of* Noster cetus

Let our joyful assembly sing together with consonant sound.

HISTORICAL ROLE OF ST. MARTIAL POLYPHONY

The School of St. Martial has traditionally been regarded as the birthplace of melismatic organum, which was then taken over and brought to full flower at the School of Notre Dame in the second half of the twelfth century. This view needs some correction. In the first place, the manuscript sources do not confirm this chronology. Of the three St. Martial manuscripts that contain polyphony, the oldest dates from the very beginning of the twelfth century. The other two belong to the last half of the century, perhaps even to its last decades. The London manuscript, which does not come from Limoges but duplicates a number of the St. Martial pieces, dates from the beginning of the thirteenth century. It is clear, therefore, that the St. Martial repertory we now possess is representative of the entire twelfth century, and much of it must be contemporary with works of the Notre Dame School.

From the chronology of the manuscript sources we can also learn something of the stylistic development that took place in Limoges during the course of the twelfth century. The traditional view of St. Martial polyphony would lead us to expect a continuing development of melismatic style. What we find is quite the opposite. Melismatic organum predominates in the oldest manuscript, but later sources show a growing preference for the developed–discant style. To account for this shift of emphasis, we must examine the considerations that governed the choice of which style to use. Chants in syllabic style, including the older sequences and *Benedicamus* tropes, consistently received melismatic treatment as organa. If the monophonic chant alternated syllabic style with melismas, however, the latter were given a note-against-note or discant setting. Both styles might thus appear in the same piece, as they do in *Viderunt Hemanuel* (They have seen Emanuel), a trope of the Christmas Gradual.[18] Such an admixture of styles is perhaps not characteristic of the St. Martial repertory as a whole, and *Viderunt Hemanuel* probably represents a transitional stage leading to the later, more consistent application of discant style to poetic texts. As rhymed and rhythmic verse became the dominant form of religious poetry during the twelfth century, composers evidently felt that the structural regularity of the texts called for a musical regularity that only discant style could give. In their different ways, but working together to some extent, poetry and music developed the technical devices that reflect the spirit of their age, the spirit that also produced the regularity, symmetry, and balance of early Gothic cathedrals.

It is, then, the tradition of polyphonic performance for versus, tropes, and sequences that explains the later emphasis on discant style in St. Martial polyphony. The same tradition also distinguishes the School of St. Martial from the School of Notre Dame in Paris. In the latter, composers first concentrated on setting the prose texts of standard liturgical chants. As a result, they produced greatly expanded forms of melismatic organum before beginning to explore the possibilities for musical development inherent in discant style. By the thirteenth century, polyphonic composition no longer flourished in Limoges and southern France, probably for the same reasons that brought the activity of the troubadours to a close (see Chapter XI). The center of musical activity shifted to Paris, and the School of Notre Dame became the starting point for the development of new polyphonic forms in the later Middle Ages.

POLYPHONY AT SANTIAGO DE COMPOSTELA

Before we consider the contributions of the Notre Dame School, we must look at a collection of polyphony from Santiago de Compostela in the northwestern Spanish province of Galicia. Because the Cathedral of Santiago (St. James) sheltered the reputed relics of James the Apostle, Compostela rivaled Rome and Jerusalem as a place of pilgrimage throughout the Middle Ages. The Cathedral Library of Santiago still preserves a *Liber Sancti Jacobi* (Book of St. James) that has been described as propaganda to promote the pilgrimage. From the social historian's viewpoint, one of the most interesting sections of the manuscript is a guide for twelfth-century tourists, where we find descriptions of the main roads to Compostela, of important buildings and shrines to visit en route, and of the character—good or bad—of people living in the regions along the way. For us, the *Liber Sancti Jacobi* is interesting be-

18. HAM, No. 27a.

Detail from the Portico de la gloria (1166–88) of the Cathedral of Santiago de Compostela. Two elders are depicted playing the hurdy-gurdy.

cause of its preservation of the complete services, with their music, for the Vigil and Feast of St. James as they were performed in the middle of the twelfth century.[19] We have already mentioned these services in connection with the creation of new plainchant settings for Offices (see Chapter VII). Now we find that the same manuscript provides an important collection of twelfth-century polyphony.

Because the *Liber Sancti Jacobi* credits Pope Calixtine II (d. 1124) with the authorship of the Offices and Masses for the Feast of St. James, the manuscript is often called the Codex Calixtinus. Just how much Calixtine had to do with creating these services remains unknown, but it is highly unlikely that he compiled all of their texts and composed their plainchant settings. Perhaps the attribution is no more than a graceful compliment to the Pope, who recognized the importance of Compostela by raising it to the rank of an archiepiscopal see in 1120. Additional items, such as sequences and tropes, versus and conducti, and all the polyphonic pieces, are credited to a number of different authors— mostly bishops—from places as widely separated as Jerusalem, Rome, Paris, and Galicia. Unfortunately, scholars also believe these attributions are unreliable. It may be significant, nevertheless, that the men whose names are attached to polyphonic pieces came, almost without exception, from cities in central and northern France.

19. For modern editions of this manuscript and its music, see the Bibliography.

The entire repertory of the Codex Calixtinus possesses great historical as well as musical interest. The monophonic settings of liturgical items tell us much about the state of plainchant composition in the twelfth century. Tropes and sequences give a clear picture of the way the liturgy was expanded and embellished on great Feast Days. The Mass of the Day, for example, includes elaborate tropes of the Introit and the Epistle, as well as troped versions of all items of the Ordinary except the Credo. Processional versus, or conducti, add to our knowledge of the history of that genre. Here, however, our primary concern is with the polyphony that forms an appendix at the end of the manuscript. Scholars date the Codex Calixtinus about 1140, but the appendix may be a somewhat later addition. Nevertheless, its contents clearly represent the state of polyphonic composition around the middle of the twelfth century.

The polyphonic repertory of Santiago de Compostela consists of twenty-one pieces, twenty of which appear in the concluding appendix of the Codex Calixtinus. The twenty-first piece is a monophonic conductus in the main body of the manuscript to which a second voice has been added. One other monophonic conductus receives the same treatment, but that one also appears in the collection of polyphony. Of the total of twenty-one pieces, then, two are definitely identified as conducti, and three more may belong to this category, since they consist of strophic poems that do not seem to have a specific liturgical function. *Benedicamus* tropes (four) and untroped settings of *Benedicamus* melodies (three) constitute exactly one third of the repertory. In addition there are two settings of well-known Kyrie tropes.[20] More unexpected are polyphonic settings of the solo portions of six responsorial chants, including the Gradual and Alleluia from the Mass of the Day and four of the twelve Office responsories. To the last of these—the final responsory of Matins that was also sung at Second Vespers—is appended a "prose" that adds words and an organal voice to the final melisma of the respond.

The emphasis on responsorial chants in the polyphony of Compostela establishes a primary distinction between its repertory and that of St. Martial. Other differences between the two repertories are much slighter. Again we find the sustained-note and discant styles, now used with even greater consistency. The poetic texts of conducti and *Benedicamus* tropes are invariably set in discant style. Just as invariably, settings of untroped *Benedicamus* melodies and of responsorial chants are in sustained-note style. In the latter, it is important to note, the two styles rarely appear together. Even the long melismas of the plainchant are further extended by being set in sustained-note style. This is less evident in the Office responsories than in the Gradual and Alleluia of the Mass, where we find a sustained-note setting of a melisma with no

20. For the setting of *Cunctipotens genitor* in sustained-note style, see HAM, No. 27b.

fewer than thirty-seven notes. As we shall see, this stylistic consistency in the setting of responsorial chants distinguishes the repertory of Compostela from that of the School of Notre Dame, which we must probably regard as a later development. For the rest, however, the same principles govern the application of polyphony to responsorial chants in both repertories. We may see these principles at work in *Huic Jacobo* (To this James), one of the Office responsories of the Codex Calixtinus (AMM, No. 31). Of the opening respond, only the short solo intonation receives a polyphonic setting. The choir then sings the remainder in its original monophonic form. The solo verse again receives a polyphonic setting that also serves for the Doxology, and the choir answers each time with the closing section of the respond. This characteristic alternation of organum and plainchant reveals one of the most fundamental characteristics of medieval polyphony in general. Rather than being choral, it is essentially music for a small ensemble of soloists. From our greater exposure to music of later times, we normally expect choral performance of polyphony, and we think of solo song as being a single melody against a harmonic background. We must not forget that the situation is approximately reversed in the Middle Ages. Throughout the period, soloists retain almost exclusive rights to the performance of polyphony, their primary vehicle for the demonstration of improvisatory skill and vocal virtuosity.

The sustained-note style of *Huic Jacobo* and of the other polyphonic settings of responsorial chants in the Codex Calixtinus raises particularly difficult problems of vertical alignment. Perhaps the only procedure that we can follow consistently in performing this music is to have the two voices begin each new syllable together. But this does not help in places where the tenor has two or more notes for one syllable. Sometimes the alignment in the manuscript suggests possible solutions, but it too often fails to answer all the questions. What do we do, for example, in the frequent instances when a two-note ligature in the tenor appears against two or more ligatures in the organal voice?[21] Some believe that the tenor should move to its next note when it can form a consonance with the other voice. To accomplish this, the tenor notes sometimes sound with the first, sometimes with the last, and sometimes with a middle note of a ligature. The inconsistency of this procedure and the jerky movement of the tenor that is its result make it somewhat less than satisfactory. The music itself provides considerable evidence that contemporary performers and composers were not afraid of momentary dissonant clashes. Let us be as bold.

In the transcription of *Huic Jacobo,* then, the voices are aligned so that each tenor note coincides with the first note of a ligature in the organal voice, which should probably be performed in relatively even note val-

21. See the second measure of AMM, No. 31.

An example of two-part organum from the Codex Calixtinus, Santiago de Compostela. *Vox nostra resonet,* a trope of *Bendicamus Domino,* is attributed to a Magister Johannes Legalis, c. 1155.

ues. The style must remain free and rhapsodic, however, with no hint of rhythmic rigidity. For this reason, the transcription does not use modern note values, but the notation in score makes it easier for the singers to keep together. Additional help comes from the barlines that are present in the manuscript. As a rule, these lines mark the beginning of a word or syllable, but many of them also appear to indicate musical phrases that, with rare exceptions, begin and end on perfect consonances. Thus the phrases establish the essential harmonic relationships between the voices and give shape to a melismatic flow that might otherwise seem formless and undirected.

DISCANT STYLE IN THE COMPOSTELA REPERTORY

Discant style in the repertory of Compostela differs scarcely at all from that of the School of St. Martial. Indeed, there is one instance of a musical concordance between the two repertories.[22] The setting of *Noster cetus* (Example VIII–9) that appears in three St. Martial sources turns up at Compostela with a different *Benedicamus* trope, *Ad superni Regis decus* (In honor of the King on high).[23]

22. NOHM, 2, pp. 298–99. Discovery of this concordance disposes of Anselm Hughes's assertion that *Ad superni* represents the normal "Spanish" treatment of consonance and dissonance as opposed to "Anglo-French."

23. A complete transcription of *Noster cetus* is available in J. Marshall, "Hidden Polyphony in a Manuscript from St. Martial de Limoges," JAMS, 15 (1962), p. 142. For *Ad superni,* see Treitler, "The Polyphony of St. Martial," p. 36.

The discant style of Compostela, then, will not be new, but we may illustrate its application to a different type of text, the versus or conductus (AMM, No. 32). *Nostra phalans plaudat leta* (Let our company praise joyfully) is the first polyphonic piece in the Codex Calixtinus.[24] The text does not appear to have a specific liturgical function, although the word "Domino" in the final stanza, with a resulting irregularity in the rhyme scheme, suggests that the poem could be another trope of *Benedicamus Domino*. In any case, the text is clearly related to celebrations at Santiago de Compostela. Each of the poem's four stanzas consists of four lines plus a one-line refrain which rhymes with the preceding line except in the final stanza. In every other respect, the four stanzas of *Nostra phalans* are identical in structure and are sung to the same music. This use of strophic form is common but not invariable in settings of conducti and often makes them musically indistinguishable from hymns. They resemble hymns too in the variety of their internal structure. *Nostra phalans,* for example, appears at first glance to be a continuous form with no pattern of phrase repetitions. More careful examination reveals that the third phrase, after a different beginning on the first two syllables, continues as a variation of the first. Thus, *Nostra phalans* falls into the pattern *aba'c D,* in which the capital letter indicates the refrain. We should note, finally, that the piece has no extended and systematically organized melismas such as are found in other examples of discant style. In later conducti, the presence or absence of such melismas creates two distinct types of musical settings.

We cannot leave the Codex Calixtinus without brief mention of its most famous composition, the first example of three-voice polyphony. *Congaudeant Catholici* (Let Catholics rejoice together) follows *Nostra phalans* on the first page of the polyphonic collection.[25] One voice appears alone on the upper staff, but the lower staff contains two voices, one written in red, the other in black ink. This difference is not evident in most photographic reproductions, and when it has been recognized it has been assumed that one voice was added later. However, the use of different colored inks to distinguish two voices on the same staff appears to have been an accepted, if not very common, device for saving space. There is really no reason to doubt, therefore, that *Congaudeant Catholici* was originally created as a three-voice composition. To judge by the musical style, moreover, one would suspect that the upper voice was created last. The two lower voices move in note-against-note counterpoint that might have served to illustrate theoretical descriptions of free organum. The third voice, more elaborate and flowing, has from one to five notes for each syllable of text or each neume of the final melisma in discant style.

24. Facsimile in Parrish, NMM, Pl. XXIII.
25. Same Plate (XXIII) in Parrish, NMM, with various rhythmic interpretations on pp. 69–71. Numerous transcriptions are available; see Reese, MMA, p. 268 and NOHM, 2, p. 305.

King David, the creator of psalms, is depicted playing a three-string vihuela de arco (rebec). The Cathedral of Santiago de Compostela.

Congaudeant Catholici is sometimes called a "pilgrim's song," with the suggestion either stated or implied that it might have been sung on the way to and from Compostela as well as in the cathedral. For a number of reasons we should not take the suggestion too seriously. The complete text of *Congaudeant* shows that it is a *Benedicamus* trope cast in strophic form with a refrain. Each of its seven stanzas, all sung to the same music, consists of two lines plus the words "die ista" (this day). This simplicity of form is perhaps the only element of the song that would make it suitable for untutored singers. It is unlikely, however, that they would perform three-voice polyphony in an age when even two-voice settings of secular or "popular" songs were unknown. They could have sung the tenor alone, of course, if it ever existed as an independent setting of the text. We cannot know whether returning pilgrims hummed or sang melodies they had heard in Compostela, but there is no evidence that any of the pieces in the Codex Calixtinus originated as pilgrim songs or were intended for performance by the general populace. Indeed, *Congaudeant Catholici* calls for rejoicing by Catholics and citizens of heaven, but directs the clergy to devote itself to beautiful songs and chants this day.[26] It is to the Codex Calixtinus that we owe our knowledge of the songs and chants the clergy sang on the Feast of St. James at Santiago de Compostela.

26. The second "stanza" reads: "Clerus pulcris carminibus / studeat atque cantibus / *die ista.*"

The origin of the Compostela repertory remains unknown, but it is probably wrong to regard it as music by Spanish composers. A remark on the page before the collection of polyphonic pieces (fol. 184v) states that the manuscript was written in a number of different places, but principally at the great Benedictine Abbey of Cluny. The other places listed correspond with the names and titles of the authors to whom the musical items are attributed. Although these attributions are thought to be apocryphal, they suggest that the musical repertory was not the unified product of composers working together in Compostela or any other single locality. Supporting evidence for this view comes from the presence of the one item from St. Martial and the settings of responsorial chants, a class of polyphony that is notably absent from the St. Martial repertory. There might even be some significance in the attribution of *Congaudeant Catholici* to a Magister Albertus of Paris, the city that was soon to take the lead in the further development of polyphony. The Codex Calixtinus as a whole appears to be of French origin, and the musical notation is of the type found in contemporary plainchant manuscripts from the region of central France. Perhaps the Benedictines of Cluny, who greatly influenced the religious establishments of northern Spain in the twelfth century, did prepare the Codex Calixtinus for the Cathedral of Santiago and did assemble the collection of polyphony from a variety of sources. That collection, at any rate, must preserve much more than an isolated and purely local tradition of polyphonic performance. Instead, the Codex Calixtinus provides us with a priceless record of the general state of religious music, both polyphonic and monophonic, about the middle of the twelfth century.

CHAPTER IX

The School of Notre Dame, I: Organum

During the twelfth century, northern France, with Paris as its natural center, gradually assumed the cultural and intellectual leadership of western Europe. Many factors contributed to this development, but among the most important were the growth and prosperity of the cities, the increasing power and prestige of the French kings, and the expansion of the cathedral schools that led to the formation of the University of Paris in the early years of the thirteenth century. The economic recovery of Europe in the eleventh century brought with it a great increase in population and provided a new basis for the organization of society. Hitherto rural and feudal, that society became increasingly urban and commercial. The renewed vigor of the cities and the wealth of their middle-class citizens, the bourgeoisie, made possible the architectural monuments of the twelfth and thirteenth centuries that are still the glory of Europe. The same factors, in combination with the increased population, swelled attendance at the schools and universities, whose intellectual achievements were perhaps even more important than cathedrals in determining the course of Western civilization. By the end of the twelfth century, the schools at Bologna and Paris had won the renown that was to make them the "mother universities of Europe." Bologna emphasized the study of jurisprudence, while Paris concentrated on theology and the liberal arts. It is no surprise, therefore, to find that the authors of many thirteenth-century musical treatises were associated with the University of Paris. The medieval habit of preserving anonymity in musical sources keeps us from knowing whether the Parisian theorists were also composers. Paris so dominated the field of polyphonic composition, however, that a tendency exists to regard as "peripheral" all music of the late twelfth and thirteenth centuries that originated elsewhere in Europe. Yet peripheral styles and conservative practices in both the improvisation and composition of organum probably give a more accurate picture of the general state of contemporary polyphony. Paris and the School of Notre Dame stood far out in front in the development of new musical forms and styles, and—as is often the case with avant-garde composers—their music opened up new paths for succeed-

The Cathedral of Notre Dame, consecrated in 1182, rises in the background of this fifteenth-century miniature by Jean Fouquet (Robert Lehman Collection, Metropolitan Museum of Art).

ing generations to follow. It fully deserves, therefore, the emphasis it usually receives in studies of medieval music.

In 1160, the energetic Maurice de Sully became Bishop of Paris and immediately set about replacing the old Romanesque cathedral of Notre Dame. The cornerstone of the present cathedral was laid in 1163, and work progressed rapidly during Maurice's thirty-six years as bishop. Construction of the apse and choir in less than twenty years made it possible to dedicate the main altar on the Feast of Pentecost, May 19, 1182. The old basilica could then be demolished to make way for the transept and nave, which were completed around 1200. Major construction ended some fifty years later with completion of the facade. During the first forty years of work on the cathedral, two generations of Parisian composers were producing a large body of sacred polyphony that we now credit to the School of Notre Dame. The master builders of the magnificent edifice—perhaps the best-known of all Gothic cathedrals—remain unknown. It is one of the ironies of fate, therefore, that we know the names of two composers, Leonin and Perotin, who made major contributions to the predominantly anonymous musical repertory of Notre Dame.

Information about the lives of Leonin and Perotin is almost nonexistent. Leonin's name has not been found in any records of the cathedral or of any other religious establishment in Paris. On the other hand, if one assumes that Perotin is a diminutive of Peter (Petrus), there are so many candidates for his role that it is impossible to determine which, if any, was the composer. What we know about the musical activities of both composers comes from an anonymous treatise written in the latter half of the thirteenth century, long after Leonin and Perotin were dead. This treatise, commonly known as Anonymous IV from its numbering in the edition of Edmond de Coussemaker, appears to consist of information gathered by an English student at the University of Paris.[1] Thanks to the student's unusual interest in historical developments, we learn that Magister Leoninus was known as the greatest composer of organum (*optimus organista*). He it was who wrote a *Great Book of Organum* (*Magnus liber organi*) from the *Gradual* and *Antiphonary* for augmenting the divine service. This book was in use until the time of Perotin the Great (*Perotinus magnus*), the best composer of discant (*optimus discantor*), who shortened the organa and composed new and better substitute sections called *clausulae* (or *points*). Perotin also wrote organa for three and four voices, as well as monophonic and polyphonic conducti. Anonymous IV names examples of each type and concludes with the statement that, at the time of writing, the book or books of Magister Perotinus were still in use in the great Parisian church of the Blessed Virgin. This is the only recorded suggestion—and it is slight indeed—that Leonin and Perotin were associated with the Cathedral of Notre Dame.

As students' notes are not usually remarkable for their accuracy, the statements of Anonymous IV—though interesting—would be of little value unless confirmed by other sources. Such sources do exist in several manuscripts that preserve the repertory of the School of Notre Dame. Two of the three main sources of Notre Dame polyphony are now in the Ducal Library of Wolfenbüttel in northern Germany. One of these manuscripts, Wolfenbüttel 677 (*W*₁), belonged to St. Andrews Priory in Scotland in the early years of the fourteenth century. The other, Wolfenbüttel 1099 (*W*₂), appears to have come from France. The third and largest of the Notre Dame sources is Pluteus 29.1 at the Biblioteca Medicea-Laurenziana in Florence (*F*). This lavishly illuminated manuscript was probably copied in France in the thirteenth century for

---

1.   Coussemaker, CS, 1, pp. 327–65. An English translation of Anonymous IV has been published by L. Dittmer, MTT, 1.

A noted teacher lecturing to a group of students in a medieval university.

the library of some wealthy patron. By the middle of the fifteenth century it belonged to Piero de' Medici, father of Lorenzo the Magnificent. A fourth and smaller manuscript, Madrid Bibl. Nac. 20486 (*Ma*), probably came from Toledo; and several fragments containing Notre Dame polyphony are preserved in various other European libraries.[2]

None of the Notre Dame manuscripts identifies the *Magnus liber organi* or names any composers. Nevertheless, the correspondence between their contents and the statements of Anonymous IV is extraordinary. The core of the repertory consists of two-voice settings of responsorial chants for the great feast days of the Church year. All manuscripts arrange these settings in two groups, each of which follows the order of the Church calendar beginning with Christmas Day. The first group consists of Great Responsories for the Offices. In its earliest form, the *Magnus liber* probably contained only Vesper responsories, the most elaborate chants of this Office in the Middle Ages. Later practice extended the application of polyphony to the final responsory for each Nocturn in Matins. The second group of two-voice settings includes the responsorial chants of the Mass, both Graduals and Alleluias. Other sections of the Notre Dame manuscripts preserve the substitute clausulae to which Anonymous IV referred, and the collections of conducti and of three- and four-voice organa include the pieces he attributed to

2. Facsimile editions of the major Notre Dame sources are listed in the Bibliography.

Perotin. Musical sources thus vindicate the reputation of Anonymous IV as a historian. They make it possible to reconstruct Leonin's *Great Book of Organum* from the *Gradual* and *Antiphonary,* to follow Perotin's process of revision and improvement, and to study the first polyphonic pieces that can be attributed with certainty to an individual composer.

Before examining the music of the Notre Dame School, let us consider some aspects of its historical development. Writing in the latter half of the thirteenth century, Anonymous IV implies that Leonin composed the *Magnus liber* some three or four generations earlier. This is not much help in dating the activities of the Notre Dame composers. More precise suggestions come from two decrees of Odo de Sully, who succeeded Maurice de Sully as Bishop of Paris. In 1198, Odo forbade the traditional New Year's celebration known as the Feast of Fools and laid down rules for solemn ceremonies to replace the many irregularities and shameful acts that had sullied the holy places. The bishop's rules specified that the responsory and *Benedicamus Domino* of Vespers, the third and sixth responsories of Matins, and the Gradual and Alleluia of the Mass might be sung in simple (two-voice), triple, or quadruple organum. A year later, the second decree permitted the same kinds of organal performance for the Feast of St. Stephen (December 26). From these decrees we may draw two obvious conclusions: Odo would not have mentioned three- and four-voice organum if compositions of this type did not exist; permission to perform organum on New Year's Day and for the Feast of St. Stephen implies that the practice was already established on other, more important feasts such as the Nativity. Other conclusions drawn from Odo's decrees are more problematical. Scholars generally agree that Leonin must have composed the *Magnus liber organi* between the years 1160 and 1180. Shortly thereafter, presumably, Perotin began his revisions of Leonin's work. Odo's decrees then establish the approximate time when Perotin wrote the four-voice settings of the Graduals for Christmas and St. Stephen that Anonymous IV attributes to him. How much longer Perotin's activities continued is subject to dispute. The text of his monophonic conductus *Beata viscera* (Blessed offspring) was by Philip the Chancellor, one of the last great writers of Latin lyric poetry, who died in 1236. The collaboration of poet and composer suggests that Perotin himself must have lived until some time after 1220. Whatever the truth may be, it is reasonably certain that the years between 1160 and 1225 saw the composition of nearly all the Notre Dame repertory of organa and conducti.

We cannot assume, of course, that Leonin and Perotin wrote all of the Notre Dame polyphony, or that the entire repertory came from Notre Dame composers. The composition of two-voice organum did not end with the introduction of organum for three and four voices, and completion of the *Magnus liber organi* may have taken fifty or sixty years. Research has shown that the oldest items followed the liturgical prac-

tices of the Paris cathedral and used its version of the chant melodies.[3]
Many of the later additions also came from Notre Dame, but some came
from other religious establishments, both within and outside of Paris.
Just as architectural features of Notre Dame reappear in cathedrals from
Cyprus to Sweden, so its music turns up in churches from Toledo in
Spain to St. Andrews in Scotland. As far as we can tell, however,
foreign centers took over the Parisian repertory with relatively few
changes or local additions. Notre Dame thus remained the fountainhead
of the new polyphony, and we may justifiably credit the entire repertory to Leonin, Perotin, and their anonymous disciples.

THE MUSIC OF THE *MAGNUS LIBER ORGANI*

In the form that we now possess, the *Magnus liber organi* consists of
about thirty-five responsories and a dozen settings of *Benedicamus Domino* for the Offices, twenty Graduals and forty Alleluias for the Mass.
In addition, two of the Notre Dame manuscripts preserve a total of
nearly 500 substitute clausulae. As in the Compostela repertory, these
settings are applied only to the solo sections of responsorial chants. All
three classes of chants—responsories, Graduals, and Alleluias—begin
with a polyphonic setting of the short solo introduction, after which the
choir completes the opening respond in plainchant. The verses of these
chants, on the other hand, are not all treated the same way. In the Office
responsories, the entire verse receives a polyphonic setting that is also
used for the doxology; the choir answers both verse and doxology with
the closing section of the respond in plainchant. In Graduals and Alleluias, however, the polyphonic settings of the verse are not complete,
and the choir sings the final phrase in plainchant. We should not be
misled by the fact that the Notre Dame manuscripts—and some modern
transcriptions—include only the polyphonic sections of responsorial
chants. The manuscripts were for the soloists' use; the choir would naturally sing from its regular chantbook. In liturgical performance, alternation of solo polyphony with choral plainchant is the result.

A second characteristic alternation of musical styles occurs within the
solo polyphony itself. In discussing the music of St. Martial we noted
that composers on occasion treated the plainchant tenor in two different
ways. Where the chant was syllabic, or nearly so, they used sustained-
note or organal style. Plainchant melismas were set in note-against-note
or discant style. The lengthy melismas characteristic of responsorial
chants led Notre Dame composers to distinguish even more clearly between these two styles. In sustained-note sections, single notes of the
chant are extended, sometimes to incredible lengths, beneath the elabo-

---

3.   H. Husmann, "The Origin and Destination of the *Magnus liber organi*," MQ, 49
      (1963), p. 311. See also Husmann's article "The Enlargement of the *Magnus liber
      organi* . . . ," JAMS, 16 (1963), p. 176.

rate melismatic flow of the upper voice. This flow continues in the discant sections, but now the tenor moves at a regular and much faster pace. As a rule, the two voices still do not move in strictly note-against-note counterpoint, and several notes may appear in the upper voice against one in the tenor. Nevertheless, both voices are sufficiently active to give the impression of being two simultaneous melodies rather than a single melody above a drone. The sections in discant style are the clausulae of which composers wrote so many different settings. Before we go further in examining the development of organal and discant styles, however, we must consider a third characteristic, and most important innovation, of Notre Dame polyphony: its use of rhythm and meter.

MODAL NOTATION AND THE RHYTHMIC MODES

As polyphony became more and more complex, composers had to find some means of indicating how the voices fit together. Difficulties had already arisen in the music of St. Martial and Compostela, where writing in score no longer provided a completely satisfactory solution. What was needed was a system of notation that would show the relative values of notes, both within a single melodic line and in the different voices of a polyphonic composition. The development of such a system, imperfect as it may have been, was one of the most significant achievements of the School of Notre Dame.

In essence, the Notre Dame School's unique contribution consisted of replacing the even, unmeasured flow of earlier polyphony (and plainchant) with recurrent patterns of long and short notes. The different patterns of these notes are known as *rhythmic modes,* and they are identified by what we now call *modal notation.*

The introduction of rhythm and meter may be credited to Leonin, but the complete system of rhythmic modes and modal notation took longer to develop. Theoretical descriptions of the system do not appear until the thirteenth century, when the composition of organum had all but ceased. Indeed, the organization of the rhythmic modes into a "system" may be the work of theorists rather than of composers. Certainly the treatises describe details and set up situations that far exceed what occurs in the music itself. We may therefore ignore theoretical complexities and concentrate on the basic forms of the rhythmic modes and how they were indicated by the notation.

THE SIX RHYTHMIC MODES

Most theorists list six rhythmic modes or patterns that correspond to the feet of quantitative meters in classical poetry. The names and structure of these meters are given in Table 8, but the rhythmic modes are usually identified by number alone. It is thought that their development was inspired by the description of quantitative meters in the treatise *De musica* by St. Augustine (354–430).[4] In that description, Augustine used only two units of measurement, a long (*longa*) and a breve (*brevis*), and he made it clear that a long equals two breves. Using these units, which may be indicated as ♩ and ♪ , we can formulate the first, second, and sixth rhythmic modes with no difficulty. The other three modes, however, introduce a longer value (♩.) not found in Augustine's units of measurement. To understand the reasons for the introduction of this longer note, we must look briefly at the chronological development of the rhythmic modes.

Table 8: *The Six Rhythmic Modes*

Mode	Meter	Musical equivalent
1	Trochaic: long short	♩ ♪
2	Iambic: short long	♪♩
3	Dactylic: long short short	♩. ♪♩
4	Anapaestic: short short long	♪♩ ♩.
5	Spondaic: long long	♩. ♩.
6	Tribrachic: short short short	♪♪♪

The first rhythmic mode seems to have been the first to come into general use. It is overwhelmingly preponderant in the oldest items of the *Magnus liber,* and it retained its dominance even after the other modes were introduced. Once the idea of the first mode had become established, reversal of its values to produce the iambic meter of the second mode would be a natural development. The sixth mode apparently originated as an ornamented version of the first or second mode before it was classified as a mode in its own right. To describe the values of longs and breves in these three modes theorists used the term "correct" (*recta*). The longer longs of the other three modes they described as "beyond the measure" (*ultra mensuram*). The origin of these longer notes is probably to be found in older discant clausulae, where the tenor has a series of even notes, one for each foot of the first rhythmic mode. Characteristic examples may be seen in *Alleluia: Nativitas* on the words "glorio(se)" and "virginis" (AMM, No. 33). In later developments, these series of undifferentiated notes evolve into recurring patterns of the fifth rhythmic mode. A similar process of combining different modes in different voices undoubtedly produced the seemingly illogical changes of note values in the third and fourth modes. According to the theorists, these modes still consist of long-short-short or short-short-

4.   For arguments in support of this belief, see W. Waite, *The Rhythm of Twelfth-Century Polyphony,* p. 29 ff.

long values, but these values must be modified in two different ways. The longs become *ultra mensuram,* and the second breve in each mode is doubled in value to make it "the other" or altered breve (*brevis altera*). As a result of these changes, a foot of the third and fourth modes—and also of the fifth—equals two feet of the first, second, and sixth modes. Units of three thus became the basis of all modal rhythms, and only the conflicting patterns of those rhythms restricted the simultaneous use of different modes. Any combination of the last five modes was possible, but the first mode was normally used only with the fifth and sixth.

The units or feet of the rhythmic modes are, of course, only building blocks for the construction of larger musical units. Just as a succession of feet creates a line of poetry, so the repeated patterns of a rhythmic mode create a musical phrase. The medieval name for such phrases was *ordines* (sing. *ordo*), a term that indicates a series in a definite and controlled order. We may define an *ordo,* then, as one or more statements of a modal pattern ending with a rest. The theorists developed an elaborate classification of ordines according to the number of complete patterns they contained and the position of the concluding rest. The second ordo of any mode, for example, would contain two complete statements of its rhythmic pattern. The ordo would be "perfect" if it concluded with a third, incomplete statement in which a rest replaced the second part of the pattern (♩ ♪♩ ♪♩ ⁊). An "imperfect" ordo would end with the last note of a complete pattern, followed by a rest equal to the first part of another statement (♩ ♪♩ ♪♩⁊). Imperfect ordines appear to be largely a theoretical concept. In practice, most ordines are perfect, ending on the first note of their modal pattern, which is completed by a rest (see Table 9, p. 224).

THE NOTATION OF RHYTHMIC MODES

Because ordines consisted of successive repetitions of a modal pattern, it was possible to identify the mode of each ordo by a particular arrangement of successive neumes. This system was much more natural and logical than knowledge of modern notation would make it seem. Composers of organum necessarily began with the only notation they knew, that of plainchant. In melismatic passages, plainchant notation, both for the sake of appearance and to save space, "bound" notes together in neumes or ligatures. Moreover, single notes in plainchant had no mensural significance. Whenever a distinction was made in their use, the virga (⁊) and punctum (•) still indicated higher and lower rather than longer and shorter notes. Musicians of the twelfth century, therefore, would never have considered writing the long melismas of organum in single notes. Instead, they naturally adopted the standard forms of ligatures that they knew and used in the notation of plainchant.

These ligatures too had no mensural significance in themselves, but they provided an ingenious yet simple solution to the problem of notating the rhythmic modes. Because the notes of a melisma may be grouped in distinctive patterns of ligatures, those patterns could be used to identify the different rhythmic modes. If a composer wanted to indicate performance in the first mode, for example, he would write a three-note ligature followed by a series of two-note ligatures. Similarly, a series of two-note ligatures ending with a three-note ligature indicated performance in the second mode. Vertical lines of indeterminate length marked the ends of ordines and called for the appropriate rests. The characteristic patterns of ligatures that identify the rhythmic modes are shown in Table 9, together with their equivalents in modern note values.

Table 9: *Ligature Patterns of the Rhythmic Modes*

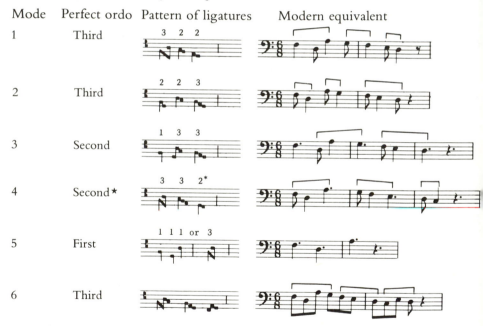

Mode	Perfect ordo	Pattern of ligatures	Modern equivalent
1	Third	3 2 2	
2	Third	2 2 3	
3	Second	1 3 3	
4	Second*	3 3 2*	
5	First	1 1 1 or 3	
6	Third		

*By analogy with the third mode, some writers end the fourth with a single note. Apel, NPM, pp. 222 and 225, gives both versions. As the fourth mode was rarely used, the matter is of little importance.

Examination of Table 9 will show that the form of a ligature has nothing to do with the note values it represents. Two-note ligatures, it is true, were normally sung as breve-long, but three-note ligatures had at least five different meanings. Theorists of the thirteenth century recommended modifying the forms of ligatures to indicate different values, but this is really a development of mensural notation. The manuscript sources of modal notation rely almost exclusively on the normal ligature forms of plainchant, and the meaning of those forms depends on the modal pattern in which they occur. This determination of note values on the basis of the position rather than the form of ligatures is one of the primary distinctions between modal and mensural notation.

The basic patterns of modal notation are clear enough, but the system suffered from disadvantages more serious than the varied meanings of ligatures. Even with strict adherence to the rhythm of a mode, repeated notes in a melody may disrupt the normal notation because they cannot be written in ligatures. When they cause a temporary break in the pattern of ligatures, the reason is usually obvious; but a sufficient number of repeated notes can make it impossible to tell which mode should be used. More difficult problems arise when changes occur in the rhythmic patterns of the modes themselves. Fortunately for the musical interest and artistic value of Notre Dame polyphony, its composers were not long content with unvaried repetitions of a basic modal pattern. They could and did achieve variety by changes of mode from one section of a composition to another, but they also avoided monotony by modifying the successive patterns of a single rhythmic mode. A process known in the thirteenth century as *fractio modi* (breaking of the mode) subdivided the notes of a modal pattern into smaller values—longs into breves and breves into semibreves. The reverse process, now called by analogy *extensio modi* (extension of the mode), combined notes of a modal pattern into a larger value. The long and breve of the first mode, for example, might become a single long equal to three breves. Some methods of notating these modifications did little violence to the normal ligature patterns. Others made those patterns almost unrecognizable. Because fractio and extensio modi play an important role in giving organum its characteristic melodic style, we must look more closely at some of the devices composers used to vary the patterns of the rhythmic modes.

THE PLICA

The *plica* (fold) is a notational sign that evolved from the liquescent neumes of plainchant and continued to be used well into the fourteenth century. The sign itself is no more than an upward or downward stem added to single notes or to the final note of a ligature. It indicates the addition of an ornamental note above or below the note to which the plica is attached.[5] Both the pitch and the rhythmic value of the added note must be determined by the context. As far as pitch is concerned, the added notes usually function as upper or lower neighbors, or as passing

5.   Downward plicas on a single note require a stem on each side of the note.

tones that fill in the interval of a third. When the two written notes lie more than a third apart, however, the pitch of the added note becomes uncertain. Decisions as to rhythmic values are somewhat less problematical. The added note always takes its value from the note to which the plica is attached. If that note has a triple value, it gives up a third to the added note. If the note is duple, it gives up half its value. In this way the plica provided a convenient means of producing fractio modi in Notre Dame polyphony. Occasional use of the plica merely introduces welcome variety without destroying the essential character of a rhythmic mode. Consistent and continued use, however, can change one mode into another. It is just in this way, indeed, that the sixth mode apparently developed from the first. As may be seen in Example IX–1, plicas on the ligatures of a first-mode pattern produce the sixth mode on all but the first foot of the ordo. Because plicas cannot be attached to the first or middle notes of ligatures, a four-note ligature was needed to indicate subdivision of the first long. The later use of three-note ligatures to continue the ordines of the sixth mode apparently resulted from a desire for more definite pitch indications than plicas could provide.

Example IX–1: *Fractio Modi Produced by Plicas*

or e?

Medieval treatises tell us that the ornamental note indicated by a plica received special vocal treatment, but their descriptions of that treatment are not particularly enlightening. Although we can only guess at the original method of performance, we know that the added note was not optional and that it had a definite rhythmic value. Modern transcriptions must therefore give both the written and unwritten notes. The latter is usually identified by means of some special sign such as the one used here: a diagonal line through the stem of the added note. In performance, treatment as ordinary notes will probably produce the most satisfactory results.

SINGLE NOTES

Single notes call for comment because they can have so many different values. Scribes apparently made no distinction in their use of the shapes ¶ and •, although the note with a stem—usually very short—is by far the more common of the two. In the tenors of discant clausulae, single notes normally indicate longs of triple value (♩.), either in a continuous series or in a repeated pattern of the fifth mode. Occasionally, however, single notes may be duplex longs with twice the normal value ($\d.$). Duplex longs are sometimes written as slightly larger notes, but in many cases they can be recognized only by the way the voices fit together. Single notes in the upper voice or voices of organum result from repeated notes in the melody or from extensions of the mode. Thus they may represent the value of a breve ($\eighthnote$), a longa recta ($\quarternote$), or a longa ultra mensuram ($\quarternote.$). The reason for their appearance is usually clear and their value easy to determine, as long as repeated notes and extensio modi do not occur simultaneously. When they do, decisions as to the values of the single notes become more difficult. In discant clausulae, again, the way the voices fit together will ordinarily solve the problem. No such help is available in passages above a sustained-note tenor, and the intended rhythm may remain forever in doubt.

THE CONJUNCTURA OR CURRENTES

A special form of ligature, the *conjunctura* or *currentes* (running notes), consists of a descending series of diamond-shaped notes attached to a single note or to the final note of a ligature. The form occurs in plainchant notation for ligatures of three or four notes, but Notre Dame composers also used it for descending scale passages up to an octave or even a ninth in range. Such passages, indeed, appear so frequently that they become a distinctive feature of Notre Dame style. Conjuncturae of more than four notes obviously have no place in the ligature patterns of modal notation. Their primary effect on the rhythm, as the alternate designation currentes suggests, is to break up the modal pattern into a series of rapid or running notes that not only divide longs into breves but also breves into semibreves (Example IX–2). The later use of diamond-shaped notes to indicate semibreves may thus have been suggested by conjuncturae, although they themselves do not always give the notes this meaning. Contrary to appearances, in fact, the final note of a conjunctura is normally a long, the penultimate a breve, and faster notes, if any, come at the beginning of the descent. Despite the general applicability of these rules, the correct rhythmic interpretation of conjuncturae often remains uncertain. They occur most commonly in sections of sustained-note style, where the tenor is of no help in determining their length. Moreover, we cannot always tell whether a conjunctura begins on the first note or in the middle of a modal pattern. Modern transcriptions of conjuncturae, therefore, need not be accepted without question. It seems probable that these ligatures represented vocal flourishes that were, and should now be, performed with considerable freedom and flexibility.

Example IX–2: *Some Conjuncturae and Possible Transcriptions*

As if the difficulties introduced by plicas, single notes, and conjuncturae were not enough, the presence of either fractio or extensio modi often results in irregular groupings of ligatures that admit of several interpretations. It is no wonder, therefore, that different transcriptions of the same organum rarely agree in all rhythmic details and may even use different rhythmic modes in some ordines. And it is not only the modern transcriber who finds modal notation confusing and uncertain. Some theorists who described the system complained that its indefiniteness led different singers to interpret a passage in different ways. Two transcriptions of the same piece will usually agree, therefore, when the modal notation is unequivocal, but they may differ considerably when irregular patterns of ligatures leave the "correct" solution in doubt.

SUSTAINED-NOTE STYLE AND MODAL RHYTHMS

In describing two-voice organum, thirteenth-century theorists distinguish between discant style, in which both voices are measured, and *organum purum,* in which the sustained notes of the tenor are unmeasured. The upper voice of organum purum, they insist, is modal, a statement they immediately qualify by adding that the mode may be abnormal (*non rectus*) or irregular. The nature of the irregularities is not entirely clear, but they seem to consist largely of willful departures from the normal note values of the rhythmic modes. Individual singers might lengthen or shorten notes according to their personal preference, but the notation remained the same as for the regular rhythmic modes. Modern scholars have assumed—perhaps too readily—that these modifications of note values did not destroy the underlying organization of modal patterns in units of three. The irregular first mode, for example, would be sung as ♩ ♪♪ instead of ♩ ♪. Also based on theoretical descriptions is the assumption that the organal voice was consistently and continuously modal from the very beginning of Notre Dame polyphony. Both of these assumptions might well be reexamined. Reliance on theoretical descriptions even of contemporaneous practice can be dangerous. It becomes even more so when we project those descriptions backward and apply them to music written fifty or more years earlier. Both the musical style and the notation of organum purum should make us suspect that thirteenth-century theorists were trying to explain a rhapsodic and improvisatory manner of performance in terms of their fully developed system of rhythmic modes.

In two-voice organum, the exuberant melismas above a sustained tenor seem almost Oriental in style and suggest a relationship with the expansive melismatic tropes that embellished responsorial chants in earlier times (see Chapter VI). Now, of course, the sustained tenor notes provide a foundation that controls the melodic flow to some extent. The melismas of the organal voice break up into phrases that usually begin and end on a consonance with the tenor. Departures from this procedure result chiefly from the introduction of melodic sequences, one of the first devices Notre Dame composers used to organize a melody. Whatever control the sustained notes may have exercised over the melodic direction of the organal voice, they certainly exercised none over its rhythmic organization. Completely unhampered by any need to consider the note values of another voice, no singer, then or now, would be likely to maintain an unyielding triple meter, even if the notation of that meter were precise and unmistakable. But this is just where the notation in the practical sources departs most strikingly from theoretical descriptions. Instead of the normal ligature patterns of modal notation, we find more often than not that the arrangement of ligatures gives no indication of a particular rhythmic mode. This situation results in part from the many conjuncturae, but other ligatures may also contain from four to six or seven notes. Even in ordines with nothing but two- and three-note ligatures and single notes, the grouping is often so irregular that several different rhythmic interpretations are possible. Faced with such a notation, singers could hardly be expected to recognize and use an underlying rhythmic mode. It is even less likely that they would group the patterns of that mode—assuming it was the first—into pairs that conveniently produce 6/8 measures in modern transcriptions. The music must nevertheless be transcribed if it is to be studied and performed, and scholars will undoubtedly continue to use the patterns of the rhythmic modes as their starting point.[6] This will do no harm if singers remember that many passages are open to different rhythmic interpretations and that even regular patterns in unequivocal modal notation were probably performed with a certain amount of freedom. Medieval theorists were fond of emphasizing the difference between musicians who "know" and singers who merely "do." In performing the extravagant vocalises of organum purum, however, the instincts of singers may be a surer guide than the knowledge of theoretical musicians. Both at least deserve consideration.

6.   For an unmeasured transcription as done by "the more cautious transcribers," see NOHM, 2, p. 344.

DISCANT STYLE AND MODAL RHYTHMS

The introduction of modal rhythms in the upper voice of sections in sustained-note style may well have been a gradual process that was never fully completed in the two-voice organa of the *Magnus liber*. Discant clausulae, on the other hand, seem to have used modal rhythms much sooner. Modal notation was not yet fully developed or wholly consistent—indeed, it never became so—and metrical patterns are often fractured beyond recognition. Nevertheless, the mode is usually identifiable, and the presence of measured values in both voices solves most of the rhythmic problems. It is primarily in the discant clausulae, therefore, that we can observe both the development of the rhythmic modes and the way that development changed the character of Notre Dame polyphony.

In the earliest form of the *Magnus liber organi,* presumably by Leonin, sustained-note style is overwhelmingly predominant. When discant clausulae do appear, they tend to be short and undeveloped. More often than not, the modal patterns of the upper voice are broken up into shorter values, and the tenor moves in a series of undifferentiated longs. These longs usually have a triple value equal to a foot of the first mode, but they may also be duplex longs of twice that value. In later substitute clausulae, the chief development lies in a clearer definition and more systematic use of the rhythmic modes. The upper voice sacrifices some of its rhythmic freedom and adheres much more consistently to the pattern of the mode. The tenor goes even further in the systematic organization of its rhythmic structure. Instead of the series of even longs, the notes of the tenor melody are now arranged in a rhythmic pattern that is repeated throughout the clausula. The most common pattern is the first ordo of the fifth mode, but the tenors of clausulae may also use short ordines of the first or second mode. Other and longer patterns may result from the alternation of duplex longs with the fifth mode or of normal (triple) longs with the first. As the characteristic patterns in Example IX–3 make clear, tenors of clausulae usually move in units that can best be transcribed as measures of 6/8, or more rarely, 9/8 meter. Above such

Example IX–3: *Characteristic Tenor Patterns of Clausulae*

5TH MODE, 1ST ORDO	
1ST MODE, 1ST OR 2ND ORDO	
2ND MODE, 1ST OR 2ND ORDO	
ALTERNATIONS	

patterns, units of the first, second, or sixth mode will also appear in pairs, and it is for this reason that these modes are normally transcribed in 6/8 rather than 3/8 meter. The consistent application of this procedure to melismas above sustained notes is more questionable, as we have seen. Regular phrases built in 6/8 measures appear to have developed along with the system of the rhythmic modes and to be another feature that distinguishes the later discant style from the earlier and freer style of organum purum.

The growing interest in musical structures based on repeated rhythmic patterns in the tenor apparently led composers to seek ways of extending the length of clausulae. Because the tenor normally used all the notes of a plainchant melisma, it could rarely be extended by including more notes of the original chant. The only solution, then, was to lengthen the tenor by repeating all or part of its melody within a single clausula. This composers frequently did. The repeat may have the same rhythms as the first statement of the melody, or it may be varied in different ways. In some clausulae, the tenor maintains one rhythmic pattern throughout, but the repetition of the melody begins on a different note of the pattern. The repeat is thus disguised by the new melodic figures of the tenor patterns. Other clausulae emphasize the structure and at the same time introduce an element of contrast by combining the repeat with a new rhythmic pattern in the tenor. Both methods of varying melodic repetitions in the tenor of clausulae are illustrated in Example IX–4. Such combined repetitions of melodic and rhythmic patterns became an important constructive principle in the thirteenth and later centuries. This principle, therefore, is one of the most significant innovations of the Notre Dame School and one that we may attribute with some certainty to Perotin. Quite obviously it belongs with the other characteristic features of the "new and better clausulae" that won the praise of Anonymous IV and led to the designation of Perotin as the best composer of discant.

Example IX–4: *Melodic Repetition in Tenors of Discant Clausulae*

a. EX SEMINE, FROM ALLELUIA: NATIVITAS (AMM, No. 33)

b. MULIERUM (from *F,* fol. 164; Apel, NPM, facs. 52a)

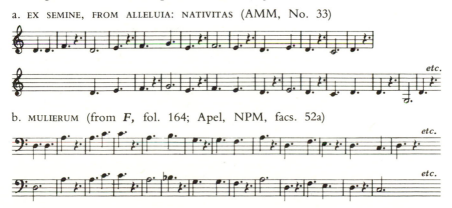

DIFFERENT VERSIONS OF *ALLELUIA: NATIVITAS*

The remark of Anonymous IV concerning Perotin's abbreviation and improvement of the *Magnus liber* has led to the assumption that substitute clausulae originated as optional replacements either of another discant clausula or of a passage originally composed in sustained-note style. In some cases, however, more clausulae were composed on the same tenor melisma than could possibly have been needed and some may have been intended for use as independent pieces. Yet we do find that clausulae have been interchanged in different manuscript versions of the same composition. The way in which this process remodeled an earlier composition will become clear in the ensuing discussion of the two-voice organum *Alleluia: Nativitas* and its dependent clausulae (AMM, No. 33).

Two of the Notre Dame manuscripts contain a two-voice setting of *Alleluia: Nativitas* for the Nativity of the Virgin Mary, and three have a three-voice setting, presumably the one attributed to Perotin by Anonymous IV. The older of the two-voice settings occurs in the manuscript from St. Andrews Priory in Scotland (W_1).[7] The later one comes from the manuscript now in Florence (*F*). (It is this later setting that is transcribed in AMM together with the substitute clausulae contained in the same manuscript.)

The two versions of the opening Alleluia in sustained-note style differ only in minor details. This situation is nearly reversed in the two settings of the verse. Beginning with the second tenor note, the melismas of sections in sustained-note style almost seem to be different compositions, with only a few short passages that are identical in both versions. It is the treatment of the clausulae, however, that is most instructive. The setting of "gloriose" is new in *F* and has a shorter closing melisma, but both versions use the same clausula for the word "Virginis." One of the most striking differences occurs on the following word, "Marie." In *F,* a clausula of only seven measures replaces a passage in sustained-note style that consists of no fewer than thirty-three measures of 6/8 in Waite's transcription from W_1. The next clausula in the series, on "ex semine," is equally interesting. The setting of W_1—thirteen measures with the tenor in even note values—is replaced by a longer clausula with a repeated rhythmic pattern in the tenor, which has been extended by melodic repetition as was shown in Example IX–4a. The older setting was not simply discarded but was preserved in *F* among the substitute clausulae (fol. 176v; see AMM, No. 34a). The new setting, curiously enough, proves to be the two lower voices of the clausula in the three-voice *Alleluia: Nativitas* attributed to Perotin. After all these changes,

---

7.   Waite, *Rhythm,* p. 195 ff. (of music). This version is included in Waite's transcription of the complete *Magnus liber organi* as it appears in W_1.

An example of organum triplum, *Alleluia: Nativitas* by Perotin, from *W₂*.

the second version returns to almost complete identity with the first for the remainder of the verse. Only at the very end do we find still another substitution. Both versions have the same short clausula on "Ju-" of "Juda," but the version of *W₁* then concludes with a melisma above a sustained note. In place of this ending, the version of *F* extends the clausula by repeating the tenor with a new countermelody and a short melisma on the penultimate note. Following the verse, *F* provides another setting of the opening Alleluia. This procedure is common to a number of Alleluias in *F* but does not occur in other Notre Dame sources. It apparently represents another way in which later composers modified and added to the original form of the *Magnus liber organi*. In this instance, a discant clausula on the syllables "-le-lu-" results in a considerably shorter setting than the first Alleluia, which is entirely in sustained-note style.

The extensive modifications in the second version of *Alleluia: Nativitas* are not the only ones that can be observed from material contained in the Florence manuscript. Of two clausulae on "Ex semine," one came from the older version of *W₁*, as we have seen. The other (AMM, No. 34b) appears to be new, although its tenor has the same rhythmic pattern and the same melodic repetition as the first twenty-two measures of

Perotin's clausula in the complete organum. In the substitute clausula, however, the tenor makes a further repeat of all twenty-two measures before going on to the closing notes of the original melisma. The result is a striking difference in the lengths of the three clausulae on "Ex semine." The shortest has only thirteen measures; Perotin's has thirty-two; the longest has fifty-four. This longest clausula, incidentally, can be substituted in the complete organum as easily as the other two were interchanged.

The greatly increased length of the later and more highly organized discant clausulae would seem to belie the statement that Perotin shortened the organa of Leonin. We may assume—if we wish—that these are the "better" clausulae of which Anonymous IV spoke, but they are not the only new ones. More than 150 very short clausulae constitute the last two cycles of discant settings in *F* (fols. 178–84v). Like the others, these cycles are arranged in liturgical order, and the clausulae for a particular chant appear in correct succession. These short clausulae can have no other function than to replace passages in sustained-note style. We have already noted one such replacement on the word "Marie" in the second version of the complete setting of *Alleluia: Nativitas.* Now, we find four more clausulae for this chant on the words or syllables "-le-lu-," "-ti-vi-," "Marie," and "Abra-."[8] The third of these provides a substitute for the replacement just mentioned. Each of the others, however, converts an extended melisma above sustained notes into a much shorter discant clausula. Although we may sometimes question how much of the original should be replaced, the difficulties of inserting these clausulae are by no means insuperable. And there can be no question that they were meant to be so inserted.

The net result of using all four of these clausulae in *Alleluia: Nativitas* is twofold. The condensation they effect more than compensates for even the longest clausula on "Ex semine," and discant style now predominates over the older organum purum. It is this development—characteristic of all Notre Dame polyphony—that corroborates the testimony of Anonymous IV. That Perotin probably did not compose all the substitute clausulae is immaterial. The School of Notre Dame, like the School of St. Martial, showed an ever increasing preference for discant style that undoubtedly reflected their increasing concern for musical organization and design. In modifying organum by means of discant clausulae, the Notre Dame composers developed many of the structural principles and techniques that characterize polyphonic composition throughout the thirteenth century.

8.   These four clausulae are inserted above the score in AMM, No. 33. All four, together with an incomplete transcription of *Alleluia: Nativitas,* are printed in W. Waite, "The Abbreviation of the Magnus liber," JAMS, 14 (1961), pp. 153–56. Assuming that the syllable "-ti-" is misplaced in the manuscript, I have divided the first two clausulae differently. As a result, the melisma of "-le-lu-" is now complete, and it is not necessary to assume that the first three notes of "-ti-vi-" are repeated.

ORGANUM TRIPLUM AND QUADRUPLUM

Organum for three or four voices is called *organum triplum* or *organum quadruplum* to distinguish it from simple *organum duplum* for two voices. Used alone, however, the terms *duplum, triplum,* and *quadruplum* refer to single voices as they appear above the tenor. In an organum quadruplum, for example, the four voices from the bottom to the top of the score would be called the tenor, duplum, triplum, and quadruplum. According to theoretical descriptions and the evidence of practical sources, the voices were composed successively in this numerical order, and each stage of the process resulted in a composition that was musically self-sufficient. It is for this reason that Perotin's three-voice clausula on "Ex semine" could be adapted for use in the two-voice setting of *Alleluia: Nativitas* simply by omitting the triplum. Or did Perotin compose the two-voice version of the clausula when he remodelled the older organum duplum and then add a third voice when he composed the complete organum triplum? Either procedure was possible and both were common in the later Middle Ages.

The addition of a third and fourth voice did not alter the overall form of organum, but the musical style changed in a number of ways. Although the tenor still alternates between sustained notes and repeated rhythmic patterns, the upper voices make scarcely any distinction between the two styles. The need to coordinate and the desire to organize these two or three voices above the tenor undoubtedly account for the characteristic features of organa tripla and quadrupla. The expansive and wide-ranging melismas of organum duplum give way to shorter and more regular phrases. Because the singers were men, all the voices lie at about the same pitch-level and frequently cross. Individual melodies tend to become narrow in range and to move around perfect consonances above the tenor. As a result, interest shifts from melodic outline to rhythmic and chordal structure. The first mode still predominates, and long passages maintain the modal pattern almost unbroken. From the combination of regular and persistent rhythms with consonant chords on each strong beat, organum for three and four voices gains a strangely hypnotic power that composers evidently appreciated and exploited.

HARMONIC STRUCTURE

The harmonic structure of three- and four-voice organum still depends in large part on perfect consonances—the unison, fourth, fifth, and octave. Theoretically, these consonances should appear at the beginning of each pattern of the rhythmic mode. No restrictions were placed on dissonant combinations produced by the intermediate note or notes. In practice, however, we find numerous deviations from this rule of consonant treatment. In the first place, the fourth becomes less and less common as a consonant interval above the lowest note, although it remains acceptable between upper voices. The result is a predominance of chords containing a fifth and octave above the bass. Such chords occur almost invariably at the beginning and end of phrases; but, in a second deviation from the rule, thirds sometimes appear as consonances within phrases. We thus have a curious situation—for modern ears—in which complete triads are less stable and less conclusive in effect than triads without the third. Another deviation from the expected consonant treatment results from the rules for the successive composition of voices. As the triplum and quadruplum were added, they were supposed to be consonant with one but not necessarily with all of the voices already existing. In consequence, sharply dissonant combinations sometimes occur on strong beats. Other accented dissonances can only be regarded as appoggiaturas that resolve to consonances. Such appoggiaturas often ornament the final note of a phrase or the sustained interval or chord with which organum invariably begins. That their use in this position may have been optional is suggested by variants in the different manuscripts. *Alleluia: Nativitas,* for example, begins with an unadorned octave in W_1 but has a major seventh resolving to an octave in F. The theorists evidently disapproved of this opening appoggiatura and recommended that the dissonance be avoided by delaying the entry of the tenor. They also disapproved of the many dissonances that occur above sustained tenor notes. To avoid these dissonances, they say, the tenor may either be silent or move to a consonant tone. To what extent singers followed these instructions we cannot know. Examination of both *Alleluia: Nativitas* and *Sederunt* (AMM, Nos. 33 and 35) will show that removal of the dissonances would require frequent interruptions or changes of the sustained notes. This free treatment of the plainchant tenor may have been normal practice in performance, but modern editors are understandably reluctant to suggest it in their transcriptions. The possibility remains that composers and performers accepted and even cultivated the free treatment of dissonance recorded in the music as it stands. It is not unreasonable to suspect that, lacking an explanation for these dissonances, theorists tried to eliminate them. In so doing, they could make organum conform to their later standards of harmonic propriety.

STRUCTURAL DEVICES IN ORGANA TRIPLA AND QUADRUPLA

The powerful effect of organa tripla and quadrupla does not result solely from the reiteration of rhythmic and chordal patterns. Melodic repetition and organization also play an important role. In organum duplum, the contrasting rhythmic structures of the two voices gave composers little opportunity to establish melodic relationships between them. Two or three voices above the tenor, on the other hand, made it possible and indeed necessary to develop procedures for relating the simultaneous melodies and for shaping the melodic material into comprehensible musical structures. It is only natural, therefore, that the emphasis on constructive devices already noted in later discant clausulae should become even stronger in organum for three and four voices.

One device that was also found in organum duplum is the use of melodic sequences to give direction to the phrases of a single melodic line. A particularly rich source of such sequences is the three-voice setting of the Christmas Responsory *Descendit de caelis* (He descended from heaven), from which Example IX–5 is taken. This excerpt follows the syllable "-quam" near the beginning of the verse. It is interesting to remark, first of all, the different rhythmic modes of the three phrases and the textbook regularity of their notation. In the second place, all three sequences in the triplum are variations of the basic melodic progression from **f′** down to a cadence on **c′** above the sustained **f** in the tenor. That only the triplum is consistently sequential makes it more interesting and important than the duplum and raises doubts as to which of the two was composed first. If the triplum really were written last, it must have existed in the composer's mind, at least, before he created the less highly organized duplum.

Example IX–5: *Melodic Sequences from* Descendit de caelis (**F**, *fol. 14*)

The process of composing individual voices one after the other seems even less credible when exchange of voice parts is involved. This device

The opening page of one of the most sumptuous of medieval manuscripts, Pluteus 29.1 (Biblioteca Laurenziana, Florence).

The beginning of the organum quadruplum *Viderunt* by Perotin (Biblioteca Laurenziana, Florence).

had already appeared in a few St. Martial pieces in discant style, but its use was virtually impossible in two-voice organum. With two or three voices above the tenor, however, voice exchange became one of the most common structural devices, particularly in the extended melismas of organum quadruplum. The opening section of Perotin's four-voice setting of *Sederunt* (AMM, No. 35) provides many characteristic examples. Beginning in measure 13, the duplum and triplum exchange two-measure motives in a way that must have been planned in advance. Moreover, the eleven measures from 13 to 23 must have been completed in all three upper voices before they could be repeated exactly with voice exchange in measures 24 to 34. In the next eighteen measures the application of voice exchange is somewhat less rigid. A six-measure pattern appears first in the quadruplum, then in the triplum, and again in the quadruplum. Beneath this pattern—which is itself like an ostinato— the other voices vary in both melodic outline and phrase structure. Examples such as these make it clear that the successive composition of voices cannot have been an invariable procedure. At least some sections must have been composed with foreknowledge of what all the voices would do, and the exchange of melodies among three voices means that no voice can be omitted without destroying the musical design. We may safely assume, therefore, that Perotin conceived *Sederunt* as a four-voice organum and that he planned in advance the complex interrelationships of its different voices.

Imitation and canon are other constructive devices that appear occasionally in the upper voices of organa tripla and quadrupla. In a few instances, imitative entries occur at the beginning of sections, as happens on the syllable "-de-" of *Sederunt* (mm. 57–58). This imitation rarely extends beyond the first few notes and is little more than an incidental detail in the overall structural plan. More often, imitation results from the transfer of motives from one voice to another in what might be called incomplete voice exchange. In measures 71–128 of *Sederunt,* for example, short motives move from voice to voice, begin on different pitches, follow each other in melodic sequence, and appear in simultaneous inversion. The result is a remarkable illustration of the various ways in which motives may be used to unify a polyphonic texture. Nevertheless, the relationship between this kind of motivic development and the practice of voice exchange is still clearly evident. That more extended imitations and canons derived from the same practice is possible but less certain. One of the longest canons occurs in *Viderunt,* Perotin's other four-voice organum.[9] A melody of twelve measures in 6/8 that appears first in the triplum is repeated by the duplum beginning

---

9.   For an excerpt that includes the canon, see Reese, MMA, p. 305 (Ex. 88). The complete organum is published in *Die drei- und vierstimmige Notre-Dame Organa,* which also contains *Sederunt principes* and Perotin's three-voice setting of *Alleluia: Nativitas.*

one measure later at the fifth below. Canonic writing of such length and strictness is unusual, but the short phrases into which the melody is broken lend a less complicated appearance to the passage. The total effect, indeed, is one of incomplete voice exchange that is varied by transposition and compressed by overlapping of motives. We shall probably not be far wrong in regarding voice exchange as the basic device from which the Notre Dame composers evolved ways of organizing and integrating the simultaneous melodies of polyphony.

It is clear that brevity was of no concern to the composers of organa tripla and quadrupla. Even the abbreviations of the *Magnus liber* resulted primarily from a desire to replace old-fashioned organum above a sustained tenor with more up-to-date discant style. In organa for three and four voices, the upper parts were in discant style throughout, and the exploitation of structural devices produced works of almost unblievable length. After the opening chord, the first tenor note of *Sederunt* is sustained beneath a melisma that lasts for fifty-six measures of 6/8 meter. The complete setting of just this one word, the solo intonation of the Gradual, extends for a total of no fewer than 142 measures, and a performance of the entire composition would take about twenty minutes. Never before had musical structures attained such astonishing dimensions. It would seem that, as the nave of Notre Dame neared completion, the cathedral's unprecedented size and magnificence stirred Perotin to fill the vast space with music of equal splendor. For his successful achievement of this goal he well deserves to be remembered as Perotin the Great.

CHAPTER X

The School of Notre Dame, II: Conductus and Motet

THE CONDUCTUS

Large as the repertory of organum is, it by no means constitutes the entire output of the Notre Dame composers. All of the manuscript sources contain settings of Latin poems that do not belong to the official liturgy of the Church. The most extensive collection of such settings appears in the Florence manuscript (*F*), where we find 130 two-voice, 56 three-voice, and 3 four-voice compositions. In addition, two sections of *F* contain a total of 143 monophonic settings of Latin poems. Whatever their subject matter may be—and it covers a rather wide range—these pieces are commonly assigned to the class of composition known as *conductus*.[1] In *The Play of Daniel,* pieces identified as conducti were processional songs, presumably the original meaning of the term. The repertory of Santiago de Compostela from the mid-twelfth century also contains conducti—both monophonic and polyphonic—that probably served the same function. By the thirteenth century, however, conductus had become a general term with approximately the same meaning as the versus of St. Martial. Some conducti have semiliturgical texts that commemorate a specific festival of the Church or honor an individual saint. A few are tropes of *Benedicamus Domino*. Many texts of a more topical nature refer to political events, celebrate the coronations of kings or bishops, mourn their deaths, or issue summonses to a crusade.[2] Still others teach moral lessons or attack social evils, often with bitter satire that spares no one, not even the clergy itself. This textual variety makes the conductus difficult to define and its function difficult to determine. Some conducti could, and probably did, serve as unofficial additions to the liturgy. A more appropriate use for others might have been the musical and moral instruction of the young or the leisure entertainment of clerics and scholars. As the texts move away from obviously sacred

---

1.   *Conductus* is properly a fourth-declension noun (pl. *conductus*). It is more convenient, however, to follow the many medieval writers who treated it as second declension (pl. *conducti*).

2.   See L. Schrade, "Political Compositions in French Music of the 12th and 13th Centuries," ÀnM, 1 (1953), pp. 9–55.

subjects, they begin to overlap with secular Latin song, and a clear line between the two is impossible to draw. This is particularly true of monophonic songs, with which we shall deal in the following chapter. Here, the polyphonic conducti preserved in the Notre Dame manuscripts will be our primary concern.

In their musical forms and styles, conducti vary almost as widely as does the subject matter of their texts. Nevertheless, their distinguishing musical characteristics are somewhat easier to describe. As a starting point, we may take the directions that the thirteenth-century theorist Franco of Cologne gives for composing a conductus. Franco states that "he who wishes to write a conduct ought first to invent as beautiful a melody as he can."[3] He then treats this melody as a tenor against which he writes a duplum in discant style. If he wishes to write a triplum, he must keep the tenor and duplum in mind, so that if the triplum makes a discord with the tenor it will be concordant with the duplum, and vice versa. The same principle applies in adding a quadruplum. If it makes a discord with one voice, it should be concordant with the others. From this description we see again that the successive composition of voices was the normal procedure, and we may infer that each successive version of a conductus—beginning with the monophonic tenor—was complete in itself. That this inference is true in many cases is proved by the differing versions of conducti that have been preserved. The conductus *Veri floris* (Of the true flower) provides one of the most striking instances. What is essentially one setting of this text appears in no fewer than nine manuscripts in versions for one, two, and three voices.[4] Numerous conducti appear in one source with only two voices and in another with an added triplum. This situation is characteristic of much music in the thirteenth and fourteenth centuries, and we cannot always tell which version was the original. In some cases it seems that third and fourth voices were added later, perhaps even by different composers.

Another inference that has been drawn from Franco's prescription for composing conducti is that their melodic material is entirely new. As a result, we frequently read that conducti are the first completely original polyphonic compositions. The statement may be generally true, but it needs qualification. According to a sightly later theorist, Walter Odington, the tenors of conducti might be either previously known or newly invented melodies. In fact, some tenors of conducti also appear as monophonic secular songs in the vernacular. One of the best-known examples is the three-voice conductus *Veris ad imperia* (By the power of spring), the tenor of which is a transposed version of a troubadour dance song, *A l'entrada del tens clar* (At the entry of fair weather), which also

---

3. Strunk, SR, p. 155.
4. For a transcription with melodic variants from several sources, see NOHM, 2, p. 330. A two-voice version from the Madrid manuscript (**Ma**) may be found in Parrish, NMM, Pl. XXIX.

celebrates the return of spring.[5] Other uses of borrowed material involve the quotation of plainchant fragments and even of complete clausulae in some of the longer conducti.[6] The full extent of such borrowings has yet to be investigated, but at the very least they show that complete originality was not an essential feature of the conductus. Moreover, the established relationships of conducti with secular song, with plainchant, and with organum are, in Bukofzer's words, "eloquent and vigorous evidence for the amazing inner consistency and stylistic unity in the music of the 13th century."[7]

THE TWO CLASSES OF CONDUCTI

On the basis of musical style, thirteenth-century theorists recognized and described two distinct classes of conducti. In the first class, known as *conductus simplex* or *simple conductus,* the tenor melody is syllabic or nearly so, and the added voices proceed in the note-against-note or neume-against-neume counterpoint characteristic of discant style. Many such conducti have strophic texts, and the music is repeated for each stanza. Thus, in both their musical form and the melodic style of their tenors, simple conducti resemble hymns as well as contemporary secular songs. The second, more elaborate class of conducti is the *embellished conductus,* sometimes called *conductus with caudae.* The term *cauda* (tail) is more familiar to us in the Italian form of the word, *coda,* which designates a terminal section; but the thirteenth-century cauda is a melismatic passage—sometimes of astonishing length—that may appear anywhere in a conductus. Although some pieces have a short melismatic extension only at the close, the typical embellished conductus has caudae at the beginning and in the middle as well as at the end. As a rule, the melismas occur on the first and either the penultimate or last syllables of poetic lines. In the most extreme cases, caudae produce a predominantly melismatic style that subordinates the text to the musical development in sharp contrast to the hymnlike character of simple conducti. Yet the setting of a text as a simple or embellished conductus seems to have been determined independently of either its subject matter or its poetic form. Perhaps the intended function, now uncertain, was the determining factor. One clue to that function would then be the degree of simplicity or embellishment in the setting of a particular text.

5. For the conductus, see J. Knapp, *Thirty-five Conductus for Two and Three Voices,* p. 36. The troubadour song is printed in NOHM, 2, p. 241. See also Gleason, EM, pp. 12 and 41.
6. See M. Bukofzer, "Interrelations between Conductus and Clausula," AnM, 1 (1953), pp. 65–103.
7. Ibid., p. 103.

PERFORMANCE PRACTICE AND RHYTHMIC INTERPRETATION

Before we turn to a more detailed study of the two classes of conducti, we must deal briefly with the general problems of performance practice and rhythmic interpretation. Polyphonic conducti were normally written in score with the text beneath the lowest voice. This disposition has led some scholars to assume that the upper voices were sung as melismas or played by instruments. Instrumental performance of the caudae in embellished conducti has also been assumed. Although conducti might have been performed in these ways, the assumptions do not rest on very solid ground. With two, three, or even four voices in score there was surely no need to write the text beneath each voice to indicate that it was to be sung by all. Moreover, the scribes took care to make clear which notes in the different voices go with each syllable of the text. As to the caudae, there seems to be no reason why they might not have been sung in an age when the vocal performance of melismatic organum was commonplace. We must admit, however, that both the style and the function of a particular conductus might affect the manner of its performance. The more elaborate conducti with caudae were surely intended for soloists, but simple conducti might have been sung by larger groups. Pieces that served as additions to the liturgy would naturally have been performed without instrumental participation, except possibly by an organ, the only instrument sanctioned for use in the services of the Church. Other instruments, of course, were commonly used for secular entertainment, and they might well have doubled or even replaced voices in the performance of conducti unconnected with the liturgy. Performance practices in the Middle Ages and the Renaissance were much more flexible than we are accustomed to in the music of later times, and we may therefore sing or play conducti—as their contemporaries undoubtedly did—with any available combination of appropriate voices or instruments.

The rhythmic interpretation of conducti raises more controversial problems. Modal notation, with its characteristic patterns of ligatures, can be used only in melismatic passages. In conducti, therefore, only the caudae are written in a notation that can be transcribed with reasonable certainty as to the intended rhythm. Simple conducti and the syllabic sections of conducti with caudae are notated with a single neume—either one note or a ligature—for each syllable. These neumes use the normal forms of plainchant notation and give no indication of mensural values. Two possible solutions have been proposed: one is to give each syllable the same time value, which is divided into smaller values when ligatures of two or more notes occur; the other is to transcribe syllabic sections in one of the rhythmic modes. In the latter solution, the text normally maintains the modal pattern while ligatures introduce fractio modi. Current opinion seems to favor the second solution but often stops short of agreement on which rhythmic mode to use. In embellished conducti, the prevailing mode of the caudae often proves suitable for the syllabic sections as well, and some caudae even begin by repeating part or all of the music that has just been sung with the text. Such instances have been taken as proof that the syllabic section must have the same modal rhythm as the cauda. This argument is somewhat weakened by the phenomenon known as *modal transmutation*—the repetition of caudae in different rhythmic modes—which is an established technique in the conductus.[8] There seems to be no reason to assume, then, that a syllabic passage, say in the fifth mode, could not have been repeated immediately in the first or second. Moreoever, the caudae themselves are not always notated with sufficient clarity to prevent differing opinions as to the correct rhythmic mode.

With simple conducti, of course, it becomes even more difficult to determine which rhythmic mode should be used, if any. Details of the notation sometimes indicate the position of long values, but decisions usually rest on considerations of both textual and musical characteristics. The length of the poetic lines and their predominant metrical patterns may make one mode more appropriate than another. The alternation of single notes and ligatures, or the consistent appearance of ligatures on odd- or even-numbered syllables may suggest a recurrent pattern of long and short values. For melodies with many ligatures irregularly placed, only the fifth rhythmic mode may prove to be suitable. Transcriptions in the fifth mode, incidentally, produce nearly the same result as the system that rejects the use of modes entirely and gives each syllable the same time value. Finally, combinations of details may indicate an irregular rhythm that is comparable to the use of extensio modi. In a prevailing first mode, for example, some syllables might require longs of triple rather than duple value.

In the historical development of conducti, it is probable that the earliest examples employed equal values for each syllable. With the development of the rhythmic modes, these equal values would have become triple in the fifth mode to provide a more consistent organization of the smaller values introduced by ligatures. Later conducti would then have applied the rhythmic patterns of other modes to settings of the texts themselves as well as to the melismatic caudae. Unfortunately, the steps in this probable development are difficult to trace. Few conducti can be dated with precision, and all have the same unmeasured notation in their sections with text. Even the occasional appearance of conducti in later sources in mensural notation cannot be taken as proof of their original rhythmic organization. Modern transcriptions follow the same procedure of imposing definite time values that are not indicated in the earlier

8.   See M. Bukofzer, "Interrelations between Conductus and Clausula," p. 90 ff.

notation. Strong as our conviction may be that the procedure is necessary, we can never be completely sure that we have recaptured either the composers' intent or the practice of medieval performers.[9]

FORMS AND STYLE OF SIMPLE CONDUCTI

Closely related to the contrasting styles of simple and embellished conducti are the different bases of their formal organization. Even in the relatively few conducti available for study, a wide variety of procedures makes generalization hazardous; but the two classes of conducti are sufficiently divergent, at least in their extreme manifestations, to require separate discussion. We shall therefore consider the characteristic relationships of form and style in simple conducti before proceeding to the more complex organizational procedures in extended examples of conducti with caudae.

We have noted that simple conducti are hymnlike in both their melodic style and their use of the same music for each stanza of a strophic poem. Now we find that conducti and hymns also have the same musical forms. One of these, the so-called hymn form, a continuous series of different musical phrases, is perhaps the most common.[10] Many conducti, however, repeat phrases to produce patterns such as *aabc, abab,* or *aabb.* Because the stanzas of conducti are usually longer than the normal four-line stanzas of hymns, each section of these forms may include two or more phrases, yet they are obviously nothing more than expanded versions of already familiar patterns (see Chapter IV). The same forms occur in secular songs, both in Latin and in the vernacular, and the presence of refrains in a number of conducti establishes an even closer relationship with contemporary secular song (see Chapters XI–XIII). These further proofs of the homogeneity of all medieval music are fascinating, but they make it impossible to disentangle mutual influences and to associate the introduction of particular forms and styles with a specific musical genre.

The tenors in polyphonic settings of simple conducti naturally have the same structural patterns as the monophonic songs. The added voices, on the other hand, may or may not reflect those forms. They normally cannot introduce exact repetitions of phrases above a continuous tenor, but they may themselves be continuous above a tenor's clear pattern of phrase repetitions. The first eight measures of *Sol sub nube latuit* illustrate this rather common procedure (Example X–1).[11] It is in-

9.   For three rhythmic interpretations of *Hac in anni janua* (At the beginning of the year), see HAM, No. 39 (even time values); Gleason, EM, p. 49 (the 5th rhythmic mode); and Knapp, *Conductus,* p. 38 (the 2nd mode). See also Apel, NPM, p. 260 ff.

10.   An example is *Veri floris,* NOHM, 2, pp. 330–32.

11.   For a facsimile of this conductus as it appears in W_1, see Parrish, NMM, Pl. XXVIII. A complete transcription of the version in F is available in Knapp, *Conductus,* p. 122.

teresting to note also that the repeated four-measure unit in the tenor consists of two similar phrases with open and closed endings. In cases such as this it almost seems that the composer made a deliberate effort to show his skill in writing different counterpoints to the same melody.

Example X–1: *Varied Counterpoint above a Repeated Melody*
(*F, fol. 354v*)

**These two notes are *d–e* in *W₁*.

The sun was hidden under a cloud but not eclipsed when the Son of the highest Father became flesh.

Instead of combining repetitive and continuous forms in different voices, composers sometimes chose to emphasize the structure of the tenor by reproducing it in the other voices. They often repeated sections exactly, but they might also take advantage of successive statements of a tenor phrase to introduce voice exchange in the duplum and triplum. *Veris ad imperia* presents a characteristic example in which, above four statements of the tenor's opening phrase, the upper voices exchange parts at each successive repetition.[12] Another simple conductus, *Procurans odium* (Earning hatred), includes the tenor in an unusually complex exchange of parts among all three voices (see AMM, No. 36).

FORMAL ORGANIZATION IN EMBELLISHED CONDUCTI

Procurans odium is perhaps an extreme example of the constructivist tendency already noted in the later works from St. Martial and in Notre Dame organum. The normal process of composition would account for the rarity of such a tour de force in simple conducti, but the caudae of

12.   For modern editions, see above, fn. 5.

embellished conducti provided more opportunities for systematic integration of voices and organization of large-scale musical forms. Pieces with a melismatic extension only at the close—a true coda—differ in no other respect from simple conducti and follow similar methods of formal construction. Characteristic examples already cited are *Hac in anni janua* and *Sol sub nube latuit*. The latter is interesting for several reasons. The eight-line stanzas have a musical setting in *aabb* form; a four-line refrain with a continuous setting returns after each stanza; and the single cauda at the close begins by repeating the final phrase of the refrain. The monophonic conductus *Beata viscera* (Blessed offspring), attributed to Perotin by Anonymous IV, also uses caudae in connection with a refrain, but in a different manner. Here again we have an eight-line stanza with a four-line refrain. This time, the stanza has a musical setting in *aabc* form. The refrain then begins with a melisma that is repeated on the first word of the final line. The two appearances of the same cauda thus distinguish the refrain from the stanzas in the style of simple conducti.[13]

Some embellished conducti have a melismatic introduction as well as conclusion, with the complete text set in simple style. More characteristic forms introduce melismas within the setting of the text itself. Typical examples of moderate length are the monophonic *Sol oritur* (The sun rises) and the two-voice *Roma gaudens* (Rome rejoicing).[14] In these pieces, the caudae again function as introductions and conclusions, but now to segments rather than to the whole of the text. A syllabic or slightly neumatic style is still the predominant feature, and the caudae remain ornamental appendages. This situation is nearly reversed in more extended examples of embellished conducti. Now, caudae predominate, and short phrases with text give an impression of being slightly incongruous interpolations. To illustrate this reversal of function we may cite a two-voice setting of *Ave Maria* from the Florence manuscript.[15] The total length of the conductus is 162 measures in 6/8 meter, and the opening and closing caudae consist of 35 and 30 measures respectively. Of the intervening 97 measures, only 27 are used in setting the text. The remaining 70 are divided among five caudae that range from eleven to eighteen measures in length. Melismas thus account for more than three-quarters of the total composition and overwhelm the setting of the text with a multiplicity of tails.

In part, at least, we must regard the size of some conducti with caudae as a reflection of the composers' delight in a newly acquired freedom. With no preexistent chant to determine the shape of their compositions,

13. This function of the caudae is obscured in transcriptions that give only one stanza of text, as HAM, No. 17c, and Gleason, EM, p. 7.

14. See HAM, Nos. 17d and 38. For another transcription of *Roma gaudens,* see Reese, MMA, p. 309. Both transcriptions are based on the version in W_1. Reese, MMA, Pl. VI (facing p. 300) includes a facsimile of the version in F.

15. Transcription in Knapp, *Conductus*, p. 81.

they now indulged—sometimes to excess—their inclination to develop complex integrative and structural devices. And they could use these devices in conducti for two, as well as for three and four voices. Long as some conducti are, no single composition can give an adequate picture of the variety and ingenuity displayed in hundreds of different caudae.[16] To give some idea of those characteristic procedures, however, we may examine *Soli nitorem . . . addo* (I add brilliance to the sun), an embellished conductus of moderate length from the Florence manuscript (AMM, No. 37).

A later manuscript of Spanish origin also preserves *Soli nitorem,* but in mensural notation that clearly indicates rhythmic values—primarily the first mode—for all passages with text.[17] The first cauda introduces this mode and firmly establishes **G** as the tonal center. It also presents an example of canonic writing, with the tenor following the duplum at a distance of one measure. The relation of such writing to voice exchange is evident in the alternate appearances of the motive **G–F–G** in the two voices. The second cauda further emphasizes the tonal center by repetition of two-measure phrases with open and closed endings. The second section with text might be called a variation of the first, and both end with the same two-measure unit but with the voices interchanged. (Measures 16–17 equal 34–35.) The third cauda makes the relationship of these two sections unmistakable by bringing together the last four measures of each, so that measures 36–43 equal measures 14–17 plus 32–35. The setting of the last six lines of text proceeds without melismatic interruption, but several cadences on **C** provide a measure of tonal contrast before the final extended cauda. This, we find, is nothing more nor less than a slightly varied recapitulation of the third, followed by the second cauda, both of which are transmuted into the fifth rhythmic mode. (Measures 59–74 correspond to 36–43, and measures 75–90 to 18–25.) New but related melodies in the final ten measures lead to the same cadential flourish that completed the second cauda. Throughout the composition, indeed, recurrent rhythmic and melodic figures add to the effectiveness of a formal organization that unifies both syllabic and melismatic sections to an extraordinary degree.

Conducti with such highly organized forms force us to modify our views about the successive composition of voices, just as we did because of similar structural procedures in some examples of organum. Quite obviously, no composer could have completed the tenor of *Soli nitorem* before he had created some sections of the duplum, at least in his mind. The tenor could scarcely reproduce a preceding duplum melody before

16.   Knapp, *Conductus* contains numerous other examples of conducti with caudae.
17.   H. Anglès, *El Còdex musical de Las Huelgas* (Barcelona, 1931), Vol. 2, facsimile, fol. 138; Vol. 3, transcription, p. 324.

that melody had been composed, and complete voice exchange cannot occur until both melodies exist. In canonic writing, moreover, both voices must have been conceived together rather than successively. From these and other bits of evidence in the music itself, it is apparent that composers did not always follow the procedures recommended by Franco of Cologne. Perhaps he intended them primarily for beginners in the art of writing simple conducti. They can have been of little use, certainly, to the finished artists who used the embellished conductus as a vehicle for the display of their highest technical achievements.

Rational organization and technical achievements are by no means the sole reasons for our interest in embellished conducti. The caudae in particular furnish some of the most attractive music of the Middle Ages, music that, as Dom Anselm Hughes has said, "only needs to be known and interpreted to be widely appreciated."[18] Much of this attractiveness derives from the lively rhythms and the frequent use of two- and four-measure phrases with open and closed endings, an organizational procedure that music of later times has made familiar and comprehensible. In all probability, it is these characteristics that led Hughes to suggest that some caudae may incorporate older dance and song tunes. Such quotations would certainly not be foreign to the practices of medieval musicians, but we have no proof as yet that they did use this kind of preexistent material. Indeed, the structural ingenuity of most caudae would seem to deny the presence of contemporary dances or popular songs. Artless music of this type may have influenced the style and phrase structure of caudae, but it is also possible that our judgments are influenced by later concepts of what constitutes popular song and dance. Conducti, after all, were written by highly sophisticated composers for equally sophisticated audiences. We can only marvel that such composers could pursue their interest in formal constructivism and at the same time produce music so fresh and direct in its appeal.

By the middle of the thirteenth century, however, interest in constructive devices and in the conductus itself had begun to wane. Originating as an offshoot of liturgical organum, a new form—the motet—first developed within the shadow of the conductus and then replaced it as the chief type of nonliturgical polyphony. Much longer lived than the conductus, the motet remained one of the most important musical types of the later Middle Ages and the entire Renaissance. Nevertheless, we may join Jacques de Liège, a reactionary theorist of the early fourteenth century, when he said, in referring to the conductus, that he regretted that songs "so beautiful, so charming, and so full of art" should have disappeared.[19]

18. NOHM, 2, p. 333.
19. CS, 1, p. 429a.

CREATION OF THE MOTET

It should be evident that the medieval attitude toward music differed considerably from ours. Neither theorists, nor composers, nor performers regarded a piece of music as fixed and unchangeable, something to be preserved and always presented in exactly the form given it by its first creator. To this attitude we owe even more than the differences—from minor variants to major changes—that occur in different manuscript versions of the same composition. Most of the major changes observed thus far have been purely musical: the addition or subtraction of voices in conducti; the abbreviation and "improvement" of organa by means of substitute clausulae. Poets collaborated in the modification of conducti only to the extent of writing a small number of contrafacta for pieces that had been composed to other texts. They made a much more significant contribution when, in a continuation of the old practice of troping, they added words to the upper voice or voices of organum. It is to this activity, literary rather than musical, that we owe the creation of a new musical genre, the motet. The name itself comes from the French for *word* (*mot*), and the term *motetus* came to signify both the composition as a whole and the voice above the tenor—the duplum—to which a text had been added. One or more additional voices, when present, were still called triplum and quadruplum.

The addition of texts to melismatic organum need occasion no surprise. Textual and musical embellishment of the liturgy had already produced both monophonic tropes and polyphony itself. Responsorial chants in particular had often been extended by musical tropes in the form of lengthy melismas, to which words—textual tropes—were added later (see Chapter VI). Nothing, then, could have been more natural than to provide the melismatic upper voice of an organum with words that troped the text of its plainchant tenor. Two of the oldest examples of this procedure occur in the St. Martial repertory. These pieces are different settings in sustained-note style of the same *Benedicamus Domino* melody. In one, the trope appears only above the word "Domino." In the other, *Stirps Jesse* (The lineage of Jesse), the upper voice has text throughout, a complete poem of five four-line stanzas. Above the sustained tenor, this upper voice with text looks very much like a piece in discant style. The setting of some lines is completely syllabic, others are neumatic, and several end with rather extensive melismas.[20] From the musical point of view, as we shall see, this trope of *Benedicamus Domino* resembles the later motet scarcely at all. It does, however, introduce one of the chief features of the form—two different texts sung together.

A few tropes of organa in sustained-note style also turn up in the Notre Dame repertory, the most notable being a series of texts that

---

20.   The beginning of *Stirps Jesse—Benedicamus Domino* is printed in Gleason, EM, p. 33.

were added to Perotin's four-voice organa *Viderunt* and *Sederunt.* The four-voice settings of these tropes in *Ma* are of particular interest because modifications of the triplum and quadruplum permit all three upper voices to sing the text. As a result, the three upper voices move together as in a simple conductus. Motets of this type, in fact, are known as *conductus motets,* although they differ from true conducti in having tenors with a different text and a different rhythmic organization. In the motets we have been discussing, all the added texts unmistakably betray their ancestry. The text of the tenor, be it one word or several, almost invariably appears somewhere in the trope. With equal consistency, moreover, the poetic rhymes of the trope are assonant with the syllable being sung concurrently by the tenor. The lengthy texts added above the words *Viderunt* and *Sederunt* make extended use of very few rhymes.

The recurrence in motets of these characteristic aspects of texts added to melismas is sufficient proof that well-known and long-established principles of troping lay behind the creation of the new musical form. In the process of that creation, however, motets with tenors in sustained notes must be regarded as an unsuccessful, or at least unfruitful, experiment. The real development of the motet as an independent form begins with the addition of tropes not to complete organa, but only to discant clausulae. This limitation relieved poets of the necessity of writing inordinately long texts and at the same time opened the door for the later creation of texts unrelated to a specific liturgical occasion. It also meant that composers could now participate in the production of motets by setting new texts in the style of substitute clausulae. In this way, the typical motet of the early thirteenth century became a relatively short composition based on a plainchant melisma arranged in repeated rhythmic patterns in the tenor, with a nearly syllabic setting of a related text or texts in the upper voices. In some instances, we do not know whether a motet is completely original or whether it is the result of adding words to a preexistent clausula. Many clausulae, however, including those that form part of complete organa, do reappear as motets that trope the text of the plainchant tenor.

To illustrate the creation of motets from preexisting clausulae we may return to Perotin's setting of *Alleluia: Nativitas* and the clausula on the words "Ex semine." In AMM, No. 38, the various texts that were added to this clausula have been brought together with the musical version that most nearly reproduces the original form of the setting in the three-voice organum. Minor variants of both melodic and rhythmic details have not been recorded because they rarely affect the way the words fit the music. The older of the two Latin tropes begins with the complete phrase of the chant *Ex semine Abrahe* (From the seed of Abraham) and returns to the word "semine" at the close. Within the text, rhymes on "-ine" and assonance with the vowel sound of the tenor melisma (E) continue the old tradition of trope composition.[21] Motets using the text *Ex semine Abrahe* occur in three different forms. In *F*, a setting for tenor and motetus corresponds with the clausula that was substituted in the two-voice setting of *Alleluia: Nativitas* in the same manuscript. The second form is a three-voice conductus motet in which both duplum and triplum sing the text. This version, curiously, functions as a substitute clausula in a three-voice setting of *Alleluia: Nativitas* that is otherwise newly composed and appears to be of English origin.[22] The third form, found in motet collections of the later thirteenth century, still has the text *Ex semine Abrahe* in the duplum but adds a new trope, *Ex semine rosa,* to the triplum. This new text follows the older one in its return to the word "semine" at the close and in its use of rhymes with "-ine" and assonance with the tenor vowel.

The intended function of motets that trope the plainchant text remains uncertain. As they did with discant clausulae, the Notre Dame manuscripts group motets together in separate collections. Now, however, the arrangement is by alphabetical order of the added texts instead of the liturgical order of the tenors. Such an arrangement suggests that motets has become independent pieces with no assigned place in the liturgy. It seems probable, nevertheless, that motet-tropes were originally written for use in the liturgical performance of a complete organum; the *Ex semine* motet in the English source offers proof that the practice was not unknown. Another possible function is the one that had also been proposed for clausulae. Both they and motets with sacred texts, whether tropes or not, would provide independent pieces appropriate for the services of particular feasts. This may well have become their chief function, but we must remember that both types originated as musical improvements or textual expansions of already existing liturgical polyphony.

The Latin tropes of *Ex semine* are not the only texts that were added to Perotin's clausula. Very early in the history of the motet, apparently, poets began writing secular French texts to fit already existing clausulae. The second Notre Dame manuscript now in Wolfenbüttel (*W₂*) contains a large collection of early French motets, among which the music of *Ex semine* appears three times with two different texts. In a version reduced to two voices—tenor and duplum—the upper voice has the text *Hyer mein trespensis erroie* (Yesterday morning, pensive, I wandered). The second French text, *Se j'ai amé* (If I have loved), occurs twice: once with the duplum of the two-voice reduction, and once as a conductus motet

---

21.   Similar procedures may be seen in the motets on the tenor *Domino* in HAM, Nos. 28f and 28g.

22.   L. Dittmer, *The Worcester Fragments* (MSD, 2, 1957), p. 155.

with both duplum and triplum of the complete three-voice clausula.[23] Neither of these texts has anything to do with the liturgical function of the clausula or with the words "Ex semine" in the tenor. *Hyer mein* is a miniature pastourelle of the type cultivated by the troubadours and trouvères (see Chapters XI and XII). *Se j'ai amé* is a love song couched in such vague terms, characteristically, that it might express devotion either to an earthly lady or to the Virgin Mary. It is obvious, in any case, that the two French texts have no connection with tropes beyond the fact that they were written to fit a preexisting melisma.

We should probably relate the appearance of motets with French texts to the medieval penchant for making contrafacta rather than to the process of troping. In the present instance, French contrafacta gave the motet a new social function as a secular amusement and established a close relationship between it and contemporary forms of secular song. We must therefore turn back to investigate the rise of monophonic songs in both Latin and the vernacular. Armed with knowledge of earlier literary and musical activity, we can better understand the sudden emergence of secular polyphony in the thirteenth century and better follow the development of the motet into an independent musical form.

23. For these motets, see the facsimile edition of *W_2*, fols. 233v, 247, and 136.

CHAPTER XI

Secular Monophonic Song, I: Latin and Provençal Lyrics

The accidents of history have made it seem that music remained for centuries the exclusive property of the Church. It is highly improbable, however, that song and dance played no part in secular amusements at all levels of society. Unfortunately, information about these amusements before A.D. 1000 is scanty indeed, and whatever music there was has vanished almost without a trace. Not until the rebirth of European civilization in the eleventh century did conditions become favorable for the development and preservation of secular songs. Even then, scribes often copied the poetry without the music or used a notation that cannot now be read. But we do begin to have tangible evidence that the secular spirit, as well as the religious, stimulated the creation of poetry and song. From this time on, the influence of that secular spirit on the development of music will be enormous. Its most immediate effect will be the additional insight we have into the pains, pleasures, and vices of medieval man, so vividly recorded in the lyric poetry of the Middle Ages.

LATIN SONGS

The origin of Latin lyric poetry in the Middle Ages is probably to be found in the hymns of the Church rather than in the classical poetry of antiquity. Verses of Horace, Vergil, and others occasionally received musical settings, but for the most part the development of secular songs in Latin paralleled the later history of liturgical poetry. Indeed, the dividing line between sacred and secular lyrics is often difficult to determine. Here, as everywhere, the two aspects of medieval life were inextricably entwined.

We may begin to explore the limits of the two areas of Latin songs in the works of Venantius Fortunatus, "the oldest medieval poet of France." Born in Italy about 530, Fortunatus "had his youth and learning in Ravenna."[1] Hence, he has also been called the last of the Italian poets. Why Fortunatus came to the North we do not know, but from his poetry we learn that he spent some years at Frankish courts before

---

1. Helen Waddell, *The Wandering Scholars*, p. 25.

Castle-fortresses, such as the famous one at Sully, dominated the medieval land-scape, providing the setting for the courtly art of secular song.

settling in Poitiers, where he became a priest and eventually Bishop of Poitiers. He died in 609. Perhaps it is not just a coincidence that, after several centuries had elapsed, the region of western France south of the Loire valley should also produce both the sacred lyrics of the Limoges school and the secular art of the troubadours. Because of his years as a courtier-poet, indeed, Fortunatus has won still a third title: "the first troubadour of the Western world."[2]

Much of Fortunatus's poetry may be classified as occasional, brought forth by specific events, situations, or personal relationships. Even his magnificent *Vexilla Regis prodeunt* (The banners of the King go forth; LU, p. 575) celebrated the arrival of part of the True Cross in Poitiers. This "greatest Processional of the Middle Ages"—the favorite hymn of the Crusaders five centuries later—may well be regarded as the ancestor of the conductus. Other types of subject matter that Fortunatus established as worthy of poetic treatment reappear in later Latin lyrics. Poems extol the virtues of kings and queens or celebrate their coronations and marriages. Princes of the Church and the ceremonies of their installation received similar honors. Epitaphs subsequently enjoyed considerable importance. Apparently intended for the funeral service, rather than for engraving on a tombstone, they anticipate the later *planctus* (lament) on the death of a famous person. Laments too may have formed part of funeral or commemorative services. In some cases, at least, the presence of a doxology or prayer at the close, followed by an Amen, suggests a liturgical function.

However, laments soon outgrew this rather limited function when

2. L. Schrade, "Political Compositions in French Music of the 12th and 13th Centuries," AnM, 1, p. 12.

the range of lamentable subject matter was broadened. They became an important element in liturgical drama and appear in the twelfth and thirteenth centuries in the vernacular poetry of the troubadours and trouvères. Occasional examples, in Latin or the vernacular, continue to receive musical settings throughout the Middle Ages and the Renaissance. With the rise of opera in the seventeenth century, laments once again become a conventional element in dramatic forms. In the same period, lute and keyboard composers, especially in France, transformed the lament into the instrumental *tombeau* (tombstone or memorial).[3]

This long and varied history of the lament makes it doubly regrettable that we do not know more about the earliest examples. Several planctus from the seventh to the eleventh centuries exist in various manuscripts, but their melodies, when present, are written in staffless neumes. Two of the oldest, each of which is still called an *epitafion,* commemorate the Visigothic king of Spain Chindasvinthus (641–652) and his queen, Reciberga (d. 657).[4] A more famous example is the *Planctus Karoli,* a lament for Charlemagne that must have been written shortly after his death in 814.[5] Despite the neumatic notation of these early laments, we are not left entirely in the dark as to the nature of their melodies. As we noted in Chapter VI, a few sequences with double cursus are actually laments. Their melodies, too, are lost to us; but other sequences with double cursus, such as *Rex caeli,* suggest what their musical characteristics may have been. More positive evidence comes from a number of sequence melodies that are entitled *Planctus.* A particularly instructive example is the *Planctus cygni* (Lament of the swan), a melody mentioned as early as the third quarter of the ninth century which served for several different texts in the years 950–1200. Formally, the *Planctus cygni* is a regular sequence, with eight double verses framed by single verses at the beginning and end. The distinctive aspect of the melody is its almost excessive reiteration of a single motive in slightly varied forms. This motive stands at the beginning of phrase 1, but it does not begin to dominate the melody until after the material has been transposed up a fifth in phrase 5. As may be seen in Example XI–1, the motive in its original form and in the four- and six-note variants (a^1 and a^2) provides almost the entire substance of phrases 6–8.[6] Such dependence on one motivic figure—not at all characteristic of sacred chant—may well represent the contemporary style of secular song, at least for texts similar to the lament in form and content.

---

3.   A more recent example is *Le Tombeau de Couperin,* a suite for piano by Maurice Ravel.

4.   For facsimiles from a tenth-century manuscript, see H. Anglès, *El Còdex musical de Las Huelgas,* 1, p. 26.

5.   See E. de Coussemaker, *Histoire de l'harmonie au moyen âge* (Paris, 1852), Plate I.

6.   For the complete melody, see B. Stäblein, "Die Schwanenklage. Zum Problem Lai—Planctus—Sequenz," *Festschrift Karl Gustav Fellerer* (Regensburg, 1962), p. 494.

Example XI–1: *Motivic Reiteration in the* Planctus cygni

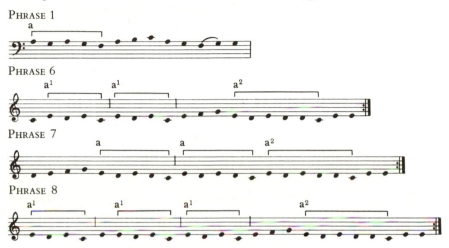

PHRASE 1

PHRASE 6

PHRASE 7

PHRASE 8

The real development of secular Latin poetry intended for singing begins in the eleventh century. Probably we should regard it as a by-product of the secular spirit that increasingly pervaded monastic and cathedral schools. Study of pagan poets—Vergil, Horace, and Ovid among them—became commonplace. Ostensibly this study was for the purpose of learning to write poetry in classical meters. In reality, it seems to reflect the more worldly interests that characterized the period. Certainly the study of ancient authors often resulted in poetry that was anything but sacred. What was particularly prized was "a mixture of scholarship with a measure of obscenity."[7] Indeed, the obscenity sometimes got out of hand, and medieval scholars did not shrink from writing verses that modern editors have not dared to publish, even in the decent obscurity of Latin. The great bulk of poetry in classical meters—and it was produced in enormous quantities in the eleventh and twelfth centuries—was not intended for singing. Nevertheless, its authors acquired a skill in versification that they put to good use when they came to write lyric poetry in the new rhythmic forms. The development of these forms parallels the development of sacred poetry touched on in previous discussions of tropes, sequences, and liturgical drama.

THE CAMBRIDGE SONGS

One of the oldest collections of Latin songs is found in an eleventh-century manuscript now in the University of Cambridge library—hence the more than forty poems in this collection are commonly called the "Cambridge Songs." This is somewhat of a misnomer. Earlier, the

7.   F. J. E. Raby, *A History of Secular Latin Poetry in the Middle Ages,* 2 vols. (Oxford, 1934), 2, p. 177.

manuscript belonged to the Augustinian monastery at Canterbury, and the songs themselves seem to be of continental origin. With few exceptions, the melodies of these songs have been lost to us; but the texts illustrate the wide range of subject matter that the Latin lyric was now able to encompass. Religious poems mingle with laments, songs in praise of kings and bishops, comic folk tales, and erotic poems that the good Augustinians evidently felt obliged to erase or blot out with varying degrees of success.[8]

Several of the Cambridge Songs appear in another manuscript with titles that include the word *modus*. This term evidently indicates a well-known melody to which the poem is to be sung, but the titles are now generally attached to the poems themselves. The subject matter of these pieces varies greatly. A purely religious poem bears the title *Modus Qui et Carelmanninc,* which means that it and a song on Charlemagne are sung to the same melody. The *Modus Ottinc*—which phrase appears in the opening lines—glorifies the Saxon Emperors Otto I (936–973), Otto II (973–983), and Otto III (983–1002). It may have been written for the imperial coronation of Otto III in 996 and is perhaps the oldest of the Cambridge Songs. The poem sung to the *Modus Liebinc* (Melody of the song of Liebo) puts into learned language the facetious legend of the Snow-Child, a tale that has been judged fit for the Decameron. This story, together with a fourth poem, a liar's tale, involves Swabians, and both poems bear amusing witness that ethnic jokes are nothing new. The real interest of these poems, however, lies in a relationship that their disparate texts fail to suggest. Their titles remind us of those for sequence melodies, and all four of the poems are written in the form of a sequence.[9] Thus the texts clearly establish a close relationship between sacred and secular song, even though the melodies remain unknown.[10] We may even regard these secular sequences adapted to preexisting tunes as supporting evidence for the theory that elements of popular song found their way into the melodies of liturgical sequences.

One of the Cambridge Songs is of particular importance because a happy chance has preserved its melody. *O admirabile Veneris idolum* (O lovely image of Venus) is a lovesong to a boy, apparently written in the neighborhood of Verona on the Adige River. Each of the three stanzas has a single rhyme, and the learned style and Greek expressions "stamp it as a typically monkish tour de force."[11] This poem is one of only two that have musical notation in the Cambridge manuscript,

8.   K. Breul, *The Cambridge Songs,* includes a facsimile of the manuscript.
9.   The four poems are printed in ibid., but *Modus Ottinc, Modus Liebinc,* and *Modus Florum* are more readily available—with English translations—in E. H. Zeydel, *Vagabond Verse,* pp. 212–31.
10. For a facsimile of the opening lines of *Modus Ottinc* with the melody in staffless neumes, see Coussemaker, *Histoire,* Plate VIII.
11. Zeydel, *Vagabond Verse,* p. 213.

where staffless neumes appear above the first two stanzas. A Vatican manuscript (Vatican, lat. 3327) couples this poem and a pilgrim's song, *O Roma nobilis* (O noble Rome), with the same poetic form and the same melody, again in staffless neumes. Still a third manuscript, this time from Monte Cassino, preserves the more respectable text with its melody notated in letters of the Guidonian hexachord.[12] It thus becomes possible to "restore" the melody of *O admirabile Veneris idolum* as it appears in the Cambridge Songs (Example XI–2).[13]

Example XI–2: O admirabile Veneris idolum

1. O ad-mi - ra - bi - le · Ve- ne-ris i - do - lum,
2. Cu-ius ma - te - ri - e ni-hil est fri - vo - lum,
3. Ar-chos te pro - te - gat qui stel-las et po - lum,
4. Fe - cit et ma - ri - a con-di - dit et so - lum.

5. Fu-ris in - ge - ni - o non sen-ti - as do - lum,

6. Clo-to te di - li - gat, que ba-jo - lat co - lum.

> O lovely image of Venus, in whom there is no flaw, may Archos, who made the stars and the heavens, the earth and the seas, protect you. May you not suffer from thievish cunning. May Clotho who bears the distaff love you.[14]

The melody in Example XI–2 is of considerable interest for a number of reasons. Because it remains within the hard hexachord (on **G**) and also ends on **G**, it seems to be in the major mode, an effect that will be characteristic of many troubadour and trouvère songs. The simple, almost completely syllabic style of the melody seems to reduce the pretentious learning of the text to the level of a popular song. In this connection, it is noteworthy that the later versions in the Vatican and Monte Cassino manuscripts provide a more elaborate and extended cadence for the final phrase.[15] The rhythms and note values in modern transcriptions, of course, represent no more than editorial opinions. Probably the melody should be sung freely, with the rhythms adapted to fit the sometimes different word accents of the individual lines. This

12. Facsimile in NOHM, 2, facing p. 221.
13. The version given here differs in some details from Ex. 86 in NOHM, 2, p. 221. The latter purports to be a transcription of the Cambridge version, but it introduces some variants from the Monte Cassino manuscript.
14. The complete text with a poetic translation may be found in Zeydel, *Vagabond Verse*, p. 235.
15. For *O Roma nobilis*, see Gleason, EM, p. 7.

repetition of several poetic lines to the same melody is the most interesting aspect of O admirabile and one of the surest indications of its age. In
the first stanza the first four lines are sung to phrase a, and the last two,
to phrases b and b'. The second stanza has seven lines, and phrase a now
serves the first five. These multiple repetitions recall procedures in the
sequence with double cursus, but they also suggest a relationship with
the method of performing long narrative poems such as the chansons de
geste (see Chapter XII). With a minimum of musical material, the wandering entertainer, goliard, or jongleur could sing poems or stanzas of
any length. The melody of O admirabile may well be characteristic of
popular song both in its own and in later times. When more aristocratic
and sophisticated levels of society began to cultivate the secular song,
the musical forms became much more varied and complex.

WANDERING SCHOLARS, GOLIARDS, JONGLEURS

The question of who created and who performed the Latin lyrics of the
later Middle Ages is difficult to answer. Many of the poems are anonymous, and it has long been the custom to use the terms "wandering
scholars" and "goliards" as interchangeable designations for their unknown authors. In reality, the two terms are not synonymous. The
wandering scholars might more properly be called wandering clerics
who failed to procure a permanent position in the Church or who preferred an independent and vagabond life. We may regard them as free-
lance writers whose talents were at the disposal of whatever patron
would provide them with a livelihood. Nevertheless, they remained
clerics; and, however badly some of them may have behaved, they enjoyed the privileges of their class and the protection of the Church. The
goliards, on the other hand, were dropouts from the religious life. The
name is believed to derive from a combination of gula (gullet) and Golias
(Goliath), reflecting the goliards' reputation for gluttony. Golias thus
became the mythical head of an equally mythical Order of Goliards and
figures as the supposed author and hero of many songs which celebrate
the pleasures of the tavern—eating, drinking, and gambling—or the
delights of amorous adventures. By the thirteenth century, goliardus was
a term of reproach and of contempt, but it did not apply to men such as
Philip the Chancellor or to the three great poets of the twelfth century:
Hugh Primas of Orléans, Walter of Châtillon, and the Archpoet.[16]
Their subjects may often have been unscholarly, but these were educated men, poets of great skill and power who were rightfully proud of
their artistry.

Even lower than the goliards in the social scale stood the wandering

16.   Zeydel, Vagabond Verse, gives information about these men with examples of their
      poems.

entertainers known in Latin as *joculatores* or *histriones* and in French as *jongleurs*. The literal meaning of *jongleurs* is "jugglers," but these men—and women—were much more than that. Jacks-of-all-amusements, the jongleurs functioned as dancers, singers, and instrumentalists; as acrobats, mimes, and storytellers; as performers of sleights of hand, and trainers of dancing bears. Such varied entertainment was enthusiastically received in ecclesiastical and secular courts as well as in the marketplace, but the entertainers themselves remained social outcasts. Better a cleric should become a grocer or a baker than a jongleur. Nevertheless, the jongleurs performed a useful function in society that went beyond mere diversion. As a rule uneducated and neither poets nor composers, the jongleurs were singers of other men's songs, and their vagrant life gave those songs the widest possible dissemination. In this way, at least, the jongleurs contributed to the flowering of both the Latin lyric and the vernacular songs of the troubadours and trouvères.

THE *CARMINA BURANA*

Of all the manuscripts that preserve secular Latin songs, the largest and most notorious is the so-called *Carmina Burana*. This collection was apparently assembled late in the thirteenth century at the Benedictine monastery of Benediktbeuern, south of Munich. Commissioned by some wealthy patron, perhaps an abbot or bishop, the manuscript remained in the library of Benediktbeuern until 1803. It was then confiscated and brought to Munich, where it is now Codex latinus 4660 in the Bavarian State Library. In 1847, the librarian J. A. Schmeller published the poems and gave his edition the title *Carmina Burana* (Songs of Bene-

One of the less serious aspects of medieval life, as represented in the *Carmina Burana* (Munich, Bavarian State Library).

diktbeuern), by which the collection has been known ever since. An undetermined number of pages are missing from the manuscript, but even so it contains over 200 poems.

The notoriety of the *Carmina Burana* rests largely on its gambling and drinking songs, its irreverent and sometimes blasphemous parodies of religious songs and services, and its love songs that often flaunt an "unmatched obscenity." But other, more serious kinds of poems are also included. Some 55 songs belong in a class generally described as "moral-satiric," and the manuscript contains six religious plays. The bulk of the collection, however, consists of 35 vagabond songs and 131 love songs.[17] Within these large categories, the songs are divided into more than twenty smaller groups. On the whole, related subject matter determines the contents of these groups, but occasionally poetic form is the deciding factor. Many groups close with a "versus" in classical Latin meter after a series of poems in the rhymed and rhythmic forms found in sacred poetry and liturgical drama. Another peculiarity of the *Carmina Burana* is its inclusion of about forty-eight songs in German. The dialect of these songs is Bavarian, and some are based on poems by Minnesingers of the late thirteenth century. While the German texts thus help to establish the manuscript's place and date of origin, the Latin songs represent the poetic activity of all of western Europe over a much broader span of time. Other copies of the Latin texts occur chiefly in manuscripts of French and English origin, and some of the poems were written in the twelfth century or even earlier. It is the international and all-inclusive aspects of the collection that give the *Carmina Burana* its importance in the history of medieval Latin song.

We know very little about the melodies for the poems in the *Carmina Burana,* but we may assume that all or most of them were meant to be sung. Several poems have melodies notated in staffless neumes, and in some cases space has been left for musical notation. Fortunately, a number of poems appear in other sources with a notation that can still be read. From these few examples, we may gain some idea of the musical forms and styles associated with Latin lyric poetry.

Most of the *Carmina Burana* poems that occur elsewhere with a legible musical notation are found in manuscripts devoted primarily to sacred music. Occasionally, a love song found its way into a collection of tropes and sequences, but chiefly settings of moral-satiric poems have been preserved. No fewer than eighteen such poems turn up in the Notre Dame manuscripts. Some are polyphonic conducti for two or three voices, but the large collection of monophonic pieces in **F** also includes a few poems from the *Carmina Burana.* One of these will demonstrate how close the relationship between sacred and secular song could be.

17. The count is Zeydel's (ibid. p. 38).

Olim sudor Herculis (Once the sweat of Hercules; AMM, No. 39) is preserved in several sources; and in both the *Carmina Burana* and the Florence manuscript it appears among other poems in sequence form. It is significant that the *Carmina Burana* designates these poems as *jubili.* Evidently the scribe still recognized the connection between sequences and the melismas of Alleluias, no matter what the subject matter of his poems might be. Although it appears among love songs in the *Carmina Burana, Olim sudor Herculis* is actually a "song against love." In typically learned fashion, the poet uses the classical story of Hercules to make his point. Entanglements with women dimmed the renown Hercules had won by his twelve great labors. A refrain then drives the moral home: Love tarnishes glory. The lover does not regret time squandered but rashly dissipates himself under the yoke of Venus. Moral as the poem is, we are far from the normal subject matter of the religious sequence.

In its poetic and musical form, *Olim sudor Herculis* also differs strikingly from the contemporary sequence as exemplified by the works of Adam de St. Victor. Indeed, the differences are perhaps more notable than the similarities. To justify classification as a sequence, four double stanzas—or pairs of stanzas—have four different melodies, each of which is repeated for the second member of the pair. But there the resemblance to the sequence ends. The first and most obvious departure from the norm is the presence of a refrain, although there is some doubt as to when and where it should be sung. Some sources indicate its performance after each half-stanza, eight times in all. In **F,** the refrain—with its music—follows stanza 1a; thereafter, the text incipit of the refrain occurs only after stanzas 1b, 2b, and 4b. Its omission after stanza 3b may have resulted from lack of space. In any case, we have some justification for assuming that performance of the refrain after each pair of stanzas was an acceptable procedure. The resulting combination of sequence structure with a refrain would give the form *aaR bbR ccR ddR.*

Closer inspection of *Olim sudor Herculis* reveals other ways in which it differs from religious sequences. Instead of the formal simplicity and regularity of later sequence texts, the individual stanzas of this poem are longer and more complex. Moreover, each pair of stanzas has its own rhyme scheme and its own distinctive arrangement of long and short lines. The variety and complexity of these different forms may be seen in the schematic representation below where letters indicate lines and rhymes, and subscript numbers the number of syllables in each line. Use of the same letters in each rhyme scheme is merely a convenience and does not mean that the same rhymes recur in all stanzas or even in both members of a pair. A few rhymes do appear in different stanzas, and in the first two pairs some rhymes in the first member recur at the same place in the second. This procedure evidently proved too difficult to maintain, and the rhymes in the last two pairs of stanzas are completely independent.

Stanzaic Forms in Olim sudor Herculis

Stanzas	Forms
1a & b	a_7 b_7 b_7 a_7 c_4 c_7 d_7 d_7 d_7 e_7
2a & b	a_7 a_7 b_8 c_4 d_7 d_7 b_8 c_4 c_7 b_8
3a &b	a_6 b_6 a_6 b_6 b_7 b_7 c_7 d_7 d_4 e_7 e_4 c_3
4a & b	a_7 a_4 b_7 b_4 c_4 c_7 d_7 d_4 e_3 f_7 f_4 e_3
Refrain	a_7 b_3 a_7 b_3 c_4 c_4 c_4 b_3

The intricacy of poetic structure in *Olim sudor Herculis* naturally affects the musical setting, but the differing phrase lengths do not always correspond with the poetic lines. Because lines of three or four syllables do not make satisfactory musical phrases in syllabic style, they are generally combined or attached to longer lines. The end result, however, is an irregularity of phrase structure in sharp contrast to the equal phrases of the later religious sequence. Both textually and musically, *Olim sudor* more closely resembles the forms of the vernacular lai (see Chapter XII).

Motivic repetition does not play an important role in organizing the melody of *Olim sudor Herculis,* but we should note the four sequential phrases at the close of stanza 1 and the exact repetition in the fourth and fifth phrases of stanza 2. Stylistically, the melody retains at least some of the syllabic character of the sequence. The most obvious departure occurs in the opening melisma, but ornamental figures from two to six notes in length appear frequently throughout the piece.

Not all nonliturgical sequences are equally restrained in their use of vocal ornament. As an extreme example, we may cite *In hoc ortus* (In this garden), the sequence that follows *Olim sudor* in **F** (fol. 417v). Shorter melismas occur in all of the different melodies for the three double stanzas, but the closing melisma of the second stanza reaches a peak of vocal extravagance (Example XI–3). We might almost conclude that the piece was written to show off the coloratura singing of a virtuoso performer.

Example XI–3: In hoc ortus, *Closing Melisma of Second Stanza (**F**, fol. 418)*

To illustrate a completely different kind of Latin song, a setting of one of the finest love poems in the *Carmina Burana* is included in AMM, No. 40. *Sic mea fata canendo solor* (Singing thus I ease my sorrows) appears to be a typical song of youth and love. Yet the poem can hardly be the product of a callow dropout from school. Years of experience must lie behind such craftsmanship. Comparable skill and sensitivity went into the fashioning of the unexpectedly simple melody. By subtly varying a minimum of musical material, the composer enhanced the emotional content of the poem without disguising its complex structure. The net result is music of haunting beauty that ranks among the great achievements of lyric song in the Middle Ages.

In the *Carmina Burana, Sic mea fata* has a third stanza that modern editors reject as a later addition. An older and better version of only the first two stanzas appears with music in a manuscript from the Abbey of St. Martial in Limoges.[18] One would like to imagine that the monks devoted their spare moments to the creation and enjoyment of such beguiling poetry and music. In any case, the presence of *Sic mea fata* in a manuscript from Limoges brings us back to the region of southwestern France that had already seen the creation of the vernacular love lyric by the troubadours.

THE TROUBADOURS

Why the region of France south of the Loire and west of the Rhone river valleys should have become the birthplace of vernacular song remains a mystery. Like all mysteries, it has received many and often divergent explanations: the relative peace and prosperity of the region as a whole; the wealth and luxury enjoyed by the aristocracy; the survival of Latin culture; contact with the Moslems in Spain; even an opposition to Catholicism stemming from the monotheistic heresy of the Visigoths. Whatever the truth of these explanations may be—and they all may have some measure of validity—it is undeniable that the history of lyric poetry in the modern languages of western Europe begins with the troubadours. (The name comes from the Provençal verb *trobar,* meaning "to find" or "to compose in verse.")

The first known troubadour is William IX, Count of Poitiers and Duke of Aquitaine (1071–1127). William's technical skill as a poet suggests that he had models from which he learned the art of versification, but the nature and identity of those models remain controversial. Almost equally controversial are questions concerning the literary language in which the troubadours wrote and what that language should be called.

The one demonstrable antecedent for both the poetic forms and the melodic style of the early troubadours is the Latin repertory of St. Martial, particularly the versus.[19] Significantly, *vers* was the first general

18. Paris, Bibl. Nat., lat. 3719, fol. 88.
19. J. Chailley, *L'École musicale de Saint-Martial de Limoges* (Paris, 1960), p. 370 ff.

designation of troubadour songs in the vernacular. That vernacular goes by several names: one is *langue d'oc,* which distinguishes it from the *langue d'oïl* of northern France on the basis of the different words for *yes: oc* and *oïl (oui* in modern French). Another name commonly given to the language of the troubadours is *Provençal.* Objections to both names arise from the existence of former provinces in southern France known as Provence and Languedoc. Few troubadours had any connection with Provence, and langue d'oc was spoken far beyond the boundaries of both provinces (see Map 4, p. 269). The French have recently adopted a third name, *occitan,* as the official designation of both the medieval and modern language of southern France. This name has the advantage of applying to the entire area south of the linguistic boundary with French, but it has yet to win general acceptance outside of France. Particularly in English-speaking countries, the name Provençal remains so firmly entrenched that its continued use here should cause no confusion. It need only be remembered that we are talking about Old Provençal and that the region of Provence was far from being the center of troubadour activity.

William IX's titles already suggest that the troubadour movement began in the westerly regions of southern France, and most of the early activity took place at aristocratic courts in the areas surrounding Poitiers, Limoges, and Toulouse—the provinces of Poitou, Limousin, and western Languedoc. It was in these regions that the troubadours created a literary language and a poetic style that were adopted wherever Provençal was spoken and imitated in many other languages. These developments came quickly, but not quite as soon as might have been ex-

Portraits of two early troubadours, William IX of Aquitaine and Folquet of Marseilles (Paris, Bibliothèque Nationale).

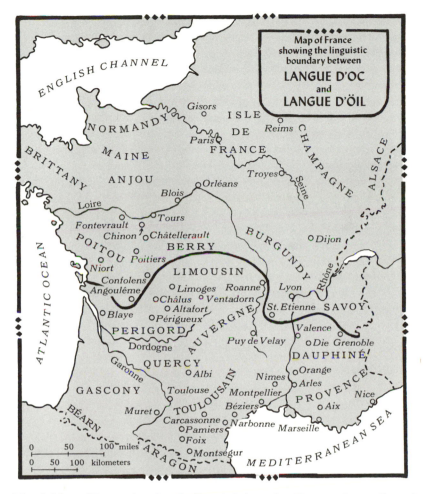

Map 4: Map of France showing the linguistic boundary between *langue d'oc* and *langue d'oïl*.

pected. William IX of Aquitaine stands alone as the only known troubadour in the first quarter of the twelfth century. Eleven of his poems survive, but without music except for one incomplete melody. Poetic activity and the number of troubadours increased only slightly in the twenty years after William's death. From this period, the names of three important poets are known to us: Cercamon, Marcabru, and Jaufre Rudel. Although their medieval biographies say that Marcabru learned his trade under Cercamon, the two men seem to have flourished at approximately the same time. Marcabru must also have known Jaufre Rudel, for he closes one poem with the wish to send "both words and tune to Jaufre Rudel beyond the sea." Rudel apparently took part in the second Crusade (1147–49), from which he did not return.

Of Cercamon, some eight poems without music survive, whereas we have over forty poems and four melodies of Marcabru, seven poems and four melodies of Rudel. Even this increase of productivity scarcely prepares us for the tremendous outpouring of troubadour poetry that occurred in the second half of the twelfth century. During this time, the Provençal lyric reached the high point of its development and began to make its influence felt outside of southern France. Before the activity of the troubadours came to a close in the latter part of the thirteenth century, they had produced an astonishing amount of poetry. We cannot know how much has been lost, but approximately 2600 poems by more than 450 authors have been preserved. The music for these poems, unfortunately, did not fare as well. About 275 melodies by 42 troubadours are all that have survived.[20] In Table 10, some of the most important troubadours are listed in approximately chronological order. The periods of activity are also approximate and necessarily overlap to some extent.[21] Additional numbers in the last column indicate melodies that have been "discovered" because they appear with other texts, usually Latin or French, that have the stanzaic forms of particular troubadour songs. There is no proof, however, that we are dealing with contrafacta whose melodies originated for use with the Provençal texts.

Table 10: *The Poetic and Musical Legacy of Important Troubadours*

Period of Activity	Troubadours	Number of Poems	Number of Melodies
1086–1127	William IX of Aquitaine	11	¼ + 1
1130–1150	Cercamon	8	—
	Marcabru	40	4 + 3
	Jaufre Rudel	7	4
1140–1190	Bernart de Ventadorn	45	19 + 1
	Berenguier de Palazol	12	8
	Arnaut de Maroill	26	6
	Guiraut de Borneill	80	13
1180–1220	Bertran de Born	45	1 + 3
	Peire Vidal	50	13
	Pons de Capdoill	27	4
	Folquet de Marseilla	27	13
	Arnaut Daniel	18	2
	Raimbaut de Vaqueiras	32	7
	Gaucelm Faidit	64	14
	Peirol	34	17
	Raimon de Miraval	47	22

20. F. Gennrich has published 302 melodies with Provençal texts in *Der musikalische Nachlass der Troubadours,* SMMA, 3 and 4. Not all qualify as troubadour songs, however. Some are sacred; some are taken from a *Mystery of St. Agnes;* a few are polyphonic motets.

21. Figures for the number of poems come from A. Pillet and H. Carstens, *Bibliographie der Troubadours* (Halle, 1933). The count of melodies is from Gennrich, *Nachlass.*

1220–1290	Peire Cardenal	70	3
	Uc de Saint Circ	44	3
	Guiraut Riquier	89	48
	Anonymous	about 250	23

The concentration of names between the years 1140 and 1220 clearly reveals the period when the art of the troubadours was at its height. The sudden decline and disappearance of that art must be blamed in large part on the so-called Albigensian Crusade against heretics in southern France (1209). One of the more infamous episodes in the history of Christianity, this misnamed war between the North and South utterly destroyed the civilized society in which the troubadour movement had flourished. With few exceptions, those troubadours who survived found shelter and patronage in Sicily, northern Italy, and at the courts of Spanish kings. Their influence on vernacular song in those countries will become apparent in Chapter XIII. The latter part of the thirteenth century produced only one great Provençal poet, Guiraut Riquier (c. 1254–84), "the last of the troubadours," who spent much of his short life in Spain.

The appearance of troubadour poetry marks the beginning of a new era in the history of Western literature and music. Vernacular song now flourishes side by side with Latin, which it first stimulates and then replaces. The influences that vernacular and Latin secular song exercised on each other are difficult to trace, for many of the same poetic forms and themes appear in both. There can be little doubt, however, that the troubadour movement contributed much to the brilliant flowering of the Latin lyric in the twelfth and thirteenth centuries. Even more important was the influence of the troubadours on the development of vernacular song in other regions of western Europe. In addition to stimulating the production of such song, they developed many of its poetic forms and techniques and established most of its literary themes.

TYPES AND FORMS OF TROUBADOUR POETRY

Until the end of the twelfth century, the troubadours most often used the term *vers* to designate any poem destined to be sung. During this same period, however, they began to attach more precise names to particular types of poems. By far the most important of these types was the love song, known as *canso,* or *chanso* in the northern dialects (*chanson* in French). We now tend to think of chansons as being merely songs in general, but for the troubadours the canso was exclusively a love song. In it they established the conventions of *l'amour courtois* (courtly love); to it they devoted their best efforts; and from it they won their greatest acclaim.

The next most important type of song, at least from the point of view of quantity, was the *sirventes*. Because a sirventes normally adopted the poetic form—and melody—of a preexisting canso, one explanation of the name sees the song itself as a servant. In the more generally accepted view, the sirventes was originally a "song of service" for the noble lord in whose household the troubadour was a retainer (*sirven*). Later, the term was used for a song on almost any topic except love. Many sirventes were devoted to personal, literary, or moral satire. Personal and literary satire often sank to the level of insults, invective, and ridicule of physical defects; but some of the moral satires give a vivid picture of contemporary life and manners. Other sirventes deal with political subjects or call for volunteers in the Crusades. Even the infamous Albigensian Crusade found apologists to write some of these propaganda pieces. More impassioned and more moving are the sirventes of later troubadours, such as Peire Cardenal, which deplore the aftermath of the Crusade. With bitter irony, these sirventes attack clerks, the French, and—above all—the Inquisition as the causes of their distress. The most famous author of sirventes, however, was the earlier troubadour Bertran de Born, who left us some twenty-five poems in this genre. Perhaps the strength of Bertran's partisan attacks was partly responsible for the severity with which Dante meted out his infernal punishment (see p. 285, fn. 2).

Two subspecies of sirventes worthy of mention are the *enueg* and the *planh*. In the enueg (French, *ennui* = "annoyance" or "nuisance"), the poet vents his spleen on aspects of life he finds particularly irritating. The enueg thus gives another and often highly personal view of contemporary social conditions. Even more personal, though in a different way, was the planh, the Provençal form of the Latin planctus. In some cases, these laments express grief with a sincerity and an emotional intensity that many other poems fail to achieve.

After the canso and sirventes, a third category of troubadour poetry includes several species that make use of dialogue in one way or another. Among these, poetic debates were especially popular. When the argument developed freely, the poem was usually identified by the general term *tenso* (dispute). Many tensos are the work of two troubadours who reply to each other in alternate stanzas, sometimes with a good bit of personal invective and ridicule. Disputes with supernatural beings, allegorical figures, animals, or inanimate objects, on the other hand, are obviously the work of a single poet. Closely related to the tenso is the *partimen* or *joc parti* (a divided or shared "game"). The partimen more closely resembles a modern debate in that the poet proposes alternatives and allows his adversary to choose which he will defend. Such debates often close with an appeal to arbiters who decide the winner of the argument.

An entirely different kind of debate occurs in the *pastorela,* a type of pastoral poetry that enjoyed an astonishing vogue. A knight, riding in the countryside, meets a shepherdess whom he addresses with frankly dishonorable intent. After a more or less extended discussion between the two, virtue usually—but not always—succumbs. Such a stereotyped pattern could have interested so many poets and, presumably, so many audiences only because it was the manner of presentation, not the subject itself, that mattered. Perhaps too the attraction lay in devising new arguments for seduction and new ways of countering them. The possibility of failure on the part of the knight may also have introduced an element of suspense. We may presume that the encounters described in pastorelas are usually imaginary. If they do represent knightly manners of the time, it is no wonder that the shepherdess so often has a father, brother, or lover within hailing distance.

Another important type of troubadour poetry is the *alba* or dawn song. Its traditional theme was the separation of two lovers at dawn (*alba*), after they had been wakened by the call of a watcher or the singing of birds. The poems generally concentrate either on the regrets of the lovers at parting or on the urgent warnings of the watcher. Usually, each stanza ends with a refrain that announces the coming of dawn. In the famous *Reis glorios* (Glorious King) of Guiraut de Borneill,[22] for example, the refrain is "et ades sera l'alba" (and soon it will be dawn). It is symptomatic of twelfth-century morals that in *Reis glorios* a watching companion asks God's care for his amorous friend. Also symptomatic—and even more curious—are thirteenth-century albas that reveal the influence of the Inquisition. Night, the dawn, and the day now become Christian symbols of purity and salvation. But such aberrations could not erase memories of the alba's original content and meaning. Shakespeare recalls it in the tender dispute between Romeo and Juliet as to whether they heard a nightingale or a lark, "the herald of the morn" (Act III, scene 5). And Richard Wagner, writing an opera on the medieval legend of Tristan and Isolde, appropriately makes the second act an alba almost as long as the night itself.

DANCE SONGS

A final poetic type is the dance song, called *balada* or *dansa*. These were often put in the mouth of a woman and commonly issue gay and carefree invitations to enjoy life, to love, and to revile the jealous, that is, husbands. Some of their texts suggest a connection with May Day festivities in which choral song and dance played a prominent part. The troubadours produced only a small number of dance songs celebrating the joys of returning spring, but two are among the most famous Pro-

22. HAM, No. 18c.

vençal songs. *Kalenda Maya* (The first of May), by Raimbaut de Vaqueiras, is in the form of an instrumental dance known as *estampida,* or *estampie* in French (see Chapter XIV). The medieval account of Raimbaut's life is probably correct in reporting that he wrote the poem to fit the tune of a dance he heard two French jongleurs play at the Court of Montferrat. *Kalenda Maya* is actually a love song addressed to a lady to whose husband the poet wants to give real cause for jealousy. A more typical dance song is the anonymous poem *A l'entrada del tens clar* (At the beginning of the fair season). To show how much she is in love, a queen described as "April-like" (*avrilloza*) invites all maids and bachelors to join the joyous dance.[23]

POETIC AND MUSICAL FORMS OF TROUBADOUR SONGS

To a large extent the structure of troubadour poems is independent of their content. With few exceptions, poetic types are not associated with particular poetic or musical forms. Whatever the poetic type, the form is almost invariably strophic, with an indefinite number of stanzas identical in structure and sung to the same melody. After the regular stanzas, many poems conclude with one or more *tornadas* (*envois* in French), usually addressed to some person: a lady, a patron, or the arbiter of a debate. As a rule, a tornada consists of three or four lines with the same forms and rhymes as the concluding lines of the last complete stanza. They would therefore be sung to the corresponding phrases at the close of the melody. English poetry has adopted the term *envoy* from the French *envoi* with its meaning unchanged. The Provençal and French terms *cobla* and *couplet,* on the other hand, refer to complete stanzas and do not correspond to the English *couplet,* a pair of verses that rhyme with each other. The terms *cobla* and *couplet* frequently occur in discussions of troubadour and trouvère poetry, but to avoid confusion only the term *stanza* will be used here.

It would be a mistake to regard the constant use of strophic form as evidence of monotonous sameness in the structure of troubadour poetry. On the contrary, poets sought to create a new structural pattern for the stanzas of each new poem and to devise new ways of linking those stanzas together. In so doing, they managed to produce an incredible number of stanzaic forms that anticipated almost all later methods of organizing lyric poetry.[24] The striking contrast between the variety of forms and the sameness of themes in troubadour poetry clearly shows

23. For both *Kalenda maya* and *A l'entrada,* with their complete texts, see F. Gennrich, *Troubadours, Trouvères,* pp. 16 and 22.

24. The forms are catalogued in I. Frank, *Répertoire métrique de la poésie des troubadours,* 2 vols. Bibliothèque de l'École des Hautes Études, 302 and 308 (Paris, 1953–57).

that what mattered was not the subject itself but the manner of its presentation. The language of love is limited, after all, and the conventions of l'amour courtois further restricted the content of troubadour love poems. It is precisely in these poems—the cansos—that the troubadours exercised the greatest ingenuity in devising new stanzaic forms. As a rule, poems on subjects other than love are structurally less complex and use simpler rhymes and rhyming patterns. Many sirventes, it is true, adopted the form and melody of a canso, but even then the identity of rhymes was not always strictly maintained. This use of preexisting melodies for the sirventes probably accounts for the small number that have been preserved with music.

Narrative and dance songs generally have simple rhyme schemes and stanzaic forms that often include refrains of one or more lines. Refrains are particularly characteristic of dance songs, where, presumably, the entire group sang the refrains in alternation with a soloist who led the dance. A characteristic example is the balada cited above, *A l'entrada del tens clar* (see p. 274 and footnote 23). The first three lines in all five stanzas end with the refrain word "eya" (an interjection expressing joy and exhortation, such as "hey!" or "come!"). In addition, a complete refrain of indeterminate poetic structure closes all the stanzas. In some baladas, the refrain appears within the stanza and also at the beginning and end. Dansas, on the other hand, rarely have refrains, but when present, they are introductory and closing, not internal. The troubadours do not seem to have developed fixed patterns for their dance songs—partly, perhaps, because they wrote so few of them.[25] It remained for the trouvères of northern France to standardize the poetic and musical forms of dance songs with refrains.

A completely different kind of poetic and musical form is represented by the *lai* and *descort*. The distinction between these names is unclear and is usually based on identifications in the texts themselves. Also unclear is the intended meaning of *descort,* a term that seems to have been a troubadour invention. It has been variously interpreted as referring to the presentation of a sentimental disagreement (*descort*), to the use of different stanzaic forms within a single poem, or to some other irregularity. In a famous descort by Raimbaut de Vaqueiras, each of five stanzas is written in a different language: Provençal, Italian, French, Gascon, and Portuguese. The usual determining characteristic common to both lai and descort is a succession of stanzas that differ from each other in rhyme scheme and rhythmic structure. Each stanza, therefore, must have its own melody. Individual stanzas are normally subdivided into two or more units that have the same poetic structure and can be sung to

25. Ibid., 2, p. 70. The author lists only nine baladas and thirty dansas, of which some half dozen survive with their melodies. A dansa of Guiraut d'Espanha is published in Gennrich, *Troubadours,* p. 20. Frank's list (2, p. 58) of troubadour songs with refrains includes only three dansas.

the same music. The resulting overall form resembles that of the Latin sequence, particularly as it appears in such secular poems as *Olim sudor Herculis,* discussed earlier in this chapter. The texts of some descorts also suggest a relationship to the sequence with double cursus. Unfortunately, very little of the music for these poems has survived. Out of twenty-eight descorts and four lais in Provençal, we possess the melodies for only two descorts and two lais.[26] It seems best, therefore, to delay further consideration of the form until we find more numerous examples with music in the repertory of the trouvères.

To illustrate some of the ways in which the troubadours organized and related the stanzas of a poem, we shall examine the three songs included in AMM: Nos. 41–43. The first, *Quan lo rius de la fontana* (When the flow of the fountain), is a vers by Jaufre Rudel, famous for his fidelity to a distant love. (The second stanza of the poem, incidentally, destroys the myth that Rudel's love was strictly platonic.) Each of the five seven-line stanzas uses the same five rhymes: "-ana," "-ol," "-ina," "-am," "-anha." In the first two stanzas, these rhymes appear in the pattern abcdace; but in the last three, they are rearranged in the order cdabcae. Further subtleties include the similarity of the feminine rhymes ("-ana," "-ina," and "-anha") and the assonance of "-ana" and "-anha" with the masculine rhyme "-am."

Non es meravelha s'eu chan (It is no wonder if I sing), is a typical canso of Bernart de Ventadorn. It has a simpler, more symmetrical stanzaic form in which all eight lines of the stanza have eight syllables and end with masculine rhymes in the pattern abbacddc. Again the same rhymes occur in all stanzas, and again their order differs. In this case, however, only the similar rhymes "-an" and "-en" (a and c) are constantly interchanged so that the last rhyme of each stanza becomes the first rhyme of the next. The following diagram will clarify Bernart's method of linking the successive stanzas of his poem:

Stanza 1	a b b a c d d c
Stanza 2	c b b c a d d a
Stanza 3	a b b a c d d c
	etc.
Stanza 7	a b b a c d d c
Envoy	d d c

Marcabru found still another means of relating the stanzas of *L'autrier jost' una sebissa* (The other day by a hedge-row). In this pastorela, twelve stanzas are grouped in pairs (*coblas doblas*), with the same rhymes in both stanzas of each pair. Using a simple scheme with only two rhymes, aaabaab, Marcabru changes the first rhyme in each new pair of stanzas.

---

26.   The four melodies are published in Gennrich, *Nachlass,* Nos. 184 and 280–82.

The b rhyme ("-ana") thus functions as a refrain rhyme in all twelve stanzas. Moreover, the fourth line of every stanza ends with the refrain word "vilana," while stanzas 2, 4, 6, 8, and 10 expand the refrain to include the entire line " 'Senher,' so dis la vilana" ("My lord," said the peasant girl). In typically paradoxical fashion, Marcabru places the shepherdess in the better light. Her cutting and often enigmatic retorts to the banal proposals of the knight eventually reduce him to despair and silence. The complete rhyme scheme of this charming poem is as follows:

Stanzas	1 & 2	a	a	a	b	a	a	b
Stanzas	3 & 4	c	c	c	b	c	c	b
Stanzas	5 & 6	d	d	d	b	d	d	b
Stanzas	7 & 8	e	e	e	b	e	e	b
Stanzas	9 & 10	f	f	f	b	f	f	b
Stanzas	11 & 12	g	g	g	b	g	g	b
Envoys						g	g	b
						g	g	b

It should be apparent that the understanding and appreciation of troubadour verse depend on the careful examination of complete poems. Students of troubadour melodies have long faulted literary scholars for neglecting or ignoring the musical side of troubadour art. But musical scholars err in the other direction when they present only the first stanza of a poem with its melody. However valuable the practice may be as a space saver, it does a grave disservice to the poetry. We get a false impression of the music if we fail to recognize the repetition of rhymes or the presence of a refrain. To give the poet-composers all the credit they deserve, let us not overlook the intricate and subtle structures that the troubadours gave to their best poems. By combining these structures with the lovely sounds of the language, Provençal poetry becomes marvelous music by itself. Sensitivity to that music can only enhance our enjoyment of the melodies that the troubadours regarded as essential and worthy of their best efforts.

MUSICAL FORMS AND STYLES

Troubadour melodies are on a par with the poems in the ingenuity and diversity of their formal structures. Some melodies are continuous, with a different musical phrase for each line of text. Others repeat one or more phrases in a variety of patterns that often have little to do with the structure and rhyme scheme of the poems. In this regard, it will be instructive to compare the musical and poetic forms of the three pieces from AMM that we have just discussed.

In Jaufre Rudel's *Quan lo rius de la fontana,* repetition of musical phrases results in the pattern *ababcb'd* . We might even regard phrase *c* as a variation of phrase *a.* Its closing notes echo those of phrase *a* and provide the same link with phrase *b',* which now accommodates a feminine rather than a masculine rhyme. Only the final phrase stands in complete contrast to the others and thus enhances the effect of the seventh line's refrain rhyme. The differences between musical form and poetic rhyme scheme may be seen in the following diagram. (Letters indicate musical phrases and rhymes; figures, the number of syllables in a line. For feminine rhymes, a prime sign—'—follows the figure.)

Quan lo rius de la fontana

Poetic form:	a_7,	b_7	c_7,	d_7	a_7,	c_7,	e_7,
Musical form:	a	b	a	b	c	b'	d

In *Non es meravelha s'eu chan* of Bernart de Ventadorn, repeated phrases produce an entirely different form: *abcdaefd.* Similarities of range and melodic contour relate phrases *e* and *f* to phrases *b* and *c,* but it is the exact repetitions of phrases *a* and *d* that give the melody its distinctive form. Here, that form obviously reflects the poetic form, at least in part. As the a and c rhymes change places from stanza to stanza, they remain attached to the same two musical phrases. Each half-stanza is set to a continuous melody, however, despite its rhyme scheme of abba. A diagram will make clear these correspondences and divergences:

Non es meravelha s'eu chan

Poetic form:	1.	a_8	b_8	b_8	a_8	c_8	d_8	d_8	c_8	
	2.	c_8	b_8	b_8	c_8	a_8	d_8	d_8	a_8	etc.
Musical form:		a	b	c	d	a	e	f	d	

Phrase repetitions in Marcabru's pastorela contrast with the rhyme scheme in another way. The simplicity of that scheme in no way suggests the sophistication of the musical form *ababccd,* in which only the repetition of phrase *c* reflects a repeated rhyme. The music completely ignores the refrainlike function of the b rhyme, particularly in the fourth line of each stanza. Again, a diagram will clarify the discrepancies between poetic and musical structures.

L'autrier jost' una sebissa

Poetic form:	a_7,	a_7,	a_7,	b_7,	a_7,	a_7,	b_7,
Musical form:	a	b	a	b	c	c	d

Attempts to classify the forms of troubadour song tend to be more confusing than enlightening. By trying to reduce the many different forms to a few basic types, modern scholars tend to obscure the diversity that the troubadours took such pains to create. To designate musical forms by the names of poetic types can also be misleading. Many writers identify continuous melodies as vers or hymn form, and they also use the term *canso* for melodies in which a repetition of the first section produces an overall *aab* form. The result is utter confusion. As we have seen, *vers* was a general name for early troubadour poetry, and *canso* specifically designated a love song. Neither term implied a particular musical form, and the forms they supposedly represent may appear in any type of poetry. Of the three songs in AMM, the canso of Bernart de Ventadorn has its own special form, Rudel's vers and Marcabru's pastorela use variants of *aab* form. These variants, indeed, prove that the designation *aab form* is itself a misleading oversimplification. The form is not really tripartite, for, as a rule, the first section with its repeat (*aa*) is approximately the same length as the *b* section. Morever, the *b* section may be organized in a variety of ways. We have already found the forms *ab ab cb'd* and *ab ab ccd*. Other variants may result in patterns such as *ab ab cde* or *ab ab cdb*. With longer strophes of eight or ten lines, the possible number of variants is greatly increased. To clear up the confusion, then, it seems best to avoid using the names of poetic types to designate musical forms.[27] Only with the later development of fixed poetic forms (*formes fixes*), may we safely give the same name to both the texts and the equally fixed musical forms (see Chapter XII). For the troubadours, neither poetic nor musical forms were fixed. On the contrary, the infinite variety of formal structures—both poetic and musical—in troubadour song constitutes one of its greatest charms.

As has already been noted, the predominant influence on melodic style must have been the music of the Church. The relationship is most obvious in settings of the rhymed poetry of hymns and versus, but in range, melodic direction, intervallic progressions, and cadential formulas, troubadour melodies scarcely differ from Gregorian Chant in general. Moreover, a surprisingly large number of melodies adhere to the system of eight church modes. For the most part, the style is basically syllabic, with occasional ornamental figures of two to four or five notes. These figures tend to come near the close of phrases, where they emphasize rhymes and strengthen the cadential feeling. Thus they seem to serve a musical function rather than being associated with particular words. It is significant, however, that variants of the same melody in different sources most frequently involve the ornamental figures. Such variants suggest that singers felt free to modify vocal ornaments, or in-

27. Personal experience of the confusion has come from trying to explain why an alba, *Reis glorios,* is labelled "Canzo" in HAM, No. 18c. The melody of the five-line stanza has the form *aabcd,* but the last line of text is a refrain. A more accurate indication of the form would show the refrain by a capital letter (*aabcD*). Its presence goes unrecognized, of course, when only the first stanza is given.

troduce new ones, as they saw fit. Perhaps they even varied the ornamentation from stanza to stanza as they sang the melody to different
words.

Whether or not singers took liberties with the ornamentation of melodies, they were forced to decide for themselves what the rhythms of
those melodies should be. As in plainchant, indeed in all contemporary
monophonic song, the notation of troubadour melodies gave no indication of note values. Musical scholars have been almost unanimous in ac-
cepting the hypothesis that the secular songs were sung in the triple
meters of the rhythmic modes. They often disagree, however, as to
how those meters should be adapted to specific texts. Literary scholars,
when they considered the matter at all, have tended to reject the use of
triple meters in the monophonic songs of the time, whether in Latin,
Provençal, or French. In none of these languages does versification depend on the regular alternation of strong and weak syllables—on the use
of poetic meters, in other words. The number of syllables in each line,
the total number of lines, and the rhyme scheme were the only criteria
for making the succeeding stanzas of a poem correspond with the first.
Within these limits, constant variation of metrical patterns proves to be
one of the subtlest techniques of troubadour verse. Carl Appel has
shown, for example, that no two lines in the first stanza of *Non es
meravelha* (AMM, No. 42) have the same distribution of accented and
unaccented syllables.[28] To devise a single metrical pattern to fit all eight
lines is an obvious impossibility. This situation is typical of Bernart de
Ventadorn's poems, and Appel strongly opposed metrical transcriptions
in which melodic and textual accents do not correspond. The scholarly
editor of Bernart's poetry and melodies argued that regular meters and
even measured note values should not be used in modern transcriptions.
Instead, the performer should reproduce the natural rhythms and accents of the text.[29] That medieval performers probably did so may be
inferred from the continued use of unmeasured notation for some time
after clear ways of indicating note values had been developed in polyphonic music.

PERFORMANCE WITH INSTRUMENTAL ACCOMPANIMENT

From both literary and pictorial evidence it seems that instruments participated in the performance of troubadour and trouvère songs. Unfortunately, the evidence tells us little as to the degree or manner of that
participation. Musical sources are of no help, for they contain only the

28. C. Appel, *Der Singweisen Bernarts von Ventadorn*, p. 18.
29. Ibid., pp. 2–4. Similar arguments are advanced in H. Van der Werf, *The Chansons of
the Troubadours and Trouvères*, pp. 35–44.

vocal melodies. Suggesting appropriate instrumental accompaniments therefore becomes difficult. We know that *vièles* (fiddles) and small harps were used, and one of the easiest solutions would be to accompany troubadour songs with a bowed string instrument playing in unison with the voice. The instrument might also play the opening phrases of the melody as a prelude. The closing phrase or phrases could then serve as interludes between the stanzas and as a postlude at the end. Should a singer accompany himself on the harp, especially if he had had some ecclesiastical training, he might well improvise a simple form of free organum. Drones—sustained notes in the manner of melismatic organum—are still another possibility. In any case, it is well not to be dogmatic in this matter. Performance practice in the Middle Ages was surely flexible enough to permit singing these pieces either with some sort of instrumental accompaniment or as unaccompanied solo songs.[30]

It is obvious that the troubadour melodies as they have been preserved give a most inadequate picture of how they were performed. They must be given rhythmic life, instrumental accompaniment, possibly a varied ornamentation from stanza to stanza of the text. Contributions of this nature can probably not be expected of most present-day performers. It is to musical scholars that we must look for practical editions that will bring troubadour song to life without doing violence to the spirit or the musical techniques of the Middle Ages. Of all medieval music, the monophonic secular songs are perhaps the most difficult to reconstruct, yet the task is worthy of successful and satisfactory completion. Only then can we fully appreciate and enjoy this attractive legacy of a vanished culture.

LIVES OF THE TROUBADOURS

It is commonly said that the troubadours—as well as their French and German counterparts, the trouvères and Minnesingers—were aristocratic poets who composed their own melodies but left the performance of their songs to jongleurs. Almost every aspect of this statement demands qualification. Among the poets, it is true, we find kings, princes, counts, even bishops. Yet most of these men were no more than gifted amateurs. Really significant contributions to the art came primarily from professionals, men who placed their talents at the service of powerful and wealthy patrons. Numbers of these men too belonged to the aristocracy; but they were often younger sons, and therefore without inheritance, or lesser nobles with no fiefs, and therefore without income. Belonging to the nobility was by no means a prerequisite for

30. Van der Werf, *Chansons,* pp. 19–21, argues that the songs should be unaccompanied on the grounds that their texts do not refer to the use of instruments and that literary and pictorial evidence is ambiguous.

becoming a troubadour, however. Some of the best and most famous troubadours were men of humble birth. By their poetic and musical gifts these men gained an entry to the aristocratic society that fostered and enjoyed their art.

Much of our knowledge about the lives of the troubadours comes from medieval biographies (*vidas*) that appear in manuscript collections of the songs. Supplemental information comes from the commentaries (*razos*) that relate some poems to the events of a troubadour's life. Neither the lives nor the commentaries are completely reliable sources of information. Most were written long after the troubadours themselves had died, and fancy is often indistinguishable from fact. In their reporting, however, the biographies are sometimes consistent enough to make clear what men of that time believed to be true. If they are in part responsible for romantic notions about the troubadours, they also provide a good deal of information that contradicts those notions. In the matter of birth and social status, for example, we learn that Cercamon was a jongleur whose name showed that he had "roamed the whole world" (*cerquet tot lo mon*). Marcabru was a foundling "left at the door of a rich man." Bernart de Ventadorn was the son of a servant in the castle of the Count of Ventadorn. Gaucelm Faidit was the son of a bourgeois and became a jongleur after he lost all his possessions playing dice.[31]

In addition to information about the lives and loves of the troubadours, the biographies also provide contemporary critical judgments. Gaucelm Faidit wrote very good tunes and poems but sang worse than any man in the world. Jaufre Rudel wrote good tunes but poor poems. Pons de Capdoill was a good singer, composer, and player of the vièle. Guiraut de Borneill, known as the "master of the troubadours" because he was better than any who came before or after him, spent his winters studying. During the summer, he travelled from court to court with two jongleurs to sing his cansos. Peire Cardenal also travelled with a jongleur, although he "read and sang well."

Statements such as these—and many more could be cited—clarify several aspects of troubadour life. In the first place, numerous references to the composition of *mots et sons* make it obvious that troubadours usually wrote both the words and the melodies of their songs. It is exceptional to find that Uc Brunet "did not compose tunes." We should remember, however, that the medieval practice of adapting old tunes to new texts—making contrafacta, in other words—also occurs in the repertory of the troubadours and trouvères. A single text, moreover, may appear with different melodies in different sources. We therefore cannot say categorically that every melody was written by the author of the poem with which it is associated. Nevertheless, it remains true that the

---

31.   The vidas and razos in Provençal are collected in J. Boutière and A.-H. Schutz, *Biographies des troubadours*, rev. ed. by J. Boutière (Paris, 1964).

troubadours normally functioned as both poets and composers. Many also functioned as performers. Even when the biographies make no mention of singing ability, there is no reason to suppose that noble amateurs never entertained—or bored—their households and friends with performances of their own songs. We should probably assume that most of the troubadours did sing, some with considerable skill.

It is worth noting that the biographies designate a number of troubadours as jongleurs and speak of their wandering life. What raised these men above the lowly and anonymous ranks of mere performers—what made them troubadours, in other words—was their creative ability. They continued to perform, however, and by their travels they helped to spread the influence and example of troubadour song beyond the confines of southern France.

CHAPTER XII

Secular Monophonic Song, II: The Music of the Trouvères

It would be strange indeed had song in the vernacular remained the exclusive property of the troubadours. Yet we may feel some astonishment at the speed with which their poetry inspired imitation and emulation in other lands and languages. Several factors contributed to this rapid development. The cultural influence of the Crusades has perhaps been overemphasized, but they undoubtedly did bring the ruder men of England, northern France, and Germany into contact with the more civilized life and pleasures of the South. More important in the spreading abroad of troubadour poetry were the travels of the troubadours themselves. Many found patrons among the Christian kings in Spain, at various courts in northern Italy, and even to some extent in northern France. Others travelled from court to court, sometimes with jongleurs to perform their songs. The independent activities of jongleurs must also be counted among the most important factors in the rapid growth and dissemination of secular song. Constantly on the move, they kept the courts of western Europe abreast of both the latest news and the newest songs. It is impossible to measure the extent of their influence, but there is no reason to disagree with the statement that "the jongleurs were one of the earliest factors in bringing North and South together and promoting the social unity of France."[1]

At a higher level, marriages among the aristocracy promoted the social unity of France and contributed to the diffusion of troubadour song. Perhaps the most influential such marriage was that of Eleanor of Aquitaine (c. 1122–1204) to Louis VII of France (1120–80). Eleanor was the granddaughter of the first troubadour, William IX, Duke of Aquitaine. Her father, William X, was not himself a troubadour; but his support of others, including Marcabru, contributed to Eleanor's becoming a patroness of troubadours by both tradition and inclination. Eleanor and Louis were married in 1137, the year he became king of France. Louis was apparently not in sympathy with the game of l'amour courtois as it was played in the South. At any rate, "the flirtatious habits of his wife" ultimately led him to secure an annulment of their marriage in

---

1. P. Aubry, *Trouvères and Troubadours*, trans. C. Aveling, p. 102.

1152. Eleanor promptly married Henry of Anjou, who was already Duke of Normandy and two years later was to become King Henry II of England. The famous troubadour Bernart de Ventadorn was at her court while she was Duchess of Normandy (1152–54) and may have gone to England with her for a short time. Bertran de Born also spent some time at the Court of Normandy, but his later relationships with the English kings seem to have been more political than poetic.[2]

Eleanor of Aquitaine passed her enthusiasm for secular song on to her children. Her most famous son, Richard the Lionhearted, has long been associated with its history. According to the romantic story, Blondel de Nesle discovered Richard's whereabouts by singing one of Richard's songs outside the castle where the king was imprisoned. The story has proved to be only a pretty legend, but Richard did write songs, if somewhat mediocre ones. Even more important were the activities of Eleanor's two daughters by Louis VII, Marie and Aelis, who became countesses of Champagne and Blois respectively. Aelis, it is said, inspired the poet Gautier d'Arras; but it was Marie who gave the court of Champagne its place in the early history of trouvère song. Chrétien de Troyes, Marie's favorite poet, was primarily an author of chivalric *romans* (romances) in verse, some of which were based on Arthurian legends. Perhaps at Marie's suggestion, Chrétien may have tried his hand at transferring the spirit and forms of troubadour poetry into langue d'oïl. Several collections of French songs—called *chansonniers*, from *chanson*, meaning "song"—attribute some half dozen courtly love songs to him, but their authenticity is doubted. Other poets to whom Marie gave encouragement and support were the young trouvères Conon de Béthune and Gace Brulé. The court of Champagne thus became the most flourishing center of poetic activity in northern France during the last third of the twelfth century. In the first half of the next century, that center was to produce one of the most prolific and best of the trouvères, Marie's grandson Thibaut, Count of Champagne and later King of Navarre.

After its first flowering in northeastern France, the art of the trouvères quickly found practitioners wherever langue d'oïl was spoken. With creative activity cut off in the South by the Albigensian Crusade, the trouvères took the lead in the development of secular song. As a result of different and changing social conditions, that development followed unexpected paths.

In the North, as in the South, lyric poetry and song began as an aristocratic art. It is true that many of the first trouvères, like some of their southern counterparts, were men of humble birth; but it was the courts of the nobility that provided these men with patronage and an audience

2.   For sowing discord between Henry II and his sons, Dante condemned Bertran to carry his severed head like a lantern in the eighth circle of Hell. *Inferno*, Canto XXVIII, lines 118–42.

The solemn ceremony of the investiture of a knight is depicted in a fourteenth-century miniature from the *Roman de Troie* (Paris, Bibliothèque Nationale).

for their songs. Early in the thirteenth century this situation began to change, as the growing prosperity and power of the cities produced new creators and consumers of secular song among the bourgeoisie. In the first half of the century, many trouvères were still members of the nobility: Hugues de Lusignan, Comte de la Marche (d. 1249); Jehan le Roux, Comte de Bretagne (d. 1250); and, most important of all, Thibaut de Champagne, Roi de Navarre (d. 1253). At the same time, however, a number of trouvères were university-bred and members of the clergy, such as Pierre de Corbie, Simon d'Autrie, Guillaume li Viniers, Gille li Viniers, Andrieu Contredit, and Richard de Fournival. Several of these men belonged to the diocese of Arras in northern France, a city that became a major center in the final period of trouvère activity (1250–1300).

The last half of the thirteenth century still produced a few aristocratic trouvères, but the great majority were members of the bourgeoisie who established guilds or "brotherhoods" of poets and singers in various towns and cities of northern France. These brotherhoods conducted assemblies known as *puys,* in which a "prince" presided over contests to choose the best new songs. The Puy d'Arras was especially famous, and we know something about its operations from registers that list the members of the brotherhood and give the dates of their deaths.[3] Of the many trouvères whose names are thus made known to us, two are particularly important. Jehan Bretel (d. 1272), who was Prince of the Puy d'Arras, has left over forty songs. Adam de la Hale (d. 1288) was even more prolific and is better known because Edmond de Coussemaker, a

3. R. Berger, *Le Nécrologe de la confrérie des jongleurs et des bourgeois d'Arras (1194–1361),* 2 vols., Mémoires de la Commission Départementale des Monuments Historiques du Pas-de-Calais, 11² and 13² (Arras, 1963 and 1970).

pioneer in the study of medieval music, published his complete works in the latter part of the nineteenth century.[4] The transfer of trouvère activity from aristocratic to bourgeois circles marks the final stage of secular monophonic song in France. Adam de la Hale, indeed, is often called the last of the trouvères. The further development of secular song belongs to the history of polyphonic music, and, as we shall see, Adam himself took the first step in that direction.

The total repertory of trouvère song has yet to receive the careful and complete study accorded the melodies of the troubadours. In part this situation results from the much greater amount of material that has been preserved. It is not possible to give exact figures, but numerous chansonniers contain approximately 2400 poems and 1700 melodies. Much of this material is available, but modern publications have tended to concentrate on special aspects of the repertory: facsimiles and transcriptions of individual manuscripts; songs of a particular type; or the works of a single trouvère. For this reason it is difficult to evaluate the relative importance of the various types and forms of songs. Generalizations as to musical style must also rest on an incomplete knowledge of the repertory as a whole. Much that has been said about troubadour music is equally applicable to the songs of the trouvères. Here, we need only note the somewhat different emphases that the northern composers placed on certain poetic types and musical forms.

CHANSONS DE GESTE AND RELATED TYPES

Vernacular song in northern France did not suddenly appear with the trouvères as it had with the troubadours in the South. From the tenth century onward, writers in langue d'oïl had been producing poems known as *chansons de geste* (songs of deeds), of which the most famous and one of the best is the *Chanson de Roland*. The chansons de geste are epic rather than lyric poetry, but they were sung, apparently, with an accompanying harp or vièle. This tradition of combined poetry and song undoubtedly made it easier for the trouvères to adopt the forms and types of lyric poetry that were the special contribution of the troubadours. Northern poets did not forget the chanson de geste, however, and they cultivated several related poetic types to a much greater extent than their southern counterparts.

The chansons de geste normally consisted of ten-syllable lines grouped in stanzas, or *laisses,* of irregular length. Each laisse, like a paragraph, concerned itself with a single thought or incident and achieved unity through the use of assonance or rhyme. In a very few poems, a shorter final line marks the close of each laisse. Poems constructed in this way, with hundreds or thousands of lines, obviously demanded

4.   See Bibliography for the editions by Coussemaker and N. Wilkins.

simple and adaptable musical material. The material appears to have been so simple, indeed, that no manuscripts preserve chansons de geste with their melodies. It is important to note, however, that recent opinions postulate a small number of melodic formulas or phrases—perhaps no more than three—which would have different functions and would be distributed according to the sense and sentence structure of the text.[5] The result, obviously, would be a highly repetitive form, but one that permitted the creation of musical units to correspond with the laisses into which the poems were divided. Significantly, the suggested musical scheme for the chanson de geste is in accord with later procedures in related types of poetry. The literary ancestry of these related types has long been recognized. Now we may include the chanson de geste in their musical ancestry as well.

LAIS AND DESCORTS

Among the songs related to older forms of narrative poetry are the lai and descort, which were briefly considered in the previous chapter. The beginnings of the lai are obscure and have occasioned a good deal of controversy. Perhaps the most common theory holds that it is of Celtic origin, coming to France by way of Brittany or through Anglo-Norman contacts in the twelfth century. One of the first French poets to write lais was Marie de France, about whom little is known except that she belonged to the court of Henry II and Eleanor of Aquitaine. The lais of Marie de France are narrative poems, or romans, some of which draw their material from the legends of King Arthur and the Knights of the Round Table. Written in rhymed couplets, these poems were apparently not meant to be sung. With the advent of lais intended for singing, narrative texts began to give way to lyric effusions of considerable length on the inexhaustible subject of love. A few lais deal with religious subjects or are addressed to the Virgin Mary, but in most of the texts the poet has some cause for complaint about a harsh, disdainful, or simply unresponsive lady who leaves his love unrequited. It is this "sentimental disagreement" or discord that may account for the popularity of the name *descort* among the troubadours, who left twenty-eight pieces with that designation but only four lais. No more than four of these thirty-two poems, it will be remembered, survive with their music (Chapter XI, p. 276). Among the trouvères the situation is different. Here we find thirty melodies with French texts from the twelfth and thirteenth centuries. Only nine identify themselves as descorts, thirteen as lais. The others belong to the group because of their formal

---

5.   See J. Chailley, "Études musicales sur la chanson de geste et ses origines," *Revue de musicologie,* 27 (1948), pp. 1–27. A more recent survey of the problems is J. Van der Veen, "Les Aspects musicaux des chansons de geste," *Neophilologus,* 41 (1957), pp. 82–100.

structure.[6] As has already been noted, it is the use of different stanzaic forms within a single poem that distinguishes lais and descorts from all other troubadour and trouvère songs. To simplify further discussion, therefore, the term *lai* may serve as a generic name for all of these pieces.

It is only to be expected that lais from the late twelfth through the thirteenth century should vary greatly in their overall structure. Neither the number of stanzas nor the number of lines within each stanza is fixed in any way. Stanzas range from four to fifty-six lines in length, with the average, according to Jeanroy, being twenty to twenty-five lines. Stanzas with eight to sixteen lines are also common, however. As in all types of lyric poetry at this time, lines of seven and eight syllables predominate, but a special characteristic of the lai is the frequent use of shorter lines with three to six syllables. Still another variable results from the degree of formal "discord" among the stanzas of a lai. In some poems, each stanza has a different poetic form. Others use the same form for two or more stanzas that may appear consecutively or be scattered throughout the poem. In the fourteenth century, the form of the lai became standardized to the extent that it usually consisted of twelve stanzas, of which the first and last are identical in structure and are sung to the same melody (see Chapter XVII). Some earlier lais foreshadow this development, but modern efforts to find twelve stanzas in the highly irregular poems of the thirteenth century are not always convincing.

The melodies of the lais naturally reflect the variability of their poetic structure. Nevertheless, common structural procedures relate the different stanzaic forms and give the lais their distinctive musical characteristics. As a starting point for examining those characteristics, let us observe the two ways in which the manuscripts preserve the melodies. As a general rule, the scribes copied the melody for the complete text. In a few cases, however, only scattered portions of the text appear with music. Apparently the notated phrases were meant to serve for all succeeding lines and stanzas with the same poetic structure. From the historical point of view, the incompletely notated lais are particularly interesting and instructive. Differences of opinion may arise as to the patterns of melodic repetition, but we can still tell a good deal about the musical origin of the lai and its relationship to other types of narrative song.

The most obvious characteristic of the partially notated lais is their use of a small number of melodic formulas for texts of considerable length. A simple, generally syllabic style and the recurrence of similar if not identical formulas in different lais further contribute to the family resemblance displayed by all members of the group. This recurrence of characteristic formulas suggests that the partially notated lais drew on an

---

6.   The thirty pieces are published in A. Jeanroy, L. Brandin, and P. Aubry, *Lais et descorts français du XIIIe siècle.*

ancient fund of melody that could be adapted to various poetic forms and modified at the discretion of the composer or performer. Increasing the probability of this hypothesis is the fact that the partially notated lais belong among the oldest examples of the form and are anonymous except for two by Ernoul de Gastinois. Little is known about Ernoul, but he appears to have been active in the first half of the thirteenth century. Although the subject matter of Ernoul's two lais is pious rather than profane, they faithfully reflect the characteristic poetic and musical structures of the older secular form.[7]

The first stanza of the *Lai de Notre Dame* by Ernoul de Gastinois illustrates one method of singing a lengthy text to a minimum of musical material. Only two basic formulas serve twenty-six lines of text, but a slight elaboration of the second formula marks the division of the stanza into two not-quite-equal sections. The manuscript source does not provide the melody for the lines enclosed in brackets in Example XII-1. It is clear, nevertheless, that the musical form of the stanza is *ab ab ab ab bbbbbb' ab ab ab ab bbbb'*.[8] The relationship between this form and the procedures postulated for the chanson de geste is self-evident.

Example XII–1: *The First Stanza of the* Lai de Notre Dame *by Ernoul de Gastinois*

1. *En en-ten-te cu-ri-eu-se*	2. *De quer-re ma vi-e,*	
3. *L'a-mor de la glo-ri-eu-se*	4. *Ne lai-se-rai mi-e,*	
5.*[(Ka) la vir-ge pre-ci-eu-se*	6. *Ne re-querre a-i-e*	
7. *Ki fu si tres sa-ve-reu-se*	8.*C'on-ques en sa vi-e]*	
	9. *Ne li prist en-vi-e*	
	10. *De car-nel fo-li-e*	
	11. *Or ne m'es-con-di-e*	
	12. *De rien ke je di-e*	
	13. *La do-ce, la pi-e*	14. *La vir-ge Ma-ri - e;*
15. *Vir-ge boine a-ven-tu-reu-se*	16. *Sain-te caste et pu-re*	
17. *De tos les biens e-u-reu-se*	18. *Plai-ne de me-su-re*	
19. *Sain-te virge a Dieu es-peu-se*	20. *Pu-celle a droi-tu-re*	
21. *Do-ce ro-i-ne pi-teu-se*	22.*[(De) boi-ne na-tu-re*	
	23. *To-te cre-a-tu-re*	
	24. *S'en vos met sa cu-re*	
	25. *Puet es-tre se-u-re*	26.*De boine a-ven-tu - re.]*

*The note f appears only in the first statement of this phrase.

Eager to claim my (full) life, I shall never abandon the love of the glorious (Virgin); nor seek aid except from the precious Virgin who was so saintly that never in her life did carnal folly tempt her. Now may the tender, pious Virgin Mary not reject anything I say. Fortunate Virgin, holy, chaste, and pure, above all the saints full of measure, Holy Virgin, spouse of God, justly a maiden, tender queen, merciful and kind, every creature, if he puts his trust in you, can be sure of good fortune.

7.   All that is known of the life and works of Ernoul is assembled in J. Maillard, "Lais et chansons d'Ernoul de Gastinois."

8.   A fascimile of the original notation for the opening stanzas of Ernoul's *Lai de Notre Dame* follows the title page of Jeanroy, *et al., Lais et descorts.*

In their efforts to discover the parentage of the lai, some scholars have claimed that it is the secular counterpart of the liturgical sequence. Certainly there is little evidence of any relationship between the variable poetic structures of the thirteenth-century lai and the almost hymnlike regularity of contemporary sequence texts. Even when the overall structure of the lai becomes standardized to some extent in the fourteenth century, the differences between the two types remain more striking than the similarities. Yet the older lais do use structural procedures encountered in the special form known as the sequence with double cursus (see Chapter VI). The most obvious and extensive application of the double-cursus principle is to be found in the *Lai de l'Ancien et du Nouveau Testament,* the second of the two lais by Ernoul de Gastinois.

A noticeable departure from the style of the older lais occurs in some pieces by thirteenth-century composers. Successive repetitions of one or two formulas disappear, and the melodic poverty gives way to more expansive and lyrical phrases. Both individual phrases and complete melodies cover a wider range and contain many more ornamental groups of two to four notes per syllable. With these developments, the lai loses its archaic and popular character and approaches the more sophisticated style of contemporary trouvère song.

OTHER NARRATIVE SONGS

Perhaps under the continuing influence of the chanson de geste, northern poets cultivated narrative song much more than did the troubadours. The French *pastourelle* followed in the same tradition as the troubadour pastorela, but it often placed greater emphasis on the depiction of rustic manners and customs than on the attempted seduction. Indeed, in the pastourelle by Jehan Erars discussed below, the contest between knight and shepherdess is missing entirely. In another type of narrative-dramatic poem, the principal character is a lady with some cause for complaint: the absence of her lover, the presence of her husband, or the obstinacy of her parents in preventing her marriage to the man of her choice. Poems of this sort are known as *chansons de toile,* sometimes mistranslated as "spinning songs." It is true that the lady may voice her complaint while sewing or weaving, but she may also be reading a book or simply doing nothing. In the Middle Ages, as now, the word *toile* had several meanings. Used generically, it meant any woven fabric, but it could specifically denote a scene depicted in a tapestry. Today, among other things, *toile* can mean either the cloth on which a picture is painted or the painting itself, like the word *canvas* in English. A correct, if not particularly elegant, translation of *chansons de toile* would therefore seem to be "picture songs," which normally begin by describing the scene in which the lady finds herself. As a genre, the chanson de toile had become extinct by the early thirteenth century. A lateral descendant may have been the songs of the *mal mariée* (ill-mated wife), in which a lady's woes arise from marriage to an old and justifiably jealous husband. Centuries later, incidentally, the mal mariée was still a favorite theme in French literature and song.

The chanson de toile is apparently one of the oldest forms of French lyric poetry, and analogies between it and the still older chanson de geste have often been noted. Each stanza of *En un vergier,* for example, has the same rhyme and uses the same melody for all four of its ten-syllable lines (Example XII–2). Only the cadence is altered in the fourth line to introduce the two-line refrain that concludes every stanza. The resulting musical form—*aaaa'BC*—seems primitive, but the melodic style is more elaborate than in other types of narrative song.

Example XII–2: *The First Stanza of an Anonymous Chanson de Toile in a Metrical Transcription*

In an orchard beside a little spring with crystal water and white sand a king's daughter sat, her hand on her cheek. Sighing, she recalls her tender friend: Alas, Count Gui, my friend, your love takes away my solace and my laughter.

Another anonymous chanson de toile, *Bele Doette,* is even more ornately expressive (see AMM, No. 44). The refrain, in particular, seems to reflect the lady's personal grief. As if to offset the ornateness of its style, *Bele Doette* has a relatively simple form—*ababC*. This use of two phrases for the body of the stanza and a third, concluding phrase for the refrain recalls Ernoul's structural procedure in the first stanza of his *Lai de Notre Dame* (Example XII–1). Perhaps the distinctive phrase concluding each stanza or laisse suggested textual repetition and the introduction of refrains in narrative songs. Dance songs and other kinds of popular and folk music may also have suggested the use of refrains and may even have provided some of those found in more literary forms.

Whatever the origin of refrains may have been, they also play a prominent role in the French pastourelle. Perhaps because of the subject matter, the trouvères usually wrote pastourelles in a simple style with highly repetitive forms. *Au tems pascor* (In paschal time), by Jehan Erars, provides a characteristic example (AMM, No. 45). Its poetic and musical forms may be outlined as follows:

Poetry:	$a_4a_4b_6$,	$a_4a_4b_6$,	c_8c_8	d_6,d_6,	e_8e_8	f_6,	G_8F_6,
Music:	*a*	*a*	*b b*	*c c*	*b b*	*d*	*A*

As is often the case, however, letters fail to indicate the homogeneous character of the melody as a whole. The opening phrase (*a*) is, in reality, the generating force of the entire song. It defines the range of a fifth within which all the phrases move; it provides the motives and melodic progressions that are fragmented and recombined to form the internal phrases (*b*, *c*, and *d*); and it returns intact for the refrain. Whether the simplicity of this and other pastourelles resulted from the use of folk melodies or from sophisticated parody remains an unanswered question. Certainly pastourelles were intended for aristocratic, or at least bourgeois, audiences who delighted in poking fun at rustic manners. For such audiences, composers may well have taken pride in skillful imitation, rather than direct quotation, of popular song. The melodic setting of *Au tems pascor,* at any rate, creates a fittingly popular tone for this charming description of a rural party that ends in a noisy row.

REFRAINS

Although refrains are particularly common in narrative songs such as the chanson de toile and the pastourelle, they also appear in other poetic types in a great variety of stanzaic forms. It is textual repetition, of course, that creates a refrain; but for the musician it is the relationship between the refrain melody and the rest of the stanza that is of primary interest. In *Bele Doette* and *En un vergier,* the refrains have new melodies. The refrain of *Au tems pascor,* on the other hand, repeats the melody of the opening phrase. Such repetitions of material from the body of the stanza produce many forms that are impossible to classify. Some writers designate as *rotrouenges* songs in which the melody for the final phrase or phrases of the stanza also serves for the refrain. This usage rests on somewhat shaky evidence, for the term seems to have originated as a loose designation for French songs not of courtly inspiration. Neither poetic nor musical procedures were uniform, and the most we can say is that rotrouenges usually combined a refrain with a simplicity of poetic structure that is either genuinely old or deliberately archaic. A late example that has been called a rotrouenge is *De moi dolereus vos chant* (Of my sad self I sing to you; AMM, No. 46) by Gillebert de Berneville, a member of the Puy d'Arras in the second half of the thirteenth century. The stanzaic form of this song, with its refrain, is $a_7 a_7 a_7 b_3 B_8$. The musical form is less easily described. An opening phrase is repeated for the second line, after which a new phrase (*b*) and a three-note motive (*c*) complete the stanza. The refrain takes as its melody the notes of the last eight syllables of the stanza but gives them a different phrase structure. Thus stated, the musical relationship between stanza and refrain sounds simpler than it actually is. Motive *c* is also the first three notes of phrase *b,* and it thus serves the double function of ending the melody of the stanza and beginning a repetition of *b* and *c* that continues as the melody of the refrain. The subtlety of this overlapping repetition belies the apparent simplicity with which Gillebert sings the blues.

It has sometimes been said that an audience would join in singing refrains, after a soloist had sung the body of the stanzas. Such audience participation may have been normal for dance songs, but it seems unlikely in the case of chansons de toile, where the refrain usually expresses a very personal emotion. It is even more unlikely in a type of song known as *chansons avec des refrains* (songs with refrains). These songs have no single refrain in the usual meaning of the term. Instead, each stanza ends with a different refrain taken from a well-known song. Composers evidently expected audiences to recognize the familiar quotations and to appreciate the ingenuity of their introduction. It does not seem probable that audiences were also expected to sing the refrains when they did not know in advance what those refrains would be.

The practice of quoting refrains was so widespread in the thirteenth and early fourteenth centuries that it almost seems a distinguishing characteristic of the period. Scholars of medieval literature have long recognized the existence of this practice, and in 1904 Alfred Jeanroy listed fifty-four chansons with "refrains foreign to the text."[9] Many of these pieces are pastourelles, but other types of songs, including *chansons d'amour,* are also represented. All of the songs apparently belong to the thirteenth century, and many were produced by later generations of trouvères in Arras and other cities of northern France. As a rule, composers adopted the same general procedure for introducing foreign refrains. All the stanzas of a song have the same poetic structure, except that each closes with an additional line to introduce the rhyme of the refrain. In some cases, the additional lines also have different melodies that lead into or even anticipate the melodies of the refrains.

Penser ne doit vilenie (One should not think evil; AMM, No. 47) pro-

---

9.   A. Jeanroy, *Les origines de la poésie lyrique en France* (Paris, 1904), p. 102 and fn. 1.
      Gennrich, who expanded the list to about eighty pieces, published all the refrain
      texts and any melodies that appear with them in RVB, 2, pp. 255–91.

vides a characteristic example of the ways in which foreign refrains might
be related to the main body of a chanson.[10] All four stanzas of the poem
have the same rhymes and the rhyme scheme a'ba'bba'a' for their first
seven lines. The eighth line of each stanza then introduces the final
rhyme of the refrain. Borrowing a device common in troubadour poetry, the poet further integrates the text of each refrain by using its final
word to begin the following stanza. The musical setting of the poem is
organized somewhat differently. Now the first eight lines constitute a
unit with the form *aa' aa' bc aa'*. In addition, phrase *a'* reappears at the
close of the first refrain and again, lacking its first two notes, at the close
of the second. The melody of the third refrain seems unrelated to the
rest of the chanson. Its opening phrase resembles the beginning of the
first refrain, but it then turns to a surprise ending on **c'**, a fourth above
the final that the chanson as a whole has led us to expect.

The fourth stanza of *Penser ne doit* presents a problem because it appears only in manuscripts that do not give the melody of its refrain.
Three quotations of the same refrain in other contexts do have melodies,
but they still leave unanswered questions. All three versions are included in AMM, No. 47. The first two closely resemble the melody of
the third refrain, especially at the beginning and end. Either one would
therefore produce a second pair of related refrain melodies to match the
first two quoted in *Penser ne doit*. This seems to prove that we have discovered the right melody for the fourth refrain, although we still do not
know which transposition should be used. The version ending on **c'**
would confirm the surprise cadence of the third refrain and emphasize
the relationship of the two melodies. On the other hand, the transposition down to **g** would bring back the expected final without destroying
the melodic resemblances between the third and fourth refrains. Which
of these solutions was intended will probably always remain unknown.
We also cannot know whether the musical relationship between the
chanson and the first two refrains results from modification of their
original melodies or from a deliberate use of preexistent phrases in constructing the melody of the chanson. Other sources quote both refrains
with completely different melodies, however, and we may therefore assume that the composer was responsible for relating them to his melody
for *Penser ne doit*.

It must already be clear that the practice of quoting refrains spread
beyond the limits of trouvère song. Indeed, all four of the refrains in
Penser ne doit turn up in different motets (see Example XIV–2). As the
predominant form of thirteenth-century polyphony, the motet and the
frequent quotation of refrains within it will be discussed in Chapter
XIV. Here we need only note that motets provide our chief source for

---

10.   Different manuscripts attribute *Penser ne doit* variously to Guiot de Dijon, Andrieu
      Contredit, and Jehan Erart. Two other examples of chansons with refrains may be
      found in Gennrich, *Grundriss einer Formenlehre,* pp. 55–59.

the melodies of refrains. To what extent they transmit the original form of these melodies must often remain in doubt.

Little is known about the texts from which thirteenth-century poets drew the refrains that they quoted so freely. Some may have come from narrative songs, especially the pastourelle, but most were apparently taken from dances or other songs of popular origin. Few of the complete texts from which these refrains came have been preserved. Those few suggest that perhaps we need not regret too much the loss of so many pieces from what must have been a much larger repertory. Neither the poetry nor the music of dance songs is particularly distinguished or distinctive. Conventional formulas and clichés abound in the texts, while the melodies tend to be simple, short, and highly repetitive. For many songs the refrain includes the entire melody to which the other lines of text were sung. Nevertheless, dance songs of the thirteenth century occupy an important historical position. From them came the more literary *formes fixes* (fixed forms) of later French poetry and song: the rondeau, the ballade, and the virelai. The early history of these forms and of their interrelationships presents a confused and confusing picture. They did not, in fact, become "fixed" until late in the thirteenth century, when the activity of the trouvères was drawing to a close. This establishment of the fixed forms coincides with their transformation from simple dance tunes into polyphonic songs. Once that transformation had been accomplished, the three distinctively different forms dominated French lyric poetry almost to the end of the fifteenth century.

THE RONDEAU

In northern France, *carole* and *ronde,* together with various diminutives such as *rondet, rondel,* and *rondelet,* seem to have been more or less synonymous terms designating round dances in which group performance of refrains alternated with lines sung by the leader of the dance. In view of modern usage, this original meaning of the word *carol* is worth noting. Rather than the birth of Christ, many of the early dance songs celebrate the joys of returning spring, and May Day festivities may well have been the origin of the species. In any case, a thirteenth-century round dance might be called either a *carole* or, more commonly, one of the diminutives of *ronde* from which eventually came *rondeau,* the spelling we use today.

Many thirteenth-century rondeaux had only six lines with an internal and concluding refrain. In the simplest version of the later "fixed" form, the refrain also introduced the rondeau, which then became a poem of eight lines with only two rhymes. Lines 1 and 2 constitute the entire refrain, which returns as lines 7 and 8. Line 1 also returns as line 4.

The remaining lines have different texts but use the same rhymes as the refrain. (In later poetry, both French and English, this form is given the somewhat misleading designation *triolet*.) The musical setting of such a rondeau consists of only two phrases, and all lines with the same rhyme are sung to the same melody. We may therefore indicate both the poetic and musical form as *ABaAabAB*. (Capital letters indicate the refrain lines—repetitions of words and music. Lower-case letters indicate rhymes as well as melodic repetitions with different words.) A characteristic rondeau of the late thirteenth century is *De ma dame vient* by Guillaume d'Amiens (Example XII–3).[11] The numbering of the lines in this example indicates the order in which they are to be sung. The translation of *De ma dame vient* should make its poetic form even clearer.

Example XII–3: *Rondeau of Guillaume d'Amiens*

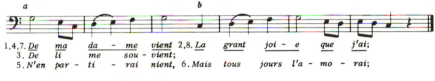

1,4,7. *De*	*ma*	*da*	-	*me*	*vient*	2,8. *La*	*grant*	*joi* - *e*	*que*	*j'ai;*
3. *De*	*li*	*me*		*sou* -	*vient;*				
5. *N'en*	*par* -	*ti*	-	*rai*	*nient,*	6. *Mais*	*tous*	*jours l'a* - *mo* - *rai;*	

1. From my lady comes
2. The great joy that I have;
3. I remember her;
4. From my lady comes.
5. I shall never leave her
6. But shall always love her;
7. From my lady comes
8. The great joy that I have.

The artificial restrictions of the eight-line rondeau and the simplicity of its melodic style would seem to make it an unlikely candidate for further development. Nevertheless, composers managed to retain its basic structure, while at the same time they increased the length of the poems and provided them with elaborate musical settings. These developments occur, however, not in the songs of the trouvères but in the polyphonic songs of the fourteenth and fifteenth centuries.[12]

THE BALLADE

As we saw in the preceding chapter, the troubadours generally called their dance songs *dansas* or *baladas*. The name *balada* passed into the musical terminology of both France and Italy, but it came to designate different forms in the two countries. The Italian *ballata* kept a refrain at

---

11. After Gennrich, RVB, 1, p. 36. For further examples see HAM, Nos. 19d and 19e, and Gleason, EM, pp. 10–11.

12. As a result of structural modifications in sixteenth-century rondeaux, modern descriptions of the form do not always agree with medieval practice.

the beginning of the poem and after each stanza and corresponds in form to the French virelai (see below). The French *ballade* apparently began with much the same form but developed in a different way. Under the influence of the chanson, the opening refrain disappeared, and the ballade adopted a fixed *aab* form. We have already encountered this form in some cansos of the troubadours, and it is even more common in trouvère chansons. The many chansons in *aab* form normally do not have refrains, however, and are clearly distinguishable from the few examples of contemporary dance songs. It is a mistake, therefore, to identify these chansons as ballades.[13] Not until the fourteenth century did the ballade take on the formal and stylistic characteristics of the more sophisticated chanson. Once the transformation had been completed, the ballade with refrain became the most common form of French secular song.

In contrast to the numerous stanzas of cansos and chansons, the "fixed" literary form of the ballade consisted of only three stanzas plus an envoy, which is almost always missing, however, in ballades provided with a musical setting. With the reduction in the number of stanzas went a corresponding increase in their length and the intricacy of their rhyme schemes. From the chanson d'amour, the ballade borrowed a characteristic arrangement of the first four lines as a pair of couplets, usually with alternating rhymes (abab). The rest of the stanza normally consisted of three or four lines, including the refrain, in which no consistent rhyme scheme prevailed. Most of the refrains consisted of a single line, but some were expanded to include the penultimate, as well as the final line. In some cases, the stanza itself was expanded to a total of ten lines. From these remarks it is obvious that the stanzaic form of the ballade was by no means as fixed as the form of the rondeau. Yet it is possible to show typical forms for stanzas of different lengths, with the warning that the rhyme schemes given for the final portions of the forms are common but not invariable:

7-line stanzas:	ab	ab	bc C
8-line stanzas:	ab	ab	ccd D
10-line stanzas:	aab	aab	bcb C
Musical form:	*a*	*a*	*b* C

From these stanzaic patterns, it can be seen that any ballade text will fit a musical form divided into three sections, of which the first is repeated—usually with open and closed endings—and the third serves as a refrain. Again, and even more than with the rondeau, the emergence of the ballade as an important literary and musical form is a fourteenth-century phenomenon. Further discussion must therefore be reserved for later chapters (see especially Chapter XVII).

13.   In HAM, for example, Nos. 19a and 36a are characteristic chansons, not ballades. The presence or absence of a refrain, of course, cannot be determined from a single stanza.

THE VIRELAI

The third fixed form, the virelai, was the last to achieve recognition as a distinct poetic and musical genre, and the name did not come into general use until the fourteenth century. Both its derivation and original meaning remain obscure. Spelled *vireli* or *virenli,* the word appears in early poetic texts with reference to a dance or to some dance movement. Current opinion explains *vireli* as "turn her" and *virelai* (=*vireles*) as "turn them." The final spelling, *virelai,* may reflect the influence of the lai, but the two forms are otherwise unrelated. A fifteenth-century suggestion—sometimes repeated by modern writers—that a virelai is a lai turned (*viré*) on itself seems to be the kind of false etymology that appears when the original meaning and use of a word has been long forgotten.

In both poetic and musical structure, the virelai is obviously related to other dance songs with refrains. It begins with a refrain; but then, as in the ballade, the stanzas fall into three parts, of which the first two are sung to the same melody. In the virelai, however, the third part of the stanza repeats the melody of the refrain. The complete form of a virelai in several stanzas thus becomes *AbbaA bbaA bbaA* etc. If we regard the virelai as a kind of ballade that kept the refrain at the beginning of the first stanza, it becomes clear how the identical forms of the French virelai and the Italian ballata evolved out of the older French ballades or Provençal baladas and dansas. In its further evolution, the virelai followed the ballade in reducing the normal number of stanzas to three. It remained even more flexible, however, in the number of lines that might be included in each section of its stanzas. Sections sung to the same music naturally had to have the same poetic structure, but in other respects poets had considerable freedom. Only the formal pattern of the virelai as a whole was fixed.

The later predominance of fixed forms in polyphonic secular song should not lead us to overemphasize the importance of those forms in the repertory of the trouvères. By far the larger part of that repertory consists of the same kinds of song that we find in the work of the troubadours: love songs (chansons), debates (jeux partis), lais and descorts, pastourelles, and aubes (albas). French contributions include the chanson de toile and songs of the mal mariée. Even in the output of a composer as late as Adam de la Hale (d. 1288) these kinds of song still predominate. Adam's complete works include thirty-four chansons, seventeen jeux partis, sixteen "rondels," and five motets. In addition, his famous *Jeu de Robin et Marion* (Play of Robin and Marion) is a dramatized pastourelle with incidental music. Earlier composers showed even less interest in dance songs, which are conspicuously rare in the great manuscript collections of trouvère songs.[14] The virelai and ballade in

14. The Manuscrit du Roy, for example, contains only one dance song, the ballade *En tous tans,* in its original repertory. Thirteen pieces added on blank pages and in measured notation include four rondeaux. See Gennrich, RVB, 2, pp. 186–88 and 228.

The composer Adam de la Hale depicted in a miniature from the *Chansonnier d'Arras.*

particular did not develop into forms that we recognize as fixed until the fourteenth century. Even at the close of the previous century, the term *rondel* covered a multitude of different forms. To cite Adam de la Hale again, the manuscript copy of his works gives the title *Li Rondel Adan* to a group of sixteen pieces that are among the first polyphonic settings of dance songs. Most of these pieces are, in fact, rondeaux, although the forms and rhyme schemes are still not completely standardized. One of the pieces has the form of a virelai, however, and another is a ballade with an opening refrain.[15] Yet to come, evidently, was the separation of these forms into the three major types of polyphonic song.

GENERAL CHARACTERISTICS OF TROUVÈRE SONG

Secular song in northern France received its chief impetus from the South, and the repertories of the troubadours and trouvères naturally share many common characteristics. Yet the trouvères were not content merely to follow in the footsteps of the pioneers. Instead, they struck out on new paths and stamped their music with its own distinctive qualities. Many French songs, it is true, imitate the serious style and subtle refinement of the Provençal canso. But many display a spontaneous gaiety and an elegant frivolity that we think of as being typically French. Naturally most obvious in the texts, these traits also make themselves felt in the music.

Much more than the troubadours, the trouvères cultivated a simplicity and directness of melodic form and style that gave their songs an almost folklike character. The extent to which that character results from

15. The two pieces, together with a rondeau of Adam, are published in Gennrich, *Troubadours, Trouvères,* pp. 39–41; the virelai and another rondeau, in Gleason, EM, pp. 74 and 76; the ballade and still another rondeau, in HAM, Nos. 36b and 36c.

the influence of folk song cannot be determined. We can see, however, that the popular kinds of song already discussed provided many traits characteristic of the trouvère repertory as a whole. From the chanson de geste and related narrative songs must have come the trouvères' preference for repetitive rather than continuous melodic structures. Reinforcing this preference was an obvious fondness for refrains. As a result, balance and clarity of formal design become a conspicuous characteristic of trouvère songs. Another characteristic that probably derives from the same sources is a preference for simple, essentially syllabic, melodies. In this respect, of course, the trouvère repertory as a whole displays considerable variety. The chanson de toile *Bele Doette* represents one extreme in its extensive ornamentation for expressive purposes. Normal chansons, especially of the earlier trouvères, tended to use vocal ornaments in the more restrained and abstract way characteristic of the troubadour canso. At the other extreme lie almost completely syllabic songs like *Au tems pascor* of Jehan Erars, in which repeated phrases, narrow in range but distinct in outline, produce a decidedly popular tone. The many melodies of this type are perhaps the most important and attractive contribution of the trouvères to the art of secular song.

The role of rhythm and meter in creating the popular tone of many trouvère songs again remains problematical. Some scholars accept without question the application of triple meter to all trouvère songs. The results, in many cases, are neither musically satisfactory nor historically justified. It is unlikely, for example, that the first generation of trouvères in the latter half of the twelfth century would have consistently followed the system of metrical organization being developed at that time in the field of sacred polyphony. A highly ornamented song such as *Bele Doette* illustrates the musical problems. Forced into the straitjacket of triple meter, both melody and text become strained and unnatural.[16] The structure of the text, moreover, suggests the necessity of some freedom in performance. The poetic lines consist of ten syllables divided by a caesura into four plus six, but both the caesuras and the complete lines may have either masculine or feminine endings. As is customary, the manuscript source gives the melody for the first stanza only, and it provides variants for the feminine and masculine endings at the caesuras in lines 1 and 3 respectively (see AMM, No. 44). We do not know, however, how to handle masculine endings at caesuras in lines 2 and 4, or feminine rhymes at the close of complete lines. The underlaying of the text in AMM is merely a suggested solution to these problems.[17] It seems obvious that only a free rhythmic performance based

16. See, for example, the transcriptions of *Bele Doette* in Gennrich, *Exempla,* p. 8, and J. Beck, *La musique des troubadours,* p. 103.
17. There is also no provision for the added refrain lines in the last three stanzas.

on the changing accents, structure, and meaning of the text can do justice to the expressive qualities of this song.

As the thirteenth century progressed, a number of developments made the use of triple meters in trouvère songs both more probable and more appropriate. Although for the most part only their refrains survive, the many dance songs that must have existed had of necessity to be metrical. Quotation of these refrains in chansons, therefore, may have led to metrical organization of the entire melody. Similarly, a regular triple meter seems called for in a song like *Au tems pascor,* in which the popular style of rustic dances is probably imitated. Yet even here textual and musical accents sometimes bump awkwardly together (see AMM, No. 45, lines 9 and 10 of the first stanza). Another development that may have led the trouvères to adopt triple meters was the quotation of refrains and the use of French secular texts in the thirteenth-century motet (see Chapter XIV). Here, at any rate, the fluctuating and fluid rhythms of the texts were subordinated to regular metrical patterns. We must remember, however, that trouvère songs continued to be written in unmeasured notation long after a precise means of indicating note values was available. It is surely significant that the manuscript collection of Adam de la Hale's complete works used unmeasured notation for the monophonic chansons and jeux partis but adopted the contemporary measured notation for the polyphonic "rondels" and motets. The conclusion seems inescapable that the trouvères still wanted freedom of performance and provided for it by the notation they chose for their melodies. Not until the fourteenth century do we finally encounter monophonic songs with clearly indicated note values and regular metrical patterns. By this time, however, the age of the trouvères had passed, and secular song had begun a new phase of its development.

Continuous development, indeed, is perhaps the most striking aspect of French secular song, which never ceased to play an important part in cultural and social life. Among the chief reasons for this prolonged vitality must be the continuing assimilation of influences from a wide variety of sources. Both musical and textual influences on trouvère song came from contemporary plainchant and polyphony, from Latin and vernacular poets, from churchmen and vagabonds, from aristocrats and country folk, from troubadours and Celtic bards. Musically, these influences are developed within the narrow limits of monophonic song. When those limits became too confining, composers opened up new possibilities by adopting the procedures of contemporary polyphony. More than anything else, perhaps, this crucial step assured the future life of French secular song. Of almost equal importance, however, was the diversity of its subject matter. As with the troubadours, the serious love song formed the core of the trouvère repertory. The spirit that produced the Albigensian Crusade, the Inquisition, and the piety of Saint

Louis (Louis IX, 1226–70) again resulted in numerous songs to the Virgin Mary and in the ideal of l'amour courtois as faithful servitude without thought of physical reward. But the trouvères found various ways to counteract the sterility of this concept. Spring songs celebrated the joys of love, and pastourelles created lively pictures of rustic pleasures. The manners and morals of society as a whole occasioned much wry humor, and neither churchmen nor lay officials were safe from satirical attack. On the completely frivolous side, jeux partis debated amorous dilemmas, and *sottes chansons* (foolish songs) imitated the serious chanson in parodies that were ribald when they were not obscene. The trouvères, in short, established both the persistent themes and the ready acceptance of stylistic innovations that characterized French secular song throughout the subsequent course of its uninterrupted history.

CHAPTER XIII

Secular Monophonic Song, III: The Diffusion of Vernacular Song in Other Countries of Western Europe

SECULAR SONG IN GERMANY

In Germany, as in northern France, secular song in the vernacular existed before the influence of the troubadours made itself felt. From the time of the migrant German tribes, singers known as *scops* had been active in social, military, and religious life. As the peoples of Germany adopted a more settled and stationary way of life, wandering entertainers (*Spielleute*) replaced the scops. Counterparts of the jongleurs, the Spielleute ranked very low on the social scale, but they played an important role in the preservation of Germanic traditions and the dissemination of Germanic culture. Some of the oldest secular songs, as we might expect, are in Latin. It is probable, however, that folk tales such as those in the Cambridge songs (see above, p. 260) also appeared in the vernacular repertory of the wandering entertainers. Another part of their repertory consisted of epic poems, comparable to the chanson de geste, that preserved the ancient legends and pre-Christian mythology of the Germanic peoples. Unfortunately, none of the music for this early repertory has survived, and again we are left with only a few hints as to the nature of an important musical tradition.

THE MINNESINGERS

Despite the existence of this older tradition, the history of German secular song really begins with the development of lyric poetry by the *Minnesingers,* the German equivalent of the troubadours and trouvères. The name reflects their preoccupation with the subject of courtly love (*Minne*), a concept evidently taken over from their Provençal and French predecessors and contemporaries. Depending on their nationality—and degree of chauvinism—European scholars have either emphasized or played down the extent to which the Minnesingers imitated the troubadours and trouvères. Yet the art of the Minnesingers obviously owes much to French influences. Quite apart from their subject matter, which was not totally restricted to courtly love, the Minnesingers adopted the poetic types, imitated the techniques and forms, and even borrowed the melodies of French and Provençal songs. This debt cannot be ignored.

Most of the poetic types that we have observed in the troubadour and trouvère repertories reappear in the songs of the Minnesingers. Laments of women (*Frauenstrophe*) over the absence or infidelity of lovers are comparable to the chanson de toile. Lovers part in songs announcing the dawning of the day (*Tagelied*). The Provençal tenso and the jeu parti find their counterpart in the *Streitgedicht* (dispute-poem). The pastourelle influenced, if it did not provide the chief inspiration for, the many songs that describe rustic revels celebrating the return of spring. The Crusades produced the *Kreuzlied,* and numerous songs deal with other religious or political topics. The German *Leich* corresponds to the French lai, both in its treatment of sacred or secular subjects and in its formal characteristics. And finally, of course, there are the songs of courtly love that gave the Minnesingers their name.

Acceptance of the French concept of courtly love in Germany depended upon the existence of an aristocratic society that lived—at least in principle—according to the code of chivalry. Such a society came into existence in the latter half of the twelfth century, particularly at the courts of the Hohenstaufen line of Holy Roman Emperors: Frederick Barbarossa (1152–90), his son Henry VI (1190–97), and grandson Fred-

Two knights in combat illustrate a manuscript of *Parzifal,* by Wolfram von Eschenbach (National Library, Vienna).

erick II (1197–1250). In 1156, Frederick Barbarossa married Beatrix of Burgundy and thus established a direct link with the French. At least one trouvère, Guiot de Provins, is known to have been a member of Beatrix's court. (A small town east and somewhat south of Paris, Provins is not to be confused with Provence.) The imperial court also knew the Latin songs of the Archpoet, author of *The Confession of Golias* and perhaps the greatest of the vagabond poets.[1] The Archpoet's patron from about 1161 to 1166 was Reginald von Dassel, Archbishop of Cologne and Chancellor to Frederick Barbarossa.[2]

These cultural crosscurrents inevitably stimulated the development of German poetry. Henry VI was himself a Minnesinger and—in one of the ironies of history—held the royal trouvère Richard the Lionhearted for ransom after saving him from death at the hands of the duke of Austria. French influence and the development of the Minnesong were not confined to the imperial court, however. In 1161, the Count of Thuringia sent his sons to the court of Louis VII to receive the education of French princes. One of these sons, Hermann, became an enthusiastic admirer of French poetry and an equally enthusiastic patron of Minnesingers.

The first period of Minnesinger activity extends roughly from 1160 to 1220, the same years that saw the first flowering of trouvère song in France. During this time, interest in the production of lyric poetry and song spread throughout Germany, and Minnesingers came from many different and widely separated places. Dietmar von Aist was an Austrian nobleman, Heinrich von Veldeke came from the region near Maastricht, now in southeastern Holland. Between these extremes, Friedrich von Hausen came from the Rhineland near Mainz; Hartmann von Aue was a Swabian; Rudolf von Fenis was a Swiss count; Heinrich von Morungen came from Thuringia, Wolfram von Eschenbach from Bavaria, and Walther von der Vogelweide from the Tyrol. At one time or another, several of these men were associated with Count Hermann of Thuringia or with the Hohenstaufen emperors. Minnesingers from the higher levels of the aristocracy had their own courts, of course, and did not depend on patronage. Members of the lesser nobility, however, often travelled from court to court as some of the troubadours had done before them. Of these wandering singers, perhaps the most notable and certainly one of the best poets was Walther von der Vogelweide (c. 1170–1228). Despite the widespread activity of these and other men, almost no melodies from the first period have survived. Some of the poems obviously imitate or paraphrase Provençal or French models, and

1. Original text and translation of the *Confessio* in H. Waddell, *Medieval Latin Lyrics* (Baltimore, 1952), p. 182.

2. Reginald's request that an epic poem celebrating the emperor's Italian campaign be completed in a week drew an indignant refusal, but the Archpoet on one occasion did receive Frederick's applause. Ibid., p. 338.

A portrait of Walther von der Vogelweide, from the *Manessische Handschrift* (Heidelberg).

scholars have reconstituted a repertory of early Minnesongs by adapting the melodies of these models to the corresponding German texts.[3] This procedure is somewhat dubious, especially when similarity of poetic form is the only indication that the German text is a contrafactum. Even more dubious is the application of triple meters to the Minnesinger versions. German prosody, unlike Provençal and French, was based on the number of accented syllables in each line. Unaccented syllables could be added or subtracted, either within or at the beginning of a line. Thus the number of syllables in each line does not remain constant, and notes must be added or combined in ornaments to make the French melodies fit the German poems. These difficulties, and the uncertainty as to whether the Minnesingers actually did borrow their melodies from the troubadours and trouvères, make examination of the early repertory somewhat pointless. One of the few poems for which we possess the complete melody is the famous *Palestine Song* of Walther von der Vogelweide.[4] According to Gennrich, even this melody is based on one by Jaufre Rudel. In reality, the two melodies bear only slight resemblance to each other, and Gennrich's claim seems a bit extravagant.[5] We may perhaps allow that here, at least, we have an original Minnesinger tune.

3.   In Gennrich, *Troubadours, Trouvères*, the first ten German songs are listed as contrafacta of troubadour or trouvère songs. Similarly, in Seagrave and Thomas, *Songs of the Minnesingers*, all but two or three of the first fifteen songs are contrafacta.

4.   The piece has been many times reprinted: NOHM, 2, p. 253; HAM, No. 20b; and Seagrave and Thomas, *Songs*, pp. 89–91, in three different rhythmic versions.

5.   Gennrich, *Troubadours, Trouvères*, note 6b on p. 71. The two pieces appear on pp. 12 and 51.

Walther von der Vogelweide represents the high point in the "classic" period of Minnesinger activity, yet his poems already depart from the classic ideal of courtly love. The artificiality of this ideal had produced a "deadlock in the love-lyric" that Walther broke "by removing its prime cause—the unattainable lady."[6] Love, as with the Latin poets, again became mutual and human. The same humanity pervades Walther's political and moralistic songs, and it has been said that his chief contribution lay in raising such songs to a high literary level.[7] Known as *Sprüche* (proverbs), songs of this type are obviously related both to the moral-satiric poems of the *Carmina Burana* and to the sirventes of the troubadours. During the thirteenth century, Sprüche became increasingly popular with German poets, who—like their French counterparts—came more and more from bourgeois rather than aristocratic circles. With this development, interest in courtly love declined still further, and other types of songs began to appear. Monophonic song in Germany was embarking on the path that would lead to the Meistersingers of the Renaissance.

The trend away from songs of courtly love is even more evident in the poetry of Walther's younger contemporary Neidhart von Reuenthal (c. 1190–after 1236). A knight of limited means, Neidhart sang at courts in Bavaria and Austria, but he used the techniques and forms of aristocratic poetry to depict rustic life and manners. Almost all of Neidhart's poems fall into two classes: summer songs or winter songs. In these poems, as a rule, a description of the season precedes a realistic narrative of some incident in which the poet often participates. The final stanzas usually take a more personal turn, sometimes give Neidhart's name, and provide the little information that we have about his life. Because the summer and winter poems often describe revelry and dancing, many scholars have assumed that the songs themselves were intended as music for dancing. The assumption seems unlikely for a number of reasons. Refrains may not be an essential feature of dance songs, but their complete absence in the poems of Neidhart already arouses suspicion. Furthermore, neither the length and content of the poems nor their sophisticated poetic and musical forms resemble in any way the known dance songs of the time. If anything, Neidhart's poems suggest a mocking, perhaps semidramatic portrayal of rustic manners by a skilled soloist for the amusement of an audience conscious of its superiority.

Whatever their function may have been, Neidhart's summer and winter poems established a vogue that lasted for many years and produced many imitators. As a result of this popularity, Neidhart is the first Minnesinger for whom we possess a relatively large number of melodies. The most extensive collection of songs attributed to him dates

6.   A. T. Hatto and R. J. Taylor, *The Songs of Neidhart von Reuental*, p. 3.
7.   Seagrave and Thomas, *Songs*, p. 81.

from the fifteenth century. It contains 132 poems, each of which is preceded by staffs for the melody; but the copyist entered only forty-five melodies. Of these, fifteen belong to poems generally acknowledged as genuine Neidhart. The rest, classified as pseudo-Neidhart, are by later and inferior imitators. Two or three more genuine poems with melodies appear in other manuscript sources.[8]

The summer songs are generally regarded as belonging to the earlier period of Neidhart's activity. Their poetic stanzas tend to be short and relatively simple in form, and the two surviving melodies for these poems are continuous with no pattern of phrase repetition. The winter songs, on the other hand, have longer stanzas as a rule with elaborate triparitite forms. The melodies reflect these forms by their use of the pattern *aab,* the so-called *Bar form* that characterizes German song for several centuries to come. (The German names for the *a* and *b* sections are *Stollen* and *Abgesang.*) Bar form is obviously related to the canso and chanson of the troubadours and trouvères, but it never led to forms that included refrains, such as the French ballade. Instead, composers contented themselves with creating different patterns of phrase repetition within the overall *aab* structure. The *b* sections might be entirely new, or they might repeat one or more phrases from the *a* section. When both sections close with the same phrase or phrases, the result is known as *rounded Bar form.*

Two examples of Neidhart's songs will illustrate the differences between the two types (AMM, Nos. 48 and 49). The summer song *Ine gesach die heide* (I never saw the heath) has stanzas of eight, rather short lines. The first two pairs of lines could be sung to the same music to produce a tripartite form. However, each of them, and each of the remaining four lines, has its own musical phrase. Thus the melody ignores the structural pattern suggested by the rhyme scheme ab ab ccdc. The stanzas of the winter song *Owê, lieber sumer* (Alas, dear summer) are more complex. Their ten, considerably longer lines have the rhyme scheme abc abc deed and a melody in typical Bar form. The large aspects of this form are obvious, but the subtle interrelationships of the internal phrases lend themselves to different interpretations.

The German method of notating Minnesongs often confronts the modern editor with many problems, a fact that accounts for the variants one finds in transcriptions of the same song from the same manuscript. Unlike French chansonniers, which set the first stanza under the melody, German manuscripts normally put the melody—without words—in a blank space above the poem. Single notes predominate, with occasional two-note ligatures. With only a few exceptions, note values are unmeasured, and the ends of phrases are not indicated. The repeated section in Bar form is often not written out. Even when the melodic style

---

8.   See Bibliography for various editions of both genuine and pseudo-Neidhart songs.

Neidhart von Reuenthal depicted with his followers in the *Manessische Handschrift* (Heidelberg).

is almost completely syllabic—as is the case with Neidhart's songs—such a notation presents problems for the modern editor. The number of notes and the number of syllables rarely agree, and adjustments of some kind must be made. As a result, we are even less sure than with the troubadours and trouvères that published versions of the Minnesinger repertory present a true picture of what medieval performers actually sang. The lateness of most manuscript sources only adds to this uncertainty.

It is possible, nevertheless, to make some comments about the musical style of Neidhart's songs and about German songs in general. The accentual nature of German poetry—in contrast to French and Provençal—makes the application of regular meters much easier, although it is uncertain whether those meters should be duple or triple.[9] In either case, the rhythmic solidity and stiffness of German song contrasts sharply with the more fluid grace of French and Provençal. German songs also tend to be more angular in outline, with more and wider skips and frequent triadic progressions. These characteristics may be related in part to the frequent use of scales that are essentially or completely pentatonic. On the other hand, it is sometimes said that the Minnesingers adhered more closely to the system of the church modes than did the troubadours and trouvères. To some extent this too may be true, but modal purity may also be the result of revisions by later generations of singers. Some of the older melodies are modally ambiguous,

9. See the three rhythmic versions of Walther's *Palestine Song* in Seagrave and Thomas, *Songs*, pp. 89–91.

with phrases that seem to alternate between different modes, none of which agrees with the final of the piece. Neidhart's *Ine gesach* is typical. On the whole we may say that, despite certain Germanic traits, the melodies of troubadours, trouvères, and early Minnesingers have much in common. More than anything else it is the different languages with their different types of prosody that distinguish the three groups of poets and composers.

MINNESONG IN THE LATER THIRTEENTH CENTURY AND BEYOND

Some fifty melodies belong to poems that Neidhart's German editors consider to be the work of inferior imitators. Already evident in these pieces is the tendency toward stereotyped musical forms that became even more marked in succeeding centuries. More and more, composers were content to work slight variations on the rounded Bar form. They carried this formal principle so far, indeed, that the second section often consists of but one new phrase, followed by still another repetition of the complete first section. One of the more successful examples of this form, which we may indicate as *aaba,* is the well-known *Maienzit* (Maytime), a strictly pentatonic, pseudo–Neidhart song that is often included in musical anthologies.[10] On the whole, however, use of the form suggests poverty of invention rather than economy of means.

In addition to the anonymous imitators of Neidhart, the thirteenth century produced numerous Minnesingers whose names and songs are known. Only slightly younger than Neidhart were Reinmar von Zweter and Tannhäuser. The latter's songs are of interest primarily for the information they give about his life. The second half of the thirteenth century, in Germany as in France, saw the production of monophonic song pass largely from aristocratic to bourgeois poets and composers. Among these men, some of the more important are Meister Alexander (also known as "wild"), Konrad von Würzburg, Herman der Damen, Der Unverzagte (The Undaunted), and Heinrich von Meissen (d. 1318), better known as Frauenlob. The most famous Minnesinger of his day, Frauenlob travelled widely throughout Germany but spent the last years of his life at Mainz, where he was buried in the cathedral. According to an unfounded legend, Frauenlob established the first singing school of the Meistersingers, at Mainz.

Despite the predominance of bourgeois composers, some members of the aristocracy continued to write songs even in the fourteenth and early fifteenth centuries. Prince Wizlaw von Rügen (c. 1268–1325) was a contemporary of Frauenlob. Nearly a century later, Count Hugo von

---

10. Gleason, EM, p. 21; Gennrich, *Troubadours, Trouvères,* p. 55. The songs in HAM (Nos. 20c and 20d) are also pseudo-Neidhart.

Montfort (1357–1423) wrote poems but retained a musician, Burk Mangolt, to compose the melodies. At about the same time, an otherwise unknown "Monk of Salzburg" was writing songs for the aristocratic court of Archbishop Pilgrim II von Puchheim (1365–96). Finally, the long line of Minnesingers ends with one of its most colorful figures, Oswald von Wolkenstein (1377–1445).[11] Both Wolkenstein and the Monk of Salzburg wrote polyphonic as well as monophonic songs. Thus they conclude the development of medieval monophony and begin the history of the German polyphonic Lied in the Renaissance.

The history of the Meistersingers also belongs primarily to the Renaissance. Descended from the bourgeois fraternities of poets and composers (confréries in France), the guilds of the Meistersingers established rigid rules for determining the status of their members, for judging the quality of songs, and for governing their singing schools. The inevitable result of such rules was a "sterile and mechanical craftsmanship" that delighted in highly complex poetic forms and rhyme schemes. Gennrich cites a poem of Michel Behaim in which every syllable somewhere has its rhyme "as a curiosity which nevertheless mirrors the spirit of the time." [12]

For the student of medieval music, the songbooks of the Meistersingers are important because they preserve tunes (Weisen or Töne) attributed to well-known Minnesingers of earlier times. It is impossible to tell, of course, whether the tunes are genuine, or how much they have been ornamented with the Meistersingers' characteristic melismas known as Blumen (flowers). Matching these tunes with their presumedly original texts is an uncertain process at best and usually requires considerable manipulation of the melodies. By this means the song repertory of early Minnesingers has been increased, but the authenticity of the result is open to serious question.[13] For this and other deficiencies in the manuscript tradition, then, German song remains one of the most enigmatic—and, at the same time, most fascinating—areas of medieval secular monophony.

MONOPHONIC SONG IN ITALY

The kingdom of Sicily, which included Naples and the southern third of Italy, saw the birth of Italian poetry during the reign of Frederick II (1197–1250). Son of Henry VI, Frederick was the last of the great Ho-

---

11. For a brief account of Oswald's life and adventures, see GD, 9, p. 351, and Seagrave and Thomas, *Songs*, p. 213 ff.

12. Gennrich, *Troubadours, Trouvères*, p. 11.

13. See Seagrave and Thomas, *Songs*, pp. 93–96, for the textless version of Walther's *Lange Ton* and the "free adaptation" of this melody to his poem *Ich saz ûf eine steine* (I sat upon a stone).

henstaufens to become Holy Roman Emperor (1220–50), yet a king less German would be difficult to imagine. Inheritor of Sicily through his mother, Frederick grew up in the South and did not even visit Germany until 1211. Throughout his life, Sicily and southern Italy remained the scene of Frederick's major interest and activity. His court won fame and notoriety for its almost Oriental splendor, and his personal gifts won him the designation *stupor mundi* (wonder of the world). More than on the material magnificence of his court or even on his achievements as a statesman, Frederick's claim to lasting fame rests on the intellectual pursuits that he stimulated and in which he participated. Scholars of all sorts—Christians, Jews, and Moslems; philosophers, scientists, and men of letters—made the Sicilian court the most cultured of its day. Frederick himself wrote a learned treatise on birds and, in lighter moments, joined other writers in the production of lyric verse.

Pope Gregory IX (1227–41) once complained that political expedience rather than conviction accounted for Frederick's seemingly orthodox belief. The accusation may have contained some element of truth, for, in addition to tolerating Jews and Moslems, Frederick sheltered troubadours who had fled from the horror of the Albigensian Crusade and the terror of the Inquisition. These were not men to spread abroad the concept of love as platonic service, but they did introduce the conceits and conventional themes of troubadour poetry, which the members of the "Sicilian" school then used for frankly sensual expression. Unfortunately, the melodies of these first Italian songs do not survive.

A somewhat different situation prevailed in northern Italy. Here the influence of the troubadours was so strong that Provençal remained the poetic language of choice throughout most of the thirteenth century. For a time, even Dante (1265–1321) debated whether he should write in Provençal or Italian. Of the Italian troubadours who did write in Provençal, the most famous and influential was Sordello of Mantua. Famous for the number of his mistresses and as a seducer of married women, Sordello influenced poets who wrote in the vernacular by his devotion to the concept of spiritual love for an unattainable lady. Faithful but fruitless service to a lady glimpsed briefly, preferably at Mass in the homeland of the troubadours, became an accepted poetic convention. Guido Cavalcanti had his Mandetta; Dante, his Beatrice; and Petrarch, his Laura. The first poets of northern Italy regarded themselves as exponents of a *dolce stil nuovo* (sweet new style), but love—now metaphysical and ethereal—remained the exclusive theme of their lyric verse. This disembodied love seems to have provided little inspiration for composers, and—to the detriment of both poetry and music—the two began to go their separate ways. The tradition of the troubadour as poet-composer declined. Few, if any, of the major Italian poets set their verses to music or even intended them to be sung. *Canzoni* and *sonetti* (little songs) became songs in name only. Not until the fourteenth century did secular poetry—usually of a less exalted nature—attract the attention of composers. This development belongs primarily to the history of polyphonic rather than monophonic song (see Chapter XVIII).

LAUDE SPIRITUALI

Although Italy produced little secular monophony, we do possess about 150 vernacular songs known as *laude spirituali* (literally, "spiritual praises"). (The word appears in two forms: *lauda,* singular, and *laude,* plural; or *laude,* singular, and *laudi,* plural.) These songs of praise are religious in nature; but, with their Italian texts, they are obviously non-liturgical. They apparently originated in a curious way. From about 1250 to 1350, the devastation of wars and of plagues led to the formation of wandering bands of penitents who sought to atone for the sins of the world by practicing flagellation and, perhaps not simultaneously, by singing laude. Some of the older songs in a thirteenth-century manuscript in Cortona are simple and folklike in character and might well have been sung as processional or marching songs. Later songs in two fourteenth-century manuscripts in Florence are considerably more elaborate and suggest performance by expert soloists.[14]

Melodically, the laude spirituali reveal the influence of Gregorian Chant, of the troubadours, perhaps also of folk song. A popular element is evident too in the obvious derivation of formal characteristics from the round dance with refrain. The basic structure of all laude includes an opening refrain (*ripresa*) that recurs after each stanza. However, the laude display considerable variety in the internal organization of their melodies and the different ways they relate the stanza to the refrain. The two sections may be completely independent or almost identical. Stanzas longer than the refrain may close with all or part of the refrain melody. When the stanza begins with a new melody that is repeated and then concludes with all of the refrain melody, the form becomes that of the Italian ballata or the French virelai (*AbbaA*).[15] It is probably a mistake, however, to regard the forms of the laude as variants of, or deviations from, the fixed form of ballate and virelais. They represent, rather, the developmental stage already observed in French secular song during which round dances with refrains evolved their distinctive and finally "fixed" forms. In Italy, that development is much more evident in the laude spirituali than in the secular ballate, which did not make their ap-

---

14. F. Liuzzi, *La lauda e i primordi della melodia italiana,* contains facsimiles and transcriptions (rhythmically dubious) of laude from the Cortona and Florence manuscripts.

15. For characteristic examples of different formal patterns, see the three laude in NOHM, 2, pp. 268–69 and three others in HAM, No. 21.

pearance in musical sources until about the middle of the fourteenth century.

A particularly charming lauda from the Cortona manuscript, *Laude novella sia cantata* (Let a new song of praise be sung), is addressed to the Virgin Mary (AMM, No. 50). The form of the poem is typical. Stanzas of four lines alternate with a two-line refrain that has the same rhyme for both lines. The first three lines of the stanzas use one rhyme, different each time, but the fourth line always returns to the rhyme of the refrain. The musical form is somewhat less typical. Each line of the refrain has its own melody, but the stanza does not begin with repeated phrases. Instead, it opens with the first phrase of the refrain and closes with the second, both slightly modified. Only the two middle lines of the stanza introduce new phrases. The combination of these poetic and musical procedures may be represented as follows:

> Rhyme scheme: AA b bba AA c cca AA d dda etc.
>
> Musical form: *AB a'cdb'* *AB a'cdb'* *AB a'cdb'* etc.

Even more remarkable than the form of *Laude novella* is its tonal organization. The mode is Dorian throughout, except in phrase *d,* which descends into the Hypodorian range. Phrases *a* and *b* both begin with upward skips of a fifth, **d–a**, while phrases *c* and *d* have downward skips, **d'–f** and **f–d**. This emphasis on the notes **d–f–a** continues within the phrases and becomes even stronger in the cadences, which end only on these notes in the order **ad affd ad**, etc. The careful balance of this structure makes the tonal center as obvious as it is in any nineteenth-century tune. Analysis of the way phrases are at once related and contrasted will reveal equal care and artistry. Only the most skillful craftsmanship can have fashioned this little masterpiece of melodic art.

THE GEISSLERLIEDER

The penitential fever soon spread from Italy to Germany, but it did not become particularly virulent north of the Alps until the great plague known as the Black Death devastated most of Euope in 1348–49. Hoping to avert the plague—but probably helping to spread contagion—bands of *Geissler* (flagellants) travelled from town to town throughout Germany. A contemporary chronicle by Hugo von Reutlingen describes a visit of the Geissler and records the words and music of some half dozen songs (*Geisslerlieder*).[16] Other manuscripts preserve the

---

16. The complete chronicle is published in P. Runge, *Die Lieder und Melodien der Geissler des Jahres 1349* (Leipzig, 1900), pp. 24–41.

words but not the melodies of a few more Geisslerlieder. Such a small repertory would scarcely be worthy of mention were it not for its sociological and historical interest. That the flagellants represented a popular religious movement may seem incredible, but that movement was only one expression of an extreme and often excessive piety in the later Middle Ages. And to the Geissler, at least, we owe some of our oldest examples of religious folk songs.

Three of the songs quoted by Hugo von Reutlingen were used as processional or "traveling" songs. The other three accompanied the actual flagellation ceremony. Some scholars have professed to find an influence of the Italian lauda on the Geisslerlieder, but that influence, if it existed at all, must have been very slight. The sophisticated diversity of the laude spirituali contrasts sharply with the simplicity and sameness of the German songs. Rhymed couplets constitute the basic structural element of all the texts, and a limited number of musical phrases are repeated in pairs (*aabb*) or in alternation (*abab*). The songs for the flagellation ceremony illustrate both procedures as well as the general style of all the melodies (Example XIII–1). In the opening stanza of the first song, *Nu tret herzuo,* three lines of text are sung to the first musical phrase, an irregularity that recurs on the second phrase of the fourth stanza. The remainder of the poem is entirely in rhymed couplets, and all stanzas except the last use only phrases *a* and *b*. In the final stanza a new phrase (*c*) alternates with phrase *b* transposed up a fourth (*b'*). The distribution of these three different phrases in the seven stanzas of *Nu tret herzuo* is as follows:

I.	*aaa bb*
II.	*aa bb*
III.	*aa bb bb bb*
IV.	*aa bbb*
V.	*aa bb bb*
VI.	*aa bb bb bb*
VII.	*aa cb' cb' cb' cb'*

The second and third flagellation songs use the melodic phrases of the first. The third includes textual and, of course, musical quotations from both of the first two; and all three end with the same final stanza (VII above). This "refrain" serves both a musical and ceremonial function, for it occurs each of the three times that the flagellants prostrated themselves in the form of a cross. In the third song, a new phrase in the penultimate stanza (*d* in Example XIII–1) adds to the climactic effect. Repetitive in itself, phrase *d* is stated three times in the middle of the stanza, the complete form of which is *aa ddd b'b'b'*.

Example XIII–1: *Phrases of Flagellation Songs, with First Stanza of* Nu tret
herzuo

a

Nu tret her-zuo der bös - sen wel-le
Flie-hen von die hais - sun hel-le
Lu - ci - fer ist bös ge - sel - le

b

Wen er be-hapt mit bech er lapt
Des flihn wir in hab wir den sin.

b′

c

d

Now approaches the deluge of evil. Let us flee from burning Hell. Lucifer
is an evil companion. Whomever he seizes, he besmears with pitch. Therefore we want to shun him.

The melodic phrases of the processional songs are equally short and
simple. Two of the songs are musically related and use repetitive formal
patterns such as *abcb* or *abcbcb*. [17] The third consists of fifty-seven rhymed
couplets that are all sung to the same two phrases, each of which is followed by a different refrain. The first line of every couplet concludes
with "Kyrie eleyson"; the second, with "Alleluia: Globet sis du, Maria"
(Praise be to thee, Maria). The first couplet of this song is given in
Example XIII–2. It seems likely that one or two leaders sang the
changing texts of the rhymed couplets and the entire group responded
with the refrains. This manner of performance would emphasize the
close relationship of the song to the Latin litany, a liturgical chant with
congregational responses that was sung on more orthodox occasions.
To a lesser extent the influence of the litany is evident in the repetitive
forms of all the *Geisslerlieder*. It is these forms, together with the folklike quality of the melodies, that distinguish the Geisslerlieder from the
more elaborate and more consciously artistic laude spirituali. Although
the Italian songs may have absorbed some popular elements, they owe
much more to the sophisticated art of the troubadours.

17. Reese, MMA, p. 239, gives one of the processional songs (incomplete).

Example XIII–2: *Processional Geisslerlied (First of 57 Couplets)*

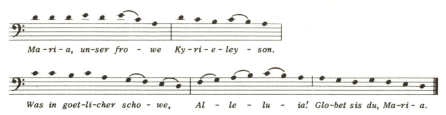

Ma - ri - a, un-ser fro - we   Ky - ri - e - ley - son.

Was in goet-li-cher scho - we,   Al - le - lu - ia! Glo-bet sis du, Ma-ri - a.

Mary, our Lady, *Kyrie eleison.*
Who, in godly sight, *Alleluia. Praise be to thee, Maria.*

THE SPANISH AND GALICIAN-PORTUGUESE CANTIGAS

Monophonic song in Spain, even more than in Italy, must be regarded as a direct outgrowth of the troubadour movement. From the time of William IX, contact between the ruling families of southern France and the Christian kings of Spain was frequent and close. The large retinues that accompanied these rulers on their many visits to each other naturally included troubadours and jongleurs, who also travelled widely on their own. French troubadours found a ready welcome at Spanish courts, and Provençal became the language of poetry south of the Pyrenees as it did south of the Alps. In the thirteenth century, however, songs in the vernacular speech of the Iberian peninsula began to make their appearance. The oldest examples are seven *canciones de amor* (love songs) by Martin Codax, for which six melodies survive. Codax came from the Galician town of Vigo on the west coast of Spain just above Portugal, and the language of his poems is Galician-Portuguese. Both texts and music are simple in form and style and suggest a derivation from folk idioms or dance songs rather than from the more sophisticated love songs of the troubadours.[18]

A much larger and more important collection of songs in Galician-Portuguese, the *Cantigas de Santa Maria,* was assembled at the court of Alfonso the Wise, King of Castile and León (1252–84). A patron of learning and letters, of troubadours and jongleurs, Alfonso himself may have contributed some of the more than 400 anonymous songs in the collection. In any case, the *Cantigas* originated in a cultured and aristocratic society that numbered troubadour song among its many amusements.

Among the more unusual aspects of the *Cantigas de Santa Maria* are

---

18.   The songs are published in I. Pope, "Mediaeval Latin Background of the Thirteenth-Century Galician Lyric," *Speculum,* 9 (1934), pp. 3–25. One song is available in NOHM, 2, p. 261.

A portrait of King Alfonso the Wise and his musicians, from a manuscript of the *Cantigas de Santa Maria* (Madrid, Escorial).

the unity of their subject matter and the systematic arrangement of the collection as a whole. The great majority of songs recount miracles performed by the Virgin Mary, one song for each miracle. Every tenth song, from No. 10 to No. 400, punctuates the series with a more general song in her praise. The regularity of this arrangement is broken only at the beginning of the collection, where a sung Prologue precedes the first song, which is also a general song of praise. In the manuscripts of the *Cantigas,* the songs are carefully numbered; rubrics identify the subject of each; and miniatures of musicians performing on different instruments further distinguish each of the songs of praise.[19]

The texts of the *Cantigas* are not as far removed from the traditions of the troubadours and trouvères as they might at first seem. Indeed, the texts themselves establish a relationship. The Prologue, which may have been written by King Alfonso himself, lists the qualities needed to compose well (*ben trobar*), and the author of the song of praise *Rosa das rosas* (Rose of roses) would be the "trobador" of Our Lady.[20] We may note further that the last of the troubadours, Guiraut Riquier, who spent ten years or more at the court of Alfonso the Wise, celebrated the Virgin Mary in many of his songs. For the benefit of the Inquisition, other poets also proved the purity of their love by substituting Mary for a earthly lady. We need not accuse them all of hypocrisy, however. The cult of the Virgin was very strong in the thirteenth century, and many of the songs addressed to her must be sincere expressions of common religious feelings. Those feelings found further expression in accounts of the numerous miracles attributed to the Virgin Mary. More than all the other saints in heaven, Mary entered people's daily lives to provide miraculous solutions for their insoluble problems. One of her special provinces was the protection of errant women from the consequences of their sins, but men—if they were not faithless husbands—might also

19. A facsimile of a manuscript from the Escorial is included in the monumental edition of the *Cantigas* published by H. Anglès (see Bibliography).

20. For the stanza with a translation, see Reese, MMA, p. 248.

This lavishly illustrated manuscript of the *Cantigas de Santa Maria* provides a wealth of information about medieval musical instruments. Note especially the fanciful bagpipes on the right (Madrid, Escorial).

receive her aid. Mary's miraculous performances had already attracted poets before the time of Alfonso the Wise. Perhaps the most famous collection of stories was *Les Miracles de Notre Dame* by Gautier de Coincy (d. 1236), a trouvère who was also a Benedictine monk. Gautier did not mean his narrative poetry to be sung, but he varied his stories of Our Lady's miracles by introducing some thirty-seven songs with their melodies. At least in part, therefore, *Les Miracles de Notre Dame* established a literary and musical precedent for the *Cantigas de Santa Maria,* and both works evidently fulfilled contemporary needs. The survival of Gautier's *Miracles* in no fewer than eighty-four manuscripts attests to the work's enormous popularity and influence. Delight and belief in the miracles may have been genuine enough, but the detailed accounts of Boccaccio-like situations that called for Mary's intervention suggest that audiences enjoyed the sins at least as much as the salvation.

Modern scholars regard the *Cantigas de Santa Maria* as "one of the greatest monuments of medieval music," and the four different manuscripts that preserve the songs indicate an equally high regard on the part of their contemporaries. In one manuscript the staffs for the music were left blank, but the other three contain both texts and melodies. As a result of their unexpected use of mensural notation, the *Cantigas* are unique in being the only large repertory of monophonic song that can be transcribed with assurance in modern meters and note values. Many songs are in triple meter, sometimes transcribed as 6/4 or 6/8. Others are clearly duple. Songs in triple meter do not always adhere to the rhythmic modes, and some do not maintain a regular meter throughout but change from triple to duple or vice versa. Songs of this kind may reflect an older, more freely rhythmic style, or they may merely record the licenses of contemporary performance. In any case, the various meters of the *Cantigas* should probably not be used to justify the application of similar meters to repertories in unmeasured notation.

In addition to the unity of their subject matter, the *Cantigas* display a uniformity of poetic and musical form remarkable for a collection of this size. The great majority of poems begin with a refrain that is repeated before each stanza and again at the end of the poem. The music of the stanza proper begins with one or two new phrases that are repeated and then concludes with all or part of the refrain melody. The form common to many *Cantigas,* that is, may be represented as *A bba A bba A,* etc., the pattern of the French virelai, the Italian ballata, and some laude spirituali. Despite the seeming rigidity of this form, it allows for considerable freedom in the distribution and relationship of phrases within the larger sections. Thus, analysis of individual phrases reveals many variants of the basic form. *Rosa das rosas* (No. 10) has the pattern *AB ccdb AB.*[21] A much more economical form, *AB a'a' ab AB,* appears in *Aque serven todo'los celestiaes* (She whom all celestial beings serve).[22]

Santa Maria amar (We should love Holy Mary; AMM, No. 51) is almost equally economical in its setting of a much longer text. Here, three or four different phrases provide all the melody for a refrain of six lines and a stanza of twelve:

$$ABA'\ ABC\ db'a\ db'a\ aba'\ abc\ ABA'\ ABC$$

Once again, however, the letter designations are somewhat misleading because they conceal interrelationships of seemingly different phrases. The third phrase (*A'*) varies the first three notes of phrase *A* by rhythmic displacement and one change of pitch. The rhythmic pattern of phrase *A'* then begins phrase *C,* which ends with the cadential formula of phrases *A* and *A'* transposed down a fifth. Following phrase *C,* the only one to end on the final of the mode (**d**), the striking entry of phrase *d* an octave higher marks the beginning of the stanza. Yet phrases *A* and *d* are rhythmically identical, and their last two measures are melodically identical as well. Just as phrase *C* is the only one to end on the low **d**, phrase *A* is the only one to begin on that note and phrase *d* is the only one in which the melody reaches the upper octave (**d'**). By the placement and restricted use of these pitch extremes, the unknown composer has shaped the simple yet subtly varied and interrelated phrases into another masterpiece of melodic art.

Both the origin of the form common to so many *Cantigas* and the sources of their melodic style have been the subject of speculation and controversies. It must be stressed here, however, that the *Cantigas de Santa Maria* are the first songs to make extensive use of the form that later became fixed in the French virelai and Italian ballata. In melodic style the *Cantigas* are simple, concise, and essentially syllabic. Ornamental figures are few in number and rarely exceed two or three notes to a syllable. Melodic motion is chiefly stepwise, with occasional skips of a third. Larger skips usually occur only between phrases. The relatively

21. Reese, MMA, p. 247.
22. HAM, No. 22c. Two more *Cantigas* in HAM and five in NOHM, 2, pp. 262–66 provide further examples for analysis.

short phrases that result from the syllabic style are defined by clear cadences, by their rhythmic shape, and by the repetitive nature of the forms. All of these characteristics combine to produce melodies that are often dancelike, almost popular in tone. Some writers find in the *Cantigas* "a flavour which is unmistakably Spanish."[23] Usually, however, the ingredients that create the flavor are left unspecified. One wonders how much it depends upon the presence of a Spanish text. Whatever one's answer may be, the *Cantigas* bestow upon us some of the most attractive and tuneful melodies in the entire repertory of monophonic song. If we accept in the proper spirit the naive accounts of miracles and the situations that called them forth, we can experience today the pleasure and amusement that the *Cantigas de Santa Maria* provided for the court of Alfonso the Wise.

MONOPHONIC SONG IN ENGLAND

For a number of reasons, England contributed little to the history of medieval secular monophony. Eleanor of Aquitaine, it is true, patronized troubadours and trouvères, but their art apparently gained little foothold in England. In the twelfth century, we must remember, England was only a small part of a much larger continental empire that included Normandy, Anjou, and Aquitaine. Eleanor's husband, Henry II (1154–89), spent more than half his reign on the continent. Their son, Richard the Lionhearted, was in England for only six months during his ten years as king (1189–99). Moreover, the language of the court was Norman-French, and any songs produced there would belong to the literature of the trouvères. Even after much of the continental territory passed from the English to the French kings, French remained the language of the English court throughout the thirteenth century and much of the fourteenth as well. Only scattered examples of vernacular poetry and prose survive from the period preceding the first flowering of English literature in the second half of the fourteenth century with Wycliffe's Bible, William Langland's *Vision of Piers Plowman* (c. 1370), and the works of Chaucer (c. 1340–1400). We need not be surprised, therefore, to find that the Middle Ages produced only a handful of songs with English texts.

The oldest English lyrics that survive with their melodies are three songs attributed to St. Godric, a Saxon hermit in northern England who died in 1170. Legend has it that the songs were dictated to Godric in angelic visions, and they give an impression of being liturgical songs in the vernacular. Two are prayers—one to the Virgin Mary and one to St. Nicholas. In the third, angels sing "Kyrie eleison," before and after a

23.   NOHM, 2, p. 263.

song by Godric's dead sister, who tells of her treatment in heaven.[24] The notation of these songs is unmeasured, and they should undoubtedly be sung in the free rhythms of the liturgical music they resemble.

English songs of the thirteenth century are only slightly more numerous. One of the best, *Worldes blis,* has been published a number of times.[25] The pessimistic tone of this lament for the transience of earthly joys is matched by another song that reminds man of the brevity of life itself: *Man mei longe him lives wene* (Man may think his life will be long).[26] In both poems, the first four lines of the stanzas have the rhyme scheme abab, which the melodies reflect by repetitions that remind us of the form often used in the continental canso and chanson. The repetition is exact (*abab*) in *Man mei longe.* The first phrases of *Worldes blis* have the pattern *abcb,* but phrase *c* twice repeats a motive from phrase *a.* Both songs also end with modified versions of their opening phrases. More purely secular, but scarcely more joyous, is the fragmentary song *Mirie it is while sumer ilast.*[27] One of the rare English love songs that has been preserved with its melody is *Byrd one brere* (Bird on a briar; AMM, No. 52). The song was copied on the back of a twelfth-century papal bull, but its mensural notation proves that it must date from the late thirteenth or early fourteenth century.[28] Although longs, breves, and semibreves are clearly differentiated, transcription is still problematical because the written values do not always result in regular meters. The version in AMM follows the values of the original and makes no attempt to achieve metrical uniformity by means of editorial changes. Only the text of the first stanza was placed under the melody, and further difficulties arise from discrepancies in the number of syllables in some lines of the second and third stanzas. In the fourth line, for example, the upbeat apparently serves only the first stanza. If it is not omitted in the others, it must become the first beat of a measure in 4/4. Another problem arises from the notation of the second staff in the original, which begins with the word "Rewe" (mercy). The unusual upward skip of a sixth in the middle of a phrase suggests that the scribe may have used the wrong clef. If he did, the melody from this point onward should be read a third lower. Finally, the disposition of text and music in the manuscript indicates that the song may have been intended as a polyphonic piece. The first part of the text—to "Rewe" again—has

24. For the prayer to the Virgin, see HAM, No. 23a. The song of Godric's sister is printed in Reese, MMA, p. 241. All of the songs are in J. B. Trend, "The First English Songs," ML, 9 (1928), pp. 120–23, with a facsimile on p. 119.

25. HAM, No. 23b; NOHM, 2, p. 251. Facsimile in Parrish, NMM, Pl. XIX.

26. Reese, MMA, p. 243.

27. Facsimile in Stainer, *Early Bodleian Music,* 2, Pl. 3. The melody is in part illegible, in part completely missing.

28. Facsimile in J. Saltmarsh, "Two Medieval Love-Songs set to Music," *Antiquaries Journal,* 15 (1935), facing p. 3. (The other "medieval" song dates from the reign of Henry VIII in the sixteenth century!)

two staffs drawn above it, with the lower left blank. The rest of the text has only one staff above it, but the two lines of text are separated by enough space to accommodate another complete staff. It would seem that the scribe who copied the text anticipated a two-part piece written in score in the characteristically English manner (see Chapter XX).

Despite these uncertainties with regard to *Byrd one brere,* the attractiveness of both its text and its melody makes us wish that the English had been less reticent in giving musical expression to their amorous moods. Indeed, from the quality of the extant songs it is evident that England must have enjoyed a high level of vernacular musical culture in the thirteenth century. How many pieces have been lost we shall never know, but none of those that do exist can have been the only work of an inexperienced composer. It is unfortunate—and frustrating—that we should possess such scanty remains of an obviously rich heritage.

CHAPTER XIV

Sacred and Secular Polyphony in the Thirteenth Century

The thirteenth century witnessed a new relationship between musical activities that had hitherto followed separate paths. From the beginning, polyphony had been the province of church musicians, who used it as an ornament of liturgical chant, including tropes and sequences, and for settings of religious or moral Latin poetry. Purveyors of music for secular entertainment in the vernacular had confined themselves almost entirely to monophonic song. With the appearance of the secular French motet in the thirteenth century, the two paths began to cross. Monophonic songs continued to be written, even into the fourteenth and fifteenth centuries, but they were soon overshadowed and eventually stifled by the luxuriant growth of secular polyphony that quickly followed the creation of the motet. The effect of this new form on liturgical polyphony was even more immediate and therefore more dramatic. By 1225 the composition of organum appears to have ceased, and by the middle of the century the conductus too was nearly extinct. The motet was now, and for the next fifty years remained, not merely the preeminent, but almost the sole form of polyphonic composition. We are adopting the attitude of its contemporaries, therefore, when we regard the sacred or secular motet with Latin or French texts as the representative form of thirteenth-century polyphony.

The addition of secular French texts to discant clausulae appears to have followed closely on the creation of motets as sacred tropes (see Chapter X). This is evident from both the oldest motet repertory and the name of the form itself. In the thirteenth century, *mots* (words) commonly designated the text of a secular song. Hence the Latinized form *motetus* was an appropriate name for a clausula with a secular French text. This derivation of the name from French rather than Latin is an indication that the early motet with Latin text was not yet regarded as an independent form. At that time, a clausula with an added Latin trope would have still been a clausula, but now *cum littera* (with text), a phrase that applied to any polyphony in syllabic rather than melismatic style. From the beginning, presumably, clausulae with French texts were intended for secular entertainment and had no functional connection with organum. As pieces with Latin texts more gradually lost that connection, they too came to be known as motets. By the time of the Renaissance—such are the paradoxes of language—the name derived from French was applied almost exclusively to polyphonic settings of sacred Latin texts.

LATIN AND FRENCH MOTETS

To some extent, Latin and French motets developed along parallel lines during the course of the thirteenth century. It seems advisable, therefore, to deal with those characteristics common to both types before considering special features that relate French motets to the secular songs of the trouvères. Both began with the addition of texts to preexistent clausulae, and the same clausula often provided the music for Latin tropes of the tenor's text and for French secular songs. The different texts added to Perotin's clausula *Ex semine,* for example, illustrate this early procedure (see above, Chapter X, and AMM, No. 38). The next step in creating a repertory of motets, logically enough, was the composition of new music in the style of discant clausulae. Composers used the familiar tenors of Notre Dame clausulae for many of their new motets, but they also began to draw tenors from chants that had not previously been given polyphonic settings. In these cases, we are sometimes faced with problems of priority. We do not always know whether a motet is newly composed or whether it was based on a clausula now lost. Even the existence of one piece as both a clausula and a motet does not always solve the problem, for in some cases, original motets may have been converted into clausulae by removal of their text.[1] There would seem to have been little need to expand the already extensive collections of clausulae in this fashion. That such a claim can be made, however, is striking proof that the clausula and motet were musically identical in the first half of the thirteenth century.

CONDUCTUS MOTET

Whether newly composed or derived from preexistent clausulae, the great majority of early motets were for two voices only. In a much smaller number of pieces for three and four voices, all voices above the tenor sang the same text, resulting in a form known as the *conductus motet.* A few of these are French motets, but most have Latin texts, many of which trope the text of the tenor. Perotin's clausula *Ex semine* once again provides characteristic examples, this time of a conductus motet that exists with both Latin and French texts (see Chapter X, pp.

1. See E. Thurston, *The Music of the St. Victor Manuscript,* p. 1 of Introduction: also, W. Waite, *The Rhythm of Twelfth-Century Polyphony,* p. 101.

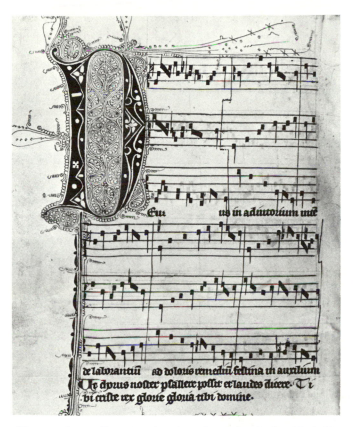

The conductus *Deus in adjutorium* from the Codex Vari 42 (Turin, Royal Library).

253–55). The term *conductus motet* is something more than a convenient modern label for this type of composition. There can be little doubt that the idea of having two or three voices sing the same text came from the conductus, and confusion between the two forms evidently existed in the thirteenth century. Collections of true conducti in the Notre Dame manuscripts, particularly **W₁**, sometimes included conductus motets *without their tenors.* Whether they were so performed we do not know. The result would be musically satisfactory in some cases, but less so in others.[2] The upper voices of a conductus motet were normally written in score, with the text beneath, while the tenor appeared by itself at the end. It is possible that the scribes who entered these pieces in collections of conducti either mistook their true nature or simply forgot to copy the tenor parts. At any rate, the intermingling of conducti and conductus motets clearly justifies describing the latter as settings in conductus style above a plainchant tenor.

2. For part of a four-voice conductus motet without the tenor and arguments for performance in this way, see NOHM, 2, p. 365 ff. and Ex. 197. See also H. Tischler, "English Traits in the early 13th-century Motet," MQ, 30 (1944), pp. 470–71. Tischler's statements are not entirely accurate. In the Florence manuscript (**F**), the final note of the tenor *Manere* is **C**, not **A**, and is perfectly concordant with the other voices.

As a musical form, the conductus motet proved to be short-lived. Its disappearance is probably related in some way to the disappearance of the conductus itself, but the difficulty of adding the same text to more than one voice may well have speeded its demise. Conductus style demanded phrases of equal length with an approximately equal number of notes. Passages in which phrases began or ended at different times or overlapped in imitation and canon would require extensive modification for use with a single text.[3] Such modifications were made in the conductus motets created from Perotin's four-voice setting of *Sederunt* (see Chapter X), but the practice did not win general acceptance. Instead, the obstacles to adding words to more than one voice were overcome by abandoning the conductus motet altogether. The solution adopted by poets and composers may seem strange to us, but it was perfectly logical given the problems they faced. They simply gave each voice above the tenor its own text. As a result, we now regard use of more than one text (polytextuality) as an essential characteristic of the thirteenth-century motet. This view somewhat overlooks the conductus motet, but it is certainly accurate for the last half of the century. Moreover, polytextuality remains characteristic of the motet throughout the rest of the Middle Ages and into the Renaissance.

POLYTEXTUAL MOTETS

The advent of polytextuality in the motet introduces a new and somewhat confusing terminology. *Double motets* have two upper voices, and *triple motets* have three, each with its own text. In addition, of course, double and triple motets have tenors, so that each class has one more voice and one more text than the name seems to imply. In the older manuscripts, the placement of syllables beneath the tenor usually agrees with the original chant. Later sources tend to ignore this placement and give the text as an identifying tag at the beginning of the tenor part. This practice suggests that motets had lost any functional connection with liturgical chants and that tenors may have become instrumental rather than vocal parts. Both developments would follow naturally on the appearance of French motets with secular texts and might then have influenced the performance of sacred motets. In any case, the terms *double* and *triple motet* designate the number of voices with different texts above the tenor, not the complete number of voices in the composition. Two-voice motets with a tenor melisma and a motetus would presumably be termed *single,* although they are not usually so called.

In the older repertory of the Notre Dame manuscripts, two-voice

3.   See HAM, No. 28i, for a three-voice clausula, *Flos filius,* and the motet with two different texts that the structure of the upper voices required.

motets far outnumber those for three voices, most of which are conductus motets. Four-voice motets are extremely rare. This situation
changes radically in motet collections from the second half of the thirteenth century, and the three-voice double motet becomes the standard
form.

Apart from this shift of emphasis to the double motet, the chronological development of the form in the later thirteenth century is difficult to
trace. Unlike the manuscript collections of trouvère songs, motet
manuscripts almost never give the names of composers. Moreover,
they group motets in ways that inextricably mix old and new pieces,
motets based on clausulae and original compositions. Even in sections of
manuscripts that contain later additions to the repertory, such as the last
two fascicles of *Mo*, many motets still resemble the tropes and contrafacta of clausulae, although they are not known to exist in that form.
In these cases it is impossible to tell whether a motet is really old or
merely the product of an old-fashioned composer. Not all composers
were conservative, however, and some motets reveal that the development of polyphony was beginning to take a new direction. That these
pieces may be relatively few in number in no way detracts from their
historical importance. Then, as always, the experiments of a progressive
minority introduced new concepts of style and technique that would
become traditional for later generations.

The new direction in the development of polyphony becomes particularly obvious when motets are compared with conducti. For uniformity of style and the constructivist devices that integrate the voices of a
conductus, the motet substitutes diversity of style by giving each voice
a distinctive rhythmic and melodic character. To some extent, of
course, this diversity was inherent in the motet from its beginnings.
Repeated rhythmic patterns and the frequent use of the fifth rhythmic
mode already differentiated tenors from the upper voice or voices of
clausulae, and structural differences between those voices were responsible, at least in part, for their being given different texts. In itself, this
process emphasized the distinctive character of each voice and led composers to seek ways of achieving still greater diversity. The origin of the
motet as a trope probably accounts for the use of related texts in double
or triple motets. At any rate, the relationship is particularly obvious
when texts are genuine tropes. It is sometimes less obvious in motets
with texts that appear to be related only because they are secular and in
French. The height of textual disparity is reached in a few motets with
texts in different languages. One fascicle of *Mo* has eleven such motets
with sacred Latin dupla and secular French tripla, and a few more bilingual motets appear elsewhere in the manuscript.[4] The intended function
of these pieces is difficult to imagine. Many exist in other sources with

4.   See G. Anderson, "Notre Dame Bilingual Motets."

Latin texts in both voices, but this is not necessarily their original form.[5] If they represent an attempt to achieve diversity of style by textual means, they must now be regarded as another short-lived experiment that did not win general approval. The great majority of motets employed different but related texts in the same language. As a starting point for the development of musical diversity, the presence of these different texts was quite sufficient.

RHYTHMIC DEVELOPMENTS IN THE LATER THIRTEENTH CENTURY

Because early motets naturally followed clausulae in their dependence on modal rhythms, the use of different modes for the tenor and the upper voices was already common. The logical and, indeed, the only possible means of distinguishing the upper voices from each other was to apply the same procedure to them. Thus we find motets with a tenor in the fifth mode, a triplum in the sixth, and a duplum in the first or second. The simplicity of this solution made it immediately attractive, but it would not long have remained so had it not offered opportunities for further development. As a first step in this development, the breves of the sixth mode in the triplum were subdivided into shorter values. Semibreves had been used before, but only in ornamental figures on syllables that received the full value of a long or breve. The new departure made each semibreve an independent note by giving it a syllable of its own. A French motet, *Pucelete—Je languis—Domino,* illustrates an early stage in this development.[6] The tenor has phrases of irregular length but moves in the even note values of the fifth rhythmic mode, while the duplum is primarily in the second mode with one long phrase in the fifth. In the Florence manuscript, these two voices exist as a clausula, to which the triplum is obviously a later addition. It moves consistently in a rhythmic pattern, ♪ ♪ ♩   ♩ , that would be no more than a variant of the sixth mode were it not for the separate syllables on each semibreve (eighth note). The result is a charming and lively evocation of the maiden for whom, presumably, the singer of the duplum languishes.

The use of semibreves as independent notes with separate syllables of text is an indication that composers were seeking to break away from the rigidity of the rhythmic modes. A slightly different attempt in this direction is evident in another French motet, *Dame de valur—Hei Diex! cant je remir—Amoris* (AMM, No. 53). In this piece the voices are less

---

5.   See HAM, No. 32b, for a double motet with a Latin duplum and a French triplum in **Mo**, but with a Latin triplum related to the duplum in **Ba**.

6.   Grout, HWM, pp. 104–05, Ex. III–12, and HAM, No. 28h 2. Motets are usually identified by the incipits of their texts, beginning with the topmost voice and reading down to the tenor. Some writers, however, list the incipit of the duplum first.

An example of a thirteenth-century motet, *Ave Virgo—Ave gloriosa—Domino* (Bamberg Staatsbibliothek).

sharply differentiated but more irregular within themselves than was the case in *Pucelete—Je languis—Domino*. The tenor comes from the verse of *Alleluia: Veni Sancte Spiritus* (LU, p. 880) and consists of four statements of a fifteen-note melody, with the last two notes of the final statement omitted to permit an ending on **C**.[7] Both the first and last statements have two three-note groups in the fifth rhythmic mode. The rest of the tenor moves in three-note groups in the first mode. Apart from a few measures in the fifth mode, the duplum is a characteristic example of a text set to the note values of the first mode with those values frequently broken into ornamental figures of two or three shorter notes. Much of the triplum is also in the first mode and follows the same procedure but with an even greater number of ornamental figures. In addition, however, several measures have the same rhythmic pattern as the triplum *Pucelete,* and in one case (m. 35) the first breve of the sixth mode is subdivided into three semibreves, each with its own syllable of text.

Dame de valur—Hei Diex! cant je remir—Amoris is of particular interest, not only in itself but also because of the prior history of its musical setting. The Florence manuscript preserves the tenor and duplum both as a clausula and as a two-voice Latin motet *Veni, salva nos* (Come, save us) that paraphrases the text of the Alleluia verse from which the tenor comes. Its irregular and inaccurate modal notation may lead one to believe that this clausula was created from a motet rather than vice versa.[8]

7. The tenor is actually two statements, slightly modified, of the melisma, which itself includes one repetition of the basic phrase.
8. Waite, *Rhythm,* p. 101. The clausula is No. 141 (fol. 163v) in Ludwig's catalog of clausulae in **F** (*Repertorium,* p. 83). The motet appears on fol. 411 in **F**.

The opening of a motet by Pierre de la Croix, *Aucun ont troveit—Lonc tens—Annuntiantes* (Turin, Royal Library).

At any rate, one of the versions in **F** must represent the original musical form. Franco of Cologne quotes the beginning of the tenor and duplum with another Latin text, *Virgo Dei plena* (Virgin, pregnant of God).[9] A manuscript from Lille preserves the duplum with still a third Latin text, *O quam sollempnis legatio* (O how solemn an embassy). It was as a French double motet, however, that the music received its widest distribution. The tenor and motetus with French text appear five times in four manuscripts, but with two different triplum melodies and texts.[10] The older triplum *Por vos amie criem* (I fear for you, friend) betrays its age by its rather rigid adherence to the patterns of the first rhythmic mode. Replacement of this triplum by *Dame de valur,* with its freer and more flexible rhythms, modernizes the motet and brings it into line with contemporary stylistic trends. Together with its previous incarnations, then, the motet epitomizes almost the entire history of the form from its beginnings to the end of the thirteenth century.

Before the century closed, however, composers had taken a further step in freeing themselves from the restrictions imposed by the rhythmic modes by breaking up more breves into even smaller note values. With fine disregard for linguistic logic, the theorists called all of these smaller notes *semibreves,* although from two to seven or eight might replace a single breve. Jacques de Liège, in his encyclopedic *Speculum musicae* (Mirror of Music), written in the early part of the fourteenth century, credits Pierre de la Croix with being the first to subdivide the breve into four or more semibreves. Furthermore, Jacques quotes examples from motets by Pierre de la Croix and thus rescues at least some of his works from the general anonymity of the thirteenth century.[11] Pierre de la Croix was active as a composer and theorist at least until 1298, and he therefore represents the final stylistic developments of the century. We cannot assume, however, that every motet in the new style is one of his compositions. Other composers must have been quick to exploit the innovations that broke through the limitations of the rhyth-

9. CS, 1, p. 130 and Strunk, SR, p. 154.

10. The motet with the triplum *Por vos amie* occurs in **Mo** (No. 86) and **Cl** (No. 48). It reappears with the text *Dame de valour* in the later repertory of the seventh fascicle of **Mo** (No. 281) and also in **Ba** and **Tu** (see Bibliography).

11. HAM, No. 34, is one motet of Pierre de la Croix cited in the *Speculum musicae.* HAM, No. 35, is another, but anonymous, example of the same style.

mic modes and made it possible to attain extremes of melodic diversity.

Even a moderate application of the new techniques, as in the motet *Aucun vont—Amor qui cor—Kyrie* (AMM, No. 54), produces striking contrasts of style in the different voices. That the tenor melody is a Kyrie (from Mass IX, LU, p. 40) rather than a melisma from a responsorial chant is already an indication that the piece as a whole does not belong to the first period of motet composition. A second indication comes from the two statements of the tenor melody in unbroken series of long notes. These aspects of the tenor suggest that the three-voice setting is probably the original form of the motet, although one source omits the triplum. The setting of the duplum text adheres strictly to the note values of the second rhythmic mode, but the frequent use of fractio modi gives greater flexibility and freedom to the melody itself. True freedom comes in the lively triplum, however, which only once settles down to match the slower pace of the duplum (mm. 9–14). For the rest, the triplum moves in unpatterned successions of single and divided breves. Most of the latter are replaced by only two or three semibreves, but a few groups of four, five, and six semibreves also occur. To organize this capricious flow of melody in the triplum, the composer has grouped the lines of text into phrases of irregular length, all of which end with the rhymes "-ment" or "-gent." In so doing, he established yet another contrast with the duplum, which consists entirely of regular four-measure phrases. The two voices, moreover, never begin or end their phrases together except at the beginning and end of the motet.

Medieval music, as a rule, makes little effort to reflect either the emotions or the meanings of its texts. In the present instance, however, it is impossible not to feel that the musical setting of *Aucun vont—Amor qui cor—Kyrie* is a witty commentary on the motet's textual disparities. The Latin duplum, in commonplace rhymed couplets of seven-syllable lines, indicts love that generates carnal passion as a transient thing displeasing to the Lord. The triplum, in lines of uneven length with irregularly placed rhymes, defends love against its detractors in highly voluble French. To these contrasts of language, form, and sentiment the diversity of melodic styles forms a perfect complement. The music even adds a third dimension to the humor by staging the debate above a tenor melody in the even, but here greatly retarded, rhythm of plainchant. In this range from liturgical solemnity through moral rectitude to irreverent gaiety, the motet preserves in miniature the spirit of its time.

FROM MODAL TO MENSURAL NOTATION

It is evident that the different note values in the triplum *Aucun vont* could not have been expressed in modal notation. Indeed, the limitations of modal notation prevented its use in motets long before the many subdivisions of the breve began breaking down the system of the rhythmic modes. As in the conductus, the syllabic setting of texts in the upper voices of motets meant that single notes, or groups of two or three notes on one syllable, replaced the regular ligature patterns of modal notation. What was needed, of course, was a means of indicating the values of these single notes, and we cannot help but wonder that it took so long to find the obvious solution to the problem. It seems extraordinary, for example, that the large collections of conducti and motets in the Notre Dame manuscripts should have been written almost entirely in unmeasured note values. Performers then must have often been in doubt as to the correct rhythmic interpretation of these pieces, just as transcribers are now. Clearly this was the case, or the system of measured note values that we know as mensural notation would never have developed.

During the second quarter of the thirteenth century, various theorists began advocating the use of differently shaped notes to indicate specific rhythmic values. It remained for Franco of Cologne, however, to build a system in which the value of every note could be expressed by a distinctive notational sign. This he did in his treatise *Ars cantus mensurabilis* (The Art of Measurable Song), written about 1260.[12] Useful as the system was, it did not win immediate acceptance, and several manuscripts of the later thirteenth century[13] still use older, pre-Franconian forms of mensural notation. Nevertheless, the principles established by Franco provided the starting point for all future developments in the notation of Western music. In addition to their great historical interest, those principles both reflected and to some extent controlled the rhythmic characteristics of music in their time. It is necessary, therefore, to examine briefly the bases of Franconian notation.

In Franco's time, we must remember, the system of rhythmic modes still governed the metrical organization of motets, even though modal notation could not be used. Thus we again face the strange fact that individual notes, despite their distinctive shapes, may have different values according to the context in which they appear.[14] Influenced by the ever-present triple meter, theorists came to regard the longa ultra mensuram, equal to three breves, as the normal or perfect long; a long equal to only two breves was therefore imperfect. Franco attributed the perfection of the number three to its association with the Holy Trinity, but we should not assume that the almost exclusive use of triple meter in the thirteenth century resulted from a deliberate attempt to represent the Trinity in musical terms. Both the historical development of the rhythmic modes and the earlier terminology for describing them deny any such assumption. Triple meter we must regard as a more or less un-

12.   Strunk, SR, pp. 139–59.

13.   Notably *Ba* and much of *Mo*.

14.   See Chapter IX for a discussion of this problem in connection with the rhythmic modes and modal notation.

foreseen consequence of the modal system and its adaptations of rhythmic patterns to permit their simultaneous use. Moreover, the idea that three is the most perfect number because it is the first to have a beginning, middle, and end goes back to the Pythagorean philosophers and thus antedates the advent of Christianity by several centuries. It was probably not theological symbolism but rather the place of music as a mathematical discipline in the quadrivium of university studies that was largely responsible for equating perfection with the ternary units of the rhythmic modes. Be that as it may, the ternary longs of the third, fourth, and fifth modes were perfect in both Franconian and later terminology, while the imperfect longs of the first and second modes required an additional breve to complete the perfections of the mode. These breves are said to imperfect the longs that they precede or follow. In the third and fourth modes, the pairs of breves consist, as before, of a *brevis recta* and a *brevis altera*. The duration of the "correct" or proper breve is described as being one *tempus* (time), and the altered breve equals two *tempora*. None of this is really new, but Franco did make an important innovation when he established the principle that the tempus, the duration of the breve, was itself a ternary value. It could thus be divided into three minor semibreves of equal value or into two unequal semibreves, of which the first was minor and the second, twice as long, was major. These subdivisions of the breve together with its use as a measure of duration make transcription in measures of 3/4 meter more appropriate than 6/8 for motets from the latter part of the thirteenth century. For the sake of consistency, and because it is often difficult to decide when to make the change, it has been common practice to transcribe all motets of this period in 3/4, even those derived from clausulae that would be transcribed in 6/8.[15] As used in motets, then, the note shapes and relative values of Franconian notation produce the modern equivalents shown in Table 11.

Table 11: *Single Notes and Values of Franconian Notation*

Name and shape of note		Value (in tempora)	Modern equivalent
Duplex long	▬▐	6	o·
Perfect long	▜	3	♩·
Imperfect long	▜	2	♩
Breve	▪	1	♪
Altered breve	▪	2	♩
Semibreve:			
Minor + major	◆ ◆	⅓ + ⅔	♪♩ (3)
Three minor	◆ ◆ ◆	⅓ + ⅓ + ⅓	♪♪♪ (3)

15. See, for example, the clausula and motet in HAM, No. 28h.

Except for the concept of the ternary breve, Franco invented neither the note shapes of mensural notation nor their values. His great contribution in this line lay in the establishment of rules for both the correct notation of rhythms and the correct reading of that notation. It thus became possible to determine with absolute certainty when longs should be perfect or imperfect and when breves should be altered. The first and most basic of Franco's rules states that a long before a long is perfect. Taking this invariable rule as a starting point, Franco then details the situations in which breves may imperfect longs or must themselves be altered. A single breve must form part of a perfection (a 3/4 measure) and may therefore imperfect either a preceding or following long. When two breves stand between longs, the second must be altered so that the two together form a perfection. (The need for this procedure results from Franco's first rule, which prevents writing the values ♩ ♩ ♩. as breve-long-long.) Three breves between longs will normally form a perfection by themselves. Series of four or more breves between longs may be treated in different ways. If one breve remains after dividing the series into groups of three, it will imperfect the preceding or following long. When two breves remain at the end of the series, the second will again be altered. To prevent the normal application of these rules, or to clarify situations that might be interpreted in different ways, Franco used a sign known as a *divisio modi* or *signum perfectionis* (division of the mode or sign of perfection). The two terms are simply different names for the same sign—a short vertical line that later practice transformed into a dot (*punctus*) of division or perfection. Placed between two notes, the sign prevents their belonging to the same perfection and thus functions somewhat in the manner of the modern barline. The notes ¶ ⸱⸱ ⸱ ¶, for example, must be read as ♩ ♩ | ♩ ♩ instead of ♩. | ♩ ♩ | ♩., which they would be without the sign of perfection. Franco used the same sign to separate groups of two and three semibreves, a practice that made it possible to notate the rhythmic innovations of Pierre de la Croix.

More detailed knowledge of Franco's rules is scarcely necessary for an appreciation of their effect.[16] Even when it used nothing but longs and breves, mensural notation could introduce rhythms such as ♩ ♩ | ♩ ♩ or ♩ ♩ | ♩ ♩ ♩ | ♩ ♩ | ♩. that broke down the rigidity of the rhythmic modes. As Franco himself said: "Observe also that all the modes may run together in a single discant, for through perfections all are reduced to one. Nor need one attempt to determine the mode to which such a discant belongs, although it may be said to belong to the one in which it chiefly or frequently remains."[17] Still greater freedom

16. For fuller discussions of Franco's principles and rules, see Reese, MMA, p. 289 ff.; Apel, NPM, Part 3, Chapters 4 and 5; and Parrish, NMM, Chapter 5.
17. Strunk, SR, p. 151.

came, as we have seen, in the post-Franconian division of the breve into four or more semibreves. The rhythmic modes had given birth to a notational system by whose potential for further development they would ultimately be destroyed.

Franco's contributions to the development of a precise notation were not limited to his treatment of single notes. He also devised, or standardized, signs that indicated the exact values of rests, and he established a system for identifying the values of notes written in ligatures. The signs for rests depended on the principle that a line through one space on the staff represented the duration of a breve or one tempus. It thus became possible to indicate rests that correspond with the different values of individual notes (Example XIV–1).[18] With these signs available for rests of any value or combination of values, mensural notation gained both in precision and in its ability to express new and more flexible rhythmic patterns.

Example XIV–1: *Rests in Franconian Notation*

1. Duplex long (maxima)
2. Perfect long
3. Imperfect long or altered breve
4. Breve
5. Semibreve

The problem of ligatures was more complex and less easy to solve. Pre-Franconian notation anticipated to a large extent Franco's principles for the treatment of single notes and even of rests. In the matter of ligatures, however, the forms of modal notation were commonly used with only slight modifications. Theorists recognized rather quickly that changes in the form of a ligature could indicate different combinations of long and short notes, but the various meanings of three-note ligatures in modal notation made it difficult to reduce those changes to a system. Franco overcame this difficulty by taking the normal forms of two-note ligatures in plainchant notation as his standard (▍ and ▐). From their use in modal notation, these forms acquired the meaning breve-long and were described as being "with propriety" and "with perfection." Changing the form of the first note by adding or omitting a tail removed its propriety and it became a long. An upward tail gave it "opposite propriety," and both notes became semibreves. Similarly, changes in the form of the second note removed its perfection, and it became a breve. Here, because the use of tails was impractical and might be confused with plicas, the descending ligature was written as an oblique bar. In the ascending ligature, turning the head

---

18. Franco proposed major and minor semibreve rests that covered ⅔ and ⅓ of the space above a line (see Strunk, SR, p. 150, and Reese, MMA, p. 290). These proved to be impractical and were soon replaced by the semibreve rest shown in Example XIV–1.

of the second note to the right instead of the left indicated lack of perfection. These various changes gave each two–note ligature five different forms, one for each of the five possible combinations of notes (see Table 12). In dealing with ligatures of three or more notes, Franco used exactly the same procedures for indicating the values of the first and last notes. All notes in between were breves except in ligatures with opposite propriety, which began with two semibreves. The rules that governed single notes determined the *values* of longs and breves, but the *kinds* of notes in ligatures of any length could now be identified as certainly as if they stood alone. By this achievement, Franco of Cologne completed the liberation of mensural notation from its dependence on the modal system and made it a self-sufficient system of its own.

Table 12: *The Forms and Values of Two-Note Ligatures*

With propriety and with perfection			B	L
With propriety and without perfection			B	B
Without propriety and with perfection			L	L
Without propriety and without perfection			L	B
With opposite propriety			Sb	Sb

THE MOTET ENTÉ

After this digression into notational problems, we may get back to the music itself and to one of the most distinctive practices in thirteenth-century French motets: the quotation of texts and melodies that presumably originated as refrains of monophonic songs. In a few cases, the entire text of a motet appears to consist of nothing but refrains. As a more usual procedure, however, a refrain is grafted (*enté*) onto a new text and melody (or vice versa) to produce what is known as a *motet enté*. The grafting was often so skillfully done that neither the text nor the melody suggests the presence of a refrain, and recognition of a motet enté depends upon discovery of the quotation in some other source.

As we saw in Chapter XII, two valuable sources for the identification of refrains are the trouvère "chanson with refrains" and contemporary narrative poems. The four refrains quoted in *Penser ne doit vilenie* (AMM, No. 47) have already been discussed in some detail, but we may return to them here because each occurs in a number of other sources, including motets. For convenient comparison, all appearances of the first three refrains with music are assembled in Example XIV–2. The first seems to have enjoyed the greatest literary popularity, for it is quoted exactly—but without music—in several different poems. Its ap-

Example XIV–2: *Refrains in* Penser ne doit *and Quotations with Music in Other Sources*

Penser ne doit, I
Mo, No. 42, triplum, measures 8–11

I. I have loves in my heart that keep me gay.
   (Then loves sting me that keep me gay.)
II. To the most delightful one in the world have I given my heart.
III. I have a love, pretty little love, so I shall love.

pearance in a motet, however, may be open to question. The texts of the refrain and the quotation in the motet correspond only in part, and musical resemblances are even slighter. The text of the second refrain, on the other hand, appears unchanged in a motet, but with a melody that has been both transposed and considerably altered. The melody with the refrain in *Le Roman de Renart le Nouvel* (The Story of the New Renard the Fox) is even more divergent. In motets, evidently, textual quotation was more important than musical, and composers felt free to modify the melodies to make them fit the polyphonic context. Nevertheless, many musical quotations introduce no more variants than are to be found in different monophonic versions of the same melody. This is true of the third refrain in *Penser ne doit,* which appears in measures 20–26 of the triplum in the motet *Dame de valur—Hei Diex!—Amoris* (AMM, No. 53). The fourth stanza and refrain of the chanson, as noted in Chapter XII, occur only in manuscripts that do not give the melody, but three quotations of the refrain with music provide alternate endings for the transcription in AMM.

The grafting of refrains onto motets takes place in a number of different ways. In many cases, a refrain is introduced at an appropriate point within the motet text, as happened with the refrain quoted in the triplum *Dame de valur.* More often, refrains appear at the beginning or end, and two-line refrains may provide the first and last lines of a motet text. A motet enté, of course, was not limited to the quotation of a single refrain. Unrelated refrains may appear at the beginning and end of a single text; the two texts of a motet may simultaneously quote different refrains; and still other quotations may occur within the same texts. Diligent scholarship over the years has identified a great many such quotations, and modern editions of motets usually indicate their presence by printing them in italics. We can now appreciate, therefore, the extent to which composers adopted the practice of quoting refrains and the skill with which they made those refrains an integral part of their polyphonic compositions.

RELATIONSHIPS BETWEEN THE MOTET AND SECULAR MONOPHONY

The inclusion of refrains in longer texts was by no means the only musical connection between the motet and secular monophonic song. A number of motets consist of nothing but a plainchant tenor combined either with a complete dance song or simply with a refrain. Motets of the latter sort are short, and the few that have been preserved are in nonmensural notation, leaving considerable doubt as to their rhythmic interpretation. The transcription offered in Example XIV–3, therefore, need not be accepted as definitive.[19] Motets in which an upper voice is a complete six- or eight-line rondeau were more common and evidently more attractive to thirteenth-century composers. Among these pieces, one of the most interesting is *C'est la jus—Pro patribus* (AMM, No. 55). The duplum melody of this motet can be traced back to a Notre Dame clausula in yet another illustration of the tangled but fascinating interrelationships that bind together all medieval music.

19.   For a facsimile of *Renvoisiement* and two different rhythmic interpretations, see Apel, NPM, pp. 277–79.

Example XIV–3: *A Refrain as a Complete Motet*

Happily I go there to my friend. So should one go to one's friend.

Literary and musical relationships between motets and trouvère chansons are not limited to the quotation of refrains or the use of complete dance songs. In a number of instances, a complete stanza of a trouvère chanson appears with its melody as the duplum of a motet. Which of the two came first is often difficult to determine, but the existence of some of these motets as textless clausulae suggests that some trouvères participated in writing motet texts, if not the music itself. Both dance songs and trouvère chansons also appear as the tenor parts of some thirty motets in the thirteenth-century repertory. Some of these French tenors have the complete text underlaid; others have only textual incipits and were presumably played by instruments. Four of the textless tenors seem to be excerpts from instrumental dances known as *estampies* (see below). In one well-known motet, the tenor *Frese nouvele* (Fresh strawberries) is believed to be a Paris street vendor's cry. Above four repetitions of this tenor melody, two upper voices celebrate the joys of life in Paris, evidently much the same then as now.[20]

POLYPHONIC SECULAR SONGS

In describing the state of music as he knew it around 1300, Johannes de Grocheo remarked that the motet was not suited for the common people but only for the educated and those who sought subtlety in art. Thus it was, says Grocheo, that motets were sung at festivals for the edification of the educated, just as rondeaux were sung at festivals of the folk. The common practice of quoting refrains in motets makes it clear that the educated knew the music of the folk and took pleasure in recognizing its subtle appearance in their own art. The use of a complete dance song, either as the tenor or upper voice of a motet, may also have been an admired subtlety, but it also suggests a desire to provide polyphonic

20. HAM, No. 33b.

settings for the more popular kinds of song. To satisfy that desire, composers naturally turned to the motet, almost the sole polyphonic form then being cultivated. The solution presented obvious difficulties. Plainchant tenors could rarely be combined with a long preexistent melody, and they tended to discourage if not to prohibit the use of repetitive musical forms in an upper voice. Placing the dance song in the tenor removed this difficulty but increased the complexity of the motet by adding another active voice, which might have a complete and different text. After following both of these paths, composers evidently came to realize the basic incompatibility between popular polyphony and the subtle art of the motet. They continued to write secular motets, but they also sought to develop an independent type of polyphonic secular song.

For being the first to create a form of secular polyphony unrelated to the motet, credit must apparently be given to the trouvère Adam de la Hale. As we noted in Chapter XII, the bulk of Adam's musical output consisted of monophonic chansons (34) and jeux partis (17). However, he also composed five motets and sixteen polyphonic settings of secular songs that the manuscript collection of his works calls *Li Rondel Adan* (see above, p. 300). All sixteen polyphonic songs are for three voices, and all bear a striking resemblance to the simple conductus, even to the point of being notated in score. It was probably this obsolete style, indeed, that suggested to Adam an appropriate means of providing a simple dance with a polyphonic setting. One new development is curious, however. Instead of the tenor, the middle voice seems to be the most important of the three. The melody of this voice, at any rate, usually appears when a motet or a poem with refrains quotes one of Adam's rondeaux. Adam did this himself when he used the refrain of *A Dieu commant amouretes* (To God I commend my love) to frame the duplum text and melody of a motet.[21] The same procedure was applied to the rondeau *He, Diex!* (Example XIV–4), which illustrates in its short span all the essential features of Adam's polyphonic songs. Two different motets, both anonymous, quote the refrain of this rondeau with the melody of the middle voice exactly as, it appears in Adam's three-voice setting.[22]

The simplicity of Adam's polyphonic rondeaux makes it reasonable to assume that they were meant to be used as music for dancing. In performing round dances of this type, the entire group sang the refrains, but the leader of the dance presumably sang the intervening lines alone. This characteristic procedure could have been accommodated to the polyphonic settings in several ways. Three-part singing of the choral

21.   N. Wilkins, *The Lyric Works of Adam de la Hale,* Rondeau No. 5 and Motet No. 1.
22.   *Mo,* No. 291, triplum, mm. 53–57, and No. 302, duplum, mm. 67–71. Both motets are included in Wilkins, *Lyric Works* (Nos. 9 and 10).

Example XIV–4: *Rondeau of Adam de la Hale*

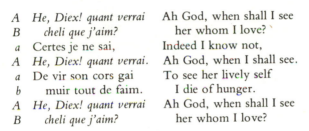

He, Diex! quant ver - rai che - li que j'aim?

A	*He, Diex! quant verrai*	Ah God, when shall I see
B	*cheli que j'aim?*	her whom I love?
a	Certes je ne sai,	Indeed I know not,
A	*He, Diex! quant verrai.*	Ah God, when I shall see.
a	De vir son cors gai	To see her lively self
b	muir tout de faim.	I die of hunger.
A	*He, Diex! quant verrai*	Ah God, when shall I see
B	*cheli que j'aim?*	her whom I love?

refrain might be answered by the soloist's singing of the principal melody, either alone or with instrumental performance of the other voices. It is even possible that both chorus and soloist sang only the middle voice, while instruments played the tenor and triplum. Indeed, these polyphonic rondeaux may represent the first attempt to write down instrumental accompaniments that had hitherto been improvised. The simplicity of the tenors, in particular, suggests the kind of melody that a skilled improviser could easily add to a well-known refrain. The resemblance of these rondeaux to the simple conductus would then be explained by their common ancestry in the practice of improvising and writing note-against-note counterpoint.

Short as they are, and whatever their ancestry and manner of performance, the polyphonic rondeaux of Adam de la Hale mark a turning point in the history of secular song. Released from the hampering conventions and polytextual complexities of the motet, secular polyphony could now develop an individual and more appropriate musical style. This it did with astonishing rapidity and with results that were perhaps unexpected. After being almost the only type of solo song for some two hundred years, secular monophony dwindled in importance until it all but disappeared by the middle of the fourteenth century. In the same span of about fifty years, the rondeau, ballade, and virelai lost their connection with the dance and became elaborate art songs for highly skilled singers. These songs were now polyphonic pieces with one vocal melody and one or more additional parts to be played by instruments. Emphasis on polyphonic as opposed to monophonic secular song brought with it other changes as well. The technical skills required for the composition of polyphony made the traditional poet-musician increasingly obsolete. Composers became professionals known for their music alone, and vast quantities of lyric poetry began to be produced with no thought that it would ever be sung. Only one man, Guillaume de Machaut (c. 1300–77), delayed this separation of lyric poetry from song. No later composer is known to students of literature as an important poet, and no later poet is known to students of music as an important composer. For this, if for no other reason, Machaut has deservedly been called the last of the trouvères. But Machaut looked forward as well as back; and, by both the quantity and quality of his work, he set the standards for French poetry and song and determined the direction of their future development. It will therefore be no surprise to find that a discussion of French music in the fourteenth century must be largely devoted to one of the greatest and most influential figures in the history of music.

MINOR FORMS AND COMPOSITIONAL DEVICES

Before beginning to consider fourteenth-century French music and the works of Machaut, we must mention some less common musical forms and compositional techniques of the thirteenth century. The forms are minor because they occur in a relatively small number of pieces, and the techniques may also be classed as minor because they rarely form the basis for an entire composition. Both the forms and techniques are important, nevertheless, for they continued in use beyond the thirteenth century and provided a starting point for the development of more sophisticated methods of musical organization.

HOCKET

Medieval theorists defined *hocket* as a "truncation" in which one voice sings while another is silent. An obvious reference to the musical effect, the name *hocket* comes from the Latin and French words for hiccup (*hoquetus* and *hoquet,* in a variety of spellings). As a device, hocket appears to have evolved from short overlapping phrases, often combined with voice exchange, in the upper voices of triple and quadruple organum and the caudae of conducti. In later thirteenth-century usage, however, the simplest form of hocket alternated single notes and rests, usually in the two upper voices of a motet. The notes and rests may be of the same or different values, but the notes of each voice fill in the rests of the other. As may be seen in Example XIV–5, the net result of two such hiccuping voices is often a single melodic line.

As a rule, longer hocket passages are reserved for melismatic polyphony; passages with text are usually short and introduce a momentary contrast to the normal motet style. In neither case, however, is hocket introduced to no purpose, although that purpose may sometimes be difficult to determine. Some hocket passages are exclamatory or descriptive; others function as structural elements by underlining the organization of the tenor, a use of hocket that becomes increasingly important in the next century. In a few motets, hocket appears in melismatic extensions and conclusions, where it creates a free variation of previously heard melodies. In some instances, finally, hocket technique is applied throughout a piece. This is the case in all but one of the seven "instrumental motets" at the end of the Bamberg manuscript, from one of which Example XIV–5a was taken.[23] Pieces of this sort, in both medieval and modern terminology, are called *hockets,* and the name thus designates a genre as well as a technique.

Example XIV–5: *Two Excerpts Illustrating the Use of Hocket*

a. *Ba*, NO. 106, MEASURES 17–23

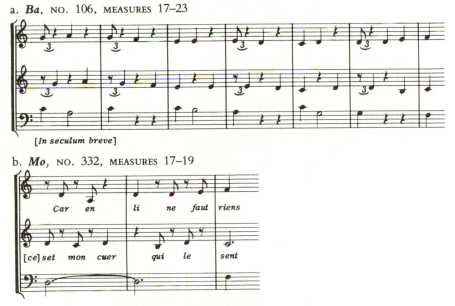

[*In seculum breve*]

b. *Mo,* NO. 332, MEASURES 17–19

Triplum: For in her nothing is lacking.
Duplum: [This] my heart knows, which feels it.

23.   The pieces are Nos. 102–08 in *Ba.* A facsimile of No. 106 is available in Parrish, NMM, Pl. XXXVI. No. 108 is published in HAM, No. 32e, but the transcription of semibreve notes and rests as equal values is incorrect. Instead of the rhythms and , rests in the original clearly indicate that the correct values should be and .

RONDELLUS

The compositional technique known as *rondellus* is much less common than hocket but is interesting and important nonetheless. Cultivated primarily but not exclusively by English composers, the rondellus was described by the English theorist Walter Odington (c. 1300) as consisting of two or three simultaneous melodies sung by each voice in turn. The example he cites is for three voices and has six melodies or phrases in the following arrangement:

Triplum	*b c a*	*e f d*
Duplum	*c a b*	*f d e*
Tenor	*a b c*	*d e f*

Clearly, a rondellus is no more than an elaborate and complete form of voice exchange, which presupposes the equal voices of conductus style. Odington says, indeed, that unless all the voices sing the melodies in order, the piece is a conductus and not a rondellus. Thus, although rondellus technique may be used throughout a piece, the term designates a method rather than a type of composition. An interesting example occurs in a cauda of a much longer conductus, where three melodies are used, and the set of three combinations is repeated exactly.[24] In this way, the rondellus becomes a round, which successive instead of simultaneous entries would convert into a normal circular or perpetual canon:

$$\begin{bmatrix} a & b \\ & a \end{bmatrix} \left\| \begin{array}{ccc} a & b & c \\ : c & a & b : \\ b & c & a \end{array} \right\|$$

From rondellus technique, obviously it is but a short step to the most famous of all medieval compositions, *Sumer is icumen in*. The piece is a four-part canon at the unison above a two-part *pes* (foot), a term the English often used in place of *tenor*. The canon differs from a rondellus in having the voices enter one after another and also in being a nonrepetitive melody in the leading voice. Instead of true voice exchange, therefore, the shifting combinations of four parts always include one new melodic phrase, as the following diagram will show:

$$\begin{array}{l} a\ b\ c\ d\ e\ f\ g \\ \quad a\ b\ c\ d\ e\ f \\ \qquad a\ b\ c\ d\ e \\ \qquad\quad a\ b\ c\ d \end{array} \text{ etc.}$$

---

24.   Cited in part by Anselm Hughes, NOHM, 2, p. 376, Ex. 203.

The pes, on the other hand, is a perfect example of a two-part rondellus as defined by Walter Odington. Throughout the entire piece, the voices do nothing but interchange two short phrases in an ostinato pattern that oscillates continuously between chords on **F** and **G** (Example XIV–6). This harmonic structure might seem monotonous, but it provides a firm support for the lively rhythms and ever-changing combinations of melodic phrases in the four-part canon. Although the use of six voices results in a full sound that supposedly reflects English taste, it does not produce six-part harmony. Instead, unison doublings reduce the number of notes actually sounding at one time to a maximum of four, more often to three, sometimes to only two. All of these characteristics, together with the F-major sound of the canonic melody, lend the piece a popular air that seems to deny its structural complexity. It is undoubtedly this ingenious simplicity that makes *Sumer is icumen in* so attractive to modern audiences.[25]

Example XIV–6: *Pes of* Sumer is icumen in

INSTRUMENTAL MUSIC

The dearth of manuscript evidence for instrumental music in the Middle Ages is both astonishing and mysterious. Writers and theorists make countless references to instruments and their practical uses. Manuscript illustrations and cathedral sculptures depict a wide variety of instruments, often in connection with singing or dancing, but sometimes in ways that suggest either solo or ensemble performance. Peasants reportedly played instruments for their rustic dances.[26] Jongleurs were expected to play as many as ten instruments according to the *Conseils aux Jongler* (Advice to Jongleurs) written by Guiraut de Calanson in 1210. Troubadours and trouvères presumably sang their songs to instrumental accompaniment. In short, there is abundant evidence that instruments played a vital role in medieval musical life at every social level, yet only a handful of purely instrumental pieces has been preserved. Several factors probably account for this situation. Instrumental performance seems to have been largely the province of jongleurs, whose music has either been lost or, as is more likely, was never written

25.   Problematic aspects of the *Sumer* canon and its dating will be considered in the essay on minor forms and techniques of the thirteenth century.
26.   For example, in the text of *Au tems pascor,* AMM, No. 45.

Various instruments are shown in this depiction of King David with scribe and musicians (by permission of Zentral Bibliothek, Zurich).

down. Peasants too probably had a repertory of both song and dance tunes that were passed on solely by oral tradition. And at all levels of society, apparently, vocal music provided the chief source of material for instrumental performance. Numerous poems speak of musicians playing chansons or lais or ballades on a variety of instruments, and Johannes de Grocheo says that "a good artist plays on the viol every *cantus* and *cantilena* and every musical form in general."[27]

Most of the references to instrumental performance, either in poems or in theoretical treatises, are concerned with monophonic songs and dances. It is probable, however, that players provided troubadour and trouvère songs with simple improvised accompaniments. We have also noted the likelihood that instruments took over the performance of motet tenors and thus introduced accompanied duets and trios as well as solo songs. Instrumental doubling of the vocal lines is a further probability from which it is but a short step to the substitution of instruments for voices. It has been suggested that the caudae of conducti were designed for instrumental performance and "may prove to be a valuable source for thirteenth-century dance music."[28] Such an assumption is a bit farfetched, perhaps, but vocal polyphony undoubtedly did provide music for instrumental ensembles. A few pieces in vocal forms even appear to have been intended for instrumental performance.

27.   Reese, MMA, p. 327.
28.   NOHM, 2, p. 337. Examples are recorded as independent instrumental pieces in HMS, 2.

One group of such pieces may be the clausulae in the St. Victor manuscript (see above, p. 326, fn. 1). In many cases, the short texts are incorrectly placed under the tenor melismas and seem to function merely as identifying tags. It has sometimes been assumed, therefore, that these clausulae were not meant to be sung in spite of their existence as motets, which some scholars believe to be their original form. Yet the state in which the pieces are preserved in the St. Victor manuscript is really independent of their origin, either as motets or clausulae. If the text placement is not simply the result of scribal carelessness, it does suggest an intent to use the melismatic form of these pieces for instrumental performance.

Much less problematical are the already-mentioned "instrumental motets" in the Bamberg Codex (Nos. 102–08). The designation is paradoxical, of course, but it seems more appropriate than "clausula," which these seven pieces also resemble. They are all notated in score with two parts above a plainchant tenor in a repeated rhythmic pattern. Like the later secular motets, these pieces would seem to have lost all connection with organum, and their textless state, together with their use of hocket, makes the assumption of instrumental performance unavoidable.

INSTRUMENTAL DANCES

A favorite pastime in the Middle Ages, dancing obviously required some form of musical accompaniment. Dance songs provided much of that accompaniment and may sometimes have been played by instruments alone, although in manuscript sources they exist only as songs. One dance, the estampie, does occur as both an instrumental piece and a poetic form. Unfortunately, poems identified as estampies are without music, except for the famous *Kalenda Maya* (The first of May; see p. 274, fn. 23), by the troubadour Rambaut de Vaqueiras (fl. 1180–1207). This piece antedates by about one hundred years the first trouvère poems and the first instrumental dances that scribes identified as estampies.[29] We also have theoretical descriptions of the estampie as both a poetic and musical form. Despite this combination of seemingly happy circumstances, many aspects of the form remain obscure and even controversial. What can be given here with reasonable certainty is a description of pieces that medieval scribes labelled *estampie*.

The first such pieces were added in mensural notation to the manuscript of trouvère songs known as the *Chansonnier du Roy*.[30] They ap-

29. The poetic estampies are published in W. Streng-Renkonen, *Les Estampies françaises* (Paris, 1930).
30. The dances appear on pp. 7 and 176v–77v of the published facsimile (see Bibliography to Chapters XI–XII). The last page, with four estampies and the dansse real, is reproduced in Parrish, NMM, Pl. XLII.

The various musical forms derived from the dance attest to its popularity throughout the Middle Ages (from a fifteenth-century German woodcut).

pear as a group of eight dances, each of which is numbered and identified as an *estampie royal*. A *dansse real* follows the estampies, and two other textless dances were added elsewhere in the manuscript. One is unidentified; the other is called simply *danse*.[31] All of these dances are monophonic, and each consists of several repeated sections or *puncta*. The estampies have from four to seven puncta; the two dances and the unidentified piece have only three.

Because the repetitive structure of these dances is usually indicated in letters as *aa bb cc dd* etc., it is easy to see why the estampie, like the lai, is often said to be derived from the sequence. In many respects, however, the estampie stands apart from both vocal forms, which themselves differ in essential ways (see above, p. 291). The most distinctive aspect of the dance form becomes obvious when we note that the puncta of an estampie are not entirely different melodies. They all will have the same open and closed endings and usually the same preceding phrase or phrases. In the fourth estampie, for example, only the opening phrases of four or six measures are different in each of the seven puncta.[32] If the letter indication of such a form is not to be misleading, it must show the repeated material, perhaps in the following way: aXY_o aXY_c bXY_o bXY_c cXY_o cXY_c etc. Of the eleven dances in the *Chansonnier du Roy,* only the *Dansse real* gives no clear indication of repeated puncta, and the piece has been said to lack first and second endings. Given the form of

31. The danse is published in HAM, No. 40a, as a "Danse Royale." No. 40b, also called a "Danse Royale," is the fourth estampie royal.

32. HAM, No. 40b.

the other ten dances, however, it is probable that repeats were intended, with endings as suggested in AMM, No. 57. In any case, the three puncta again differ only in their opening five-measure phrases. Rather than treating the estampie and the lai as derivatives of the sequence, therefore, we should probably regard the three forms as different applications of a common structural principle that may well be much older than any of its medieval manifestations. That principle—repetition of each musical section—might even have originated in connection with the recurrent movements of a dance. It would then be the vocal forms that adapted the principle to their varying needs.

Other medieval dances take us beyond the chronological or geographical limits of the present chapter, but they should at least be mentioned here. English sources from the thirteenth century preserve four untitled pieces presumed to be dances and sometimes even called estampies. Only one is monophonic, and three are two-part pieces in modal notation.[33] All four pieces have repetitive structures, but none corresponds exactly with the form of the French estampie. In both style and structural procedures, indeed, the three polyphonic pieces more closely resemble the caudae of conducti and may have provided the basis for the suggestion that caudae are a repository of contemporary dance music (see p. 348).

Another English source, a fragmentary manuscript known as the Robertsbridge Codex, dates from around 1325 and preserves the earliest known music for a keyboard instrument. The collection consists of three dances, the first incomplete, and three transcriptions of motets, the last also incomplete.[34] In this case, the complete dances, although not identified as estampies, do correspond exactly with the monophonic French form. The vocal forms of the complete motets, moreover, appear among the interpolations in the French *Roman de Fauvel* (see Chapter XV). Whether the music is of English origin is therefore problematical. Perhaps the greatest significance of the Robertsbridge Codex lies in its inclusion of both dances and transcriptions of vocal pieces, two types of composition that have contributed ever since to the repertory of keyboard instruments.

A final collection of medieval dances is included in an Italian manuscript devoted primarily to fourteenth-century secular polyphony.[35]

33. The monophonic dance is HAM, No. 40c; of the two-part pieces, the first two are in HAM, No. 41a and b; the third is in Gleason, EM, p. 56. Facsimile in Apel, NPM, p. 239.

34. For the entire contents of the Robertsbridge Codex, together with the two *Fauvel* motets, see W. Apel, *Keyboard Music of the Fourteenth and Fifteenth Centuries* (AIM, 1963), pp. 1–9.

35. The manuscript is now in the British Museum (Add. 29987). For a facsimile with Index and Introduction by G. Reaney, see MSD, 13. The dances appear on fols. 55v–58 and 60–63v. Transcriptions, some incomplete, may be found in J. Wolf, "Die Tänze des Mittelalters," AMW, I (1918–19), pp. 24–42.

Heading this collection of fifteen monophonic pieces is the designation *istanpitta,* which evidently applies to the first eight dances. The term is not repeated, but a note on fol. 58 indicates the continuation of "this *istanpita"* (the fifth dance) on fol. 60. After the eighth dance, the collection continues with seven pieces including four *saltarelli,* one *trotto,* and two entitled *Lamento di Tristano* and *La Manfredina.*[36] An interesting aspect of the collection is its similar use of titles for the eight estampies: Some appear to be names (Ghaetta, Isabella, Belicha), others are phrases such as *Chominciamento di gioia* (Beginning of joy) and *Principio di virtu* (Source of virtue). Whatever connection there may have been between these titles and the music is now unknown, but they foreshadow the fanciful titles in dance suites of the seventeenth and eighteenth centuries.

All fifteen dances in the collection follow the structural principles of the earlier French dances in the *Chansonnier du Roy.* Each consists of a series of puncta, usually four to six, that have different opening phrases but close by repeating some or all of the first punctum, with its open and closed endings. There are significant differences, however, between the Italian istanpitte and the earlier French estampies and also between the two groups of Italian dances. Indeed, the istanpitte stand alone in having long and complex puncta. These characteristics make them seem unsuitable for dancing, and they should probably be regarded as pieces to be played for a listening audience. The other seven Italian pieces have much shorter and simpler puncta and could well have served as music for dancing. Although the trotto is the only dance of its kind, it is typical of the group as a whole in both form and style (AMM, No. 58). The dance consists of five puncta or *partes* (sing. *pars*), the last four of which provide new introductions to repeats of part or all of the *prima pars* (first part). The third part expands the introduction of the second, and both lead into the third measure of the first. Similarly, the fifth part expands the beginning of the fourth, but these two lead to repetitions of the complete first part. Each part, of course is to be played twice, with open and closed endings.[37]

One further aspect of the Italian dances should not pass unnoticed. Instead of being single pieces, the *Lamento di Tristano* and *La Manfredina* are pairs of related dances. The opening dance in each pair consists of three partes that are followed by a second set of three entitled *La Rotta* and *La Rotta della Manfredina* respectively. The meaning of the designation *rotta* is unclear, but it is certain that each one belongs with and completes the dance it follows. Thus the fourteenth century introduced the pairing of related dances that became common in the Renaissance and created a nucleus for the development of the Baroque dance suite.

36. For the *Lamento* and a saltarello, see HAM, No. 59a and b. Another saltarello is available in GMB, No. 28.

37. Wolf and, following him, Gleason (EM, p. 57) ignored the explicit indications of partes in the manuscript.

CHAPTER XV

The Ars Nova in France

Cultural historians often speak of the thirteenth century as the high point, or the classic period, of medieval life and art. They emphasize its stability, its reconciliation of divine revelation and human reason, its religion-centered unity of spirit. To these and other factors we owe magnificent achievements in architecture, literature, and music. But the classic spirit is essentially static, and the dynamic forces that reject classicism lead inevitably to new and different achievements. In the realm of music, the early fourteenth-century Frenchmen implied their scorn of the outmoded and old-fashioned music of the previous century when they called their own music an *ars nova,* a new art. The term has since come to signify, somewhat unjustifiably, the music of western Europe in the fourteenth century. Looking back over six and a half centuries, we may find this music less novel than its creators did. Yet the same spirit that produced the Ars Nova animated the Italian creators of the Nuove Musiche in the early seventeenth century and the creators of the more obviously "new music" of the twentieth century. As always, that innovative spirit opened up new horizons and gave a new direction to the art of music.

Evidence that musicians recognized the novelty of early fourteenth-century music appears around 1320 in the form of two treatises: the *Ars nove musice* (Art of New Music) by Johannes de Muris, and the *Ars nova* of Philippe de Vitry. The *Ars nove musice* is probably the older of the two, but Vitry's work gave its name to the music of the fourteenth century. This fact and our scanty knowledge about Johannes de Muris have tended to obscure his greater importance and influence as a musical theorist.[1] He apparently spent his young manhood in Paris, first as a student and then as a teacher, and it was at this time that he produced "a body of theoretical writings far more substantial and distinguished than Philippe's."[2] He does not seem to have been active as a composer of music, and later in life he devoted himself primarily to studies in mathe-

---

1. For information about J. de Muris, see L. Gushee, "New Sources for the Biography of Johannes de Muris," JAMS, 22 (1969), pp. 3–26.
2. Ibid., p. 3.

matics and astronomy. Nevertheless, his treatises on music formed an essential part of the university curriculum in the fourteenth and fifteenth centuries, and even as late as 1528 at the University of Prague.[3] Philippe de Vitry, on the other hand, was celebrated in his own time as a poet and musician, "the flower and gem of singers," and "the flower of all the world of music."[4] Despite the high esteem of his contemporaries, few of his compositions have been preserved. Of fourteen motets ascribed to him by modern scholars, four can be authenticated with reasonable certainty. Various reasons account for the belief in his authorship of the other ten, but documentary proof is lacking.[5] Whether Vitry was in reality a more prolific composer we shall probably never know. Yet these few pieces, together with his epoch-making treatise, confirm the judgment of his contemporaries and justify the high position accorded to him by posterity.

THE INNOVATIONS OF PHILIPPE DE VITRY

Before turning to the music of the fourteenth century, then, we should examine what it was that the theorists regarded as new. Strangely enough, the novelty of the Ars Nova proved to be almost entirely a matter of notational principles. The motets of Pierre de la Croix, with their groups of from two to nine semibreves, had clearly shown the need for some means of organizing and distinguishing smaller note values. This Philippe de Vitry accomplished by providing rules for determining which of the semibreve shapes were truly semibreves, which were minims, and even which were semiminims. In so doing, he extended the Franconian rules that governed the relationships between longs and breves by applying them to the relationships between breves and semibreves and between semibreves and minims in triple mensurations. An even more far-reaching innovation, however, was the establishment of duple mensurations on a par with triple. Occasional examples of duple meter appear in the thirteenth century, but with the treatises of Vitry and Muris duple meters become fully acceptable. Moreover, duple and triple mensurations at different levels may now be combined to produce a variety of meters that would have been inconceivable to an ars antiqua musician brought up in the Franconian system of notating the rhythmic modes.

The effect of combining mensurations at different levels of organization is most easily understood in the terms used by fourteenth-century theorists themselves. As in the rhythmic modes of the thirteenth cen-

3. Nan C. Carpenter, *Music in the Medieval and Renaissance Universities* (Norman, Oklahoma, 1958), p. 317.
4. Reese, MMA, pp. 336–37.
5. See Schrade, PMC, 1, pp. 29–41.

tury, *modus* (mood) applies to the relationship of longs and breves. The mood is perfect if the long equals three breves, imperfect if it equals two. Similarly, *tempus* (time) refers to the subdivision of the breve into semibreves and may be perfect or imperfect, depending on whether the breve equals three or two semibreves. *Prolatio* (prolation) refers to the semibreve and is the lowest level at which both triple and duple subdivisions are possible. Prolation too is perfect (or major) when the semibreve equals three minims, imperfect (or minor) when it equals two. In music with note values from the long to the minim, then, the mensuration at each level—mood, time, and prolation—could be either perfect or imperfect. Music of the thirteenth century, as we have seen, moved almost entirely in triple groups of longs and breves—in perfect mood, in other words. With the increasing use of shorter notes, the breve naturally become a longer value, and music of the fourteenth century moves primarily in breves, semibreves, and minims in one of the four possible combinations of time and prolation shown in Table 13 together with their identifying mensuration signs and modern equivalents. Many pieces restrict themselves to one of these combinations and make no use of mood, which would combine units of time and prolation into groups of two or three measures. As we shall see, however, mood and time do commonly appear in the lower parts of fourteenth-century motets, while the upper voices move in time and prolation. As an addition to this hierarchy of mensural organization, longs together with the duplex long—now called a *maxima*—could be grouped together to form a major mood (*maximodus*) that could also be either perfect or imperfect. This organization of the longest note values remained largely theoretical, although it does occur in a few motets of the fourteenth and the early fifteenth centuries.

Table 13: *The Four Combinations of Time and Prolation and Their Modern Equivalents*

From the note values given in Table 13 it is evident that the breve instead of the long has now become the unit of the musical measure. Thus the breve is no longer "short" in fact as well as name. Its value varies according to the mensuration, and it is the *minima* (♩), the "shortest" or "least" note, that is now a constant value in all mensurations. Despite the superlative of its name, the minima too was soon subdivided into semiminims (♪). Even the *Ars nova* of Philippe de Vitry mentions semiminims, but this may have been a later addition to his treatise, because the note value did not come into common use until late in the fourteenth century. The minim was always considered to be duple, divisible into only two semiminims, and therefore the introduction of this smaller note did not produce another level of organization that might be either perfect or imperfect. That introduction, however, marks a further step in the already well advanced development that ultimately reversed the meaning of the word *breve*. In music of the last two or three centuries, the whole note is the equivalent of the semibreve, and the breve is now such a long note that it is almost never used. It is for this reason that modern transcriptions must reduce the values of medieval notation. To use the modern breve, semibreve, and minim (◻, ♦, ♩) in editions of fourteenth-century music would totally misrepresent the effect it had for its contemporaries. As far as we can tell, a moderate tempo for the metrical equivalents given in Table 13 most nearly reproduces that effect.

The mensuration signs created in the fourteenth century are also of considerable historical interest. They are, in fact, time signatures, one of which is still in use today. Perfect time was indicated by a circle, and perfect prolation, by a dot. Thus, it was only natural to indicate imperfect time by a half circle and imperfect prolation by the absence of a dot. The half circle we now think of as being the letter C, perhaps because of its association with what we call "common time" (4/4). We have also shifted the unit of time from the breve to the semibreve (♦), but ¢ means now—as it did in the fourteenth century—the duple division of that unit and of all smaller note values. The signature ¢ is nearly as old. During the fifteenth and sixteenth centuries it meant that the beat fell on the breve (*alla breve*) instead of on the semibreve. Now, of course, it means that 4/4 becomes 2/2, with the beat falling on the half note (minim) instead of on the quarter. Nevertheless, we still speak of pieces with the signature ¢ as being alla breve.

After this brief look at some future developments, we may return to the fourteenth century. It should be evident that the notational system established by Philippe de Vitry did indeed constitute a new art of rhythmic organization. Other elements also contributed in some degree to the novelty of fourteenth-century music, but the real break with the music of the ars antiqua came in the field of rhythm. Never before had composers had at their disposal a notation that gave them such freedom of rhythmic expression in a variety of different meters. Nor were they slow in exercising that freedom. In large part we may say that concern for rhythmic organization is the chief characteristic of French music in the fourteenth century. That concern manifests itself both in the development of large-scale forms based on rhythmic repetitions and in the creation of rhythmic complexities unequaled in any period of Western music before the twentieth century. Neither of these things happened all at once, of course, and we can follow their gradual evolution as we examine the music left to us by the French Ars Nova.

THE *ROMAN DE FAUVEL*

The first collection of music with pieces reflecting the innovations of the Ars Nova is known as the *Roman de Fauvel*. In reality, this is the title of a lengthy poem in two parts by Gervais de Bus, a clerk in the chancellery of the kings of France from 1313 to 1338. The poem is a characteristic medieval satire on social corruption symbolized by an ass or horse named Fauvel. As the poem explains, the name Fauvel is full of hidden meanings. Taken as a whole it indicates that Fauvel's color is a dingy reddish-yellow (*fauve*) because he is unworthy of being one of the bright colors that represent human virtues. The two syllables Fau-vel refer to his veiled falsehood, while the spelling of his name comes from the initial letters of *Flaterie, Avarice, Vilanie, Variété, Envie,* and *Lascheté*. Beginning with popes and kings, men of all classes display these common vices when they eagerly rub down and curry Fauvel. It is a measure of the poem's popularity that this activity gave rise to the parallel French and English expressions "étriller Fauvel" and "to curry favel." Only when memory of the poem had dimmed was the English expression transformed into the one we now use, "to curry favor."

Another measure of the popularity of the *Roman de Fauvel* is its preservation—in whole or in part—in no fewer than twelve manuscripts. Only one of these manuscripts, however, contains the musical interpolations that have made the *Roman de Fauvel* familiar to students of medieval music.[6] Gervais de Bus had completed the first part of his poem (1226 lines) in 1310 and the second part (2054 lines) in 1314. By 1316, one Chaillou de Pesstain had apparently completed the musical additions. Nothing is known about him, unless he is the Raoul Chaillou who was also in the service of the French court. If this is true, Chaillou and Gervais may even have collaborated on the version of the *Roman de Fauvel* that somewhat alters and expands the original poem to introduce the numerous musical items. Those items come from a variety of sources and represent an astonishing range of musical types. Thirty-four

6. Paris, Bibl. Nat., f. fr. 146. See Bibliography.

Two pages from the *Roman de Fauvel,* including the motet *Tribum—Quoniam secta—Merito,* by Philippe de Vitry (Paris, Bibliotheque Nationale, f. fr. 146).

motets account for the bulk of the collection, although monophonic songs appear in far greater numbers.[7] Despite the language of the *Roman de Fauvel,* the great majority of musical interpolations have Latin texts. Over fifty of the monophonic songs are liturgical chants that the original index identifies as Alleluias, antiphons, responses, hymns, and versets. Latin texts also occur in a group of twenty-five monophonic conducti and sequences. Complete songs with French texts include four lais, four rondeaux, and nine "ballades," two of which have the musical and poetic form of the virelai. Among shorter musical interpolations with French texts we find fifteen refrains and twelve brief quotations of sottes chansons (foolish songs). Finally, a complete duplum with French text has been extracted from a motet and broken into eleven fragments, each of which is followed by a textual interpolation.[8]

What part Chaillou de Pesstain played in choosing and adapting these musical interpolations remains unknown, but it would be a mistake to regard them as nothing more than an anthology of music popular around 1315. Their obvious purpose was to provide a running musical commentary on the *Roman de Fauvel,* and individual pieces were selected solely on the basis of their relation to the poem. Some were taken over without change. Others, even among the liturgical chants, were remodelled to fit the new situation or were extended to include specific references to Fauvel. Still others have new texts adapted to older musical sources—clausulae, motets, and the melismas of conducti. In a few pieces, finally, both words and music appear to have been newly composed.

MOTETS IN THE *ROMAN DE FAUVEL*

The motets in the *Roman de Fauvel* are characteristic of the repertory as a whole in their range of musical styles. Of the thirty-four pieces, only one is a four-voice motet; twenty-three are for three voices; and ten are for two. As in the monophonic songs, Latin texts predominate in the motets. Only four are French double motets with secular French tenors as well. Three more mix French and Latin texts in various ways.[9] In the

---

7.   All the motets are published in Schrade, PM, 1. The complete musical contents of the *Roman de Fauvel* are listed in PMC, 1, pp. 57–101. The monophonic music is available in G. Harrison, *The Monophonic Music in the* Roman de Fauvel (Ph.D. dissertation, Stanford, Univ., 1963, University Microfilms 64–1613).

8.   Schrade, PMC, 1, p. 85, lists these fragments as eleven different "motets entés" (No. 57).

9.   **Fauv** 15 (32) has a French triplum and Latin motetus; **Fauv** 28 (121) has Latin texts in the two upper voices with a French rondeau as a tenor; and **Fauv** 9 (12) presents a curious alternation of Latin and French phrases in both upper voices. NB: The first of the two identifying numbers are those of Schrade's edition cited in fn. 7 above. The numbers in parentheses indicate the position of the motets in the complete series of 130 pieces.

case of the motets, it would be true to say that they constitute an anthology—but one that represents all stages in the development of the form
up to 1315. We find pieces from the early thirteenth century in strict
modal rhythms, pieces from mid-century in the freer rhythms described by Franco of Cologne, and pieces from the end of the century in
the style of Pierre de la Croix. Most important of all, however, are a few
motets contemporary with the *Roman de Fauvel* itself. In these works,
we can follow the early development of the Ars Nova and observe its
first fruits. Some of the motets, indeed, are cited in the treatise of Philippe de Vitry and are believed to be his own compositions. It becomes
doubly important, therefore, to see how these first examples of the
fourteenth-century Ars Nova differ from the music of the ars antiqua.

The opening measures of *Adesto—Firmissime—Alleluya* (Example
XV–1) illustrate some of the possible combinations of mensurations at
different levels. Attributed to Philippe de Vitry, this motet is cited in
his *Ars nova* as an example of imperfect mood and time; and we can see
that both the long (♩) and the breve (♪) are duple in value. At higher
and lower levels, however, the mensurations are perfect. Longs and
maximas in the tenor combine to produce perfect maximodus, indicated in the transcription by measures in 3/2 meter. At the other end of
the scale, semibreves and minims in triplet patterns (♫) show that the
prolation is also perfect.[10]

Example XV–1: *Fauv 30 (124)—Philippe de Vitry (?)*

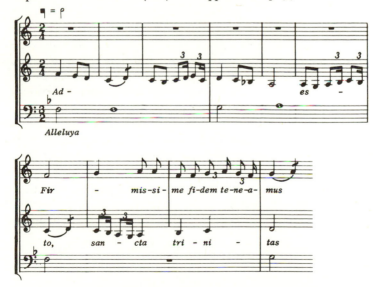

Come, holy Trinity—Let us keep the faith most firmly.

10. Schrade, PMC, 1, p. 95, inexplicably states that the prolation is imperfect (minor),
but his transcription always subdivides the semibreve into triplets.

The musical effect of *Adesto—Firmissime–Alleluya* is much simpler than the complexity of its mensural organization would seem to suggest. We are primarily aware of the duple rhythms produced by the imperfect longs and breves, and it is this aspect of the music, of course, that makes it new. Interest in metrical organization has also led to a more regular treatment of the smaller note values. Instead of the many different subdivisions of the breve that characterize the style of Pierre de la Croix, we now find it replaced only by groups of two, three, or four notes (♩♫, ♩♫♫, ♫♫♫). The resulting rhythmic consistency makes a further contribution to the simplicity and attractiveness of this music.

Another *Fauvel* motet, *Garrit gallus—In nova fert* (AMM, No. 59), is attributed to Philippe de Vitry largely on the basis of his having cited it in the *Ars nova* for its use of red notes in the tenor. According to Vitry, coloration—either red or hollow notes in place of solid black—may have several different meanings. Most commonly, however, it indicates that perfect notes lose a third of their value—become imperfect, in other words—with a resulting change in mensuration. This is exactly what happens in the tenor of *Garrit gallus—In nova fert,* although the use of coloration was so new that an explanatory canon (rule) was added to indicate that the mood was perfect with black notes, imperfect with red. The already imperfect value of the breve remains unchanged by the coloration.

ISORHYTHM

Coloration in the tenor of *Garrit gallus—In nova fert* is only one aspect of the motet's modernity. Of much greater importance is the organization of the entire tenor melody in what we now call *isorhythm*. *Iso-* means "same," and the essential characteristic of isorhythmic structure is the repetition of identical rhythmic patterns called *taleae* (cuttings). As a rule, the tenor melody—now called a *color*—contains several statements of the rhythmic talea and usually is itself repeated at least once. In *Garrit gallus—In nova fert,* three statements of the talea shown in Example XV–2 complete the tenor melody, which is then repeated with its rhythmic organization unchanged. The overall organization of the tenor may therefore be indicated by the formula 2C = 6T. A further subtlety indicative of the motet's modernity is the symmetrical structure of the

Example XV–2: *The Tenor Talea of* Garrit gallus—In nova fert

*The passage between incomplete brackets (⌐   ¬) is in coloration.

talea itself. The two halves of the pattern are perfectly balanced around the rest in the middle of the passage in coloration, which changes the mood from perfect to imperfect. The final rest is more a separation than an integral part of the taleae and is omitted at the end of the motet.

Philippe de Vitry is often regarded as the inventor of isorhythm, but it is obvious that the principles of isorhythmic construction are not new in themselves. Taleae are no more than expanded forms of the repeated rhythmic patterns in the tenors of clausulae and thirteenth-century motets, in which repetitions of the melody were also commonplace. In a gradual process, the repeated patterns of tenors grew longer and freed themselves from the restrictions of the rhythmic modes. At the same time, tenor melodies continued to be repeated in a variety of ways, either with the same or with different rhythmic relationships. We do not ordinarily speak of isorhythm in thirteenth-century music, but it is there that we find its seeds as well as its first flowers.

Isorhythmic construction, then, was neither an invention of Philippe de Vitry nor his exclusive property in the early fourteenth century. The talea of *Garrit Gallus—In nova fert* has a more complex rhythmic structure than earlier examples or than other motets in the *Roman de Fauvel*, but some motets attributed to Vitry have simpler tenor patterns than their thirteenth-century prototypes. Moreover, Vitry's taleae closely resemble those in other *Fauvel* motets not attributed to him. For comparative purposes, four rhythmic patterns of taleae from the *Roman de Fauvel* are assembled in Example XV–3 together with the formulas that show the complete form of the tenor in each case.

Example XV–3: *Rhythms of Taleae in Four* Fauvel *Motets*

Motet	Talea	Form of tenor
Fauv 4	♩. | ♪♪ | ♩. | ♩. ♩. | ♩. | ♪♪ | ♩. | ◼. |	2C = 10T
Fauv 9 (12)	♩. | ♪♪ | ♩. | ◼ ♪ | ♪♪ | ◼. |	1C = 7T
Fauv 12 (22) (Ph. de Vitry, No. 1)	♪♪ | ♩. | ♪♪ | ♪♪ | ♩. |	3C = 9T
	x 4 + y	
Fauv 16 (33)	♩. | ♪♪ | ♩. | ♪♪♪ | ♪♪ | ♩. | ◼.:‖ ♩. | ♩. | ◼. |	2C = 2(4T + Y)

Composers sometimes gave variety to their isorhythmic structures by repeating the color with smaller note values in either free or strict diminution. This procedure undoubtedly stems from the older practice of repeating a plainchant tenor (color) with a different rhythmic pattern. One of the more striking examples of this practice occurs in *Ave, Virgo—Ave gloriosa Mater—Domino,* a motet that must have enjoyed great popularity in the thirteenth century.[11] The tenor is stated twice,

11.   It occurs in variant forms in some nine different manuscripts, including **Ba** (No. 1), **Mo** (No. 53), and Las Huelgas (No. 101). See also Parrish, NMM, Pl. XXXII and XXXIII.

each time as a free and different variation of the original melody, the melisma of a *Benedicamus Domino* (LU, 124). It is the rhythmic contrast between the two statements that is of particular interest, however. The melody is first divided into three-note units in the common pattern of the fifth rhythmic mode (♩. ♩. ♩. ♪·). With the second variation of the melody, the rhythm shifts to a five-note pattern in the first mode (♩ ♪♩ ♪♩. ♪.). In a motet written just before the *Roman de Fauvel,* Pierre de la Croix produced a similar increase of rhythmic activity but in a different way.[12] He divided the first appearance of his color into nine statements of the same common fifth-mode pattern. For the repetition of the color, he did not change the note values but created a feeling of urgency and condensation by omitting all the rests. From practices such as these it is but a short step to free diminution in isorhythmic motets of the early fourteenth century.

One of the earliest instances of such diminution occurs in *Adesto—Firmissime,* the fourth of Vitry's motets in the *Roman de Fauvel.* As we saw in Example XV–1, the tenor of this motet uses the pattern of the second rhythmic mode but transferred to the level of maximodus. The notes, that is, are longs and maximas instead of breves and longs. The color extends through eight statements of the five-note talea and is then repeated with the five notes reduced to even breves followed by a breve rest. As a result, the talea now occupies three instead of nine measures in 2/4 meter (Example XV–4).

Example XV–4: *The Tenor Talea of* Adesto—Firmissime

Color - 3 x $\frac{2}{4}$ ρ o | ρ o | ρ - | x 8 —

is diminished to

$\frac{2}{4}$ ρ ρ | ρ ρ | ρ ♪ | x 8

Another motet of Vitry, *Garison—Douce playsence—Neuma quinti toni* (Recovery [from a sickness]—Sweet pleasure—Melisma in the fifth [Lydian] mode; No. 6), illustrates the results of diminishing both perfect and imperfect longs. In the seven-note talea, each perfect long equals three measures of 9/8 meter, and each imperfect long equals two of 6/8. When the color is repeated in diminution, however, the perfect longs lose two-thirds of their value, while the imperfect longs lose only one-half of theirs. Omission of the first rest from the diminished talea further shortens its first part. In Example XV–5, double dots (:) indicate the values of measures in 9/8.

Before summarizing the various ways in which Philippe de Vitry treated isorhythm, we must digress to consider the characteristic distribution of voices in fourteenth-century motets. In the first half of the

12. HAM, No. 34.

Example XV–5: *The Isorhythmic Structure of the Tenor in*
Garison—Douce playsence

Color – 3 x $\frac{9}{8}$ 𝅗𝅥·♪: | 𝅗𝅥·♪: | 𝅗𝅥·♪: |▬:▬:| 2 x $\frac{6}{8}$ 𝅝· |𝅝· |𝅝· |𝅝· | ▬· | ▬· | x 4 –

is diminished to

$\frac{9}{8}$ ♪: |♪: |♪: |$\frac{6}{8}$ ♩· |♩· |♩· |♩· | ▬ | ▬ | x 4

century, the majority of motets—whether isorhythmic or not—had
three voices: a duplum and triplum with different texts, and a presumably instrumental tenor. When a fourth voice was added, it was no
longer a quadruplum with its own text, as in the thirteenth-century
motet. Instead, the added voice now has no text, lies in the same general
range as the tenor, and is identified as a *contratenor*. This development
reflects a growing tendency to stratify the voices at different pitch levels
in contrast to the equal voice ranges often found in earlier polyphony.
Thus, in the typical four-voice motet of the fourteenth century, the
upper two voices move in approximately the same range a fifth or an octave above the range of the supporting tenor and contratenor. As we
have already seen in three-voice motets, the upper voices are further differentiated from the lower by their mensural organization. They usually
move in units of time and prolation, while the tenor, now accompanied
by the contratenor, moves in units of mood and time. This stratification
of the voice pairs with regard to both range and rhythmic character is
one of the distinctive features of the later isorhythmic motet.

From our knowledge of previous practices in the successive composition of voices, we might expect that a four-voice motet could be reduced to three simply by omitting the contratenor. This may have been
done at times, but there is evidence that the lower parts were coming to
be regarded as a unit, neither member of which was complete without
the other. A number of four-voice motets, including two of the three
by Philippe de Vitry, are provided with an optional *solus tenor* (single
tenor) to replace both the tenor and contratenor. Because these voices lie
in the same range, they cross frequently; and one often complements the
other by filling in its rests in the isorhythmic pattern. To function as a
replacement for the tenor and contratenor when three-voice performance was desired, the solus tenor had to provide approximately the
same harmonic support for the upper voices. The process of achieving
this support was not invariable, but for the most part it consisted of taking the succession of lowest-sounding notes to create a new and nearly
continuous tenor melody. The results of this process are noteworthy
for a number of reasons. In the first place, a solus tenor cannot always
maintain exact repetitions of the isorhythmic talea and color. Furthermore, because the solus tenor inevitably departs from the original tenor
melody, it suggests the possibility of a supporting bass freed from the
restrictions imposed by a preexistent plainchant. This dawning recogni-

tion of the importance of the bass line as a harmonic support represents one of the most significant new developments of the fourteenth century.

In most isorhythmic motets, one or both of the upper voices begin together with the first note of the tenor's talea, but four of Vitry's motets have an introduction, or *introitus,* before the isorhythmic structure commences. As a rule, the tenor does not participate in such introductions, and the upper voices enter successively, sometimes in imitation. One exception occurs in a late motet of Philippe de Vitry, *Petre Clemens—Lugentium* (No. 12), which honors Pope Clement VI (1342–52). Here, the tenor provides a rhythmically free accompaniment for the upper voices throughout the fourteen-measure introduction. It then leads without a break into the beginning of the isorhythmic talea in measure 15.

Because Vitry's isorhythmic motets foreshadow almost all future developments of the form, it is important that his procedures be summarized here. Throughout the history of isorhythm, we find three different ways of organizing the tenor taleae and colores. The least common procedure divides a long melody with no repeats into several taleae. Only one motet ascribed to Vitry is in this form, the above-mentioned *Petre Clemens—Lugentium,* in which the tenor melody extends over the introitus and seven taleae with no repetition of a color.[13] Tenors of this type occur more frequently in later motet collections, and many appear to be newly composed rather than taken from plainchant melismas. In the second way of organizing isorhythmic tenors, the talea is also repeated unchanged throughout the motet but with one or more repetitions of the melody. This color often equals a round number of taleae, so that the total structure of a tenor may be indicated by such formulas as 2C = 8T or 3C = 9T. In some cases, however, the end of the color does not coincide with the end of a talea, and we find tenors in which 2C = 3T or 3C = 4T. This practice, common in the works of Machaut and later composers, occurs only once in somewhat irregular fashion in the motets of Philippe de Vitry. In *Colla jugo—Bona condit* (No. 9), the color begins to repeat with the second note in the fourth of seven taleae. At the end of the first section of the motet, three added notes complete the melody, and a rhythmic extension follows the seventh talea before the whole is repeated in diminution. Such diminutions, found in six of Vitry's motets, constitute the third way of organizing isorhythmic tenors. As we have seen, Vitry sometimes used free diminution that altered the relative values of notes in the talea, but he also wrote motets in which the color and talea are repeated with all note values exactly halved.[14] This latter procedure is by far the more com-

13.   For a similar subdivision of a single color into seven taleae, see the *Fauvel* motet in HAM, No. 43.

14.   E.g., in PM, 1, Nos. 9, 10, and 14.

mon in motets that introduce diminution in the tenor and contratenor parts, but later composers often added the subtlety of successive repetitions in different combinations of mood and time or of time and prolation. Thus, for example, the notes long–breve–breve–long would have the values of ♩. | ♩ ♩ | ♩. |, ♩ | ♩ ♩ | ♩ |, ♩. | ♩ ♩ | ♩. |, and ♩ ·| ♩ ♩ | ♩ |, when read successively in perfect and imperfect mood, perfect and imperfect time. The result appears to be a combination of the strict and free types of diminution used by Philippe de Vitry. Repetition with the change from perfect to imperfect mood reduces the total length by one third, but it also changes some of the relative note values within the pattern. The last two statements in perfect and imperfect time then diminish the first two exactly by half. Exact diminutions were sometimes written out in smaller note values. More often, the melody was written only once, with a canon (rule) prescribing the different mensurations or degrees of diminution to be used in successive statements of the original color and taleae.

In addition to establishing the normal methods of isorhythmic organization in the tenor and contratenor parts, Philippe de Vitry began applying isorhythm to the upper voices and using hocket both for structural clarity and climactic effect. Later composers expanded and refined the application of these procedures without changing any of the fundamental principles. Four-part writing became more and more common, and all voices were often strictly isorhythmic throughout an entire motet. At the same time, the taleae tended to become longer and consequently fewer in number. Isorhythmic upper voices normally followed the structure of the tenor and contratenor, except when these lower voices were repeated with changes of mensuration or in exact diminution. With rare exceptions, the duplum and triplum in such cases repeated nothing but introduced new melodic progressions in new taleae that matched the reduced length of the taleae in the lower parts. Reflecting the growing interest in rhythmic complexity, hocket continued to be used, but in conjunction with more sophisticated devices such as syncopation, rhythmic sequence, imitation, and canon. In the latter part of the fourteenth century, isorhythm occasionally appeared in forms other than the motet, such as Mass movements and secular songs. It was the isorhythmic motet, however, that became the most intricate and most highly organized musical form ever created by medieval composers.

THE SONGS OF JEHAN DE LESCUREL

The manuscript that preserves the *Roman de Fauvel* with musical interpolations also contains a small group of pieces identified as "ballades, rondeaux, and poems grafted onto rondeau refrains, which Jehannot de

Lescurel made" (*balades, rondeaux et diz entez sus refrois de rondeaux, les quiex fist Jehannot de Lescurel*). The author of these songs is believed to be the same Jehan de Lescurel who was hanged on May 23, 1304, together with three other "children" of wealthy Parisian families. Convicted of debauchery and crimes against women, the four delinquents were tonsured clerks apparently connected with Notre Dame cathedral, where we may assume that Jehan received his musical training. His songs, however, are neither religious nor debauched. On the whole, they are inoffensive poems in the tradition of courtly love, although a few texts do name specific ladies.[15]

The collected works of Jehan de Lescurel comprise thirty-four pieces, of which the last two are "diz entez," lengthy poems of twenty-four and twenty-eight stanzas respectively, with a different refrain at the end of each stanza. The manuscript provides melodies for all of the refrains, but the poems themselves remain without music. They are therefore of limited interest except as they augment the repertory of quoted refrains.

Lescurel's settings of thirty-one lyric poems possess much greater musical and historical interest. Although the index of the manuscript mentions only ballades and rondeaux, the collection includes five virelais, fifteen ballades, and eleven rondeaux, of which one appears in both polyphonic and monophonic versions. These texts display considerable variety in the details of their internal structure, but they clearly establish the large structural patterns that differentiate the three poetic types and determine their characteristic musical forms. One of these forms had yet to receive its distinguishing name, but Lescurel's songs confirm the existence of all three at the beginning of the fourteenth century. By adopting only these forms, Lescurel departed from the more traditional types of trouvère chansons. On the other hand, he continued one tradition in his preference for monophonic song. Only the first piece in the collection, a rondeau refrain, is set in three-part polyphony. It is somewhat more melismatic than the conductus-like pieces by Adam de la Hale but is written in the same neume-against-neume style. Moreover, the middle voice again proves to be the basic melody of the setting. It reappears alone with the complete rondeau text as the third piece in the collection. Like the two versions of this rondeau, the monophonic songs in general tend to be more highly ornamented and to have more and longer melismas than the trouvère chansons of the later thirteenth century. Lescurel's works also differ from older chansons in being written in mensural notation. Unfortunately, that notation represents a transitional stage between the innovations of Pierre de la Croix and the fully developed system of the Ars Nova. It therefore leaves in doubt the correct interpretation of semibreves in groups of two to four, or occasionally five notes. As a result, various modern transcriptions differ considerably in

15. For a modern edition with a facsimile of the manuscript, see N. Wilkins, *The Works of Jehan de Lescurel.*

Triplum and Tenor of a motet by Philippe de Vitry from the Ivrea
Codex: *Tuba sacrae fidei—In arboris—Virgo sum* (Biblioteca
Capitolae, Ivrea).

their rhythmic details.[16] Nevertheless, the distinctive character of Lescurel's melodic and rhythmic style remains clear enough. It would seem
that the fixed forms became the predominant types of French secular
song only when they had lost or were in the process of losing their original connection with the dance. By their melodic elaboration, the songs
of Jehan de Lescurel show that the process was well under way even
before the advent of fourteenth-century secular polyphony. It remained
for Guillaume de Machaut to devise an appropriate style that would
transform the ballade, rondeau, and virelai into accompanied art songs
far removed from their humble origins.

THE IVREA CODEX

After the *Roman de Fauvel* the next important source of fourteenth-
century polyphony is a manuscript now in the Chapter Library at Ivrea,
a small city near Turin in northwestern Italy. The Ivrea Codex (*Iv*) apparently originated around 1360 in the musical environment of the papal
court at Avignon, and its contents form a representative anthology of
music composed during the first half of the fourteenth century. As
might be expected, nearly half of the more than eighty pieces are double

16. In addition to the publication of N. Wilkins, the songs of Lescurel are available in
    Gennrich, RVB, 1, pp. 307–72. See also, RVB, 2, pp. 246–54.

motets, most of them isorhythmic. There are twenty-one motets with Latin texts, fourteen with French, and two with one Latin and one French text. It is more surprising to find that the next largest group of pieces consists of twenty-five settings of texts from the Ordinary of the Mass (see Chapter XVI). French secular songs are relatively few in number—six rondeaux, five virelais, and four canons or chaces. The manuscript does not identify any composers of this music, but it proves to be the primary source for the later motets attributed to Philippe de Vitry.[17] It also contains three motets and one rondeau by Machaut. Three-part writing prevails in the great majority of these pieces, and individual differences largely result from the degree to which isorhythm is present in the upper voices. Machaut's more complex application of isorhythmic procedures and his contributions to the development of polyphonic ballades, rondeaux, and virelais will be considered in Chapter XVII, devoted to his complete works. The one type of secular song in *Iv* that demands discussion here is the chace.

THE CHACE

Earlier discussions of polyphonic techniques in organum, the conductus, and even the motet, have cited instances of canonic writing and have noted its close relationship to the technique of voice exchange. Apart from *Sumer is icumen in,* however, canons as complete compositions do not appear before the four chaces in the Ivrea Codex. One of these pieces is called a *chace* in the instructions that indicate the manner of its performance, and the name was probably intended as a description of the way one voice chases another in a musical canon. Slightly later terminology shifted the emphasis from the pursuer to the pursued and gave it the name *fuga* (flight). The double meaning of the word *chace*—a simple pursuit, or a hunt—undoubtedly suggested the use of canonic technique to depict hunting scenes, and one of the Ivrea pieces does depict such a scene. The other three treat different subjects and offer the first but not the only evidence that it was the technique and not the musical description of a hunt that gave the chace its name.

The French chaces were first thought to be for two voices only, and some were published and performed in this way, even after it was discovered that they are three-part canons at the unison.[18] The origin of this sort of canon remains open to question, but it may well have devel-

---

17. As the motets of Vitry have already illustrated the various methods of isorhythmic construction, the other motets in *Iv* need not be discussed in detail. They are published, together with other motets from the middle and later fourteenth century in Harrison, PM, 5.

18. Credit for the discovery goes to N. Pirrotta, who announced it in "Per l'origine e la storia della 'caccia' . . . ," *Rivista musicale italiana,* 48 (1946), p. 317 ff.

oped from a popular or folk practice of singing rounds rather than from sporadic appearances of canonic writing in learned polyphony. The simplest and perhaps the oldest of the Ivrea chaces seems to bear out this supposition. *Talent m'est pris* is a short melody of twenty-one measures that is to be sung as a circular canon or round in which the voices enter at seven-measure intervals (Example XV–6). The text confesses a desire to sing like the cuckoo, presumably resulting from the return of "pretty weather." Cuckoo calls in hocket passages promptly appear, with a punning insinuation (cuckoo—cuckold) that betrays an age-old French preoccupation with the bird's domestic habits. *Talent m'est pris* possesses further interest because it exists in several variant forms.[19] Even in the Ivrea Codex it appears twice in slightly different versions, and copies in manuscripts of Germanic origin are even more divergent. One version is entirely in duple meter—2/4 instead of 6/8—and two have different German texts, one of which begins *Der Summer kummt* (Summer is coming). Together with its intrinsic qualities, these several versions of *Talent m'est pris* suggest that it was indeed a widely known "popular" song that learned musicians adapted and revised for their collections of "classical" polyphony. The many similarities between this round and the *Sumer* canon are obvious, but they do not justify any assumption of a direct relationship between the two pieces. Probably they both stem from medieval equivalents of *Frère Jacques* and *Three Blind Mice*.

Example XV–6: *Chace,* Talent m'est pris

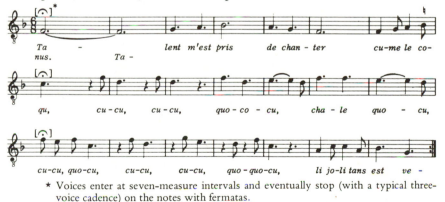

* Voices enter at seven-measure intervals and eventually stop (with a typical three-voice cadence) on the notes with fermatas.

I am seized by a desire to sing like the cuckoo. Pretty weather has come.

The other three canons in the Ivrea Codex are longer and more complex pieces that illustrate the features generally regarded as characteristic of the chace. Their texts depict lively scenes of various kinds and often use nonsense syllables to imitate natural sounds, but only *Se je*

19. See J. Handschin, "The Summer Canon and its Background," MD, 3 (1949), p. 80 f. Apel, FSC, 3, No. 291, gives three different versions.

chant mains que ne suel (If I sing less than usual) describes a hunt (AMM, No. 60). For these long and partly narrative texts, circular canons were no longer appropriate, and the three voices continue their chase until they are stopped by a strong final cadence that cuts off the second and third voices before they have sung the complete melody. However, the canons follow the example of *Talent m'est pris* in their use of hocket and lively rhythmic figures for descriptive purposes. Passages that introduce these devices become much more extended and complex, and it is evident that poetic and musical description was now of primary importance.

The emphasis that writers have placed on *Se je chant* must be held partly responsible for the common notion that a chace normally describes a hunt. If it is kept in mind that the notion holds true for only one of the French chaces, that one may still serve to illustrate the general characteristics of the type. More than the other chaces, *Se je chant* clearly and successfully contrasts quiet and slow-moving sections at the beginning and end with the lively descriptive scene that forms the central portion of the piece. The sectional divisions are clearly defined in the melody, but they naturally overlap in canonic performance. Thus a gradual involvement of all voices in the hunt creates a mounting excitement, which then subsides as one by one the voices return to calm. The realism of the hunting cries is obvious and rather naïve, but the broader treatment of rhythm in the hunt achieves a more sophisticated level of musical description. The piece as a whole is written in perfect mood with imperfect time and major prolation. This has been transcribed (AMM, No. 60) as 3/2 with triplet subdivisions of the quarter note (♩♪ and ♪♩). Near the climax of the hunt, however, the meter loses its stability when units equal to two or three breves appear in irregular alternation. In such a situation, the barring of a modern transcription might be done in several ways, all of which would be somewhat arbitrary. Nevertheless, some measures of 2/2 must be introduced to accommodate the irregular placement of the mensural units. Whatever barring is chosen for the individual voices, their combination produces a rich counterpoint of rhythms that subtly suggests the confusion of a hunt, a confusion that gradually diminishes as each voice resumes a straightforward triple meter. By this skillful exploitation of canonic technique for pictorial effect, the unknown composer of *Se je chant* turned what might have been an intellectual exercise into a masterpiece of descriptive music.

Although the canonic technique of the chaces sets them apart from other polyphonic forms, their texts show that they do not stand entirely outside the traditions of French secular poetry. The duplum of a motet in the Bamberg Codex (No. 92) begins "Talent m'est pris de chanter," but in this case the poet wants to sing of a much beloved lady rather than like a cuckoo. Similarly, the duplum of Motet 277 in the Montpellier

Codex begins with the line "Se je chante mains que ne sueil," but again the continuation is different. Here, it is not the love of falcons and hunting but unrequited love for a lady that has caused the singing to lapse. In neither of these two instances do the identical lines of text have the same melody, and there is no reason to assume a direct connection between the chaces and the presumably older motets. More probably they were both following the usual practice of quoting familiar lines and refrains. This supposition seems to be borne out by the fact that the first line of *Se je chant* appears in two other songs. Once it is the first line of a ballade, unfortunately without music, in the Oxford collection of song texts (Douce 308).[20] Even more interesting and thought-provoking is Guillaume de Machaut's use of the line as the refrain of his ballade No. 12. Moreover, the cantus of the ballade's refrain is melodically identical with the opening phrase of the chace except in the fourth measure, which Machaut presented in its unadorned and perhaps original form (Example XV–7). It seems improbable that the two pieces can have originated as independent quotations of a well-known refrain. Yet if they are directly connected we cannot tell whether Machaut quoted the beginning of the chace or its composer took Machaut's refrain as his starting point. In addition, the text of *Se je chant* perfectly expresses the love of falcons and of hunting that Machaut revealed in some of his longer poems. These connections and coincidences would normally be more than enough to attribute an anonymous work to a specific medieval composer. In this case, however, such an attribution is precluded by the absence of *Se je chant* from the manuscript collections of Machaut's works that were prepared under his supervision (see pages 399–401). If we must therefore assume an unknown composer for the chace, we may at least conjecture that he and Machaut were comrades in the cultivation of both music and the chase.

Example XV–7: *First Phrase of Chace and Refrain*
of Machaut's Ballade No. 12

The four examples in the Ivrea Codex comprise the entire repertory of complete and independent chaces that have been preserved. However, the form was more popular and important than these few pieces would

20. Gennrich, RVB, 1, No. 171, and 2, p. 113.

seem to imply. The several versions of *Talent m'est pris* indicate that it was widely known, and a second copy of *Se je chant* is preserved in a manuscript fragment of northern French origin.[21] The same fragment contains the close of a fifth chace that is also found without its beginning in still another remnant of a larger manuscript. How many other examples have been lost we cannot know, but the evidence suggests that chaces were not uncommon in the early part of the fourteenth century. Subsequently, the chace retained its canonic technique but lost its descriptive function. In Machaut's Lai 11, the even-numbered stanzas are three-voice canons identified as chaces. The stanzas of the following lai (No. 12) lack the identifying label, but all twelve are set as three-voice canons. A similar canon occurs in Machaut's Ballade 17, with a different text for each voice. Although hocket passages appear in some of these nineteen canons, they have no programmatic relationship with the texts, which are normal examples of their poetic types (see pages 407–09). Toward the end of the fourteenth century the descriptive and programmatic aspects of the chace reappear in a number of French virelais.[22] One of these pieces, *Or sus vous dormez trop* (Get up, you sleep too much), is included in the Ivrea Codex, but probably as a later addition to the original contents. For the most part these virelais deal with pastoral themes and confine their descriptive effects to imitations of the songs of birds— the lark, the nightingale, and the inevitable cuckoo. The transfer of programmatic music from the chace to a form that was free of the restrictions imposed by canonic writing seems sensible enough, but it had to wait on Machaut's development of an appropriate style and distribution of voices for the polyphonic secular song.

The French chace was not without its counterparts in other countries during the fourteenth century. Its relationship with the Italian caccia is somewhat problematical and will be considered in connection with the emergence of Italian secular polyphony (Chapter XVIII). A more direct connection seems to exist between the chace and three pieces labelled *caça* in a Catalonian manuscript known as the *Llibre Vermell* (Red Book) from its red-velvet nineteenth-century binding. These pieces have Latin texts in praise of the Virgin, and rubrics indicate that they may be performed as either two- or three-part canons. Two are short rounds that involve little more than voice exchange. The other is a longer, noncircular canon with a chantlike melody in unmeasured notation.[23] All three serve as a final reminder that musical description was only a secondary and nonessential characteristic of the chace.

21. Paris, Bibl. Nat., Coll. de Picardie 67, fol. 67 (**Pic**). Facsimile in MGG, 1, cols. 715–16.

22. They are all available in W. Apel's publications of fourteenth-century French secular pieces (see Bibliography). *Or sus* is No. 70 in FSM and No. 212 in FSC, 3.

23. See O. Ursprung, "Spanisch-katalanische Liedkunst des 14. Jahrhunderts," *Zeitschrift für Musikwissenschaft,* 4 (1921–22), pp. 153–55.

CHAPTER XVI

Liturgical Polyphony in the Fourteenth Century

The appearance of polyphonic Mass movements in the fourteenth century obliges us to consider the contemporary state of liturgical music. Historians in general tend to regard the period as one of increasing secularization in all the arts, and they account for this situation on both religious and economic grounds. With the "Babylonian captivity" of the popes in Avignon (1305–78) and with two and finally three rivals contending for the papal throne during the Great Schism (1378–1417), the power and prestige of the Church sank to a new low. On the other hand, the increasing wealth of the cities and their inhabitants created a vast new market for secular architecture, painting, and sculpture as well as music. Certainly these factors were in part responsible for the advance of secular culture, but even at its lowest ebb the Church—or individual churches and churchmen—did not entirely cease to patronize the arts. More than most, perhaps, historians of music had some excuse for over-emphasizing secular composition. The accidents of history decided which of the fragile monuments of music should survive and which should first become known in modern times. Thus it was that the over-whelming preponderance of secular polyphony in the works of Machaut and of Italian composers came to be regarded as typical of the entire fourteenth century. By an unlucky chance, a famous decree of Pope John XXII (1316–34) provided a too-convenient explanation of this phenomenon. Issued in 1324 at Avignon, the decree used strong language to condemn composers who overloaded their music with a multitude of small notes—semibreves and minims—and who distorted the melodies of the Church with hocket and elaborate polyphony. Singers too were censured for their vocal display and for using gestures to express the sentiment of the music. The decree forbade all of these practices and prescribed penalties for failure to observe the prohibition. Only on solemn occasions might plainchant be enriched by a few concords—octaves, fifths, and fourths—as long as the established melodies remained unchanged and undisturbed.[1]

As a contemporary record of reactionary opposition to the innova-

---

1. For the text in both Latin and English, see *The Oxford History of Music*, 1, 2nd ed. (London, 1929), p. 294 ff.

The fortress-like Palace of the Popes in Avignon (courtesy of the French Cultural Services, New York).

tions of the Ars Nova, Pope John's decree possesses considerable interest, but its effect on the course of musical development has been greatly overemphasized. In the usual view, the Church now permitted only the simplest forms of improvised organum, and the production of sacred music all but ceased as composers turned their attention to secular forms. Holders of this view seem to overlook much that had happened in the thirteenth century. The large repertory of trouvère chansons and the many motets with secular French texts contradict any assumption that interest in secular music had to await the stimulus of John's decree. As far as we know, moreover, the composition of liturgical polyphony had been almost totally neglected during the preceding hundred years. In at least a few places, Notre Dame organum continued in use until the fourteenth century, and Latin motets undoubtedly found a place in church services. Even secular French motets were sometimes performed, as the complaints of religious authorities prove. Whatever new music may have enriched or debased the liturgy, that music evidently did not include new polyphonic settings of strictly liturgical texts. At least such settings are almost nonexistent in the musical sources that have come down to us from the period between the School of Notre Dame and the middle of the fourteenth century. It seems scarcely correct, therefore, to say that Pope John's decree caused a decline in the composition of sacred music. We might better stress its ineffectiveness. Within twenty or twenty-five years, as the Ivrea Codex bears witness, liturgical polyphony had not only been reborn but was flourishing in Avignon itself. Another and somewhat later source of music from Avignon is now preserved in the nearby city of Apt. This manuscript and *Iv* have several pieces in common, but *Apt* also includes pieces by composers whose activities extended into the early years of the fifteenth century. A number of smaller collections of liturgical polyphony apparently originated in musical establishments outside of Avignon, yet almost without exception these sources contain at least one piece that is also found in *Iv* or *Apt*. We may safely assume, therefore, that the papal chapel and the rival chapels of noble and wealthy cardinals took the lead in making Avignon the central source of liturgical polyphony. Recent publications of that polyphony make it clear that the music of the fourteenth century was by no means as predominantly secular as had once been thought.[2]

MASS MOVEMENTS

When composers returned to setting liturgical texts after a lapse of a century or more, their music differed in many ways from the older forms and styles of liturgical polyphony. Almost without exception, the School of Notre Dame had limited the composition of organum to the solo sections of responsorial chants for the Offices and the Proper of the Mass. But in the fourteenth century, it is the texts of the Ordinary of the Mass that received exclusive attention. This shift of emphasis must have resulted in part from the greater usefulness of Ordinary texts as compared with Proper texts that would be sung but once during the course of the Church year. However, the shift also reflects—or anticipates—a change in the nature and function of liturgical polyphony itself. Unlike responsorial chants, the texts of the Ordinary were sung by the choir after short solo intonations. We do not know whether the polyphonic settings of these texts were still performed in the old way by a group of soloists, but it seems probable that in some circumstances they may have been sung by a small choir with several singers for each part. In any case, the Mass movements of the fourteenth century foreshadow the conversion of soloistic polyphony that would culminate in the choral Masses of the Renaissance.

Also, in the fourteenth century the word *Mass*, as applied to music, took on the specialized meaning that it still has today. In liturgical usage, of course, the Mass includes everything that is spoken or sung in both the Proper and the Ordinary. As a musical composition, however, a Mass normally consists of the five sung items of the Ordinary—Kyrie, Gloria, Credo, Sanctus, and Agnus Dei. Some of the Machaut manu-

---

2. The most inclusive publication of liturgical polyphony from *Iv*, *Apt*, and other sources is H. Stäblein-Harder, *Fourteenth-Century Mass Music in France*, 2 vols. Two "companion" volumes contain 78 compositions (CMM, 29) and a "Critical Text" (MSD, 7), which is primarily a study of the sources and the music. I wish to thank Dr. Armen Carapetyan for granting permission to take most of the examples in the present chapter from this publication.

scripts already use the word with this restricted meaning when they give his Mass the title *Messe de Nostre Dame*. As the only complete Mass by one composer to have been written in the fourteenth century, the *Messe de Nostre Dame* may best be considered in connection with the other works of Machaut (Chapter XVII). Our primary concern here, however, is with the collections of polyphonic Mass movements, independent and unrelated settings of individual items from the Ordinary. Although such settings can be found almost from the beginning of polyphonic writing, they are scattered and few in number, and most are the shorter items of the Ordinary, particularly the Kyrie. The Ivrea Codex represents a new departure in being a rather large collection of Mass movements in which the Gloria and Credo predominate. Its twenty-five pieces include only four settings of the Kyrie, two of the Sanctus, and none of the Agnus Dei. The remainder is divided almost equally between Gloria and Credo, with nine polyphonic settings of each plus one monophonic Credo. In performing these two texts, it should be recalled, the officiating priest sang the opening phrases "Gloria in excelsis Deo" and "Credo in unum Deum." Composed settings therefore begin with the next phrase of each text—"Et in terra pax" and "Patrem omnipotentem." This practice, which continued throughout the Middle Ages and Renaissance, accounts for the fact that these Mass movements are often listed and referred to as *Et in terra* and *Patrem* rather than as Gloria and Credo.

THREE STYLES OF POLYPHONIC MASS MOVEMENTS

The lapse of Notre Dame organum and the new interest in setting texts of the Ordinary meant that fourteenth-century composers of Mass movements had no continuing tradition of liturgical polyphony to follow. They were equally unhampered by any feeling that sacred polyphony called for a particular and distinctive musical style. It is no surprise, therefore, to find them writing Mass movements in the styles they were accustomed to using for other types of contemporary polyphony. One of these styles derives from the motet; a second adopts the new style of the polyphonic secular song. The origin of the third style is less certain. It is sometimes called "conductus style" because all the voices sing the text more or less together, but its derivation from the long obsolete conductus is unlikely. More probably, this "simultaneous style" represents in written form the contemporary practice of improvised polyphony. The opening measures of three Glorias in the Ivrea Codex (Example XVI–1) will illustrate these three styles and will also serve as a starting point for a more detailed discussion of their identifying characteristics.

Example XVI–1: *Excerpts from Three Glorias in* **Iv**

a. MOTET STYLE (**Iv**, No. 45)

b. SONG STYLE (**Iv**, No. 25)

c. SIMULTANEOUS STYLE (**Iv**, No. 62)

MOTET STYLE

As the only type of polyphonic music widely cultivated in the early years of the fourteenth century, the motet naturally exerted a predominating influence on the composition of Mass movements. This influence is clearly evident in the twenty-five movements in **Iv**, of which no fewer than fifteen are written in motet style. Ten have a duplum and triplum with text above an untexted tenor, while the remaining five add a contratenor, also without text, as a fourth voice. Most of these movements differ from true motets in having the same text in both upper voices, but in some cases, the presence of tropes gives partially or completely different texts to each voice. One unusual example occurs in a

Gloria that has the official text in the triplum while the duplum has a longer Latin poem in praise of Pope Clement VI (1342–52).[3] More often it is the shorter items of the Ordinary that have different tropes added to the original texts, and the upper voices then alternate between singing the same and different words. At times the resemblance to a motet is so strong that pieces have been classified in different ways. This is especially true of motets on *Ite, missa est* and *Benedicamus Domino*. One such piece in Ivrea (No. 34) has a French triplum, a Latin duplum, and a tenor with the text *Ite, missa est*.[4] In this case, neither text refers to the liturgical situation, and neither, therefore, can be regarded as a trope. Both are edifying, however, and their moral injunctions might not be too out of place at the conclusion of a Mass. The same function is much more obviously intended for the Ivrea "motet" *Post missarum sollemnia—Post misse modulamina* (After the ceremonies of the Mass—After the songs of the Mass).[5] Both texts are extended tropes that end with the words "Deo gratias," the response to *Ite, missa est* or *Benedicamus Domino*. In musical structure, the piece is a four-voice isorhythmic motet with an additional solus tenor that permits performance by only three voices. The original tenor has no identifying text, and its plainchant source, if any, remains unknown. There can be no doubt, nevertheless, that the motet belongs with other examples of fourteenth-century liturgical polyphony.

Most Mass movements in motet style are much further removed from the contemporary motet than the two pieces just cited. Plainchant tenors and isorhythmic construction are rare, and both upper voices usually sing the same text, as has already been noted. The lower parts move in longer note values than the upper, but all voices tend to cadence together. Thus, the individual voices in a Mass movement display less rhythmic diversity and independence than in a true motet, and the tenors appear to have been composed to fit particular settings of the texts. As a rule, Mass movements also differ from motets in being sectional rather than continuous forms. The repetitive texts of the Kyrie and Agnus Dei naturally suggest three musical sections, and the Sanctus is usually subdivided into at least two, of which the second begins with the words "Benedictus qui venit." Almost without exception in these movements, the sections end with a cadence on longs in all voices followed by double bars. In most cases, Glorias and Credos are similarly divided, but in a less systematic way. A common treatment of both texts creates three large sections plus the Amen. The divisions do not always occur in the same places, however, and a few movements have more and shorter sections. One curious feature of several Glorias and

3.   *Iv* No. 42; *Mass Music*, No. 22.
4.   Besseler called this piece a motet in his index of *Iv*, AMW, 7 (1925), p. 189. It also appears after the Agnus Dei as the final item in the so-called Mass of Tournai.
5.   *Iv* No. 11; *Mass Music*, No. 73.

Credos is their use of one- and two-measure textless interludes as a sort of musical punctuation within the larger sections of the movement. These interludes usually involve only two voices in varying combinations that, in three-voice movements, must include one upper voice and may include both duplum and triplum. They are sometimes assumed to be instrumental, but it is also possible that the upper voice or voices sang them as short melismatic interjections. Much longer melismas close the large sections of several movements, particularly Credos, and the Amen of both Gloria and Credo normally receives an extended melismatic setting. An almost excessive use of hocket in many of these melismas proves how quickly Pope John's censure of the device had been forgotten (Example XVI–2).

Example XVI–2: *Closing Melisma of Second Section in Credo,* **Iv,** *No. 57*[6]

6.   *Mass Music,* No. 42.

SONG STYLE

The creation of a distinctive polyphonic style appropriate for secular song was largely the achievement of Guillaume de Machaut in the first half of the fourteenth century. As will be seen in the following chapter, Machaut's ballades, rondeaux, and virelais illustrate the formative stages of this style as well as its fulfillment in the three-voice disposition that remained standard for a century or more after his death in 1377. In essence, the new style consists of a solo song (*cantus*) above a supporting tenor part without words. This two-part framework can and sometimes does stand alone, but more often another part without text, a contra-tenor, gives added strength and harmonic richness to the accompaniment of the solo song. The newness of this song style undoubtedly accounts for its appearance in only six of the Ivrea Mass movements.[7] In sources from the latter part of the fourteenth century, it replaces motet style as the favorite type of liturgical polyphony.

Of the six pieces in **Iv** in secular song style, two are Kyries for which only the music for the first section has been preserved complete. Both are simple two-part pieces for cantus and tenor. The other four, two Glorias and two Credos, have the standard distribution of three voices. One Gloria is a continuous setting of the text except for separate sections at the close on "Cum sancto spiritu . . ." and "Amen," and one Credo is continuous up to the separate Amen. In both pieces, the two lower parts punctuate the text with the one- and two-measure interludes we have already noted in movements in motet style. Such interludes, indeed, are common in motet and simultaneous styles but rare in song style. They are not found in the other Gloria and Credo, which are subdivided into many short sections. These sections, like the longer ones in motet style, end with strong cadences on longs and are set off from each other by double bars. It is difficult to account for the fact that multiple subdivisions of Glorias and Credos became typical of movements in song style. Perhaps the style was used for antiphonal performance by a divided choir or by two small groups of singers. Plainchant Glorias were normally sung in this way, and the practice was sometimes adopted for the Credo as well. It would have been natural, therefore, to introduce antiphonal singing in polyphonic Mass movements when the style permitted. Choirs of the time were small and might well have had difficulty in providing two groups to alternate in singing the two voice parts of motet style or the three or four parts of simultaneous style. The single vocal melody of song style would present no such difficulty. We cannot be sure, of course, how Mass movements in any style were performed in the fourteenth century, and practices must have varied ac-

---

7. *Mass Music,* Nos. 6, 8, 27, 28, 47, and 50. Stäblein-Harder uses the designation "discant style" for these pieces, but it seems preferable to speak of song (chanson or cantilena) style to avoid confusion with the quite different style of English discant (see Chapter XX).

cording to the musical resources available at any given time or place. It seems certain, nevertheless, that movements in song style did not long remain—if, indeed, they ever were—music for a solo singer. By the middle of the century the solo song in secular polyphony had already developed an elaborate and highly melismatic style that was soon to be joined with tremendous rhythmic complexity. In liturgical polyphony, on the other hand, song style retained a characteristic simplicity of rhythm and a nearly syllabic text setting except for the Amens. Few, if any, movements in the style could not be performed with ease by choirs of very modest ability. Documented evidence of choral performance comes early in the fifteenth century, along with obvious proof of a new kind of antiphonal or responsorial performance (see Chapter XIX).

SIMULTANEOUS STYLE

The designation *simultaneous style* has two important implications: that all the parts are vocal, and that, with minor exceptions, all voices sing the words of the text together. From the latter characteristic, it follows that the rhythmic structure of all voices will be similar if not identical. This lack of rhythmic differentiation between the upper and lower voices is the primary *musical* characteristic that distinguishes simultaneous from motet and song styles. In movements with lengthy texts, Glorias and Credos, the voices often move together in note-against-note counterpoint to produce a chord on each syllable. At times, however, one or more voices may add rhythmic variety with ornamental figures that break up longer note values. All voices, moreover, sometimes have short melismas, usually on either the first or the penultimate syllable of a phrase. A few movements are less various and adhere more consistently either to syllabic or to slightly ornamented settings of the text.[8] As in motet style, Glorias and Credos in simultaneous style may be continuous movements, but more often they are divided into several large sections plus a melismatic Amen. In both styles, as we have already noted, short textless interludes commonly create subdivisions within the large sections of the movements.

MELISMATIC MOVEMENTS AND HYBRID STYLES

The method of performance—whether one, two, or all voices sing the text—may seem to be the primary basis for distinguishing the three styles of liturgical polyphony. It must be remembered, however, that different dispositions of the text produce different rhythmic and pitch relationships among the voices and thereby give each style a distinctive

8.   Compare, for example, the two Credos, Nos. 53 and 54 in *Mass Music*.

musical structure. In Glorias and Credos, which always tend to be syllabic, a high degree of correspondence between musical structure and method of performance makes determination of the style relatively simple. Melismatic movements, such as the Kyrie and Sanctus, are often more difficult to classify. Careless or incomplete underlay of the text may leave doubt as to whether a part is intended to be vocal or instrumental. The structure of the musical fabric may also be ambiguous or may fluctuate between different styles. In some movements, finally, the disposition of text and the musical structure simply do not correspond. One of the most obvious examples occurs in a Sanctus found in **Iv** (No. 58).[9] All voices sing the text, but the musical structure resembles a three-voice motet with lively upper parts above a tenor moving in longer note values (Example XVI–3). This piece is typical of most movements for which the stylistic classification may be subject to differences of opinion. It is usually the lower part or parts that differ from the expected style and about which questions arise as to vocal or instrumental performance. The existence of these ambiguities suggests that, regardless of its musical structure, a Mass movement might be performed by various combinations of voices and instruments or by voices alone. That performance practices did vary in this way is proved by the appearance of a few movements in different manuscripts with different dispositions of text. One of the best known examples is a Credo that appears in three sources, including **Apt** and the Mass of Tournai, as a three-voice movement in simultaneous style. A fourth manuscript preserves the same music with text only in the top voice.[10] Although the version in song style is apparently the oldest of the four that have been preserved, it does not necessarily represent the original form of the composition. In cases such as this, it is often impossible to establish the priority of one version over the other. As a rule, however, the characteristics of the musical structure, rather than the disposition of text, provide a better guide to the composer's original intent.

Example XVI–3: *Sanctus in Motet Style with Text in All Voices* (**Iv**, *No. 58*)

9.   Ibid., No. 64.
10. All four versions are published in C. van den Borren, *Missa Tornacensis,* CMM, 13 (AIM, 1957), pp. 9–28.

MASS CYCLES

Most fourteenth-century Mass movements are independent pieces and show no evidence of being composed to provide a complete polyphonic setting of the Ordinary. The Ivrea and Apt Codices, both large collections that preserve the repertory of musical circles in Avignon, are somewhat haphazard in their arrangement, but they tend to group together settings of the same text (Glorias, Credos, etc.). Neither manuscript presents five movements as a unit that forms a complete Mass; indeed, one cannot be formed from Ivrea, which lacks any setting of the Agnus Dei. We have already noted that the *Messe de Nostre Dame* by Guillaume de Machaut is the only fourteenth-century example of a complete Mass by one composer. However, the existence of four other Masses from this period suggests that polyphonic performance of the entire Ordinary was gradually becoming an accepted practice. These four Masses are known by the present location of their manuscript sources in Tournai, Toulouse, Barcelona, and the Sorbonne. The last-named was once called the Mass of Besançon from its presumed place of origin.[11] Later writers have disputed that origin and have generally adopted the designation Mass of the Sorbonne to be consistent with the naming of the other three Masses. The present location of a manuscript, be it remembered, does not necessarily indicate its place of origin, which—in turn—is not necessarily the source of its contents. Whatever the origin of the four Masses may have been, they all prove to be related in some way to the repertory of Avignon preserved in the Ivrea and Apt manuscripts. Nevertheless, they all differ from one another in a number of ways. Short descriptions of each Mass will therefore complete the picture of liturgical polyphony in the fourteenth century.

THE MASS OF TOURNAI

A manuscript in the library of the cathedral of Tournai preserves what is thought to be the oldest of the polyphonic Masses. It consists of the five movements of the Ordinary followed by a motet on *Ite, missa est*. A later hand has added a Sanctus and a Kyrie, neither of which has any connection with the original Mass. The Kyrie is for three voices in simultaneous style, but the Sanctus is monophonic except for a three-voice setting of the words "in excelsis" at the close of each *Osanna*.[12] The rest of the Tournai manuscript consists of five sections devoted to portions of the plainchant repertory. These sections appear to be fragmentary and are unrelated to each other or to the polyphonic Mass.

11. J. Chailley, "La messe de Besançon et un compositeur inconnu du XIVe siècle: Jean Lambelet," AnM, 2 (1954), pp. 93–103.
12. The two movements are Nos. 17 and 62 in *Mass Music*. The complete Mass is also published in Schrade, PM, 1, and the Van den Borren edition cited above in fn. 10.

The nature of this odd collection of music makes it clear that the Mass of Tournai was copied as a unit to provide a completely polyphonic performance of the Ordinary. It is equally clear, however, that the Mass was not composed as a unit. The Kyrie, Sanctus, and Agnus Dei use Franconian notation of longs and breves in note-against-note counterpoint with modal rhythms that suggest a possible origin in the latter part of the thirteenth century (Example XVI–4). Freer rhythms and the notational innovations of the Ars Nova characterize the other three movements, particularly the Gloria (Example XVI–5). This movement applies the principles of Philippe de Vitry in ways that would have been impossible before the second quarter of the fourteenth century. Even for this period the Gloria seems unusually advanced in its occasional use of parallel triads in first inversion to approach a cadence (Example XVI–5b). Only at a somewhat later time do such progressions become frequent, and they are still likely to be regarded as a distinctive trait when they appear in fifteenth-century music. To judge from their divergent styles, then, the movements of the Tournai Mass may have been composed over a time span of nearly fifty years. Further evidence that the Mass was not composed as a unit comes from the presence of two of its movements in other manuscripts. The Credo must have been widely known, for—as noted above—it is found in three other sources, including the Avignon repertory preserved in **Apt**. Similarly, the related repertory of the Ivrea Codex includes the motet on *Ite, missa est*. All of this evidence marks the Mass of Tournai as a compilation of independent movements that were brought together to permit polyphonic performance of the complete Ordinary. By his choice of movements, however, the compiler of the Mass did achieve a degree of artistic and stylistic unity. All of the movements are for three voices, and all but the final motet are in simultaneous style. This unity remains superficial, nevertheless, and scarcely blunts the sharp contrasts of musical style that are illustrated by the Kyrie and Gloria excerpts in Examples XVI–4 and 5. The Mass as a whole thus provides another demonstration that the same method of performance may be used with widely differing musical structures.

Example XVI–4: *Mass of Tournai, Kyrie I*

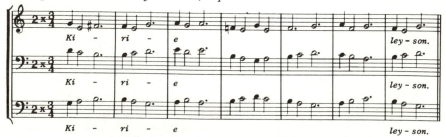

Example XVI–5: *Mass of Tournai, Gloria*

a. MEASURES 1–7

b. MEASURES 43–45

THE MASS OF TOULOUSE

The Mass of Toulouse has been preserved in a strange way that leaves some doubt as to whether it was intended to be a complete polyphonic setting of the Ordinary. The municipal library of Toulouse now owns a large manuscript devoted entirely to the texts and plainchants of the Mass. This missal dates from the first half of the fourteenth century, but much later—probably around 1400—someone entered the polyphonic movements that constitute the Mass of Toulouse. These movements were copied in empty spaces throughout the manuscript, and only the Sanctus and Agnus Dei appear together. After the latter movement, the scribe noted where the "motetus super *Ite missa est*" could be found and thus suggested that he was copying a complete Mass. There is no trace of a Gloria, however, and all that exists of a Credo is the tenor part from *Crucifixus* to the end. This fragment is sufficient to establish its identity with a widely known Credo that appears in both *Iv* and *Apt* as an independent movement and that also forms part of the Barcelona Mass. The only other movement of the Toulouse Mass that might establish a connection with the repertory of Avignon is the Agnus Dei, which also appears in a fragmentary manuscript now in the archives of the cathedral of Gerona in northeastern Spain. Of the three other Mass movements in this fragment, a Kyrie and a Kyrie trope are also found in *Iv* and *Apt* respectively. As it stands, then, the Mass of Toulouse consists of four movements—Kyrie, Sanctus, Agnus Dei, and a motet on *Ite, missa est*—plus a Credo that can be completed from other sources.[13] Why the scribe failed to complete the Credo himself or to provide a Gloria remains unknown. Perhaps the Mass, like some in plainchant, never included these two movements.

Despite differences in age and style, the Tournai and Toulouse Masses resemble each other in two important ways. Both are compilations of musically independent movements, and each is unified to some extent by having the same disposition of voices in all movements. The Toulouse Mass, however, is in song rather than simultaneous style. This is true of the incomplete Credo and even of the misnamed "motet" on *Ite, missa est,* which has only one voice with text above textless tenor and contratenor parts. The designation probably reflects the tradition of such motets and the fact that the one text—*Laudemus Jesum Christum* (Let us praise Jesus Christ)—ends with the word "gratias" and may be regarded as a trope. One wonders whether the scribe or compiler of the Mass simply ignored the musical structure or whether he omitted the triplum of a four-voice motet to bring the piece into stylistic agreement with the other movements. The Sanctus of the Mass also suggests the possibility of such an adaptation. Its contratenor lies in the same range as the cantus, and both voices use the same rhythmic and melodic figures above a tenor in longer note values (Example XVI–6). Only the absence of text in the contratenor prevents classification of this movement as three-voice motet style.[14] In the other movements, the contratenor lies in a lower range than the cantus and is somewhat less active rhythmically, although the two parts often engage in hocket patterns. Whatever the original form of the Sanctus may have been, it again illustrates the difficulty of classifying highly melismatic styles. In the Agnus Dei,

13. In PM, 1, Schrade published only the four complete movements in the Mass of Toulouse, but the Credo is included in the Mass of Barcelona. Harder included a transcription of the Credo from *Iv* in "Die Messe von Toulouse," MD, 7 (1953), p. 119 ff. In *Mass Music* (No. 47), the transcription is from *Apt*. The other movements of the Toulouse Mass in this publication are Nos. 5, 58, 67, and 74.

14. In *Mass Music,* the movement (No. 58) appears with other Sanctus settings in motet style.

with the trope *Rex immense pietatis* (King of infinite mercy), a syllabic setting of the text in short note values clearly differentiates the cantus from the lower parts. Here, song style is unmistakable, as it is in the final "motet" and the Credo.

Example XVI–6: *Mass of Toulouse, Sanctus, measures 1–6*

THE MASS OF BARCELONA

The Mass of Barcelona differs from the Masses of Tournai and Toulouse in several important ways. In the first place, the source in which it is found has no connection with plainchant. Instead, the five movements of the Barcelona Mass—it has no motet on *Ite, missa est*—appear in succession at the beginning of a small manuscript that is completed by two Latin motets and two other Mass movements, an anonymous troped Kyrie and a Gloria by Peliso. The quality of the handwriting and decoration in the twelve folios that contain these pieces makes it probable that the manuscript is only the first section of what must have been a large and important collection of late fourteenth-century polyphony. What has been preserved, however, is enough to show that the repertory is more closely related to Avignon than either the Tournai or Toulouse Mass.[15]

The compilers of the Tournai and Toulouse Masses, it will be remembered, achieved a measure of unity by choosing movements that already had, or could be reduced to, a common disposition of voices: three-part simultaneous style in Tournai, three-part song style in Toulouse. In the Barcelona Mass, a quite different principle seems to have determined the choice of movements. Instead of being in the same basic style, each of the five parts of the Mass presents a different arrangement of vocal and instrumental parts.[16] The Kyrie is a short setting in simultaneous style, with an obvious correspondence between musical structure and the prescribed manner of performance. For the most part, the three

15. See *Mass Music,* Critical Text, p. 98.
16. The Mass is published as a unit in Schrade, PM, 1, pp. 139–64. In *Mass Music,* it is Nos. 19, 25, 47, 56, and 72.

voices move together in rhythms that are similar when not identical. A somewhat more independent contratenor in the *Christe* adds variety to the texture, as does the imitative use of a three-note figure in Kyrie II.

Example XVI–7: *Mass of Barcelona, Kyrie II*

In the Apt manuscript, the Gloria and Credo are both in song style, and each has tenor and contratenor parts that are rhythmically similar and lie in the same range beneath the cantus. As it appears in the Barcelona Mass, however, the Gloria has a different contratenor, which lies in the same range and uses some of the same rhythms as the cantus.[17] The musical structure thus resembles a three-voice motet or a secular song with a textless triplum instead of a contratenor (see Chapter XVII). Whether or not this modification resulted from a deliberate effort to enhance the stylistic contrasts of the Barcelona Mass, it does distinguish the Gloria from the more usual song style that is retained in the Credo. In quite different ways, the Sanctus and Agnus Dei form a second pair of movements that are stylistically related, yet clearly distinguished from one another. With its two paraphrase-tropes, the Sanctus appears at first glance to be a normal motet in which all three voices are quite strictly isorhythmic throughout six statements of a nineteen-measure talea. A closer look at the structure reveals that what seems to be the motetus is actually the tenor part. It is the lowest of the three voices, and with the cantus it forms a two-voice framework for the composition. The textless third part completes that framework when the tenor or cantus

17. *Mass Music*, No. 25, gives both contratenors plus a third from still another version of the Gloria in a different Barcelona fragment.

rests, but at other times it functions as a contratenor and justifies its being so named in the manuscript. In form, then, the Sanctus is an isorhythmic motet, but the distribution of vocal and instrumental parts is one that first appears in Italian secular songs of the later fourteenth century (see Chapter XVIII). A similar distribution occurs in the Agnus Dei, where the tenor and cantus are again the two voices that have the text. Now, however, there are two textless contratenors, a higher that lies in the range of the cantus and a lower in the range of the tenor.[18] The resulting texture differs from a normal four-voice motet not only in having a vocal tenor and cantus, but also in the rhythmic similarity of all four parts. Every part, moreover, is essential to the musical structure, and none could be omitted without damage to the harmonic and rhythmic organization. The increased sonority of four-part polyphony in the Agnus Dei does more than provide a fitting climax for the Barcelona Mass. By its style and structure, that polyphony foreshadows fifteenth-century developments, including the emergence of an international musical style that will be discussed in the final chapters of this book. The entire Mass, indeed, might have been designed as a survey of musical styles from simultaneous, through secular song, to the newest hybrid styles of the closing fourteenth century. It is this aspect of the Barcelona Mass that makes it both the most unusual and most interesting of the early Mass compilations.

MUSICALLY RELATED MASS MOVEMENTS AND THE SORBONNE MASS

Most fourteenth-century Mass movements appear to have been composed as independent pieces with no thought of establishing musical relationships among the various parts of the Ordinary. Indeed, the stylistic contrasts in the movements brought together to form the Barcelona Mass stand in direct opposition to the concept of a musically unified Mass cycle. Even the superficial unity of the Tournai and Toulouse Mass compilations probably reflects no higher artistic consideration than a desire—or need—to maintain one method of performance throughout the service.

In the Sorbonne Mass, however, the Agnus Dei quotes sections from both the Kyrie and the Sanctus and thus gives evidence of an attempt to create some measure of unity in the Mass as a whole. This is by no means the only peculiarity of the Sorbonne Mass. On the basis of a "signature in the middle of the Kyrie," the entire Mass has been attributed to one Johannes Lambuleti.[19] Whether Lambuleti was responsible for

18. *Mass Music,* No. 72, adds text to the higher contratenor part.
19. The Mass was first described, with a complete facsimile and partial transcriptions, by J. Chailley in the article cited in fn. 11 above. All movements are published in *Mass Music,* Nos. 3, 36, 63, 70, and 75.

the composition or compilation of all the movements, or even of the Kyrie, remains somewhat doubtful. If the Mass is indeed his work, Lambuleti, following Machaut, would become the second fourteenth-century composer to write what was probably a complete polyphonic setting of the Mass Ordinary.

As it now stands, the Sorbonne Mass lacks a Credo but ends with a fifth movement in the form of a two-voice *Benedicamus Domino*. With possibly this one exception, every movement is incomplete to some extent, but enough has been preserved to establish that they all draw some part of their musical material from other sources, primarily the older Avignon repertory of the Ivrea Codex. Such borrowings from preexistent polyphony are not without precedent, and in a few other instances the same or similar material appears in different Mass movements. We may use the Sorbonne Mass, however, to illustrate some of the ways in which composers used borrowed material to create related but different Mass movements.

For the Sorbonne Kyrie in motet style, Lambuleti took the tenor of a two-voice Kyrie in *Iv*[20] and added two upper voices, neither of which resembles the cantus of his source. Both Kyries are tropes, but with different texts and a curious discrepancy of position. The Ivrea Kyrie is sung to the first three stanzas of the trope *Sol justicie* and is therefore Kyrie I. (The Christe and Kyries II and III are either missing or illegible in the three versions copied in *Iv*.)[21] The text of the Sorbonne Kyrie, on the other hand, is the ninth stanza of a widely known trope, *Kyrie Rex genitor*. It seems probable, therefore, that the Sorbonne Mass originally began with a much more extended Kyrie in four sections—Kyrie I, Christe, Kyrie II, and Kyrie III—of which only the last survives.

The Gloria in simultaneous style is also for three voices and is incomplete at the end rather than at the beginning. All of the upper voice has been preserved (132 measures), but the tenor is missing after measure 29 and the middle voice after measure 55. This movement opens with an almost exact quotation of the first two measures of a Credo in *Iv* (Example XVI–8). Thereafter, the two movements go their separate ways, and the claim that one is a "parody" of the other rests on a few and scattered similarities that might be found in any two movements written in the same mensuration and mode.[22]

The correspondence between the opening measures of the Sorbonne Gloria and the Ivrea Credo must have been deliberate, but it is the only link between the two movements that can be established with any certainty. That link makes it probable, nevertheless, that the Sorbonne Mass once included the Ivrea Credo.

Despite the fragmentary state of the Sorbonne Sanctus, it clearly

20. *Mass Music,* No. 6.
21. See *Mass Music,* Critical Text, p. 26.
22. Ibid., pp. 48, 54, and 90, with n. 176.

Example XVI–8: *Opening Measures of Sorbonne Gloria and Ivrea Credo*

SORBONNE GLORIA

Ex   in   ter - ra   pax   ho-mi-ni - bus

IVREA CREDO No. 48 (*Mass Music*, No. 43)

Pa - trem   om - ni-po -ten-tem,   fac-tor-em ce - li et   ter-re,

Pa - trem   om - ni - po-ten-tem,   fac-tor-em ce - li et   ter-re,

TENOR

derives from an Ivrea Sanctus, which, in turn, is a reworking of an Agnus Dei in a manuscript now in the municipal library of Cambrai.[23] The relationships of the three movements are again complex, but the order of their composition is unmistakable. In the Sorbonne Sanctus, literal quotations from the Ivrea Sanctus include parts of an introduction that this intermediate movement added to the Cambrai Agnus Dei. Interspersed among these quotations we find other, more or less varied excerpts from the Ivrea Sanctus and a few passages that appear to be entirely new.

Only two voices of the Sorbonne Agnus Dei have been preserved, but in Agnus I they fit perfectly with the single voice of the Sanctus, measures 1–12.[24] Confirming this restoration is the resulting literal quotation of the first four measures of the Ivrea Sanctus. Thus we can be sure that both the Sanctus and Agnus Dei of the Sorbonne Mass were originally three-voice compositions and that the surviving parts of the latter movement are the upper voice and the tenor. The second Agnus is unrelated to any surviving part of the Sorbonne Mass, but the outer voices of the Kyrie return with only slight changes in Agnus III. It seems probable, therefore, that Agnus II also quoted preexistent material, perhaps from an earlier portion of the Kyrie.

23. See *Mass Music*, No. 66 for the Ivrea Sanctus, and No. 71 for the Agnus Dei.
24. The three voices are reassembled in ibid., No. 63.

Following the Agnus Dei, a two-voice setting of *Benedicamus Domino* seems to conclude the Sorbonne Mass. Whether it was meant to fulfill this function is somewhat doubtful. The text normally replaced *Ite, missa est* only when the Gloria was not sung, and the setting is stylistically incongruous with the rest of the Mass. The upper voice is the well-known plainchant *Benedicamus II* (LU, p. 124) transposed up a fourth. With this melody, the added voice moves almost entirely in contrary motion and in strict note-against-note counterpoint with only two note values, longs and breves. More than two-thirds of the intervals are perfect consonances—unisons, fifths, and octaves—and the rest are either thirds or sixths. In effect, therefore, the *Benedicamus Domino* differs scarcely at all from free organum as described and illustrated by John of Afflighem some three centuries earlier. It suggests, indeed, that counterpoint of this sort—probably improvised more often than written down—continued to be used when more elaborate compositions were not available.

The Sorbonne Mass has been hailed both as an early example of parody technique and as a forerunner of the unified cyclic Mass. Neither claim can be accepted without qualification. The sixteenth-century parody Mass drew on a preexistent polyphonic composition—motet, chanson, or madrigal—for the musical material that unified its five movements. Composers displayed their ingenuity and craftsmanship by the ways in which they adapted and expanded this basic material to meet the formal requirements of the different liturgical texts. The fourteenth-century use of borrowed material seems to have had other goals. In its simplest form it is but another instance of the common medieval practice of providing old music with new words. The first and third Agnus of the Sorbonne Mass, in fact, are no more than contrafacta. More elaborate reworking of borrowed material in the Sorbonne Sanctus does resemble the later parody techniques to some extent. What was common practice in the sixteenth century, however, was extremely rare in the fourteenth, and there is no evidence of continuous development or indeed of any historical connection between the two.

A consideration of musical unity in the Sorbonne Mass imposes much the same conclusions. Four of the five movements—if we include the *Benedicamus Domino*—draw to some extent from outside sources wholly unrelated to each other. Thus, although the Sorbonne Mass consists of arrangements rather than ready-made movements, it too is essentially a compilation and not a composed musical entity. Only the Agnus Dei introduces a measure of unity by its quotations from the Sanctus and the Kyrie. This process does not mean that the Kyrie and Sanctus are themselves related. Indeed, the Agnus Dei emphasizes diversity rather than unity in a way that almost seems intentional. Its three sections are in different modes, or at least end on different notes—**G**, **D**, and **C**—and Agnus II contrasts with the outer sections by being in triple rather than duple mensuration. Even more than the Mass as a whole, therefore, the Agnus is a pastiche of unrelated material, and its unifying effect is largely offset by its own lack of artistic unity. We cannot know, unfortunately, whether the complete Mass revealed more interrelationships than the existing fragments indicate. It seems unlikely, nevertheless, that Lambuleti—if he was indeed the sole arranger and compiler—was greatly concerned about the musical unity of his Mass. As we shall see in the next chapter, neither tonal nor melodic nor even stylistic unity is to be found in the one fourteenth-century Mass known to be wholly original and the work of a single composer, Guillaume de Machaut. It remained for composers of the following century to develop the concepts and techniques that would make the musically unified Mass cycle the crowning achievement of Renaissance choral polyphony.

CHAPTER XVII

Guillaume de Machaut

Important as Philippe de Vitry was in establishing both the mensural principles of the Ars Nova and the structural principles of the isorhythmic motet, he still stands in the shadow of his somewhat younger and considerably more prolific contemporary Guillaume de Machaut. In large part, the relative positions of the two men must be the result of their personal interests and preferences. To some degree, however, those positions reflect the superficially similar, but in reality profoundly different, circumstances of their lives. It will be useful, therefore, to review those circumstances before we examine the music of the greatest French poet and composer in the fourteenth century.

Both men came from the province of Champagne, where Philippe was born—presumably in one of six villages named Vitry—on October 31, 1291, according to his own account. The date of Machaut's birth is generally believed to have been around 1300.[1] Almost nothing is known about the childhood and early youth of either man. Documented evidence of Vitry's life begins with his appointment as a canon of the Church in 1323 and his service to the French kings from the time of Charles IV (1322–28) until 1351. As a responsible and trusted official of the royal household, Vitry twice went on diplomatic missions to the papal court in Avignon, where he became a friend of Petrarch. Two letters from the Italian poet to Philippe praise him as a musician, poet, and man of inquiring spirit. In 1351, probably in recognition of his services both to the French kings and to the papacy, as well as for his other merits, Philippe was appointed Bishop of Meaux by Clement VI (the subject of Philippe's motet *Petre clemens—Lugentium;* see p. 366). This high position Philippe held until his death on June 9, 1361.

How much of Philippe de Vitry's poetry and music has been lost we do not know, nor can we be sure to what extent his contemporary reputation rested on his position and personal qualities. Certainly the motets attributable to him do not belie that reputation, but it is strange indeed

---

1.   A. Machabey, in his two-volume study *Guillaume de Machault* (Paris, 1955), adopted the modern spelling of the town in Champagne for Guillaume's surname. This attempt to replace the spelling long accepted by historians of both literature and music has not been generally successful.

that more did not survive from the creative output of a man so important and so esteemed. It is also strange that more than half of the motets as well as the theoretical treatise must have been completed by the time Philippe was about thirty years of age.[2] That poetry and music did not occupy a primary place in Philippe's concerns during the last forty years of his life seems an inescapable conclusion.

With Guillaume de Machaut the situation is quite different. He too appears in historical documents in the service of a king—John, Count of Luxembourg and King of Bohemia—and ends his life in the Church, but in the less exalted position of canon at Reims Cathedral. Apart from these similarities, the activities and interests of the two men seem scarcely to correspond at all. Throughout his life, Machaut remained a practising musician, a composer, and a prolific poet who supervised the preparation of several manuscript collections of his works.

Documentary evidence of Machaut's existence dates from a series of papal bulls of 1330 that identify him as a "clerk, secretary, and familiar" (i.e., in the household) of John of Bohemia. At the request of King John, these bulls granted Machaut various church benefices and canonicates with the expectation of a prebend when a vacancy occurred. By this common medieval practice, popes sought to gain the loyalty and support of powerful noblemen who, in turn, found it a convenient means of providing supplemental income and future social security for their protégés. In one of the most important bulls, Pope Benedict XII made Machaut a canon of Reims—still in expectation—and allowed him to retain a canonicate at St. Quentin and a chaplaincy in the diocese of Arras. This bull also states that Machaut had been in John of Bohemia's household for about twelve years and thus establishes 1323 as the approximate date of Machaut's entry into the king's service. That service continued for some time after the vacancy of a prebend led to Machaut's installation by procuration (*in absentia*) as a canon of Reims late in January, 1337. Being in the service of the king, Machaut was not required to live in Reims, but he seems to have established a residence in that city by 1340. From then until John's death in 1346, Machaut probably remained on call and may sometimes have rejoined the king for short intervals.

The duties and restrictions imposed on the seventy-two canons of Reims were far from onerous, although around 1350 they were forbidden to wear long hair. Their primary function was to sing in the Offices, and each canon was also expected to sing for a minimum number of Masses during the course of a year. For fulfilling these duties they received a regular stipend plus a fee for each service in which they took part. In addition, their prebends provided daily or periodic dis-

---

2.   Five of the fourteen motets Schrade attributes to Vitry appear in the *Roman de Fauvel* (1316). Three more (Nos. 6, 9, and 10) are mentioned in the *Ars Nova* treatise (c. 1320).

tributions of bread, wine, vegetables, and wood. The canons did not have to be ordained priests, and Machaut seems never to have been more than a tonsured clerk. Moreover, he did not live in the cloister but had his own house, where he was later joined by his brother Jean de Machaut, who also became a canon at Reims after serving with John of Bohemia. In theory, canons were to be in residence at all times, but Machaut's position as secretary to John of Bohemia permitted him to be absent at the king's pleasure and perhaps also at his own. After the king's death, connections with other members of the highest nobility still gave Machaut freedom to travel, a freedom of which he did not fail to take advantage.

The exact nature of Machaut's relationships with his later patrons remains somewhat conjectural. Most of our information comes from Machaut's poems rather than from official records and often fails to describe the way in which he "served" these patrons. Nevertheless, we know that Machaut was first associated with Bonne of Luxembourg, John of Bohemia's daughter, who married the son of Philippe VI, King of France. After Bonne's death in 1349, Machaut found a new Maecenas in the person of Charles, King of Navarre and pretender to the French throne, who came to be known in history as Charles the Bad. Machaut was apparently not involved in Charles's intrigues and conspiracies with the English against the French royal house. Instead, the poet remained

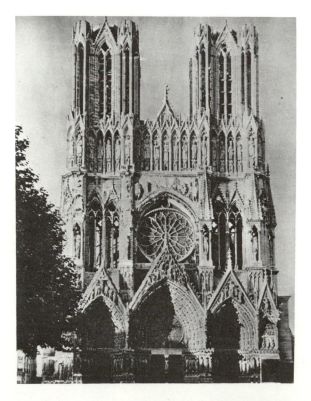

The Cathedral at Reims where Machaut spent many years as a canon.

Machaut is depicted writing at his desk (from a fifteenth-century manuscript in the Morgan Library).

on good terms with both parties and later served King Charles V of France (1364–80) as well as his brother John, Duke of Berry.

In addition to revealing much about Machaut's associations with his royal patrons, his poetry gives many details about himself and the life he led in Reims. We learn, for example, of his infirmities—gout and blindness in one eye; of his personal experiences in more universal afflictions such as the great plague, the Black Death that ravaged Europe in 1348–49; and of the hardships that resulted from the English invasions and siege of Reims in the early part of the Hundred Years' War (1337–1453). In a happier vein, Machaut's poetry reveals his enthusiasm for falconry, his delight in horseback riding, and his pleasure in the beauties of the French countryside. Somewhat surprisingly, Machaut tells next to nothing about his activities in connection with the Church. We can only conclude that those activities occupied but little of either his time or his thoughts. Instead, as the most celebrated poet and composer in France, Machaut led a rather worldly life. Almost without interruption throughout his career, he enjoyed the confidence and patronage of kings and shared their pleasures.

THE COMPLETE WORKS

One of the most complete and reliable of the Machaut manuscripts begins with an inscription that reads in translation "Here is the order that G. de Machaut wishes to have in his book." A listing of Machaut's works as they appear in this manuscript will therefore reveal both the scope of his creative activity as he wished it to be presented and the place of music in his total output (Table 14).[3] Of all Machaut's pieces that have been preserved, only five are missing in this manuscript. Presumably, they are his last musical compositions. With some exceptions, the other Machaut manuscripts arrange his works in much the same order and for this reason are thought to have been prepared under his direct or indirect supervision.

3.　The numbering of musical works in Table 14 and throughout this chapter is that of Schrade in PM, 2 and 3. Ludwig's numbering of the lais and virelais differs because he included the poems without music. Rondeau 16 has no music in any source (see fn. 33 below).

Table 14: *Machaut's Works in the Order They Appear in Paris, Bibl. Nat., f. fr. 1584*

Poetry
1. *Prologue* (1371?) on 4 of 6 unnumbered leaves added at beginning
2. *Le Dit du Vergier*   fol. 1
3. *Le Jugement du Roi de Behaigne* (before 1346)   fol. 9v
4. *Le Jugement du Roi de Navarre* (1349)   fol. 22v
5. *Remède de Fortune* (1342–49?)   fol. 49v
6. *Dit du Lyon* (1342)   fol. 80v
7. *Dit de l'Alerion* (before 1349)   fol. 96v
8. *Confort d'Ami* (1357)   fol. 127
9. *Dit de la Fonteinne Amoureuse* (c. 1361)   fol. 154
10. *Dit de la Harpe*   fol. 174
11. *La Louange des Dames* (268 lyric poems)   fol. 177v
12. *Dit de la Marguerite*   fol. 213v
13. *Les Complaintes* (8 texts)   fol. 214v
14. *Livre du Voir Dit* (c. 1365)   fol. 221
15. *La Prise d'Alexandrie* (not before 1369)   fol. 309
16. *Dit de la Rose*   fol. 365v
17. *Les biens que ma dame me fait*   fol. 366

Musical compositions
18. Lais (22—6 without music; Nos. 17 and 18 missing)   fol. 367
19. Motets (23)   fol. 414v
20. The Mass   fol. 438v
21. *Hocket David*   fol. 451v
22. Ballades (38; Nos. 39 and 40 missing)   fol. 454
23. Rondeaux (19; Nos. 16 and 21 missing)   fol. 475
24. Virelais (38—6 without music)   fol. 482–94v

In compiling his collected works, Machaut appears to have arranged his longer poems in approximately chronological order except for the *Prologue,* the final version of which, fittingly enough, was written last. He then completed the collection with his musical works grouped according to formal types. It is generally assumed that within each type the pieces again appear in more or less chronological order, and comparative studies of the different manuscripts confirm this view to some extent. At any rate, the more complete Machaut manuscripts generally repeat the series of pieces in the different groups before adding new and presumably later compositions to each group. Further information as to the chronology of Machaut's music is extrapolated from stylistic considerations and the relationships between musical compositions and

Fortune and her wheels, a persistent medieval theme (from a fifteenth-century manuscript in the Morgan Library).

datable poems. Yet even when all these factors are taken into account, the results are somewhat disappointing.[4] Only a relatively small number of pieces can be dated with any precision. For the rest, any assigned dates remain conjectural and must allow for a wide margin of error. It is not very helpful, for example, to suspect that the first sixteen ballades were written before 1349, when Machaut was nearly fifty. Linking stylistic development with precisely dated works adds something to our knowledge of chronology, but the results must always be accepted with great caution. New stylistic features in a dated composition do not necessarily mean that they were first used in that piece or that all subsequent pieces abandon older procedures. Because of differing styles in the different musical types, moreover, determining dates and chronology for one type yields little or no information about the others. Interesting and important as they are, questions of chronology can therefore be dealt with only incidentally in discussing the different types of Machaut's musical compositions. Before doing so, however, we must mention several of the poetic works that in one way or another are particularly related to music.

Written about 1371, the *Prologue* in its complete form was apparently Machaut's last important poem. In 184 lines and four ballades, the poet sets forth his artistic principles and, despite the absence of music for the ballades, lays more stress on music's importance than in any other work except the *Remède de Fortune*. The latter is a typical medieval treatise on Love and Fortune that Machaut enlivened by framing it in a realistic nar-

4. See G. Reaney, "Towards a Chronology of Machaut's Musical Works," MD, 21 (1967), pp. 87–96 and the references there given in notes 1 and 2.

rative of a personal love affair.[5] This narrative provided an opportunity for the introduction of songs; but, true to his didactic purpose, Machaut illustrated the style, poetic construction, and musical setting of seven different lyric forms. Four of the songs are monophonic: a lai, a virelai, and the less common forms of *complainte* and *chanson royal* (see below). The three polyphonic pieces illustrate the rondeau and two forms of the ballade. The date of the *Remède de Fortune* has been much discussed, but there now seems to be general agreement that it must have been completed before 1349, possibly even by 1342. At any rate, the poem stands among Machaut's first major works, and the illustrative pieces must be among his earlier compositions. That Machaut regarded music as an essential part of the *Remède de Fortune* is indicated by the fact that all manuscripts place the pieces within the poem rather than at the end with the other musical works.

The *Remède* is also noteworthy for its detailed description of a day of pleasure that included singing and dancing, both out of doors and in the manor after dinner. At this latter time, the entry of minstrels gave Machaut an excuse for naming more than thirty different musical instruments.[6] Medieval poets took naïve delight in catalogues of this sort, and Machaut compiled an even longer list of instruments in his extended narrative poem *La Prise d'Alexandrie* (The Taking of Alexandria).[7]

Another long and important work directly related to Machaut's own music is *Le Livre du Voir Dit* (The Book of the True Story). In this book we learn of a love affair—largely conducted by correspondence—between the sexagenarian canon of Reims and Peronne, a rather madcap girl in her late teens. Peronne had become enamored of the aging poet after hearing her friends sing his praises and after reading his ballades and rondeaux. Flattered by the girl's interest, Machaut answered her initial letter and thus began an association that lasted for three or four years, from about 1362 to 1365. During these years the "lovers" saw each other only on rare occasions, but they continued to correspond until, after the usual recriminations and reconciliations, the affair dwindled to an amicable conclusion. Meanwhile, Machaut had begun Peronne's "book," the *Voir Dit,* in which over 9000 lines of poetry link together forty-six of their letters in prose. In addition to providing a narrative background for the letters, the poetry includes eight musical compositions—one lai, four ballads, and three rondeaux—that Machaut sent to Peronne or at least included in the *Voir Dit.* One rondeau (No. 4) was probably an earlier work, and of another (No. 13?) Machaut says that he wrote the text and melody long ago but has now added tenor and contratenor parts—an interesting comment on his method of com-

5.   Machaut himself called the *Remède* a "traitie" (line 4257).
6.   Lines 3960–98. Reprinted in Ludwig, *Machaut,* 1, p. 102.
7.   M. L. de Mas Latrie (ed.), lines 1140–77. The passage is also published in Ludwig, *Machaut,* 2, p. 53★.

posing secular songs. The other six pieces in the *Voir Dit* appear to have been written for enclosure with Machaut's letters to Peronne and can thus be dated with unusual accuracy. In the rondeau *Dix et sept, cinc, trese* (No. 17), it is interesting to note, the numbers in the text produce an anagram of Peronne.[8]

THE MUSIC

The succession of types and forms that Machaut himself prescribed (Table 14, above) seems to provide the most satisfactory means of organizing any discussion of his music. Machaut's reasons for this arrangement remain somewhat obscure, and all other manuscripts differ from it to some degree. Despite a few irregularities, however, most of the manuscripts present the important musical types and the individual pieces within them in approximately the same order. In so doing, they reveal to us the extraordinarily wide range of Machaut's musical accomplishments.

THE LAIS

As we have seen, the trouvères cultivated the lai continuously, if not extensively, throughout the thirteenth century. Four more complete lais appear among the monophonic secular songs in the *Roman de Fauvel*, and in these later examples Machaut found models for some of his own compositions. Because of these and other links with the past and also because later composers abandoned the form, Machaut's nineteen lais are often said to be his most backward-looking musical works. The judgment may be accurate enough, but it should not obscure the developments—both poetic and musical—that made his lais representative of their time. They also represent one of the high points of medieval song and, as models of melodic construction, are worthy of detailed and individual analysis. We must be content, however, with pointing out their general and more salient characteristics.

POETIC AND MUSICAL FORM OF THE LAIS

In Machaut's treatment of the lai as poetry, he characteristically systematized earlier procedures in order to make it almost a fixed form, at least in its larger outlines. The number of stanzas became set at twelve, and Machaut made it a principle that each stanza should have a different po-

8.   With no *j* in the alphabet, numbers 17, 5, 13, 14, and 15 correspond to the letters *r, e, n, o, p.*

Dame Nature presents her three children, Sense, Rhetoric, and Music, to Machaut (from a fifteenth-century manuscript in the Morgan Library).

etic structure except the twelfth, which returned to the form and rhymes of the first stanza. Structural differences resulted from changes in the number and lengths of lines, and in the rhymes and rhyme schemes. These changes did not affect the normal practice of dividing stanzas into structurally equal halves, and Machaut further subdivided many stanzas into structurally equal quarters. By forming stanzas only in these two ways, Machaut eliminated the irregularity of earlier lais without sacrificing the variety achieved by giving each stanza a different internal structure.

It is obvious that the poetic structure of the lai must determine the larger aspects of its musical form. The different stanzaic forms require different music, and only the last stanza can, and does, repeat the melody of the first. Similarly, the melodic structure of each stanza reflects the division of the text in equal halves or quarters. In the former case, the two halves are sung to the same melody, usually with no change in the final cadence. With fourfold statements of a melody, Machaut almost invariably used open and closed endings in the pattern $a_o a_c a_o a_c$. He thus distinguished the four sections of text and at the same time emphasized the customary half-stanzas.

Within the limits imposed by the standardized poetic structure of the lai, Machaut achieved an astonishing diversity of musical styles and forms. For his first two lais, he apparently had yet to establish that standardized structure, and each is irregular in a different way. Lai 1 has the usual twelve stanzas, but they all have approximately the same poetic form and were meant to be sung to the same melody. Lai 2 more nearly approaches Machaut's normal treatment of the form but has only seven instead of twelve stanzas. Of the seventeen lais with the standard twelve-stanza form, four are polyphonic and will be dealt with separately. That Machaut deliberately sought diversity of form in the remaining thirteen monophonic lais is shown by the fact that no two have the same distribution of stanzas with duple and quadruple subdivisions. One lai (No. 6) has nothing but quadruple subdivisions with fourfold statements of each melody. Several have no more than one or two stanzas in which the two halves are sung with only one melodic repetition.[9] And no monophonic lai is without quadruple subdivisions in some of its stanzas. It is clear, therefore, that the usual designation of lai form as *aa bb cc dd . . . aa* is misleading and incomplete. It suggests a resemblance to the sequence that both the poetic structure of the lai and the many fourfold melodic repetitions contradict, and it implies a structural simplicity never found in Machaut's lais and rarely, if ever, in any other examples of the form.

MELODIC AND RHYTHMIC STYLE OF THE LAIS

The aspects of melodic and rhythmic style that distinguish Machaut's lais from his other musical works result in the main from the nature of their texts. Twelve stanzas with many lines in each almost force the adoption of a nearly syllabic setting with occasional melodic ornaments of no more than four or six notes. As a natural result of such a setting, rather short and clearly defined musical phrases correspond either with a single longer line of text or with a group of two or three shorter lines. Thus the different stanzaic forms in Machaut's lais produce equally various phrase patterns that are welded together and unified with astonishing ingenuity. Indeed, one of Machaut's chief distinctions as a composer of lais comes from the many ways in which he shapes individual stanzas into complete and self-sufficient musical entities. This achievement results in part from skillful manipulation of both rhythmic and melodic motives, in part from careful attention to contrasts of pitch level and melodic direction in successive phrases. Melodic movement within phrases is largely by step, and the occasional skips rarely exceed the intervals of a fourth or fifth. Both large and small skips occur more

9.   In the lai from the *Remède,* only stanzas 1 and 12 have the duple division; in Lai 2, only stanzas 1 and 7; in Lai 5, only stanza 10; and in Lai 7, only stanzas 10 and 11.

often between phrases, where their use facilitates the creation of balanced structures within the stanza as a whole. Of the innumerable examples that might illustrate these characteristics, one of the simplest is the fifth stanza of the *Lay mortel* (Example XVII–1). For the text of this stanza, Machaut wrote twenty lines of three, four, and five syllables with only a single rhyme, a virtuoso performance that cannot be duplicated in translation. In the musical setting of these lines, Machaut's use of rhythmic motives, transposed phrases, contrasts of pitch level, and balance of upward and downward motion can all be easily discovered. Also to be noted is the rhythmic identity of the melody's two halves. Machaut often set lines or groups of lines of equal length to the same rhythmic pattern and thus gave many stanzas a structure that is partially or completely isorhythmic. Yet he always managed to avoid monotony in these lengthy pieces—and to match the rhythmic variety of their texts—by his skillful distribution of similar and contrasting rhythmic patterns within single stanzas and from stanza to stanza.

Example XVII–1: *Stanza 5 of Machaut's* Lay mortel *(No. 8)*
(Paris, Bibl. Nat., f. fr. 1584, fol. 388v)

5a.   "Sorrowing, unhappy heart, tell me, what will you do, what say, where go, when you see that you are unwanted? You will have no other solace than to say 'Alas!'

5b.   You will be brought down from the heights to the depths. There you will lament your poignant sorrows. There you will break, wherever you may go. So shall you die without relief in the bonds of love."

Changes of pitch level perform similar functions in organizing and contrasting successive stanzas, with the added peculiarity that lais often end on a higher pitch level than they began. All of Machaut's display the characteristic use of the same melody for the first and last stanzas, but in eleven lais that melody is transposed up a fifth when it returns in stanza 12. In one lai (No. 6), the transposition is up a fourth, and in the polyphonic Lai 18 it is down a fourth (see p. 409). Only five lais in addition to the first begin and end at the same pitch level (Nos. 2, 3, 8, 12, and 17). The last two of these are polyphonic and are therefore unusual in other ways as well.

Transposition of the final stanza is by no means the only contrast of pitch level in Machaut's lais. Even those that begin and end at the same level have internal stanzas at different levels and with different final notes. Typically, Machaut seems to have deliberately sought a new and different succession of pitch levels and final notes for each lai. Only in Lai 5 and in Lai 19 from the *Remède de Fortune* is that succession the same. Every other lai is unique in its arrangement of these contrasting elements.

Different pitch levels within a lai and the transposition of the melody for its final stanza raise questions as to the manner of its performance. Single stanzas have a normal range of an octave or a ninth, but the changes of pitch level give the lai a total range that often falls only one or two notes short of two full octaves. Pieces with such a wide range and of such length are so exceptional, either in polyphony or in other forms of monophonic songs, that one wonders whether Machaut intended his lais to be sung by only one performer. Literary sources abound in references to lais played on instruments alone or sung to the accompaniment of a harp.[10] Perhaps it is not too fanciful to suggest that two performers spelled each other in singing a lai, each taking the stanzas best suited to his voice while the other improvised a simple accompaniment in discant style. That two of Machaut's seemingly monophonic lais are in reality polyphonic increases the plausibility of this suggestion. It would at least make the lais easier for modern singers and more attractive for modern audiences.

THE POLYPHONIC LAIS

Four of Machaut's lais prove to be polyphonic, although their appearance in the manuscripts differs not at all from the monophonic pieces. It has long been recognized, however, that Machaut called for canonic performance of Lais 11 and 12, which are found together in all manuscripts. In the first of these pieces, each even-numbered stanza is prefaced by the designation *Chace* and followed by the remark "a second time without pause" (*iterum sine pausa*). As a result of the canons, which are assumed to be for three voices in the manner of the French chace (see Chapter XV), monophonic and polyphonic stanzas alternate throughout the lai. This procedure has another and more unexpected result: the single melody of stanza 1 becomes a three-voice canon when it returns transposed

10. Machabey, *Machault*, 1, pp. 100–06.

up a fifth in stanza 12.[11] None of the stanzas in Lai 12 is called a chace, but canonic performance is implied by a remark that the second half of the first stanza, like all the others, is to be sung at once and without pause.[12] Unfortunately, the manuscripts give no hint as to the number of canonic voices or where they should enter, and in some stanzas, at least, unusual and inexplicable dissonances suggest that the published transcriptions as three-voice canons may not have correctly realized Machaut's intentions.

The other two polyphonic lais, Nos. 17 and 18, appear in only one manuscript and are presumed to be Machaut's last compositions in the genre. The *Lay de Consolation* (No. 17) is unique in having different melodies for the two halves of each stanza. The first stanza (Example XVII–2) will suffice to illustrate the simple, almost note-against-note style that prevails throughout the lai when the two melodies for each stanza are combined in two-part polyphony.[13] Seven more stanzas, including the last, end on a unison **c'**, while four have closed endings on the fifth **g–d'** (stanzas 5 and 8–10). The effect is almost modern in its shift to the dominant and subsequent return to the tonic.

Example XVII–2: *Machaut,* Un Lay de Consolation, *Stanza 1 (Paris, Bibl. Nat., f. fr. 9221, fol. 125v)*

1a. Because one more properly speaks of his own feeling than of others' thoughts, I should like, Love, lovingly to make a lai of what is in my heart, if it pleases you.

1b. And if I do this clumsily, my lady, may you graciously pardon the work as sincerely as my heart is devotedly all yours without demur.

11. Schrade errs in indicating that stanza 12 lies an octave below the written pitch.
12. Schrade, PMC, 2 and 3, p. 66.
13. Both Ludwig and Schrade published this lai as a monophonic piece. For the polyphonic transcription, see R. Hoppin, "An Unrecognized Polyphonic Lai of Machaut," MD, 12 (1958), pp. 93–104.

Also published as a monophonic piece by Ludwig and Schrade, the "hidden polyphony" of Lai 18 is produced in still another way.[14] Here, the melodies of the first three stanzas combine in three-part polyphony, a procedure which is repeated in groups of three through stanza 12. Thus the melody of stanza 1 is combined with two different melodies when it returns, transposed down a fourth, in stanza 12.

The four polyphonic lais raise further questions as to the manner of performance. We need only note here that the required performing group might well include instrumentalists to play the accompanying polyphony while the melodies of the stanzas are sung in the proper order. The resulting repetitions would take no longer than a normal monophonic lai.

If we assume that Machaut's polyphonic lais represent an effort to revitalize and modernize the form, we must admit that the effort was unsuccessful. The lais themselves stand out as high points of Machaut's creative activity, but they inspired no successors. In the later fourteenth and fifteenth centuries, treatises on the art of poetry describe the form of the lai much as Machaut established it, and poets continued writing lais. As far as we know, however, none of these later poems was ever set to music. The lai as a musical form was evidently the victim of changing times and tastes. Monophonic song was no longer palatable in large-scale works, and poets who could write lais lacked the knowledge and technical skill to provide them with polyphonic settings. Composers, on the other hand, preferred the shorter lyric forms for their polyphonic songs. As specialists in music they were no longer capable of writing the text of a lai, and they may well have shrunk from the difficulty of providing one with an adequate musical setting. Few composers, certainly, could have matched the supreme artistry with which Machaut accomplished this task.

COMPLAINTE AND CHANSON ROYAL

Machaut's lyric poems include a number of complaintes and chansons royaulx, but he provided musical settings only for the one example of each type that he included in the *Remède de Fortune*.[15] The primary interest of these monophonic songs lies in the evidence they provide, together with the older lais, of Machaut's links with the past. His *Complainte* bewails the trickery of both Fortune and Love in no fewer than thirty-six stanzas, all of which have the same sixteen-line form and are sung to the same melody.

Although the implication of the title *Chanson royal* is uncertain, its

14. The discovery was announced, with a transcription, in M. Hasselman and T. Walker, "More Hidden Polyphony in a Machaut Manuscript," MD, 24 (1970), pp. 7–16.
15. Schrade, PM, 2, pp. 106–07 and Ludwig, *Machaut*, 1, pp. 96–97.

connection with the trouvère tradition is obvious. Indeed, it proves to be a typical "solemn and majestic" song in praise of love with five stanzas and an envoy. The melody of the chanson is also typical in its use of the *aab* form in which thirteenth-century trouvères cast most of their love songs. Conversion of this poetic and musical form into a ballade required only a reduction to three stanzas and the addition of a refrain. The melodic form of Machaut's *Complainte*, $a_o a_c b_o b_c$, also turns up, but as a less common structural pattern, in his and other composers' ballades. This fusion of chanson and ballade seems to have occurred early in the fourteenth century, at least as far as composers were concerned. The characteristic features of the ballade now prevailed, and the true chanson had almost ceased to exist as a separate musical form. Perhaps Machaut gave a sly hint that such songs were outdated when he allowed "the lover" to confess that he dozed a bit during the lady's singing of the *Chanson royal* ("un petitet m'i endormi"—line 1980). One wonders if the lady may not have slept even more soundly during the lover's lengthy *Complainte*.

THE MOTETS

Like the lais that precede them in the manuscripts, Machaut's twenty-three motets are often said to represent the more conservative aspects of his musical output. This judgment can be accepted only with reservations. By the time of Machaut, the motet had existed as a musical form for more than a hundred years, and its traditional and identifying characteristics were well established. Neither Machaut nor any other fourteenth-century composer would have considered abandoning the structural and stylistic elements then regarded as appropriate for the motet. To say that this was being conservative as opposed to the "progressive" treatment of polyphonic secular songs is to overlook the essential differences between the two musical types. It is a measure of Machaut's greatness as a composer that he could adopt different musical styles and even different compositional techniques while remaining unmistakably a child of the French Ars Nova.

The one respect in which Machaut does seem to look backward in his motets is his striking preference for French secular texts. Only six of the twenty-three pieces are Latin motets, and two more have a Latin duplum and French triplum. Of the fifteen entirely French motets, three even have secular French tenors. All other tenors have Latin incipits that suggest plainchant origins, although the specific sources of some melodies have yet to be discovered. Although much of the contemporary motet literature may have been lost, it seems probable that Machaut's concentration on French secular texts reflects his own preference rather than the common practice of his time. Latin motets far outnumber French in the *Roman de Fauvel,* and they account for more than half of the motet repertory in the Ivrea Codex (see Chapter XV). Later collections usually contain a few French motets with texts that sing the praises of an unnamed lady who sometimes turns out to be the Virgin Mary. More and more, however, the motet dissociates itself from secular song in the vernacular. Its Latin texts tend to have some liturgical, or at least religious, connection or to celebrate important persons or historical events. Machaut himself foreshadowed this trend in his most elaborate and presumably latest motets (Nos. 21–23). It may well be, indeed, that Machaut's contributions to the development of a polyphonic style more appropriate for secular song led him and those who came after him to turn away from the French motet and to adopt the newer and more popular forms of the ballade, rondeau, and virelai.

If Machaut's motets may be conservative and even backward-looking in their use of French texts, the same cannot be said of their musical style. Without exception, they follow fourteenth-century notational procedures and use the different combinations of mensurations described by Philippe de Vitry and Johannes de Muris. They also follow and develop the structural procedures established by the "modern" motets in the *Roman de Fauvel* and the works of Vitry.

Nineteen of Machaut's motets have the typical three-voice arrangement of a duplum and triplum with different texts above a tenor. The remaining four (Nos. 5 and 21–23) add a textless contratenor to this arrangement. Except for one motet with a rondeau tenor, all of these pieces display the contrasts of mensural organization that we noted in the works of Vitry and that remain characteristic of the isorhythmic motet throughout its subsequent history. Tenors, and contratenors when present, normally move in the longer note values of mood and time, while the upper voices use one of the possible combinations of time and prolation. We find all four of these combinations in Machaut's motets, but imperfect time with major prolation (6/8) occurs in fifteen of the pieces. This predominance of 6/8 mensuration was so characteristic of French polyphony in the fourteenth century that contemporary Italians applied the adjective *gallica* to the corresponding mensuration in their own notation (see Chapter XVIII). Just as 6/8 predominates in the upper voices of Machaut's motets, so is perfect mood by far the most common mensuration of their tenors. It too occurs in fifteen pieces, with only four in imperfect mood.[16] In three of the four-voice motets, the tenor and contratenor combine perfect and imperfect mood in various ways.

---

16.   The four in imperfect mood are Nos. 3, 4, 7, and 13.

MACHAUT'S ISORHYTHMIC STRUCTURES

All of Machaut's motets are isorhythmic with the exception of the three that use secular French tenors, and even these reveal the influence of isorhythmic techniques. Any analysis of those techniques must consider both the structure of the lower voice or voices and the relation of that structure to the appearance of isorhythmic passages in the upper voices. Machaut's closest approach to the use of strict isorhythm in all voices occurs in Motet 4, but every motet has some repeated patterns in the duplum and triplum that clarify the structure of the tenor or create a structure that the tenor by itself leaves undefined. For the most part, isorhythmic passages in the upper voices introduce hocket or some other device, such as syncopation or rhythmic sequences, that will stand out against the normal rhythmic and melodic flow of the motet as a whole. Such passages are often framed by conspicuous cadences—long notes and full-measure rests—that also recur in the same place above each succeeding talea in the tenor. This use of isorhythm in the upper voices, of course, makes the structure of a motet more perceptible to the ear, which was undoubtedly the reason for its introduction.

In devising his isorhythmic tenors, Machaut invented no new procedures, but he applied the old ones with astonishing variety and ingenuity. Moreover, he seems to have preferred devices that rarely appeared in the motets of Philippe de Vitry and the *Roman de Fauvel*. Exactly half of Machaut's isorhythmic motets, for example, close with a repetition of the tenor color and taleae in strict diminution. Another device that appears with increasing frequency in Machaut's motets is the use of a color that does not divide into a whole number of taleae. In several tenors, a color one and one-half times as long as the talea creates a structure that may be expressed by the formula $2C = 3T$. The complete formula may be repeated in diminution—as it is in Motets 4 and 7—or it may be repeated unchanged. Three statements of the formula in Motet 9, for example, give an overall form of $6C = 9T$.

In some motets, the repeated rhythmic patterns of the tenors are so short and simple that they seem to differ scarcely at all from thirteenth-century practices. By introducing isorhythmic passages in the upper voices, however, Machaut groups two or more statements of a simple pattern into a longer talea and thus creates musical forms of considerable subtlety and sophistication. One of the most striking examples of this procedure occurs in Motet 8, *Qui es promesses—Ha! Fortune—Et non est* (AMM, No. 61). In the manuscript sources, the tenor of this motet is written out once with a sign indicating threefold performance, and its division into four statements of a short rhythmic pattern also suggests a simple and somewhat primitive isorhythmic form (Example XVII–3a). The upper voices decide otherwise, however. By treating *three* of the rhythmic patterns as one talea, they make the form of the tenor become

3C = 4T (Example XVII–3b). The resulting taleae consist of twenty-seven measures, of which the last twelve are rhythmically identical each time. In this case, the isorhythmic passages in the upper voices introduce syncopation rather than hocket and close with an obvious cadence on the final tenor note of each talea. It should also be remarked that the triplum always uses the same rhythmic and melodic figure to lead into the next statement of the talea. In some of Machaut's motets, even larger amounts of melodic repetition increase the perceptibility of his isorhythmic structures.

Example XVII–3: *Tenor Structure in Motet 8 of Machaut*

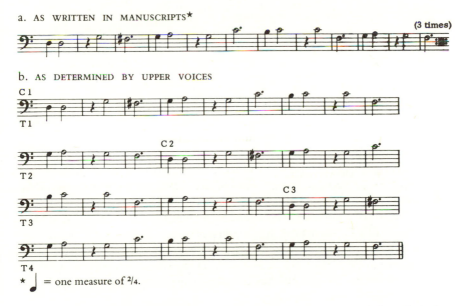

a. AS WRITTEN IN MANUSCRIPTS*

(3 times)

b. AS DETERMINED BY UPPER VOICES

C 1

T 1

C 2

T 2

C 3

T 3

T 4

* ♩ = one measure of ²/₄.

Another aspect of Machaut's motets that deserves detailed study is the internal symmetry and balance of the taleae themselves.[17] One of his common procedures was to divide the talea into equal halves with identical or related rhythmic patterns. In two of the four motets with an added contratenor (Nos. 5 and 23), Machaut applied this procedure to the combination of the two lower voices rather than to the tenor alone. The tenor and contratenor use black and red notes in each of these pieces to produce passages of perfect mood in one voice against imperfect mood in the other. In Motet 23, these passages alternate in rhythmic, but not melodic, voice exchange, so that the combination of the two parts creates a talea with rhythmically identical halves (Example

17.   An interesting, if somewhat controversial, study of internal symmetry in the motets as well as the Mass may be found in O. Gombosi, "Machaut's *Messe Notre Dame*," MQ, 36 (1950), pp. 204–24.

XVII–4a).[18] Motet 5 refines on this procedure by presenting the exchanged rhythms in reverse or retrograde order (Example XVII–4b). The result of these combined rhythmic palindromes, the same when read backward or forward, is a talea with symmetrical rather than identical halves. (The oldest verbal palindrome, obviously, is Adam's self-introduction to Eve: "Madam I'm Adam.")

Example XVII–4: *Tenor and Contratenor Taleae in*
Two Motets of Machaut

a. MOTET 23

b. MOTET 5

Further discussion of Machaut's motets cannot be undertaken here, but the above examples and citations should give some idea of his ingenuity in devising new and unexpected isorhythmic structures. Like composers before and after him, Machaut evidently regarded motets as music for connoisseurs who could understand and appreciate the subtleties of their construction. In the variety and complexity of their architecture and in the increasing penetration of isorhythmic organization into the upper voices, his motets surpass the works of earlier composers and pave the way for further developments in the late fourteenth and early fifteenth centuries.

LA MESSE DE NOSTRE DAME

Machaut's *Messe de Nostre Dame* is unique for a number of reasons. It is his largest single musical work and the only one with a strictly liturgical function. As we noted in the previous chapter, it is the first complete setting of the Ordinary that is known to have been written as a unit by one composer. In length it far exceeds any of the compilations of individual movements that make up other Masses in the fourteenth century. Machaut's Mass was the only one of its kind, and not until some fifty

18.   Apel, NPM, pp. 360–61, gives the original notation of the tenor and contratenor in color with the beginning of a transcription. For a complete facsimile of Motet 23, see Parrish, NMM, Pl. LII and LIII.

years after his death did complete Masses begin to appear in the works of early Renaissance composers.

The *Mass of Notre Dame* provides polyphonic settings for all the chants of the Ordinary, including the *Ite, missa est,* which almost never forms part of the later polyphonic Mass. All six movements are written for four voices, but in two distinctly different styles. The Kyrie, Sanctus, Agnus Dei, and *Ite, missa est* are isorhythmic motets in all but their use of the same text for each voice.[19] To their complexity, the Gloria and Credo contrast simultaneous style with short, clearly defined phrases in note-against-note counterpoint and a nearly syllabic setting of the text. Each of these movements ends, however, with a long melismatic Amen that returns to motet style and thus establishes a relationship with the rest of the Mass.

A further contrast between the movements in different styles is less readily apparent to the ear. The Gloria and Credo seem to make no use of preexisting melodies, but each of the other movements takes a corresponding chant of the Ordinary for its tenor melody.[20] Machaut's choice of chants on which to base his isorhythmic movements may have determined, or been determined by, the overall modal scheme of his Mass. The first three movements, at any rate, are all in the Dorian mode ending on **D**, while the last three have Lydian or Hypolydian tenors and end on **F**.

MUSICAL FORMS IN THE MASS— GLORIA AND CREDO

The longer texts of the Gloria and Credo undoubtedly influenced Machaut's choice of simultaneous style for these two movements. That style, in turn, demanded methods of formal organization quite different from those used in isorhythmic structures. Machaut's solution was to divide each movement into large sections of approximately equal length, as shown in Table 15. Cadences on long notes followed by double bars mark the end of each section, and they all close on **D** except the one that precedes the Amen of the Credo. In each movement Machaut organized and related the sections by similar arrangements of open and closed internal cadences and by the placement of one-measure textless interludes in the tenor and contratenor with rests in the two upper

19. The manuscripts do not give the complete text for the contratenor in the Sanctus and Agnus Dei, and it may be questioned whether this part (and perhaps the tenor too) should be vocal or instrumental in the isorhythmic sections.

20. With some variants these melodies appear in LU as follows: Kyrie IV (p. 25); Sanctus and Agnus Dei XVII (pp. 61–62). Typically, the *Ite, missa est* uses part of another Ordinary chant, but Machaut chose the opening phrase of a different Sanctus (No. VIII, p. 38).

parts.[21] As was noted in Chapter XVI, such interludes are a character-istic feature of Glorias and Credos in simultaneous style. In Machaut's hands, however, they take on greater formal significance and reveal once again his concern for structural balance and clarity. In the Gloria, the same interlude appears once in each section except the introductory five measures and the concluding Amen. The Credo has two interludes in each of its first three sections, but in this case no two are exactly alike. A further aspect of the Gloria and Credo that deserves mention is Ma-chaut's occasional use of maximas (duplex longs) in chordal style. Such passages occur on the opening phrase of the Gloria, "Et in terra pax," and twice on the words "Jesu Christe." In the Credo, only the phrase "Ex Maria Virgine" receives this special treatment. When these passages interrupt the normal rhythmic flow of the movements, the stress they place on the text could hardly be more emphatic.

Table 15: *Subdivisions of the Gloria and Credo in Machaut's Mass*

Incipits of sections	Number of measures	Incipits of sections	Number of measures
Et in terra pax	5	Patrem omnipotentem	51
hominibus	25	Qui propter nos	59
Domine Deus, Rex	26	Et in Spiritum	47
Qui tollis	27	Amen	37
Quoniam tu solus	22		
Amen	26		

The melismatic Amens of the two movements also introduce striking contrasts of style and completely different methods of formal organiza-tion. The Amen of the Gloria is not isorhythmic, but it resembles the musical style of a motet in every other way. Its twenty-six measures divide into almost equal halves, the second of which is marked by hocket, syncopation, and rhythmic sequences in the contratenor as well as in the upper voices. The Amen of the Credo, on the other hand, is strictly isorhythmic in all four voices.

THE ISORHYTHMIC MOVEMENTS

Machaut's general procedure in the Mass was to divide the original form of each chant into a number of taleae without introducing any melodic repetition. Moreover, he seems to have devised his taleae in such a way that they disguise any repetitions within the chants themselves. Almost always, the contratenor is completely isorhythmic and the upper voices partially so. The isorhythmic passages in the duplum and triplum are

21.   For more detailed analyses of these forms and of the isoryhthmic movements, see the article of Gombosi cited in fn. 17 above.

particularly interesting for their use of syncopation and hocket and for their frequent grouping of patterns in rhythmic sequences.

Some differences in the overall forms of the isorhythmic movements result from the nature of the plainchant melodies and their liturgical texts. The plainchant Kyrie has four melodic sections arranged in the characteristic pattern $A \times 3$ $B \times 3$ $C \times 2$ C'. Machaut gives each of these sections its own isorhythmic setting and indicates the repeats needed to produce the traditional nine acclamations. As written, the four parts of Machaut's Kyrie provide extended melismatic settings of the text with a total of 95 measures.[22] Performance of the indicated repeats would bring this figure to 210 measures and would make the Kyrie the longest movement in the Mass.

The Sanctus is only one measure shorter than the Kyrie without repeats, but it is one continuous movement, with a complete statement of the plainchant Sanctus in the tenor. Machaut set the opening three "Sanctus" in five-measure phrases arranged in the *aba* pattern of the chant melody. He then began his isorhythmic structure with the words "Domine Deus" and continued for ten statements of an eight-measure talea. For the most part, the taleae fall into groups that reflect the major divisions of the text. It is noteworthy, however, that they present the many melodic repetitions of the chant in constantly changing rhythmic patterns.

The three acclamations of the plainchant Agnus Dei are melodically identical except that the second has a contrasting intonation on the first two words. Machaut took advantage of this form to use the same music for his first and third settings, with the necessary change of text from "miserere nobis" to "dona nobis pacem." He thus composed only two settings, in which the opening invocations on the words "Agnus Dei" obviously had to be different. These invocations are not isorhythmic, but the identical tenors for the rest of each setting are both divided into two taleae. The taleae of the two settings differ in rhythm and length, however, so that once again melodic repetition is disguised by a change of rhythmic arrangement (Example XVII–5).

Example XVII–5: *Different Taleae in the Agnus Dei*
of Machaut's Mass

AGNUS I AND III, TALEA I

qui   tol - lis pec -   ca - ta

AGNUS II, TALEA I

qui   tol   -   lis pec   -   ca - ta   mun-

22.   The individual sections have 27, 22, 17, and 29 measures.

The final movement of the Mass has a simple isorhythmic form of two eight-measure taleae plus a final measure. The manuscripts give the two texts, *Ite, missa est* and *Deo gratias,* beneath the music, which must therefore be sung twice to complete the work. If this repeat and the repeats of the Kyrie are made, the entire Mass attains a grand total of 730 measures. No composer has left a more imposing monument of medieval music.

Whether the *Mass of Notre Dame* can be called a cycle, in the sense that its movements are musically related, has been a subject for some debate. Certainly Machaut did not anticipate the characteristic unifying devices of the fifteenth century. No single melody serves as the tenor for all the movements, and no opening motive or "motto" begins every movement in the same way. The Mass is not modally unified, as we have seen, but splits into two sections in the Dorian and Lydian modes. And the contrast provided by the Gloria and Credo suggests a deliberate effort to achieve diversity rather than unity of musical style. Much has been made of a melodic figure that appears occasionally in the Mass (Example XVII–6), but to call this motive the "generating cell" of the entire work is surely an exaggeration. The same motive appears frequently in the Mass of Toulouse (see Example XVI–6, mm. 3–5) and in many other pieces by Machaut, his contemporaries, and his followers in the fourteenth and early fifteenth centuries. Thus it proves to be part of the vocabulary of melodic figures common to all music of the period. Machaut could have used the motive as an integrative device if he had placed it consistently and conspicuously at important structural points in the Mass. This he did not do. Instead, it seems to appear at random, rather frequently in some movements or sections, rarely if at all in others. We should probably regard the motive as one of several clichés that Machaut used, almost without thinking, as a normal part of his melodic vocabulary. In a sense, of course, these clichés do contribute to the stylistic unity of the Mass, but it is a unity that we should be surprised not to find in a long work by one composer.

Example XVII–6

Given Machaut's interest in rhythmic organization, it is curious that this element has often been overlooked as a unifying factor in the Mass. Yet the use of imperfect time with minor prolation throughout the entire work can only reflect a conscious effort to achieve rhythmic unity. Machaut treated this mensuration in a rather old-fashioned way that limits minims to short ornamental figures and makes the breve seem to be the unit on which the beat should fall. The consistent grouping of breves in all voices into units of perfect or imperfect mood confirms this judgment. Measures of 3/2 (♩ = o.) and 2/2 (♩ = o), with the breve always equal to a half note, therefore become the most appropriate modern equivalents of the original mensurations.[23] The prevailing mood in the Gloria and Credo is imperfect (2/2), but occasional phrases with a value of three breves and cadences on perfect longs introduce short passages in 3/2 meter. Measures of 4/2 result when maximas are used for word emphasis.

The Gloria and Credo thus provide rhythmic variety by their departure from the perfect mood that is used exclusively in all the isorhythmic movements as well as in their own melismatic Amens. Within the limitations imposed by this mensuration (3/2), the upper voices are remarkably varied in their rhythmic patterns, while the tenor and contratenor display an even more remarkable unity. As we might expect, no two of the nine sections have identical taleae in either the tenor or contratenor parts. When the two voices are considered as a unit, however, we find that their various combinations of notes and rests produce only three arrangements of note values within a measure—| ♩ ♩ ♩ |, | ♩ o |, and | o· |. Curiously enough, the contratenor introduces the only exceptions to this statement in three measures of the talea in Kyrie I and in one measure of the talea in the *Ite, missa est.* It should also be remarked that, except in Agnus II, all of the taleae end with the three arrangements of note values in the order given above. (The final long of the pattern is sometimes the last note of one talea, sometimes the first note of the next.) Machaut's ingenuity in devising new combinations of the lower voices to produce such a limited number of rhythmic patterns should not be allowed to obscure the consistency of their use or the importance of their function. Like the basic structure of a Gothic cathedral, the rhythmic unity of Machaut's Mass provides an unobtrusive but unshakable support for its wealth of decorative detail.

We do not know for what occasion Machaut composed his one great liturgical work. The baptism of Clovis at Reims in 496 had won the cathedral its privilege of conducting the ceremonies at which French kings were crowned, and Machaut's Mass is often said to have been written for the coronation of Charles V on May 19, 1364. No shred of historical evidence supports this assertion, and the strict traditions of the ceremony made any such innovation unlikely. Machaut himself spoke of the coronation and the presence of King Peter II of Cyprus but said nothing about the music for the Mass.[24] Perhaps a clue to the time of its composition lies in the extraordinary emphasis placed on the words "et in terra pax" and their equally extraordinary separation from the continuation of the phrase, "hominibus bone voluntatis" (see above, p. 416 and Table 15). In the Hundred Years' War with England, the French military position was at low ebb discouragingly often, but for Machaut the

23. Both Ludwig and Schrade transcribe in this way.
24. *La Prise d'Alexandrie,* lines 799–817.

fighting came closest to home when the English laid siege to Reims itself in the winter of 1359–60. It is now generally agreed that the Mass is
one of the composer's late works, and there can surely have been no
more appropriate time for him to stress the need for peace on earth. We
do not know whether Machaut or someone else provided the title "La
Messe de Nostre Dame," which appears in only one of the manuscript
sources. Yet a dedication—or appeal—to the Virgin Mary would also
have been appropriate for a canon of Reims Cathedral, another Notre
Dame in which feasts of the Virgin would have been celebrated with
particular solemnity. Machaut himself left other evidence of his devotion to Mary. He and his brother were buried side by side in the cathedral, and their epitaph recorded their establishment of a fund for the
weekly performance on Saturday of a "Mass of the Virgin." A document of 1411 mentions such performances "for the late Guillaume de
Machault," and the tradition seems to have persisted, with its founders
still remembered, as late as the eighteenth century.[25] Once again, we do
not know how long Machaut's music was used for these Masses or even
if it was used at all. Nevertheless, we shall probably not be far wrong in
regarding the *Messe de Nostre Dame* as Machaut's own memorial to his
years of service in the Church of Our Lady of Reims.

THE *DAVID HOCKET*

Machaut often introduced hocket passages, as we have seen, in his
motets and the motetlike portions of the Mass, but he wrote only one
work that he specifically called a hocket. In reality, the *David Hocket* is
nothing more than a textless isorhythmic motet for three voices. The
manuscripts identify these voices as "David Tenor," "David Hoquetus," and "David triplum," but the designation *David* belongs by rights
only to the tenor melody, the plainchant melisma on that word that
completes the verse of *Alleluia: Nativitas*. In liturgical performance, this
conclusion of the verse was sung by the choir and was therefore not included in Perotin's setting of *Alleluia: Nativitas* in three-voice organum
(see above, Chapter IX). The suggestion that Machaut deliberately set
out to rival the great Parisian discantor by completing his work seems
somewhat fanciful. The *David Hocket* is archaic enough, but it resembles
the so-called instrumental motets of the Bamberg Codex more than the
clausulae of Perotin. Whether the work can be called liturgical, or even
religious, also seems doubtful. Its intended function remains unknown,
and it follows the Mass only in the one manuscript that purports to arrange the pieces according to Machaut's wishes. This arrangement prob-

25. Machabey presents the historical evidence in *Machault*, 1, pp. 69–70. See also his dis-
     cussion of the Mass, 2, p. 113 ff.

ably came after the fact because of the derivation of the *David* tenor from a chant in honor of the Virgin Mary. In the other three manuscripts that contain the hocket, it comes at the end of the musical collection. Perhaps Machaut wrote it only to provide at least one example of a musical type described by contemporary theorists.

THE SECULAR SONGS

Machaut's polyphonic songs—the ballades, rondeaux, and a few virelais—are often regarded as his most progressive works, the ones that exercised the greatest influence on his successors. This, like most generalizations, is only partially true. It is also misleading because it overlooks the state of development of the different musical types at the time Machaut began to compose. Long-established traditions determined the essential characteristics of both the lai and the motet, and Machaut needed only to bring both forms up to date by applying to them the technical devices and procedures of the Ars Nova. No such traditions provided Machaut with a starting point for the polyphonic settings of shorter lyric poems. Earlier examples known to us are limited to the sixteen conductus-like "Rondels" of Adam de la Hale and the one rondeau in similar style by Jehan de Lescurel. If Machaut knew these songs at all, he failed to imitate their style. Instead, having no other models, he developed his own method of providing lyric poetry with an appropriate polyphonic setting. Writers in the later fourteenth century credited Vitry and Machaut with inventing or beginning the new lyric forms. Since we possess none of Vitry's secular songs, we cannot assess his contributions, but we know that neither he nor Machaut invented the poetic and musical forms of the ballade, rondeau, and virelai. What Machaut did invent was an arrangement of vocal and instrumental parts that itself established a tradition, one that remained in force for a century or more after his death. In that arrangement, textless tenor and contratenor parts support an upper voice (cantus) that alone sings the words of the song. Thus the so-called polyphonic secular song of the later Middle Ages and early Renaissance is in fact a solo song with an accompaniment provided by two contrapuntal parts that presumably were played by instruments.

It is not to be expected that Machaut's invention came suddenly with his first secular songs. It came, rather, as one of several experiments in which Machaut not only created a new style but also developed a new process of composition. Instead of beginning with the tenor, as for a motet, he apparently composed the melody of the cantus and then added one or more other parts, as he said he had done for one of the rondeaux in the *Voir Dit*. In the early stages of his search for an appropriate polyphonic setting, Machaut added only a tenor part, perhaps in the way a skilled instrumentalist might have improvised an accompaniment to a trouvère chanson. The tenor usually has a greater number of long notes than the cantus and is thus a slower-moving part, but both voices move at the same level of mensural organization. In modern transcriptions, therefore, the two parts have measures of equal length, and the tenor does not group the measures of the cantus in units of two or three as in the motet. The basic harmonic structure of the two voices consists of a series of perfect and imperfect consonances in note-against-note counterpoint. Melodic figuration then breaks up the notes of this structure, particularly in the cantus, to give it rhythmic vitality and harmonic interest. The figuration naturally introduces many dissonances, most of which can be explained in modern terms as suspensions, anticipations, passing and neighboring notes, and appoggiaturas (see the ballade *Dous amis* [Gentle friend]; AMM, No. 62). Even in pieces for only two voices, a high dissonance level is one of the most characteristic features of Machaut's style.

The two-part framework established by the cantus and tenor provided the basis for all of Machaut's further experiments in the development of secular polyphonic song. The framework itself shows little influence of the older techniques of motet composition, but that influence is clearly evident in the ways Machaut expanded the polyphony to include a third and even a fourth voice. One way, perhaps the first that Machaut tried, was to add a textless triplum to the two-part framework. Except for its lack of words, this third part combined with the cantus to form a pair comparable to the two upper voices of a motet. This solution to the problem of creating three-part polyphony seems to have been less satisfactory than the other, which augmented the basic unit of tenor and cantus by adding a contratenor part. The resulting texture, quite different from that of the three-voice motet, provided a more solid support for the cantus and did not force it to compete with another upper voice. These satisfying acoustical properties undoubtedly account for Machaut's preference for the combination of cantus, tenor, and contratenor and for its acceptance by succeeding generations of composers. The creation of four-part secular polyphony is somewhat more problematical. Several of Machaut's songs have both a triplum and a contratenor, and four-part performance of some pieces was certainly intended. In other pieces, however, the triplum and contratenor do not seem to have been designed for use together. Instead, they provide alternate possibilities for performance in three-part polyphony. This situation is sometimes clarified and sometimes obscured by the songs that appear with a different number of voices in different manuscripts. Nevertheless, the stages of Machaut's development of the standard three-voice texture are clearly discernible in his three groups of polyphonic songs, and particularly in the ballades.

THE BALLADES

Machaut provided music for forty-two of his ballade texts, including the two in the *Remède de Fortune*. The collection of forty ballades is presumably arranged in more or less chronological order, and it is therefore significant that the first sixteen pieces were originally for cantus and tenor alone. (Nos. 3 and 4 have an added contratenor in one of the late Machaut manuscripts.) A textless triplum appears in eight of the forty-two ballades, but only No. 19 still has the arrangement of triplum, cantus, and tenor. In most of the others, the later addition of either a contratenor or the triplum itself seems intended to provide an alternate combination of three-part polyphony. Ballades 21 and 22 are perhaps the only ones originally composed as four-part pieces, for they alone have triplum, cantus, tenor, and contratenor parts in all sources. What was to become the standard three-part arrangement of cantus, tenor, and contratenor is now found in fifteen ballades, four of which also exist in ear-

The ballade *De toutes flours,* by Machaut (Morgan Library MS 396).

lier two-part versions. In the four-voice Ballades 31 and 41, however, the triplum may be a later addition.

It is noteworthy that the one Machaut manuscript in which most of the added parts appear is the copy prepared for the Duke of Berry. This manuscript is the least reliable in its transmission of both texts and music, and we may question whether Machaut himself made all of the additions to the ballades. In some of the later "repertory" manuscripts—collections of pieces by various composers—his songs continue to appear either with an added contratenor or with a new one in place of the original.[26]

A few of Machaut's ballades depart in one way or another from the two-, three-, and four-voice arrangements just discussed. Curiously, the only monophonic ballade comes late in the collection (No. 37). Ballade 34, on the other hand, is a four-voice piece of the type known as a *double ballade,* one in which the two upper voices sing different texts but with the same form, rhymes, and refrain. Machaut presumably maintained, or pretended to maintain, a literary practice when he said in the *Voir Dit* that he wrote one text of Ballade 34 in answer to the other, which had been sent him by a friend. He left no explanation, either fictional or real, for his two triple ballades, Nos. 17 and 29. The first, strangely enough, is a three-voice canon with a different text for each voice.[27] The second is also for three voices, but each now has a different melody as well as text. One more ballade (No. 1) should be mentioned here because of its exceptional introduction of isorhythm in both voices. The experiment apparently showed Machaut that ballade form was unsuited for isorhythmic treatment. At any rate, he never applied it again, either in his ballades or in his other secular songs.

POETIC AND MUSICAL FORM IN THE BALLADES

In their poetic and musical forms, Machaut's ballades offer little that is new. For the most part, his texts are conventional love songs that differ from older trouvère chansons only in having a refrain and in being reduced to three stanzas.[28] The envoy has also been eliminated, although it continues to appear in literary ballades throughout the fourteenth and fifteenth centuries. Because the ballade is strophic, its three stanzas are identical in form, have the same refrain, of course, and usually use the same rhymes. The stanzaic structures may vary considerably from one ballade to another, but in Machaut's hands they did become standardized to a degree. Most of his ballades have stanzas of seven or eight lines with

26.   See PMC, 2 and 3, notes to Ballades 18, 22, and 23, and Rondeau 7 (AMM, No. 63).

27.   The canon of Ballade 17 is incorrectly solved in the editions of Ludwig and Schrade. The third voice should enter in the 5th, not the 2nd, measure of 6/4 meter.

28.   All the ballades have three stanzas except No. 10, which has only one.

rhyme schemes such as ababbcC, or ababccdD. Also evident is a tendency to use longer lines of eight or ten syllables and to make all the lines of equal length. This tendency becomes almost a rule for later composers, most of whom use only a few stereotyped patterns of stanzaic construction in their ballades. Whatever poetic form Machaut chose for a ballade, it always fit one of two musical forms. The one usually called ballade form—$a_o a_c bC$—is by far the more common and occurs in 37 of Machaut's 42 ballades. In the other five pieces, the second section of music is also repeated with open and closed endings to give the pattern $a_o a_c b_o b_c$.[29] Machaut illustrated both ballade forms in the *Remède de Fortune,* where he introduced the less common type as a "baladelle." At the end of the song, however, it is called a "balade."[30] Machaut seems to have used the word *baladelle* merely to rhyme with *nouvelle* and did not mean it as a designation of the form. The technical terms for the two forms in the fourteenth century were *ballade simplex* and *ballade duplex.* These terms provide convenient distinctions so long as we do not confuse the ballade duplex with the double ballade, which has two different texts and may be in either form. Indeed, Machaut's double and triple ballades all have the form of ballade simplex.

Use of the ballade duplex form obviously depends on the presence of a particular stanzaic structure in the text. The last section of the stanza, like the first, must subdivide into equal halves that can be sung to the same music (see AMM, No. 62). It is particularly noteworthy that the refrain of a ballade duplex does not have a separate musical setting of its own but is sung to music that has already served another line of text. Perhaps this lack of musical emphasis on the refrain was one reason for the infrequent appearance of the form in the ballades of Machaut and other fourteenth-century composers.

Even in ballades with the more common $a_o a_c bC$ form, however, the separate setting of the refrain is not always entirely new. With few exceptions, the closed ending of the first section establishes the "key" in which the piece will end, and to this tonal unity Machaut often added structural unity by introducing musical rhyme. Although the device is rare in his early ballades, the later pieces almost always end with an exact repetition of music that closed the first section. Ballade 28, *Je puis trop bien* (I can too well [compare my lady]), is exceptional in repeating only the cadential progression of the closed ending.[31] More often the repetition includes the complete closed ending and sometimes even more of the first section. One of the longest repetitions occurs in *Mes esperis* (My

---

29. No melodic refrain can be indicated in this schematic pattern because the poetic refrain is sung to the final phrase of section *b,* which has already been used for an earlier line of the stanza. The form occurs in Ballades 6, 19, 38, 40, and 41 (*Remède de Fortune*).

30. Lines 2851 and 2893.

31. HAM, No. 45.

spirit, No. 39).[32] Here, the last twelve measures of the first section return to complete the five measures that begin the setting of the refrain. Such extended settings of a single line of text illustrate a process of expansion already begun in the songs of Jehan de Lescurel and carried much further in Machaut's three- and four-part ballades. To take the most extreme example, the eight-line stanzas in the upper voices of the double ballade *Quant Theseus—Ne quier veoir* (No. 34) are spread over 119 measures of 2/4 meter. The refrain alone extends for 21 measures, with a melisma of 14 measures on the penultimate syllable, and its last 12 measures repeat the end of an even longer melisma that closes the first section of the ballade. Pieces of such length and complexity could scarcely be further removed from any association with the dance. Even the poetry sometimes seems to be nearly forgotten in the exuberance of musical development that turned the ballade into the most elaborate and extended form of polyphonic secular song in the fourteenth century.

THE RONDEAUX

Almost all of the characteristics we have observed in Machaut's ballades reappear in the twenty-one rondeaux he set to music.[33] The poetic and musical forms are different, of course, but we find the same combinations of two, three, and four voices, and the same melismatic expansion that leaves little trace of an origin in simple dance songs. In describing the musical style of Machaut's rondeaux, therefore, we need do little more than document the various ways in which they resemble his ballades.

In the matter of voice combinations, we find that two-part settings again predominate in the early part of the collection. The seven rondeaux for cantus and tenor alone occur as Nos. 2–6, 12, and 20. Two pieces, Nos. 1 and 22, add a triplum to the two-part framework, and two more add both a triplum and a contratenor (Nos. 9 and 10). The remaining ten rondeaux have the "standard" arrangement of cantus, tenor, and contratenor parts. These combinations of voices are less subject to variation in the rondeaux than in the ballades, but four pieces do appear in different arrangements in the manuscript sources.[34] In all of the rondeaux, only the cantus sings the text, and Machaut did not experiment with canonic writing or with multiple texts as he did in the

32. Gleason, EM, p. 85.
33. Both Ludwig and Schrade give 21 numbered rondeaux plus the one in the *Remède de Fortune*. Rondeau 16 is without music, however, and merely provides the clue for finding the name Isabel that is only slightly disguised in the strained rhymes on "visa bel" in the preceding Rondeau 15.
34. Nos. 7, 9, 10, and 21. In the notes on these pieces (PMC, 2 and 3), Schrade lists the different combinations of voices in various manuscripts.

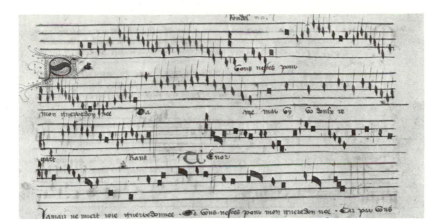

The rondeau *Se vous n'estes,* by Machaut, is a two-voiced version of AMM No. 63 (Morgan Library MS 396).

ballades. It is ironic, therefore, but perhaps typical, that Machaut's best-known composition should be the rondeau *Ma fin est mon commencement* (No. 14), the only one of all his works with retrograde motion in all parts. The manuscript sources give one melody that produces both upper voices of this rondeau. One performer reads the melody forward, while the performer who sings the text must read the melody backward. In this way, as the poem says, "My end is my beginning and my beginning, my end." The lower part, which the manuscripts label variously as tenor or contratenor, is only half as long and must be performed forward and then backward, so that it too ends with the beginning and begins with the end. As a result of these procedures, the second section of the rondeau is a retrograde repetition of the first, but with the upper voices interchanged. Machaut showed astonishing skill in achieving this playful parallel between words and music, but the piece must not be regarded as a representative work. Retrograde motion in all parts of a polyphonic complex is rare in music generally, and its appearance in this rondeau is unique in the music of Machaut.

Machaut both standardized the poetic form of the rondeau and fore-shadowed its future development. Some earlier rondeaux had lines of unequal length and number in the two sections of the refrain. Machaut abandoned this practice in favor of an eight-line rondeau with lines of equal length. Seventeen of his rondeaux with music are of this type, for which the formula *ABaAabAB* expresses the poetic form and its rhyme scheme, as well as the musical form. Rondeau 5 is unique in having groups of three four-syllable lines for each musical section. The overall form of the music remains unchanged, but the poem now has twenty-four lines arranged in eight groups, all of which use the same two rhymes in the pattern aab. Machaut's other three rondeaux, Nos. 10, 11, and 13, expand the eight-line rondeau in another way. They all add one line to the first section of the refrain and therefore must add other lines for each repeat of that section. The result is a thirteen-line rondeau that still uses only two rhymes in lines of equal length. Again the musical form remains unchanged, but the poetic form must now be expressed by another formula:

Poetic form: AB B ab AB ab b AB B

Musical form: *A* *B* *a* *A* *a* *b* *A* *B*

Later composers continued this process of expansion by adding a line to the second section of the refrain to produce a sixteen-line rondeau. By the end of the fourteenth century, this longer form had become standard for the rondeau, but the development did not stop there. Further expansion created the rondeau of twenty-one lines with a five-line refrain (divided three and two) and the rondeau of twenty-four lines with a six-line refrain. The terms *rondeau quatrain, rondeau cinquain,* and *rondeau six-ain* then came into use to identify each of these larger forms by the number of lines in the refrain.

None of these expansions affected the basic musical structure of the rondeau. Its two sections might vary in length, but they continued to be repeated in the pattern established by the old eight-line form. Machaut consistently distinguished the two sections of his rondeaux by giving the first an open ending, usually a normal cadence but on some degree of the mode other than the final. In two rondeaux, however, the last chord of the open ending is a full triad on the final instead of the empty fifths and octaves that signaled completion to fourteenth-century ears. The rondeau *Se vous n'estes pour mon guerredon née* (If you were not born to be my reward; No. 7, and AMM, No. 63) will give the modern listener a chance to adjust his own ears to this medieval subtlety.[35] Rondeau 7 also provides a characteristic example of the way a contratenor might be added to the two-voice framework established by the cantus and tenor parts.[36] Textually, too, the piece is characteristic in its use of long rhymes of several syllables that are broken up to form different words: "guerredon née," "guerredonnée" (rewarded), and "guerre donnée" (war given). Poets seem to have enjoyed increasing the considerable technical difficulty of the rondeau as a poetic form by adding to it this kind of word play. Fortunately, perhaps, the elaborate and rather forced punning is impossible to reproduce in English translation.

Apart from the parallel forms of music and poetry in the rondeau, the style and length of the musical setting appear to be independent of either the length or meaning of the text. Two of Machaut's eight-line rondeaux, Nos. 1 and 18, have very short settings, with twelve measures of 3/4 and seven measures of 3/2 respectively. On the other hand, another eight-line rondeau, No. 21, has the longest setting of all: 74 measures of

35.   The other rondeau with an open ending on a full triad is No. 11.
36.   As may be seen in AMM, No. 63, one repertory manuscript preserves Rondeau 7 with a different contratenor. Another manuscript once had an added triplum, of which only a fragment survives (see Schrade, PMC, 2 and 3, p. 127).

2/4, with melismas of more than 25 measures on the penultimate syllable of each section. It should be remembered that the number of measures in these pieces indicates only the length of the refrain. Performance of the complete text roughly quadruples that length. When all eight lines of Rondeau 21 are sung, for example, its 74 measures expand to 298. It thus becomes longer than many ballades with three stanzas of seven or eight lines. Why Machaut should have so extended some of his rondeau settings is an interesting but unanswerable question. Other composers rarely followed his lead in this direction, and on the whole the rondeau remained a shorter and less elaborate form than the *grande ballade* of four-teenth-century secular polyphony.

THE VIRELAIS

The pieces that complete the collection of Machaut's music present the curious and wholly unexpected anomaly of a return to monophonic song. Of the 33 virelais that Machaut set to music, no fewer than 25 are monophonic. Seven are in two parts, for cantus and tenor (Nos. 24, 26, and 28–32), and only one (No. 23) has both a tenor and a contratenor in addition to the cantus. The collected musical works thus end as they began, with a group of pieces that seem to look back to the older tradi-tions of the trouvères. Whether Machaut intended this arrangement as an acknowledgement of his musical ancestry or whether he merely took pleasure in its superficial symmetry we cannot say. That the symmetry was superficial becomes apparent, however, when we consider the his-torical positions of the lai and virelai in Machaut's time. The lai, as we know, had a long tradition behind it, but its history as a musical form ended with Machaut. On the other hand, the virelai did not acquire its fixed form and distinguishing name—of which Machaut disapproved—until after the beginning of the fourteenth century. There may have been no prophetic implication in Machaut's placement of the virelais at the end of his musical works, but the form did have a future as a poly-phonic secular song.

Machaut's preference for the designation *chanson baladée* instead of *virelai* may have stemmed in part from his consistent use of texts with three stanzas, as in the ballade. He may also have liked the adjective *baladée* for its implication of the origin and continued function of these songs as accompaniments for dancing. In this connection, it is interest-ing to note that the Italian ballata, with the same form as the virelai, was also a monophonic dance song that developed into an important form of fourteenth-century secular polyphony (see Chapter XVIII).

Evidence that the virelai was just emerging as an independent but not entirely fixed form can be found in Machaut's own works, which we may henceforth call virelais in the usual defiance of his wishes. Included in the collection are two pieces (Nos. 13 and 14) that do not follow the fixed forms of either the virelai or the ballade. Each of them does have three stanzas with a refrain, however, and in their poetic and musical style they resemble the simple monophonic virelais with which they appear. All of the other poems in the collection, including the six that Machaut did not set to music, display the form that we now regard as being standard for the virelai. A refrain of several lines begins the poem and then returns to conclude each of its three stanzas.[37] The stanzas themselves subdivide into three sections, of which the first two have the same form and are sung to the same melody. The third section returns to the form and melody of the refrain. Within this fixed pattern, the structure of Machaut's poems varies to a much greater degree in the virelais than in his ballades and rondeaux. The refrains, and therefore the third sections of the stanzas, range in length from three to eight lines, but the longer forms with six or more lines occur in over half of the poems. Each of the first two sections of the stanzas is shorter and usually consists of two or three lines. Further variety of poetic structure results from the characteristic use of lines of contrasting lengths combined with nearly complete freedom in the disposition of rhymes.

Machaut took full advantage of all these opportunities for creating different poetic forms within the basic structure of the virelai. He evidently liked the form of the example in the *Remède de Fortune*, for he reproduced its every detail in Virelais 24, 28, and 29.[38] The common scheme of these four pieces is as follows:

Poetry: $A_7A_7B_4B_7A_4A_7B_4$ $b_7b_7a_4$ $b_7b_7a_4$ $a_7a_7b_4b_7a_4a_7b_4$ $A_7A_7B_4B_7A_4A_7B_4$

Music: *A*   *b*   *b*   *a*   *A*

All of the other virelais differ to a greater or lesser extent in their rhyme schemes and in the lengths and number of their lines. This structural variety, which must reflect a conscious effort of the poet, makes designation of the virelai as a fixed form seem a paradox. Yet the larger formal pattern remains unchanged, however much the size and shape of its components may differ from one virelai to another. Moreover, the fixed disposition of those components determines the fixed musical form. Thus the overall form of any virelai with three stanzas can be expressed by the reduced formula *A bba A bba A bba A*.

Machaut's treatment of the virelai's musical form is not quite as standardized as we might expect. He did not change the fixed pattern of repetitions, of course, but he did follow different procedures in constructing the two musical sections and in relating those sections to each other.

---

37. Schrade's edition of the virelais is misleading in its suggestion that the refrain is sung twice between the stanzas.

38. Virelai 28 is also available in HAM, No. 46b.

One difference involves the ending of the melody for the first two parts of the stanza. In eleven of the true virelais, this melody (b) is repeated exactly with no change in its final cadence. In the other twenty virelais, the b section is provided with open and closed endings, which later composers made an almost invariable feature of the form. A more unexpected procedural difference occurs in Machaut's settings of some refrains. As a rule, both musical sections reflect the poetic structure of the text but with no internal repetitions of melodic phrases. In eight of the virelais, however, the refrain is set as a repeated melody with open and closed endings.[39] This subdivision makes the form of the first musical section correspond with the two statements of the second section $(A_oA_cb_ob_ca_oa_cA_oA_c)$. Machaut's use of this procedure seems to be independent of the poetic structure. It is true that seven of the refrains divide into formally equal halves, but others that do the same are set in the normal manner as a nonrepetitive form.[40] Moreover, in Virelai 10 (De bonté; With goodness, AMM, No. 64), the five lines of the refrain are divided three and two between the repeated sections. This kind of repetition in the first section of the virelai does not occur in Machaut's polyphonic settings or in the works of later composers. Indeed, it usually goes unmentioned in descriptions of the virelai. It is common in the Spanish Cantigas, however, and its presence in the works of Machaut is important as another indication that the French form was still in the process of becoming fixed.

Poetic and musical forms and a predominance of monophonic songs are not the only aspects of Machaut's virelais that set them apart from his ballades and rondeaux. One contrast, perhaps the most obvious, is the difference in melodic style. Many virelais are like No. 10 in being almost completely syllabic. Others introduce a few vocal ornaments of two or three notes to a syllable without losing their simple, almost folklike quality. Longer melismas occur once or twice in a small number of pieces, but they rarely extend beyond two or three measures. Even the polyphonic virelais do not stray far from this simple melodic style. Virelai 28 is characteristic in using ornaments of no more than three notes to a syllable.[41] Only Virelai 31 points toward future developments in having longer melismas that correspond with its unusually extended musical rhyme. Nowhere in the virelais do we find the spun-out phrases, the frequent and lengthy melismas that are typical of the rondeaux and later ballades.

Taken as a whole, Machaut's secular songs bring his collected musical works to a fitting close. Not only do they include some of his most attractive music, but they also represent his most original contribution to

39. In Virelais 7, 10, 12, 17–20, and 27.
40. E.g., Virelai 4, HAM, No. 46a.
41. HAM, No. 64b.

the development of musical forms and styles. Starting with the monophonic songs of the trouvères, Machaut himself created the accompanied solo song. In so doing, he developed the compositional techniques and the arrangement of vocal and instrumental parts that remained in use for more than a century. Beyond their revelation of this creative process, Machaut's songs illustrate the transformation of simple music for dancing into highly elaborated art forms. It is especially significant to note that the coexistence of all stages of this transformation rules out undeviating progress from the simplest to the most complex secular songs. Machaut apparently moved with ease from the dense four-part polyphony of the double ballade (No. 34) to the dancelike tune of the monophonic Ballade 37. Moreover, we cannot assume that the virelais belong to an earlier period than the ballades and rondeaux or than the motets, for that matter. Indeed, it is an important measure of Machaut's greatness that he could range at will between the extremes of intellectual constructivism and folklike simplicity. No other medieval composer left proof of such versatility. No other wrote with equal success in all the forms and styles of his time. Not until the beginning of the Renaissance do we find composers of comparable universality. Even then, few could match and fewer still surpass Machaut's towering achievements.

CHAPTER XVIII

The Italian Ars Nova

Italian secular polyphony suddenly appeared and flourished in the fourteenth century with no apparent antecedents. It is sometimes argued, therefore, that the term *Ars Nova* should not be applied to music that seems to have developed independently of the musical forms and the notational system that characterize the French Ars Nova. Italian music, it is true, does not form part of the new art described by Philippe de Vitry and Johannes de Muris. Moreover, it was not new in the sense of being contrasted with an older musical practice that could be called an *ars antiqua*. For this very reason, however, it was a far more radical innovation than any of the new developments in France and fully deserves to be called an *Ars Nova*.

Attempts to find the ancestry of this new polyphony in the conductus or in melismatic organum seem strained and generally lacking in credibility. A more plausible hypothesis sees the beginnings of Italian polyphony in an indigenous art of solo song with an improvised instrumental accompaniment.[1] This art has left no earlier monuments, but its existence is well documented. As we have seen in Chapter XI, the Albigensian Crusade (1209–29) drove many troubadours and jongleurs to find refuge at courts in Spain and Sicily or with members of an emerging aristocracy in northern Italy. Even before this time, moreover, the poetry of southern France had been known in Italy and emulated by Italian poets who continued to write in Provençal throughout most of the thirteenth century. Only with the coming of Dante (1265–1321) and his less well known contemporaries did Italian begin to be accepted as a proper language for lyric verse in the *dolce stil nuovo* (sweet new style). Strongly influenced by the forms and spirit of troubadour poetry, this new style was cultivated by a host of fourteenth-century poets of whom Petrarch (1304–74) is deservedly the most famous. Through the works of these poets, then, as well as through many literary references to music, we can trace a continuing tradition of monophonic song that

1. K. von Fischer, "On the Technique, Origin, and Evolution of Italian Trecento Music," MQ, 47 (1961), pp. 41–57.

Detail from *The Dormition and Assumption of the Virgin* by Fra Angelico (1387–1455) showing the angel musicians (Isabella Stewart Gardner Museum, Boston).

overlapped with the sudden blossoming of Italian secular polyphony, a blossoming that coincides with what literary and cultural historians generally regard as the beginning of the Italian Renaissance.

Rather than concern itself with conjectural antecedents, the present chapter shall deal with the actual music of the *trecento* (literally, the "three hundreds"), the Italian way of designating the fourteenth century. Instead of a collection of music, however, the earliest surviving document that deals with Italian polyphony is a treatise by Marchettus of Padua with the fanciful title *Pomerium artis musicae mensuratae* (Orchard-Garden of the Art of Measured Music). Although monophonic songs were being written in measured notation in the fourteenth century, the phrase *measured music* in the title of a treatise ordinarily implied a concern with polyphony. Moreover, the *Pomerium* was a promised sequel to Marchettus's first treatise, the *Lucidarium in arte musicae planae,* an "Explanation" of the art of plain or unmeasured music (plainchant). The dating of these two treatises has been the subject of much discussion, but it is now established that the *Lucidarium* was completed in the years 1317–18 and the *Pomerium* shortly thereafter, probably by 1319 and certainly no later than 1326.[2] The exaggerated concern over this dat-

2.   N. Pirrotta, "Marchettus de Padua and the Italian Ars Nova," MD, 9 (1955), p. 60 ff.

ing arose in large part from an effort to prove that the Italian system of measured notation described by Marchettus was independent of the French system and could not have been influenced by the French Ars Nova treatises. In reality, the *Pomerium* itself provides sufficient and more reliable evidence for judging the truth of these assertions. Marchettus cites Franco of Cologne on a number of occasions, and his comparisons of Italian and French procedures—sometimes with a stated preference for the latter—show that he was by no means ignorant of contemporary French principles of notation. Whether those principles had yet been formulated by Philippe de Vitry and Johannes de Muris is of little importance. Despite some areas of similarity between the two systems, Italian notation quite obviously was based on different principles and followed different procedures than the French. Moreover, the Italian system introduced mensural combinations unknown in French notation. Because these notational differences gave Italian polyphony a new and distinctive rhythmic style, it is important to discuss the principles of Italian notation before considering Italian composers and their music.

THE ITALIAN NOTATIONAL SYSTEM

Although no historical connection can be proved, Italian notation appears to have branched off from the procedures characteristic of Pierre de la Croix and the *Roman de Fauvel*. At any rate, the Italians continued to use the dot of division to set off groups of semibreves that equaled the value of a breve. In French notation, as we have seen, the different values of these semibreves were determined by rule until the treatises of Vitry and Muris established the principles of using semibreves and minims (◆ and ↓) in the four combinations of time and prolation. The dot of division then became unnecessary except in a few special instances, and French music was free to develop its flexible and highly complex rhythmic style. In Italian notation, on the other hand, dots of division remained an essential feature and functioned in almost the same way as modern barlines. They proved to be even more restrictive, however, for they severely limited, when they did not entirely eliminate, the possibility of tied notes or syncopation across the barline. It was undoubtedly such restraints that eventually led Italian composers to adopt the principles of French notation in a revolt against the tyranny of the barline some five hundred years in advance of the twentieth century. In the beginning, however, the Italian notational system took the breve as the unit of measure and then classified the mensurations in a series of three "divisions" according to the number of smaller notes within the breve (Example XVIII–1).

Example XVIII–1: *The Divisions of Italian Notation*

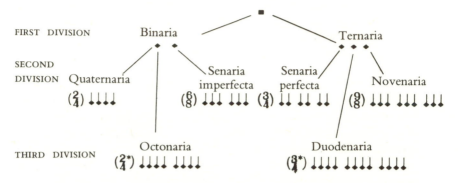

The similarities between Italian and French mensurations are obvious enough, but the differences call for some comment. The binary and ternary forms of the first division parallel the French concept of imperfect and perfect time but are rarely used alone. Normally they are further subdivided into one of the second or third divisions, indicated in the manuscripts by their initial letters: *q, si* or *i, sp* or *p, n, o,* and *d.* Although the four forms of the second division correspond with Vitry's four combinations of time and prolation, Italian composers used them much less often than the two forms of the third division, which have no counterpart in French notation. Octonaria and duodenaria are not merely subdivisions of quaternaria and senaria perfecta, which could have been obtained by the use of semiminims, nor are they simply combinations of two or three units of quaternaria. Instead, they are independent mensurations, best transcribed as 2*/4 and 3*/4, with the asterisks to distinguish them from the same meters in the second division.[3] Minims in the third division thus become sixteenth notes instead of eighths; breves still equal a full measure (𝅗𝅥 or 𝅗𝅥.); and the semibreve serves for all values in between. A later development removed this ambiguity of the Italian system by introducing the French concept of mood in the notation of octonaria and duodenaria. Now the long becomes the unit of measure; breves equal quarter notes; semibreves, eighths. That this more precise notation did not change the musical effect is proved by a few instances in which the same piece is notated in the two different ways in different manuscripts.[4] Nevertheless, modern editors usually distinguish the new manner of notating octonaria and duodenaria by using the signature 2 × 1*/4 and 3 × 1*/4.

The need for distinguishing mensurations of the third division arises from their proportional relationship to mensurations of the second. In this latter division, as in French notation, minims have the same value in

3.   Pirrotta introduced the system of signatures used here in MFCI (see Vol. 1, p. ii).
4.   In MFCI, 1, No. 9, Pirrotta gives three versions of a madrigal in duodenaria, of which two are notated in the old style and one in the new. See also Nos. 3, 12, and 14.

all four mensurations. They also maintain a constant value within the third division, but now they move at a faster pace in a slower tempo. One measure of octonaria, for example, equals a measure and a half of quaternaria, and four minims occupy the place of three. To put it another way, the quarter note of 2★/4 and 3★/4 equals the dotted quarter of 6/8 and 9/8. Numerous Italian pieces confirm this relationship by introducing measures of octonaria or duodenaria in one part against measures of senaria imperfecta or novenaria in the other.[5] Distinctive time signatures for the third division thus indicate the proportional relationship that should also apply when all voices change from one mensuration to another, as they frequently do in Italian music.

Although these tempo relationships may have been somewhat unstable in the formative stages of Italian polyphony and its notation, Marchettus's comparison of the Italian and French manners of interpreting a series of undifferentiated semibreves makes it clear that the tempo equivalence of duodenaria with novenaria and octonaria with senaria imperfecta formed part of the oldest Italian practice. The description in the *Pomerium* is so precise that a composite example showing the differences between the two manners can easily be compiled (Example XVIII–2).[6] The rules that govern the two notational systems need not concern us here, but the contrast of rhythmic style that results from the Italian interpretation is readily apparent. Marchettus himself was aware of this contrast and of its national origins. He proposed that when the French interpretation was desired the letter *g* (for *gallica*) should be used as a sign "because we had this division of imperfect time from the French." Clearly the Italians—or Marchettus—could have adopted the French manner had they so desired.[7] Instead, they showed a decided preference for the mensurations of the third division—octonaria and duodenaria—which gave their music a rhythmic style peculiarly its own.

Example XVIII–2: *French and Italian "Manners" of Reading Groups of Semibreves (After Marchettus)*

ITALIAN

FRENCH

5. E.g., the first piece cited in fn. 4 above. See Ch. XIX, p. 482 and Example XIX–5.
6. For part of the *Pomerium* in English with the examples from which Example XVIII–2 is compiled, see Strunk, SR, pp. 168–69.
7. Pirrotta, MFCI, 2, Nos. 23 and 28, are two pieces from *Rs* with the indication *s.g.* (*senaria gallica*). No. 29 alternates between *s.y.* (*senaria ytalica*) and *g*. For a facsimile of No. 28, see Apel, NPM, p. 383.

THE ROSSI CODEX AND MUSIC IN NORTHERN ITALY

The earliest extant collection of Italian secular polyphony is the Vatican manuscript Rossi 215 (*Rs*), now a fragment containing twenty-nine pieces, of which a few are incomplete. The recent discovery of four additional folios of the Rossi Codex raises this total to thirty-seven pieces. All are anonymous, but concordances in later manuscripts establish the authorship of two pieces by "Piero" and two by Giovanni da Firenze, composers whom we shall shortly meet again.[8] Despite the general anonymity of its contents, the Rossi Codex clearly originated in northern Italy and is believed to preserve the repertory of a musical circle connected with Alberto della Scala in the years between 1330 and 1340–45. Alberto was a member of the Scaliger family, the elder son of the famous Can Grande della Scala, Prince of Verona, and patron of Dante. Even more than his father, Alberto was a patron and lover of art, literature, and music. "Frail and very impatient of labor and discomfort,"[9] he preferred to live in Padua—which the Scaligeri also ruled until 1337—and to leave the burden of government in Verona to his younger brother Mastino. Numerous aspects of the songs in the Rossi Codex seem to confirm its connection with Alberto and the city of Padua. The language of the texts betrays the influence of the local dialect, and the poetic forms correspond with descriptions given by Antonio da Tempo, a poet and native Paduan who dedicated a treatise on vernacular poetry to Alberto della Scala in 1332. Two poems mention Iguane or Euguane, nymphs who were supposed to live in hills near Padua still known as the Euganean Hills (*Colli Euganei*). One poem may even be related to the Scaligeri themselves. It speaks of a brother (Mastino?) who leaves the beautiful castle of Peschiera—built on the south shore of Lake Garda by Can Grande in 1328—to seek his elder (Alberto?).[10] The musical notation of the Rossi Codex, finally, is closer to that described by Marchettus of Padua than in any other source of Italian polyphony. This must be due in part to the age of *Rs,* but it adds one more bit of evidence to support the suggestion that Padua and the court of Alberto della Scala played a primary role in the early development and diffusion of Italian polyphony.

Although its origins remain obscure, the Rossi Codex sets the stage

8.   A transcription of *Rs* (without the eight newly found madrigals) is available in Pirrotta, MFCI, 2, Nos. 9–33. The two pieces by Piero are Nos. 2 and 8 in the same volume. Those of Giovanni da Firenze are Nos. 8 and 9 in Vol. 1. For a list of the other pieces, see W. T. Marrocco, "The newly-discovered Ostiglia Pages of the Vatican Rossi Codex 215. . . ," AcM, 39 (1967), pp. 84–91.

9.   From an eighteenth-century history of Verona quoted in Pirrotta, "Marchettus," p. 67.

10.   Pirrotta, MFCI, 2, No. 12. For more historical details, see Pirrotta's Forewords to Vols. 1 and 2, and pp. 67–68 of the article cited in fn. 2 above.

for the flowering of secular polyphony that was soon to take place in northern Italy, particularly at the courts of the Visconti in Milan and the Scaligeri in Verona. Of the thirty-seven pieces that have been preserved, one is a rare example of an Italian rondeau (*rondello*). The rest of the repertory presents for the first time the three forms of secular song in the Italian Ars Nova. Twenty-nine madrigals and two cacce are polyphonic, while five ballate are monophonic songs. Both the relative importance of these forms and their musical styles changed considerably in the course of the fourteenth century, but we may describe them here because the Rossi Codex marks the beginning of their recorded history.

THE MADRIGAL

As far as we know, the first form of Italian secular poetry to receive polyphonic settings was the madrigal. The derivation of this name has been the subject of much discussion and disagreement since the earliest references to the form. Writing in 1313, Francesco da Barberino used the spelling *matricale,* apparently with the implication that the poetry was in the vernacular or mother tongue. Antonio da Tempo in 1332 derived the name *mandriale* from *mandria* ("herd" or "sheep-fold") to designate a rustic kind of pastoral poem. This etymology, no less famous than arbitrary, cannot be accepted, but it does indicate the pastoral character of many early madrigal poems. Other and later madrigals cover a wide range of subject matter, from the amorous to the moralizing and satiric. Moreover, the poetic form appears to be a wholly Italian invention. It seems probable, therefore, that the name does derive from *matricale* and that *madrigale* and other variant spellings all refer to the same thing—one of the earliest forms of a distinctively Italian poetry.

POETIC AND MUSICAL FORMS OF THE MADRIGAL

At the beginning of the madrigal's history, its poetic form was perhaps even more variable than the spelling of its name. The basic form consisted of a varying number of three-line stanzas, or *terzetti,* followed by a *ritornello* of one or two lines. The number of ritornelli might also vary, however, as might their placement. A few texts have no ritornello; others have one after each terzetto; still others have two at the end. Some early pieces even have texts in other poetic forms but are usually classified as madrigals because of their musical form and style. In all of these forms, including true madrigals, further variety results from different combinations of rhyme schemes and line lengths. With regard to the latter, it should be noted, Italian poets showed such a strong prefer-

A page from the Squarcialupi Codex containing the madrigal *Ita se n'era star nel paradiso* and a portrait of its composer, Vincentino de Arimino (Florence, Biblioteca Laurenziana).

ence for eleven-syllable lines that modern scholars indicate them by capital letters in analyzing poetic forms. Lower-case letters then identify shorter, "broken" lines, usually of seven syllables. This use of capitals in analyses of Italian poetry must not be confused with their quite different use to indicate poetic and musical refrains.

The standardized form that gradually emerged as the fourteenth century progressed consisted of two or three terzetti followed by a single two-line ritornello. Only eleven-syllable lines were used throughout the poem, and the rhyme scheme too became almost invariable: ABB CDD EE or ABB CDD EFF GG. Settings of madrigal texts reflect this poetic form by providing two separate sections of music, one that is repeated for each terzetto and another for the ritornello, which often contrasts with the first section by being in a different mensuration.

The resulting musical form of a complete madrigal may thus be expressed in letters as *aab* or *aaab*. This simplified representation of the standardized madrigal should neither lead us to forget the existence of variant forms nor be taken as an indication that the madrigal is similar, or in any way related, to the French ballade and chanson forms. To do the latter is to ignore the entirely different poetic forms of ballade and madrigal as well as the equally different structure and function of the musical sections in the two national forms. For the ballade, it will be remembered, the overall form of a single stanza is a_oa_cbC. If the music for each line of the stanza is represented by a letter, the form of a typical seven-line stanza becomes *ababcdE*. In the madrigal, on the other hand, each line of the stanza (terzetto) normally receives its own setting, often a unit complete in itself with a strong concluding cadence followed by rests or dividing barlines. The first section, therefore, consists of three subsections in an *abc* pattern. The two-line ritornello may be treated in different ways. In some madrigals both lines are sung to the same music; in others, each line has its own setting. If, then, we indicate the music for each line of a complete madrigal, we get the following patterns:

Terzetti	Ritornello
abc abc (abc)	*dd* or *de*

Comparison of these patterns with that of the ballade, which must be tripled to indicate the complete form, makes it obvious that the madrigal is no more indebted to the French secular song for its musical than for its poetic form.

Given the indigenous nature of the madrigal as a poetic and musical form, it is no surprise to find that its musical style was equally independent of foreign influence. The most obvious characteristic of that style is a two-part polyphony in which both voices sing the text. A further characteristic is the alternation of extended melismas with shorter passages that are nearly or wholly syllabic. These obvious aspects of the madrigal have led to the assumption that it derived from the conductus. The improbability of this ancestry has already been suggested at the beginning of the present chapter. It is difficult to believe that the long-neglected conductus could have been twice "revived" in such different styles as the rondeaux of Adam de la Hale and the madrigals of the Rossi Codex. The stylistic contrast between madrigals and the few, nearly contemporary Italian settings of hymns, sequences, and processional songs in conductus style is equally striking, as the excerpts in Example XVIII–3 show. The first excerpt, dating from around 1300, has been claimed as "concrete evidence" of a connection between the conductus and the madrigal.[11] That the second excerpt from an early madrigal differs radically in style is indisputable.

In addition to the obvious contrasts of meter and melodic character, Example XVIII–3 illustrates more subtle differences that distinguish the madrigal from the conductus.[12] In the normal conductus, the voices cover the same general range, move largely in contrary motion, and hence must frequently cross. As a result of the note-against-note or neume-against-neume counterpoint, moreover, the rhythmic patterns of the voices in a conductus are similar, when not identical. To all of

11. NOHM, 3, p. 42. Ex. 19 is a longer excerpt from this "concrete evidence." A comparison of this piece and the corroborating Ex. 20 (p. 44) with the later Ex. 22 (p. 55), which is presented as a "typical" madrigal, will reveal the radical differences between the two styles.

12. See the article cited in fn. 1 above.

Example XVIII–3: *An Early Madrigal Contrasted with Its Supposed*
Link to the Conductus

a. BONAIUTUS DE CASENTINO, FROM VATICAN MS. LAT. 2854 (C. 1300)

b. *Quando i oselli canta* (**Rs 5**)

a. May this treatment of the body yield the fruit of spiritual love and joy.
b. When the birds sing, shepherdesses go into the open country.

these aspects of conductus style, the early madrigal offers exact oppo-
sites. Its two voices may overlap in range, but they are clearly distinguished as upper and lower parts that rarely cross or remain crossed for
more than a few notes. Parallel motion in unisons, fifths, or octaves is
common and may occur in note-against-note counterpoint or disguised
by ornamental figures. Such figures are particularly characteristic of the

upper voice and make it generally more elaborate and melismatic than the lower, which tends to move more slowly, in longer note values. In many instances, repeated notes in the lower voice suggest that sustained notes have been broken up to accommodate the addition of a text. Another distinguishing feature of the madrigal is its decided preference for cadential progressions in which the tenor rises to the final and the harmonic interval of a third contracts to a unison. In the most common cadences of contemporary French polyphony—and of the older conductus—the tenor descends to the final. Intervals of a third therefore expand to fifths, and fifths or sixths expand to octaves. The divergent form of Italian cadences is but one more indication that the traditional process of adding voices to a tenor foundation did not provide a starting point for Italian polyphony. Only the hypothesis that the madrigal developed from secular monophony with an improvised accompaniment satisfactorily accounts for all of its idiomatic features. Conversion of the improvised instrumental part into a composed vocal melody scarcely disguised that part's function as an accompaniment to the more florid upper voice. The texture became a bit more homogeneous, perhaps, but the idiomatic features persisted. Indeed, they never disappeared entirely from this most typical form of Italian polyphony in the fourteenth century.

THE CACCIA

The second form of Italian secular polyphony to appear in the Rossi Codex is the caccia. Questions as to the origin of the form are even more complex and difficult to answer than for the madrigal. *Caccia,* of course, is merely the Italian equivalent of *chace,* and both terms designate canonic technique. Nevertheless, structural differences between the French and Italian forms seem to deny any direct relationship between the two. The chace, it will be remembered, is normally a three-part vocal canon. The typical caccia is also in three-part polyphony, but only the two upper parts form a vocal canon with words. The third and lowest part is a tenor in free counterpoint—that is, noncanonic—and usually without text. We may thus describe the polyphonic texture of a caccia as a two-voice canon supported by a presumably instrumental tenor. This texture occurs in nineteen of the twenty-six canonic pieces in the Italian repertory.[13] In addition to the differing structure of the polyphony, a formal aspect of the caccia distinguishes it from the chace and relates it to the madrigal. With only five exceptions, Italian cacce subdivide in two separate sections, of which the second is a ritornello. The first and longer section is always canonic, with the second voice fol-

13.   As with the madrigal, variant musical and textual forms of the caccia will be discussed in a supplemental essay.

lowing the first at a rather long time interval. The treatment of the ritornelli is more various. Slightly more than half are also canonic, but because of their brevity the time interval between the first and second voices is generally shorter than in the first sections. In most of the non-canonic ritornelli, the two upper voices begin together with the tenor, but a few make a pretense of being canonic by beginning with imitative entries, which may even include the tenor. The result is not a true canon, however, because each voice lapses into free counterpoint to accompany the next entry of the opening phrase.[14]

CACCIA TEXTS

In both subject matter and form, the texts of cacce show even greater variety than does the musical treatment of the ritornello. Fifteen of the twenty-six texts are descriptive, with dialogue and exclamations that provide an opportunity for programmatic effects in the musical setting. Italian poets and composers were no slower than the French in connecting the musical technique of the caccia with the hunt, but only seven pieces actually depict hunting scenes. The other eight concern themselves with such varied subjects as fishing and boating expeditions, a fire, market scenes, and walks in the country. All of these descriptive texts are cast in long stanzas with no fixed poetic form except that they usually begin and end with couplets of eleven-syllable lines. Lines of this length may also occur at irregular intervals among shorter lines of dialogue and the cries of the participating actors. In setting these texts, composers sometimes continued the canon without interruption through the final couplet, but more often that couplet forms the text of the separate ritornello. Some cacce have two or even more stanzas that require repetition of the first section before the ritornello, and a few have two stanzas with a ritornello after each. Performance of the complete text in these pieces results in *aab* or *abab* forms that reinforce the suggestion of a relationship between the caccia and the madrigal.

This relationship becomes even more obvious in cacce with texts in the poetic form of the madrigal. Pieces of this sort are often called *canonic madrigals* to distinguish them from the "true" caccia that uses dialogue and exclamatory cries for dramatic representation. With respect to both subject matter and poetic form, however, the distinction between the two groups tends to become blurred. One of the early cacce, *Con dolce brama* (With sweet longing), depicts a sailing expedition, yet its

---

14. See, for example, W. T. Marrocco, *Fourteenth-Century Italian Cacce*, Nos. 14 and 15. The ritornello of the latter is published in NOHM, 3, p. 59 (Ex. 24), where it is erroneously described as a triple canon. It may be compared with a true three-voice canon in the ritornello of Landini's *De, dimmi tu* (Alas, tell me), Marrocco, *Cacce*, No. 10, and Schrade, PM, 4, p. 216.

The caccia *Or qua conpagni* attributed to Piero, from the Rossi Codex (Rome, Vatican Library).

text is cast as a madrigal with five terzetti and no ritornello.[15] On the other hand, texts that tell of a hunt without attempting a realistic portrayal occur in two of the so-called canonic madrigals, *Per larghi prati* (Through open fields) and *Nel bosco senza foglie* (In the leafless wood).[16] The composer of both these cacce was Giovanni da Firenze, a member of the first generation of known Italian composers. His contemporary and compatriot Gherardello da Firenze, it is curious to note, set a number of similar hunting texts as normal (that is, noncanonic) madrigals.[17] Gherardello also composed one of the best-known, because most widely reprinted, of all the hunting cacce, *Tosto che l'alba* (As soon as dawn).[18] A third member of this first generation, Jacopo da Bologna, provided yet another illustration of the close connection between the madrigal and the caccia by writing an example of each form with the same text, *Oselleto selvazo* (Little wild bird). The poem itself is a madrigal that has no connection with hunting. Instead, it heaps scorn on the multitude of unskilled composers who set themselves up as the equals of Philippe (de Vitry) and Marchettus (of Padua).[19] To this already considerable variety of textual form and subject matter we may add one caccia, *Dal traditor* (From the traitor), that is a setting of a ballata and another, *Quan ye voy* (When I see), that is a French chanson![20] From the foregoing discussion it appears impossible to claim that the depiction of

15. Marrocco, *Cacce,* No. 6, and Pirrotta, MFCI, 2, No. 7.

16. Marrocco, *Cacce,* Nos. 20 and 15, and Pirrotta, MFCI, 1, Nos. 19 and 20.

17. See, for example, Pirrotta, MFCI, 1, Nos. 24, 25, 27, and 29.

18. HAM, No. 52; Marrocco, *Cacce,* No. 25; Pirrotta, MFCI, 1, No. 33.

19. For a reading of the text that proposes a third *maestro,* Fioran or Floran, see Pirrotta, MFCI, 4, p. ii. The same volume contains the two pieces (Nos. 17 and 31). See also Marrocco, *The Music of Jacopo da Bologna,* pp. 78 and 111; and PM, 6, Nos. 18 and 20a & b.

20. Marrocco, *Cacce,* Nos. 8 and 22; Pirrotta, MFCI, 5, No. 6, and 2, No. 44.

hunting scenes gave the caccia its name. Instead, as with the French chace, the name designated a musical technique—the canon—that might be and was used to set poems of widely differing form and content. We may therefore identify all canonic pieces in the Italian repertory as cacce with the same justification that Machaut had for identifying the canonic stanzas of a lai as chaces.

THE BALLATA

The third form of fourteenth-century Italian secular song, the ballata, also makes its first appearance with music in the Rossi Codex, but as a monophonic rather than a polyphonic composition. The Italian ballata is not to be confused with the French ballade, although both began as dance songs. By the middle of the fourteenth-century, however, the French ballade had become an elaborate polyphonic song with only its name to suggest its humble origin. The ballata, which still retained its close connection with the dance, was the contemporary and counterpart in both form and function of the French chanson balladée or virelai. An opening *ripresa* (refrain) was followed by a stanza that began with two *piedi* (feet), each of which was sung to the same new music. The stanza then concluded with a *volta* (turning) that used the music of the refrain with new words. Theoretically, the ripresa returned after each stanza of a ballata, but these repetitions may have been omitted in performance. In this case, the theoretical form of the ballata with several stanzas—*A bba A bba A bba A*—would have become *A bba bba bba A* in practice. In the latter part of the fourteenth century, however, the great majority of ballate have only one stanza and a refrain in the form *AbbaA*.

With regard to the sectional divisions of both its text and music, the Italian ballata may be called a fixed form; but, as in the French virelai, the number of poetic lines in each section may vary from one ballata to another. A few poems have only one line for each section. More often, the ripresa and volta have three or four lines, while each piede has two or sometimes three. Rhyme schemes and line lengths are also variable, but the ballata normally makes one use of rhyme that is not characteristic of the virelai. In most cases, the rhymes of the volta link its first line to the preceding piedi and its last line to the ripresa. The following rhyme scheme of a ballata with two stanzas illustrates this typical procedure:

ABBA cd cd deea ABBA fg fg ghha ABBA[21]

That the linking continues through stanzas with different rhymes seems to indicate that the poets, at least, expected each volta to lead into a repetition of the ripresa.

21. Pirrotta, MFCI, 5, No. 19. All lines have seven syllables. Capital letters in the scheme given here indicate the refrain.

In musical style, ballate differ from madrigals and cacce as much as they do in poetic and musical form. Not only do the two sections of the ballate tend to be nearly equal in length, but they lack the contrasts of mensuration that usually distinguish ritornelli in the other forms. Perhaps the most obvious difference, however, lies in the less elaborate melodic style of the ballata. Melismas are present in most ballate, but they are generally shorter, fewer in number, and much less florid than in the madrigal. This greater simplicity undoubtedly reflects both the origin of the ballata as a dance song and its continued fulfillment of that function in the fourteenth century. Whether or not the later polyphonic ballate were also sung and danced, they generally retained this simpler and more restrained melodic style.

The question of French influence on the origin of the ballata is difficult to resolve. Although the ballata and virelai have the same poetic and musical forms, the same holds true for some Italian laude and many Spanish cantigas. As we have seen, moreover, the virelai only came into its own as an independent musical form in the works of Machaut. Many of his monophonic virelais may well be contemporary with or even later than the ballate of the Rossi Codex. We shall probably be safe in assuming, therefore, that the ballata, like the madrigal and caccia, was not dependent on French models.

In the course of its development, the ballata takes on an importance never enjoyed by its French counterpart. Both in numbers and in musical interest, the virelai remained subordinate to the rondeau and especially to the grande ballade throughout the fourteenth century. The ballata, on the other hand, captured the attention of Italian composers to such an extent that it almost completely replaced the older forms of secular polyphony.[22] It is quite clear that the three forms of Italian secular song, though they may seem of equal interest to us, were decidedly unequal in importance to fourteenth-century composers.

LATER SOURCES OF ITALIAN POLYPHONY

Several decades separate the Rossi Codex—presumably copied before 1350—from the later sources of Italian polyphony. In addition to a number of fragmentary manuscripts, these sources include five or six large collections that, when taken together, contain almost the entire repertory of trecento music.[23] The dating of these collections has been a

22. In a catalogue of the Italian repertory, Kurt von Fischer lists 423 ballate, 177 madrigals, and only 25 cacce. The last figure does not include the canonic ballata. See K. von Fischer, *Studien zur italienischen Musik des Trecento und frühen Quattrocento* (Bern, 1956), pp. 18–73 and 82. Marrocco later discovered the eight additional madrigals from *Rs;* see fn 8 above.

23. They are listed, with summary descriptions of their contents, in Fischer, *Studien,* pp. 83 and 88 ff.

matter of much discussion, but they appear to have been copied at various times between 1380 and 1420 or a little later. The latest and by far the largest manuscript is the famous Squarcialupi Codex, so named because it belonged to the Florentine organist Antonio Squarcialupi (1417–80). It seems doubtful that it was prepared for or by Squarcialupi himself. The arrangement and scope of the collection evidence an antiquarian's interest in assembling music of the past, and the lavish illumination suggests that a wealthy aristocrat's library was its intended destination. A number of factors account for the importance of the Squarcialupi Codex. Its versions of the music are not always the most accurate, but its 352 pieces include many that are found in no other source. A miniature of each composer heads the collection of his works, and the composers themselves are presented in nearly exact chronological order. As most of the composers had been long dead, the miniatures cannot be actual portraits, but they do offer bits of information, such as membership in religious orders. The chronological arrangement of the manuscript is much more significant and is supported by information gleaned from other musical as well as historical and literary sources. It thus becomes possible to establish the historical position of Italian composers with some degree of certainty and therefore to trace the growth and development of Italian secular polyphony from its beginnings around 1330 to its unexpected disappearance in the second and third decades of the fifteenth century.

THE FIRST GENERATION OF TRECENTO COMPOSERS

The first group of composers whose names are known to us includes Maestro Piero, Jacopo da Bologna, and Giovanni da Firenze, who is also called Giovanni da Cascia, after a town near Florence. Despite the diversity of their birthplaces, the music of these men connects them with the two most powerful ruling families of northern Italy, the Visconti in Milan and the Scaligeri in Verona and Padua. Piero and Giovanni are each represented by two pieces in the Rossi Codex and presumably were with Alberto della Scala in Padua before going to Verona. Jacopo set two texts that praise Luchino Visconti and give his name in acrostics. One is the madrigal *Lo lume vostro* (Your light), and the other, *Lux purpurata radiis* (Light with rosy rays), one of the rare examples of a Latin motet by an Italian trecento composer. Another madrigal by Jacopo, *O in Italia,* celebrates the birth of twins to Isabella and Luchino and gives the date as August 4, 1346. Luchino died, suspecting that Isabella had poisoned him, on January 24, 1349; apparently Jacopo then moved to Verona, where he remained at least until the death of Mastino della Scala in 1351. In Verona, all three men engaged in a musical contest that involved settings of what amounts to a madrigal cycle. Several texts refer to a lady whose name, Anna, is hidden in the poetry but is revealed by repetitions of its two syllables in the musical settings. Later the affair turned sour, and the lady—no longer named—becomes a venomous serpent to the rejected lover. The cycle ends with a reply from the lady herself, for which Giovanni da Firenze supplied the musical setting.[24] This group of related madrigals is not the only connection that links the three composers. Giovanni and Piero set the same caccia text, *Con brachi assai* (With plenty of hounds), that speaks of hunting on the banks of the river Adda near Milan. In another pair of pieces, both Piero and Jacopo set a madrigal in praise of Margherita. Contemporary ladies of this name in Milan and Verona include a mistress of Luchino Visconti and an illegitimate daughter of Mastino della Scala.

After the deaths of Mastino and Alberto della Scala in 1351 and 1352 respectively, we find no further trace of Piero and Giovanni da Firenze. Jacopo da Bologna may have continued to be active somewhat longer. None of his works can be assigned a later date with any certainty, but the triple madrigal *Aquil' altera* (Proud eagle) suggests a possible connection with the coronation of Emperor Charles IV in Milan on January 6, 1355. By that time it appears that the importance of Milan and Verona as musical centers had begun to decline. Secular polyphony continued to be written and performed, but the earliest composers, Giovanni and Jacopo in particular, remained the most significant contributors to the music of the northern courts. In the second half of the fourteenth century, the center of activity shifted southward to Florence, which then took the lead in the further development of Italian secular song.

Before we turn to the Florentine composers, the music of our northern triumvirate calls for some comment. All three men concentrated on the typically Italian forms of the madrigal and caccia. Piero and Giovanni, indeed, composed only in these forms, and only in their cacce did they employ three-voice polyphony. All of their madrigals are for two voices that normally sing in simultaneous style. Of the three composers, Piero appears to have been the least prolific. He may have written more than two pieces in the Rossi Codex, but his name is attached to no more than four madrigals and four cacce in later sources. Two of the cacce are for two canonic voices without a tenor, while the other two have the normal free tenor below the canon. Further evidence of Piero's interest in canonic technique comes from his use of it in the ritornelli of two madrigals. Thus the works of Piero significantly represent the principal stages in the development of the caccia from the madrigal.[25] In the

24. Pirrotta, MFCI, 1, No. 5. For other pieces in the cycle, see Vol. 1, Nos. 3, 11, and 14 (Giovanni); Vol. 2, Nos. 1 and 4 (Piero); and Vol. 4, Nos. 12, 15, 18, 22, and 26 (Jacopo).
25. Pirrotta, MFCI, 2, p. i. Piero's works are Nos. 1–8 in this volume. Nos. 1 and 3 are madrigals with canonic ritornelli.

works of Giovanni, the separation of the two forms is complete. Musically, if not textually, his sixteen two-voice madrigals are quite distinct from his three cacce with two canonic voices above an instrumental tenor.[26] *Nel mezzo a sei paon* (In the midst of six peacocks) is typical of Giovanni's madrigals, which tend to be more fully developed, with more elaborate melodies and longer melismas, than those in the Rossi Codex.[27] It is in these works, as well as in the two-voice pieces of Jacopo, that the madrigal comes of age as an art form.

The compositions of Jacopo da Bologna are both more numerous and more varied in scope and style than those of Piero and Giovanni da Firenze. Whether this is the result of a more adventurous spirit, a longer life, or a greater knowledge of French music is difficult to say. Of Jacopo's 34 pieces known to us, 24 are two-voice madrigals and 3 are cacce. The remaining seven pieces include the Latin motet in honor of Luchino Visconti mentioned above, a lauda for two voices above a textless tenor, and five three-voice madrigals. In four of these madrigals, all voices sing the same text, but one has a different text for each voice. What prompted Jacopo to make these departures from the normal two-voice style of the madrigal remains unknown, but they were not to win wide acceptance among later composers. Only 18 of 185 madrigals that have been preserved are for three voices, and only Francesco Landini wrote another triple madrigal.

One aspect of Jacopo's style calls for special notice here. In most of his madrigals, as in those of Piero and Giovanni da Firenze, both voices sing the text simultaneously, despite the rhythmic and melodic contrasts between the upper and lower parts. In a few cases, however, the voices enter one after the other so that they sing part or all of a poetic line at different times. A somewhat tentative step in this direction may be seen in *Non al so amante* (Not to her lover), the only contemporary setting of a poem by Petrarch.[28] A more thorough and consistent application of the technique occurs in Jacopo's well-known madrigal *Fenice fu'* (I was a phoenix).[29] Here, only the first line of the ritornello is set entirely in simultaneous style. For each of the other four lines, the voices enter separately but return to simultaneous style near the middle of the line. Two of these entries give different melodies to each voice, but the second and fifth lines begin with melodic imitation, which continues in the second line until the beginning of the melisma (Example XVIII–4). The departure from simultaneous style and the use of imitation, perhaps reflecting the influence of the caccia, were innovations that later composers of madrigals would not ignore.

26. Giovanni's compositions are Nos. 2–20 in Pirrotta, MFCI, 1.
27. HAM, No. 50.
28. Ibid., No. 49.
29. Pirrotta, MFCI, 4, No. 5. For others in this volume that depart from simultaneous style, see Nos. 3, 6, 13, and 15 (Marrocco, *Jacopo,* pp. 36, 40, 45, 69, and 74).

Example XVIII–4: *Second Line of* Fenice fu',
by Jacopo da Bologna

And now I am transformed into a turtledove.

With the exception of Jacopo's one lauda, *Nel mio parlar di questa donn'eterna* (In my speaking of this eternal lady), no other texts in ballata form were given polyphonic settings by the first generation of composers in northern Italy.[30] It remained for Florentine composers in the latter half of the fourteenth century to make the ballata the predominant form of Italian secular polyphony. In other respects, however, the composers working in the North set Italian music on the path it was to follow throughout the trecento. Jacopo da Bologna in particular, with his experimental and somewhat eclectic style, pointed the way to future developments. In his works more than in any others, we find the first traces of that French influence by which native Italian music would be gradually changed and eventually overwhelmed.

THE FIRST GENERATION OF FLORENTINE COMPOSERS

We know almost nothing about the dates and lives of the early Florentine composers, but the oldest, Gherardello da Firenze, must have been about the same age as Jacopo da Bologna and Giovanni da Firenze. Unlike Giovanni, however, Gherardello was not a traveller and did not seek his fortune in the North. Instead, he remained "faithful to a circumscribed, localized tradition, hardly known outside Florence."[31] Gherardello died about 1362–64. Two of his slightly younger compatriots, Lorenzo Masini and Donato da Firenze (or da Cascia), appar-

30.   The ballata *Io son un pellegrin* (I am a wanderer) is sometimes attributed to Giovanni da Firenze (as in HAM, No. 51), but it is anonymous in all manuscripts.
31.   Pirrotta, MFCI, 1, p. ii.

The Cathedral of Santa Maria del Fiore in Florence, built largely during the Trecento.

ently flourished in the years between 1350 and 1370. One manuscript that contains pieces by Lorenzo calls him a priest, and the Squarcialupi Codex pictures Donato as a Benedictine monk.

Perhaps the most striking aspect of the Florentine tradition, indeed, is the number of ecclesiastical composers who made secular polyphony their almost exclusive concern. Most of the large collections of trecento music contain nothing but secular songs. Motets by Italian composers, as we have already noted, are extremely rare, and only a handful of Mass movements appear, almost as an afterthought, in a few manuscripts. Two of these movements, a Gloria and Agnus Dei, are by Gherardello. Lorenzo composed a Sanctus, and a setting of the Credo is now attributed to Bartolo da Firenze, an otherwise unknown composer who may have been the first Italian to compose a polyphonic Mass movement. A Gloria fragment and a Sanctus, both anonymous, complete the count of Italian Mass movements written before 1400. All of these pieces are for two voices, both of which sing the text. On a few occasions, the voices sing phrases of text at different times and may even alternate in singing successive phrases. For the most part, however, they sing together in what may be called a restrained madrigal style. Melismas are generally short and unobtrusive, although they become somewhat longer and more elaborate in the Sanctus of Lorenzo, which thus reflects, again in a restrained way, the melodic expansion that is characteristic of Lorenzo's madrigals.

In contrast to his limited output of sacred music, Gherardello wrote ten two-voice madrigals, five monophonic ballate, and one caccia, the well-known *Tosto che l'alba*.[32] Lorenzo's secular compositions are exactly equal to Gherardello's in number and kind, but one of his ten madrigals is for three voices. Donato wrote fourteen two-voice madrigals,

32. HAM, No. 52.

again only one caccia, and two pieces for two voices in ballata form. The text of the first is a true ballata, but Donato gave it a musical form of *AbbcA,* apparently because dialogue in the ripresa made its music unsuited for repetition with the text of the volta. For the second piece, the manuscripts give only the first words of the text in what appears to be garbled French for *Je porte amiablement* (I carry—or wear—lovingly). The musical form—two sections, of which the second is repeated with open and closed endings—makes it likely that the complete text was a virelai. So far as we know, Donato wrote no sacred music of any kind, even though he was a Benedictine.

Both Lorenzo and Donato wrote music particularly notable for its melodic expansiveness. Indeed, the two men "represent the peak of virtuoso singing in the Italian madrigal, and therefore in the Italian Ars nova as a whole."[33] Melismas become almost excessively long and ornate, especially in the upper part, which remains the more active of the two voices. In some pieces, both composers follow the lead of Jacopo da Bologna in adopting successive rather than simultaneous declamation of the text. The voices then achieve greater independence and come closer to being equal in importance. Imitation occurs frequently in these pieces and usually involves short motives and figures of one or two measures. More rarely, longer phrases imitated at a distance of several measures suggest the influence of the caccia. The same influence may account for occasional repetitions of words and phrases, which sometimes appear to reflect a descriptive or humorous intent. All of these devices are concentrated in Lorenzo's setting of *Dà, dà a chi avaregia* (Give, give to him who hoards; AMM No. 65), a madrigal by Nicolò Soldanieri. It should be noted that this is not the only occasion on which Lorenzo, Donato, and other composers chose texts from the madrigals and ballate of well-known Florentine or Tuscan poets such as Soldanieri, Sacchetti, Boccaccio, and Antonio degli Alberti. The great majority of texts remain anonymous, however. Possibly the composers themselves wrote some of these texts, although few achieved fame as poets or left separate literary works.

Of the Florentine composers, only Gherardello and Lorenzo continued the tradition of the monophonic ballata. The five such pieces that each man wrote are somewhat less florid than their madrigals, but melismas do occur, particularly on the first and penultimate syllables of poetic lines. When the intervening text is set syllabically—as it usually is—the stylistic influence of the madrigal becomes unmistakable. Also characteristically Italian are the mensurations most commonly used: duodenaria, or octonaria, or the senaria that Marchettus called *ytalica* (3/4). Lorenzo's setting of a ballata by Boccaccio, *Non so qual i' mi voglia* (I know not what I want), provides an excellent example of these purely

---

33.   Pirrotta, 3, p. ii. This volume contains all the pieces of both Lorenzo and Donato.

Italian traits.[34] Though restrained, the melodic ornamentation of this ballata contrasts strikingly with the folklike simplicity of Machaut's monophonic virelais. Once again we must conclude that the formative stages of fourteenth-century Italian song show little or no trace of French influence. That influence does not make itself widely felt until well after the advent of the polyphonic ballata around 1365 in the works of the later Florentine composers.

SECOND-GENERATION ITALIAN COMPOSERS— FRANCESCO LANDINI

Nothing in the works of the older Italian composers presages the sudden popularity of the ballata in the last third of the fourteenth century. Certainly the few monophonic examples in no way suggest that the polyphonic ballata will almost totally eclipse the madrigal and caccia in the output of the second generation of Italian composers. Of those composers, Francesco Landini was the most celebrated in his own time and is the best known in ours. He was also the most prolific by far, having left a total of 154 polyphonic songs: 11 madrigals, 2 cacce, and 141 ballate, exactly one-third of the extant ballate with music. As will become evident, Landini's preference for the ballata was by no means peculiar to him. By the quality as well as by the quantity of his works, however, Landini led Italian music in a new direction and created its most imposing monument.

For a composer as renowned as Landini was, information about his early life is surprisingly scarce. The son of a painter, he was born in the lovely village of Fiesole on the hills overlooking Florence, but the usual placement of his birth in 1325 is unsupported by documentary evidence. Apparently a victim of smallpox, Landini went blind in childhood. The affliction may have been responsible for his turning to a career in music; in any case, he became a skilled performer on several instruments, including the *serena serenorum,* a string instrument of his own invention. It was as an organist, however, that he was best known. For his excellence as a performer—so says Villani, the contemporary chronicler of famous Florentines—Landini was crowned with laurel in Venice by no less a personage than Peter, King of Cyprus. Later embellishments of the story have proved to be historically unfounded and have raised unjustifiable doubts as to the truth of Villani's simple remark. Some such coronation could certainly have taken place in Venice during one of Peter's visits in 1362, 1365, and 1368. During this decade, at any rate, Landini is believed to have travelled in northern Italy and may have spent considerable time in Venice.

34.   NOHM, 3, p. 38. All monophonic ballate, with the exception of a single example by Nicolò da Perugia, are available in Pirrotta, MFCI, 1–3.

The tombstone of Landini depicts the famous composer with a portative organ and two angel musicians above his head (Florence, The Church of San Lorenzo).

The first firmly established date in Landini's life comes from a letter of recommendation written in 1375 by Coluccio Salutati, chancellor of Florence. From this time on, it is reasonably certain that Landini remained in Florence and took an active part in the city's musical and cultural life. He died on September 2, 1397, and was buried in the church of San Lorenzo where he had served as organist. His tombstone depicts him with a portative organ, as does his portrait in the Squarcialupi Codex, where he is identified as "Magister Franciscus Cecus [blind] Horghanista de Florentia." Other manuscripts sometimes name him "Francesco degli Organi." This emphasis on Landini as a performer continues in literary reports concerning the effects of his organ playing on both feathered and human audiences. Even when his compositions are mentioned, it is the sweetness with which he played their beautiful harmonies that makes "hearts almost burst from their bosoms."[35] Now, of course, we can only know and honor Landini as a composer. Yet it is probably to his contemporary reputation as a performer that we owe the preservation of such a large amount of music.

Landini's fame and the size of his musical output are no doubt responsible for the modern tendency to regard him as the Italian counterpart of

35. Reese, MMA, p. 372.

Guillaume de Machaut. Such a view distorts the historical position and importance of both men, but to point out its falsity is not to deny either Landini's skill as a composer or the attractiveness of his music. Perhaps the most obvious difference between the two lies in the scope of their creative activities. Equally endowed as a poet and composer, Machaut cultivated almost every literary and musical form known in his time. In comparison, Landini's contributions appear surprisingly limited. He may have written a good many of the texts he set to music, but he wrote few other poems and certainly cannot be counted among the great poets of the fourteenth century. As far as we know, Landini composed no Mass movements or other liturgical music, although in 1379 he received payment "for five motets" from Andrea dei Servi (Andrea da Firenze). None of these motets has survived, if indeed they were composed by Landini himself. The only pieces that we know with certainty to be his belong to the standard forms of Italian secular polyphony, and even these three forms are most unequally represented.

THE MUSIC OF FRANCESCO LANDINI

Despite the abundance of Landini's music and the preservation of many pieces in several manuscripts, we have little to guide us in determining the chronology of its composition. Partly because of its sheer bulk, however, it provides the clearest and most complete picture of musical developments in Italy during the last decades of the fourteenth century. In examining those developments, our ignorance of chronology may prove beneficial. At least we have no reason to adopt the popular view of music history as a continuous and one-way progression. Changes do come, but gradually, and the new does not at once replace the old. Instead, a composer may alternate between divergent styles according to the musical form or type for which he deems each style appropriate. It is this situation that the music of Landini illustrates with particular clarity.

THE MADRIGALS

As might be expected, Landini's nine two-voice madrigals remain wholly Italian in style. Their texts are all in the standardized form of eleven-syllable lines arranged in two or three terzetti and a two-line ritornello. The musical forms—*aab* or *aaab*—are equally standardized. All settings are vocal duets, with melismas characteristically placed on the first and penultimate syllables of each poetic line. A few of these melismas extend for ten, fifteen, or even twenty measures, but as a rule they are both shorter and simpler than the florid expansions of Lorenzo and Donato. Although the upper voice is still the more elaborate, Landini evidently sought to make the two parts more nearly equal in rhythmic and melodic interest. Independent declamation of the text is common and often involves imitation or an exchange of motives between the parts. The same devices also relate the two voices in many melismatic passages. For the metrical organization of his madrigals, Landini relied almost entirely on octonaria and duodenaria. Six of the pieces use only these two mensurations, usually with octonaria in the first section and duodenaria in the ritornello. In two cases, however, this order is reversed. The other three madrigals begin in octonaria and have ritornelli in senaria perfecta (3/4). Thus Landini never failed to provide a metrical contrast between the first section and the ritornello. Within each section the mensuration remains unchanged, except in *Mostrommi amor* (Love showed me), where the first section begins with seven measures of 6/8 and then continues in octonaria.[36] As in most of Landini's music, the actual notation in the manuscripts is more often French than Italian, with octonaria and duodenaria expressed by means of imperfect and perfect mood. Nevertheless, the survival of these typically Italian mensurations is unmistakable.

The persistence of Italian characteristics—both melodic and rhythmic—cannot be taken as an indication that all the madrigals are early works. While it is probable that Landini began his career by writing in this form, several of the pieces display a technical mastery that can only have come with artistic maturity. Landini simply wrote in the style that tradition demanded for this oldest form of Italian secular polyphony.

No such tradition governed the composition of three-voice madrigals, which always remained exceptional in the output of trecento composers. Landini's two examples, by their differing structural procedures, make the exceptional nature of the three-voice madrigal even more explicit.[37] In *Sì dolce non sonò* (So sweetly did not sound), the nine lines of three terzetti are set continuously in the upper voices above an isorhythmic tenor with three statements of a color subdivided into three taleae ($3C = 9T$).[38] The setting of the two-line ritornello is again continuous in the upper voices, while the tenor has the same melody for each line, but with open and closed endings. Landini's other three-voice madrigal is tritextual, with a different terzetto and ritornello in each voice. In the texts of the two upper voices, Music herself weeps to see popular songs replace her sweet effects that once were prized by knights, barons, and great princes. Her only consolation is that she does not weep alone, for the other virtues too she sees deserted. The tenor text is a more general complaint that everyone wants to arrange notes

36. PM, 4, No. 146. Identification is by Schrade's continuous numbering of all Landini's works.
37. Ibid., Nos. 151 and 152.
38. HAM, No. 54.

and compose madrigals, cacce, and ballate. Landini seems here to echo the scorn of Jacopo da Bologna for "little masters" who set themselves up as the equals of Marchettus and Philippe de Vitry (see above, p. 445). Perhaps Landini's madrigal is itself a tribute to Jacopo, whose *Aquil'altera—Creatura—Ucel de Dio* is the only other tritextual madrigal.[39] It is clear, in any case, that Landini regarded the three-voice madrigal as an appropriate vehicle for experimentation with various musical techniques.

Much the same attitude is evident in *De, dimmi tu* (Alas, tell me; No. 153). The text is a normal madrigal with two terzetti and a two-line ritornello, but the musical form is an equally normal caccia. A continuous setting of the terzetti is followed by a ritornello in contrasting meter. What is unexpected is the novel structure of the canons, in which all three voices sing the text. The upper voice enters alone as though it were beginning a canon, but it proves to be a free contrapuntal part in the first section. It is the two lower voices that are canonic, and at the interval of a fifth rather than at the unison. The same relationship among the voices prevails in the ritornello, except that the upper part now begins a strict canon for all three voices. In contrast to this experimentation with canonic procedures, Landini's *Cosi pensoso* (Thus thoughtful; No. 154) is a normal caccia with a two-voice canon above a free instrumental tenor. Perhaps because the scene is of ladies fishing along the shore, the dialogue and descriptive elements in both words and music are somewhat restrained. Nevertheless, all the elements of the older descriptive caccia are present. The piece has an old-fashioned air that suggests it may have been an early work written to demonstrate the composer's skill in an already obsolete form.

THE BALLATE

French influence has sometimes been held responsible for the ballata's sudden popularity in the later fourteenth century and its overwhelming preponderance in the works of Landini and his contemporaries. Such a view is perhaps too extreme. As has been mentioned earlier, the ballata probably derived its poetic and musical form from sources other than the virelai. The latter, moreover, never became the most popular form of French secular polyphony. If French influence accounted for the near eclipse of the madrigal, we would expect Italian music to have developed a counterpart of the grande ballade. That it never did is related to one of the most puzzling aspects of the Italian Ars Nova. Almost without exception, composers ignored the more serious poems and more complex forms—canzoni and sonnetti—of even the greatest poets. In-

---

39.   Landini's ballata No. 112 also has a different text for each of its three voices.

stead, they first adopted the simpler form of the madrigal and then turned it into an elaborate and virtuosic art song. When the style of the madrigal palled, they chose another form that was still close to its popular origins—the ballata. Perhaps the preponderance of ballate in Landini's works may be taken as confirmation of Music's complaint in his tritextual madrigal that the sweet and perfect effects of music were being deserted for popular songs. The polyphonic ballata cannot have been truly popular, but it must have reached a wider audience than the older forms "prized by knights, barons, and great lords," who did not exist in republican Florence. At the villa of the wealthy Alberti family, Landini himself took part in the philosophical discussions and musical entertainments described by Giovanni da Prato in *Il Paradiso degli Alberti* (c. 1390). On one occasion two young girls danced and sang a ballata of Landini much to the delight of all, especially Francesco himself. In a similar way, the fictitious characters in Boccaccio's *Decameron* (1353) ended each day's festivities with dancing and a song that was always a ballata. These and other bits of literary evidence as well as the composers' music suggest that, rather than French influence, the interests and tastes of Florentine society were responsible for the predominance of the ballata in the second half of the fourteenth century.

That both monophonic and polyphonic ballate began as purely Italian creations is strikingly confirmed by the music itself. Only later did the gradual introduction of foreign stylistic elements transform the ballata into a replica of French secular song. We can follow this process with particular ease in the 141 ballate of Landini, even though we have only the most general knowledge of their chronology. Any discussion of stylistic development in these ballate must deal separately with the pieces for two and three voices. Slight indications in manuscript sources suggest that the great majority of the 91 two-voice ballate belong to the earlier phases of Landini's career, while nearly all of the 50 pieces for three voices are among his latest and most mature works. Beyond the different number of voices, other contrasts of style distinguish the two groups and confirm this view of their chronology. Of the two-voice ballate, 82 are vocal duets, and only 9 are solo songs with instrumental tenors. By their very number, Landini's two-voice ballate in Italian style show that the sudden popularity of the form must have been independent of French influence. Before that influence effected perceptible changes, Landini and other composers had made the ballata an integral part of the Italian polyphonic tradition. The break with tradition that came in only nine of Landini's two-voice ballate will end with the predominance of French practices in his three-voice pieces.

All ballate for three voices, including Landini's, fall into one of three classes, according to the number of voices with text. The first class, which may be identified by the symbol 3^3, comprises ballate with text in all three voices. To this typically Italian procedure, a second class opposes the typically French arrangement of a cantus with text accompanied by instrumental tenor and contratenor parts (3^1). Between these two extremes stands the third class of ballate (3^2), in which both cantus and tenor sing the text and only the contratenor is instrumental. This hybrid class appears to be a wholly Italian invention. Whether it actually developed later than the other two classes as a compromise between them is uncertain. It did have a subsequent history, however. In some movements of the Barcelona Mass, as was noted in Chapter XVI, a vocal duet of the cantus and tenor is augmented by one or two instrumental parts. More common is the use of the 3^2 arrangement by fifteenth-century composers for settings of French secular songs. Thus, although the Italian hybrid never rivaled the French arrangement in popularity, it did become an accepted part of the international style that characterizes the music of the early Renaissance.

In classifying Landini's three-voice ballate, problems arise because no fewer than 19 of the 50 pieces occur in different versions in different manuscripts. Seven of the 19 exist as two-voice ballate, which may have been the original form of at least two pieces.[40] These two must also be included with the twelve that have different distributions of text among three voices. Of these fourteen pieces, only one exists in all three versions, 3^3, 3^2, and 3^1. The alternate forms of all the others are either 3^3 and 3^2 or 3^1 and 3^2. This situation seems to confirm the origin of Class 3^2 as a hybrid offspring of the other two classes. To illustrate how this hybrid may have developed, we may note the different versions of *Questa fanciull'amor* (This girl, Love; AMM, No. 67). The arrangement of this ballata is 3^1 in a Florentine manuscript that, according to Schrade, contains the oldest collection of Landini's music and "represents the highest degree of authenticity."[41] Although he believed the 3^1 version to be the "original,"[42] Schrade chose to publish *Questa fanciull'* as it appears in two other manuscripts, including Squarcialupi, with the text added to the tenor part (3^2). In this version, which is also given in AMM, the only changes in the tenor to accommodate the text involve the separation of notes written in ligatures and the subdivision of longer values into repeated notes. Thus the tenor part may be either played or sung, but the 3^2 version at least suggests the way in which this modification of the typically French texture may have been invented, perhaps by Landini himself.

Although some doubts about the nineteen pieces that appear in different versions do remain, we may accept Schrade's edition as the basis for the following classification of Landini's three-voice ballate:

40.   PM, 4, Nos. 92 and 93.
41.   PMC, 4, p. 7.
42.   Ibid., p. 98.

Class	Total	Number in no other form
3^3	11	6
3^2	12	7
3^1	27	18

That more than half of Landini's three-voice ballate have the French arrangement 3^1 is unexpected, but it is no surprise that the group includes his one setting of a French text—a virelai rather than a ballata. We can only conclude that Landini acted with deliberate intent when he illustrated the inherent contrasts between Italian and French styles in the different classes of his three-voice ballate.

Not all composers of Landini's generation shared his enthusiasm for the French style or even his interest in writing three-voice polyphony. What they did share in differing degrees was a distinct preference for the ballata over the madrigal. They continued to compose madrigals, even into the beginning of the fifteenth century, but they all chose the ballata for a majority of their works. Of these composers, four have a sufficient number of pieces to warrant individual consideration here. A brief survey of their contributions to the Italian repertory will complete the story of trecento music and provide a better basis for judging the importance and influence of their more prolific and more famous contemporary.

NICOLÒ DA PERUGIA

Nicolò da Perugia appears to be the oldest, or at least the most conservative, of the composers whose creative years overlap Landini's. Almost nothing is known about Nicolò beyond what can be deduced from his music, which consists of 16 madrigals, 4 cacce, and 21 ballate.[43] Except for one three-voice piece (3^3), all of the madrigals are for two voices in the traditional Italian style. Their only departure from normal procedures is the continuous setting of two terzetti in the first sections of four madrigals, a peculiarity that may have been suggested by the usual treatment of madrigal texts when they were set as cacce. Indeed, the text for one of Nicolò's cacce is a trilingual madrigal (see p. 463), with two terzetti in the first musical section. All of his cacce are traditional in having a two-voice canon above an instrumental tenor, and the other three have more normal caccia texts, although none depicts a hunt. The most descriptive is *Dappoi che'l sole* (After the sun hides its rays; AMM, No. 66), a vivid portrayal of a fire in the city at night. Although the actual fire is successfully put out, the surprise ending in the ritornello suggests that the fire of love burns on in the poet's heart.

Turning to Nicolò's ballate, we find that one is monophonic, seven-

---

43. See PM, 8, for Nicolò's complete works. See also S. K. Kelly, "The Works of Niccolò da Perugia," 2 vols. (Ph.D. dissertation, The Ohio State University, 1974.)

teen are vocal duets, and only three have the text in the cantus alone above an instrumental tenor. These and other aspects of his music lead to the assumption that Nicolò began his activity as a composer shortly before the appearance of the polyphonic ballata around 1365. Further assumptions place him in Florence from about 1360 until 1375 and make him a friend of Franco Sachetti. These assumptions are based on Nicolò's use of texts that the Florentine poet wrote during the period 1354–75. Sachetti himself cited twelve of his poems—six madrigals, two cacce, and four ballate—that Nicolò set to music. Of the twelve, four madrigals, one ballata, and the two cacce have survived. There can be little doubt, therefore, that Nicolò participated in the cultural life of Florence for a good many years and made his own contribution to the development of the polyphonic ballata.

BARTOLINO DA PADOVA

The second contemporary of Landini to be considered here, Bartolino da Padova, raises many of the same problems as Nicolò da Perugia. Literary sources and a few of the texts Bartolino set to music indicate that he was active as a composer from about 1375 until 1400 or even as late as 1410. He is believed to have spent most of his life in Padua, although he may have been in Florence for a time. Both his name and his music, at least, were known in Florence around 1390 when Giovanni da Prato wrote of singing madrigals made in Padua by this so famous musician.

Given the presumed period of Bartolino's activity, some aspects of his 11 madrigals and 27 ballate make him seem almost more conservative than Nicolò da Perugia.[44] Although the preponderance of ballate confirms Bartolino's place in the last third of the fourteenth century, they show few traces of the French influence that so strongly affected the contemporary ballate of Landini. Only one of the twenty-seven pieces exists in no other form than as a vocal duet with instrumental contratenor (3^2). Four others exist as vocal duets and in three-voice arrangements, with two each in Classes 3^2 and 3^3. All the rest of the ballate (22) are vocal duets. Not once did Bartolino adopt the typical French arrangement of cantus with one or two instrumental parts. His madrigals, as might be expected, are equally in the Italian tradition. Nine are vocal duets, only two of which have alternate 3^2 arrangements that may be their original form. The remaining two madrigals appear to have been composed for three voices with the text in each voice. One of them, however, is unusual for the diversity of forms in which it appears (3^3, 3^2, 3^1, and 2^2) and for its French text, *La douce cere d'un fier animal* (The

---

44. See PM, 9, for Bartolino's complete works.

gentle aspect of a wild animal). Curiously, the one manuscript with the French arrangement of vocal and instrumental parts has the most Italianized version of this text. Although corrupt in all sources, the poem apparently refers to the Visconti family of Milan, as the trilingual madrigal *La fiera testa* (The savage head) undoubtedly does. In this poem, Italian and Latin lines alternate in the two terzetti, while the two-line ritornello is French. Both Bartolino and Nicolò set *La fiera testa* to music, the former as a two-voice madrigal, the latter as a caccia. It has been assumed that Bartolino's madrigal dates from the brief occupation of Padua by the Visconti in 1388–89. By the same reasoning, Nicolò would have composed his caccia as late as 1400–02, when Gian Galeazzo Visconti held dominion over Perugia. These dates seem incompatible with what is known or assumed about Nicolò's activity in Florence before 1375 and even more with the general style of his music. In any case, deductions from the enigmatic text of *La fiera testa* illustrate the fragility of the straws we grasp in attempting to reconstruct the lives of trecento composers.

ANDREA DA FIRENZE

Much more is known about a third contemporary of Landini, Andrea da Firenze, or Andrea dei Servi. In the Squarcialupi Codex, the main source of Andrea's works, he is called "Magister Frater Andreas Horghanista de Florentia." Another source gives the further information that he was a brother in the Servite order (*Servi di Maria*) that had been founded in Florence in 1233. Records show that Andrea entered the order in 1375 and held a number of important administrative positions before his death in 1415. With Landini as a consultant, Andrea supervised the building of a new organ for the Servites' Florentine house, and he played the instrument when it was completed in 1379. Andrea's expense accounts include payments for entertaining Landini on periodic visits to check the progress of construction and for the cost of wine during three days Landini spent tuning the organ. This last entry also records the payment "for five motets" that were presumably composed by Landini himself. The joint efforts of the two men must have been successful, because they were both consulted in 1387 about plans for a new organ in the cathedral of Florence.

Given Andrea's professional relationships with Landini, it is not surprising that the music of the two composers should be similar in many respects. In his preference for the ballata, Andrea even outdid Landini. As far as we know, he composed no madrigals at all, and his complete works consist only of ballate, 18 for two voices and 12 for three. It is possible, but by no means certain, that Andrea was the composer of one

French ballade, *Dame sans per* (Lady without peer).[45] Of Andrea's two-voice ballate, only two have an instrumental tenor. All the rest are vocal duets in the Italian tradition. As with Landini, it is in Andrea's three-voice ballate that French musical practices most frequently appear. Only three of the twelve have the text in all three voices, while three more have the text in two. Of the six that follow the French plan (Class 3[1]), four also have open and closed endings and are written in 6/8 meter.

Although Landini and Andrea both show the same effects of French influence, each man retained his own individuality. The stylistic distinctions between them seem to result in large part from different attitudes toward the problem of setting words to music. Landini often gives the impression that he regarded the text as little more than an excuse for writing expansive lyric melodies. He almost never repeats words and phrases for emphasis, so that the return of the music with a different text creates no problems. Melodic ornamentation in the upper voice is generally restrained, and melismatic extensions are neither excessively long nor highly virtuosic. Nevertheless, such extensions convert even his simplest ballate into art songs that show little trace of their origin in the dance. Rhythms are gentle and fluid, rather than vigorous; melodies move chiefly stepwise in graceful curves; consonant intervals and chords are linked in smooth harmonic progressions. With Landini, in short, Italian polyphony reached a peak of lyrical elegance and refinement. Not until two centuries later did it reach another such peak in the music of Palestrina.

On some occasions, Andrea da Firenze showed that, when he chose, he could match the refined elegance of Landini's lyric style. More often, however, he preferred an energetic and even dramatic presentation of the text. This tendency is particularly evident in his use of textual repetition combined with special musical devices. A few excerpts from Andrea's ballate (Example XVIII–5) will illustrate the kinds of dramatic effects that are almost totally lacking in Landini's music. One of Andrea's frequent devices is the combination of repeated words and phrases with fragmentary motives in imitation or hocket-like passages (XVIII–5a and b). At times, as in the setting of *Pena non n'è maggiore* (There is no greater pain), the musical device alone lays special emphasis on a line of text, (XVIII–5c). For the most part, Andrea's melodies differ little from Landini's in their predominantly stepwise motion. In rare instances, however, Andrea introduces wide leaps that are all the more dramatic for being unusual and unexpected. The most spectacular of such leaps is the augmented octave that sets the word "maladetto" (accursed) in high relief (XVIII–5d). Indeed, the disjunct and wide-ranging melody for the entire second line of this ballata stands in sharpest contrast to the gentle lyricism of Landini and to the usual melodic style of Andrea himself.

45.   Pirrotta, MFCI, 5, No. 50.

Example XVIII–5: *Dramatic Effects in the Ballate of Andrea da Firenze*

a. NO. 5

b. NO.16

c. NO. 19

d. NO.17

a. Cruel Cosa (a pun on "thing" [*cosa*] and a lady's name)
b. Mercy, to cry mercy
c. There is no greater pain
d. Burning envy will die / In its great fire and accursed ardor.

The dramatic effects illustrated in Example XVIII–5, as well as many others in Andrea's ballate, were obviously designed to fit the texts with which they first appear. When the same passages return with other words—as they all must in ballata form—they often become inappropriate or even nonsensical, especially where textual repetition is involved. Nevertheless, we may be thankful that these difficulties did not deter Andrea from his various experiments in relating textual and musical expression. His pieces thereby acquired greater diversity and individuality, if not always greater beauty, than is to be found in the more uniform and predictable style of Francesco Landini.

PAOLO TENORISTA

Another major composer among Landini's contemporaries, and the last to be considered, is Paolo Tenorista, or "Magister Dominus Paulas Abbas de Florentia," as he is called in the Squarcialupi Codex. Curiously, the thirty-two pages prepared for Paolo's music contain only his portrait in the black cassock of a Benedictine, the full designation of his name and titles across the tops of all facing pages, and tantalizingly empty staves. That his music was evidently unavailable when the manuscript was compiled supports the view that Paolo spent the later years of his life outside of Florence, presumably in the household of Cardinal Acciaiuoli (d. 1409), who had been bishop of Florence from 1383 to 1387. In 1404, "Dominus Paulus de Florentia abbas . . ." witnessed the signing of a document written at the cardinal's house in Rome. The only other date that can be associated with Paolo's life comes from his madrigal *Godi, Firenze* (Rejoice, Florence), which celebrates the victory of Florence over Pisa in 1406. Information from musical and archival sources notwithstanding, Paolo's biography remains more than usually "problematic," and even his identity is open to question.[46] Despite these difficulties, Paolo emerges as an important composer of 11 madrigals, 23 ballate, and a setting of *Benedicamus Domino.*[47] Three additional ballate are probably by him, although they are anonymous in the manuscript sources.

Now that Paolo's music is available in a modern edition, he will undoubtedly be more widely recognized as one of the most interesting and unusual of the later Italian composers.[48] No one was more conservative and progressive at the same time. No one was more eclectic in borrow-

46. For details, see N. Pirrotta, *Paolo Tenorista* (Palm Springs, 1961), pp. 20–26 ("A Problematic Biography"). In a later article, "Paolo da Firenze und der Squarcialupi-Kodex," *Quadrivium,* 9 (1968), pp. 5–24, K. von Fischer presents new evidence suggesting a close connection between Paolo and the compilation of the manuscript. He also documents Paolo's death in September, 1419.

47. A facsimile of the *Benedicamus* is printed in Apel, NPM, p. 379. It is now published in PM, 12, p. 105. The music is anonymous, but the original index of *Pit* lists the piece with the familiar monogram.

48. Marrocco, PM, 9. See Pirrotta, *Paolo,* for a perceptive discussion of the composer's artistic development. The latter publication also includes transcriptions of five ballate.

ing and combining musical practices past and present, Italian and French. And no one, therefore, achieved a richer and more various musical style.

The characteristic features of Paolo's artistic personality are as evident in the large aspects of his music as in the small details and are even reflected in the notation. It is a sure sign of his eclecticism that his works could provide examples of purely Italian notation, of the mixed notation that combined French principles with a multiplicity of Italian note shapes, and of the mannered notation that introduced new and often needlessly complex ways of expressing intricate rhythmic patterns.[49] This diversity of notational practice is no more than one would expect in the works of a composer who still treated the madrigal as the "flower of musical art," while at the same time he raised the popular ballata to a higher level of subtlety and sophistication. All but one of Paolo's eleven madrigals are vocal duets, seemingly in the traditional forms and styles. One unusual feature is the provision of open and closed endings for the ritornelli of six madrigals, in one of which the text does not require repetition of the music. The same madrigal also has open and closed endings for the first musical section. Such endings are extremely rare in the works of earlier composers, although they do occur in the ritornelli of one madrigal by Lorenzo da Firenze and one by Jacopo da Bologna.[50] It is only the frequency of their use by Paolo that is unprecedented. This departure from common practice in Paolo's madrigals is less significant than the rich variety of their rhythmic and melodic figuration. Because the musical style, particularly of the later madrigals, so clearly reflects contemporary trends at the turn of the century, it is strange that Paolo went beyond the vocal duet only in the three-voice *Godi, Firenze*. Perhaps the importance of the occasion being celebrated led him for once to abandon his conservative respect for the traditional arrangement of voices in the madrigal.

If conservative and progressive tendencies sometimes seem to conflict in Paolo's madrigals, the progressive tendencies clearly win the day in his ballate. The force of tradition was much weaker in the case of the ballata, of course; but Paolo is the first, indeed, the only major composer in whose works ballate for three voices far outnumber those for two. Of the twenty-six pieces by or attributed to Paolo, no more than six exist only as vocal duets. Ten have the French disposition of solo cantus with instrumental tenor and contratenor (3^1), and ten have the hybrid form of a vocal duet with instrumental contratenor (3^2). Three pieces in this last group also exist as vocal duets without a contratenor, but the three-voice versions probably represent their original form. That the three groups of Paolo's ballate reflect a chronological develop-

49. Apel, NPM, Facsimiles 75, 80, 81, and the fragment on p. 394. The three kinds of notation are discussed and illustrated in Part III, Chapters VII–IX.
50. Pirrotta, MFCI, 3, No. 2, and 4, No. 1.

ment to some extent is suggested by the way the manuscript source identifies the composer. Four of the vocal duets are assigned to "Don Paolo," while "P. A." is the composer of five pieces in Class 3[1] and eight pieces in Class 3[2]. It would seem that Paolo began with the traditional form of the two-voice ballata but quickly acquiesced in the then-fashionable imitation of French style. More and more, however, he adopted the hybrid form as the most appropriate vehicle for combining his own brand of intensely expressive lyricism with the rhythmic subtleties and notational devices of the contemporary mannered style.

With Landini, Andrea da Firenze, and Paolo Tenorista, the dominance of Florence over Italian musical life seems to come to an end. Indeed, if Paolo did spend the latter part of his life away from his native city, Andrea may be the last important representative of the Florentine tradition. It is perhaps significant in this connection that Andrea's works conclude the music in the Squarcialupi Codex. After the folios devoted to him, a final section of twenty-one empty folios was prepared for the music of a "Magister Johannes Horghanista de Florentia." The allotment of so much space implies that the composer was both well known and prolific, but only two pieces in other manuscripts might possibly be his.[51] Presumably, he was the Giovanni degli Organi who succeeded Landini at San Lorenzo and later became organist at the Florence cathedral. Giovanni died in 1426, and the absence of his music from the last of the Florentine manuscripts seems to symbolize the city's decline as a center of musical creativity. In the first quarter of the fifteenth century, the cities of northern Italy—particularly Milan, Venice, and Padua—again came to the fore. During these years, however, composers more and more turned away from the traditional forms of Italian polyphony. Madrigals and cacce disappeared almost completely from their works, and even the ballata became increasingly scarce. In place of these forms, and in addition to adopting French musical styles, many Italian composers now chose French texts—ballades, rondeaux, and virelais—for most of their secular polyphony. They also wrote Mass movements and ceremonial motets in much greater numbers than before. These changed interests of the northern composers mark the end of the Italian Ars Nova and the beginning of a new age.

Striking as may be the changes that took place in Italian music at the beginning of the fifteenth century, they were less sudden than they at first appear. We find occasional examples of mixed French and Italian or wholly French texts from the time of the Rossi Codex to Paolo Tenorista's *Soffrir m'estuet* (I must suffer), a ballata that has French for the ripresa and volta, Italian for the two piedi. For the most part, however, trecento composers set Italian texts, even when they adopted the superficial aspects of the fashionable French style. Little in their music fore-

---

51.   See Pirrotta, MFCI, 5, p. iii, and Nos. 47 and 49.

shadows the preference of later Italians for setting French texts or for composing motets and Mass movement. To observe the early stages of this development we must go back in time to the latter part of the fourteenth century and the contacts between French and Italian musicians at the papal court in Avignon. It was here, and later at the courts of schismatic popes and in other religious establishments in northern Italy, that the divergent musical traditions of the two countries met and began the process of blending into an international style. It will be the objective of the last two chapters to follow this process to the point at which it provides Renaissance composers with a richly varied but common musical language.

CHAPTER XIX

Transition to the Renaissance

Periods of transition from one historical age to another are always complex and difficult to define. The various aspects of human life that characterize an age—political, economic, social, and cultural—do not change overnight. Neither do they all change at the same time. Some fundamentals never change. The Middle Ages may have "waned" during the fifteenth century, but they had already contributed many ideas and institutions that were to persist for centuries. It is wholly arbitrary, therefore, to take the year 1500 as the "time-honored boundary between the medieval and modern periods."[1] The division may be convenient and workable for historians who are primarily concerned with the political, economic, and social aspects of Western civilization. It does not work for cultural historians, who insist on following the Middle Ages with a Renaissance. The impetus for this Renaissance came in the field of literature with a new and passionate concern for the "more humane letters" of classical antiquity. Beginning with Petrarch and some of his fourteenth-century contemporaries, Italian humanists scorned both the vernacular language and the "barbaric" Latin of the Middle Ages. Instead, they devoted themselves to the rediscovery and reinterpretation of classical literature and learning. That they themselves could think of their activities as a "rebirth" implies a supercilious disdain for the achievements of the immediate past. And the continued use of the term *Renaissance* implies that the Middle Ages were much darker than they really were. Humanism was an intellectual movement that became an academic fad. As such, it profoundly changed the course of university studies both for good and for ill. Its influence on the arts was less direct and often long delayed. Vernacular literature not only survived but flourished. Architecture, painting, even sculpture showed the effects of humanism in their secondary, much more than in their primary, characteristics. In all fields of artistic endeavor it is not the slavish imitations of classical models that we remember and most admire.

Music, of course, had no classical models at hand to imitate. There can

---

1. C. Stephenson and B. Lyon, *Medieval History: Europe from the Second to the Sixteenth Century,* 4th ed. (New York, 1962), p. 399.

A scene of aristocratic music making portrayed in this fourteenth-century Gobelin tapestry (Paris, Musée de Gobelins).

be no question, therefore, of a renaissance that abruptly changed the course of musical development. Music in the fifteenth century continued the practices it had inherited from the past, while transforming itself at the same time by the introduction of new compositional procedures and techniques. Even less direct than on the other arts, the influence of humanism on music made itself felt scarcely at all before the beginning of the sixteenth century. How then can we justify the common practice of making the first decades of the fifteenth century the dividing line between the music of the Late Middle Ages and the Early Renaissance? The answer to this question lies in the attitude of fifteenth-century musicians themselves toward the music of their own time. The most explicit statements of that attitude appear in the dedications of two treatises by Johannes Tinctoris (c. 1435–1511), a practicing musician, mathematician, and the first author who deserves to be called a Renaissance musical theorist. In his treatise on musical proportions, written no later than 1476, Tinctoris remarked that "the possibilities of our music have been so marvelously increased that there appears to be a new art, if I may so call it, whose fount and origin is held to be among the English, of whom Dunstable [d. 1453] stood forth as chief."[2] According to Tinctoris, the "moderns" of his own time followed directly on Dunstable's contemporaries Dufay (c. 1400–74) and Binchois (c. 1400–60). Now, however, it is the French who "contrive music in the newest manner for the new times." In the dedication of *The Art of Counterpoint*,

2. Strunk, SR, p. 195.

which is dated October 11, 1477, Tinctoris reaffirmed the excellence of contemporary composers who had learned their art from Dunstable, Dufay, and Binchois. He also made the surprising statement that no music composed more than forty years earlier was regarded as worth hearing.[3]

From these remarks we may draw a number of important conclusions. Composers in the latter part of the fifteenth century were evidently aware that their music was a new art, that it represented, in other words, a new period in the development of musical forms, techniques, and styles. For Tinctoris, at least, that period began about 1435. He perhaps overstated his case when he assigned the origin of the new art to the English, but he obviously recognized the importance of English contributions to the formation of that art. He also recognized its continuing development by composers who were chiefly French by culture, if not always so by birth. Tinctoris himself came from Nivelles, near Brussels, and wrote his treatises in Naples, where he was attached to the court of Ferdinand, King of Sicily.

Modern historians generally agree with Tinctoris's evaluation of the state of music in the fifteenth century. They may find the beginnings of the new art to be less sharply defined and to occur somewhat earlier than Tinctoris suggests, but they too regard it as the starting point for the development of what has been called "the central musical language of the Renaissance."[4] Whatever name we may give to this new style period in the history of music, its continuation through the sixteenth century and the amount of music it produced make it the proper subject of another book. The task of the present chapter will be to survey the transitional period from the death of Machaut in 1377 to the years 1420–25 when Dufay and Binchois became active as composers.

THE MANNERISTIC STYLE OF THE LATE FOURTEENTH CENTURY

The final decades of the fourteenth century witnessed one of the strangest developments in the entire history of music. Characterized primarily by extremes of notational and rhythmic complexity, this development resulted in what are now usually known as *mannered notation* and *manneristic style*. To counter any derogatory implications in these terms it has been suggested that, compared to the earlier subtlety of the French Ars Nova, the music of the late fourteenth century should instead be called an *ars subtilior* (more subtle art).[5] With regard to the his-

---

3.   See ibid., pp. 193–99, for English translations of both dedications.

4.   Reese, MR, Part I is entitled: "The Development of the Central Musical Language of the Renaissance in France, the Low Countries, and Italy."

5.   See U. Günther, "Das Ende der *Ars Nova,*" *Die Musikforschung,* 16 (1963), pp. 105–20.

tory of Western music as a whole, we might more appropriately use the superlative, *ars subtilissima*. Not until the twentieth century did music again reach the most subtle refinements and rhythmic complexities of the manneristic style.

Before describing this end-of-the-century phenomenon, we should pause to note the geographical regions and centers in which it flourished. We have already seen that, during the "Babylonian captivity" of the papacy (1309–77), Avignon was the most important center for the cultivation of sacred polyphony (see Chapter XVI). That importance continued after the Great Schism (1378–1417) produced rival popes in Avignon and Rome, but now we find that the city on the lower Rhone had also become a center for the composition of French secular songs. Two other centers with close musical ties to Avignon were situated just south and north of the Pyrenees: the courts of Peter IV (1335–87) and John I (1387–96), Kings of Aragon, and of Gaston Phebus, Count of Béarn and Foix (1343–91).

Our chief source for the secular repertory of Avignon, Aragon, and Foix in the last quarter of the fourteenth century is a manuscript from Chantilly.[6] Only a few of the thirteen motets and one hundred secular songs in **Ch,** including three ballades by Machaut, came from northern France or from the older Avignon repertory of the Ivrea Codex. Most of the newer pieces that can be dated with some precision refer to historical events or persons connected with one of the three courts during the papacy of Clement VII (1378–94). Taken as a whole, the collection may be said to exemplify the complex manneristic style cultivated and prized at both ecclesiastical and secular courts in southern France and Spain.

Although it tended to be simpler and more restrained, the music of northern France and even of England (see Chapter XX) did not escape the influence of southern mannerism. When composers from northern France became attached to one of the southern courts, however, they wholeheartedly adopted the manneristic style. So too did a number of Italians who devoted themselves to the composition of French secular polyphony of extreme rhythmic complexity. In all likelihood some of them came in contact with the manneristic style in Avignon, but the style itself seems to have been transplanted to northern Italy in the first decades of the fifteenth century. In part, at least, this development is related to the election of still a third pope by the Council of Pisa in 1409. Intending to bring the Great Schism to an end by deposing both the Roman and Avignonese popes, the Council chose as their successor Pietro Filargo, cardinal archbishop of Milan and patron of the composer Matteo da Perugia (see below). The other two popes—as might have been expected—refused to step down, and Filargo, who took the name Alexander V, died less than a year after his election. His place was im-

6.   Musée Condé, 564 (formerly 1047)—**Ch.**

In this fifteenth-century miniature, instrumental accompaniment is provided for a round dance in the garden (Paris, Bibliothèque Nationale).

mediately filled, however, by the election of Cardinal Baldassare Cossa as John XXIII. (Because the Church considers this first John XXIII an antipope, there could be another in the twentieth century.) Established primarily in Bologna, the court of these northern Italian popes became the focal point for an already flourishing musical life in such other cities as Genoa, Milan, Venice, and Padua. Even after the Council of Constance successfully disposed of all three papal contenders, the newly elected Martin V (1417–31) stayed in Florence and Bologna as much as in Rome itself. It is undoubtedly to the widespread and continued musical activity in all of these cities that we owe the many manuscripts of northern Italian origin in which so much of western Europe's music from the waning Middle Ages and the early Renaissance has been preserved.

Our concern with these manuscripts must be limited to the one source in which we can see both the flowering and fading of manneristic style on Italian soil, a manuscript now in Modena.[7] In the kinds of music it includes, the repertory of **Mod** is unusually diverse. French secular songs account for exactly 66 percent of the 100 complete pieces—17 rondeaux, 18 virelais, and 31 ballades. Five more songs in ballade form and one virelai have Latin texts. Italian secular songs are sparsely represented by two madrigals, one caccia, and six ballate. Two three-voice canons—one with Latin text, one with French—complete the secular

7. Biblioteca Estense, α, M. 5, 24 (formerly Lat. 568)—**Mod.**

polyphony. More unexpected is the presence of religious and liturgical polyphony in the form of five motets, the Christmas hymn *Puer natus in Betheleem* (A Boy is born in Bethlehem), and eleven Mass movements (eight Glorias and three Credos). This motley collection reflects the diverse origin of both the music and the composers who are represented. The preponderance of French songs, which include twelve concordances with *Ch,* and the presence of three texts in honor of Pope Clement VII suggest an origin in Avignon for some of the repertory, if not for the manuscript itself. Yet many of the French texts were set to music by Italian composers who are not known to have been outside of Italy. Much of the music, moreover, must date from the first ten or fifteen years of the fifteenth century. A good deal of evidence—both documentary and circumstantial—connects this later music and its composers with Genoa, Milan, Padua, and the courts of Alexander V and John XXIII. It seems probable, therefore, that the compilation of *Mod* began in Bologna around 1410. Presumably, all the music in the manuscript had been composed by the time the Great Schism came to an end in 1417.[8]

Having briefly introduced the two largest and most typical collections of music in manneristic style, the Chantilly and Modena manuscripts, we may now examine the constituent elements of that style in some detail. One of its goals (or results) was the creation of polyphony in which the individual lines achieved a maximum of rhythmic independence. In this respect, French secular songs, the primary vehicle for displaying the full measure of manneristic complexity, recall the motet style of Pierre de la Croix at the end of the previous century. The tenor of a chanson was newly composed; but, by maintaining the basic mensuration with few metrical changes and with relatively simple rhythmic patterns, it provided the same kind of stable foundation as the plainchant tenors of the earlier motets. This foundation enabled the cantus to indulge in a wide variety of rhythmic complications, sometimes to the point of destroying all feeling of a consistent metrical organization. Neither as complex as the cantus nor as simple as the tenor, the contratenor established its own distinctive character and moderated the contrast between the two extremes. It seems clear that the differentiated lines in manneristic style resulted at least in part from the practical necessity of supporting a virtuoso singer who could read and perform the most extravagant notational and rhythmic complexities that composers could devise. In addition to the mensural stability of the tenor, however, counterpoint based on progressions of consonant intervals also holds the seemingly independent voices together. Almost without exception, the rhythms of

8. A supplemental essay will deal more fully with the schismatic popes and their relationships with composers represented in *Ch* and *Mod*. See also the discussion of Matteo da Perugia below.

all voices converge in strong cadences at the end of phrases. In between, the tenor and cantus still constitute a two-voice framework that can be reduced to traditional progressions of perfect and imperfect consonances. As in the music of Machaut, ornamentation of these consonances by a variety of nonharmonic tones often disguises the intervallic structure and creates a highly dissonant effect. Devices such as syncopation and the lateral displacement of an interval's constituent tones raise the dissonance level to even greater heights and sometimes make the individual lines seem as independent harmonically as they are rhythmically. Yet despite all appearances, the traditional consonances and mensurations of the French Ars Nova provide the twin bases on which the intricacies of the style depend.

Overemphasis on the manneristic exaggerations of a few composers has tended to bring the artistic movement as a whole into disrepute. To some extent, this judgment must be regarded as a survival of the nineteenth-century romantic notion that a composer's primary function was to express his emotions and to arouse similar emotions in the listener. In dealing with medieval music, we must remember that its composers were at least equally concerned with stimulating the mind. Some may have gone too far in their search for intellectual *subtilitas,* but the music they produced was by no means all bad. Listened to without prejudice, many songs in manneristic style prove to be both fascinating and attractive. Moreover, they provide one of the clearest reflections of the sophisticated society for whose amusement and delight they were created. Finally, the experiments with notational and rhythmic complexities developed many of the devices that were to become the common property of Renaissance composers. For its own sake, then, as well as for its historical importance, the music of the mannerists deserves close scrutiny.

As was suggested in connection with the music of Paolo Tenorista (Chapter XVIII), composers drew on both Italian and French practices in their efforts to notate the rhythmic complexities of manneristic style. They have been accused, indeed, of greater interest in notational puzzles than in rhythmic complexity for its own sake. It is true, certainly, that relatively simple rhythms were often notated in needlessly complex ways. By thus presenting the performer with problems that did not affect the musical result—unless the performer solved them wrongly— the notation itself deserves the epithet "mannered." Yet the music too presents problems that only a virtuoso in the performance of difficult rhythms could solve. Notational devices that affect only the performer and most of those that affect the music need not concern us here. It is more important to classify and illustrate the kinds of rhythmic complexities that characterize the manneristic style. To do so will deepen our understanding and appreciation of the ways medieval subtilitas expressed itself in music. It will also explain why the products of this ars subtilissima are so rarely performed today.

RHYTHMIC COMPLEXITY WITHIN THE NORMAL MENSURATIONS OF FRENCH NOTATION

One of the most common means of achieving rhythmic complexity involved the combination of patterns that suggest different mensurations. Perhaps the simplest manifestation of this practice is the fluctuation, either apparent or specifically indicated, between imperfect time with major prolation (6/8) and perfect time with minor prolation (3/4). Fluctuation of this sort had already appeared in some pieces by Machaut, and may have stimulated later composers to seek even greater contrasts between individual melodic lines. In a few cases, they wrote each voice in a different mensuration, sometimes with shifting combinations as the composition progressed. More often they exercised their ingenuity in devising independent or conflicting rhythms and meters while remaining within one basic mensuration.

The variety of their achievements in this regard makes illustration difficult, but we may single out the repetition of conflicting rhythmic patterns as a particularly characteristic device. In many cases only the note values of the pattern are repeated in what may be called a rhythmic sequence. It is not uncommon, however, to find that one or more voices also repeat the intervallic progressions at different pitch levels to create a melodic or even harmonic sequence. The seven measures from Trebor's ballade *Hélas, pitié* (Example XIX–1) present an unusual concentration of sequences with different and unexpected rhythmic patterns. Although the basic mensuration is perfect time with minor prolation (3/4), the contratenor seems to be in 6/8 throughout the passage. It states the pattern of the first measure four times in a purely rhythmic sequence before becoming a series of undifferentiated dotted quarter notes. The syncopated pattern of the cantus in the first measure shifts to the tenor for a three-measure rhythmic sequence and then back to the cantus for another three-measure sequence that is both rhythmic and melodic. Still another sequence begins in the cantus on the second half of measure 2. This sequence too is both melodic and rhythmic, but the pattern has a value of only four eighth notes and thus suggests 2/4 instead of 3/4 meter.[9]

If the concentration of sequences in Example XIX–1 is unusually dense, the passage nonetheless typifies the mannered achievement of complexity within essentially simple mensurations. Particularly in the first four measures, indeed, any feeling for the original mensuration is almost totally lost. To obtain this effect in a variety of ways seems to have been one of the tests of a composer's skill. One of the favorite devices was the sequential repetition of figures longer or shorter than the units of mensuration. Such a figure in the cantus of Example XIX–1

---

9.   For complete transcriptions of *Hélas, pitié,* see Apel, FSM, No. 42, and FSC, 1, No. 109.

Example XIX–1: *Trebor,* Hélas, pitié, *measures 48–54* (**Ch**, *fol. 42*).

(mm. 49–51) merely creates a temporary change of mensuration in that one voice. If the figure is of irregular length, however—say, five or seven minims—the effect is more disturbing and more complex. Still further complexity results when patterns in all voices are of different and irregular lengths.

A particularly instructive example of the complexity possible in even the simplest mensuration—imperfect time and prolation (2/4)—occurs in the ballade *Le point agu* (The sharp point) from the French repertory of the Court of Cyprus (Example XIX–2). Using only breves, dotted and undotted semibreves, and minims, the unknown composer created completely independent rhythms in all three voices. Only the tenor maintains a strict sequence of a rhythmic pattern that Bartók might have notated as $\frac{3+2+3}{8}$. The other two voices have shifting patterns of irregular lengths that finally return to rhythmic stability with a cadence on

Example XIX–2: *Rhythmic Complexities in the Ballade*
Le point agu (measures 21–33)

F at the close of the tenor's sequence. Transcription of such a passage in 2/4 facilitates reading the score but obscures the rhythmic structure of the individual lines. A "modern" barring according to the rhythmic patterns, on the other hand, could be done in several ways but would make the score extremely difficult to read. Perhaps the original notation in separate parts without barlines was the best solution after all. Apart from rhythmic problems, it should be remarked that both the tenor's descent through a full octave and the progression from a C-major triad to a cadence on **F** are characteristic tonal procedures in music of the early fifteenth century.[10]

DISPLACEMENT SYNCOPATION

The rhythmic complexities illustrated thus far are also characteristic in their introduction of syncopated notes in both 2/4 and 3/4 meters. Syncopation of this sort differs in no way from later practices and was already a normal procedure in the works of Machaut. For fourteenth-century theorists, however, *syncopa* included a special device that has no modern counterpart. This involved separating the notes of a triple unit or "perfection" by the insertion of one or more perfections. In relation to the other voices, they would thus be displaced from their normal position by one or two notes. This displacement syncopation was first described—in somewhat enigmatic terms—by Philippe de Vitry and Johannes de Muris.[11] It first appears in its simplest form in a few pieces by Machaut, although his modern editors sometimes failed to recognize its existence. A characteristic pattern that occurs several times in Machaut's Motet 20 may be seen in the third measure of the duplum, Example XIX–3a. Here, a minim (♪) displaces two perfect semibreves (♩. ♩.) before its perfection is completed by an imperfect semibreve

Example XIX–3: *Displacement Syncopation in Machaut*

a. MOTET 20, MEASURES 1–4

---

10.   The passage occurs near the close of the ballade's first section (mm. 21–33) and returns in the refrain (mm. 76–88). Complete transcription in Hoppin, CFR, 3, p. 80 (No. 47).

11.   See Apel, NPM, p. 395.

b. LAI 12, MEASURES 501–06

(♩) at the end of the measure. Two similar but longer passages, each with five displaced semibreves, occur in the tenth stanza of the canonic Lai 12 (Example XIX–3b).[12]

Compared with later developments, Machaut's treatment of displacement syncopation was simple in the extreme. It was characteristic, however, in applying this kind of syncopation to the triple units of perfect prolation. Machaut's successors generally followed the same practice and only rarely applied it to the larger units of perfect time with imperfect prolation (3/4). What they did do was to extend the length of the displaced passages and to include all the note values and normal rhythmic patterns of the basic mensuration. The result is one of the most common and distinctive features of late fourteenth-century mannerism. It is also one of the most difficult to indicate clearly in a modern transcription. We may illustrate the problem with the opening phrase of a rondeau, *Dame gentil* (Gentle lady), by Anthonello da Caserta (Example XIX–4). The excerpt is particularly complex because both the cantus and contratenor have displaced passages but at different time intervals above the tenor, which, as is usually the case, maintains a stable rhythmic foundation to support the syncopations. To notate all three voices within the 6/8 measures of the tenor gives the false impression that the displaced passages have syncopations within themselves. The alternate barring and notation above the staffs indicates the way performers would have understood the rhythmic organization of their melodies. As in Example XIX–2, the three voices of Anthonello's rondeau resolve their differences on the final chord of the cadence that completes the phrase. The cantus immediately begins another displacement, however, and the entire piece becomes a prime example of the way this kind of syncopation could be used to achieve extremes of medieval subtilitas.[13]

---

12. The passages are incorrectly transcribed in Schrade, PM, 2, Lai 12, but are correct in Ludwig, *Machaut,* 4, Lai 17 (mm. 248–49, 251–52).

13. Complete transcriptions in Apel, FSM, No. 29, and FSC, 1, No. 10; facsimile of the original notation in Apel, NPM, p. 415.

Example XIX–4: *Displacement Syncopation in* Dame gentil
by Anthonello da Caserta

PROPORTIONS

The devices for achieving rhythmic complexity that we have thus far examined have all depended for their effect on the equality of the minim (♪) in the four mensurations of French notation. This equality provided a stable basis for the performance of rhythmically independent lines, including those created by displacement syncopation or by the simultaneous use of mensurations with measures of different lengths. Composers in the latter half of the fourteenth century added another dimension to the subtlety of their art by introducing combinations of mensurations that replaced equality of the minim with proportional values. Medieval theorists had developed an elaborate system for classifying and naming what they called proportions and what we would call ratios. In earlier centuries, these ratios had been put to musical use primarily to determine and describe intervals such as the octave (2:1), fifth (3:2), fourth (4:3), and so on. Now, the ratios began to be applied in a so-called proportional notation that continued in use throughout most of the Renaissance.[14] We need not concern ourselves with theoretical excesses that constructed proportions far beyond the limits of musical practicality. Nor need we consider such simple proportions as 2:1, which merely called for the written note values to be diminished by half in performance.

As their most common audible result, proportions reduce to equal length mensural units that are normally unequal. This use of proportions obviously contrasts with the combination of mensurations in which the minims remain of equal value, although both procedures may have been suggested by the mensurations that produce 3/4 and 6/8 meters. In these mensurations, the six minims in each breve create measures of the same length, but three imperfect semibreves in 3/4 equal two

14. See Apel, NPM, p. 145 ff.

perfect semibreves in 6/8. The combination of these mensural units, because it was so easily achieved and because the minim remained a constant value, is not usually regarded as an example of proportions. Yet it played an essential part in developing the rhythmic complexities of manneristic style, and it remained a characteristic feature of music throughout much of the fifteenth century.

If the alternation and combination of patterns in 3/4 and 6/8 seems to have been primarily a French procedure, the principles of Italian notation gave rise to a similar treatment of 2/4 and 6/8, *but in measures of equal length.* As was indicated in Chapter XVIII, three minims in senaria imperfecta (♩♩♩) were the equivalent of four minims in octonaria (♩♩♩♩). Or, stated another way, the dotted quarter in 6/8 and the quarter in 2*/4 covered the same span of time. Similarly, of course, units of novenaria (9/8) and duodenaria (3*/4) were also equal in length. The theoretical examples given by Marchettus of Padua already imply this relationship, and one of its earliest practical applications appears in the madrigal *Nascoso el viso* (With my face hidden), by Giovanni da Firenze, who belonged to the first generation of Italian trecento composers (Example XIX–5a). Here, the upper voice shifts from duodenaria to novenaria and back, while the lower continues with unchanging values in duodenaria. The later composer Bartolino da Padova frequently exploited this equality of mensural units in more complex ways. In his three-voice ballata *Per un verde boschetto* (Through a green wood), for example, the shifts between senaria imperfecta and octonaria occur in all voices, sometimes together, sometimes separately. As a result, the contrasting metrical patterns of the two mensurations appear in simultaneous combination as well as in successive alternation (Example XIX–5b).[15] Although Bartolino did not here use minims in the passages in octonaria, there can be little doubt that the 4:3 proportion of minims was an Italian contribution to the complexities of manneristic style. It did not take long, however, for composers of all nationalities to make equal measures of 6/8 and 2/4 one of the hallmarks of that style.

Example XIX–5: *Proportional Mensurations in Italian Polyphony*

a. GIOVANNI DA FIRENZE, *Nascoso el viso*

15. Facsimile in Parrish, NMM, Pl. LV. The confused discussion and erroneous conclusion (p. 175 ff.) could have been avoided by checking the version in the Squarcialupi manuscript where the alternations between senaria imperfecta and octonaria (not quaternaria, as Parrish says) are specifically indicated.

b. BARTOLINO DA PADOVA, *Per un verde boschetto*

a. Above a spring
b. With an almost human voice

A second commonly used proportion (3:2) replaces two minims with three to produce measures of 9/8 against either 3/4 or 6/8. This proportion completed the devices that permitted writing the four mensurations of French notation in measures of equal rather than different lengths. Composers rarely combined all four at the same time, however, probably because they reserved the extremes of manneristic style, as has already been noted, for the cantus in three-voice secular songs.

Without being excessively complex, the anonymous ballade *Medee fu en amer veritable* (Medea was true in loving) illustrates the common proportions as well as the other features of mannered style that have previously been discussed (AMM, No. 68). The tenor has unusually simple rhythms and remains in 6/8 from beginning to end. The contratenor changes a few times from 6/8 to 3/4 or 2/4 with equal minims and also makes extensive use of the 4:3 proportion. For the most part, the units of this proportion correspond with, and thus emphasize, the divisions of the tenor's imperfect time, but unusual rhythms and syncopations in measures 12–14 produce a more complex effect. In a longer passage (mm. 28–33), the cantus makes equally complex use of the same proportion. This voice also introduces the 3:2 proportion of minims, usually in the normal rhythms of 9/8 meter. In measure 9, however, displacement syncopation adds to the subtlety of the proportion. The same kind of syncopation occurs in normal 6/8 meter (mm. 2–4), and in combination with irregular rhythmic patterns of various sorts (see especially mm. 25–26 and 55–59). In addition, the cantus illustrates a problem that frequently arises in connection with the use of proportions. In this voice, all of the measures in the modern transcription that have sixteenth notes in 6/8 meter were written in duple proportion—that is, with a minim equal to ♪ instead of ♪ . Where we find nothing but minims, as in measure 23, their rhythmic organization in groups of two or three remains ambiguous. In measure 34, on the other hand, the use of displacement syncopation proves that the composer thought of duple proportion as producing two units of 6/8 in the time of one. Whenever he used this proportion, therefore, a correct transcription and performance would be in measures of 6/16 (or 12/16). The distinction is slight, perhaps, but it adds one more subtlety to this typical example of a most subtle art. It is interesting to note that the text of this ballade—like many others in the later Middle Ages—introduces characters from classical Greek and Roman stories to exemplify the conventions of courtly love.

From the foregoing examples of manneristic style it is obvious that composers freely combined the various rhythmic devices we have been discussing. Unusual and conflicting rhythmic patterns, syncopations of duple note values, and displacement of triple units occur in both normal and proportional mensurations. Moreover, different proportions often appear in combination or successively in a single voice. Not content with these seemingly limitless possibilities, a few composers achieved even greater complexity by introducing unusual proportions—such as 9:8, 5:2, 7:3—or by applying the more common proportions to unexpected mensurations. An example of the latter practice occurs in the first measures of the rondeau *Amans, ames secretement* (Lovers, love secretly) by Baude Cordier.[16] In perfect time and prolation (9/8), a duple proportion in the cantus results in two measures of 9/16 (Example XIX–6). In other words, it divides a 9/8 measure into equal halves! At the same time, the contratenor is written in triple proportion (3:1), which produces no

Example XIX–6: Amans, ames secretement, *by Baude Cordier, measures 1–4* (**O**, *fol. 123*)

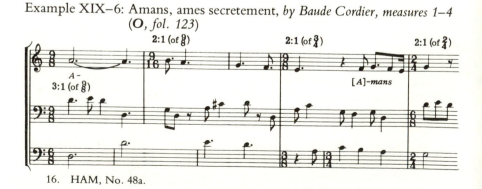

16.   HAM, No. 48a.

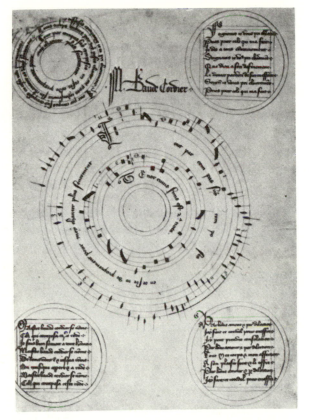

The famous perpetual canon *Tout par compas suy composé* by Baude Cordier (Chantilly).

visible effect in a modern transcription and no audible effect in performance. The rondeau is very short, but, in the equivalents of fourteen measures of 6/8 and four of 2/4, its three voices manage to introduce all four basic mensurations in their normal values as well as in six different combinations with duple and triple proportions.[17]

The concentration of proportions in Cordier's rondeau is almost unparalleled and contrasts strikingly with his much simpler rondeau *Belle, bonne* (Beautiful, good [lady]). The more flowing melodic line of this rondeau and its opening bit of imitation in all three voices probably reflect the Italian influence that helped to bring manneristic excesses under control at the beginning of the fifteenth century. At any rate, the relative simplicity of *Belle, bonne* points toward a new musical era and makes it one of Cordier's most attractive songs.[18] Its chief claim to fame, however, arises from its original notation in the form of a heart, a symbol of the poet-composer's gift to his lady of his own heart together with his "new song."[19] Visual representations of this sort were more common in poetry than in music, and they must be regarded as another, if rare, manifestation of manneristic tendencies. Cordier himself provided another example when he used circular staffs to notate the perpet-

17. For a facsimile and explanation of the proportions, see Apel, NPM, p. 175.

18. Cordier's known works—1 ballade, 9 rondeaux, and 1 Gloria—are published in Reaney, EFCM, 1, pp. 1–18.

19. Facsimiles in Apel, NPM, p. 427, and Grout, HWM, p. 135.

ual canon *Tout par compas suy composés* (All by compass am I composed).[20] The music resembles an Italian caccia in having two canonic voices above a free tenor, but its text is a three-line rondeau refrain. The remainder of this rondeau's text appears—again written in a circle—in the upper left-hand corner of the page and includes directions for performing the canon. Three more rondeau texts in the other three corners of the page are written in squares within circles. One of these is of special interest because it asserts that Baude Cordier composed the round, that he came from Reims, and that his music was known in Rome. We know nothing else about Cordier except the eleven pieces that have been preserved. The heart and circle appear together as additions to the Chantilly Codex, but his name is found with other pieces only in two later manuscripts of northern Italian origin. It seems probable, therefore, that Cordier was one of the many northern composers who made Italy a French musical province in the early decades of the fifteenth century.[21]

Much less well known than the heart and circle pieces of Cordier is a virelai written in the form of a harp, *La harpe de melodie,* by Jacob Senleches or Selesses (see jacket of this book and AMM, No. 69). Like Cordier's circle canon, this virelai has two canonic voices above a free and textless tenor. Although the scribe of **Ch** copied *La harpe de melodie* in the normal way on staffs, both its text and an added rondeau that explains the method of performance prove the notation within a harp to be the composer's original intent. Written on the ribbon spiraling down the curved right side of the harp, the explanatory rondeau indicates somewhat enigmatically that the lines represent strings and notes are not written in the spaces as on a normal musical staff. The rondeau also indicates the beginning pitch of the canonic voices, the time interval between them, and the diminution by one half of all their black and white (hollow black) notes. The values of red notes are not diminished, and they function as usual to produce measures of 3/4 against the normal 6/8 meter of the tenor. To the unnecessary—because inaudible—mannerism of the 2:1 diminution in the canonic voices, Senleches added a number of special note shapes with downward stems, both straight and hooked. When the riddle of their meaning has been solved, the chief

---

20. Facsimile in Parrish, NMM, P1. LXII. For corrections of all previously published transcription, see R. Meylan, "Reparation de la roue de Cordier," MD, 26 (1972), p. 70 (lowest example).

21. Craig Wright, in "Tapissier and Cordier: New Documents and Conjectures," MQ, 59 (1973), pp. 177–89, has conjectured that Baude Cordier was the Baude Fresnel (d. 1397–98) who was a harper and chamber valet to Philip the Bold, Duke of Burgundy, and a companion of the composer Tapissier, who was also in the duke's employ. As Wright has shown, the name Tapissier appears in numerous archival references, both alone and in connection with his "real" name, Jean de Noyers. Thus, the absence of the name Cordier in the same archives that refer to both Tapissier and and Fresnel argues strongly against the likelihood of Wright's conjecture.

function of these note shapes proves to be the introduction of short figures in either 3:2 or 4:3 proportion. As a result, the smaller note values
in a modern transcription appear in a wide variety of unusual and irregular rhythmic patterns. Such patterns make *La harpe de melodie* typically
manneristic in style, but they are particularly characteristic of Senleches,
one of the most mannered of all composers.[22]

COMPOSERS REPRESENTED IN THE CHANTILLY AND MODENA MANUSCRIPTS

Because they preserve the names of so many composers, the Chantilly
and Modena manuscripts clearly reveal the cosmopolitan nature of the
society that produced mannered notation and the ars subtilior.[23] In addition to Baude Cordier, some thirty-one composers of secular songs are
named in *Ch,* twenty of whom are represented by only one or two
works. The remaining eleven are credited with from three to ten songs
apiece. Many of the names are otherwise unknown, and some are given
in shortened forms that make it difficult to connect them with archival
references to singers in the papal chapel or to men in the service of
various princes. Most of the texts are conventional love songs, and
therefore they too give no information about their composers. It is well
to remember, moreover, that even a song in honor of a particular person
need not have been written by a member of that person's household. Its
composer might equally well have honored a visiting prince in the hope
of receiving a princely reward. All of these difficulties notwithstanding,
a number of composers represented in *Ch* have been identified and their
affiliations with princes or popes determined with reasonable certainty.

It is probable that at least half, if not a majority, of the composers
came from various regions of northern France. We have no indisputable
information about Cordier's life beyond his own statement that he came
from Reims, but we do know a good bit more about some other song
composers in the original repertory of *Ch.* Brief consideration of two
men—Philipoctus de Caserta and the already-mentioned Jacob Senleches—will illustrate both the diverse origin of maneristic composers
and the ways in which their association with courts in southern France
and Spain can be established.

Jacob (or Jacomi) Senleches probably came from Senlecques in the
Pas-de-Calais province of northwestern France.[24] From the rich ar-

22. All six of Senleches' known pieces are published in Apel, FSC, 1, Nos. 88–93 (see
    also FSM, Nos. 47–51). Unfortunately, the first section of *La harpe de melodie* (only
    in FSC, No. 92) is wrongly transcribed (see note to No. 69 in AMM).
23. Apel, FSC, 1, includes all French secular songs in *Ch* and *Mod* that are ascribed to a
    composer, except the two by Cordier in *Ch.*
24. Senleches's name appears, with some variant spellings, as J. Senleches, Jacomi, Sen-
    leches Jakob, and Jakob de Senleches in *Ch,* and as Jacopinus Selesses in *Mod.*

chives of Aragon, we learn that in 1378 "Jacomi" was attached to that court or to the household of the future King John I. That same year and again in 1379, he traveled to the minstrels' schools in Flanders. Returning to Spain, Jacomi was sent by John I to his sister Eleanor, wife of another John I, King of Castile. After Eleanor's death in 1382, Senleches wrote a famous lament, the ballade *Fuions de ci* (Let us flee from here). The future for musicians in Castile evidently looked bleak—as the ballade's refrain says—"since we lost Eleanor," and by August 1383 Senleches was in the service of Pedro de Luna, cardinal of Aragon and future Benedict XIII.[25] How long he remained with the cardinal is unknown. He was not in the papal choir in Avignon when Benedict succeeded Clement VII in 1394, and no further clues as to his activities can be found in any of his other songs. Senleches' works in *Ch* consist of the virelai *La harpe de melodie* and three ballades, to which list *Mod* adds two more virelais.

Of all the composers' names in *Ch,* only that of Philipoctus de Caserta is clearly of Italian origin. It is unexpected, therefore, to find that his seven pieces in *Ch* are all settings of French texts—six ballades and one rondeau—and comprise all of his known compositions. Four of the ballades also appear in *Mod,* thereby correcting the ascription of one ballade in *Ch* to Jo. Galiot. How an Italian composer from a town near Naples came to Avignon—if that is where Philipoctus was—remains uncertain. Perhaps he joined the papal court when Queen Joanna of Naples welcomed and supported Clement VII shortly after the Great Schism began. At any rate, Philipoctus's ballade *Par les bons Gedeon et Sanson* (By the good Gideon and Samson) mentions the Schism and praises "the sovereign pope who is named Clement." Another ballade refers in enigmatic terms to the expedition of Louis, Duke of Anjou, to restore Joanna to her throne, usurped by her nephew Charles Durazzo. Joanna and Charles are disguised as Ariadne and Theseus, and Louis's name is hidden in the riddle of the refrain, "Qu'avoir ne puet sanz O couvert de Lis" (That she cannot have without O covered by the lily). As the emblem of French royalty, the lily was applicable to the duke of Anjou, brother of King Charles V, and when the *lis* covers O it yields Lois (or Loys), common medieval spellings of the duke's name.[26] With the spiritual blessing and financial support of Clement VII, Louis set out from Avignon in March of 1382, and Philipoctus's ballade probably dates from about this time. Certainly it could not have been written much later, for Charles Durazzo had Queen Joanna strangled with a silken cord in March of 1382, and Louis's campaign ended in total failure.

25. U. Günther, "Zur Biographie einiger Komponisten der *Ars subtilior,*" AMW, 21 (1964), p. 195.

26. For a full discussion of this text and the connection with Naples, see N. Wilkins, "Some Notes on Philipoctus de Caserta," *Nottingham Mediaeval Studies,* 8 (1964), p. 84 ff.

The ballade *Le saut perilleux*, by J. Galiot, found in the Chantilly manuscript.

Perhaps the strangest circumstance connected with three of Philipoctus's ballades is the quotation of their incipits—words *and* music—in the virelai *Sus un fontayne* (Above a spring) by Johannes Ciconia of Liège.[27] The quantity and variety of Ciconia's music make him—for us—a much more important composer than Philipoctus, and his act of homage therefore seems inconceivable unless the two men were personal friends. Yet we have no evidence that they were ever associated, even though we are unusually well informed about Ciconia's life and works (see below, pp. 493–500). Moreover, Ciconia was the first northern composer to be so strongly influenced by Italian music that he wrote numerous madrigals and ballate, but only this one virelai in the manneristic style. Philipoctus, as we have seen, did just the reverse. All of his preserved music reveals him as a mature and skillful composer who wholeheartedly adopted the French style current in Avignon in the 1380s.

Several composers whose works appear in **Ch** are also represented in the Modena Codex. Some of these composers' names were unknown to the scribe of **Mod,** but the works that he left anonymous include pieces by Hasprois (1), Galiot (1), Matheus de Sancto Johanne (2), and Machaut (4). He did know the names of Jacob Senleches and Philipoctus de Caserta, however, to each of whom he ascribed four French songs. Among all these pieces we find Senleches's lament for Eleanor of Aragon and ballades by Matheus and Philipoctus that honor Clement

27. In the order of their quotation, the three ballades of Philipoctus are: *En remirant* (While watching); *En attendant* (While waiting); and *De ma dolour* (From my sorrow). The scribe's error in attributing *En attendant* to Galiot in **Ch** probably arose because Galiot did set a different text that also begins *En attendant* (**Ch,** No. 59). Apel still attributes both pieces to Galiot (FSC, 1, xxxiv, note to No. 14) and makes the improbable suggestion that Philipoctus and Galiot extracted internal passages from Ciconia's virelai to begin the three ballades. To quote the opening words and music of three already existing pieces is surely a far more likely procedure.

VII. Another ballade that honors Clement as the rightful pope, *Courtois et sages* (Courtly and wise), appears only in **Mod** and a Paris manuscript (**PR**) that originated in northern Italy.

MATTEO DA PERUGIA

Although the relationships with Avignon and the music of **Ch** might suggest French origin, at least 30 percent and perhaps more of the repertory in **Mod** is devoted to compositions by Matteo da Perugia, who has no known connection with southern France or Spain. All of Matteo's pieces in **Mod** are unica, and none sheds any light on his life. Biographical information about him is not entirely lacking, however. A singer at the cathedral of Milan in the years 1402–07 and again in 1414–16, Matteo enjoyed the patronage of Pietro Filargo, the cardinal archbishop of Milan. His generous salary was once reduced because he was "maintained with food and drink" by the cardinal, and in 1406 he accompanied Pietro on a journey to Pavia. The coincidence of Matteo's first period of service with the cardinal's residence in Milan makes it probable that the musician remained with his patron when the latter became involved in the intrigues that led to his elevation to the papacy as Alexander V. Presumably, Matteo remained at the papal court in Bologna under John XXIII and returned to Milan only when John set out to begin the Council of Constance. The last payment to Matteo recorded in the cathedral archives was for the month of August, 1416, and his subsequent history remains unknown. Although it is not certain, he is believed to have died in (or before) the month of January, 1418.

That Matteo da Perugia was somehow involved in putting the Modena Codex together is suggested by the extraordinary number of his pieces that it contains and even more by the distribution of those pieces in the five fascicles of the manuscript. The three central fascicles are devoted to a chiefly secular repertory that contains—with one exception—all of the music ascribed to composers other than Matteo da Perugia as well as some anonymous works. It is here that we find the four pieces of Machaut, all the concordances with **Ch,** and eight pieces by Matteo himself. The bulk of Matteo's compositions appear in the first and last fascicles, where no other composer is named except Grenon, the author of a ballade for which Matteo provided a contratenor. Of the twelve pieces and two contratenors in the first fascicle, Matteo is credited with only five; but of the twenty-one items in the last fascicle, his authorship is indicated for all but three: another single contratenor, a motet, and the ballade of Grenon. Whether any of the anonymous pieces in these two fascicles should be attributed to Matteo remains an open question. Some of the Mass movements resemble his style, and his habit of composing new contratenors for preexistent compositions makes it probable that he was responsible for the three examples.[28] If not prepared for or by Matteo himself, the first and last sections of the manuscript must have come from a musical circle of which he was an active member. The contratenor of Grenon's ballade and a fragmentary cantus with only the initial letter of the text aside, we still have thirty pieces ascribed to Matteo da Perugia in *Mod* and another ten that may also be his.[29] The authentic works fall into three distinct but most unequally represented categories. The only settings of Italian texts are two rather undistinguished ballate in the Italian form of vocal duets with instrumental contratenor parts. Sacred pieces with Latin texts include five settings of the Gloria and an isorhythmic motet. The remainder of Matteo's work—22 pieces in all—consists of French secular songs: 4 ballades, 7 virelais, 10 rondeaux, and one canon. We must assume that the preponderance of French songs in Matteo's output reflects the taste and interests of his ecclesiastical patron. After studying in Padua, Oxford, and Paris, Pietro Filargo taught at the University of Pavia and was a trusted counselor of Gian Galeazzo Visconti in Milan. By the time Pietro became cardinal archbishop of Milan, he was powerful and rich, a humanist and Maecenas who held a joyous court and gave much time to convivial pleasures. He might well have preferred music such as Matteo wrote, even if the general vogue of French manners and styles had not all but overwhelmed the native Italian product.

As might be expected, Matteo set most of the French texts for a solo voice (cantus) with instrumental tenor and contratenor parts. Of the six pieces that depart from this traditional pattern, one virelai and two rondeaux lack contratenors. Another two-voice rondeau has a different text in each voice, and one rondeau is a vocal duet (cantus and tenor) with an instrumental contratenor. The canon has a four-line text that reveals how it is to be sung by three voices in the manner of the French chace. A few of Matteo's French chansons show him to have been in full command of the highly mannered style.[30] In the majority of his pieces, however, he tends to moderate the complexities of that style. This is especially true of pieces in the last section of *Mod,* some of which approach the rhythmic clarity, the harmonic solidity, and the lyric grace of the early Renaissance. To what extent Matteo led the way in this return to a simpler style and whether it reflects Italian influence are difficult questions to answer. The first decades of the fifteenth century saw a general reaction against mannered complexity, and Matteo may seem a

28.   One contratenor is for a rondeau by Machaut that appears in the central portion of *Mod* (AMM, No. 63). Another is for a ballata by Bartolino da Padova; the third is for a composition now unknown.

29.   See U. Günther, "Das Manuskript Modena. . . ," MD, 24 (1970), p. 24 and index, pp. 52–67.

30.   For example, *Le greygnour bien* (The greatest good), Apel, FSC, 1, No. 51, and FSM, No. 1 and Pl. 1 (facs.). For a discussion of Matteo's stylistic development, see FSM, pp. 13b–14a and the commentary on individual pieces.

leader in this respect merely because so much of his music has been preserved.

Matteo's few sacred works also reveal his general adherence to French musical traditions. Only one of the five Glorias may be called Italian, by virtue of being written as a caccia with two canonic voices above a free instrumental tenor. Two of the remaining four Glorias are in three-voice song style with text only in the cantus; one is in four-voice motet style with text in both upper voices; and one is a curious mixture of motet and song styles. One of the two voices with text lies in the same range as the tenor and functions as a contratenor whose notes are often broken into smaller values to accommodate the words. The third voice, a fifth higher in range than the other two, resembles the cantus of a secular song in a highly ornate and manneristic style. Like this hybrid, the other two Glorias in song style are written in 6/8 meter, the most common mensuration of the contemporary French chanson, but their cantus melodies range from moderate complexity to extreme rhythmic simplicity. In contrast to the French secular songs, the simplest of the three Glorias appears in the oldest section of *Mod* (No. 40), while the hybrid and most manneristic style appears in the manuscript's fifth fascicle (No. 101), which presumably contains Matteo's latest compositions. It almost seems that, as soloist in the Milan cathedral, Matteo here provided himself an opportunity for public display of his virtuosity in the performance of intricate rhythms and elaborate vocal ornaments.[31]

It is important to note that Matteo introduced isorhythmic procedures in the tenor and contratenor of the four-voice Gloria in motet style and in the tenor of the hybrid combination of motet and song styles. Another curious hybrid that might be classed as a motet or a troped Agnus Dei (*Mod*, No. 1) is fully isorhythmic. These technical devices, as well as the song and motet styles of his sacred music, are just as obviously derived from French practices as are the forms and styles of almost all his secular songs. Despite his Italian origin and his connection with Milan, then, we need not hesitate to regard Matteo da Perugia as a typical composer of French music at the beginning of the fifteenth century.

Critics have rated him as a good craftsman of mediocre talent and have denied him a place in music history as an "epoch making" composer. These adverse judgments rest in part on the apparently limited distribution that Matteo's music achieved. They also seem to result from Matteo's position as an Italian who chose to write in French forms and styles at a time when rhythmic and structural complexities were more highly prized than sensuous melodic charm. Yet it is that choice, together with the quantity and diversity of his music, that makes Matteo an important

31. Matteo's sacred polyphony, as well as the anonymous pieces in *Mod* that may be his, are published in F. Fano, *Le Origini e il primo maestro di cappella: Matteo da Perugia*, Vol. 1 of *La Cappella musicale del Duomo di Milano* (Milan, 1956). A supplemental essay will consider the technical and formal aspects of Matteo's sacred music in some detail.

historical figure. The quality of his music may be subject to dispute; his influence may have been slight; but his significance as a representative of his age cannot be denied.

JOHANNES CICONIA

The last composer to be considered individually, Johannes Ciconia (c. 1335–1411), presents almost a reverse image of Matteo da Perugia in his reaction to the crosscurrents between French and Italian musical cultures. Coming from the city of Liège, Ciconia's musical training must have been wholly in the French tradition. Yet he wrote only two French chansons, as far as we know, and the bulk of his secular music consists of Italian songs—four madrigals and nine ballate. In further contrast to Matteo, Ciconia's settings of Latin texts make up slightly more than half of his total output. These works include nine Mass movements, (five Glorias and four Credos), eleven motets, and one canon. Another canon, but with French text, has been attributed to Ciconia because it appears beneath one of his madrigals in the only manuscript source. In addition to these thirty-seven pieces, fragments of two ballate, one Gloria, and two motets complete the list of works by or attributed to Ciconia. No other composer of the transitional period between Machaut and Dufay left such a large body of music. Only Matteo da Perugia came close to equaling it, and just as Matteo has been included with composers of French secular music, so Ciconia has often been listed as an important Italian composer. Such a designation for Ciconia is both misleading and wrong. Instead, we should regard him as the first northern composer of stature to succumb to the charms of Italian musical forms and styles.

Although Ciconia's life is unusually well documented, there are still many gaps in our knowledge of his activities. He himself attested to his origin in Liège, but the date of his birth is unknown. Presumably that event occurred between 1330 and 1335, for in 1350 he appears in Avignon as clerk and "familiar" of Eleanor of Comminges, the wife of Guillaume, Viscount of Turenne and nephew of Pope Clement VI. From 1358 to 1367, Ciconia was in Italy with Cardinal Gil Albornoz, the papal legate who was then making his second attempt to regain control of the Papal States. As clerk and dispenser of alms for Albornoz, Ciconia must have followed the cardinal-legate in his many travels throughout Italy— to Pisa and Florence, to the court of Queen Joanna of Naples, to Ancona, Cesena, and Bologna, and to meetings with his allies, including Francesco Carrara of Padua, the patron of Bartolino. During these years in which Ciconia first encountered Italian music on its native soil, he also became a priest (1362) and received a canonicate at the Church of St. John the Evangelist in his native city. Cardinal Albornoz died in 1367, and we lose track of Ciconia until 1372, when we find him residing in

Liège. Missing records from the city's archives make our knowledge of his next thirty years scanty indeed. He retained his canonicate at St. John the Evangelist until 1402, but his presence is not documented between 1372 and 1385 or in 1396, 1398, and 1400. During these years Ciconia may well have made one or more trips to Avignon or to Italy, even though he had found a "companion" in Liège by whom he had several natural children. (The circumstance was by no means unusual.) Particularly in the last years of the fourteenth century Ciconia seems to have renewed or established connections with Padua and the Carrara family. One of his two motets in praise of Francesco Zabarella appears to have been written after the eminent jurist became a professor at the University of Padua but before he was made archpriest of the cathedral in 1397. Another motet honors Stefano Carrara, a natural son of Francesco Novello. For both motets Ciconia received handsome rewards. In 1401 Zabarella granted him a benefice in a church near Padua. The next year Stefano Carrara became bishop of Padua, and Ciconia received a second prebend, this time in the cathedral itself. By April, 1403, Ciconia was in residence in Padua, where he remained until his death in December, 1411. During Ciconia's long life, then, we know that he spent at least two periods of about nine years each in Italy. Much of his music is obviously connected with these two periods, and direct evidence of his musical activity in Avignon and Liège is almost totally lacking. Taken as a whole, however, Ciconia's works present an amalgam of French and Italian elements that make him one of the most important forerunners of the new international musical style.

As might be expected, Ciconia's madrigals and ballate are his most Italianate compositions. Three of the madrigals and five of the ballate are vocal duets in the traditional forms and styles. The fourth madrigal is apparently a vocal trio, although the scribe failed to copy the first two lines of text beneath the contratenor part. Of the four ballate for three voices, two follow the model of the French solo song with instrumental tenor and contratenor parts. The other two appear to have been written in the Italian manner as vocal duets with an instrumental contratenor. In some manuscripts, however, these pieces have the text only in the cantus or lack the contratenor part. Two more ballate cannot be classified because only their cantus parts have been preserved. The adoption of song style for three-voice ballate is by no means unusual, of course, but even in his successful imitations of Italian style Ciconia betrays his own individuality, if not his northern origin and training. Perhaps he differs from his Italian models most often and most obviously in his greater concern for melodic organization and structural unity. Instead of using a variety of rhythmic and melodic patterns within a phrase, Ciconia was more apt to reiterate a small number of related figures. He often applied this procedure to sequential passages in the traditional style with a more active upper voice above a simpler tenor (Example

XIX–7a). A more distinctively personal characteristic, however, is his frequent equalization of the two voices by alternating short motives and figures in imitation (Example XIX–7b). These two excerpts from Ciconia's madrigal *Per quella strada* provide typical examples of the different procedures. The second excerpt comes from a melisma between lines of text and may have been intended as an instrumental interlude.

Example XIX–7: *Two Excerpts from* Per quella strada
                 by Ciconia

a. MEASURES 10–16

Through that milky way of the sky

b. MEASURES 28–32

Many of the same devices appear in Ciconia's two-voice ballate, although they are traditional in being smaller in scale and simpler in style than the madrigals. One of the most attractive pieces in this group—and indeed in all of Ciconia's works—is the ballata *Con lagrime bagnandome el viso* (With tears bathing my face; AMM, No. 70). In this lament on the death of his "signore," Ciconia tempers the sweetness of Italian lyricism with expressive dissonances and syncopations. Imitative figures in the two voices are perhaps more frequent than one would find in the work of a native Italian, and a motive dear to Machaut (♪♩♪) provides material for an extended melisma at the close of the second musical section.

Ciconia's only work that adopts the mannered style current in southern France is his already-cited virelai *Sus un fontayne,* which quotes the opening words and music of three ballades by Philipoctus de Caserta (see above, p. 489 and n. 27). In a different way, Ciconia's other setting of a French secular text is just as unusual. Only the upper voice has been preserved of the virelai *Aler m'en veus en strangne partie* (I would leave for foreign parts). The piece can be reconstructed, however, because it also exists as a two-voice motet, *O beatum incendium* (O blessed ardor), with the same text in both voices.[32] That the motet must be a contrafactum is proved by its retention of repeat signs after the open ending of the second musical section, although the text does not call for such repetition. The virelai, therefore, must represent the original form of the piece. Another motet by Ciconia is also for two voices of equal range, both of which sing the same text.[33] In this case, however, extensive melismas and the overall form suggest a derivation from the madrigal rather than the virelai or ballata.

That Ciconia should create motets from or in secular forms is another indication of his eclectic tendencies, but it also reflects a general trend toward simpler and more personal expression of religious feeling. We should not be surprised, then, to find other motets in which he abandoned isorhythmic techniques and four-voice writing with different texts in the two upper parts. Ciconia did write motets with this typical structure, to be sure, but they account for only five of the eleven pieces. One of the five, moreover, is not isorhythmic, and none of the tenors makes use of a repeated plainchant melody. The four motets for three voices diverge even more from traditional motet style. None is isorhythmic, and again none has a plainchant tenor. Three do have two vocal parts above the tenor, but in two pieces (Nos. 34 and 36) both voices sing the same text. Only one of the three-voice motets (No. 40) has a different text for each of the upper parts. Even this motet is unusual, however, in that the tenor is not entirely without text. Instead, it occasionally has words, phrases, and even complete lines drawn from the text of the triplum.

Ciconia's fourth motet for three voices, *Regina gloriosa* (Glorious Queen; No. 32), is like *O beatum incendium* in being a contrafactum of a virelai or ballata. An unusually short text is spread—with some repetitions—over two sections of music, the second of which again has unnecessary open and closed endings. The texture is that of a French chanson, and performance with text in the cantus only is a possibility. The manuscript source, however, gives almost all the text beneath the tenor part, and Ciconia probably intended the motet to be a vocal duet with an instrumental contratenor. Whatever the arrangement, the position of *Regina gloriosa* as a forerunner of the early Renaissance song motet is clear.[34]

Adapting sacred Latin texts to secular song forms is not the only way in which Ciconia foreshadowed future developments in motet composition. His six motets with only one instead of two or more texts presage the gradual abandonment of medieval polytextuality. By writing his own tenors instead of using preexistent melodies, he achieved

32. The two pieces are Nos. 17 and 30 in S. Clercx, *Johannes Ciconia.* Further references to Ciconia's works follow the numbering of pieces in Vol. 2.
33. No. 31: *O Petre, Christi discipule* (O Peter, disciple of Christ).
34. See Reese, MR, p. 94.

greater control over tonal organization and paved the way for the creation of counterpoint above a harmonic bass. This function of the lowest voice becomes particularly obvious in the fanfarelike passages that so often add brilliance to the close of Ciconia's motets (Example XIX–8). The reiteration and imitation of short motives in such passages—almost always above **f** and **c′** in the tenor—clearly stem from traditional ways of creating rhythmic climaxes in isorhythmic motets. Italian influence, however, probably accounts for the more general use of imitation, both of short motives and of longer melodies, throughout the motets. And when the imitation involves the tenor as well as the upper voices, Ciconia seems to anticipate the Renaissance ideal of a homogeneous texture in which all voices are of equal melodic importance.

Example XIX–8: *Melismatic Amen of* O felix templum
by Ciconia

Italian influence on the melodic style of Ciconia's motets is difficult to pin down. Many of his figures and motives belong to the common melodic vocabulary of his French predecessors and contemporaries. Yet even in the isorhythmic pieces his melodies often seem tinged with Italian sweetness and lyric charm. Indeed, Ciconia's motto as a composer may well have been the opening words of the duplum in his motet No. 41: "Melodia suavissima cantemus" (Let us sing the sweetest melody).

CICONIA'S POLYPHONIC MASS MOVEMENTS

After the combinations of new and old procedures and the mixtures of French and Italian elements encountered in Ciconia's motets, it is no surprise to find that the forms and styles of his Mass movements are equally various. That he composed such movements at all may have resulted from his early contacts with the musical life at Avignon. Some, if not all, of the movements, however, may have been written for use at Liège or Padua. At any rate, there seems to be considerable justification for regarding Ciconia as a link between the liturgical polyphony of Avignon and the more widespread composition of Mass movements and complete Masses in the early Renaissance.

Four musically unified Gloria-Credo pairs plus a single Gloria comprise all of the preserved Mass movements by Ciconia that are legible and complete. Suzanne Clercx's edition does not bring together the members of each pair, but a number of features make them easily recognizable. The usual but superficial indications of musical unity in paired movements are identity of mensuration, mode, and number and ranges of voices. More profound indications come from the identity of style and of structural procedures in both members of a pair. Ciconia's four pairs are particularly instructive in this respect, because each has its own distinctive style. Nos. 22 and 29 are in four-voice motet style (4^2) with isorhythmic repetitions of tenor and contratenor colores. Nos. 21 and 27 are in three-voice madrigal style (3^3), and Nos. 23 and 28 are in three-voice song style (3^1). The fourth pair, Nos. 24 and 26, alternates two-voice solo sections (2^2) with sections for chorus in three-voice motet style (3^2). The single Gloria (No. 20) also alternates solo and choral sections, but the latter are here in four-voice motet style. Ciconia's obviously systematic approach to the composition of unified Gloria-Credo pairs makes it probable that a matching Credo for the single Gloria is now lost.

In general, it is clear, the basic styles of Ciconia's paired movements correspond with the song, motet, and simultaneous styles of the fourteenth-century Avignon repertory described in Chapter XVI. For the second pair listed above, however, madrigal rather than simultaneous style is a much more appropriate designation. Only rarely in these two movements do all three voices sing the same syllables at the same time, and the style is clearly not related to the chordal writing of French composers as exemplified in the Gloria and Credo of Machaut's Mass. Instead, these movements adopt the more imitative style of the later madrigal and ballata, as well as their declamatory and dramatic elements. Nowhere in Ciconia's works does he exploit the dramatic effect of repeated words more tellingly than at the beginning of the Gloria (Example XIX–9). By his treatment and repetition of the word "pax," the opening phrase becomes a personal plea for peace in times that were singularly troubled by civil, political, and religious strife.

Example XIX–9: *The Opening Measures of Ciconia's Gloria in Madrigal Style*

For a number of reasons, Ciconia's paired Mass movements must be regarded as his most innovative and influential compositions. Discussion of those reasons, with analyses of the individual pairs, cannot be undertaken here, but we may at least note some of the topics such a discussion would have to consider. Because of uncertainty as to the dates of specific compositions, chronological developments are difficult, if not impossible, to determine. As far as we can tell, however, Ciconia was the first composer who consistently wrote musically related Gloria-Credo pairs. Moreover, his association of structural relationships with the unities of mode, mensuration, and basic style was a contribution of singular importance. Later composers, both on the continent and in England, continued his search for ways to establish a unity of structural procedure that could support a rich variety of surface details. Their first satisfactory solution to this problem was the cantus firmus Mass, in which one melody serves as the tenor for all five movements. With the achievement of this solution, the cyclic Mass became, in Bukofzer's words, "the most representative and extended form of Renaissance music."[35]

No less innovative, again as far as we can tell from uncertain chronology, was the introduction of what we may call responsorial polyphony in three of Ciconia's Mass movements. At any rate, most of the other composers who alternated duets with choral sections were much younger men, and examples of the practice are particularly abundant in the three decades following the death of Ciconia in 1411. Because the manuscript sources designate the alternating sections by the words *unus* or *duo* and *chorus,* it has been argued that these pieces mark the beginning of choral polyphony. That they do not has already been suggested in Chapter XVI. In the various pieces that introduce solo duets, we find choral sections in all three of the styles cultivated by composers of Mass movements in the fourteenth century. Ciconia, as we have seen, alternated duets with choral sections in three- and four-voice motet style. What was new, then, was not the style of the choral sections but the unaccompanied duets for soloists. This solo performance had to be iden-

35. SMRM, p. 217.

tified, and it therefore became necessary to label the choral passages as well. Of course, we must not think of this music in terms of modern choirs. Even in the larger religious establishments, it is unlikely that the membership of medieval choirs exceeded, or often reached, a total of twelve or at most sixteen singers. Yet there is no reason to insist that fourteenth-century Mass movements were always performed with only one singer for each vocal part. Where choirs did exist, as in the papal chapel, performance with three or four singers on a part may well have been the norm with which the innovation of duets for two soloists provided an effective contrast.[36]

ITALIAN SOURCES OF EARLY FIFTEENTH-CENTURY MUSIC

One of the more curious aspects of music from the early fifteenth century is the preponderance of manuscript sources that originated in northern Italy. Only in small part can the loss of manuscripts from other regions of Europe explain this situation. We know of musical activities at various centers in northern France and England, but apparently it was in cities from Milan to Padua and Venice in the north, and from Bologna to Florence and Lucca in central Italy, that the international polyphonic repertory of the early fifteenth century was largely created and almost wholly preserved.

The Modena manuscript, with its varied collection of both secular and sacred music, represents the earliest phase of this international activity in Italy, while a Bologna manuscript (**BL**) includes works of Ciconia in a later and much more extensive sacred repertory by many composers of widely diverse origins.[37] Some were Italians, of whom several were associated with Padua during the last years of Cicona's life or shortly thereafter. A few were Parisians, and a few more were English. By far the largest number, however, came from Liège and the regions that lie on either side of the present French and Belgian border. A good many of the younger men in this group of northern composers served in the papal chapel at one time or another between the years 1418 and 1437, and during the first half of the century—it is well to remember—the popes lived in Lucca, in Florence, and especially in Bologna far more than they did in Rome. Among the northerners most abundantly represented in **BL** are Dufay, Binchois, and other men commonly regarded as the first generation of Renaissance composers, the "school" from which sprang the "central musical language" of the Renaissance. From the evidence

36. These views conflict with M. Bukofzer, "The Beginnings of Choral Polyphony," SMRM, pp. 176–89. Bukofzer gives the impression that only song style appears in sections marked *chorus,* and he is clearly mistaken when he connects Ciconia with "choral monophony" supported by two instrumental parts (p. 179).

37. Bologna, Civico Museo Bibliografico Musicale, Cod. Q 15.

A picture of the Sainte Chapelle in Paris from a fifteenth-century manuscript now in the Musée Condé, Chantilly.

of this and other manuscripts, therefore, we may assume that school most often kept in Italy.[38] It was there, certainly, that the fusion of French and Italian musical elements—perhaps most complete in the works of Ciconia—began the development of a new and international style.

English influence on this new musical language and style came somewhat later and will be considered briefly in the closing chapter of this book. Before the effects of that influence became evident, French traits naturally predominated in the music of continental composers from the North. Few of these men—even those who spent considerable time in Italy—adopted Italian forms and styles as wholeheartedly as Ciconia had done. Few of them were untouched, however, by the "sweetness" and gentle lyricism of Italian music. Northern French composers, as we have seen, had rarely carried the manneristic style to the extremes that were reached in Avignon, Aragon, and Foix. Yet they never lost their typically French concern with structural subtlety. What was new in the early fifteenth century, then, was less a return to simplicity than a tempering of northern constructivism by an infusion of southern sensuousness. Not humanistic in the sense of reviving the classic culture of Greece and Rome, music nevertheless began to be humanized. It was now prepared to receive the English contributions that would complete the creation of Tinctoris's "new art" and thus begin the musical Renaissance.

38. One of the largest Italian manuscripts from about the same period as **BL** is now in the Bodleian Library at Oxford (Canonici misc. 213). This collection of some 325 pieces is largely devoted to secular songs, although it also includes a number of motets and Mass movements. Ciconia and other transitional composers are represented, but at least half of the repertory consists of pieces by Dufay, Binchois, and their contemporaries. See G. Reaney, "The Manuscript Oxford, Bodleian Library, Canonici Misc. 213," MD, 9 (1955), pp. 74–104; and *Early Fifteenth-Century Music,* CMM, 11, 6 vols. (AIM, 1955–75).

CHAPTER XX

An English Epilogue

Nothing in the history of European music before the fifteenth century suggests that by 1475 Tinctoris would regard English composers as the "fount and origin" of a new art. Our surprise at this statement is probably attributable to the scarcity of musical sources and information about the previous development of music in England. From the eleventh to the early fifteenth century—a period of some four hundred years—we possess only three or four sizable English manuscripts in a nearly complete state. The first of these, the Winchester Troper, testifies to the early cultivation of organum in England, although the music cannot be transcribed with any certainty and some of the pieces apparently came from the region of the Loire valley in France (see Chapter VIII). A second source is the manuscript from St. Andrews in Scotland that is now in Wolfenbüttel (**W**₁). Here, even more obviously, we have a collection that consists of a few English additions to a continental repertory, that of the School of Notre Dame. Not until the Old Hall Manuscript (**OH**), from the early fifteenth century, do we find a repertory that is almost wholly the product of English composers.[1] Fortunately, these three sources are not the only record of musical life in England during the Middle Ages. The recovery of a good many fragmentary manuscripts has filled in some of the temporal gaps and has documented the wide geographical distribution of English musical activity.[2] Yet the disconnected nature of this evidence and the lack of a dominant musical center make it difficult to get a picture of English musical developments during the thirteenth and fourteenth centuries. Taken as a whole, nevertheless, English sources reveal many elements of a musical tradition that eventually produced the influential music of Dunstable and his contemporaries.

The same sources also make clear that a distinction must be made be-

---

1.   A. Ramsbotham, *et al.*, eds., *The Old Hall Manuscript;* a new and more complete edition by A. Hughes and M. Bent has now been published as CMM, 46 (OHM). Unless specified otherwise, all future references will be to the Hughes-Bent edition and their numbering of the pieces in **OH.**

2.   See NOHM, 2, p. 315 for a list of places in the British Isles from which thirteenth- and fourteenth-century polyphony is "known or presumed to come."

tween English music and music in England. To do so, however, is not always a simple matter. The liturgical repertory of the School of Notre Dame was known and used in England throughout the thirteenth century and perhaps even later. We only presume that additions to this repertory in English sources are the work of English rather than French composers. The conductus and motet were also known in England, and again we cannot always be sure whether a particular piece is of continental or insular origin. Similarly, in the fourteenth century the innovations and at least some of the music of the French Ars Nova penetrated England with evident effects on the work of presumably native composers. The unfortunate anonymity of almost all of this music does nothing to remove our uncertainties, but even so it is possible to discern traits that are typical of English music throughout its history.

According to one eminent British scholar, it is characteristic that English composers first copied and then continued to use the styles and methods of Notre Dame music but developed them along different lines. The process illustrates another characteristic of English music: "a habit of pushing some particular set of ideas to their limit, long after they have been discarded elsewhere."[3] This habit allows us to distinguish with some degree of certainty the English contributions and practices in the thirteenth and fourteenth centuries. Finally, by naming a large number of English composers, the Old Hall manuscript confirms the existence and nature of specifically English traits as well as continuing foreign influences that now come from both France and Italy. The reverse influence of English on continental composers forms the final contribution to the international language of the musical Renaissance. Our task here is to survey the traits that contributed to the first great flowering of English music in the works of John Dunstable and his contemporaries.

Perhaps the most striking trait of English medieval polyphony is its almost exclusively liturgical function. There is evidence that popular or even folk polyphony did exist in various forms, some of which may have suggested the technique of the *Sumer* canon with its ostinato-bass support (see Chapter XIV). Nevertheless, surviving examples of polyphony with English texts are about as rare as monophonic songs, and in both cases the subject matter tends to be sacred or moralizing rather than truly secular. This probably does not mean that musical frivolity was unknown in medieval England. It is equally probable, however, that few records of that frivolity ever existed. Until the end of the fourteenth century, the language and culture of the court and the nobility remained primarily French, and their secular entertainments must have depended far more on music in England than on English music. Professional minstrels undoubtedly performed secular songs in English for the

3.   F. Ll. Harrison, *"Ars Nova* in England: A New Source," MD, 21 (1967), p. 67).

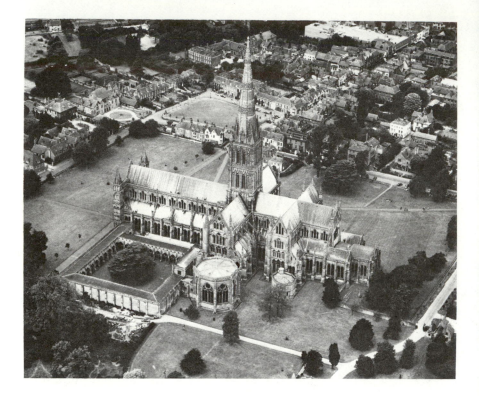

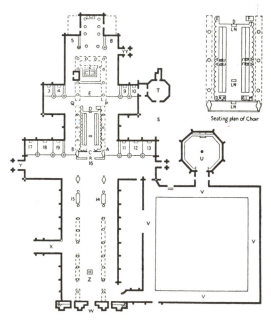

Seating plan of Choir

Above, a splendid example of English Gothic architecture, Salisbury Cathedral, source of the influential Sarum rite. At left, a plan of the Cathedral showing the seating arrangement in the choir.

middle and lower classes, but their transient life and their lack of wealthy patrons kept their music from being preserved in durable manuscript form. It cannot be purely chance, then, that sacred polyphony outweighs secular to such a great extent. As the primary cultivators of English polyphony, monastic and cathedral establishments were largely responsible for the development of its peculiarly national characteristics.

Because of its liturgical function, English polyphony long continued to use forms and styles that had disappeared from continental music. Around 1300, organa, conducti, and motets still made up the major part of the repertory in the Worcester fragments.[4] The typical pushing of this "particular set of ideas to their limit" resulted in an equally typical hybridization of forms and styles that often makes classification of individual pieces extremely difficult. Two of the ideas that contributed most to this hybridization were the fondness of the English for the process of troping and their obsession with the technique of voice exchange. Motets with texts that trope the word or words of the tenor's melisma remain a fairly distinct category, although their liturgical function may be unusual. English composers sometimes used troping motets to introduce an organal setting of an Alleluia and to separate the Alleluia from its verse, which might itself have tropes in the upper voices while the tenor sings the plainchant melody and text. One such prefatory motet in the Worcester fragments also appears in the Montpellier Codex, but as an independent piece with a different text—*Alle psallite cum luya*.[5] The use of voice exchange in the upper parts of this motet is typically English and adds a confusion of musical styles and techniques to the already great confusion of textual forms.

Whether voice exchange originated in England or on the continent is debatable, but it first came into common use in the melismatic upper parts of three- and four-voice organum and in the caudae of embellished conducti. When English composers applied the technique to music with words, they had to deal with the musical repetitions that voice exchange inevitably produces. In motets such as *Alle psallite cum luya,* one of the commonest solutions was to let one of the exchanged phrases be melismatic. The repetition of the phrase with text might then have the same or different words.[6] When all voices engage in the exchange of phrases, as in the rondellus (see Chapter XIV), the problem and the solutions become more complex. One phrase with text may combine with wordless phrases, but two or even three voices sometimes sing different lines of text at the same time.[7] As a result, the distinction between conductus and motet sometimes becomes as blurred as that between motet and organum. In longer pieces, moreover, English composers often introduced contrasting sections in different styles and techniques. It is little wonder, therefore, that modern scholars sometimes fail to agree as

4.   L. Dittmer, *The Worcester Fragments*.
5.   *Worcester Fragments,* No. 19 and *Mo,* No. 339 (HAM, No. 33a).
6.   *Alle psallite cum luya* repeats words and music; the Worcester version has different words when the voices exchange phrases.
7.   E.g., *Worcester Fragments,* Nos. 21 and 31.

to what a particular piece should be called. For our purposes, it is enough to remember that English music in the early fourteenth century created its hybrid forms and styles by applying a variety of techniques, including total and partial voice exchange, to the older continental forms of organum, conductus, and motet.

ENGLISH DISCANT

The various aspects of English music that have been surveyed briefly help to distinguish it from contemporary practices on the continent, but they do not account for the characteristic and distinctive sound of English polyphony. Of the elements contributing to that distinctive sound, the most important seem to be a large amount of parallel motion, simple and similar rhythms in all voices that often give a chordal effect, and above all an emphasis on imperfect consonances—thirds and sixths. No doubt the most influential factor in the development of these typical procedures was the continued and widespread English practice of accompanying plainchant with improvised polyphony or discant. Yet the theoretical prescriptions for such improvisation have often been misinterpreted and hence have given rise to a concept of English discant more mythical than real.[8]

There seems to be little basis for the usual description of improvised English discant as a series of parallel thirds and sixths *above* a plainchant, with perfect intervals—fifths and octaves—only at the beginnings and ends of phrases. English as well as continental theorists described discant as note-against-note counterpoint for two voices that produced only consonant intervals. They all stressed the priority of contrary motion and, as second choice, the preferability of similar to strictly parallel motion. By the mid-fourteenth century they were becoming more and more emphatic in outlawing parallel unisons, fifths, and octaves; and even the most liberal of English theorists did not permit more than five successive imperfect consonances (thirds or sixths). The more usual prescription was for no more than three or four between perfect intervals. Finally, although English treatises mention the possibility of two or even three discanting voices, they give explicit directions for only one part, which is usually above, but may also be below, the plainchant.

We cannot know, of course, to what extent improvised discant followed the theorists' rules. Yet the preserved examples of two-voice pieces show that English composers and theorists were in general accord. Thus the extensive series of parallel thirds in the thirteenth-cen-

8.   For the most lucid explanation and correction of previous misconceptions about English discant, see S. Kenney, *Walter Frye and the* Contenance Angloise (New Haven and London, 1964), Chapter 5, "The Theory of Discant."

tury *Nobilis, humilis* (Noble, humble) appear to be quite exceptional.[9] This hymn to St. Magnus, patron saint of the Orkney Islands, has been taken as an early example of the English predilection for thirds, but it more probably reflects a popular manner of singing that may have come to England with the Danish and Norwegian invasions.[10] Two settings of English texts from the latter half of the thirteenth century, a hymn and a paraphrase of a Latin sequence, illustrate more typical discant in which contrary motion and crossing of voices produce many thirds, either in succession or alternating with unisons and occasional fifths.[11] The composition and presumably the improvisation of unaccompanied duets continued through the fourteenth and into the fifteenth century, when manuscripts begin to identify such pieces by the term *gymel*, from *cantus gemellus* (twin song). The usual application of this name to earlier pieces of English origin is not wholly justified, since many of them follow the rules of discant common to all of western Europe. Nevertheless, continental composers almost never wrote in the wholly consonant style of the note–against–note discant duet, and the English emphasis on thirds and sixths in either contrary or parallel motion gave their duets a distinctive character that deserves to be known by an English name.

Most of the composed music that we now classify as English discant is for three voices in a nearly homorhythmic or chordal style. A good many pieces in this style seem to make no use of a preexistent melody, but when an identifiable plainchant is present it almost invariably appears in either the middle or, less often, the top voice.[12] The bottom voice, or *counter*, is lower in range than the tenor, and the two voices rarely cross. As in two-voice discant, they proceed in perfect and imperfect consonances with a mixture of contrary, similar, and parallel motion. The third voice has the highest range and, like the counter, rarely crosses the tenor. It does have a greater tendency, however, toward parallel motion with the tenor, most often in fourths. When these intervals occur with parallel thirds in the counter below the tenor, they produce the successions of $^6_3$ chords that have been wrongly called the essential feature of English discant. In preserved examples of composed discant, both the amount and kind of parallel motion vary considerably. Many of the older pieces use parallel fifths and octaves almost as freely as thirds and sixths, and parallel progressions with a fifth and third (or tenth)

9. HAM, No. 25c.

10. NOHM, 2, p. 316. Other duets with occasional series of parallel thirds and sixths can be found as late as the early fifteenth century, when their essentially popular nature is confirmed by their appearance in English carols. See *Musica Britannica,* 4 (London, 1952).

11. For the hymn *Edi beo u, hevene quene* (Blessed be thou, Queen of heaven), see NOHM, 2, p. 342. Reese, MMA, p. 389, gives two versicles of the sequence *Jesu Cristes milde moder* (Jesus Christ's gentle mother).

12. According to A. Hughes, "of nearly two hundred pieces noted in practical manuscripts, only one has the chant in the lowest voice"; "The Old Hall Manuscript: A Re-appraisal," MD, 21 (1967), p. 99.

One of the most famous medieval compositions, *Sumer is icumen in,* from a thirteenth-century manuscript (reproduced by permission of the British Library Board).

above the lowest voice are by no means uncommon.[13] Although the setting of a Gloria in the Worcester fragments is not based on a preexistent chant, it provides a characteristic example of English practice from the early fourteenth century.[14] At first glance, thirds and sixths seem to predominate, but closer inspection reveals an astonishing number of parallel fifths and octaves. Indeed, the emphasis on parallel motion of both perfect and imperfect intervals strongly suggests that the influence, if not the actual practice, of strict organum still survived. Only in the latter part of the fourteenth century did three-voice pieces in English discant style begin to reflect theoretical strictures against perfect intervals in parallel motion. At the same time, composers began to give the lowest voice a greater variety of melodic motion in order to comply with theoretical limitations on the number of imperfect intervals to be used in succession.

THE OLD HALL MANUSCRIPT

We may now turn to the repertory preserved in the Old Hall manuscript (**OH**), so called because it was preserved in the Library of St. Edmund's College, Old Hall, Ware. When and where the compilation of the

13. See NOHM, 3, p. 96, Ex. 44, ii.
14. HAM. No. 57b.

manuscript began remains unknown. At some time, presumably, it was acquired and used by the Chapel of the Royal Household, an institution that grew to considerable size and importance during the reign of King Henry IV (1399–1413). The presence of a Gloria and Sanctus by "Roy Henry" seems to confirm the connection with the Chapel Royal, but hot disputes have arisen over which of the three successive Henrys was the actual composer. Henry VI was only a few months old when he inherited the throne in 1422, and it is now agreed that he was not precocious enough to have written pieces that must date from the first two decades of the fifteenth century. Both Henry V (1413–22) and Henry IV still have their partisans, however. One would like to know whom to credit, of course, but the information would add little to our knowledge of the manuscript's history. Many more prolific composers are much more obscure and their identity much less certain.[15] We can be reasonably sure only that the repertory in **OH** came from several different musical centers, mostly English, but also foreign. Somewhat more conjectural is the assumption that the music was composed over a period of about fifty years, approximately 1370 to 1420.

As it now stands, the manuscript is both incomplete and mutilated. Entire folios are missing in various places, and illuminated initials have been cut out of a number of remaining pages. As a result, many of the pieces in **OH** are also incomplete. Nevertheless, the preserved contents make clear the manuscript's primary function as a collection of music for the Ordinary of the Mass. With all fragmentary pieces included, the catalog of **OH** runs to 147 items. Of these, 121 are Mass movements: 40 Glorias, 35 Credos, 27 Sanctus, and 19 Agnus Dei. All of the settings of each text appear together and thus divide the contents into four large groups, between or within which the remaining 26 pieces have been somewhat arbitrarily inserted. These pieces consist of 11 Latin motets and 15 discant settings of sacred, often liturgical Latin texts. Both the concentration on Mass movements and the exclusively religious nature of the repertory as a whole distinguish the Old Hall manuscript and English music in general from the contemporary output of continental composers.

One aspect of the Old Hall repertory that inevitably arouses curiosity is the absence of any settings of the Kyrie. Such settings were by no means common on the continent at this time, but they do occur as separate pieces, in composite Masses of the fourteenth and early fifteenth centuries, and in complete Masses by early Renaissance composers. Many of the musically unified Mass cycles by later English composers, on the other hand, omit the Kyrie and thus consist of only the four movements found in **OH.** The usual explanation of this phenomenon has been that, because of the English predilection for troped Kyries,

---

15. For the latest information as to the composers, see the article of A. Hughes cited in fn. 12. A complete inventory of **OH** by Hughes and M. Bent follows the article.

composers left them to be sung in plainchant rather than writing polyphony for texts of limited use. The recent discovery in English sources
of several polyphonic Kyries with tropes—three of them by Dunstable—has led to another hypothesis: "the rejection of polyphonic
troped Kyries by many continental scribes."[16] Unfortunately, this
proposition too cannot be wholly accepted. It does not account either
for the absence of Kyries in **OH** or for their continued absence in many
English Masses preserved in English sources up to the middle of the sixteenth century. In the period with which we are concerned, moreover,
neither composers nor scribes on the continent rejected polyphonic
troped Kyries. Ten of the nineteen Kyries found in fourteenth-century
French sources are troped,[17] as are three of sixteen in the Bologna manuscript (**BL**), which also contains a composite Mass by English composers without a Kyrie. The Old Hall manuscript might have begun, it
is true, with a group of Kyries that became detached and has now been
lost. More probably, however, liturgical polyphony in England simply
did not include the Kyrie in the years when the bulk of the Old Hall repertory was composed.

DIVERSE STYLES IN THE OLD HALL REPERTORY— ENGLISH DISCANT

In contrast to its functional unity, the stylistic diversity of the Old Hall
repertory makes it one of the most fascinating sources of late medieval
polyphony. Slightly more than half of the pieces—77 out of 147—may
be classed as English discant because of their notation in score rather
than in separate parts. Yet even in these pieces, the diversity of style is
much greater than one might expect. They all do maintain the simultaneous text declamation that must result from writing the words only
once beneath the bottom staff of the score. In the great majority, moreover, the distribution and function of the three voices remains traditional. Each voice, that is, has its own individual range, and the voices
rarely cross. Diversity sets in, however, in the rhythmic organization of
pieces written as English discant. The opening measures of two settings
of the same plainchant Sanctus will illustrate the extremes of that diversity. The Sanctus by Lambe (Example XX–1) presents the transposed
but unadorned chant in the tenor, which moves chiefly in notes of equal
value. The outer voices are only slightly more active and for the most
part produce a simple chordal texture. Short progressions of parallel intervals are common, especially in the upper two voices, but "strings of $\frac{6}{3}$

16. M. and I. Bent, "Dufay, Dunstable, Plummer—A New Source," JAMS, 22 (1969),
    p. 407.
17. Published in H. Stäblein-Harder, *Fourteenth Century Mass Music in France,* CMM, 29
    (AIM, 1962).

A setting of the Sanctus by Lambe from the Old Hall Manuscript (see Example XX–1).

chords"—the supposed characteristic of English discant—are noticeably in short supply. As may be seen at the end of the example, moreover,

Example XX–1: *Sanctus in English Discant Style*
by Lambe (**OH**, 97)

the older tolerance of parallel fifths (between tenor and counter) has not entirely disappeared.

As Lambe's Sanctus progresses, ornamental figures sometimes bring the upper voice into temporary prominence, but the style as a whole remains typical of English discant. To that style a Sanctus by Olyver presents the strongest possible contrast, although it is still written in score (Example XX–2). The most obvious novelty lies in the almost complete disappearance of chordal texture that results from the rhythmic independence of each voice. As a corollary to this development, the cantus becomes the most elaborate and melodically dominant part and is largely responsible for presenting a version of the transposed chant that is no longer rhythmically simple and unadorned. For the second Sanctus, however—the first is sung as usual in plainchant—the lowest voice has the notes of the chant at their original level, and both upper parts could be regarded as ornamental variations of the simple three-note figure. In the third Sanctus, the notes of the chant are thoroughly hidden in the ornamental figures of the upper voice, and the style has clearly become that of the treble-dominated French chanson. Indeed, Hughes classifies the Sanctus of Olyver, along with two others also written in score, as being wholly in song style. Of the 74 other pieces written in the same way, he indicates 22 in which the influence of the chanson has modified to some degree the characteristic traits of English discant.[18]

Example XX–2: *Beginning of the Sanctus of Olyver* (**OH**, *119*)

18.   In their inventory of **OH**, Hughes-Bent indicate a mixture of English discant and chanson by the abbreviation ED/CH.

As a typical example of English discant not based on a chant melody, the motet *Stella celi* (Star of heaven) by Cooke is included in AMM (No. 71). The ranges of the three voices overlap, but are nevertheless distinct: **d–d′**; **g–f′**; and **b–c″**. Although the tenor goes below the counter now and then, it usually maintains its position as the middle voice and never goes above the cantus. Parallel fourths between the two upper voices are numerous, but only twice do as many as four $^6_3$ chords occur in succession (mm. 18 and 28). For the most part, the three voices move together with only two note values, breves and semibreves (♩ and ♪). Departures from these values in the top voice are few but significant. The four red notes at the beginning of measure 9, as well as the minims in measures 9 and 18, show that the prolation is perfect in the first two sections of the piece. (The last two sections are in perfect time, presumably with imperfect prolation, although no minims are present.) It is particularly in the rhythmic elaboration of the top voice through an increasing use of perfect prolation that English discant more and more reflects the influence of the contemporary French chanson.

MASS MOVEMENTS NOT WRITTEN IN SCORE

Within each group of Mass movements in **OH,** pieces written in score appear first and are followed by settings in other styles with the voices notated separately. Although such settings account for almost half of the Mass movements, they are distributed most unequally among the four parts of the Ordinary. Movements not written in score include 26 of 40 Glorias and 25 of 35 Credos, but only 6 of 27 Sanctus and 2 of 19 Agnus Dei. In general, these movements with parts written separately derive from the continental styles of the chanson and motet, and they reflect contemporary practices on the continent much more strongly than do the movements written in score. It is typical of English composers, however, that they tended to combine elements of both styles—and of English discant as well—in ways that often make classification difficult and subject to dispute.

MASS MOVEMENTS IN SONG STYLE

Slightly more than half of the fifty-nine Mass movements not written in score might be classified as being in song style by virtue of the number and arrangement of parts. All of these pieces, that is, are in three-voice polyphony with one voice approximately a fifth higher than the tenor and contratenor, which lie in the same range and frequently cross. In many cases, however, the distribution of text among the three voices departs from the normal treatment of song style by continental composers. Only a few of the thirty-odd movements in this class maintain a

3[1] arrangement throughout. The only departure from this arrangement in some pieces results from manuscript indications that apparently call for all three voices to sing the Amen in Glorias and Credos (e.g., in Nos. 31, 32, and 79). More unexpected are movements in which one or both of the lower voices participate in singing part or all of the text. Sometimes the tenor and contratenor have only a few words here and there throughout the movement, but a number of pieces have text in both the cantus and contratenor, leaving only the tenor as a presumably instrumental part. Evidently not related to the Italian vocal duet of cantus and tenor with an instrumental contratenor, this curious procedure must represent an English adaptation of motet style to the normal texture of the chanson. The resemblance to the motet is heightened in a few of these pieces by division of the text between the two vocal parts, which thus sing different words and phrases at the same time. This practice of "telescoping" the long Gloria and Credo texts, although not exclusively English, seems to have been particularly favored by English composers.

In addition to the variety of textual treatment, about a third of the movements in song style introduce two-part sections in contrast to the basic texture. Only a few are vocal duets with text in both parts. In the majority, the cantus is accompanied by a textless tenor, even when the three-part sections have text in both cantus and contratenor (e.g., in Credo 93). This preference for a single vocal part supported by the tenor is unexpected, because it contrasts with both the vocal duets in continental Mass movements (see Chapter XIX) and the English form of two-voice discant known as gymel. It does, however, seem to confirm the derivation from song style of the pieces in which it appears.

Perhaps the most curious intermingling of stylistic procedures is the application of isorhythm to three movements in song style.[19] In addition, isorhythmic construction is found in the presumably all-vocal Amen of Gloria 32, a piece already cited as being in normal song style up to that point. As all of these pieces lead us to suspect, isorhythm will provide the structural basis for an even larger number of movements in motet style.

That the Mass movements in song style display great diversity in other aspects of their rhythmic organization should occasion no surprise. At the two extremes of this diversity stand a complexity rivaling the manneristic style of continental composers and a simplicity almost indistinguishable from English discant.[20] The resemblance to discant becomes even more striking when all voices sing the text, as in Leonel's

---

19.   Gloria 24 and Credo 84 (a related pair by Leonel), and Credo 87 with text in cantus and contratenor.

20.   Leonel's Gloria 22, for example, is a manneristic exercise in the use of proportions. Hollow black, solid and hollow red, and solid blue notes (color, not sound) introduce the proportions 2:1, 3:1, 3:2, and 4:3 in a variety of combinations.

Sanctus 116, which uses the same plainchant as the discant settings of Lambe and Olyver (Examples XX–1 and 2). Compared with Olyver's Sanctus, indeed, Leonel's seems closer to the style of English discant, even though it is not written in score. The voices are not as independent rhythmically, and the chant in the cantus is less highly ornamented, if somewhat freer in its occasional omission of notes (see the bracketed letters in Example XX–3). If the contratenor were below the tenor instead of being in the same range (**c–d'**) a fifth below the cantus (**g–b'**), and if the text declamation were simultaneous, the Sanctus of Leonel could scarcely be said to be in song style. Yet when this piece appears in later manuscripts of northern Italian origin, only the cantus has the text. Modifications of this sort are frequent in continental sources and may be indicative of a general distaste for the blurring of stylistic distinctions that is such a striking characteristic of English music.

Example XX–3: *Two Excerpts from Sanctus 116*
                    by Leonel

MASS MOVEMENTS IN MOTET STYLE

For purposes of classification here, the defining criterion of motet style is the presence of two vocal parts that lie in the same range above the tenor and are approximately equal in rhythmic activity and melodic interest. Of the twenty-seven Mass movements in **OH** that meet this criterion, all but two also have a contratenor in the same lower range as the tenor. Both lower voices—and particularly the tenor—tend to move in long note values and thus create an even stronger contrast with the vocal parts than is normal in song style.

If the 4^2 arrangement of parts is an infallible indicator of motet style, it is not the only arrangement found in that style. That two Mass movements have no contratenor has already been noted. A few have text in one or both of the lower parts, and four add a third voice with text to produce a 5^3 arrangement. Two other procedures increase the diversity of textual treatment. As in some movements in song style, telescoping the text gives many Glorias and Credos the appearance of a bitextual motet. In other movements, each voice follows its line of text with a melisma against the succeeding line in the other voice. This alternating presentation, which neither telescopes the text nor shortens the movement, must surely be a survival of the older English ways of treating text—if not music—in motets with voice exchange (see above, p. 505).[21]

Independently of differences in texture and treatment of text, differing structural procedures divide the twenty-seven Mass movements in motet style into three distinct groups or classes: isorhythmic (9); canonic (7); and, for lack of a better term, freely composed (11). This last and largest group includes three Glorias, four Credos, three Sanctus, and one Agnus Dei.[22] All of these movements are for four voices, and all but two have the standard 4^2 distribution of vocal and instrumental parts. In Sanctus 118, the tenor has a chant melody and sings the text along with the upper two voices. All four voices sing the text in Sanctus 122, which also has a plainchant Sanctus in the tenor.

The three Glorias and four Credos show none of these traces of English discant style. Only two of these movements maintain the 4^2 arrangement throughout, however (Nos. 34 and 78). The other five contrast duets for the triplum and textless tenor with the full four-part texture. A further contrast in four of these movements is of particular interest as a reflection of the English predilection for fullness of sound. In the final sections of Glorias 21 and 36 and of Credos 77 and 82, the triplum divides into two parts. The resulting five-part texture with three upper voices brings the alternation of duets with four-part sections to an effective climax and emphatic close. It should be noted, finally, that telescoping of text occurs to some degree in all but one of the freely composed Glorias and Credos in motet style. In the five-part ending of Credo 77, indeed, we might even speak of triple telescoping, because each of the three voices sings a different portion of the text.

21. For a systematic application of the procedure, see the isorhythmic Gloria 19 by J. Tyes; facsimile in Apel, NPM, p. 365.
22. Nos. 21, 34, and 36; 76–78 and 82; 117, 118, and 122; and 141. In the Hughes-Bent inventory, all eleven movements are classified as chanson style, surely an unnecessary compounding of the already great confusion of styles in the **OH** repertory.

ISORHYTHMIC MASS MOVEMENTS IN MOTET STYLE

"The greatest surprise of the Old Hall repertory is unquestionably the prominent role of isorhythmic technique, which is irrefutable proof of a strong French influence."[23] That nine of the eleven motets not written in score should be isorhythmic is not strange. The surprise comes in finding the technique applied to so many Mass movements. In addition to the three movements in song style already mentioned, four Glorias and five Credos in motet style are also isorhythmic.[24] Because Bukofzer's description of all isorhythmic pieces in **OH**—both Mass movements and motets—is easily available, only a few general comments are needed here.[25] In the nine Mass movements we find the only two pieces in motet style for three voices, Nos. 19 and 88. Although by different composers, Tyes and Queldryk, the two movements must have been intended as a Gloria–Credo pair, for they are identical with regard to mode, clefs and key signatures, mensurations, isorhythmic structure, and the alternation of text and melismas in the vocal parts. In the four-voice movements, which do not seem to form any pairs, the degree of isorhythmic organization varies considerably. Some are strictly isorhythmic in all voices; others have repeated taleae only in the tenor or in the tenor and contratenor together. Only two of the tenor melodies come from plainchants. The rest seem to be newly composed. Whatever the source of the tenors may be, their treatment usually combines subdivision into taleae with repetitions of the entire melody, either without change or, more often, with proportional diminutions.

CANONIC MASS MOVEMENTS

Despite Bukofzer's unquestionable finding that the prominence of isorhythm is "the greatest surprise of the Old Hall repertory,"[26] we may question whether the surprise occasioned by the appearance of canonic technique in seven Mass movements is not at least as great. Comparable movements in continental sources are rare indeed, and none of the few contemporary examples can match the technical ingenuity and complexity of the English pieces. Moreover, no two of the **OH** canonic movements follow the same structural procedure. This curious circumstance may somehow be related to the fact that the names of only two

23. Bukofzer, SMRM, p. 56.
24. Nos. 19, 23, 28, and 30; 85, 86, and 88–90.
25. SMRM, pp. 58–72. See also the commentaries on individual pieces in Hughes–Bent, OHM, 3. Information in the Hughes–Bent inventory (OHM, 1¹, pp. xxvi–xxix, and MD, 21 [1967], pp. 136–47) makes it possible to correlate their edition with Bukofzer's references to the earlier edition and his numbering according to an older catalog of **OH**.
26. SMRM, p. 56.

composers—Byttering and Pycard—are attached to any of the seven movements.[27]

The structural diversity that gives extraordinary interest to the seven canonic movements can be indicated here only in the most summary fashion. Although motet style with the voice parts in canon forms the basis of all the movements, only Byttering's Gloria adheres to the normal four-part arrangement (4^2). The piece is cast in two large sections, in each of which the voices sing the telescoped text in a canon at the unison.

Like Byttering, Pycard uses the normal four-voice arrangement of motet style in Gloria 26, but the text appears in three voices, leaving the tenor as the only instrumental part. After an eight-measure introduction, the contratenor, surprisingly, begins the canon, followed by the duplum at the fourth above. The canonic voices alternate between singing the same and different lines, while the free triplum has the complete text. This partial telescoping of text in the canonic voices also occurs in Pycard's other two Glorias, as well as in the two anonymous Credos. All four of these movements further resemble Gloria 26 in having three vocal parts, but in each of them a third voice is added to produce a five-part texture (5^3).

In his second Gloria (No. 27), Pycard succeeded in writing what may be the earliest example of simultaneous two-voice canons, one in the tenor and contratenor, another in the top two voices. A free duplum completes the five-part texture. His third canonic Gloria (No. 35) closely resembles the second, except that the tenor and contratenor are now free parts instead of being canonic. Although the principle of text distribution remains the same in all three Glorias, each follows a different pattern for telescoping portions of the text in the canonic voices.

Both canonic Credos differ from the five-part Glorias in having a three-voice canon above the tenor and contratenor. The two canons differ structurally, however. The one in Credo 71 is at the unison with a time interval of four measures in 2/4 between entries. Much more complex in every way, Credo 75 has a mensuration canon in the upper three voices. Each voice, that is, sings the melody in a different mensuration, in this case resulting in a combination of 2/4, 3/4, and 9/8 meters.[28] Against this combination, the tenor is in 6/8, and the contratenor has sec-

27. Byttering is credited only with Gloria 18; Pycard, with Glorias 26, 27, and 35, and Sanctus 123. Credos 71 and 75 are anonymous, but they form pairs with Glorias 27 and 35, and both must be the work of Pycard.

28. The voices do not begin together, as Bukofzer wrote in NOHM, 3, p. 168. Instead, the voice in 2/4 leads off, and the other two begin after breve rests, i.e., measures of 3/4 and 9/8. Confusingly, the entering voices are numbered 3 2 1 in the Hughes-Bent edition, just the reverse of the way they are described in an explanatory verbal canon. In addition, consistent barring of all parts together, mostly in 6/8 (or 3/4), makes the score easier to read but obscures the conflicting mensural relationships of the different parts.

tions in each of the four meters. As if this rhythmic complexity were not enough, mensuration changes are prescribed for the canonic voices; and red, black-red, and blue notes introduce various proportional or unusual note values.[29]

The evident concern for diversity of both musical and textual treatment in Pycard's canonic Glorias (and Credos?) must also be responsible for the unique scheme of his canonic Sanctus (No. 123). As it stands in **OH,** the piece has only two parts, a cantus and a textless tenor, but the cantus yields a canon at the unison for at least two voices and possibly three. Whatever the number of canonic voices, the canon itself is a rare *tour de force.* Rather than being newly composed, its melody is a rhythmic, but otherwise almost unchanged, version of a plainchant Sanctus.[30] Objections to the third canonic voice stem from its occasional introduction of strongly dissonant clashes. Such clashes are by no means foreign to Pycard's other works, however, or to the **OH** repertory as a whole. A three-voice canon in the Sanctus, with entries at the time interval of three breves, would nicely symbolize the seraphims with three pairs of wings who call to each other "Holy, holy, holy." We need not assume that the song of angelic choirs was unfailingly consonant.

FOREIGN INFLUENCES ON THE OLD HALL REPERTORY

If the isorhythmic pieces in **OH** leave no doubt as to their composers' acquaintance with contemporary French applications of the technique, the degree of foreign influence on English canonic writing is more open to question. It is often assumed, without any real proof, that any non-Italian composer of canons must necessarily have borrowed the technique from the caccia. For the composers of canonic Mass movements in **OH,** this assumption should not too readily be taken for granted. Native cultivation of such pseudo-canonic techniques as rondellus and voice exchange, possibly too the rounds of less learned music, may well have sparked the development of English canonic writing. In any case, application of the technique to Mass movements appears to have occurred more or less simultaneously, and perhaps independently, in both England and Italy. Wherever the idea may have originated, the collection of such movements in **OH** remains the largest of its time.

Similar questions of priority, of who influenced whom, arise with

29. For a facsimile in color, see the earlier edition of **OH,** 3, between pp. xxiv and xxv.
30. See Hughes-Bent, OHM, 3, p. 57 for the chant melody. In 1², p. 373, they transcribe as a three-voice canon but mark the third voice "optional." Sanctus 123 may be incomplete, however. After the two written parts on fol. 100v, one or more folios are missing. As Hughes-Bent indicate (OHM, 3, p. 39), a free vocal part and a contratenor may well have been written on the facing page that has now disappeared.

regard to the pairing of Mass movements and the alternation of solo and choral sections. Both practices, as we have seen, occur in the Mass movements of Ciconia, who died in 1411. With no precise dating of pieces in **OH,** we cannot know when the two practices first appeared in England, but it can scarcely have been early enough to have influenced Ciconia. It should be noted, moreover, that the scribe who copied the supposed pairs in **OH** gave no indication of an intended relationship. Coupled with this lack, the relatively small percentage of such pairs in the total repertory suggests that English composers were just beginning to be concerned with the musical unity of different Mass movements. In movements with solo sections, too, we find less specific directions than in later continental sources that nevertheless include works of Ciconia. Rather than using the designations *unus* (or *duo*) and *chorus* for the contrasting sections, the scribes of **OH** sometimes, but not always, wrote the duet texts in red instead of the usual black—a distinction that is only presumed to have the same meaning as the more explicit labels. Perhaps, like canonic writing, the pairing of movements and the alternation of duets with full textures represent constructive principles that were applied to Mass compositions more or less independently and at about the same time in various centers of European musical culture.

Of all the foreign influences on the repertory of **OH,** that of French music is the least problematical. Adoption of French notational practices and mensurations, particularly imperfect time with major prolation (6/8), gradually changed the rhythmic character of English discant, just as its contrapuntal structure changed under the influence of chanson style. Both this style and isorhythmic technique were French inventions, after all, and both had been adapted to Mass movements by fourteenth-century French composers. Even the mannerisms of the end-of-the-century ars subtilior make their appearance in some works—chiefly by Leonel and Pycard—that use a variety of note shapes and colors to introduce complex proportions or intricate combinations of different mensurations.

In many ways, then, the music of **OH** reveals that its composers were neither far removed from their continental counterparts nor far behind them in adopting the latest musical fashions. If the admixture and fusion of foreign with native musical styles and techniques make the repertory a characteristically English compendium of international musical practice at the beginning of the fifteenth century, there still is little to suggest that English music will shortly become the "fount and origin of a new art," the art that Tinctoris regarded as the beginning of music worth listening to and that we may regard as the beginning of Renaissance music.

Evidence that English music of the late fourteenth and early fifteenth centuries can have had little influence on the continent comes from the

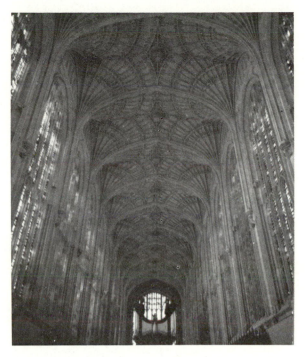

A striking example of the final phase of Gothic architecture, the great vault of King's College Chapel, Cambridge.

fact that only eleven pieces in **OH,** including a Gloria by the Italian composer Zacar (No. 33), have also been found in continental manuscripts. Of the ten English pieces, three motets are later additions to the original repertory (Nos. 66–68). They include the only work of Dunstable in **OH,** curiously, without giving his name, and two motets attributed to Forest, who is also represented by no other pieces in the manuscript.[31] Three of the seven Mass movements are by Leonel Power, and one of the two anonymous works may also be his. One of Byttering's six pieces and the only one by Gervays complete the list of works in **OH** that appear in continental sources. Small as this list is, its significance goes beyond merely negative evidence. Like the three motets, two of the Mass movements are later additions to **OH,** and all seven represent the more advanced applications of song style, sometimes with text in more than one voice, sometimes with contrasting sections for two and three voices. It seems reasonable to assume, therefore, that older, purely English styles were either unknown or unacceptable on the continent, and that English music in general only began to find its way into the international repertory of northern Italy about the beginning of the fifteenth century's third decade. The latter assumption in particular corresponds with the little we know about Leonel Power and John Dunstable, the two most prolific English composers of the time and the two whose works received the widest distribution in continental manuscripts.

31. Dunstable's piece is his famous isorhythmic motet *Veni Sancte Spiritus.* A later Italian source credits Forest's motets to other composers—one to "Polmier," the other to Dunstable.

LEONEL AND DUNSTABLE

All that we know about the life of Leonel, as he was usually called in the manuscripts, is that he became associated with Christ Church, Canterbury, in 1423, but apparently lived there only from 1441 until his death in 1445. That he was already active and well known in England during the early years of the fifteenth century is evident in his having contributed twenty-one works to the repertory of **OH,** more than twice as many as any other composer. Some thirty other pieces that appear only in continental sources are mostly later works and suggest the possibility that Leonel left England for a number of years before returning to end his life in Canterbury. The music of John Dunstable—some 60 works in all—is even more restricted to manuscripts of continental origin, with only a handful of pieces in English sources to suggest that his native land knew him as a composer. From an epitaph that records Dunstable's death in 1453, we learn that he was also a mathematician and astronomer, and from a treatise that Dunstable owned we get the further information that he was, or had been, a musician (singer?) of the Duke of Bedford. In this position we find the clue to Dunstable's musical activities on the continent. Brother of King Henry V, John, Duke of Bedford, was Regent of France from 1422 to 1429 and then Governor of Normandy until his death in 1435. During these years, England was allied with Burgundy against Charles VII of France, and in 1423 Bedford cemented the political ties by marrying the sister of Philip the Good, Duke of Burgundy. If Dunstable was in Bedford's service on the continent, as we must assume he was, he would have had ample opportunities for meeting and influencing musicians at the Burgundian court. A contemporary poet, Martin le Franc, bears witness to the influence, if not to an actual meeting, in an often-quoted passage from *Le Champion des dames* (The Champion of Ladies), an enormously long poem written in 1441–42 and dedicated to Philip the Good. After proclaiming the superiority of Dufay and Binchois over their French predecessors, le Franc credits their excellence to their having followed Dunstable and adopted the "English countenance," by which means they found a new way of using "sprightly concords" to create song of marvelous pleasure, joyous and memorable.[32]

The verses of Martin le Franc cannot be dismissed as the conventional and exaggerated praise to be expected in references to the most famous composers of the time, both of whom, moreover, were associated to some degree with the powerful and wealthy patron to whom *Le Champion des dames* was addressed. Instead, we can only admire the poet's acuity of critical judgment in putting his finger on the one aspect of English music—and of Dunstable's in particular—that was chiefly responsible for its influence on continental composers. That aspect is a new

32.   Reese, MR, pp. 12–13, gives the two pertinent stanzas with a free poetic translation.

treatment of consonance and dissonance, a new approach to the problems of combining voices in a polyphonic texture, and in it we find the departure from older practices for which we searched in vain in the original repertory of **OH.** That departure began when composers rejected medieval permissiveness in the combination of harmonic intervals in favor of a "panconsonant" style that required each voice to be consonant with all the others. Hand in hand with this elimination of dissonance from the essential tones of vertical combinations went a much more restricted and controlled use of dissonance to ornament the harmonic tones. The unprepared and accented dissonances so characteristic of fourteenth-century music now disappear almost entirely. Even prepared dissonances—those in which a note enters as a consonance, becomes dissonant when the other voices move, and then itself moves to a consonance—are used less often and with greater discretion than before. Other dissonances are limited to short note values on weak parts of the beats, what we would call passing and neighboring tones that move from and to consonances by step, or various forms of escape tones that move to a consonance by skip. From this sparing use and careful treatment of dissonance combined with total consonance in the harmonic structure came the features of the English countenance that aroused continental composers to enthusiastic admiration and successful emulation.

Neither the adoption of panconsonant style on the continent nor its development by English composers can rightfully be considered in a study of medieval music. Yet their enormous importance for the history of music means that neither can be wholly ignored. In the new consonant style we have nothing less than a fundamental change in the technique of polyphonic composition; and in this change, more than anything else, we find the dividing line between medieval and Renaissance music. Medieval music emphasized the linear aspects of polyphony, the independence and individuality of superimposed melodies that proceed with a minimum of harmonic restraint. Renaissance music shifted the emphasis to the vertical aspect of polyphony and placed melodic movement under the absolute dictatorship of successive consonant triads. As a result, the different lines in Renaissance polyphony tend to lose their individuality and become more and more homogeneous in style. Having learned to savor in earlier music the freer movement of sharply differentiated melodies and their stimulating harmonic clashes, the confirmed medievalist may sometimes find the incessantly consonant progressions of the Renaissance becoming bland and even monotonous. He cannot fail to realize, however, that Renaissance composers had turned a corner and had moved so quickly in the new direction that they soon left the music of his favorite era out of both hearing and mind.

Of the two Englishmen most responsible for that turning, Leonel Power is perhaps the more interesting from a historical point of view because he was the more transitional. His works in **OH,** like almost all the others, are still essentially medieval. Only in his later pieces in continental sources does Leonel approach and sometimes attain the consonant style that we expect to find as a matter of course in the works of Dunstable. Leonel and Dunstable were not the only English practitioners of the new style whose music circulated and was preserved on the continent, but the sheer bulk and wide distribution of their works inevitably made them outstanding figures. From the consistent excellence of Dunstable's music, it also seems both inevitable and right that he should have gained a much higher reputation. That reputation began in his own lifetime, as Martin le Franc proves, and it continued to grow until it attained the "almost mythical splendour" that dazzled a late-nineteenth-century English historian into proclaiming that English musicians, chief of whom was Dunstable, "invented the art of musical composition."[33] Were this show of national pride not a bit exaggerated, the present book could not have been written! Yet we must recognize Dunstable as the greatest English composer of his day. We must also recognize that, for perhaps the only time, the prestige and influence of English composers changed the course of music history throughout western Europe. By these recognitions we confirm the judgment of Tinctoris, although we may rephrase his statement to make English composers, with Dunstable at their head, the fount and origin of the musical Renaissance. In their works, and in the works of continental contemporaries who added the English countenance to their earlier mixture of French *subtilitas* with Italian *dulcedo,* music moves beyond the scope of the present study. For the music of the Middle Ages, the end had come.

33.   H. Davey, *History of English Music* (London, 1895), p. 50.

Appendices

APPENDIX A

A Guide to the *Liber Usualis*

PART 1: THE MAIN DIVISIONS OF ITS CONTENTS

  I. The Ordinary Chants of the Mass, pp. 11–111

   As well as the chants commonly thought of as belonging to the Ordinary of the Mass, this section includes the Alleluias for Paschal Time and various recitation tones for Lessons, prayers, etc.

 II. The Ordinary Chants of the Office, pp. 112–316

   This section begins with recitation tones for the Office, including those used for psalms (see Chapter III). The bulk of the section is devoted to psalms and canticles for the most important daytime Offices.

III. The Proper of the Time, pp. 317–1110

   By far the largest section of LU, the Proper of the Time occupies over one third of the total number of pages.

 IV. The Common of Saints, pp. 1112–1302

   This section contains chants and liturgical texts that are common to all the saints of a particular category (apostles, bishops, martyrs, virgins, etc.). If special chants are not provided for a particular saint, the services for his day draw on the Common of the category to which he belongs. Also included in the Common of Saints are services for the dedication of a church, for the Virgin Mary, and for a number of votive Masses. (Votive Masses are for special devotions or occasions, such as weddings, that have no connection with the Church calendar.)

  V. The Proper of the Saints, pp. 1303–1762

   The first important feast in this section is that of Saint Andrew on November 30, the last is for Saint Sylvester on November 26.

 VI. The Burial Service, pp. 1763–1831

   This section includes the Requiem Mass on pp. 1807–15.

A rather odd assortment of different items follows the six large sections of the *Liber Usualis:* miscellaneous chants for a variety of purposes, an Alphabetical Table of Chants, an index of Chants for Benedictions, and an Alphabetical Table of Feasts. The pagination of these items varies in the different editions of LU, but it is especially important to mention the indices because they do not come at the very end of the book. Instead, the *Liber Usualis* closes with a Supplement for Certain Religious Congregations. It is also important to mention the arrangement of the Alphabetical Table of Chants. Grouped according to type, the chants of the Mass Proper come first in the order in which they appear in the service: Introits, Graduals, Alleluia verses, Sequences, Tracts, Offertories, and Communions. Then follow the chants of the Offices: antiphons, hymns, psalms, canticles, and responsories. Within each group the chants are arranged alphabetically by the opening words of their texts. The number preceding each chant identifies its mode.

PART 2: INDICATIONS OF THE TERMINATION TO BE USED WITH EACH ANTIPHON

The designation $\begin{smallmatrix} 5. & \text{Ant.} \\ 1. & g \end{smallmatrix}$, for example, precedes the chant *Levate capita vestra* (Lift up your heads; LU, p. 365). The upper line identifies this chant as the fifth antiphon in the series (for First Vespers of the Nativity). The number and letter below indicate the mode and the termination of the psalm tone. The *Liber Usualis* indicates the mode of every chant in this way, but it specifies the termination only for antiphons that are sung with psalm tones. For such antiphons, the indication is never omitted, even for tones with only one termination, as 2. D, for example. It should be noted that the *Liber* uses capital letters for terminations that close on the final of the mode; lower-case letters indicate endings on notes other than the final. The *Liber* gives all the endings for each tone on pp. 113–17, but it also notates the termination after each antiphon. Following medieval practice, this termination appears above the letters *E u o u a e*. Especially with the old way of writing U as V, this may look like a Greek yell—EVOVAE! Instead, it is simply the vowels of "s(a)eculorum Amen," the closing words of the Lesser Doxology that lead to the repetition of the antiphon. Thus the *Liber* makes doubly sure that the correct termination is used. The absence of both indications for an antiphon means that it has lost its connection with psalmody and has become an independent chant.

PART 3: CHANTS OF THE ORDINARY OF THE MASS

Beginning on p. 16, there are eighteen Masses or Mass formularies with designations of the season or the kind of liturgical day for which each is appropriate. The first fifteen consist of Kyrie, Gloria, Sanctus, and Agnus Dei, plus the *Ite, missa est* and sometimes the *Benedicamus Do-*

mino. The last three are for ordinary weekdays of any season (ferias) and Sundays in Advent and Lent. They therefore omit the Gloria and consequently have only a *Benedicamus Domino*. The Credo is not included in any of these Masses, but six settings are given in the immediately following pages (64–78). The *Liber* remarks (p. 66) that the first "is the authentic tone for the Credo," but the others "may be used where it is customary." Finally, we find a series of "ad libitum" chants that are not grouped in Mass formularies (pp. 79–94). Instead, the section begins with eleven Kyries, followed by four Glorias, three Sanctus, and two Agnus Dei.

APPENDIX B

The System of Pitch Identification Used in This Book

C - B   c - b   c' - b' c" - g"

Although most medieval music remains within the Guidonian gamut (**G–e"**), the system given here is better known today and less cumbersome than Guido's lettering (see Example III–2).

Bibliography

What follows can only by courtesy be called a bibliography. Listings of manuscript facsimilies and modern editions by chapters or groups of chapters are relatively complete. Suggestions for further reading, however, may not include items already cited in footnotes and have been limited primarily to books and articles in English. Even in this category many studies of musical technicalities have been excluded. References to works in other languages imply the presence of music, lists of works, indices of various kinds, or other material that will be intelligible without a reading knowledge of the language in question.

Anthologies of Music   A separate *Anthology of Medieval Music* (AMM) is being published as a companion volume to the present book. Another anthology devoted to medieval music, EM, has somewhat old-fashioned transcriptions and lacks both editorial notes and translations of texts. Vols. 2, 9, and 18 of AoM are anthologies of monophonic songs, medieval polyphony, and Gregorian chant. Of anthologies broader in scope, HAM includes the largest collection of medieval music (Nos. 9–60). Smaller collections are to be found in GMB (30), MM (14), SS (30), and TEM (17). Booklets accompanying the albums of HMS also include music, but pieces are not always complete.

Reference Works   The German encyclopedia MGG contains the most extensive articles with bibliographies on the types and forms of medieval music as well as on individual composers and theorists. Good articles are also to be found in GD, but the coverage is less inclusive. Shorter articles with bibliographies in HDM are useful starting points for further investigation of medieval topics (no composer entries). Chapter bibliographies in Reese, MMA, are the most complete up to date of publication (1940). NOHM also has useful bibliographies for each chapter. Despite its title, MMBb is an annotated bibliography, "comprehensive" in scope but "selective, listing the best recent works, but referring to earlier works when appropriate." Indices of manuscripts of medieval music with incipits in the original notation are published in RISM, Series B IV.

Works cited throughout this book, e. g., MMA, NMM, NPM, and NOHM, will not be referred to in the following chapter bibliographies.

CHAPTER I, HISTORICAL INTRODUCTION

For Further Reading   Of the many historical surveys of the Middle Ages, the most comprehensive is the eight-volume *Cambridge Medieval History* (Cambridge, 1911–36). Less ambitious readers may prefer the two-volume condensation, *The Shorter Cambridge Medieval History* (Cambridge, 1952). Both sets have excellent maps, as does the useful atlas of W. R. Shepherd, *Historical Atlas,* 9th ed. (New York, 1964). A still shorter survey is H. Pirenne, *A History of Europe from the Invasions to the XVI Century* (London, 1939; repr. in paperback, Garden City, N.Y., 1958).

A number of more specialized studies deal with various aspects of the later Middle Ages and will provide a better understanding of the intellectual and cultural environment in which medieval music flourished. All but the first of the following works are available in paperback editions: E. de Bruyne, *The Esthetics of the Middle Ages* (New York, 1969); J. Evans, *Life in Medieval France,* 3rd ed. (New York, 1969); F. Heer, *The Medieval World: Europe 1100–1350* (London, 1962); G. Henderson, *Gothic* (Baltimore, 1967); J. Huizinga, *The Waning of the Middle Ages* (Garden City, N. Y., 1954); E. Panofsky, *Gothic Architecture and Scholasticism* (New York, 1957); O. von Simson, *The Gothic Cathedral* (Princeton, 1974).

CHAPTERS II–V, PLAINCHANT

Facsimiles   Primarily devoted to facsimiles of chant manuscripts with indices, PalM also includes studies of the notation and other aspects of the plainchant tradition (in French).

Walter H. Frere, ed., *Antiphonale Sarisburiense* (London, 1901–26; repr. Farnborough, 1966); and *Graduale Sarisburiense* (London, 1894; repr. Farnborough, 1966)—manuscripts of the Use of Sarum published by the Plainsong and Medieval Music Society. For further references, see MMBb, Nos. 502–34, under the heading Liturgical Books, which includes "editions, facsimiles, or major studies."

Modern Editions   The important liturgical books of the Roman Church are: *Antiphonale Sacrosanctae Romanae Ecclesiae pro diurnis horis* (Desclée, No. 820; Tournai, 1949); *Antiphonale monasticum pro diurnis horis* (Desclée, No. 818; Tournai, 1934); *Graduale Sacrosanctae Romanae Ecclesiae* (Desclée, No. 696; Tournai, 1945); *Liber responsorialis . . . juxta ritum monasticum* (Solesmes, 1895); and *The Liber Usualis with Introduction and*

Rubrics in English (LU) (New York, 1952). Page numbers in references to LU will be correct for earlier editions and also for later editions except in the Proper of the Time between Palm Sunday and the Easter Mass (pp. 578–777 in older editions). In the "restored Ordo of Holy Week" authorized by Pius XII in 1955 (pp. 579–776$_{MM}$ in later editions), the placement of some chants has changed, others have been retitled, and a few were omitted.

Music for the Mass of the Ambrosian rite in Milan has been published in the *Antiphonale missarum juxta ritum Sanctae Ecclesiae Mediolensis* (Rome, 1935).

Monumenta Monodica Medii Aevi (Kassel, 1956–). A projected series devoted primarily to specific kinds of plainchant. Vol. 1, *Hymnen I* (1956); Vol. 2, *Die Gesänge des altrömischen Graduale* (1970); Vol. 7, *Alleluia-Melodien I* (1968).

For Further Reading   History of the Liturgy: Pierre Batiffol, *History of the Roman Breviary* (London, New York, etc., 1912); L. M. O. Duchesne, *Christian Worship: its Origin and Evolution* (London, 1931); Adrian Fortescue, *The Ceremonies of the Roman Rite Described,* 8th ed. (London, 1948); id., *The Mass: a Study of the Roman Liturgy,* 2nd ed. (London, 1913; later reprints have added bibliographies); Josef A. Jungmann, *The Mass of the Roman Rite,* 2 vols. (New York, 1951–55); id., *The Early Liturgy to the Time of Gregory the Great* (Notre Dame, Ind., 1959).

Both the *Catholic Encyclopedia,* 15 vols., Index, and 2 Supplements (1907–22), and the *New Catholic Encyclopedia,* 14 vols. and Index (1967), have many useful articles on plainchant and items of the liturgy.

Willi Apel, *Gregorian Chant* (GC) (Bloomington, 1958), the most comprehensive study in English, is primarily concerned with the chant as it appears in modern publications. Its more expansive German counterpart is Peter Wagner's *Einführung in die gregorianischen Melodien,* 3 vols. (Leipzig). Vol. 1, *Ursprung und Entwicklung der liturgischen Gesangsformen* (1895; 2nd ed., 1901; 3rd ed., 1911); translation of 2nd ed., *Origin and Development of the Forms of the Liturgical Chant* (London, 1907[?]). Vol. 2, *Neumenkunde* (1905; 2nd ed., 1912), has many plates illustrating regional notations. Vol. 3, *Gregorianische Formenlehre* (1921), a study of the forms of Gregorian Chant, has many musical examples.

Dom Gregory Suñol, *Introduction à la paléographie musicale grégorienne* (Tournai, 1935; also published in Catalan, Montserrat, 1925), has plates and tables illustrating the various regional notations and the forms of neumes. J. R. Bryden and D. Hughes, *An Index of Gregorian Chant,* 2 vols. (Cambridge, Mass. 1969).

Other Liturgies and Music   A. Z. Idelsohn, *Jewish Music in Its Historical Development* (New York, 1967). Eric Werner, *The Sacred Bridge* (New York, 1959), studies the relationships between Jewish and early Christian liturgies. Egon Wellesz, *A History of Byzantine Music and Hymnody,* 2nd ed. (Oxford, 1961); id., *Eastern Elements in Western Chant* (Oxford, 1947). Oliver Strunk, *Essays on Music in the Byzantine World* (New York, 1977). Apel, GC, includes chapters on Ambrosian and Old Roman chant; see also NOHM, 2, Chapter 3.

For further bibliography on all aspects of plainchant, see Hughes, MMBb, Nos. 476–714.

CHAPTER VI, TROPES AND SEQUENCES

Facsimiles   Monumenta Musica Sacra (Mâcon-Rouen, 1952–).

I. *Le Prosaire de la Sainte-Chapelle* (1952)

II. *Les Manuscrits musicaux de Jumièges* (1954)

III. *Le Prosaire d'Aix-la-Chapelle* (1961)

IV. *Le Tropaire-Prosaire de Dublin* (1970)

The Sequences of the Archbishopric of Nidarós, ed. Erik Eggen, 2 vols. (Copenhagen, 1968)—facsimiles and transcriptions. *Troparium sequentiarium nonantulanum,* ed. G. Vecchi (Modena, 1955).

Modern Editions   Richard Crocker, *The Early Medieval Sequence* (Berkeley, 1977)—includes 118 transcriptions; the definitive study of its subject.

Paul Evans, *The Early Trope Repertory of Saint Martial de Limoges* (Princeton, 1970)—an excellent introduction to the early history of tropes, with 145 pages of music.

Nikolaus de Goede, *The Utrecht Prosarium* (Amsterdam, 1965)—one of the best editions of sequences, with a valuable historical introduction.

Dom Anselm Hughes, *Anglo-French Sequelae* (London, 1934).

E. Misset and P. Aubry, *Les Proses d'Adam de Saint Victor* (Paris 1900; repr. New York, 1969).

Carl A. Moberg, *Über die schwedischen Sequenzen,* 2 vols. (Freiburg, Switzerland, 1927; repr. Uppsala, 1970). Vol. 2 contains 69 sequence melodies.

Monumenta Monodica Medii Aevi (Kassel, 1970), Vol. 3, *Introit-Tropen I*—the repertory of southern French tropers of the tenth and eleventh centuries.

Sequence texts are published in AH, Vols. 7–10, 34, 37, 39, 40, 42, 44, and 53–55. Vols. 47 and 49 contain tropes of the Ordinary and Proper of the Mass.

For a catalogue of trope and sequence manuscripts, see H. Husmann, *Tropen- und Sequenzenhandschriften,* RISM B V¹ (1964).

For Further Reading   Willi Apel, GC, pp. 429–64.

Richard Crocker, "The Repertory of Proses at Saint Martial de Limoges in the 10th Century," JAMS, 11 (1958), pp. 149–64; id., "Some

Ninth-Century Sequences," JAMS, 20 (1967), pp. 367–402 (see also JAMS, 21 [1968], p. 124); id., "The Troping Hypothesis," MQ, 52 (1966), pp. 183–203.

Paul Evans, "Some Reflections on the Origin of the Trope," JAMS, 14 (1961), pp. 119–30.

J. Handschin, "Trope, Sequence, and Conductus," NOHM, 2, Chapter 5; id., "The Two Winchester Tropers," Journal of Theological Studies, 37 (1936), pp. 34–49, 156–72.

Hans-Jörgen Holman, "Melismatic Tropes in the Responsories for Matins," JAMS, 16 (1963), pp. 36–46.

Ruth Steiner, "Some Melismas for Office Responsories," JAMS, 26 (1973), pp. 108–31; id., "The Prosulae of the MS Paris, Bibliothèque Nationale, f. lat. 1118," JAMS, 22 (1969), pp. 367–93.

Rembert Weakland, "The Beginnings of Troping," MQ, 44 (1958), pp. 477–88.

CHAPTER VII, FURTHER EXPANSION OF THE LITURGY

Rhymed Offices

Texts are published in AH, Vols. 5, 13, 18, 24–26, 28, and 45a; also Vol. 17, pp. 1–188, and Vol. 52, pp. 329–51. The omission of prose texts makes some Offices seem incomplete.

The music of rhymed Offices has received little attention, but a few facsimiles, transcriptions, and studies are available: W. Arlt, Ein Festoffizium des Mittelalters aus Beauvais, 2 vols. (Cologne, 1970); Vol. 2 includes an edition of the New Year's Office with appended polyphony. Richard Hoppin, Cypriot Plainchant of the Manuscript Torino, Biblioteca Nazionale, J. II. 9, MSD, 19 (AIM, 1968)—facsimiles (with commentary) of Offices for St. Hylarion and St. Anne. Ewald Jammers, Das Karlsoffizium "Regali natus" (Strasbourg, 1934). Giuseppe Vecchi, Uffici drammatici padovani (Florence, 1954)—an edition of texts and music. Henri Villetard, Office de Pierre de Corbeil (Paris, 1907); id., Office de Saint Savinien et de Saint Potentien, premiers évêques de Sens (Paris, 1956)—both are editions (text and music) with introductions. R. Weakland, "The Compositions of Hucbald," Études grégoriennes, 3 (1959), pp. 155–62, includes one Office.

A few more studies of particular Offices are listed in Hughes, MMBb, Nos. 689b–703. Publications that include the polyphony as well as the Office of St. James from Santiago de Compostela are listed in the Bibliography for Chapters VIII–X.

Liturgical Drama

Modern Editions   Edmond de Coussemaker, *Drames liturgiques du moyen âge* (Rennes, 1860; repr. New York, 1964)—transcriptions of 22 plays, including the ten from Fleury. G. Tintori, *Sacre rappresentazioni nel manoscritti 201 della Biblioteca Municipale di Orléans* (Cremona, 1958), includes both facsimiles and transcriptions of the entire Fleury Play Book. Unfortunately, all the chants, including the *Te Deum,* receive unjustified and "capricious" rhythmic interpretations. Hughes, MMBb, Nos. 802–22, lists these two works together with other publications, mostly European, that are primarily studies of individual plays but also include transcriptions.

Items in the following list of performing editions (or "acting versions") vary considerably in the degree to which they have been edited or arranged:

The Play of Daniel—an acting version edited by N. Greenberg (New York, 1959); a literal transcription by W. Smoldon (London, 1960);

The Play of Herod—an acting version edited by N. Greenberg, together with a complete facsimile from the Fleury Play Book and a literal transcription by W. Smoldon (New York, 1965);

The Son of Getron—an acting version edited by C. Sterne (Pittsburgh, 1962).

Other plays edited by W. Smoldon: *Peregrinus* (London, 1965); *Planctus Mariae* (London, 1965); *Officium pastorum* (London, 1967); *Visitatio sepulchri* (London, 1964).

For Further Reading   Most historical and literary studies of medieval drama pay little or no attention to the music; therefore, only a few of the most important works will be listed here. Edmund K. Chambers, *The Medieval Stage,* 2 vols. (Oxford, 1903), discusses both secular and sacred drama and the development of the latter from the process of troping. Karl Young, *The Drama of the Medieval Church,* 2 vols. (Oxford, 1933), follows Chambers's evolutionary theory and arranges the texts of liturgical dramas according to their increasing expansion and complexity rather than in chronological order. O. B. Hardison, *Christian Rite and Christian Drama in the Middle Ages* (Baltimore, 1965), challenges the basic assumptions of both Chambers and Young (see below). Two literary studies more limited in scope are also valuable: Richard B. Donovan, *Liturgical Drama in Medieval Spain* (Toronto, 1958); and Grace Frank, *The Medieval French Drama* (Oxford, 1954). R. Axton, *European Drama of the Early Middle Ages* (London, 1974), provides an excellent introduction to the subject and discusses a number of plays in considerable detail.

Several articles by William L. Smoldon present the traditional view of liturgical drama's origin and development and provide the most extensive discussion of its music: "The Liturgical Music-Drama," NOHM, 2, Ch. 6; "The Music of the Medieval Church Drama," MQ, 48 (1962), pp. 476–97; "Medieval Lyrical Melody and the Latin Church Dramas," MQ, 51 (1965), pp. 507–17; "The Melodies of the Medieval Church Dramas and their Significance," *Comparative Drama*, 2 (1968), pp. 185–209 (reprinted "with extensive changes" in *Medieval English Drama: Essays Critical and Contextual*, ed. J. Taylor and A. H. Nelson [Chicago and London, 1972], pp. 64–80).

CHAPTERS VIII–X, POLYPHONY THROUGH THE SCHOOL OF NOTRE DAME

Facsimiles and Editions   The Winchester Troper: some facsimiles included with the partial edition of the texts by Walter H. Frere for the Henry Bradshaw Society, Vol. 8 (London, 1894; repr. New York, 1973). See also Andreas Holschneider, *Die Organa von Winchester* (Hildesheim, 1968), for more fascimiles and an index of incipits. Publication of the Winchester Tropers in the series Early English Manuscripts in Facsimile has been announced.

Polyphony of St. Martial: facsimiles of complete manuscripts and transcriptions of all the music have yet to be published. A few facsimiles are available in NPM and NMM; a number of pieces are included in the various anthologies and in articles cited in the notes to Chapter VIII.

Santiago de Compostela: P. Wagner, *Die Gesänge der Jakobusliturgie zu Santiago de Compostela* (Freiburg, 1931), transcribes both plainchant and polyphony in square notation. W. M. Whitehill, G. Prado, and J. C. García, *Liber Sancti Jacobi, Codex Calixtinus*, 3 vols. (Santiago de Compostela, 1944); Vol. 2 contains facsimiles and transcriptions of all the music. Individual pieces may be found in anthologies and in a few articles (see Hughes, MMBb, Nos. 1376–80).

School of Notre Dame: the four main sources of Notre Dame polyphony are available in fascimile editions: *F*, PMMM, 10 and 11; *Ma*, PMMM, 1; *W₁*, *An Old St. Andrews Music Book*, ed. J. H. Baxter (London, 1931); *W₂*, PMMM, 2. See also Luther A. Dittmer, *A Central Source of Notre-Dame Polyphony*, PMMM, 3; and id., "The Lost Fragments of a Notre Dame Manuscript in Johannes Wolf's Library," AMRM, pp. 122–33 and Plates 6–17. A facsimile of the St. Victor manuscript (Paris, Bibl. Nat., lat. 15139) with an introduction by Ethel Thurston is published under the title *The Music of the St. Victor Manuscript* (Toronto, 1959).

Reference Works   Three reference works are indispensable for detailed study of the Notre Dame repertory and the thirteenth-century motet: G. Reaney, *Manuscripts of Polyphonic Music, 11th–Early 14th Century*, RISM B IV¹, includes catalogs of Notre Dame manuscripts with musical incipits and an index of texts; F. Gennrich, *Bibliographie der ältesten französischen und lateinischen Motetten*, SMMA, 2; F. Ludwig, *Reper-*

torium organorum recentioris et motetorum vetustissimi stili, 1¹ (Halle, 1910)—only Vol. 1¹ (manuscripts in square notation) was published in Ludwig's lifetime, reprinted by L. Dittmer in MSt, 7. F. Gennrich later published the completed portions of Vol. 1² (manuscripts in mensural notation) and Vol. 2 (index of musical incipits) in SMMA, 7 and 8; Vol. 2 is also published in MSt, 17. From Ludwig's complex and confusing catalogs come the numberings used by modern editors to identify motet texts, clausulae, and organal settings of chants for Offices (O1–O34) and Masses (M1–M59)

Modern editions of Notre Dame polyphony are few in number. William G. Waite, *The Rhythm of Twelfth-Century Polyphony* (New Haven, 1954), includes a transcription of Leonin's *Magnus liber* as it appears in W_1. Waite also gives the most comprehensive, if controversial, explanation of modal notation and the problems involved in its interpretation.

Ethel Thurston, *The Works of Perotin* (New York, 1970), is a performing edition of all works attributed to Perotin by Anonymous IV.

Heinrich Husmann, *Die drei- und vierstimmige Notre-Dame Organa,* PAM, 11 (Leipzig, 1940; repr. Hildesheim, 1967)—the transcriptions use C-clefs.

Janet Knapp, *Thirty-five Conductus for Two and Three Voices* (New Haven, 1965).

Literature on the development of polyphony to the early thirteenth century is extensive and varied (see Hughes, MMBb, Nos. 1335–1446, and, for both monophonic and polyphonic conducti, Nos. 1105–24). Much of it is in foreign languages and often deals with specific and highly technical aspects of the different repertories, as do many of the articles in English. Some general studies of the Notre Dame repertory have been cited in the notes to Chapter IX and X. A few more are listed here:

Rebecca Baltzer, "Thirteenth-Century Illuminated Miniatures and the Date of the Florence Manuscript," JAMS, 25 (1972), pp. 1–18.

Hans Tischler, "How were Notre Dame clausulae performed?" ML, 50 (1969), pp. 273–77.

Gordon A. Anderson, "Clausulae or Transcribed-Motets in the Florence Manuscript?" AcM, 42 (1970), pp. 109–28; id., "Notre Dame and Related Conductus—A Catalogue Raisonné," *Miscellanea Musicologica—Adelaide Studies in Musicology,* 6 (1972), pp. 153–229, and 7 (1975), pp. 1–81; id., "Thirteenth-Century Conductus: Obiter Dicta," MQ, 58 (1972), pp. 349–64.

Norman E. Smith, "Tenor Repetition in the Notre-Dame Organa," JAMS, 19 (1966), pp. 329–51; id., "Interrelationships among the Alleluias of the *Magnus liber organi,*" JAMS, 25 (1972), pp. 175–202.

Ethel Thurston, "A Comparison of the St. Victor Clausulae with their Motets," AMRM, pp. 785–802.

CHAPTER XI–XII, LATIN, PROVENÇAL, AND FRENCH SONGS

Latin Songs

Facsimiles   Karl Breul, *The Cambridge Songs* (Cambridge, 1915), with introduction and edition of texts. *Carmina Burana,* PMMM, 9.

Modern Editions   A good many songs may be found in various books, articles, and anthologies, but no collection of Latin songs with music has yet been published. Of the editions of poetry listed below, all but the first include English translations.

A. Hilka and O. Schumann, *Carmina Burana,* 3 vols. (Heidelberg, 1930–41). Never completed, this critical edition of the texts gives references to other manuscripts in which poems appear with music.

Jack Lindsay, *Medieval Latin Poets* (London, 1934); John A. Symonds, *Wine, Women, and Song* (London, 1884 and numerous later editions); Helen Waddell, *Mediaeval Latin Lyrics,* 4th ed. (Penguin Classics, Baltimore, 1952); George F. Whicher, *The Goliard Poets,* 2nd ed. (New York, 1950); E. H. Zeydel, *Vagabond Verse* (Detroit, 1966).

For Further Reading   F. J. E. Raby, *A History of Secular Latin Poetry to A.D. 1300,* 2 vols. (Oxford, 1934)—the last two chapters of Vol. 2 deal with "The Latin Lyric"; Helen Waddell, *The Wandering Scholars* (New York, 1961). Neither of these valuable studies gives translations of the poems that are quoted.

Two introductory surveys of both Latin and vernacular lyric poetry in the Middle Ages may also be cited here: F. Brittain, *The Medieval Latin and Romance Lyric to A.D. 1300,* 2nd ed. (Cambridge, 1951); Peter Dronke, *The Medieval Lyric* (London, 1968). Brittain gives poems only in the original languages, but Dronke translates all texts and includes a number of melodies.

Troubadour and Trouvère Songs

Facsimiles   *Le melodie trobadoriche nel canzoniere provenzale della Biblioteca Ambrosiana R. 71 Sup.,* ed. Ugo Sesini (Turin, 1942). In addition to a facsimile, this includes transcriptions and analyses of the melodies; also published, but without the last 21 plates, in *Studi medievali* (new series), 12–15 (1939–42).

Le Chansonnier de l'Arsenal, ed. P. Aubry (Paris, 1909)—contains some transcriptions. *Le Chansonnier Cangé,* ed. Jean Beck, 2 vols. (Philadelphia, 1927; repr. New York, 1965)—includes transcriptions. *Le Manuscrit du Roi,* ed. Jean and Louise Beck, 2 vols. (Philadelphia, 1938). *Le Chansonnier d'Arras,* ed. A. Jeanroy (Paris, 1925). *Le Chansonnier français de Saint-Germain-des-Prés,* ed. P. Meyer and G. Raynaud (Paris, 1892).

<u>Modern Editions</u>   F. Gennrich, *Der musikalische Nachlass der Troubadours,* 3 vols., SMMA, 3, 4, and 15; (Darmstadt, 1958–65); a critical edition of all melodies with Provençal texts with introduction, commentary, and bibliography; id., *Lo gai saber,* MSB, 18/19 (Darmstadt, 1959)—50 troubadour songs with complete texts. Carl Appel, *Der Singweisen Bernarts von Ventadorn,* Beihefte zur Zeitschrift für romanische Philologie, 81 (Halle, 1934). H. Anglès, "Les Melodies del trobador Guiraut Riquier," *Estudis Universitaris Catalans,* 11 (1926), pp. 1–78. S. C. Aston, *Peirol, Troubadour of Auvergne* (Cambridge, 1953)—fascimiles with music. U. Sesini, "Piere Vidal e la sua opera musicale," *Rassegna musicale,* 16 (1943), pp. 25–33 and 65–95.

Anthologies of trouvère songs: F. Gennrich, *Exempla altfranzösischer Lyrik,* MSB, 17 (Darmstadt, 1958); J. Maillard and J. Chailley, *Anthologie de chants de trouvères* (Paris, 1967).

Numerous publications are devoted to a particular type of song or to the works of a single trouvère: J. Bédier and P. Aubry, *Les chansons de croisade* (Paris, 1909); J. Bédier and J. Beck, *Les chansons de Colin Muset* (Paris, 1912); A. Jeanroy, L. Brandin, and P. Aubry, *Lais et descorts français du XIIIᵉ siècle* (Paris 1901; repr. 1970); E. de Coussemaker, *Oeuvres complètes du trouvère Adam de la Halle* (Paris, 1872; repr. Ridgewood, N.J., 1965); N. Wilkins, *The Lyric Works of Adam de la Hale,* CMM, 44 (AIM, 1967); J. Maillard, "Roi-trouvère du XIIIᵉ siècle," MD, 21 (1967), pp. 7–66 (revised repirnt in MSD, 18); id., "Lais et chansons d'Ernoul de Gastinois," MD, 17 (1963), pp. 21–56, repr. in MSD, 15 (AIM, 1964); J. Chailley, *Les chansons à la Vierge de Gautier de Coinci* (Paris, 1959); F. Gennrich, *Cantilenae Piae: 31 altfranzösische geistliche Lieder . . . ,* MSB, 24; T. Newcombe, *Jehan Erart, 13th-Century Trouvère d'Arras,* CMM, 67 (AIM, 1975).

A few anthologies contain songs from various countries: F. Gennrich, *Troubadours, Trouvères, Minne- and Meistersingers,* AoM, 2 (Cologne, 1960); id., *Aus der Formenwelt des Mittelalters,* MSB, 7 (64 examples illustrating various musical forms); R. J. Taylor, *Die Melodien der weltlichen Lieder des Mittelalters,* 2 vols. (Stuttgart, 1964).

For editions of poetry with English translations, see F. Goldin, *Lyrics of the Troubadours and Trouveres* (Garden City, N.Y., 1973); and S. G. Nichols, *The Songs of Bernart de Ventadorn . . . ,* North Carolina Studies in Romance Languages and Literature, 39 (Chapel Hill, N.C., 1962); J. Wilhelm, *Seven Troubadours: The Creators of Modern Verse* (University Park, Pa., 1970)—includes many translations, but not the original poems; A. Bonner, *Songs of the Troubadours* (New York, 1972)—gives excellent short accounts of 20 troubadours and their poetry, with many complete translations but no original texts.

<u>For Further Reading</u>   Of the extensive literature on troubadour and trouvère poetry and music, only a few items can be listed here. The books in foreign languages contain numerous musical examples. P. Aubry, *Trou-*

vères and Troubadours (New York and London, 1914; repr. New York, 1969); J. Beck, *Die Melodien der Troubadours* (Strasbourg, 1908); id., *La Musique des troubadours* (Paris, 1910)—both books by Beck deal with trouvères as well as troubadours. R. Briffault, *The Troubadours* (Bloomington, Ind., 1965)—this book ignores music but presents the case for Arabic influence in a good literary and historical survey. F. Gennrich, *Grundriss einer Formenlehre des mittelalterlichen Liedes* (Halle, 1932)—a forced and arbitrary classification of forms, but valuable for the musical examples. H. Van der Werf, *The Chansons of the Troubadours and Trouvères* (Utrecht, 1972).

For further bibliography, see the somewhat confusingly arranged section "The lyric in Latin and the vernacular" in Hughes, MMBb, Nos. 1038–1236.

CHAPTER XIII, SECULAR MONOPHONY IN GERMANY, ITALY, SPAIN AND ENGLAND

Germany

Facsimiles and Modern Editions   F. Gennrich, *Die Colmarer Liederhandschrift*, SMMA, 18—a facsimile; P. Runge, *Die Sangweisen der Colmarer Handschrift und die Liederhandschrift Donaueschingen* (Leipzig, 1896)—transcription in square notation. See also F. Eberth, *Die Minne- und Meistergesangsweisen der Kolmarer Liederhandschrift* (Detmold, 1935); R. Zitzmann, *Die Melodien der Kolmarer Liederhandschrift* (Würzburg, 1944).

F. Gennrich, *Die Jenaer Liederhandschrift*, SMMA, 11—a facsimile of pages with music; K. Müller, *Phototypische Facsimile-Ausgabe der Jenaer Liederhandschrift* (Jena, 1896)—a complete facsimile; F. Saran, G. Holz, and E. Bernouilli, *Die Jenaer Liederhandschrift*, 2 vols. (Leipzig, 1901; repr. Hildesheim, 1966)—includes transcriptions in both square notation and modern note values.

H. Rietsch, *Gesänge von Frauenlob, Reinmar von Zweter und Alexander*, Denkmäler der Tonkunst in Österreich (DTÖ), 41 (Jg. 20/2; Vienna, 1913; repr. Graz, 1960)—facsimiles and transcriptions.

H. Heger, *Mondsee-Wiener-Liederhandschrift*, Codices Selecti, 19 (Graz, 1968)—facsimile.

P. Runge, *Die Lieder des Hugo von Montfort* (Leipzig, 1906).

W. Schmieder and E. Wiessner, *Lieder von Neidhart (von Reuental)*, DTÖ, 71 (Jg. 37/1; Vienna, 1930)—facsimiles and transcriptions; F. Gennrich, *Neidhart-Lieder*, SMMA, 9—an edition of 18 songs, but No. 6 is of doubtful authenticity. A. Hatto and R. Taylor, *The Songs of Neidhart von Reuental* (Manchester, 1958)—this is an edition of the 17 genuine songs that have melodies (2 summer and 15 winter). The first stanza of each poem is translated; the remaining text is only summarized.

F. Maurer, *Die Lieder Walthers von der Vogelweide,* 2 vols., Altdeutsche Textbibliothek, 43 and 47 (Tübingen, 1960 and 1962)—edition of texts with transcriptions of melodies.

In addition to these facsimiles and editions of manuscripts or individual Minnesingers, there are a number of anthologies: F. Gennrich, *Melodien altdeutscher Lieder,* MSB, 9—47 melodies; id., *Mittelhochdeutsche Liedkunst,* MSB, 10—24 melodies; id., *Troubadours, Trouvères, Minne- und Meistersingers* (Cologne, 1960). E. Jammers, *Ausgewählte Melodien des Minnesangs* (Tübingen, 1963)—131 songs; B. Seagrave and W. Thomas, *The Songs of the Minnesingers* (Urbana and London, 1966), includes an introduction, notes on composers and their songs, translations of texts, and a recording of selected items; R. J. Taylor, *The Art of the Minnesinger,* 2 vols. (Cardiff, 1968)—an edition of all songs up to 1300. W. Thomas and B. Seagrave, *The Songs of the Minnesinger, Prince Wizlaw of Rügen* (Chapel Hill, 1967), includes an introduction and complete translations of the transcribed songs.

Apart from the works with English titles, almost all studies of the Minnesingers and their melodies are in German (see Hughes, MMBb, Nos. 1237–68a and 1278–1322).

Italy

Studies of the Italian lauda are few in number and almost exclusively in foreign languages (see Hughes, MMBb, Nos. 1323–34). The single publication of facsimiles and transcriptions is F. Liuzzi, *La Lauda e i primordi della melodia italiana,* 2 vols. (Rome, 1935). Texts of both German and Italian songs are translated in F. Goldin, *German and Italian Lyrics of the Middle Ages* (Garden City, N.Y., 1973); the Italian lyrics do not include anonymous laude.

Spain

Facsimiles and Editions   H. Anglès, *La música de las Cantigas de Santa Maria,* 3 vols. in 4 (Barcelona, 1943–64); Vols. 1 and 2 contain a facsimile and complete transcription of the Escorial MS j.b.2. The two parts of Vol. 3 contain detailed studies of music in Spain up to the thirteenth century, various aspects of the cantigas, the question of Arabic influence, and relationships between Spanish and European monophonic songs (all in Spanish except for a chapter in German by H. Spanke on the poetic meters and forms of the cantigas). Vol. 3^2 includes a number of facsimiles and transcriptions of other music.

J. Ribera, *Cantigas de Santa Maria,* 2 vols. (Madrid, 1889)—a literary and historical study with an edition of the texts by a strong proponent of

Arabic influence; id., *La Música de las Cantigas* (Madrid, 1922)—facsimile of Madrid MS 10069 with unacceptable transcriptions. An abridged English version of this second publication translated by E. Hague and M. Leffingwell, *Music in Ancient Arabia and Spain* (London and Stanford, 1929), lacks most of the facsimiles.

P. Vindel, *Martin Codax. Las Siete Canciones de Amor* (Madrid, 1915)—a facsimile and transcription of the 7 songs. Some facsimiles and all transcriptions are also available in the article by I. Pope listed below.

Miscellaneous facsimiles and numerous transcriptions are also available in H. Anglès, *La Música a Catalunya fins al segle XIII* (Barcelona, 1935).

For Further Reading   R. Stevenson, *Spanish Music in the Age of Columbus* (The Hague, 1960), begins with a survey of the medieval period (pp. 1–49). An older but still useful survey is J. B. Trend, *The Music of Spanish History to 1600* (New York, 1926; repr. New York, 1965); see also id., *Alfonso the Sage, and other Spanish Essays* (London, 1926). Another survey, H. Anglès, "Hispanic Musical Culture from the Sixth to the Fourteenth Century," MQ, 26 (1940), pp. 494–528, is an abbreviated English version of the Introduction to *El Còdex musical de las Huelgas,* 3 vols. (Barcelona, 1931).

A few articles in English deal with more specialized aspects of Spanish monophonic song: E. Gerson-Kiwi, "On the Musical Sources of the Judaeo-Hispanic *Romance,"* MQ 50 (1964), pp. 31–43; A. F. G. Bell, "The 'Cantigas de Santa Maria' of Alfonso X," *Modern Language Review,* 10 (1915), pp. 338–48—literary aspects; id., "The Seven Songs of Martin Codax," *Modern Language Review,* 18 (1923), pp. 162–67—translations; I. Pope, "Medieval Latin Background of the Thirteenth-Century Galician Lyric," *Speculum,* 9 (1934) pp. 3–25.

England

Two anthologies of facsimiles contain some pages with English sacred and secular songs:

Early Bodleian Music, 3 vols. (London, 1901–13; repr. Farnborough, 1967). Vol. 1, *Sacred and Secular Music from Manuscripts in the Bodleian Library,* ed. Sir John Stainer, contains 223 facsimiles (the transcriptions in Vol. 2 are old-fashioned); Vol. 3, *Introduction to the Study of some of the oldest Latin Musical Manuscripts in the Bodleian Library,* ed. E. B. Nicholson, includes 71 facsimiles.

Early English Harmony, 2 vols. (London, 1897–1913). Vol. 1, ed. H. E. Wooldridge, gives brief descriptions of 60 facsimiles. The transcriptions by H. V. Hughes in Vol. 2 are almost unusable.

Apart from the items cited in footnotes 24–28 of this chapter and brief discussions in histories of music, studies of English monophonic song are almost nonexistent. J. H. Chaytor, *The Troubadours and England* (Cambridge, 1923), treats the troubadours purely as literary figures. For a collection of 96 poems of various kinds, both sacred and secular, see *Medieval English Verse,* trans. B. Stone, rev. ed. (Penguin Classics, London, 1971). In appendices, Stone lists modern publications of the poems in their original form and provides a short "Further Bibliography," primarily literary and historical.

CHAPTER XIV, SACRED AND SECULAR POLYPHONY OF THE THIRTEENTH CENTURY

Facsimiles and Editions   For facsimiles of the oldest motet collections, see the Notre Dame manuscripts (*F*, *Ma*, *W₁* and *W₂*) listed in the Bibliography for Chapters VIII–X. Publications of later collections are as follows:

Ba: P. Aubry, *Cent Motets du XIIIᵉ siècle,* 3 vols. (Paris, 1908; repr. New York, 1964); the transcriptions (Vol. 2) use C-clefs and are not entirely accurate; the commentary in Vol. 3 includes 13 facsimiles from contemporary sources. A new edition by G. Anderson is now available in CMM, 75 (AIM, 1977).

Cl: L. Dittmer, *Paris, 13521 [Cl] & 11411,* PMMM, 4—facsimile, with introduction and transcriptions of 2 motets. F. Gennrich, *Ein altfranzösischer Motettenkodex,* SMMA, 6—facsimile and index only. G. Anderson, *Motets of the Manuscript La Clayette,* CMM, 68 (AIM, 1975)—a complete edition.

Las Huelgas: H. Anglès, *El Còdex musical de Las Huelgas,* 3 vols. (Barcelona, 1931)—introduction (in Catalan), facsimile, and transcription in C-clefs. A new edition by G. Anderson is in preparation (CMM, 79).

Mo: Y. Rokseth, *Polyphonies du XIIIᵉ siècle,* 4 vols. (Paris, 1935–39)—facsimile, transcription, and commentary.

Tu: A. Auda, *Les Motets wallons du manuscrit de Turin: Vari 42,* 2 vols. (Brussels, 1953)—facsimile and transcription.

Other editions and anthologies: F. Gennrich, *Aus der Frühzeit der Motette,* MSB, 22/23—facsimiles and copies of two clausula cycles from *W₁* with copies of the corresponding motets in *W₂* and *F;* id., *Die Sankt Viktor-Clausulae und ihre Motetten,* MSB, 5/6—facsimiles of the clausulae and copies of the motets in their original notation; id., *Florilegium motetorum,* SMMA, 17—an edition of 53 motets presents "a cross section of the 13th-century motet repertory"; H. Tischler, *A Medieval Motet Book* (New York, 1976)—an anthology of 18 motets edited for performance with voices and instruments. Announced for publication by H. Tischler are a complete edition of the earliest motets and a new edition of *Mo.*

G. Anderson, *The Latin Compositions in Fascicules VII and VIII of the Notre Dame Manuscript Wolfenbüttel Helmstadt 1099 (1206) [W₂],* MSt,

24/1—this is a critical commentary with translations of the motet texts and historical notes. Volume 24/2 contains the complete transcriptions.

For the motets and polyphonic songs of Adam de la Hale, see the complete editions of his works listed in the Bibliography for Chapters XI–XII.

Reference works pertaining to thirteenth-century motet manuscripts are listed in the Bibliography to Chapters VIII–X.

For Further Reading   G. Anderson, "Motets of the Thirteenth Century Manuscript La Clayette," MD, 27 (1973), pp. 11–40; id., "Newly Identified Clausula-Motets in the Las Huelgas Manuscript," MQ, 55 (1969), pp. 228–45; id., "Newly Identified Tenor Chants in the Notre Dame Repertory," ML, 50 (1969), pp. 158–71; id., "Notre Dame Bilingual Motets—A Study in the History of Music (c. 1215–1245)," *Miscellanea Musicologica, Adelaide Studies in Music,* 3 (1968), pp. 50–144; id., "Notre Dame Latin Double Motets ca. 1215–1250," MD, 25 (1971), pp. 35–92; id., "A Small Collection of Notre Dame Motets ca. 1215–1235," JAMS, 22 (1969), pp. 157–96. F. Mathiassen, *The Style of the Early Motet,* Copenhagen, 1966.

Several articles deal with more specific aspects of the motet repertory: D. Harbinson, "The Hocket Motets in the Old Corpus of the Montpellier Motet Manuscript," MD, 25 (1971), pp. 99–112; id., "Imitation in the Early Motet," ML, 45 (1964), pp. 359–68. See also W. Dalglish, "The Hocket in Medieval Polyphony," MQ, 55 (1969), pp. 344–63. H. Nathan, "The Function of Text in French Thirteenth-Century Motets," MQ, 28 (1942), pp. 445–62. H. Tischler, "The Evolution of the Harmonic Style in the Notre-Dame Motet," AcM, 28 (1956), pp. 87–95; id., "The Evolution of Form in the Earliest Motets," AcM, 31 (1959), pp. 86–90; id., "Intellectual Trends in thirteenth-century Paris as reflected in the Texts of Motets," *The Music Review,* 29 (1968), pp. 1–11; id., "Why a New Edition of the Montpellier Codex?" AcM, 46 (1974), pp. 58–75.

A number of studies deal with English polyphony and practices in the thirteenth century: K. Levy, "New Material on the Early Motet in England," JAMS, 4 (1951), pp. 220–39; H. Tischler, "English Traits in the Early Thirteenth-Century Motet," MQ, 30 (1944), pp. 458–76. E. Sanders, "Peripheral Polyphony of the 13th Century," JAMS, 17 (1964), pp. 261–87, discusses supposedly English traits and their relationship to continental practices, as does the lengthy article of J. Handschin listed below.

Problems connected with the *Sumer* canon are dealt with in a series of four studies: M. Bukofzer, *"Sumer is icumen in": a Revision* (Berkeley, 1944): B. Schofield, "The Provenance and Date of 'Sumer is icumen in,' " *The Music Review,* 9 (1948), pp. 81–86; N. Pirrotta, "On the Problem of 'Sumer is icumen in,' " MD, 2 (1948), pp. 205–16; J. Handschin, "The Summer Canon and its Background," MD, 3 (1949), pp. 55–94, and 5 (1951), pp. 65–113.

CHAPTERS XV–XVI, ARS NOVA IN FRANCE AND
FOURTEENTH-CENTURY LITURGICAL POLYPHONY

Facsimiles and Editions   Le *Roman de Fauvel,* ed. P. Aubry (Paris,
1907)—a color facsimile of the MS Paris, Bibl. nat., fr. 146, the only
manuscript of the poem with the musical interpolations. L. Schrade,
PM, 1, edits all the polyphonic music in the *Roman de Fauvel,* the later
motets attributed to Vitry, and the fourteenth-century Mass cycles except the Sorbonne Mass.

N. Wilkins, *The Works of Jehan de Lescurel,* CMM, 30 (AIM, 1966)—a
facsimile and transcription. F. Gennrich, SMMA, 13, gives another edition of the music, which he also published in RVB, 1, pp. 307–72 (see
also RVB, 2, pp. 246–54).

W. Apel, in FSC, includes the few early fourteenth-century examples
of secular polyphony in addition to all the chaces, but most of the pieces
come from the last decades of the century.

F. Ll. Harrison, PM, 5, includes motets from *Iv* as well as from later
sources.

H. Stäblein-Harder, *Fourteenth-Century Mass Music in France,* CMM,
29 (AIM, 1962), is an edition with introduction and commentary in
MSD, 7. A less reliable transcription of music in *Apt* is A. Gastoué, *Le
Manuscrit de musique du Trésor d'Apt* (Paris, 1936). Another edition of the
Tournai Mass by C. Van den Borren is in CMM, 13 (AIM, 1957).

For Further Reading   L. Schrade, "The Chronology of the Ars Nova in
France," *Les Colloques de Wégimont, II—1955* (Paris, 1959), pp. 37–62;
id., "Philippe de Vitry: Some New Discoveries," MQ, 42 (1956), pp.
330–54.

On the motet: D. Harbinson, "Isorhythmic Technique in the Early
Motet," ML, 47 (1966), pp. 100–09; E. Sanders, "The Early Motets of
Philippe de Vitry," JAMS, 28 (1975), pp. 24–45; W. Apel, "Remarks
about the Isorhythmic Motet," *Les Colloques de Wégimont, II—1955*
(Paris, 1959), pp. 139–48; G. Reaney, "The Isorhythmic Motet and its
Social Background," *Bericht über den internationalen musikwis-
senschaftlichen Kongress Kassel 1962* (Kassel, 1963), pp. 25–27; U.
Günther, "The 14th-Century Motet and its Development," MD, 12
(1958), pp. 27–58.

On Related Movements in fourteenth-century Masses: L. Schrade,
"The Mass of Toulouse," RBM, 8 (1954), pp. 84–96; id., "A Fourteenth-Century Parody Mass," AcM, 27 (1955), pp. 13–39, with a
"note" in AcM, 28 (1956), pp. 54–55; R. Jackson, "Musical Interrelations between 14th-Century Mass Movements," AcM, 29 (1957), pp.
54–64.

For the early history of the secular formes fixes, see the bibliography
to Chapter XVII.

A few studies or translations of theoretical writings are available in

English: L. Plantinga, "Philippe de Vitry's *Ars Nova:* a Translation," JMT, 5 (1961), pp. 204–23; E. Warner, "The Mathematical Foundation of Philippe de Vitry's *Ars Nova,*" JAMS, 9 (1956), pp. 128–32. F. J. Smith, "Jacques de Liège, an Anti-Modernist?" RBM, 17 (1963), pp. 3–10; id., "Ars Nova—a Re-definition?" MD, 18 (1964), pp. 19–35, and 19 (1965), pp. 83–97; id., *Jacobi leodiensis, Speculum Musicae,* MSt, 13 and 22.

CHAPTER XVII, GUILLAUME DE MACHAUT

Editions of Music   F. Ludwig, *Guillaume de Machaut: musikalische Werke,* 4 vols. (Leipzig, 1926, first 3 vols. only; repr. 1954 with vol. 4 edited by H. Besseler from Ludwig's notes); L. Schrade, *The Works of Guillaume de Machaut,* 2 vols., PM, 2 and 3 (1956).

Separate editions of the Mass: J. Chailley (Paris, 1948); F. Gennrich, SMMA, 1 (facsimile); H. Hübsch (Heidelberg, 1953); A. Machabey (Liège, 1948); D. Stevens (London and New York, 1973); G. de Van, CMM, 2 (AIM, 1949). All except the facsimile are intended as performing editions.

Editions of Poetry   V. Chichmaref, *Guillaume de Machaut: Oeuvres lyriques,* 2 vols. (Paris, 1909); E. Hoepffner, *Oeuvres de Guillaume de Machaut,* 3 vols. (Paris, 1908–21)—contains the longer poems, including the *Remède de Fortune* with its music, but excluding the following two works: M. L. de Mas Latrie, *La Prise d'Alexandrie* (Geneva, 1877); P. Paris, *Guillaume de Machaut: Le livre du Voir Dit* (Paris, 1875). N. Wilkins, *La Louange des dames by Guillaume de Machaut* (Edinburgh, 1972), includes transcriptions of the 22 poems Machaut also set to music.

For Further Reading   For a short but excellent survey, see G. Reaney, *Guillaume de Machaut,* Oxford Studies of Composers, 9 (London, 1971).

Much of the literature in English is devoted to studies of the secular songs. As a preliminary to these studies, see W. Apel, "Rondeaux, Virelais, and Ballades in French 13th-Century Song," JAMS, 7 (1954), pp. 121–30; G. Reaney, "Concerning the Origins of the Rondeau, Virelai and Ballade Forms," MD, 6 (1952), pp. 155–66; id., "The Development of the Rondeau, Virelai and Ballade Forms from Adam de la Hale to Guillaume de Machaut," *Festschrift Karl Gustav Fellerer, zum 60. Geburtstag* (Regensburg, 1962).

Articles dealing with various aspects of the songs: G. Reaney, "Fourteenth Century Harmony and the Ballades, Rondeaux and Virelais of Guillaume de Machaut," MD, 7 (1953), pp. 129–46; id., "The Ballades, Rondeaux and Virelais of Guillaume de Machaut: Melody, Rhythm and Form," AcM, 27 (1955), pp. 40–58; id., "Guillaume de Machaut: Lyric

Poet," ML, 39 (1958), pp. 38–51; id., "The Poetic Form of Machaut's Musical Works," MD, 13 (1959), pp. 25–41; S. J. Williams, "Vocal Scoring in the Chansons of Machaut," JAMS, 21 (1968), pp. 251–57.

Articles on the lais: G. Reaney, "The Lais of Guillaume de Machaut and Their Background," Proceedings of the Royal Musical Association, 82 (1955/56), pp. 15–32; L. Schrade, "Guillaume de Machaut and the Roman de Fauvel," Miscelánea en homenaje a Monseñor Higinio Anglès, 2 vols. (Barcelona, 1958–61), 2, pp. 843–50; see also the articles cited in notes 13 and 14. Seven short articles dealing with various aspects of Machaut's music have been published in Early Music, 5 (1977), pp. 462–98: "a Special Issue devoted to his work."

CHAPTER XVIII, THE ITALIAN ARS NOVA

Facsimiles and Editions   I Più antichi monumenti italiani di melica mensurale, ed. G. Vecchi (Bologna, 1960)—14 facsimiles from before 1300.

Monumenta Lyrica Medii Aevi Italica—Mensurabilia (Bologna, 1966–). I: I Più antichi monumenti sacri italiani, ed. F. A. Gallo and G. Vecchi (1968)—151 facsimiles of sacred, mostly polyphonic, music from Italy up to 1400; II: Il Canzoniere musicale del Codice Vaticano Rossi 215, ed. G. Vecchi (1966)—a complete facsimile. Further publications of fourteenth-century manuscripts in this series have been "imminent" for several years.

The Manuscript London, British Museum, Additional 29987, ed. G. Reaney, MSD, 13 (AIM, 1965)—a facsimile with introduction and complete inventory of the manuscript. With an added transcription of a Gloria, the introductory material and inventory were published under the same title in MD, 12 (1958), pp. 67–91.

The complete repertory of trecento polyphony has yet to be published, and there is considerable duplication in the two major editions: The Music of Fourteenth Century Italy (MFCI), ed. N. Pirrotta, 5 vols., CMM, 8 (AIM, 1954–64). PM, 4, ed. L. Schrade, and PM, 6–9, ed. W. T. Marrocco (Monaco, 1958–75). The contents of these volumes, including all the works of the named composers, are as follows: CMM, 8, Vol. 1, Bartolomeo, Giovanni, and Gherardello da Firenze; Vol. 2, Maestro Piero, the Rossi Codex, and 11 anonymous madrigals and cacce; Vol. 3, Lorenzo and Donato da Firenze, Rosso da Collegrano, and 9 anonymous pieces; Vol. 4, Jacopo da Bologna and Vincenzo da Rimini; Vol. 5, Andrea da Firenze and seven minor composers of the Florentine circle.

Already-published volumes in the continuing PM series include: Vol. 4, Franceso Landini; Vol. 6, Magister Piero, Giovanni da Firenze, Jacopo da Bologna; Vol. 7, Vincenzo da Rimini, Rosso da Collegrano, and the Florentines Donato, Gherardello, and Lorenzo; Vol. 8, Nicolò da Perugia and anonymous madrigals and cacce; Vol. 9, Bartolino da

Padova, Don Paolo, and Egidius and Guilielmus de Francia. Vols. 10 and 11 will also contain Italian secular polyphony but have not been published at the time of this writing. Vol. 12 (1976) is devoted to sacred Italian music, mostly Mass movements and motets.

Other editions: L. Ellinwood, *The Works of Francesco Landini* (Cambridge, Mass., 1939)—old-fashioned transcriptions, but with a still-useful introduction; W. T. Marrocco, *Fourteenth-Century Italian Cacce,* 2nd rev. ed. (Cambridge, Mass., 1961); id., *The Music of Jacopo da Bologna* (Berkeley, 1954); J. Wolf, *Der Squarcialupi Codex* (Lippstadt, 1955)—the transcriptions in this posthumous edition use C-clefs and are not notable for their accuracy.

For Further Reading   Most of the editions listed above have valuable introductions, but other material in English is not abundant. In addition to items cited in the notes to this chapter, the following studies may be useful: L. Ellinwood, "The Fourteenth Century in Italy," NOHM, 3, pp. 31–81; W. T. Marrocco, "The Ballata—a Metamorphic Form," AcM, 31 (1959), pp. 32–37; id., "Integrative Devices in the Music of the Italian 'Trecento,' " *L'Ars nova italiana del trecento III: Secondo convegno internazionale, 1969* (Certaldo, 1970), pp. 411–29; C. Schachter, "Landini's Treatment of Consonance and Dissonance: A Study in Fourteenth-Century Counterpoint," *The Music Forum* (New York and London, 1970), 2, pp. 130–86.

For more detailed bibliographies, see V. L. Hagopian, *Italian Ars Nova: A Bibliographic Guide to Modern Editions and Related Literature,* 2nd rev. ed. (Berkeley, 1973); and A. Hughes, MMBb, Nos. 1631–1748.

CHAPTER XIX, TRANSITION TO THE RENAISSANCE

Facsimiles and Editions   No complete manuscript has yet been published in facsimile, but some modern editions include a few examples of the original notation as noted below:

W. Apel, *French Secular Compositions of the Fourteenth Century* (FSC), 3 vols., CMM, 53 (AIM, 1970–72); id., *French Secular Music of the Late Fourteenth Century* (FSM) (Cambridge, Mass., 1950)—81 pieces with 8 facsimiles and an extensive introduction; S. Clercx, *Johannes Ciconia: Un musicien liégeois et son temps,* 2 vols. (Brussels, 1960)—Vol. 2 includes transcriptions and 16 facsimiles; U. Günther, *The Motets of the Manuscripts Chantilly, musée condé, 564 (olim 1047) and Modena, Biblioteca estense, α. M.5, 24 (olim lat. 568),* CMM, 39 (AIM, 1965); R. Hoppin, *The Cypriot-French Repertory of the Manuscript Torino, Biblioteca Nazionale J. II. 9* (CFR), 4 vols., CMM, 21 (AIM, 1960–63)—4 facsimiles in each volume; G. Reaney, *Early Fifteenth-Century Music,* 6 vols., CMM, 11 (AIM, 1955–); C. Van den Borren, *Pièces polyphoniques profanes de provenance liégeoise* (Brussels, 1950); N. Wilkins, *A 14th-Century Repertory from the Codex Reina* (**PR**), CMM, 36 (AIM, 1966)—52 ballades, vire-lais, and rondeaux; id., *A 15th-Century Repertory from the Codex Reina,* CMM, 37 (AIM, 1966); M. Perz, *Sources of Polyphony up to c. 1500,* Antiquitates Musicae in Polonia, 13 and 14 (Warsaw, 1973–76)—presents facsimiles and transcriptions of several manuscripts that include three Mass movements and the motet *Regina gloriosa* by Ciconia.

For more information about the contents of CMM volumes, see the listing of AIM publications in each issue of MD.

Inventories of Manuscripts   Most of the editions listed above have valu-able and informative introductions in English, as do published inventori-es of manuscripts that preserve the repertory of the transitional period between Machaut and Dufay:

BL: G. de Van in MD, 2 (1948), pp. 231–57—2 facsimiles but no in-troduction.

BU: H. Besseler in MD, 6 (1952), pp. 39–65—a facsimile of this fif-teenth-century manuscript, which includes works of Dufay and Bin-chois, has been published with critical notes and transcriptions by A. Gallo in the series *Monumenta Lyrica Medii Aevi Italica III—Mensurabilia,* Vol. 3, parts 1 and 2 (Bologna, 1968–70).

Ch: G. Reaney in MD, 8 (1954), pp. 59–113 and "Postscript" in MD, 10 (1956), pp. 55–59.

Mod: U. Günther in MD, 24 (1970), pp. 17–67; N. Pirrotta in *Atti della Reale Accademia . . . di Palermo* (1946), series IV, Vol. 4, part 2, pp. 101–54. Introductions to these inventories are in German and Italian, re-spectively.

O: G. Reaney in MD, 9 (1955), pp. 73–104. Like the two Bologna manuscripts, **O** preserves the later repertory of the transitional period, up to and including works by Dufay and Binchois.

PR: K. von Fischer in MD, 11 (1957), pp. 38–78; see also N. Wilkins, "The Codex Reina: a Revised Description," MD, 17 (1963), pp. 57–73, with answer by von Fischer on pp. 74–77. Both the inventory and Wilkins's article include facsimiles from **PR**.

TuB: H. Besseler in AMW, 7 (1925), p. 209 ff.; see also the contents of the 4 vols. in Hoppin, CFR (CMM, 21) and, for the plainchant, MSD, 19.

For additional catalogs of manuscripts with incipits of the original no-tation, see RISM, B IV² and IV³.

For Further Reading   W. Apel, "The Development of French Secular Music During the Fourteenth Century," MD, 27 (1973), pp. 41–59; R. Hoppin, "The Cypriot-French Repertory of the Manuscript Torino, Biblioteca Nazionale, J. II. 9," MD, 11 (1957), pp. 79–125; N. Pirrotta, "On Text Forms from Ciconia to Dufay," AMRM, pp. 673–82; G. Reaney, "Machaut's Influence on Late Medieval Music. I: France and

Burgundy; II: The Non-Gallic Countries," *The Monthly Musical Record,* 88 (1958), pp. 50–58 and 96–101; N. Wilkins, *One Hundred Ballades, Rondeaux and Virelais from the Late Middle Ages* (Cambridge, 1969)—an anthology of texts with commentary and an appendix of music; id., "The Post-Machaut Generation of Poet-Musicians," *Nottingham Medieval Studies,* 12 (1968), pp. 40–84.

For articles on paired Mass movements, see M. Bukofzer, "The Origins of the Cyclic Mass," SMRM, pp. 217–26; P. Gossett, "Techniques of Unification in Early Cyclic Masses and Mass Pairs," JAMS, 19 (1966), pp. 205–31; C. Hamm, "The Reson Mass," JAMS, 18 (1965), pp. 5–21.

CHAPTER XX, AN ENGLISH EPILOGUE

Modern Editions   L. Dittmer, *The Worcester Fragments,* MSD, 2 (AIM, 1957); A. Hughes and M. Bent, *The Old Hall Manuscript* (OHM), 3 vols., CMM, 46 (AIM, 1969–73); A. Ramsbotham *et al., The Old Hall Manuscript,* 3 vols. (Nashdom and London, 1933–38); M. Bukofzer, *John Dunstable: Complete Works,* Musica Britannica, 8, rev. ed. (London, 1969); C. Hamm, *Lionel Power: Complete Works,* 2 vols., CMM, 50 (AIM, 1969–)—Vol. 2 not yet published.

For Further Reading   The most comprehensive account of English music and musical institutions is to be found in F. L1. Harrison, *Music in Medieval Britain* (New York, 1959)—see especially Chapters III–V. For studies of English church music in the fourteenth and fifteenth centuries, see NOHM, 3, Chapters 3 and 6.

Paired Mass movements in **OH** are discussed in A. Hughes, "Mass Pairs in the Old Hall and other English Manuscripts," RBM, 19 (1965), pp. 15–27; and D. Stevens, "Communication," JAMS, 20 (1967), pp. 516–17. The sale of **OH** to the British Library (formerly British Museum) is described in M. Bent, "The Old Hall Manuscript," *Early Music,* 2 (1974), pp. 2–14, with 4 facsimiles.

In addition to articles cited in the notes to this chapter, a few items of particular interest may be cited here: G. Reaney, "John Dunstable and Late Medieval Music in England," *Score,* 8 (1953), pp. 22–33; E. H. Sanders, "Cantilena and Discant in 14th-Century England," MD, 19 (1965), pp. 7–52; A. B. Scott, "The Performance of the Old Hall Descant Settings," MQ, 56 (1970), pp. 14–26; D. Stevens, "A Recently Discovered Source of Medieval Polyphony in England," MQ, 41 (1955), pp. 26–40.

For a much more extensive but still selective bibliography, see A. Hughes, MMBb, Nos. 1749–1815.

Index

Definitions of terms appear on pages indicated in **bold** type.